THE TWELFTH
Garfield
Fat Cat 3-Pack

Jim Davis

Ballantine Books • New York

A Ballantine Book
Published by The Ballantine Publishing Group

www.ballantinebooks.com

Library of Congress Catalog Card Number: 00-110659

ISBN 0-345-44581-3

Manufactured in the United States of America

First Edition: April 2001

10 9 8 7 6 5 4

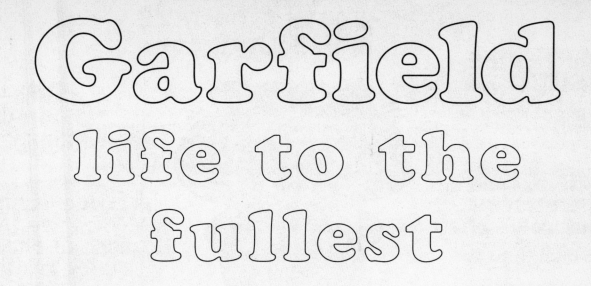

Garfield
life to the
fullest

BY: JIM DAVIS

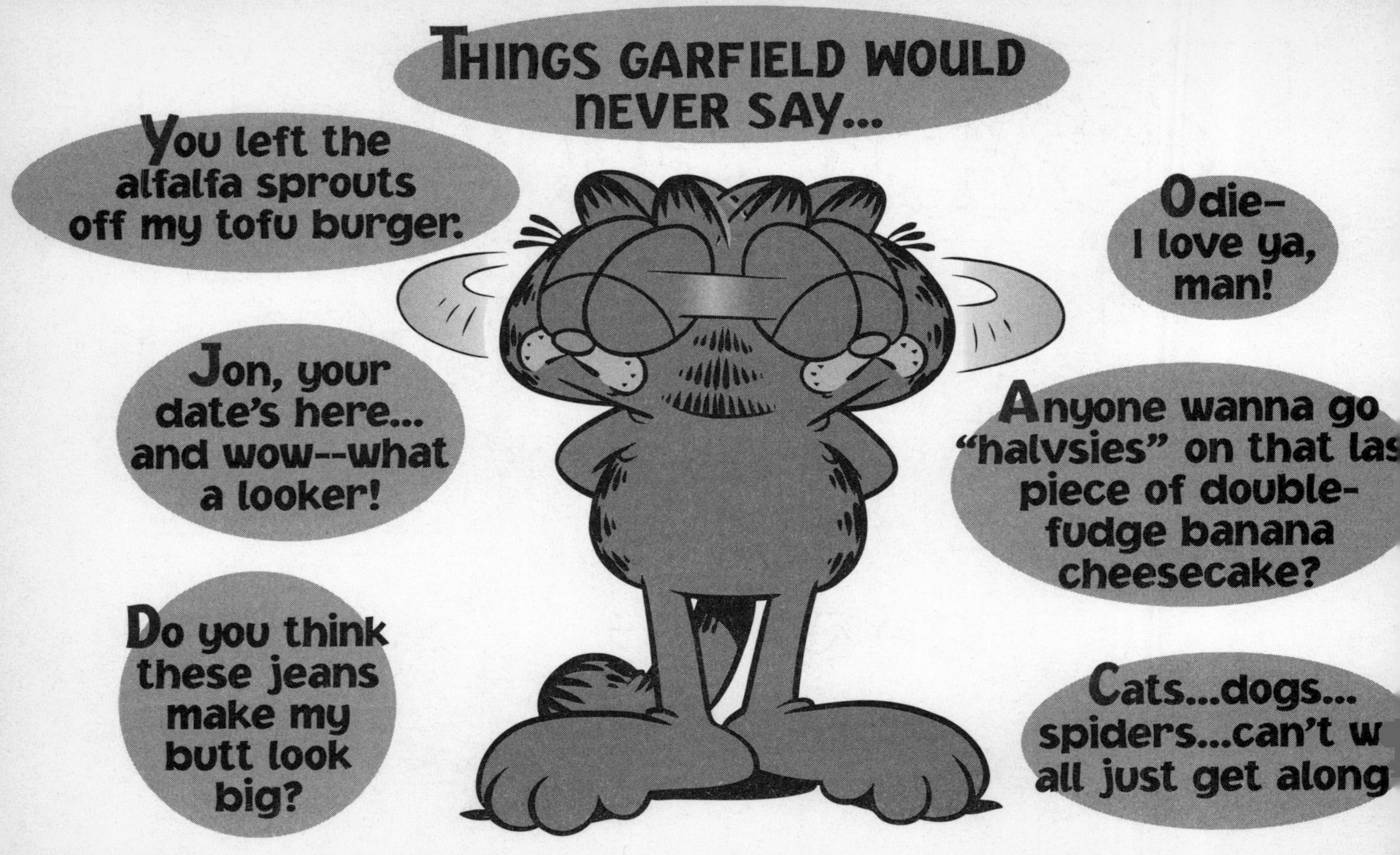
THINGS GARFIELD WOULD NEVER SAY...
You left the alfalfa sprouts off my tofu burger.
Odie- I love ya, man!
Jon, your date's here... and wow--what a looker!
Anyone wanna go "halvsies" on that las piece of double-fudge banana cheesecake?
Do you think these jeans make my butt look big?
Cats...dogs... spiders...can't w all just get along

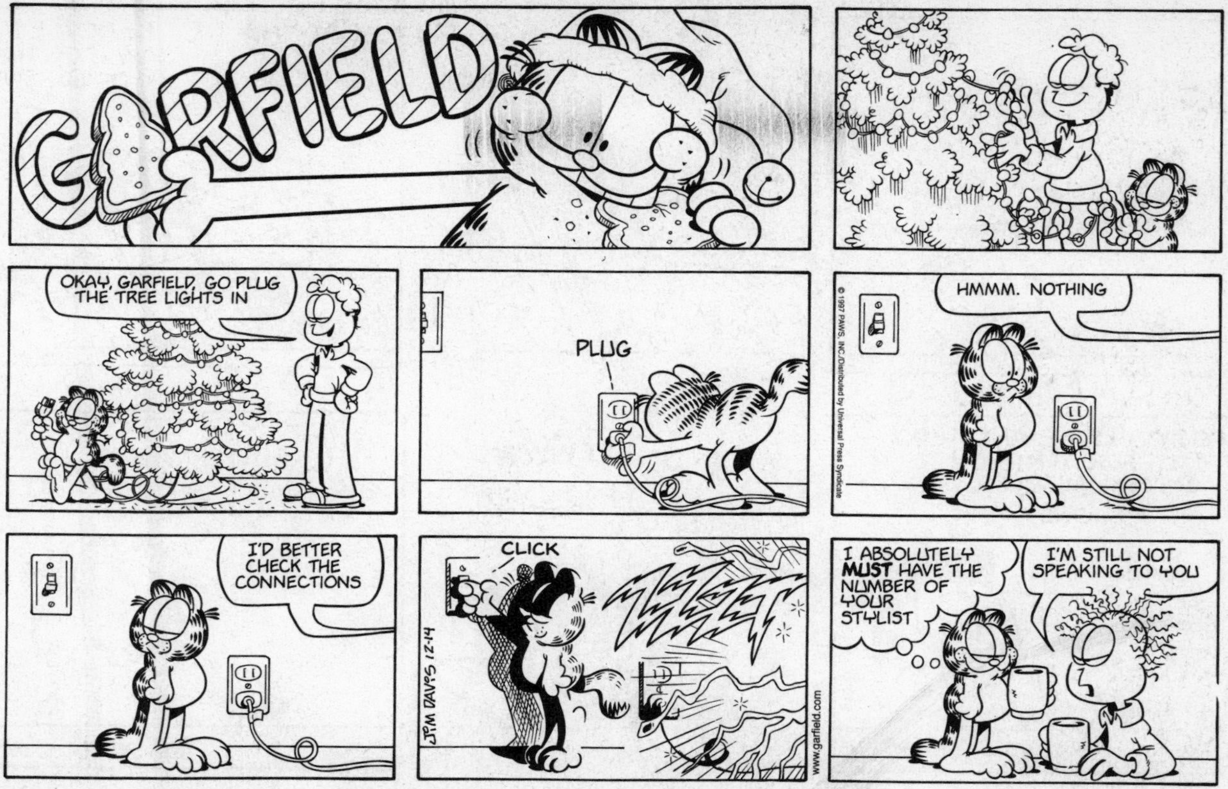
GARFIELD
OKAY, GARFIELD, GO PLUG THE TREE LIGHTS IN
PLUG
HMMM. NOTHING
I'D BETTER CHECK THE CONNECTIONS
CLICK
JIM DAVIS 12-14
I ABSOLUTELY MUST HAVE THE NUMBER OF YOUR STYLIST
I'M STILL NOT SPEAKING TO YOU
© 1997 PAWS, INC./Distributed by Universal Press Syndicate
www.garfield.com

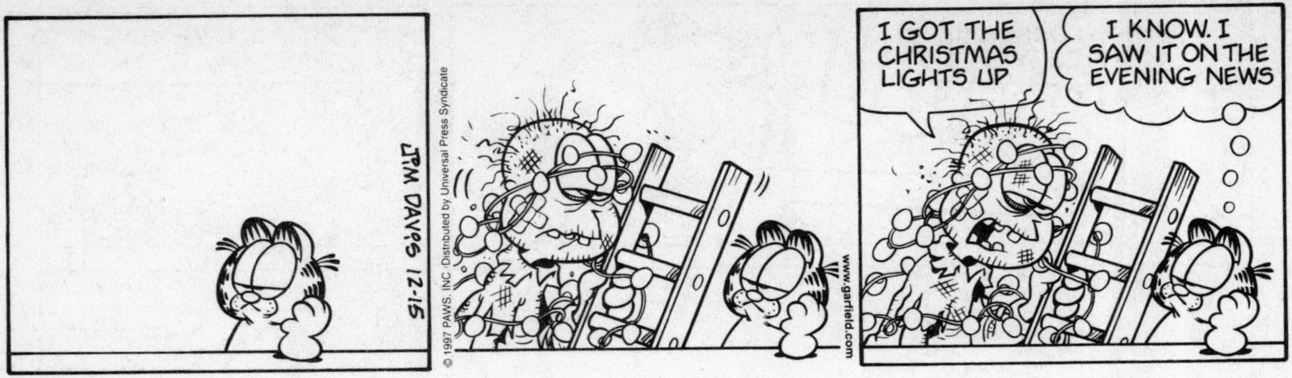
JIM DAVIS 12-15
© 1997 PAWS, INC./Distributed by Universal Press Syndicate
www.garfield.com
I GOT THE CHRISTMAS LIGHTS UP
I KNOW. I SAW IT ON THE EVENING NEWS

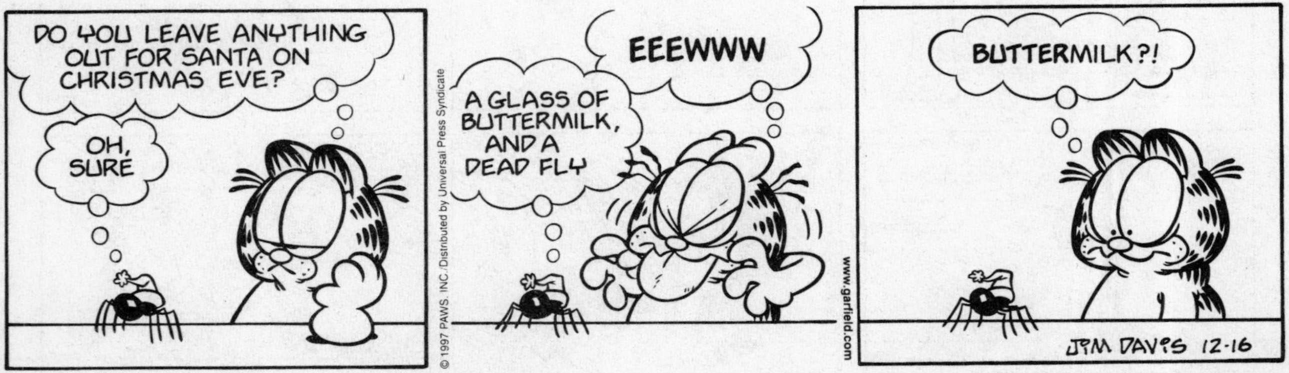
DO YOU LEAVE ANYTHING OUT FOR SANTA ON CHRISTMAS EVE?
OH, SURE
© 1997 PAWS, INC./Distributed by Universal Press Syndicate
A GLASS OF BUTTERMILK, AND A DEAD FLY
EEEWWW
www.garfield.com
BUTTERMILK?!
JIM DAVIS 12-16

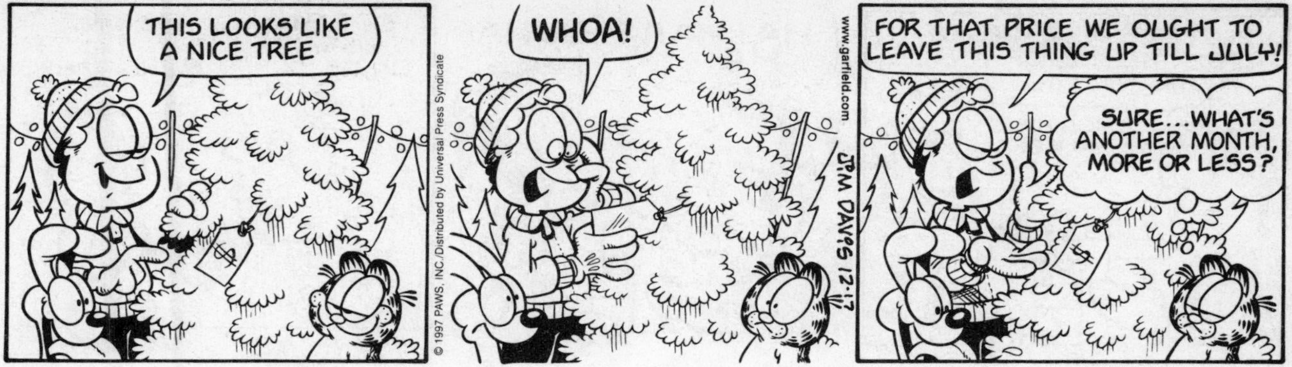
THIS LOOKS LIKE A NICE TREE
WHOA!
FOR THAT PRICE WE OUGHT TO LEAVE THIS THING UP TILL JULY!
SURE...WHAT'S ANOTHER MONTH, MORE OR LESS?
© 1997 PAWS, INC./Distributed by Universal Press Syndicate
www.garfield.com
JIM DAVIS 12-17

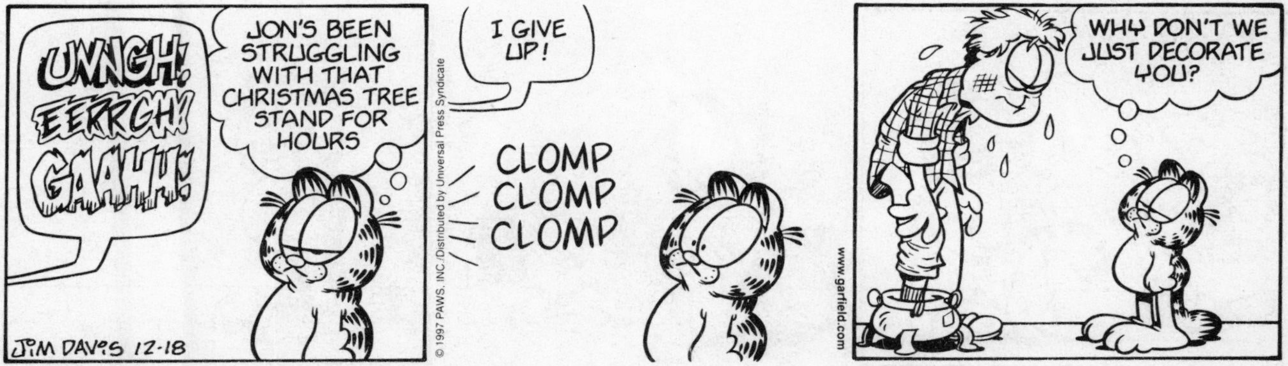
UNNGH! EERRGH! GAAHH!
JON'S BEEN STRUGGLING WITH THAT CHRISTMAS TREE STAND FOR HOURS
I GIVE UP!
CLOMP
CLOMP
CLOMP
WHY DON'T WE JUST DECORATE YOU?
JIM DAVIS 12-18
© 1997 PAWS, INC./Distributed by Universal Press Syndicate
www.garfield.com

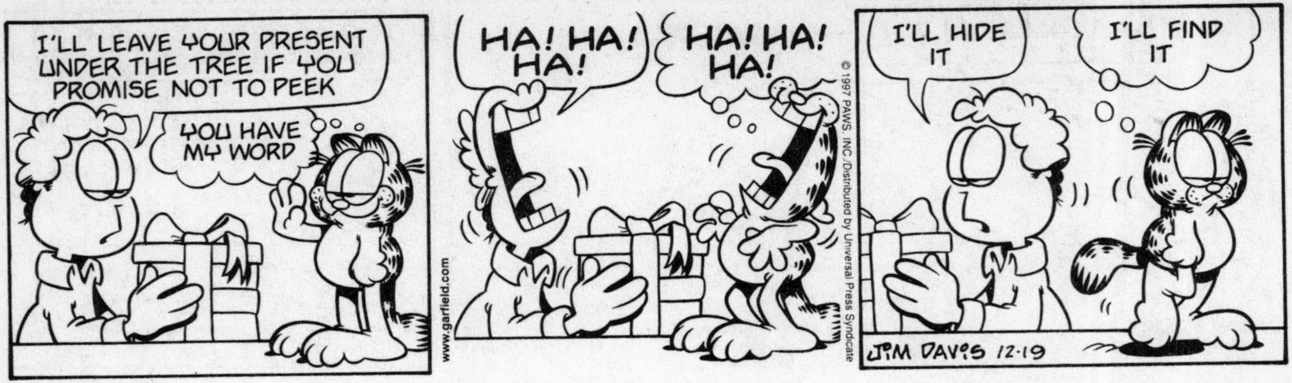
I'LL LEAVE YOUR PRESENT UNDER THE TREE IF YOU PROMISE NOT TO PEEK
YOU HAVE MY WORD
www.garfield.com
HA! HA! HA!
HA! HA! HA!
© 1997 PAWS, INC./Distributed by Universal Press Syndicate
I'LL HIDE IT
I'LL FIND IT
JIM DAVIS 12·19

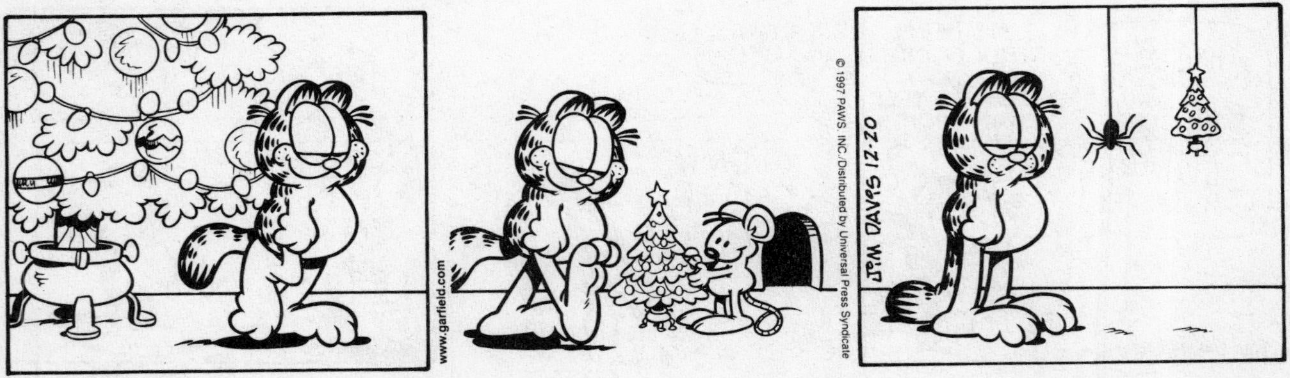
www.garfield.com
© 1997 PAWS, INC./Distributed by Universal Press Syndicate
JIM DAVIS 12·20

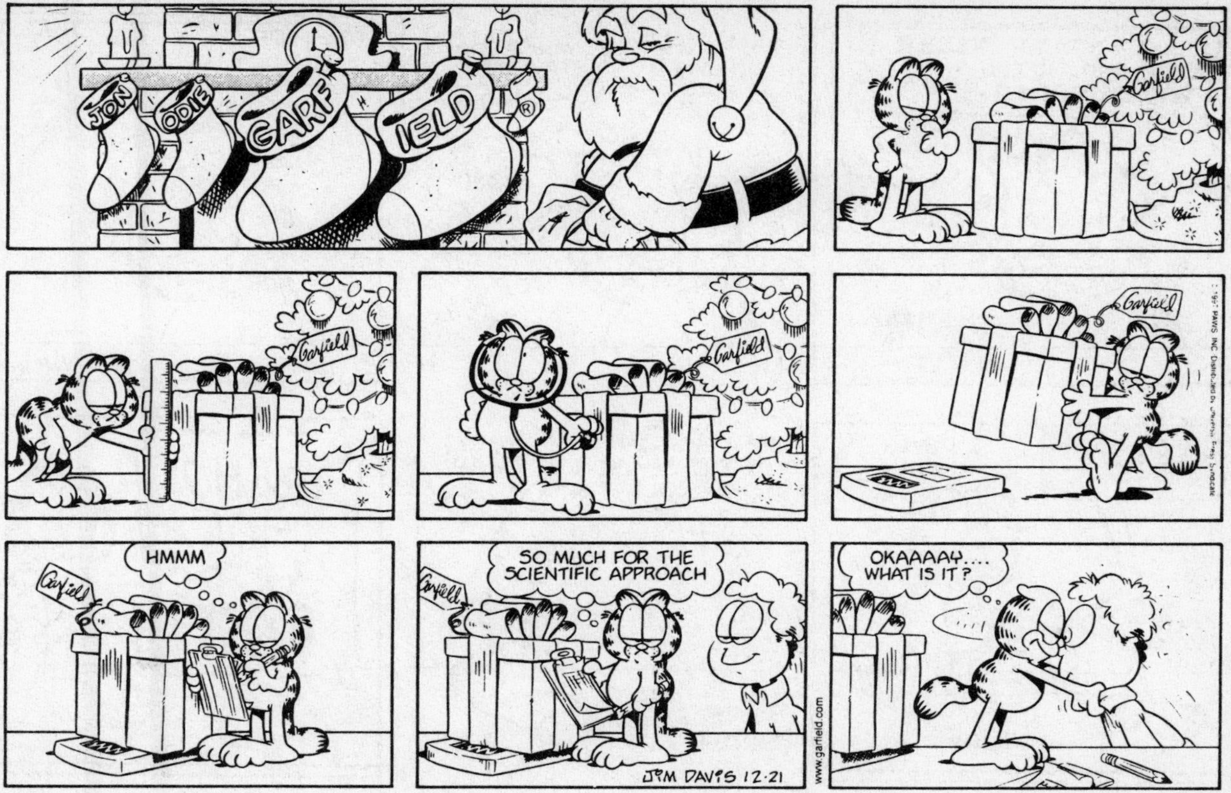
JON
ODIE
GARF
IELD
Garfield
Garfield
Garfield
Garfield
PAWS INC
Garfield
HMMM
Garfield
SO MUCH FOR THE SCIENTIFIC APPROACH
JIM DAVIS 12-21
www.garfield.com
OKAAAAY....
WHAT IS IT?

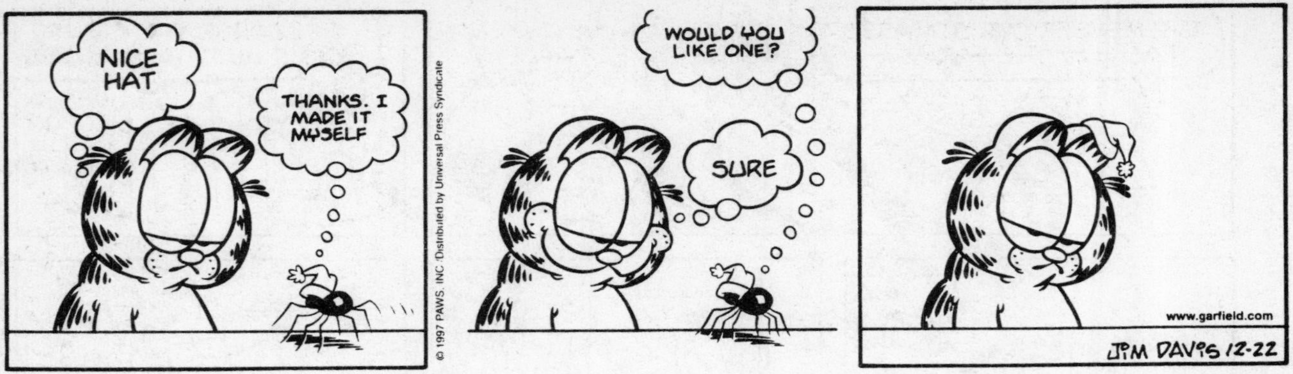
NICE HAT
THANKS. I MADE IT MYSELF
WOULD YOU LIKE ONE?
SURE
© 1997 PAWS, INC./Distributed by Universal Press Syndicate
www.garfield.com
JIM DAVIS 12-22

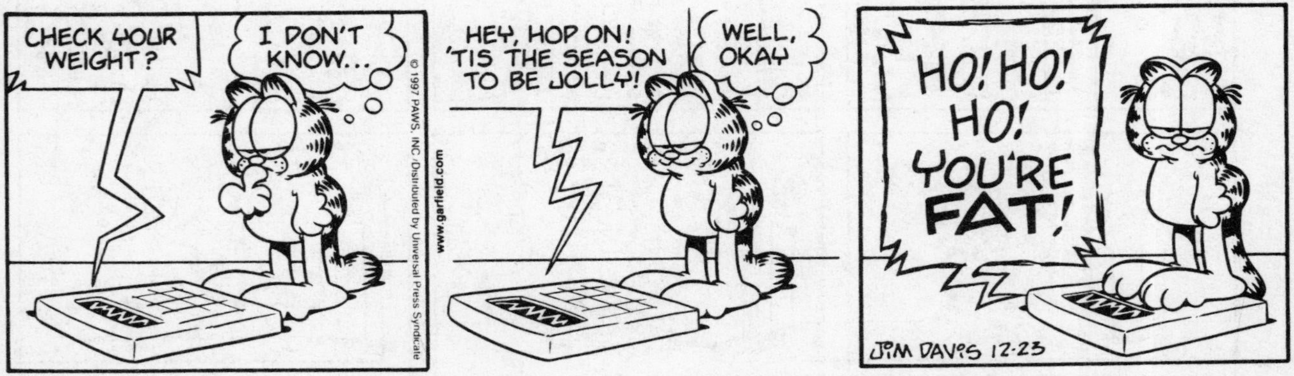
CHECK YOUR WEIGHT?
I DON'T KNOW...
© 1997 PAWS, INC./Distributed by Universal Press Syndicate
www.garfield.com
HEY, HOP ON! 'TIS THE SEASON TO BE JOLLY!
WELL, OKAY
HO! HO! HO! YOU'RE FAT!
JIM DAVIS 12-23

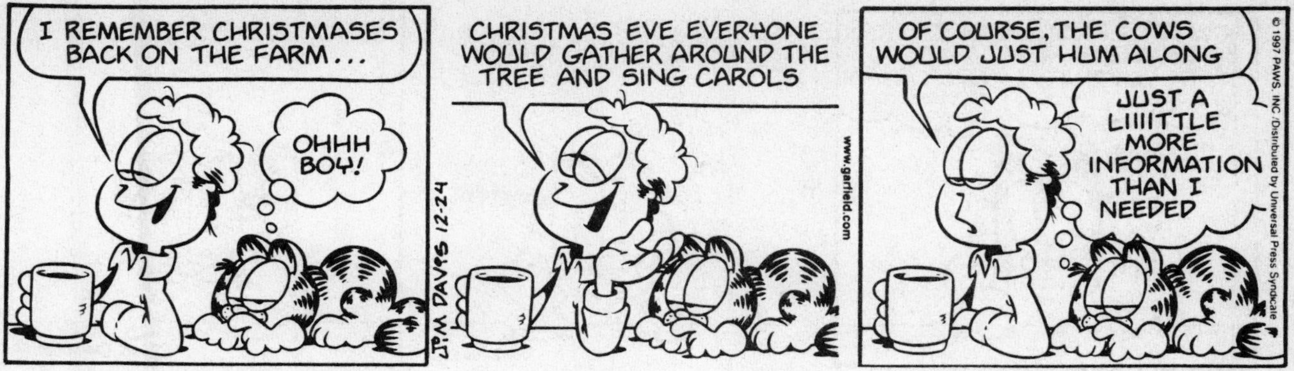
I REMEMBER CHRISTMASES BACK ON THE FARM...
OHHH BOY!
CHRISTMAS EVE EVERYONE WOULD GATHER AROUND THE TREE AND SING CAROLS
OF COURSE, THE COWS WOULD JUST HUM ALONG
JUST A LIIIITTLE MORE INFORMATION THAN I NEEDED
JIM DAVIS 12-24
www.garfield.com
© 1997 PAWS, INC./Distributed by Universal Press Syndicate

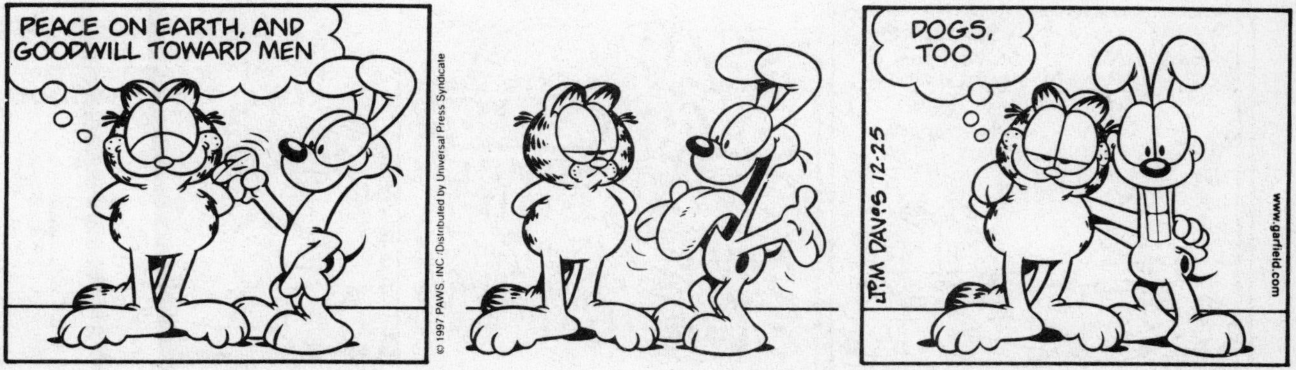
PEACE ON EARTH, AND GOODWILL TOWARD MEN
DOGS, TOO
JIM DAVIS 12-25
www.garfield.com
© 1997 PAWS, INC./Distributed by Universal Press Syndicate

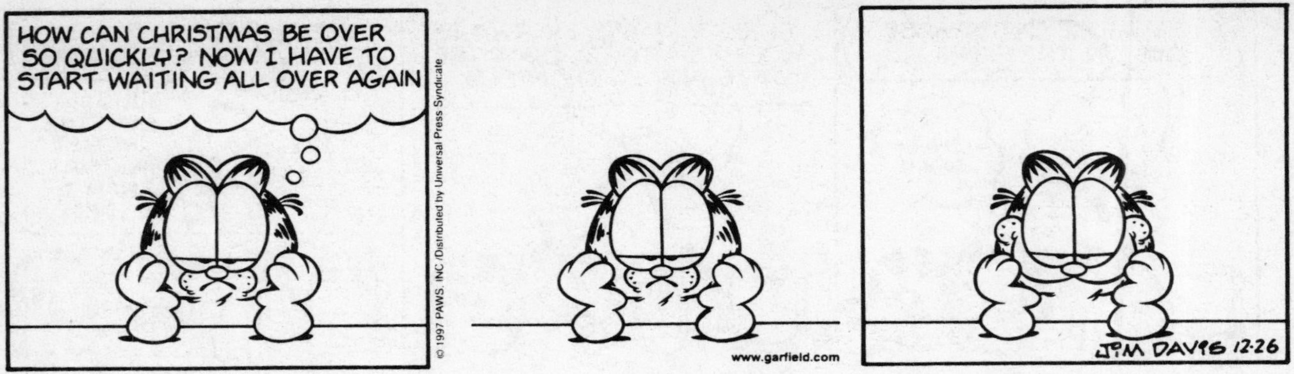
HOW CAN CHRISTMAS BE OVER SO QUICKLY? NOW I HAVE TO START WAITING ALL OVER AGAIN
© 1997 PAWS, INC./Distributed by Universal Press Syndicate
www.garfield.com
JIM DAVIS 12-26

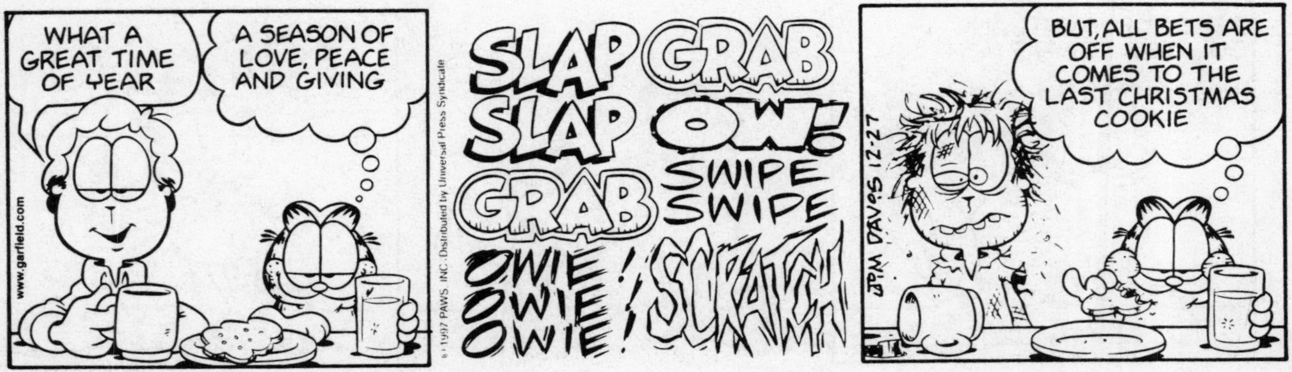
WHAT A GREAT TIME OF YEAR
A SEASON OF LOVE, PEACE AND GIVING
www.garfield.com
© 1997 PAWS, INC./Distributed by Universal Press Syndicate
SLAP GRAB
SLAP OW!
GRAB SWIPE SWIPE
OWIE! OWIE! OWIE!
SCRATCH
JIM DAVIS 12-27
BUT, ALL BETS ARE OFF WHEN IT COMES TO THE LAST CHRISTMAS COOKIE

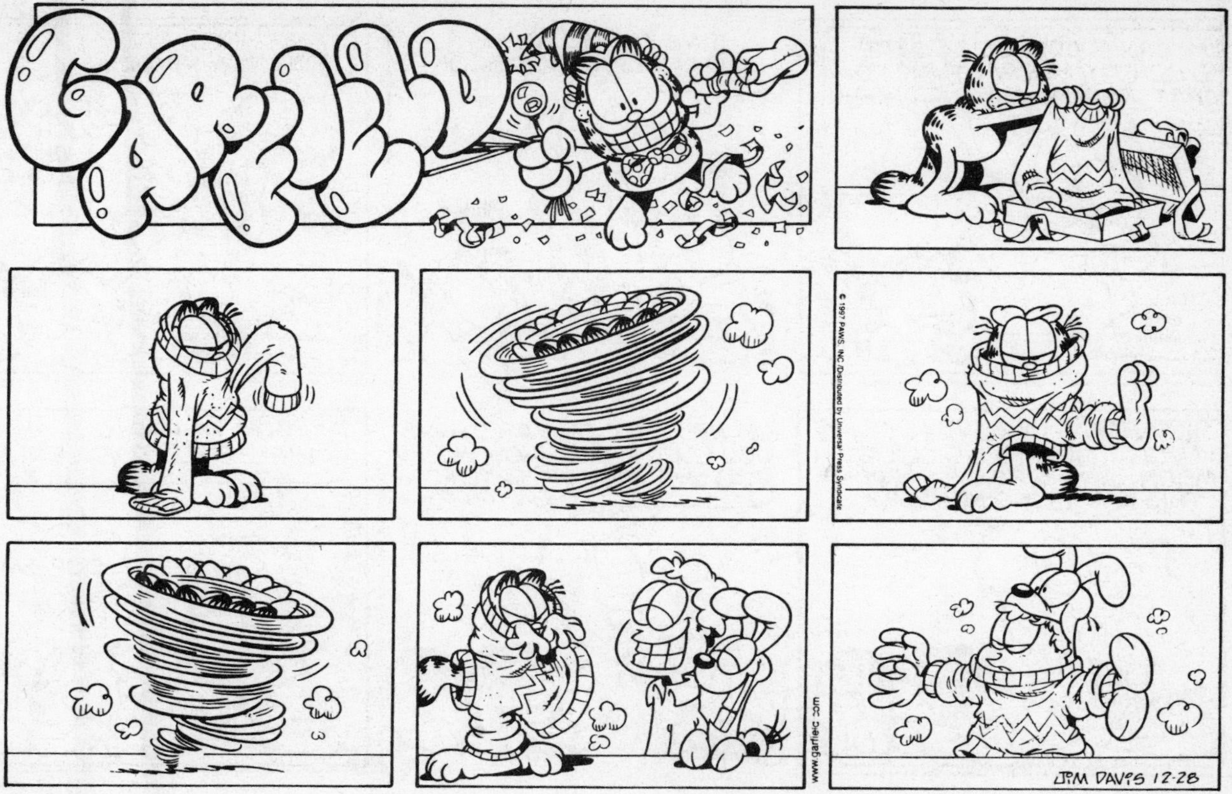
GARFIELD
© 1997 PAWS, INC./Distributed by Universal Press Syndicate
www.garfield.com
JIM DAVIS 12-28

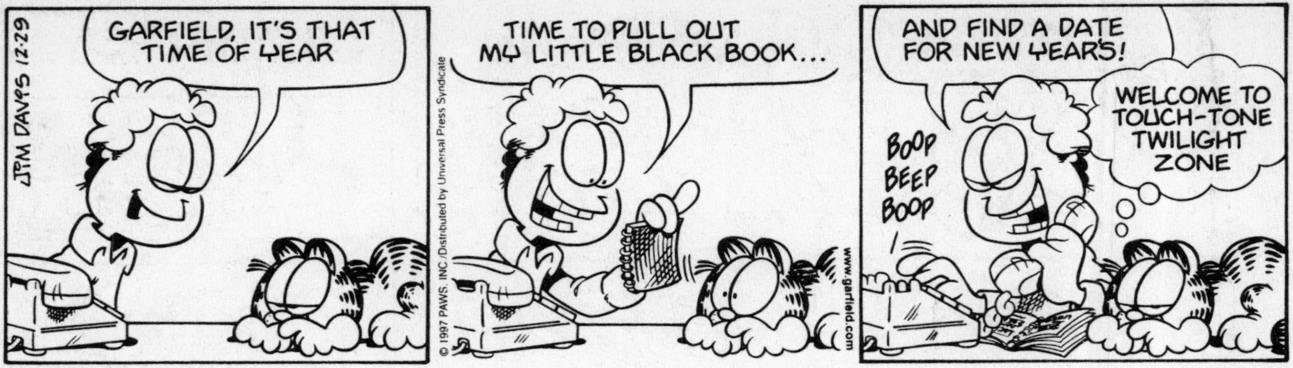
GARFIELD, IT'S THAT TIME OF YEAR
JIM DAVIS 12-29
TIME TO PULL OUT MY LITTLE BLACK BOOK...
© 1997 PAWS, INC./Distributed by Universal Press Syndicate
AND FIND A DATE FOR NEW YEAR'S!
BOOP BEEP BOOP
WELCOME TO TOUCH-TONE TWILIGHT ZONE
www.garfield.com

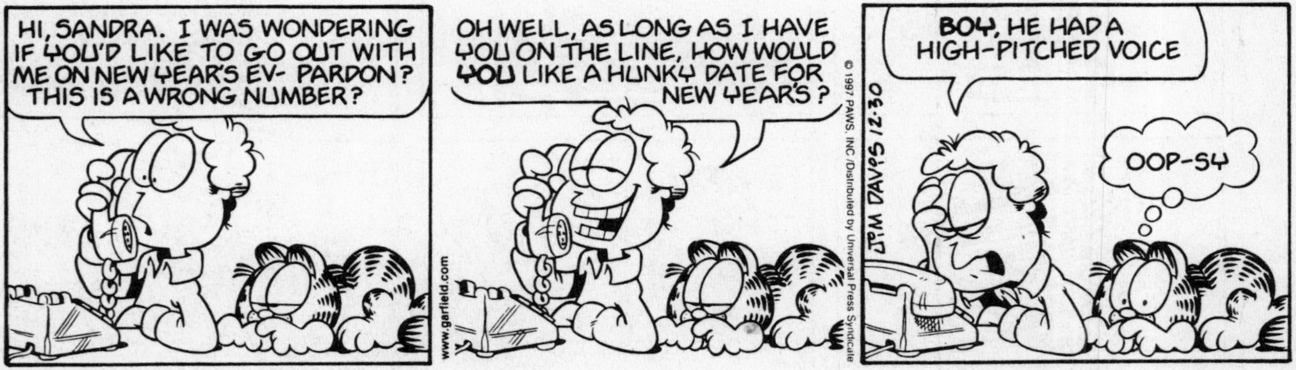
HI, SANDRA. I WAS WONDERING IF YOU'D LIKE TO GO OUT WITH ME ON NEW YEAR'S EV- PARDON? THIS IS A WRONG NUMBER?
www.garfield.com
OH WELL, AS LONG AS I HAVE YOU ON THE LINE, HOW WOULD YOU LIKE A HUNKY DATE FOR NEW YEAR'S?
© 1997 PAWS, INC./Distributed by Universal Press Syndicate
JIM DAVIS 12-30
BOY, HE HAD A HIGH-PITCHED VOICE
OOP-SY

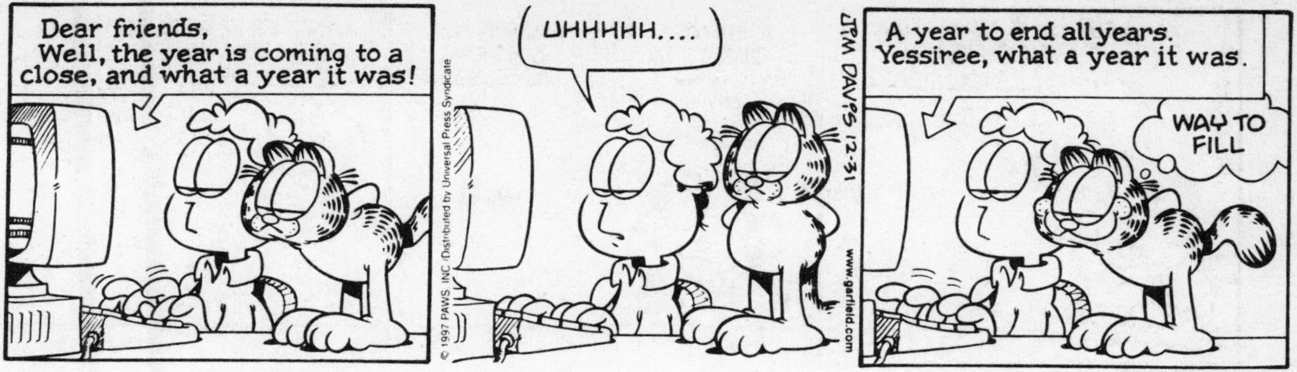
Dear friends,
Well, the year is coming to a close, and what a year it was!
UHHHHH....
© 1997 PAWS, INC /Distributed by Universal Press Syndicate
JIM DAVIS 12-31
www.garfield.com
A year to end all years. Yessiree, what a year it was.
WAY TO FILL

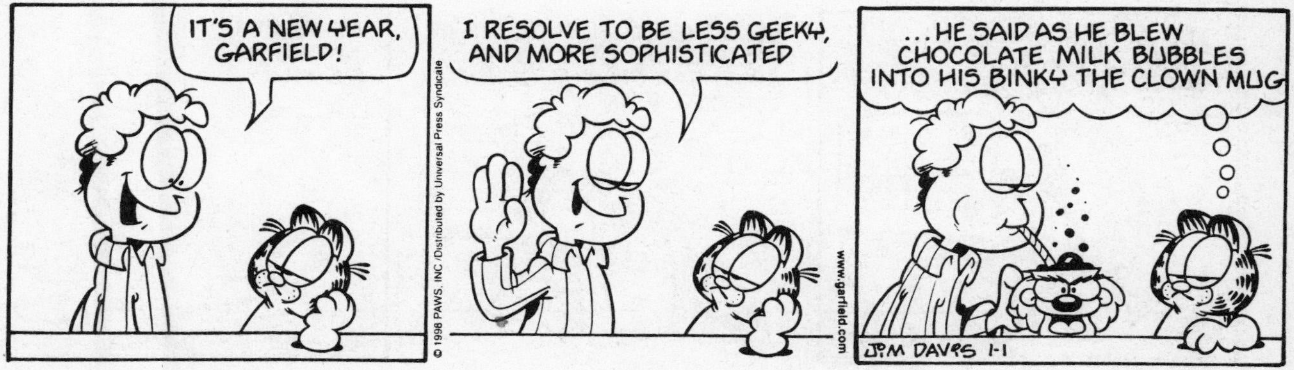
IT'S A NEW YEAR, GARFIELD!
© 1998 PAWS, INC /Distributed by Universal Press Syndicate
I RESOLVE TO BE LESS GEEKY, AND MORE SOPHISTICATED
www.garfield.com
...HE SAID AS HE BLEW CHOCOLATE MILK BUBBLES INTO HIS BINKY THE CLOWN MUG
JIM DAVIS 1-1

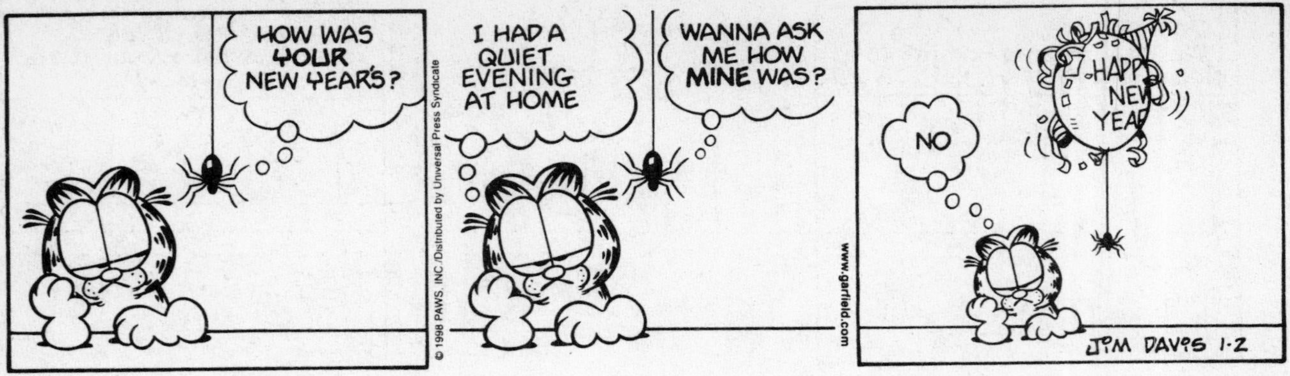
HOW WAS YOUR NEW YEAR'S?
I HAD A QUIET EVENING AT HOME
WANNA ASK ME HOW MINE WAS?
NO
HAPP NEW YEA
© 1998 PAWS, INC./Distributed by Universal Press Syndicate
www.garfield.com
JIM DAVIS 1-2

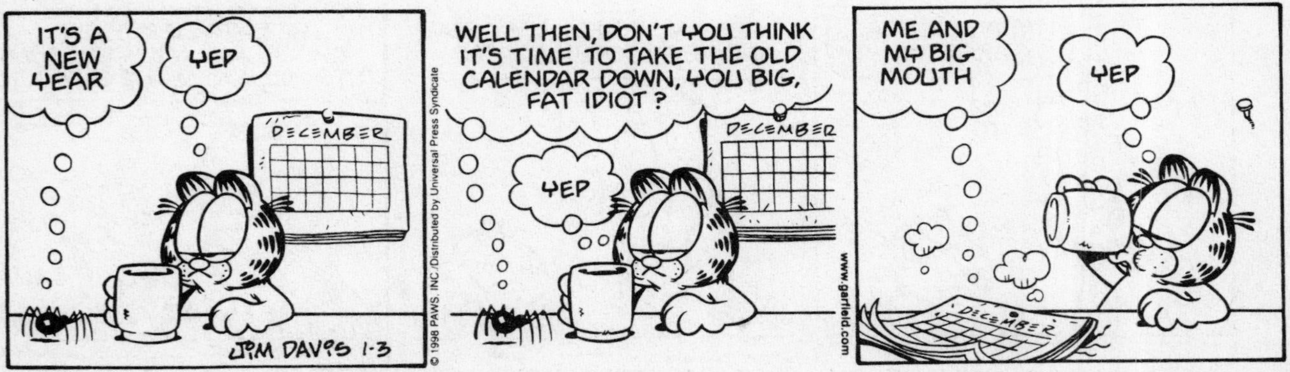
IT'S A NEW YEAR
YEP
DECEMBER
WELL THEN, DON'T YOU THINK IT'S TIME TO TAKE THE OLD CALENDAR DOWN, YOU BIG, FAT IDIOT?
YEP
DECEMBER
ME AND MY BIG MOUTH
YEP
DECEMBER
© 1998 PAWS, INC./Distributed by Universal Press Syndicate
www.garfield.com
JIM DAVIS 1-3

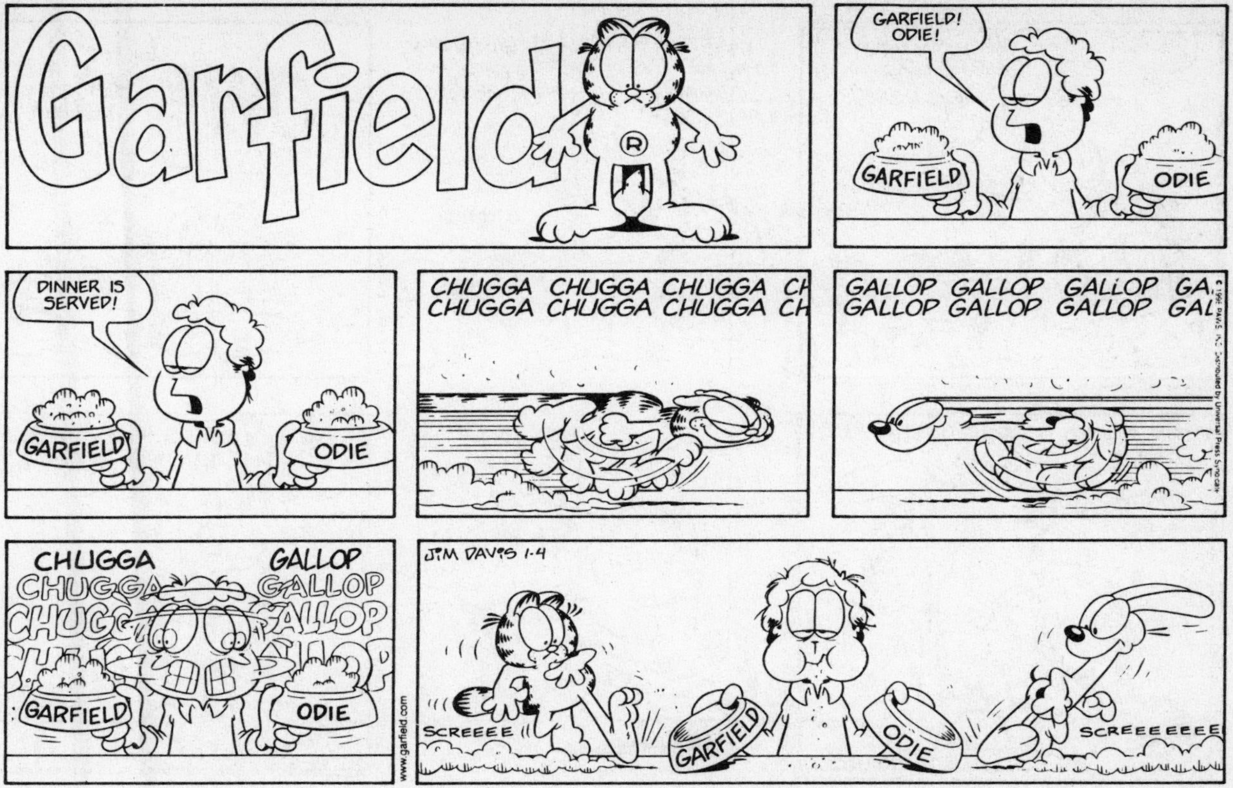
Garfield
GARFIELD! ODIE!
GARFIELD
ODIE
DINNER IS SERVED!
GARFIELD
ODIE
CHUGGA CHUGGA CHUGGA CH
CHUGGA CHUGGA CHUGGA CH
GALLOP GALLOP GALLOP GA
GALLOP GALLOP GALLOP GAL
CHUGGA
GALLOP
CHUGGA
GALLOP
CHUGGA
GALLOP
GARFIELD
ODIE
www.garfield.com
JIM DAVIS 1-4
SCREEEE
GARFIELD
ODIE
SCREEEEEEE

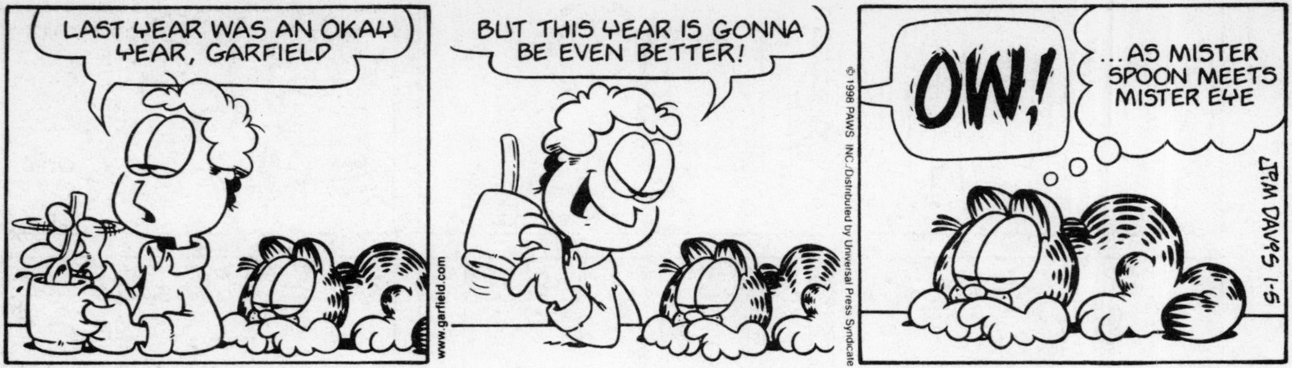
LAST YEAR WAS AN OKAY YEAR, GARFIELD
BUT THIS YEAR IS GONNA BE EVEN BETTER!
OW!
...AS MISTER SPOON MEETS MISTER EYE
JPM DAVPS 1-5
www.garfield.com
© 1998 PAWS INC./Distributed by Universal Press Syndicate

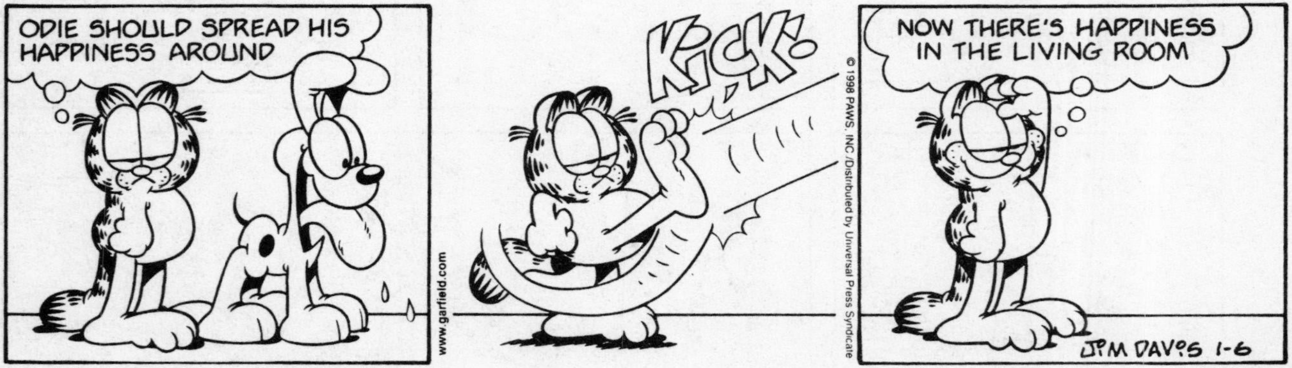
ODIE SHOULD SPREAD HIS HAPPINESS AROUND
KICK!
NOW THERE'S HAPPINESS IN THE LIVING ROOM
JPM DAVPS 1-6
www.garfield.com
© 1998 PAWS, INC./Distributed by Universal Press Syndicate

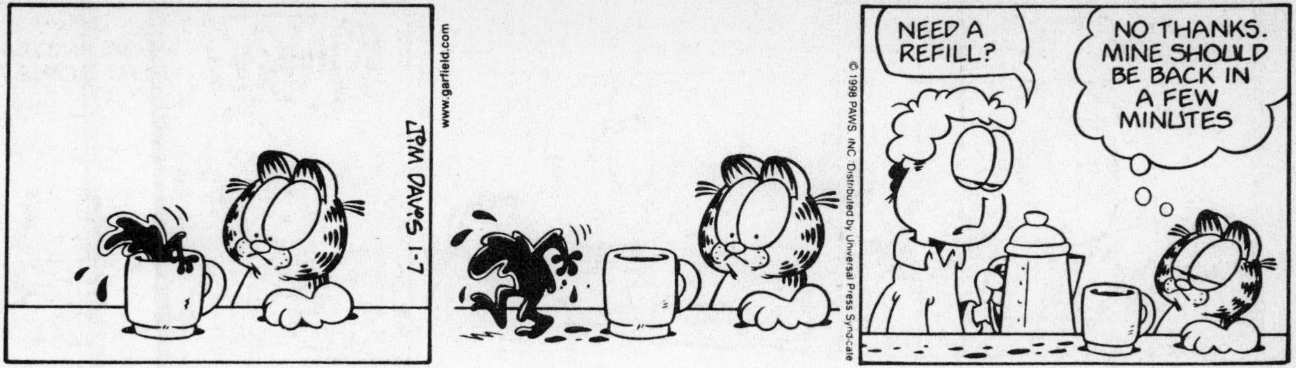
JIM DAVIS 1-7
www.garfield.com
© 1998 PAWS, INC. Distributed by Universal Press Syndicate
NEED A REFILL?
NO THANKS. MINE SHOULD BE BACK IN A FEW MINUTES

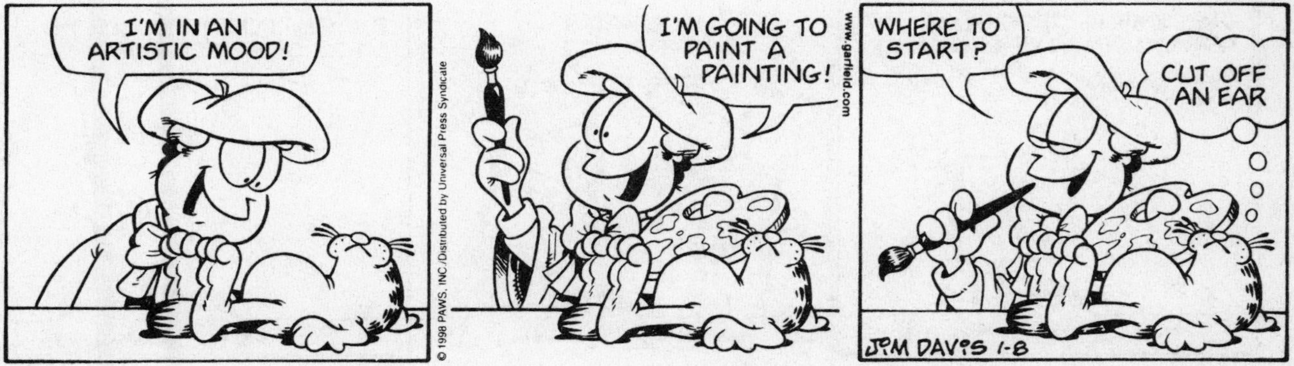
I'M IN AN ARTISTIC MOOD!
© 1998 PAWS, INC./Distributed by Universal Press Syndicate
I'M GOING TO PAINT A PAINTING!
www.garfield.com
WHERE TO START?
CUT OFF AN EAR
JIM DAVIS 1-8

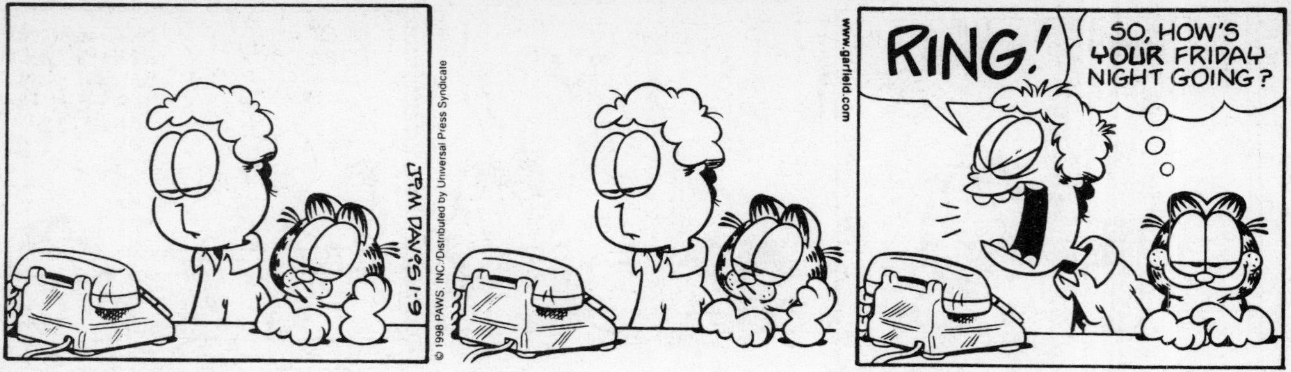
JIM DAVIS 1-9
© 1998 PAWS, INC./Distributed by Universal Press Syndicate
www.garfield.com
RING!
SO, HOW'S YOUR FRIDAY NIGHT GOING?

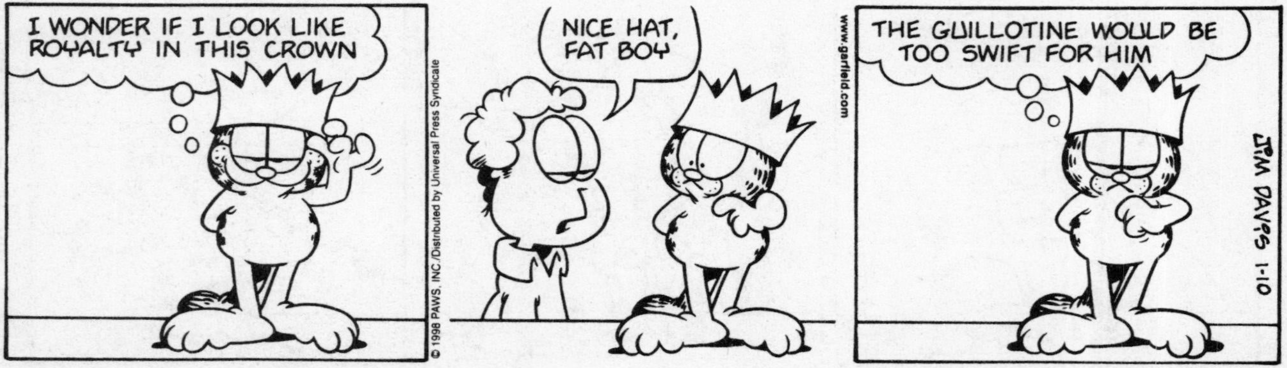
I WONDER IF I LOOK LIKE ROYALTY IN THIS CROWN
© 1998 PAWS, INC./Distributed by Universal Press Syndicate
NICE HAT, FAT BOY
www.garfield.com
THE GUILLOTINE WOULD BE TOO SWIFT FOR HIM
JIM DAVIS 1-10

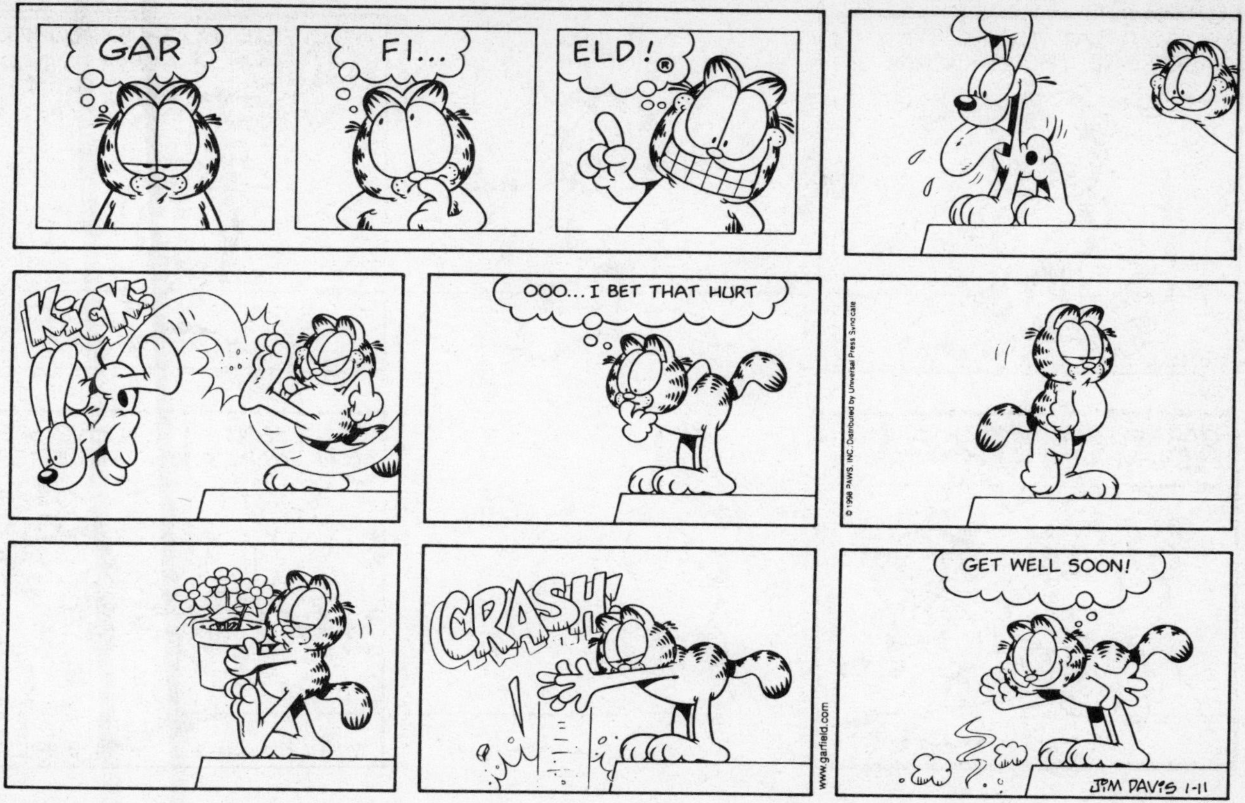
GAR
FI...
ELD!®
KICK!
OOO... I BET THAT HURT
CRASH!
GET WELL SOON!
© 1998 PAWS, INC. Distributed by Universal Press Syndicate
www.garfield.com
JIM DAVIS 1-11

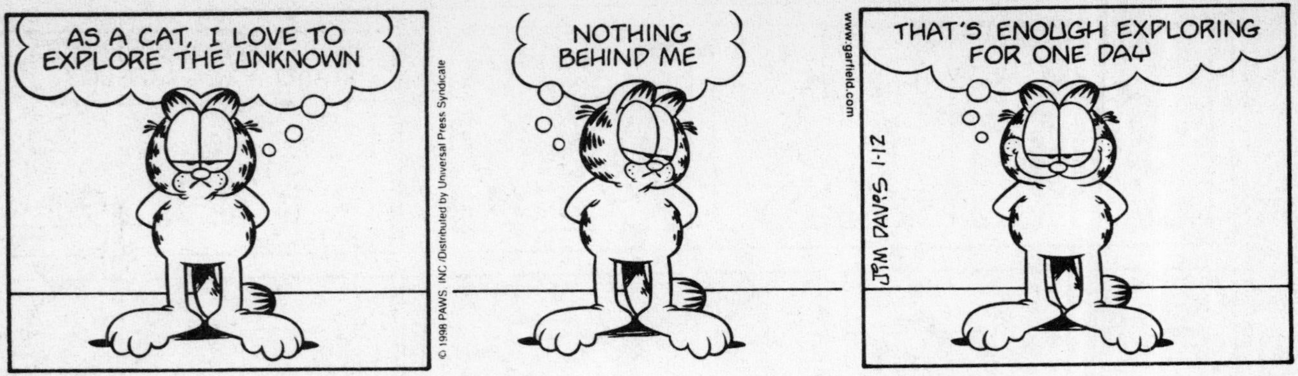
AS A CAT, I LOVE TO EXPLORE THE UNKNOWN
© 1998 PAWS, INC /Distributed by Universal Press Syndicate
NOTHING BEHIND ME
www.garfield.com
JIM DAVIS 1-12
THAT'S ENOUGH EXPLORING FOR ONE DAY

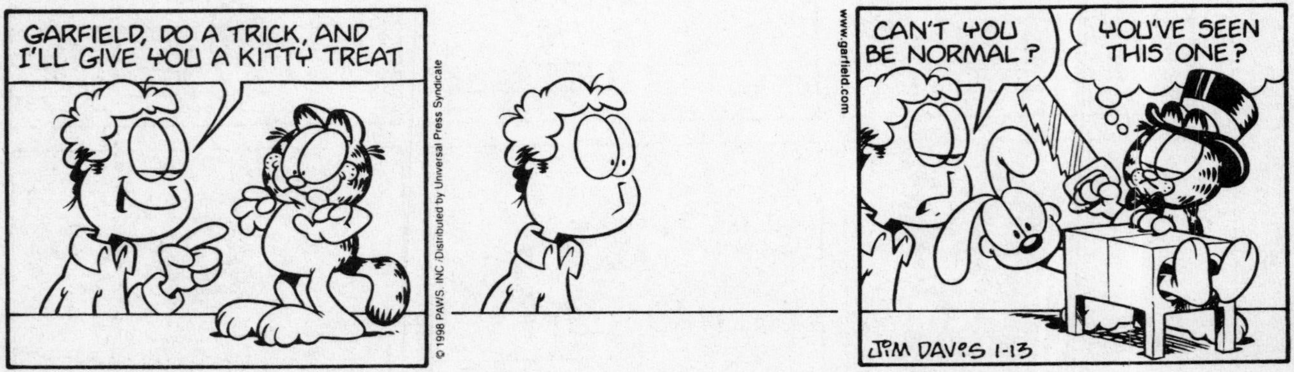
GARFIELD, DO A TRICK, AND I'LL GIVE YOU A KITTY TREAT
© 1998 PAWS, INC /Distributed by Universal Press Syndicate
www.garfield.com
CAN'T YOU BE NORMAL ?
YOU'VE SEEN THIS ONE ?
JIM DAVIS 1-13

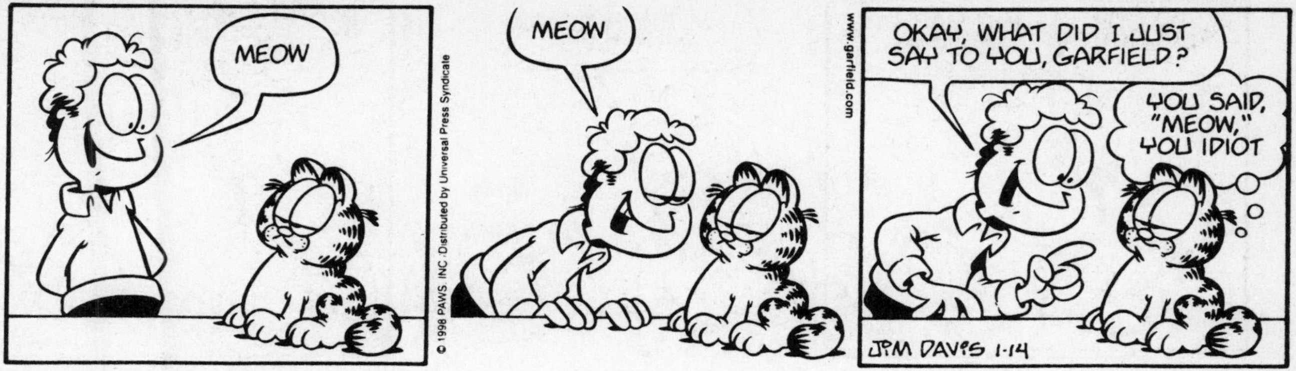
MEOW
MEOW
© 1998 PAWS, INC./Distributed by Universal Press Syndicate
www.garfield.com
OKAY, WHAT DID I JUST SAY TO YOU, GARFIELD?
YOU SAID, "MEOW," YOU IDIOT
JIM DAVIS 1-14

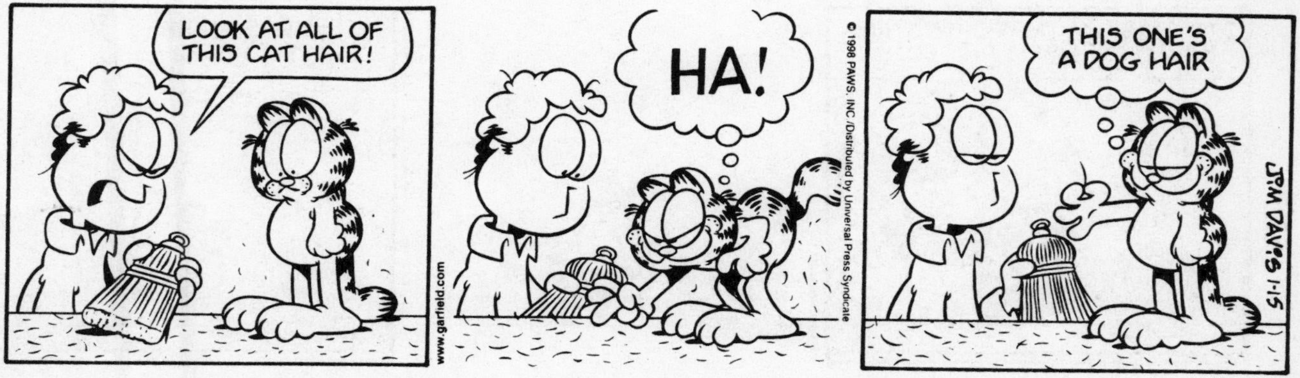
LOOK AT ALL OF THIS CAT HAIR!
www.garfield.com
HA!
© 1998 PAWS, INC./Distributed by Universal Press Syndicate
THIS ONE'S A DOG HAIR
JIM DAVIS 1-15

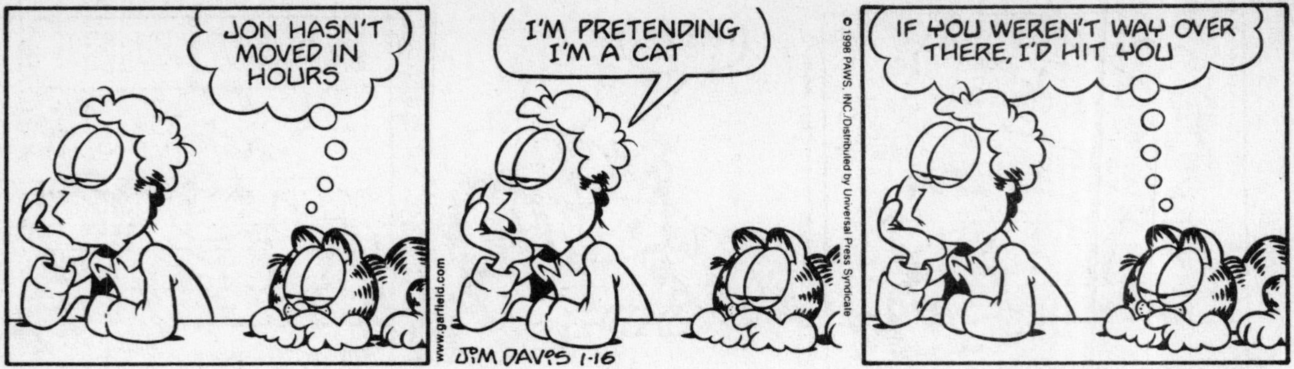
JON HASN'T MOVED IN HOURS
I'M PRETENDING I'M A CAT
IF YOU WEREN'T WAY OVER THERE, I'D HIT YOU
www.garfield.com
JIM DAVIS 1-16
© 1998 PAWS, INC./Distributed by Universal Press Syndicate

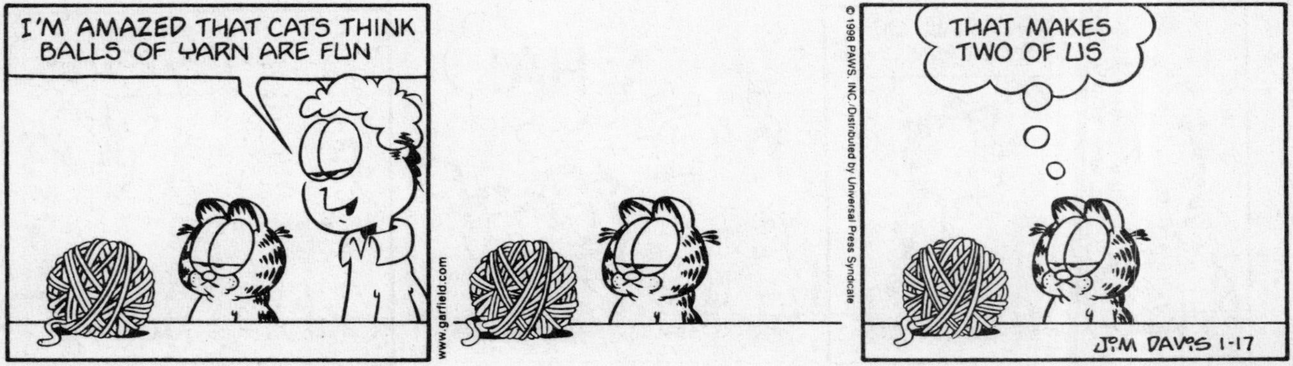
I'M AMAZED THAT CATS THINK BALLS OF YARN ARE FUN
THAT MAKES TWO OF US
www.garfield.com
JIM DAVIS 1-17
© 1998 PAWS, INC./Distributed by Universal Press Syndicate

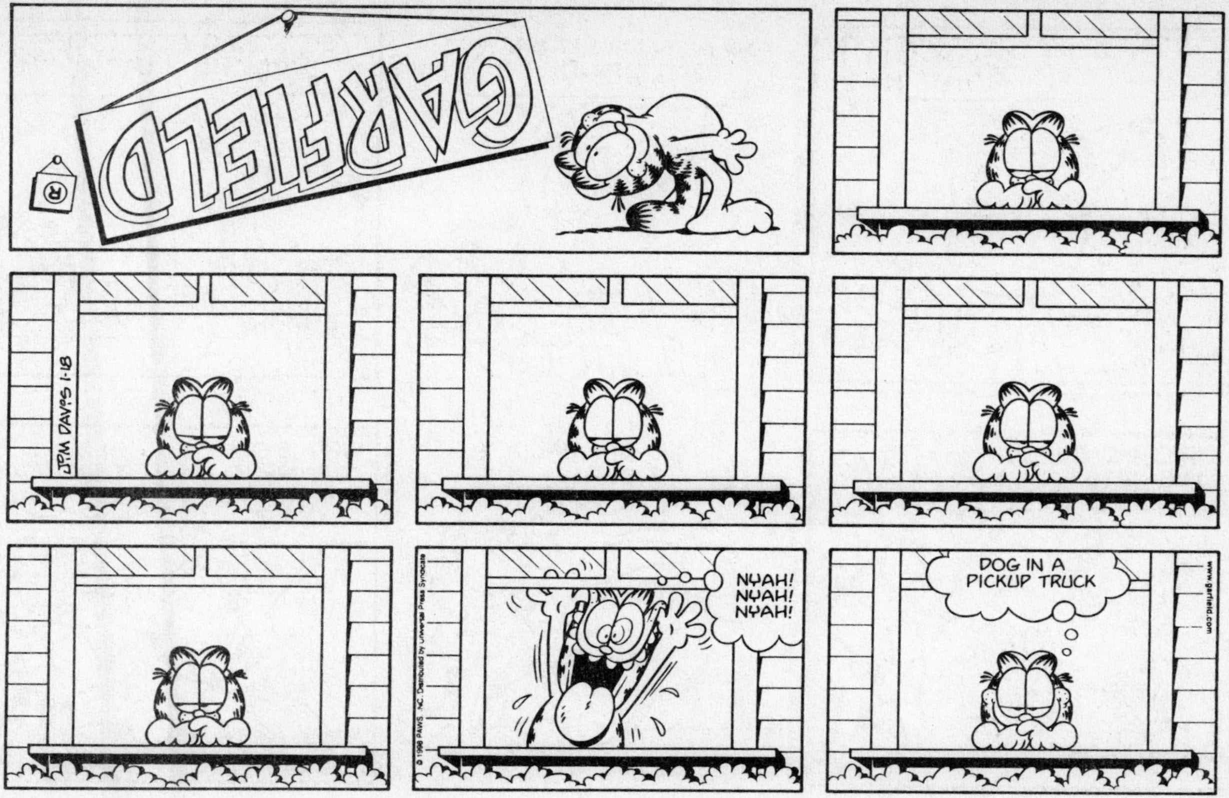
GARFIELD
JIM DAVIS 1-18
© 1998 PAWS, INC. Distributed by Universal Press Syndicate
NYAH! NYAH! NYAH!
DOG IN A PICKUP TRUCK
www.garfield.com

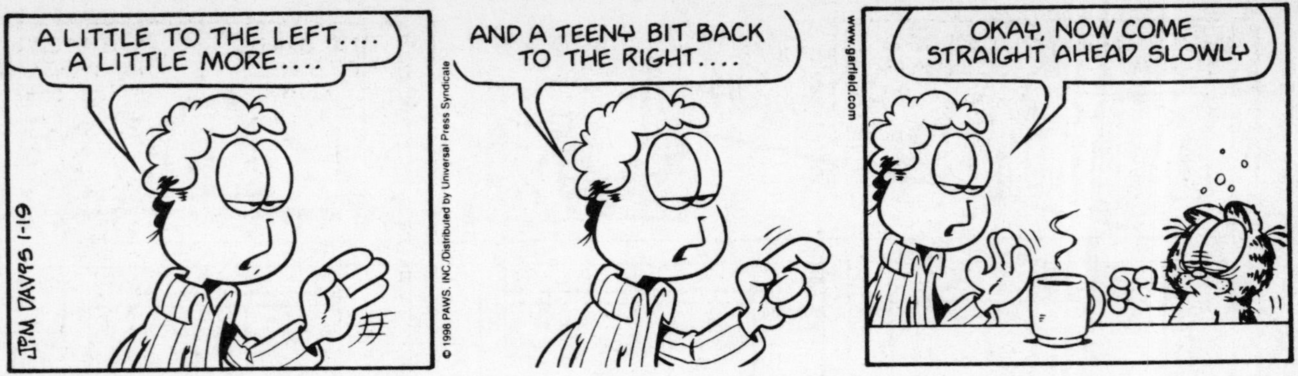
A LITTLE TO THE LEFT.....
A LITTLE MORE....
JIM DAVIS 1-19
© 1998 PAWS, INC./Distributed by Universal Press Syndicate
AND A TEENY BIT BACK TO THE RIGHT....
www.garfield.com
OKAY, NOW COME STRAIGHT AHEAD SLOWLY

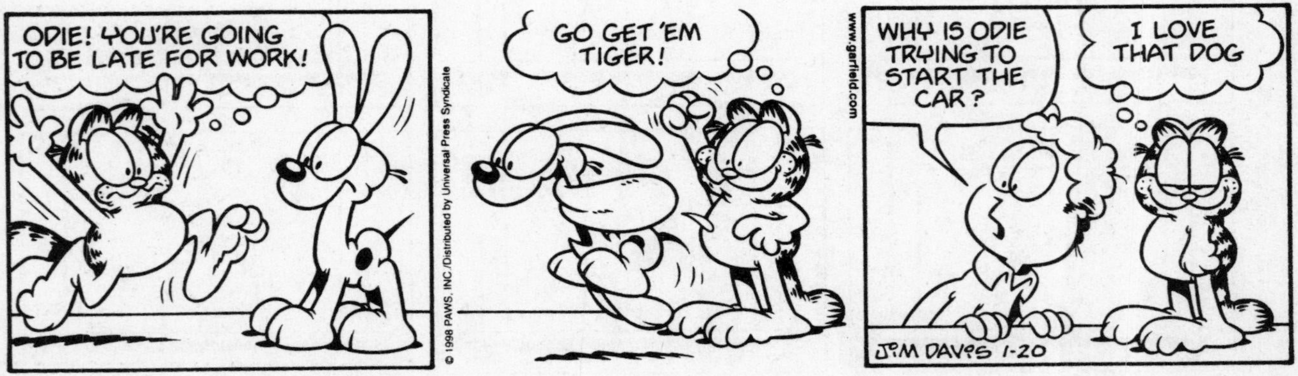
ODIE! YOU'RE GOING TO BE LATE FOR WORK!
© 1998 PAWS, INC./Distributed by Universal Press Syndicate
GO GET 'EM TIGER!
www.garfield.com
WHY IS ODIE TRYING TO START THE CAR?
I LOVE THAT DOG
JIM DAVIS 1-20

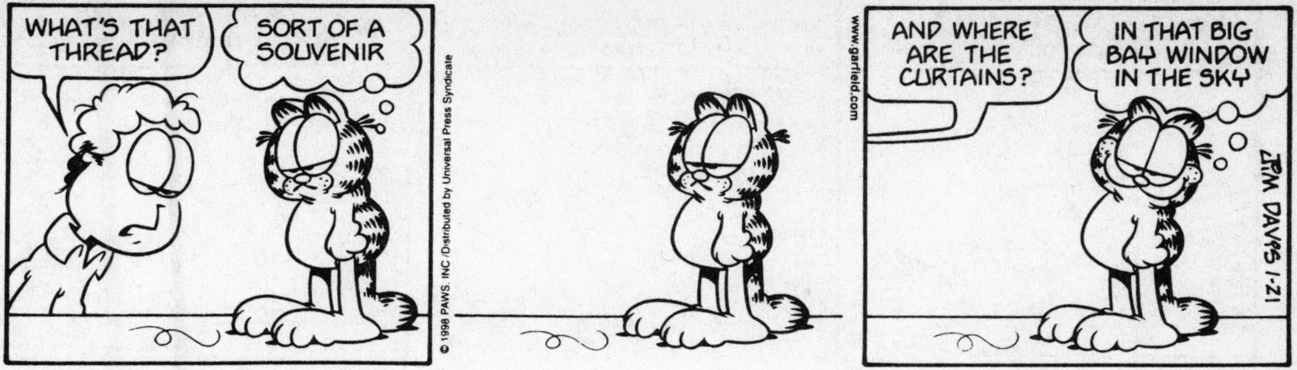
WHAT'S THAT THREAD?
SORT OF A SOUVENIR
© 1998 PAWS, INC /Distributed by Universal Press Syndicate
www.garfield.com
AND WHERE ARE THE CURTAINS?
IN THAT BIG BAY WINDOW IN THE SKY
JIM DAVIS 1-21

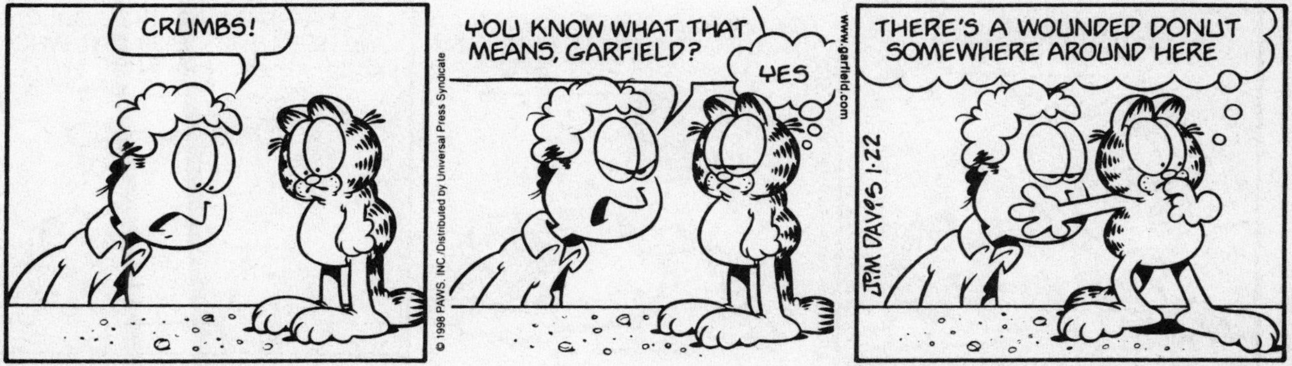
CRUMBS!
© 1998 PAWS, INC /Distributed by Universal Press Syndicate
YOU KNOW WHAT THAT MEANS, GARFIELD?
YES
www.garfield.com
THERE'S A WOUNDED DONUT SOMEWHERE AROUND HERE
JIM DAVIS 1-22

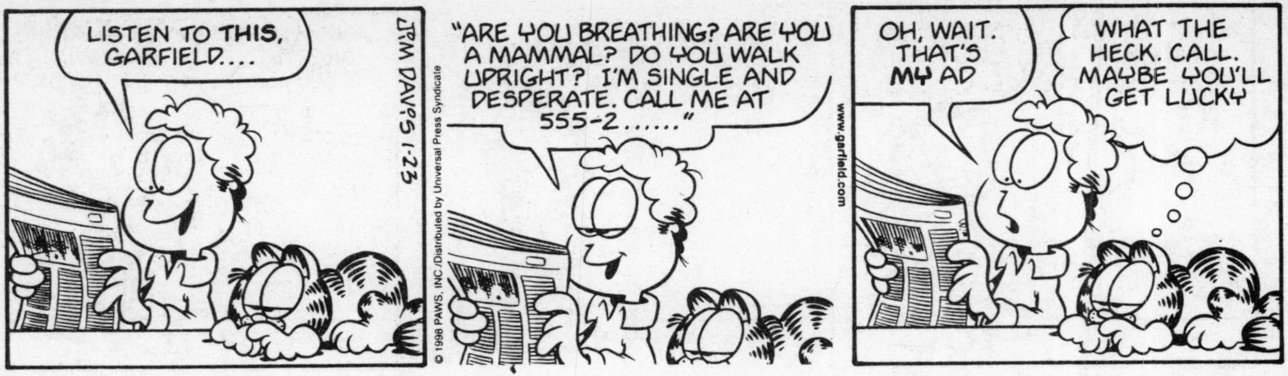
LISTEN TO THIS, GARFIELD....
JPM DAVPS 1-23
© 1998 PAWS, INC./Distributed by Universal Press Syndicate
"ARE YOU BREATHING? ARE YOU A MAMMAL? DO YOU WALK UPRIGHT? I'M SINGLE AND DESPERATE. CALL ME AT 555-2......"
www.garfield.com
OH, WAIT. THAT'S MY AD
WHAT THE HECK. CALL. MAYBE YOU'LL GET LUCKY

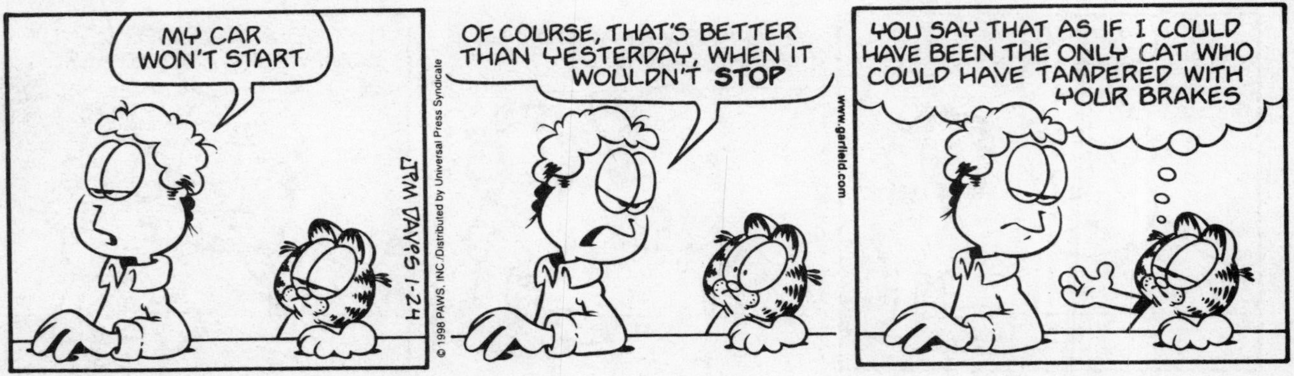
MY CAR WON'T START
JPM DAVPS 1-24
© 1998 PAWS, INC./Distributed by Universal Press Syndicate
OF COURSE, THAT'S BETTER THAN YESTERDAY, WHEN IT WOULDN'T STOP
www.garfield.com
YOU SAY THAT AS IF I COULD HAVE BEEN THE ONLY CAT WHO COULD HAVE TAMPERED WITH YOUR BRAKES

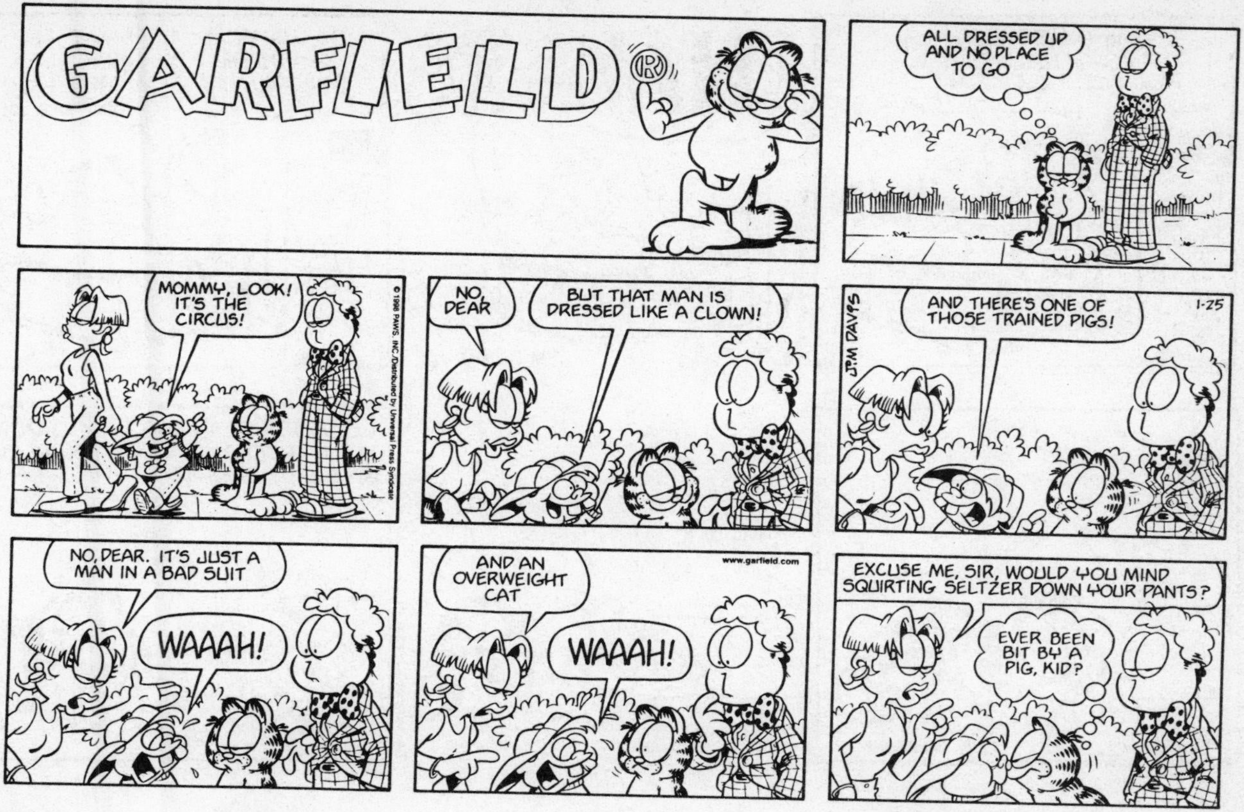
GARFIELD®
ALL DRESSED UP AND NO PLACE TO GO
MOMMY, LOOK! IT'S THE CIRCUS!
© 1998 PAWS, INC./Distributed by Universal Press Syndicate
NO, DEAR
BUT THAT MAN IS DRESSED LIKE A CLOWN!
JIM DAVIS
1-25
AND THERE'S ONE OF THOSE TRAINED PIGS!
NO, DEAR. IT'S JUST A MAN IN A BAD SUIT
WAAAH!
www.garfield.com
AND AN OVERWEIGHT CAT
WAAAH!
EXCUSE ME, SIR, WOULD YOU MIND SQUIRTING SELTZER DOWN YOUR PANTS?
EVER BEEN BIT BY A PIG, KID?

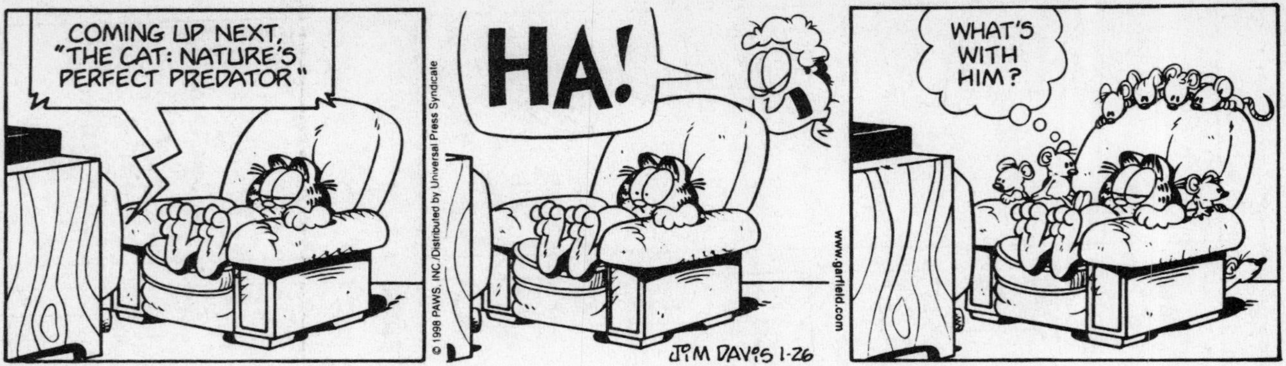
COMING UP NEXT, "THE CAT: NATURE'S PERFECT PREDATOR"
HA!
WHAT'S WITH HIM?
© 1998 PAWS, INC./Distributed by Universal Press Syndicate
www.garfield.com
JIM DAVIS 1-26

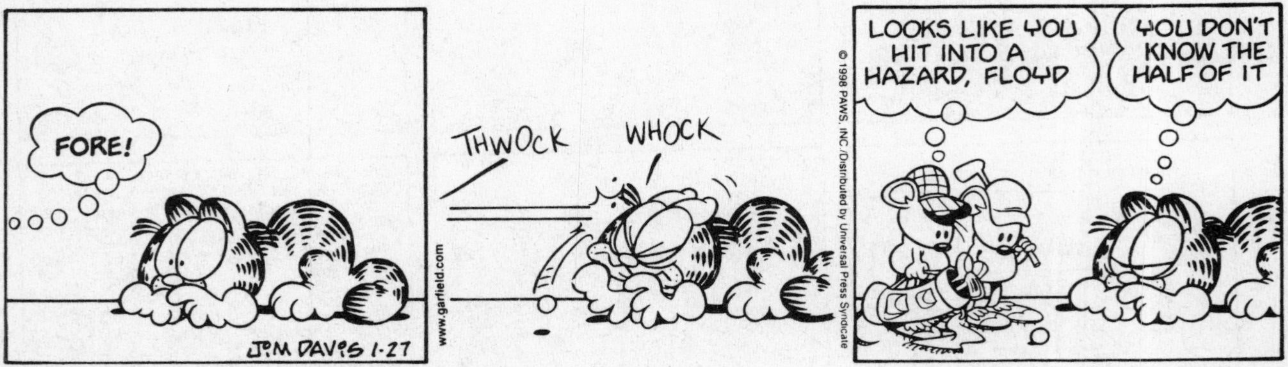
FORE!
THWOCK
WHOCK
LOOKS LIKE YOU HIT INTO A HAZARD, FLOYD
YOU DON'T KNOW THE HALF OF IT
www.garfield.com
© 1998 PAWS, INC./Distributed by Universal Press Syndicate
JIM DAVIS 1-27

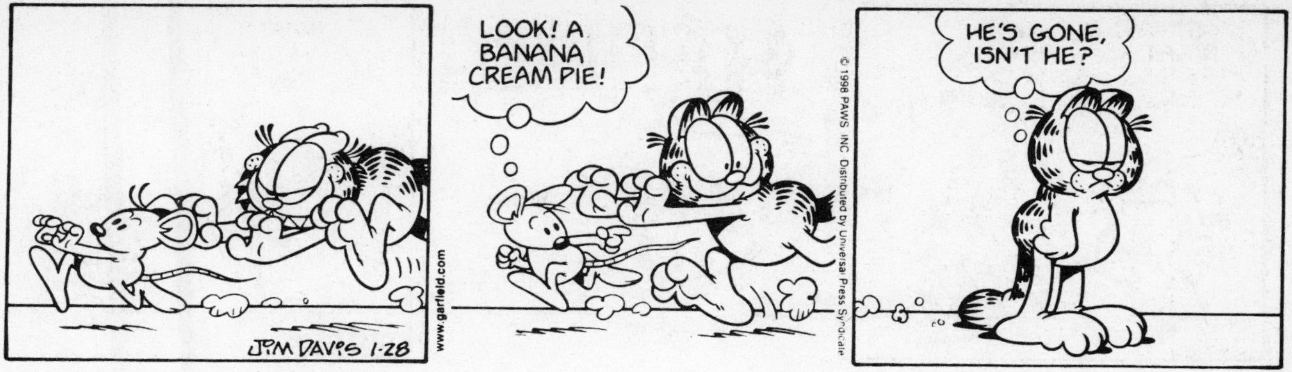
JIM DAVIS 1-28
www.garfield.com
LOOK! A BANANA CREAM PIE!
© 1998 PAWS INC Distributed by Universal Press Syndicate
HE'S GONE, ISN'T HE?

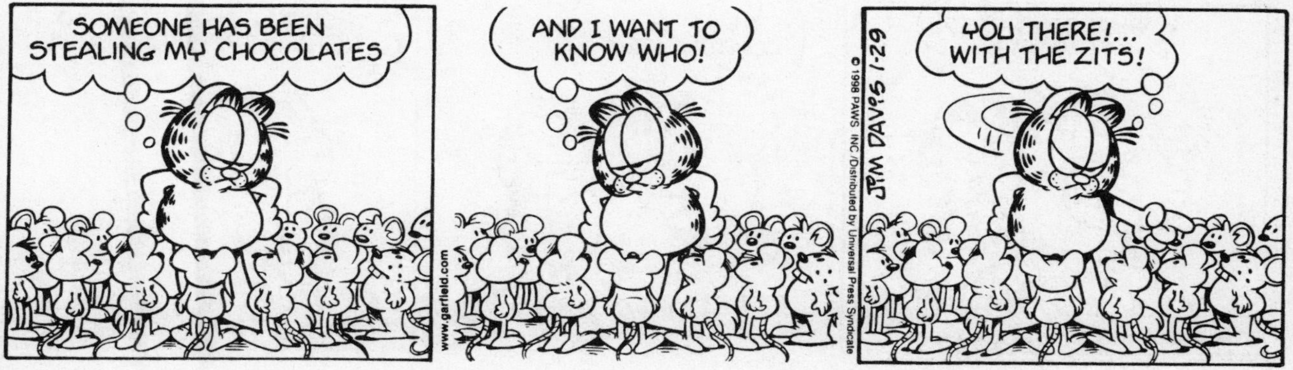
SOMEONE HAS BEEN STEALING MY CHOCOLATES
www.garfield.com
AND I WANT TO KNOW WHO!
© 1998 PAWS INC /Distributed by Universal Press Syndicate
JIM DAVIS 1-29
YOU THERE!... WITH THE ZITS!

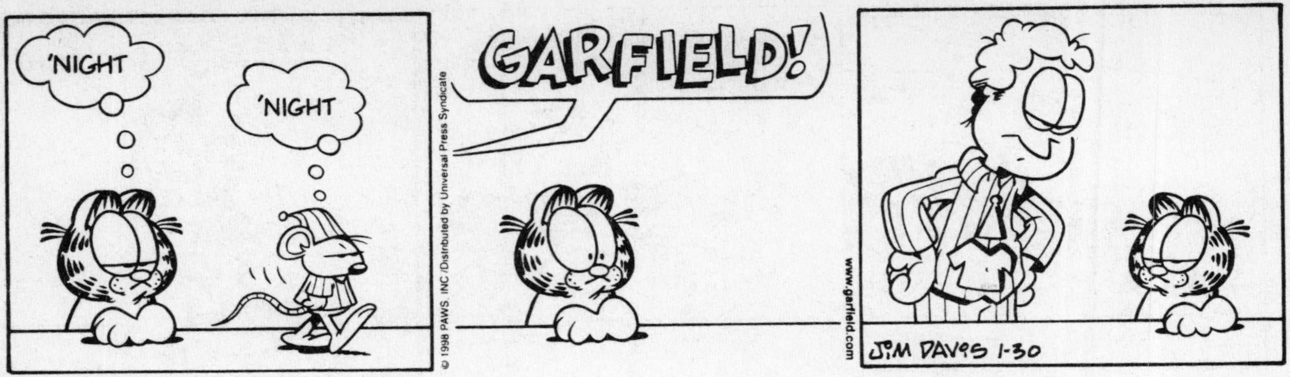
'NIGHT
'NIGHT
© 1998 PAWS, INC./Distributed by Universal Press Syndicate
GARFIELD!
www.garfield.com
JIM DAVIS 1-30

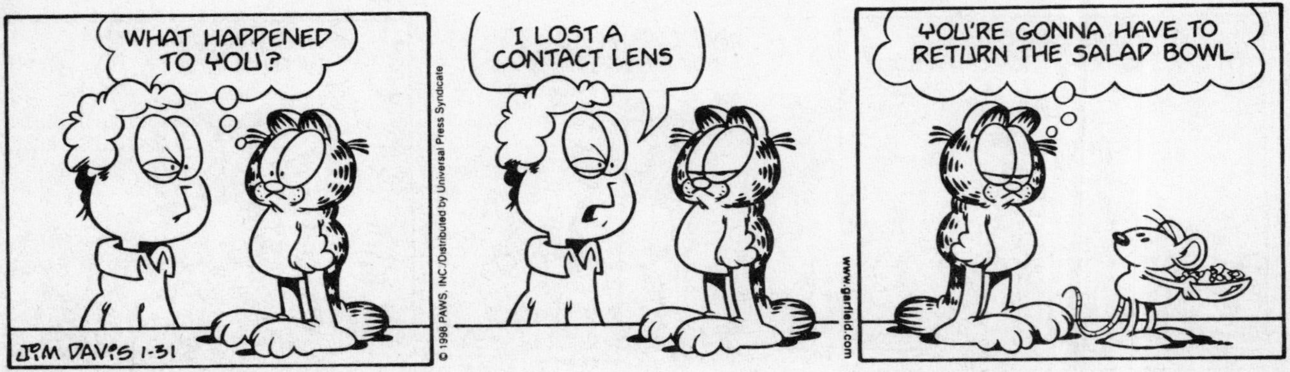
WHAT HAPPENED TO YOU?
JIM DAVIS 1-31
© 1998 PAWS, INC./Distributed by Universal Press Syndicate
I LOST A CONTACT LENS
www.garfield.com
YOU'RE GONNA HAVE TO RETURN THE SALAD BOWL

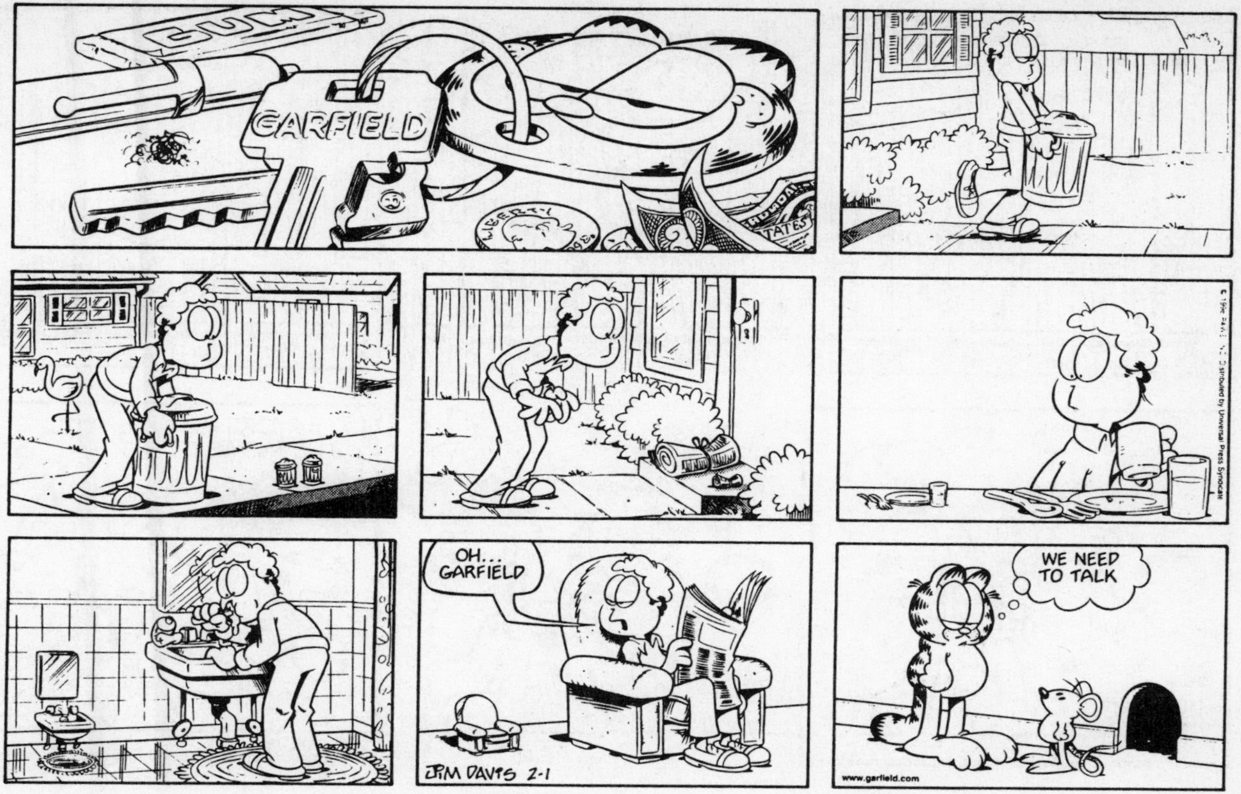
GUM
GARFIELD
OH... GARFIELD
JIM DAVIS 2-1
WE NEED TO TALK
www.garfield.com

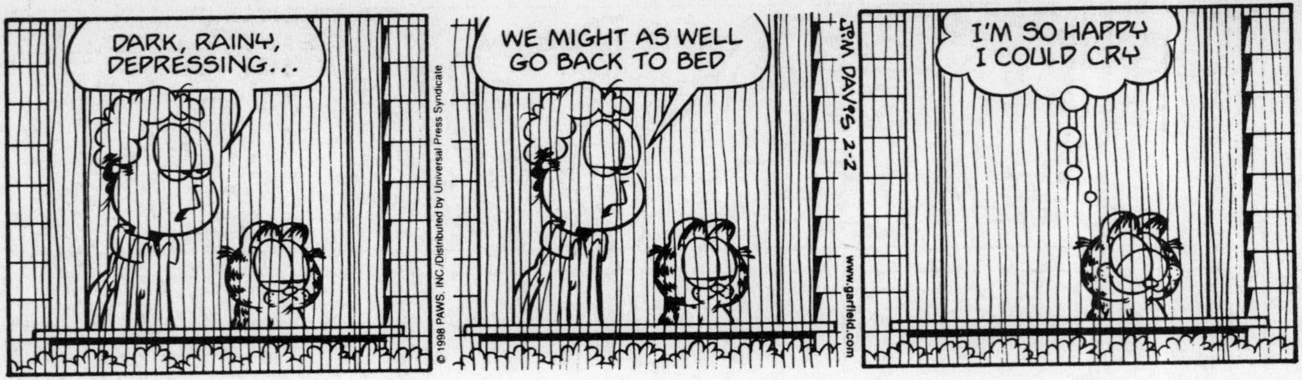
DARK, RAINY, DEPRESSING...
WE MIGHT AS WELL GO BACK TO BED
I'M SO HAPPY I COULD CRY
JIM DAVIS 2-2
www.garfield.com

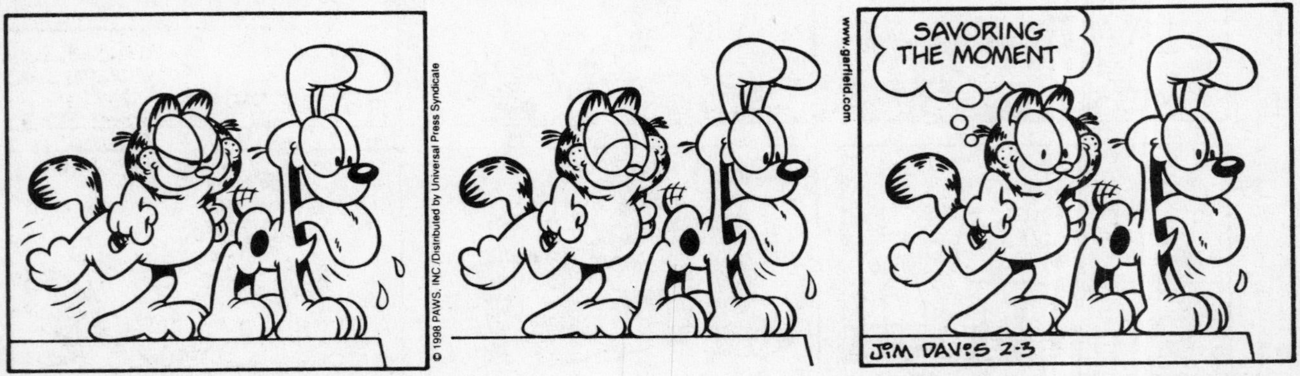
SAVORING THE MOMENT
JIM DAVIS 2-3
www.garfield.com

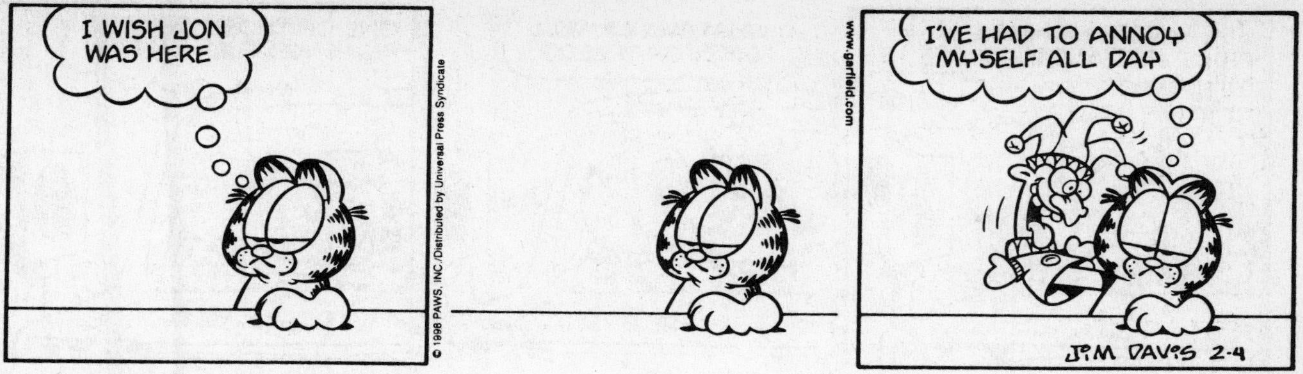
I WISH JON WAS HERE
© 1998 PAWS, INC./Distributed by Universal Press Syndicate
www.garfield.com
I'VE HAD TO ANNOY MYSELF ALL DAY
JIM DAVIS 2-4

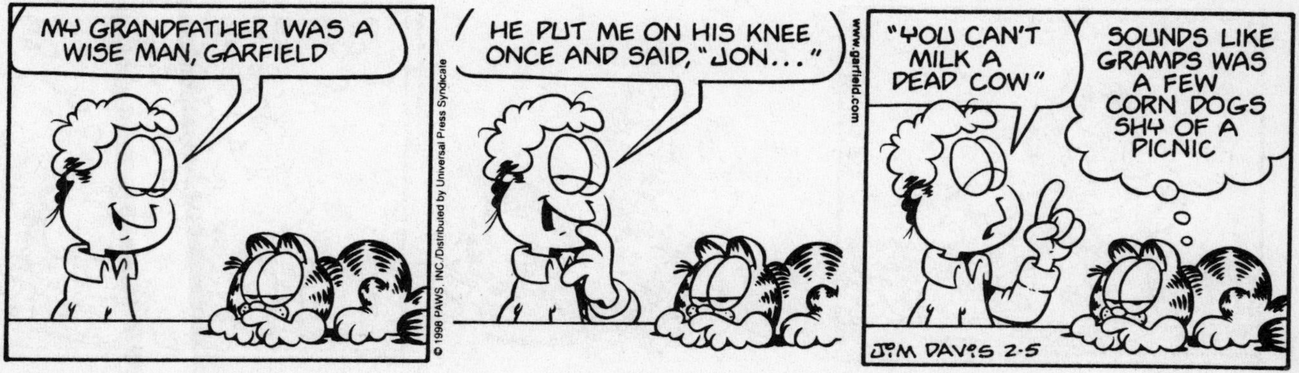
MY GRANDFATHER WAS A WISE MAN, GARFIELD
© 1998 PAWS, INC./Distributed by Universal Press Syndicate
HE PUT ME ON HIS KNEE ONCE AND SAID, "JON..."
www.garfield.com
"YOU CAN'T MILK A DEAD COW"
SOUNDS LIKE GRAMPS WAS A FEW CORN DOGS SHY OF A PICNIC
JIM DAVIS 2-5

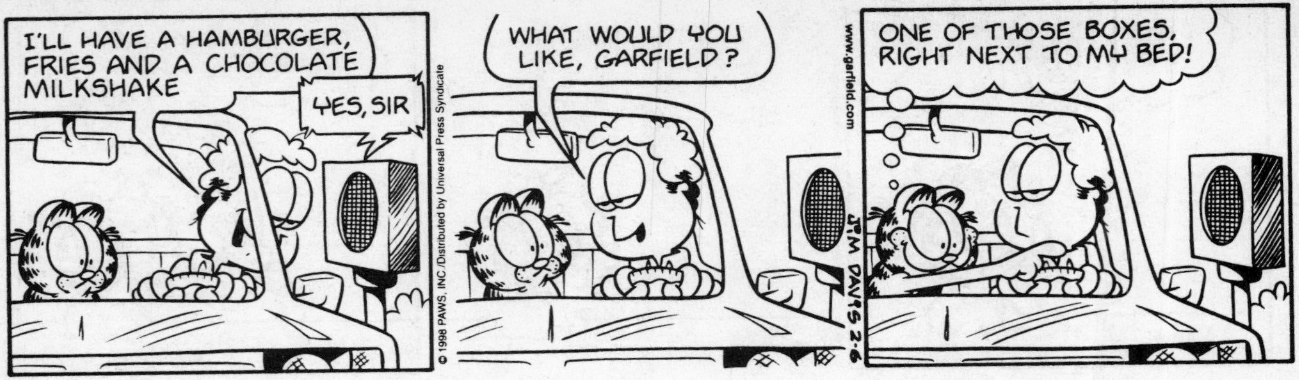
I'LL HAVE A HAMBURGER, FRIES AND A CHOCOLATE MILKSHAKE
YES, SIR
© 1998 PAWS, INC./Distributed by Universal Press Syndicate
WHAT WOULD YOU LIKE, GARFIELD?
www.garfield.com
JIM DAVIS 2-6
ONE OF THOSE BOXES, RIGHT NEXT TO MY BED!

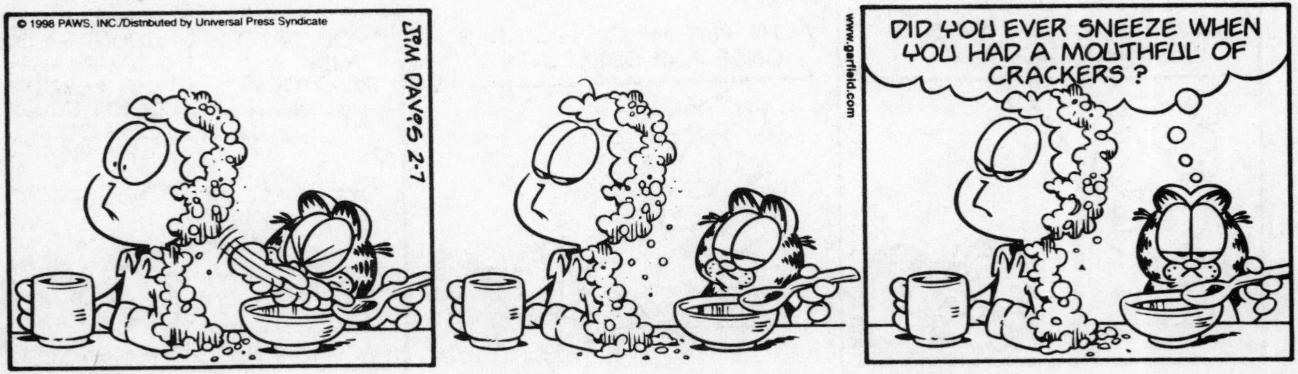
© 1998 PAWS, INC./Distributed by Universal Press Syndicate
JIM DAVIS 2-7
www.garfield.com
DID YOU EVER SNEEZE WHEN YOU HAD A MOUTHFUL OF CRACKERS?

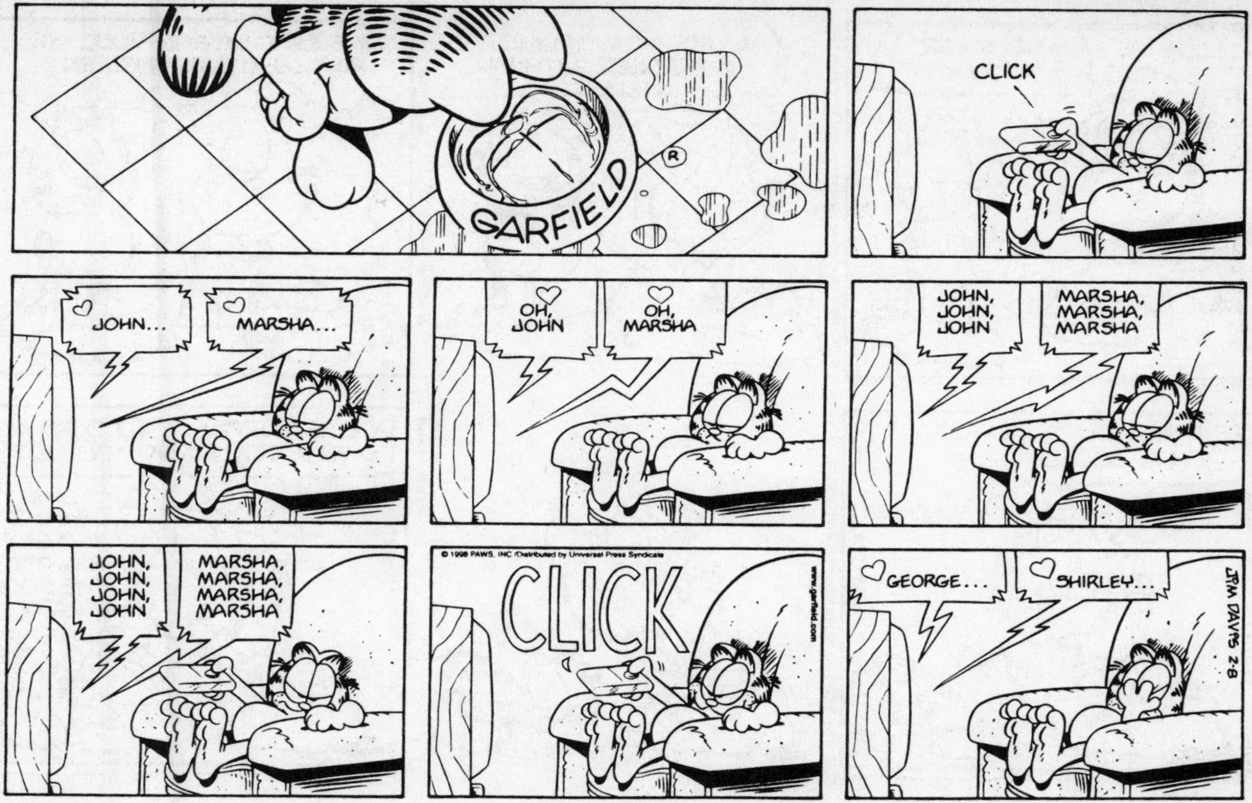
GARFIELD
CLICK
JOHN...
MARSHA...
OH, JOHN
OH, MARSHA
JOHN, JOHN, JOHN
MARSHA, MARSHA, MARSHA
JOHN, JOHN, JOHN, JOHN
MARSHA, MARSHA, MARSHA, MARSHA
© 1998 PAWS, INC./Distributed by Universal Press Syndicate
www.garfield.com
CLICK
GEORGE...
SHIRLEY...
JIM DAVIS 2-8

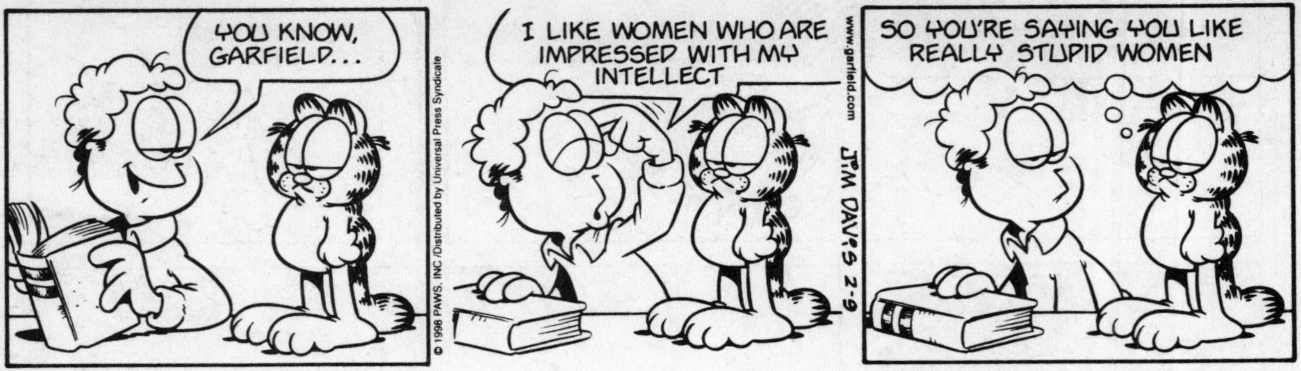
YOU KNOW, GARFIELD...
© 1998 PAWS, INC./Distributed by Universal Press Syndicate
I LIKE WOMEN WHO ARE IMPRESSED WITH MY INTELLECT
www.garfield.com
JIM DAVIS 2-9
SO YOU'RE SAYING YOU LIKE REALLY STUPID WOMEN

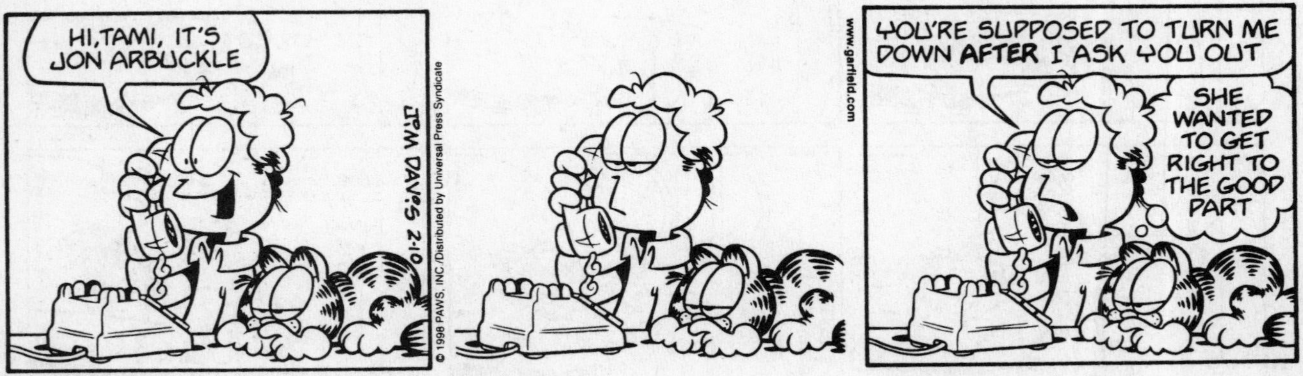
HI, TAMI, IT'S JON ARBUCKLE
© 1998 PAWS, INC./Distributed by Universal Press Syndicate
JIM DAVIS 2-10
www.garfield.com
YOU'RE SUPPOSED TO TURN ME DOWN AFTER I ASK YOU OUT
SHE WANTED TO GET RIGHT TO THE GOOD PART

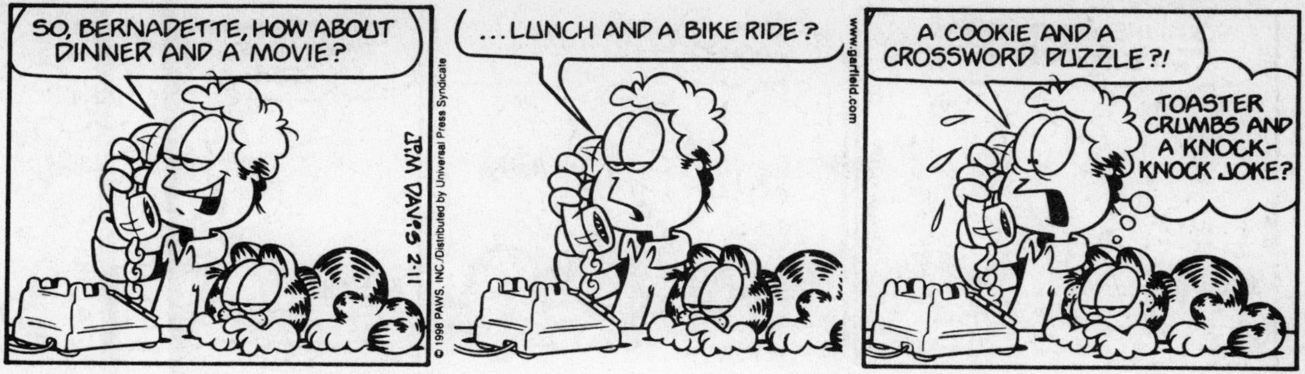
SO, BERNADETTE, HOW ABOUT DINNER AND A MOVIE?
JIM DAVIS 2-11
© 1998 PAWS, INC./Distributed by Universal Press Syndicate
...LUNCH AND A BIKE RIDE?
www.garfield.com
A COOKIE AND A CROSSWORD PUZZLE?!
TOASTER CRUMBS AND A KNOCK-KNOCK JOKE?

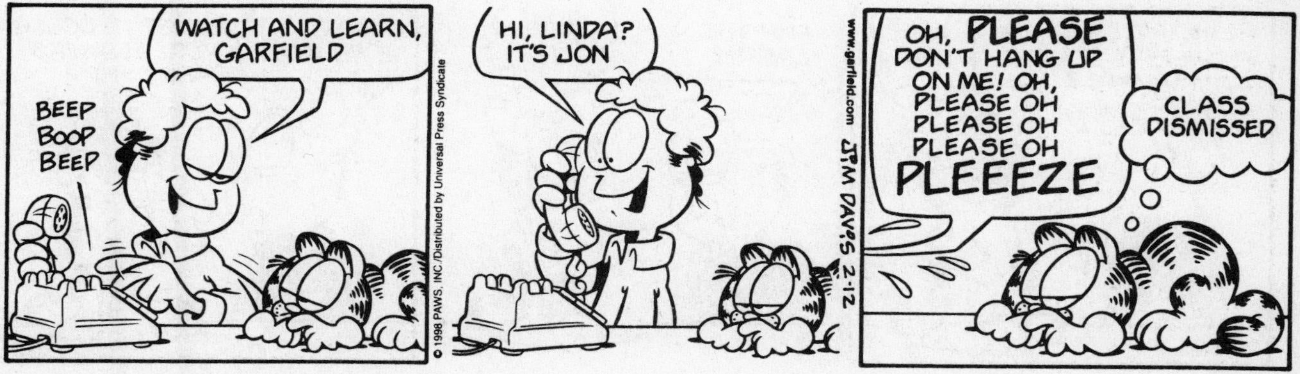
WATCH AND LEARN, GARFIELD
BEEP BOOP BEEP
© 1998 PAWS, INC./Distributed by Universal Press Syndicate
HI, LINDA? IT'S JON
www.garfield.com
JIM DAVIS 2-12
OH, PLEASE DON'T HANG UP ON ME! OH, PLEASE OH PLEASE OH PLEASE OH PLEEEZE
CLASS DISMISSED

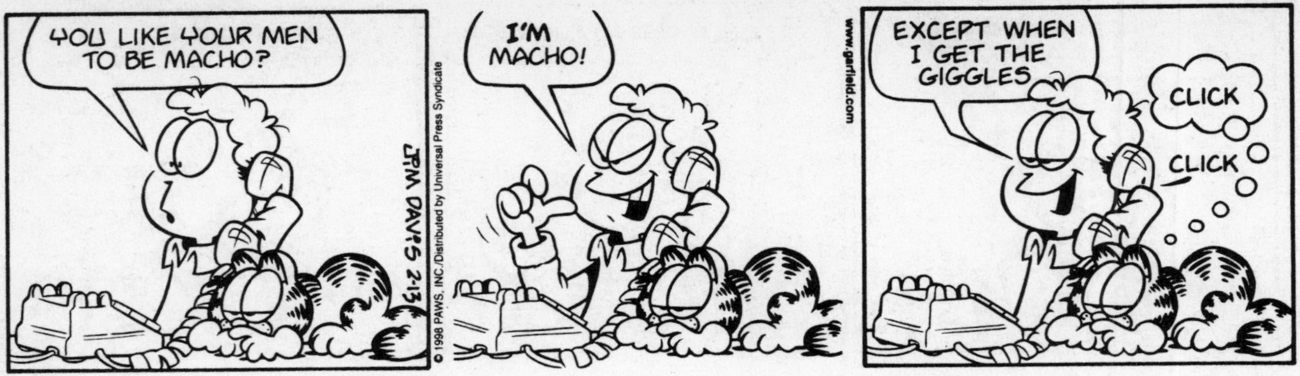

YOU LIKE YOUR MEN TO BE MACHO?
JIM DAVIS 2-13
© 1998 PAWS, INC./Distributed by Universal Press Syndicate
I'M MACHO!
www.garfield.com
EXCEPT WHEN I GET THE GIGGLES
CLICK
CLICK

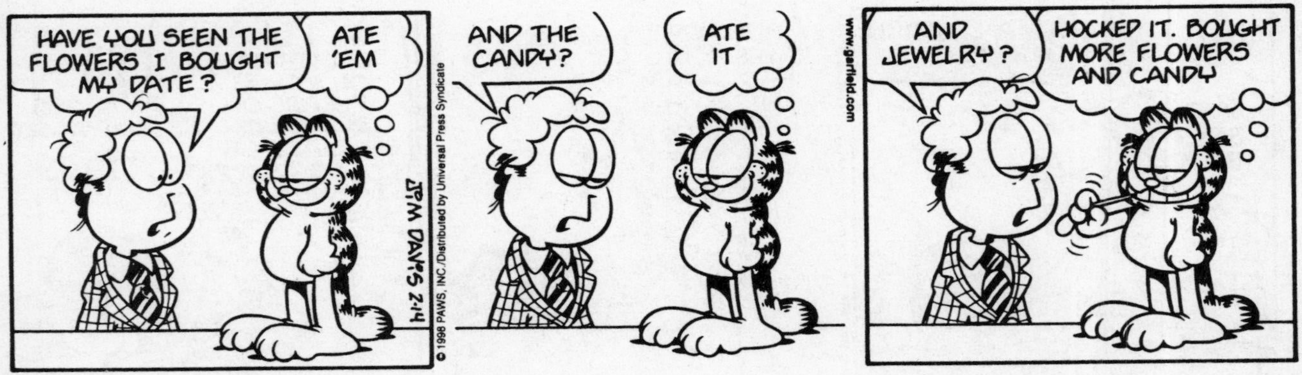

HAVE YOU SEEN THE FLOWERS I BOUGHT MY DATE?
ATE 'EM
JIM DAVIS 2-14
© 1998 PAWS, INC./Distributed by Universal Press Syndicate
AND THE CANDY?
ATE IT
www.garfield.com
AND JEWELRY?
HOCKED IT. BOUGHT MORE FLOWERS AND CANDY

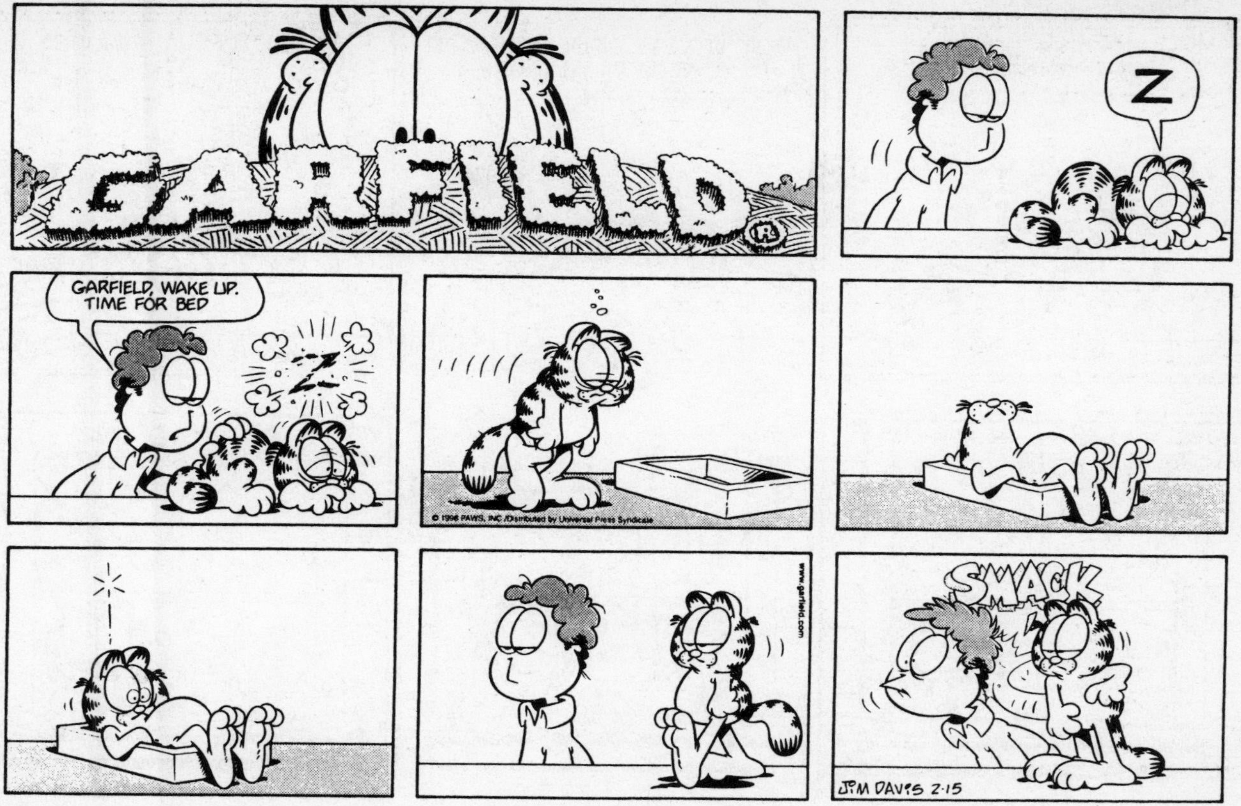
GARFIELD
Z
GARFIELD, WAKE UP. TIME FOR BED
Z
© 1998 PAWS, INC./Distributed by Universal Press Syndicate
www.garfield.com
SMACK
JIM DAVIS 2-15

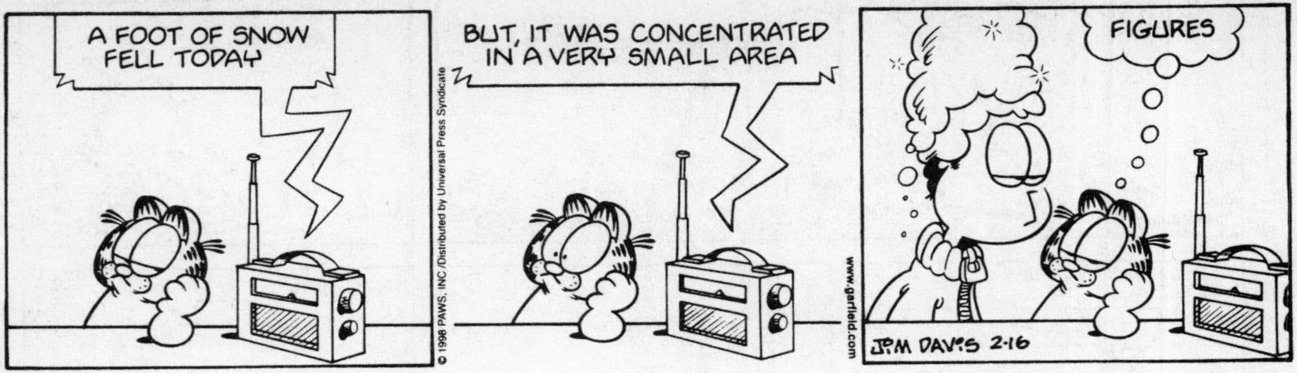
A FOOT OF SNOW FELL TODAY
BUT, IT WAS CONCENTRATED IN A VERY SMALL AREA
FIGURES
JIM DAVIS 2·16
© 1998 PAWS, INC./Distributed by Universal Press Syndicate
www.garfield.com

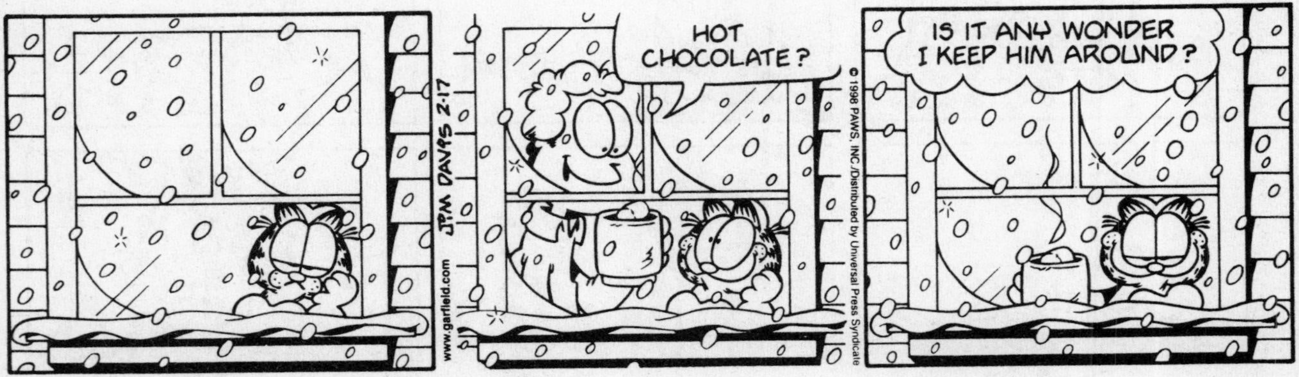
HOT CHOCOLATE?
IS IT ANY WONDER I KEEP HIM AROUND?
JIM DAVIS 2·17
www.garfield.com
© 1998 PAWS, INC./Distributed by Universal Press Syndicate

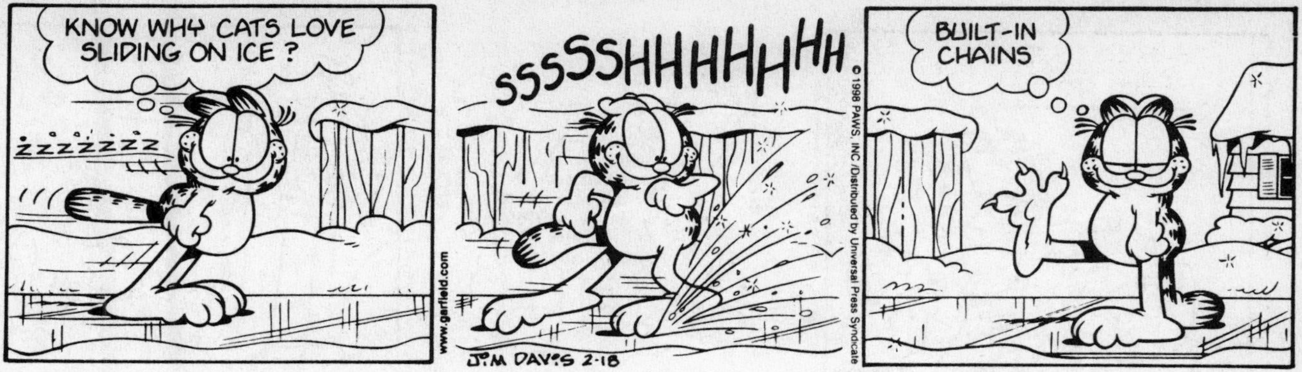
KNOW WHY CATS LOVE SLIDING ON ICE ?
ZZZZZZZ
SSSSSHHHHHHHH
BUILT-IN CHAINS
JIM DAVIS 2-18
www.garfield.com
© 1998 PAWS, INC./Distributed by Universal Press Syndicate

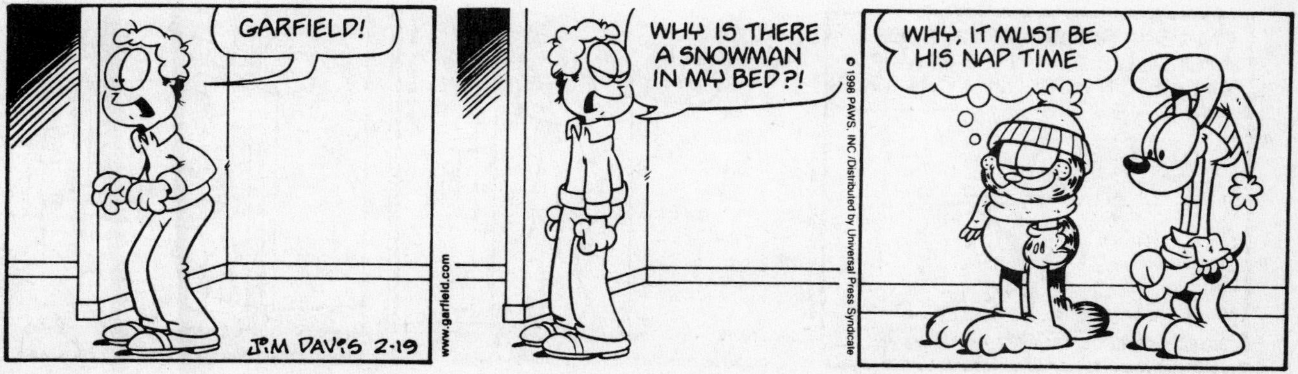
GARFIELD!
WHY IS THERE A SNOWMAN IN MY BED?!
WHY, IT MUST BE HIS NAP TIME
JIM DAVIS 2-19
www.garfield.com
© 1998 PAWS, INC./Distributed by Universal Press Syndicate

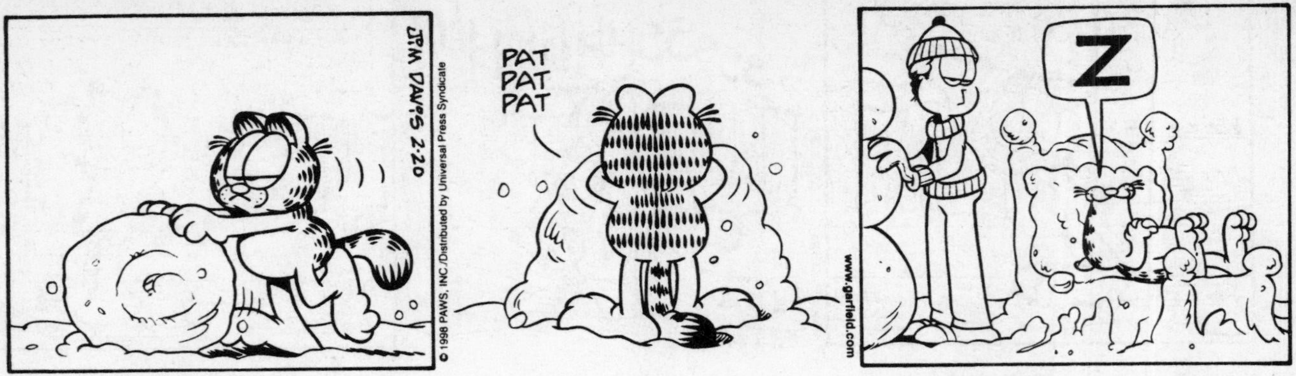
JIM DAVIS 2-20
© 1998 PAWS, INC./Distributed by Universal Press Syndicate
PAT
PAT
PAT
www.garfield.com
Z

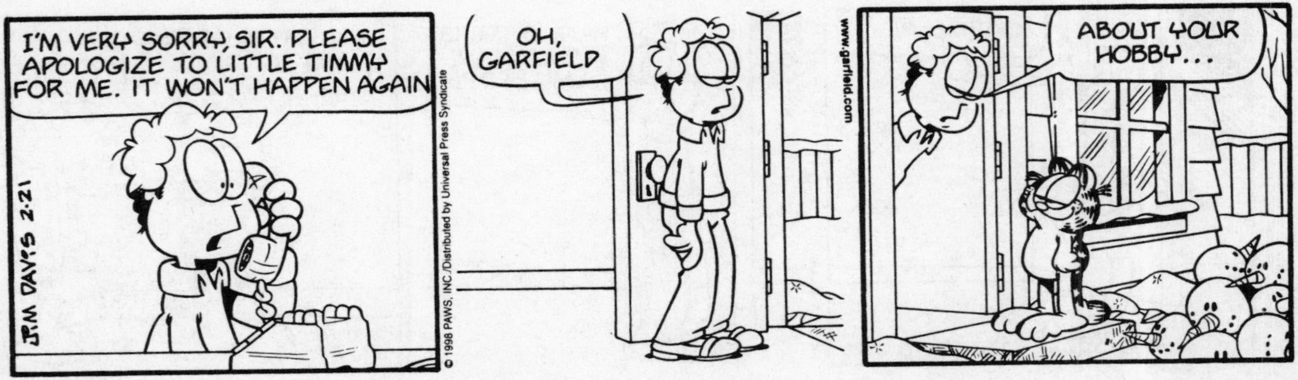
I'M VERY SORRY, SIR. PLEASE APOLOGIZE TO LITTLE TIMMY FOR ME. IT WON'T HAPPEN AGAIN
JIM DAVIS 2-21
© 1998 PAWS, INC./Distributed by Universal Press Syndicate
OH, GARFIELD
www.garfield.com
ABOUT YOUR HOBBY...

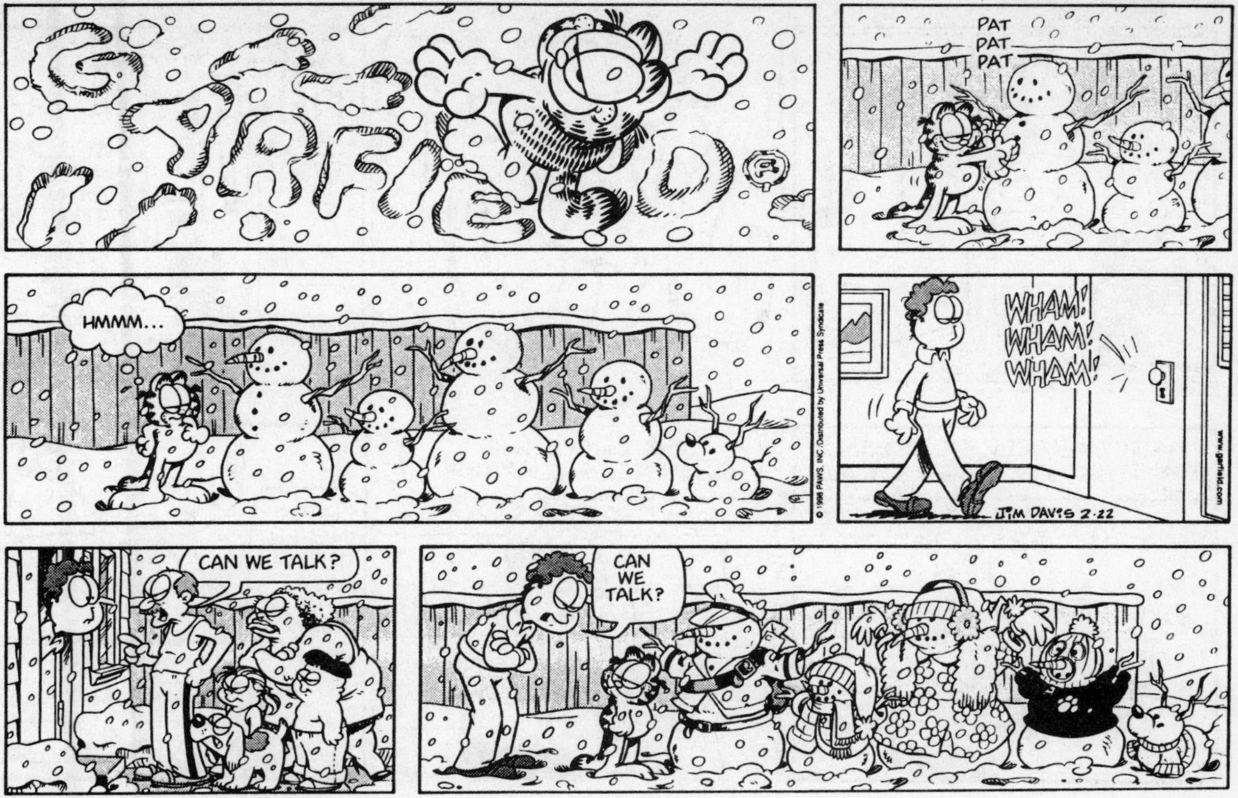
GARFIELD®
PAT
PAT
PAT
HMMM...
© 1998 PAWS, INC./Distributed by Universal Press Syndicate
WHAM!
WHAM!
WHAM!
JIM DAVIS 2-22
www.garfield.com
CAN WE TALK?
CAN WE TALK?

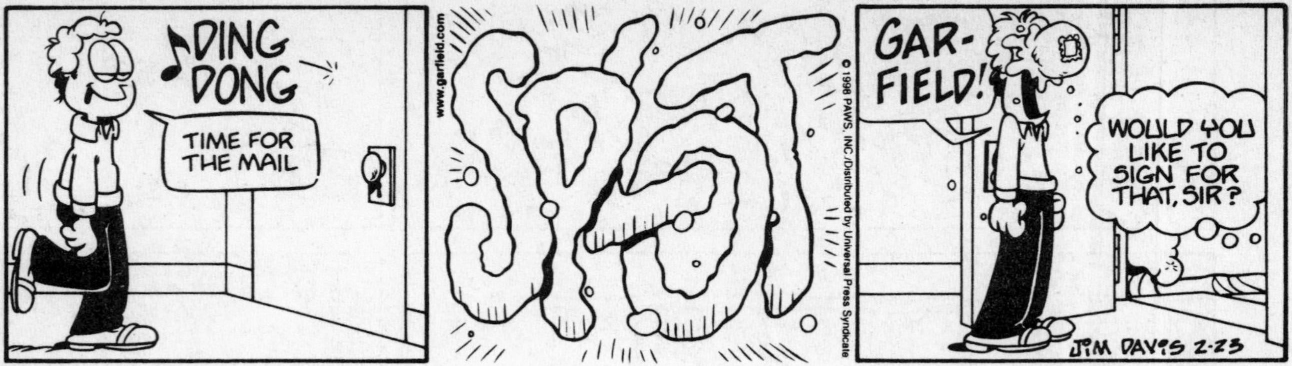
DING DONG
TIME FOR THE MAIL
www.garfield.com
© 1998 PAWS, INC./Distributed by Universal Press Syndicate
GAR-FIELD!
WOULD YOU LIKE TO SIGN FOR THAT, SIR?
JIM DAVIS 2-23

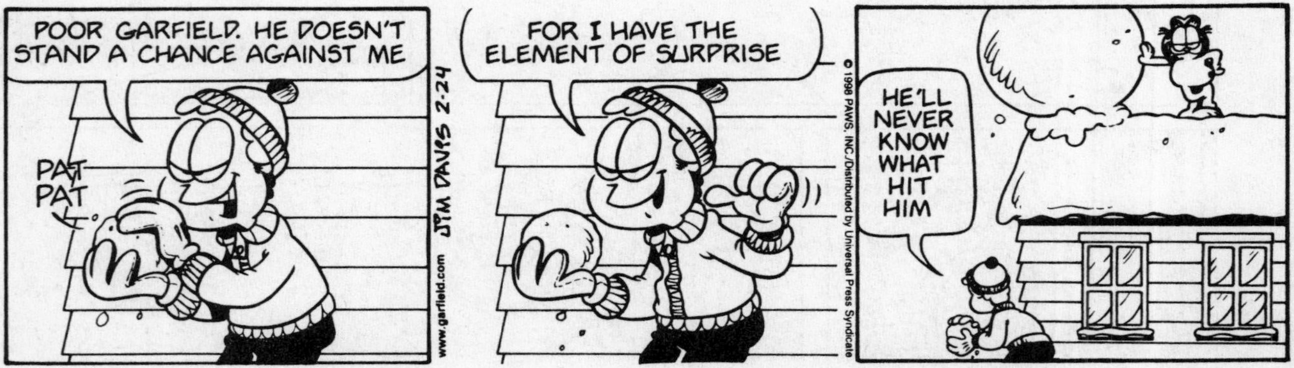
POOR GARFIELD. HE DOESN'T STAND A CHANCE AGAINST ME
PAT PAT
JIM DAVIS 2-24
www.garfield.com
FOR I HAVE THE ELEMENT OF SURPRISE
© 1998 PAWS, INC./Distributed by Universal Press Syndicate
HE'LL NEVER KNOW WHAT HIT HIM

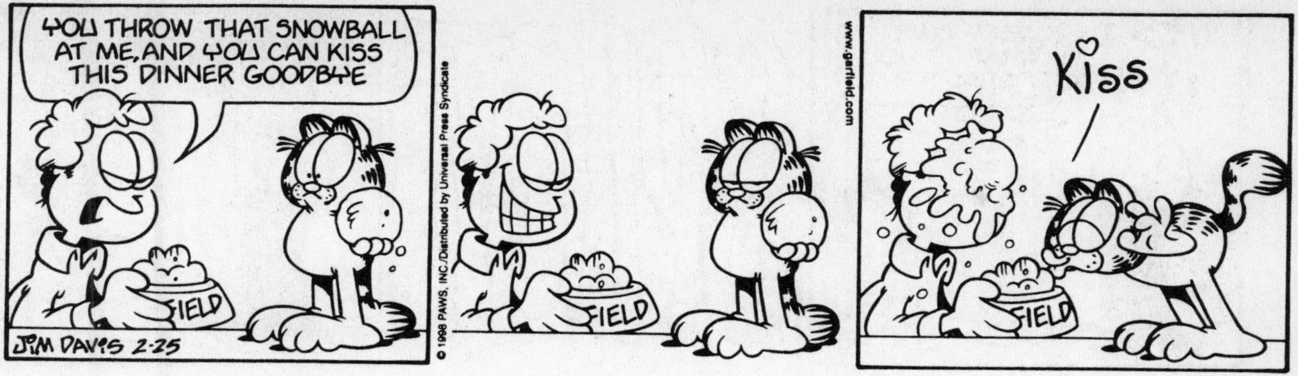
YOU THROW THAT SNOWBALL AT ME, AND YOU CAN KISS THIS DINNER GOODBYE
JIM DAVIS 2-25
KISS

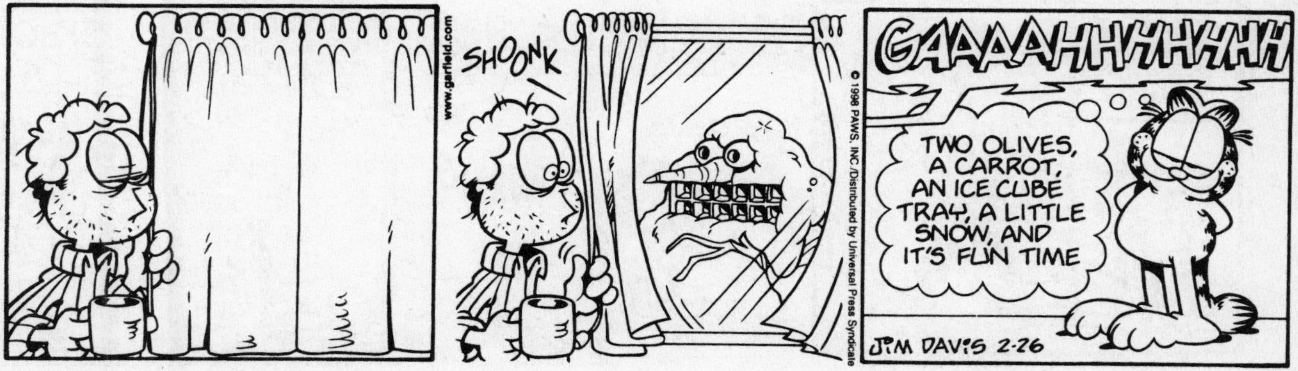
SHOONK
GAAAAHHHHHHH
TWO OLIVES, A CARROT, AN ICE CUBE TRAY, A LITTLE SNOW, AND IT'S FUN TIME
JIM DAVIS 2-26

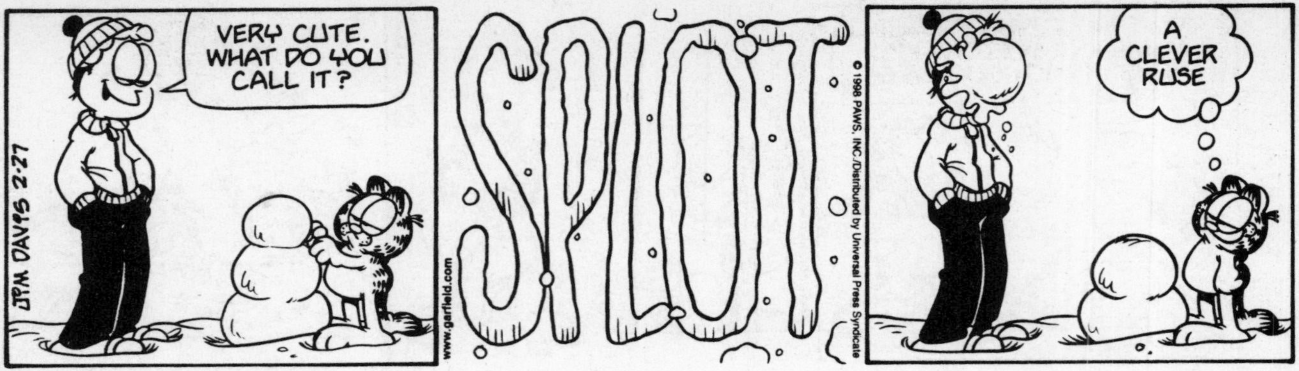
JIM DAVIS 2-27
VERY CUTE. WHAT DO YOU CALL IT?
SPLOT
A CLEVER RUSE
www.garfield.com
© 1998 PAWS, INC./Distributed by Universal Press Syndicate

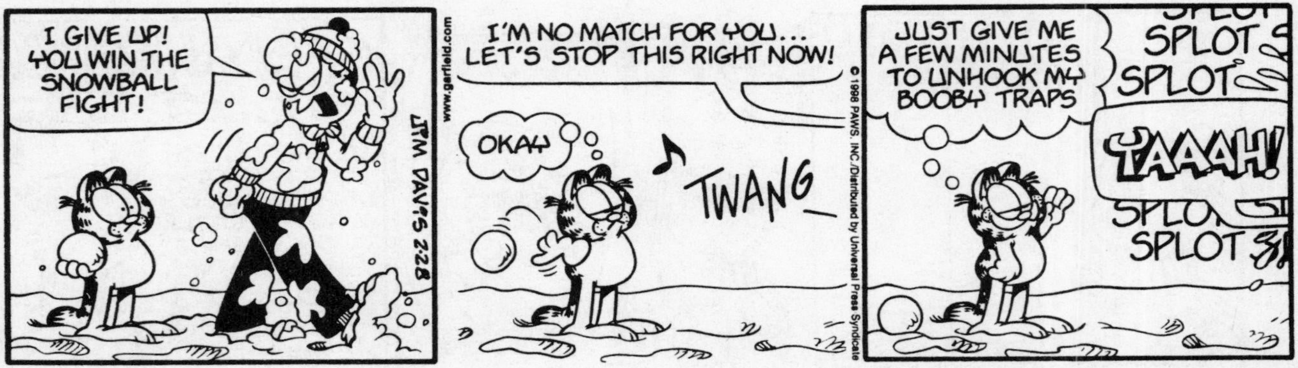
I GIVE UP! YOU WIN THE SNOWBALL FIGHT!
JIM DAVIS 2-28
www.garfield.com
I'M NO MATCH FOR YOU... LET'S STOP THIS RIGHT NOW!
OKAY
TWANG
© 1998 PAWS, INC./Distributed by Universal Press Syndicate
JUST GIVE ME A FEW MINUTES TO UNHOOK MY BOOBY TRAPS
SPLOT
SPLOT
YAAAH!
SPLOT

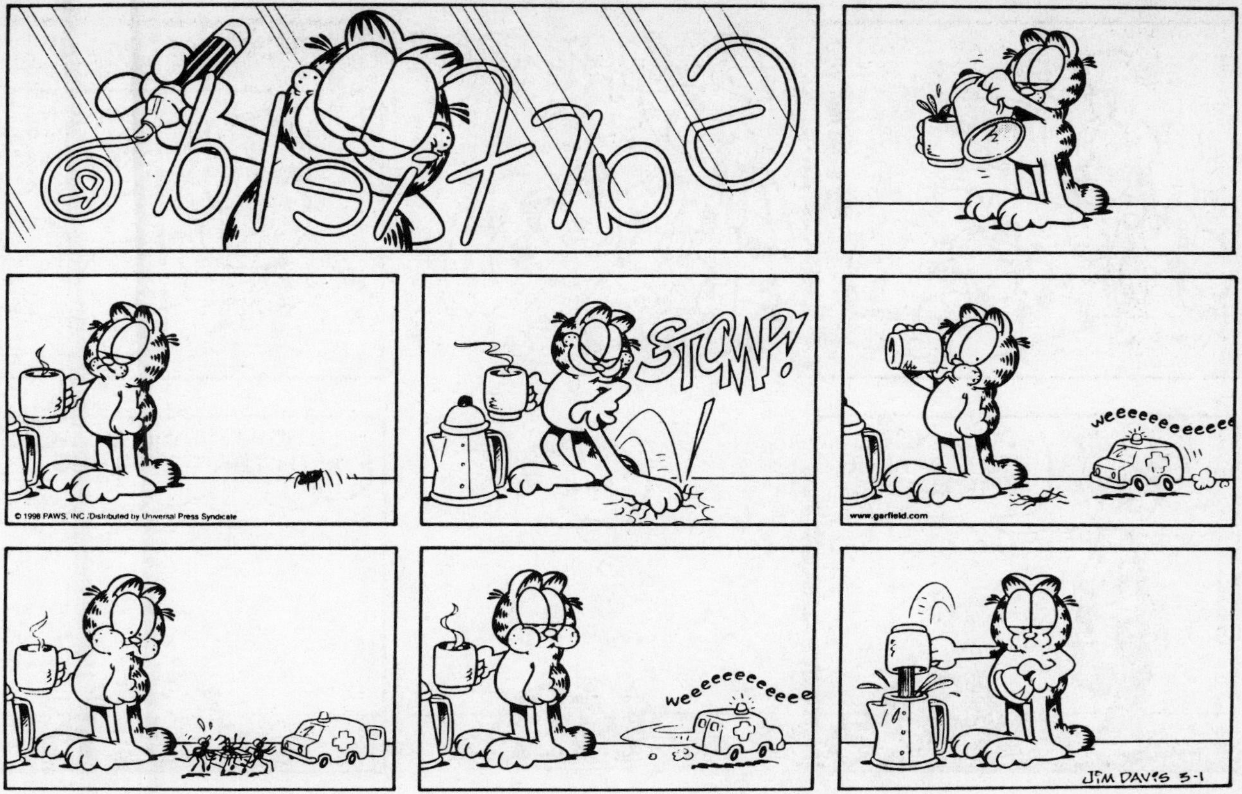
STOMP!
© 1998 PAWS, INC./Distributed by Universal Press Syndicate
www.garfield.com
weeeeeeeeeeee
weeeeeeeeeeee
JIM DAVIS 3-1

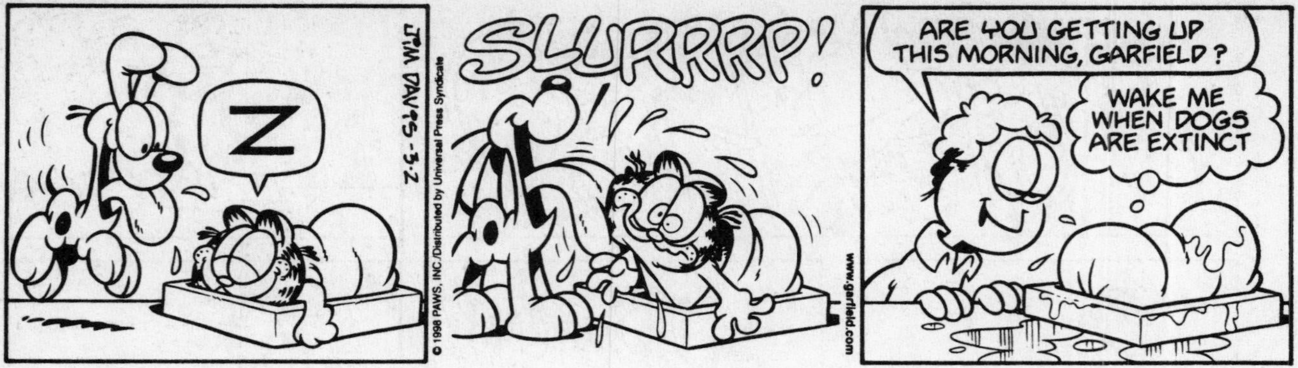
Z
JIM DAVIS 3-2
© 1998 PAWS, INC./Distributed by Universal Press Syndicate
SLURRRP!
www.garfield.com
ARE YOU GETTING UP THIS MORNING, GARFIELD?
WAKE ME WHEN DOGS ARE EXTINCT

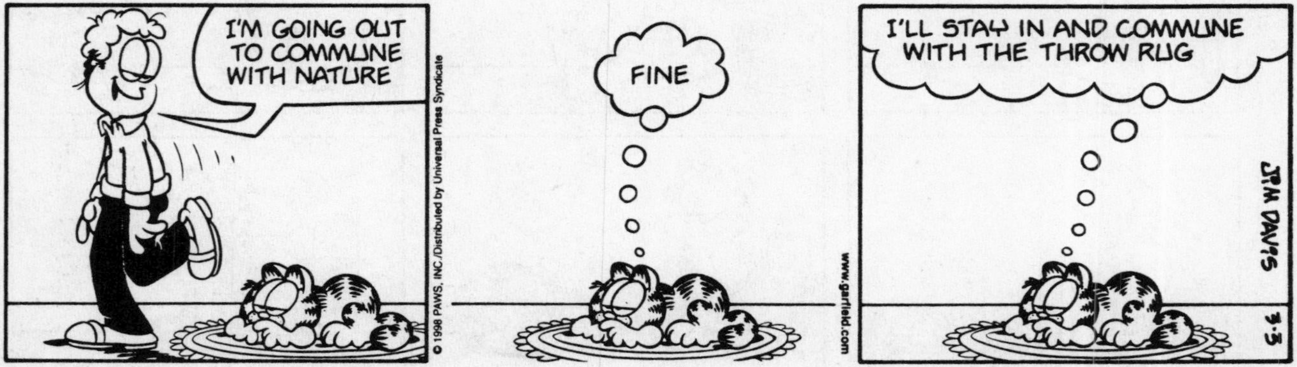
I'M GOING OUT TO COMMUNE WITH NATURE
© 1998 PAWS, INC./Distributed by Universal Press Syndicate
FINE
www.garfield.com
I'LL STAY IN AND COMMUNE WITH THE THROW RUG
JIM DAVIS 3-3

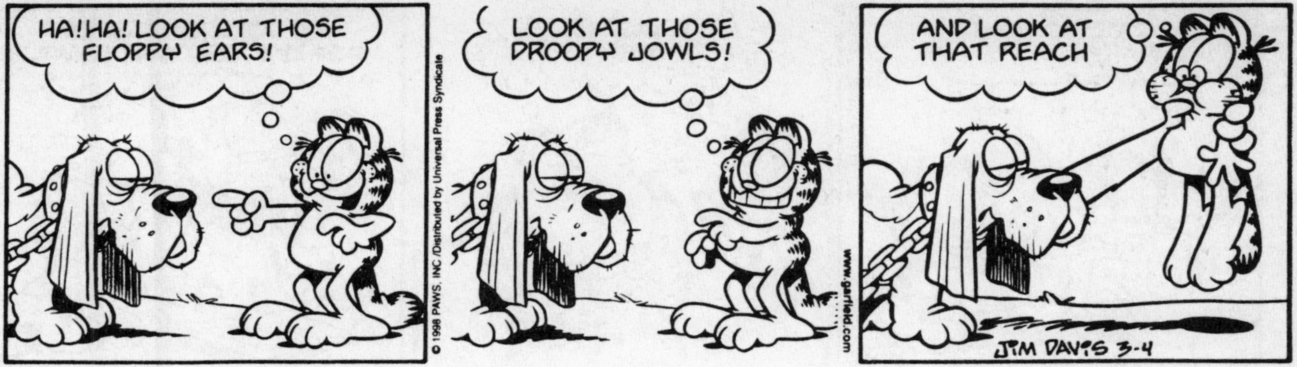
HA! HA! LOOK AT THOSE FLOPPY EARS!
© 1998 PAWS, INC./Distributed by Universal Press Syndicate
LOOK AT THOSE DROOPY JOWLS!
www.garfield.com
AND LOOK AT THAT REACH
JIM DAVIS 3-4

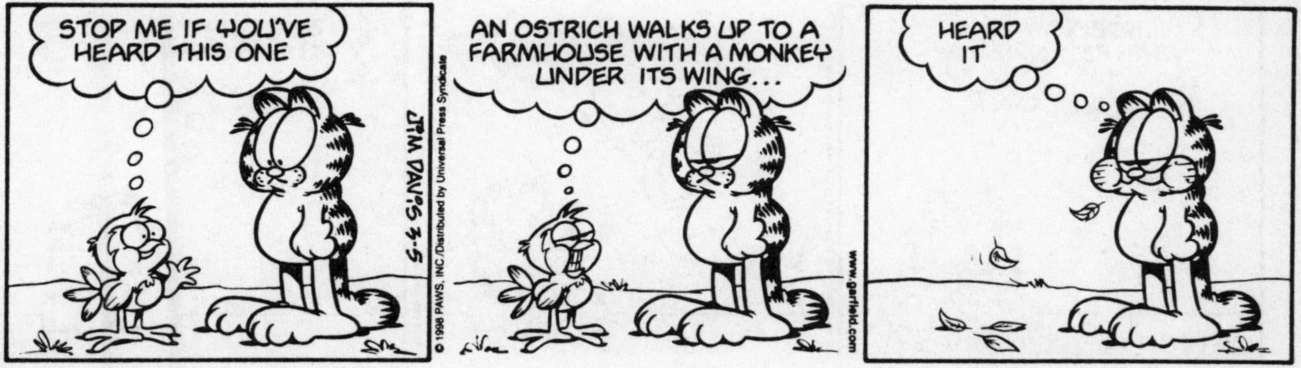
STOP ME IF YOU'VE HEARD THIS ONE
JIM DAVIS 3-5
© 1998 PAWS, INC./Distributed by Universal Press Syndicate
AN OSTRICH WALKS UP TO A FARMHOUSE WITH A MONKEY UNDER ITS WING...
www.garfield.com
HEARD IT

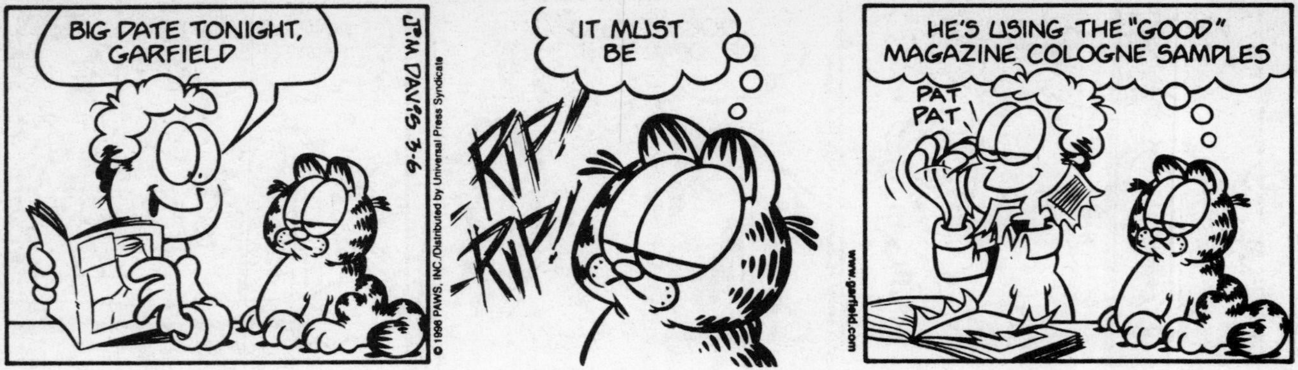
BIG DATE TONIGHT, GARFIELD
JIM DAVIS 3-6
© 1998 PAWS, INC./Distributed by Universal Press Syndicate
IT MUST BE
RIP!
RIP!
www.garfield.com
HE'S USING THE "GOOD" MAGAZINE COLOGNE SAMPLES
PAT PAT

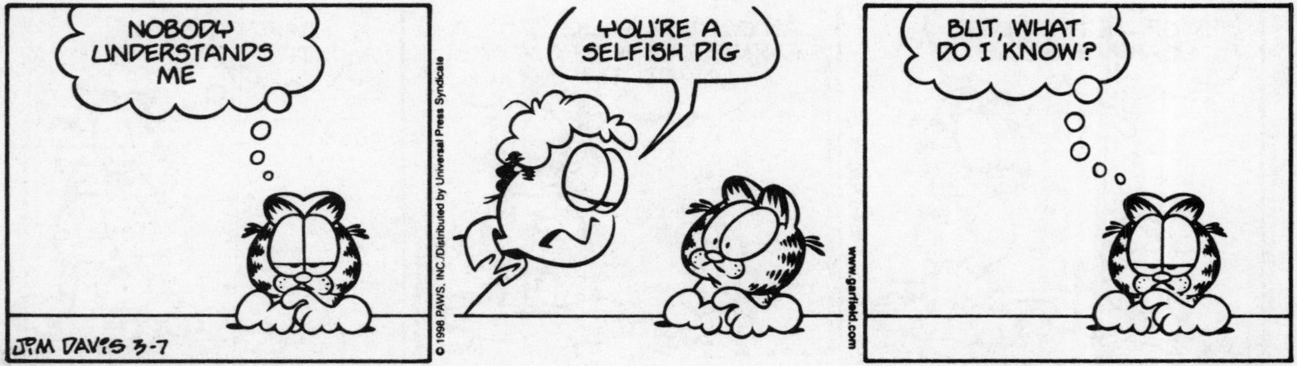
NOBODY UNDERSTANDS ME
JIM DAVIS 3-7
© 1998 PAWS, INC./Distributed by Universal Press Syndicate
YOU'RE A SELFISH PIG
www.garfield.com
BUT, WHAT DO I KNOW?

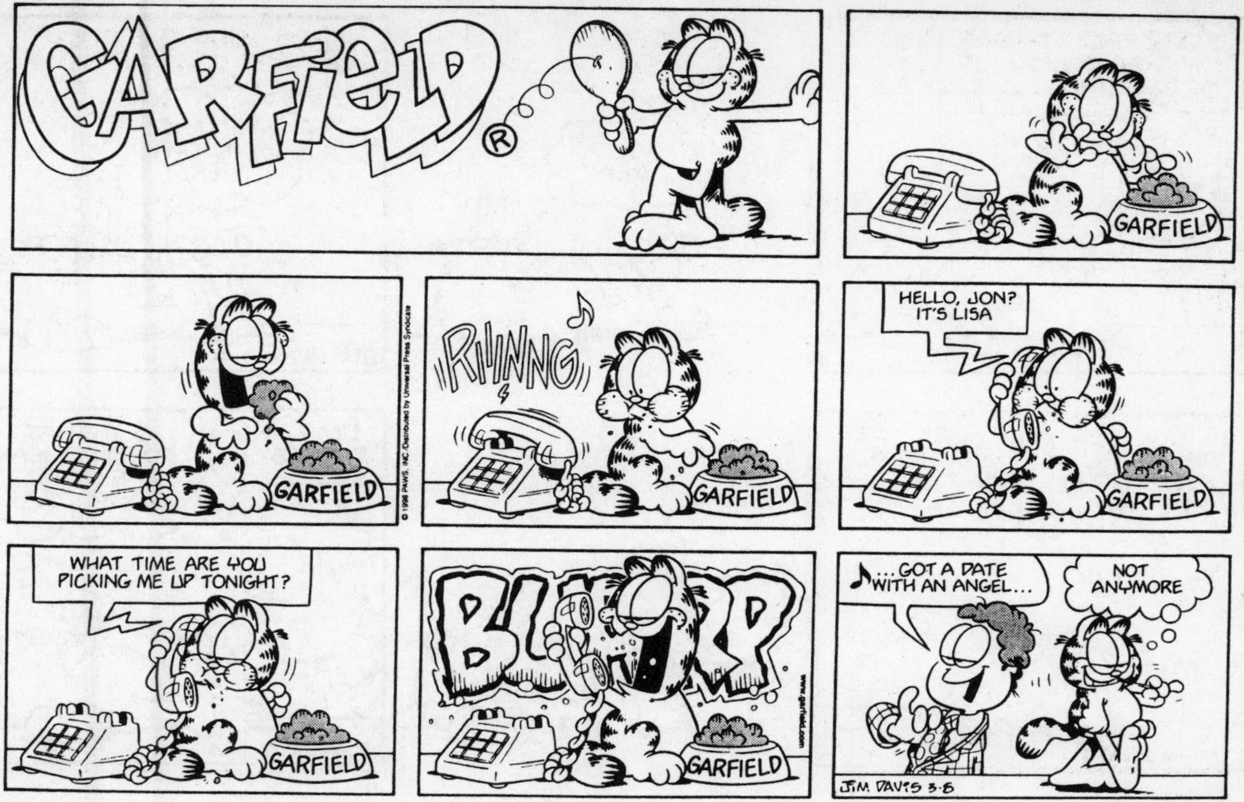
GARFIELD
© 1998 PAWS, INC./Distributed by Universal Press Syndicate
RIIINNG
HELLO, JON? IT'S LISA
WHAT TIME ARE YOU PICKING ME UP TONIGHT?
www.garfield.com
♪ ...GOT A DATE WITH AN ANGEL...
NOT ANYMORE
JIM DAVIS 3-8

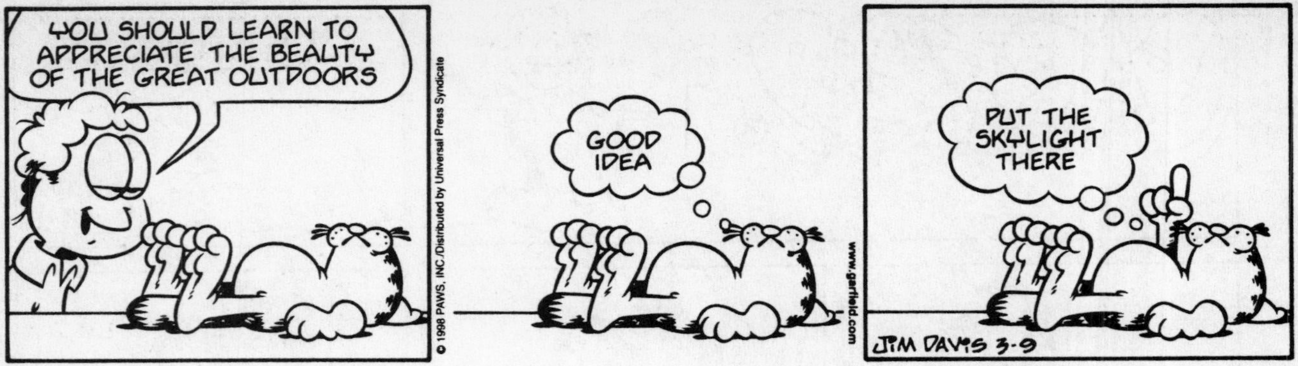
YOU SHOULD LEARN TO APPRECIATE THE BEAUTY OF THE GREAT OUTDOORS
GOOD IDEA
PUT THE SKYLIGHT THERE
JIM DAVIS 3-9

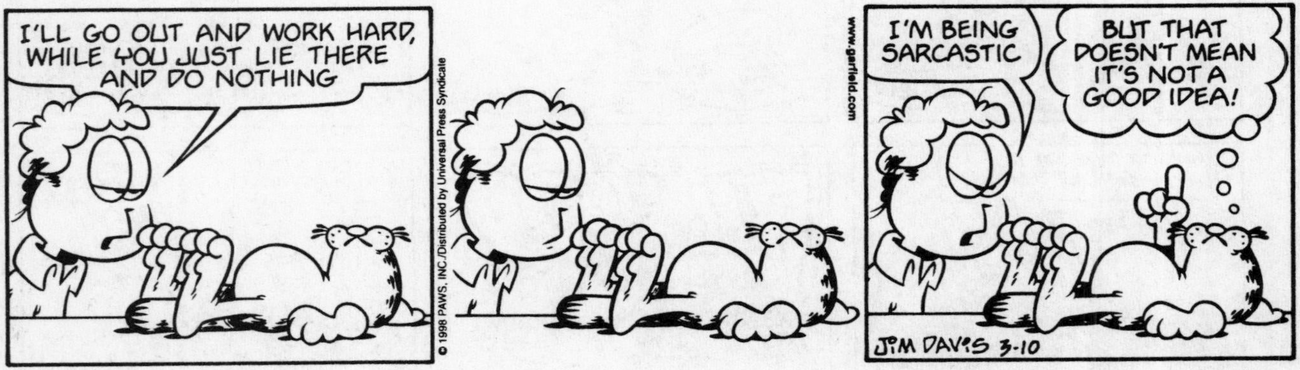
I'LL GO OUT AND WORK HARD, WHILE YOU JUST LIE THERE AND DO NOTHING
I'M BEING SARCASTIC
BUT THAT DOESN'T MEAN IT'S NOT A GOOD IDEA!
JIM DAVIS 3-10

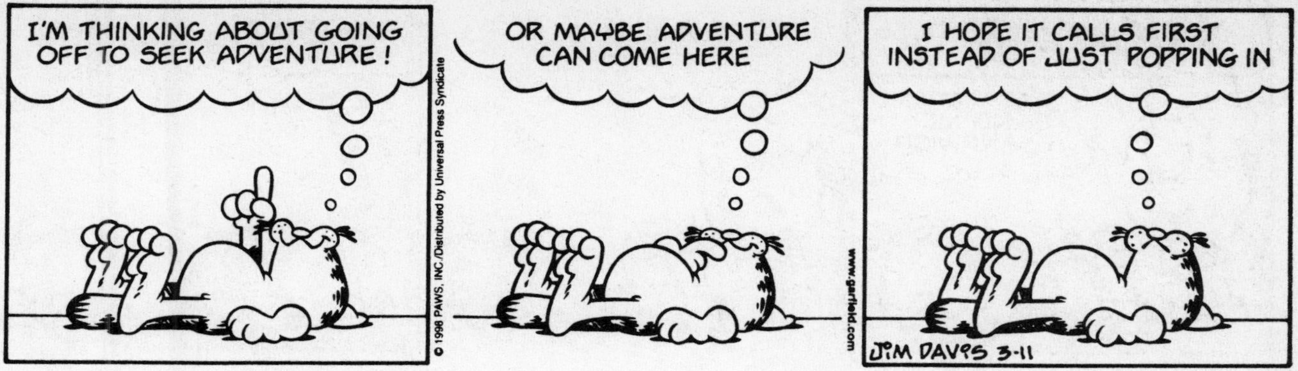
I'M THINKING ABOUT GOING OFF TO SEEK ADVENTURE!
© 1998 PAWS, INC./Distributed by Universal Press Syndicate
OR MAYBE ADVENTURE CAN COME HERE
www.garfield.com
I HOPE IT CALLS FIRST INSTEAD OF JUST POPPING IN
JIM DAVIS 3-11

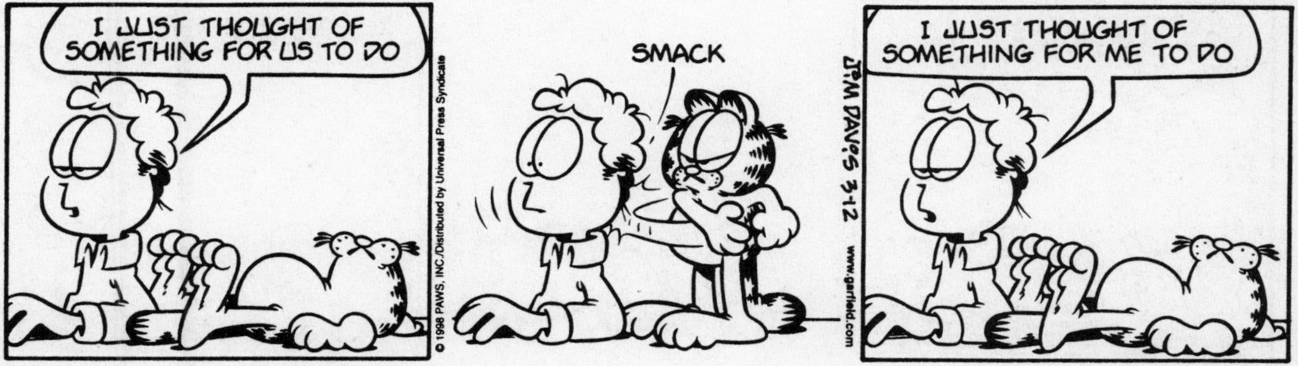
I JUST THOUGHT OF SOMETHING FOR US TO DO
© 1998 PAWS, INC./Distributed by Universal Press Syndicate
SMACK
JIM DAVIS 3-12
www.garfield.com
I JUST THOUGHT OF SOMETHING FOR ME TO DO

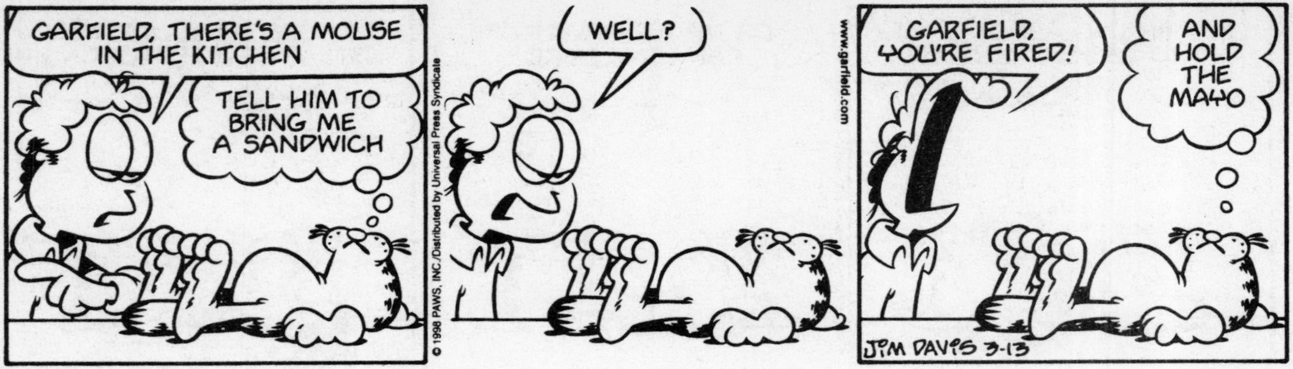
GARFIELD, THERE'S A MOUSE IN THE KITCHEN
TELL HIM TO BRING ME A SANDWICH
© 1998 PAWS, INC./Distributed by Universal Press Syndicate
WELL?
www.garfield.com
GARFIELD, YOU'RE FIRED!
AND HOLD THE MAYO
JIM DAVIS 3-13

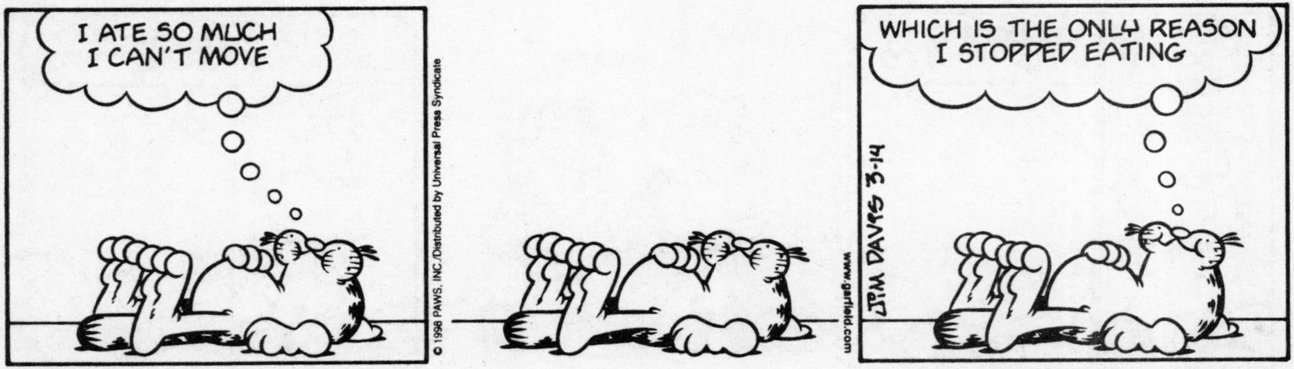
I ATE SO MUCH I CAN'T MOVE
© 1998 PAWS, INC./Distributed by Universal Press Syndicate
www.garfield.com
JIM DAVIS 3-14
WHICH IS THE ONLY REASON I STOPPED EATING

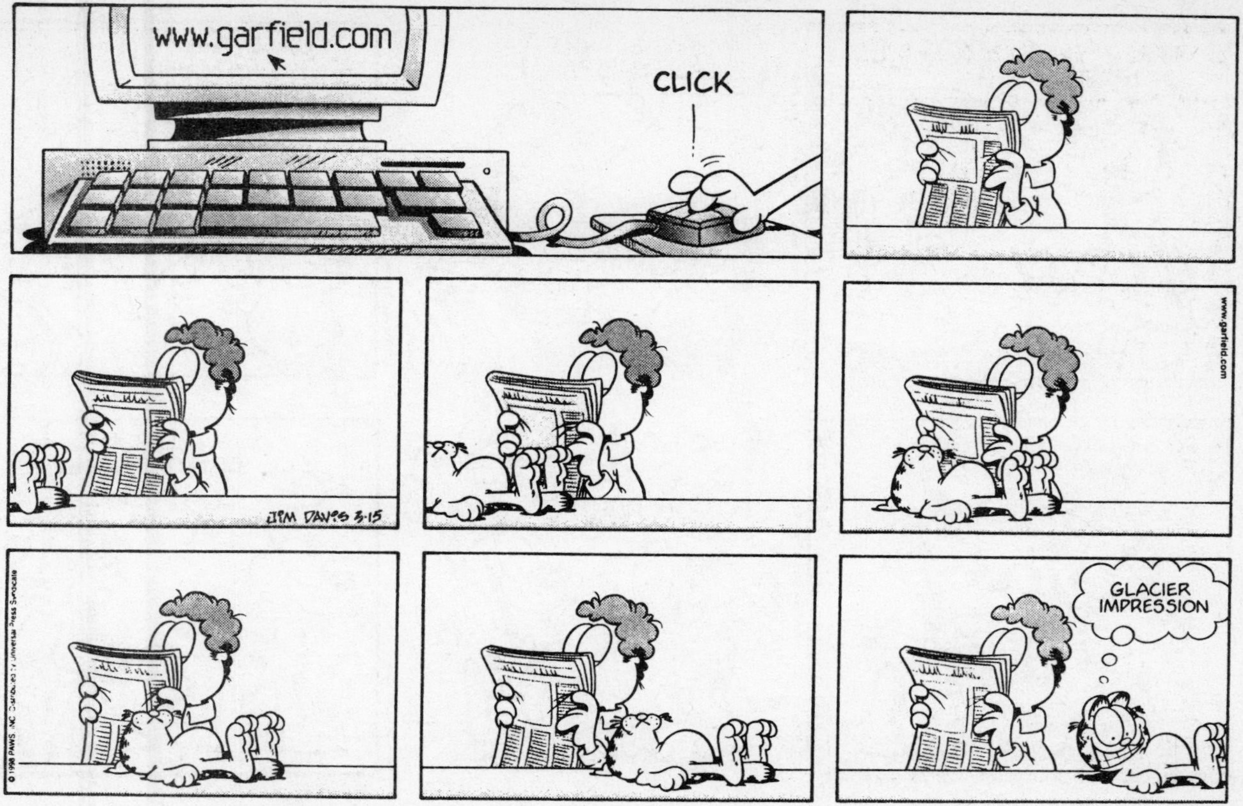
www.garfield.com
CLICK
JIM DAVIS 3-15
www.garfield.com
© 1998 PAWS, INC Distributed by Universal Press Syndicate
GLACIER IMPRESSION

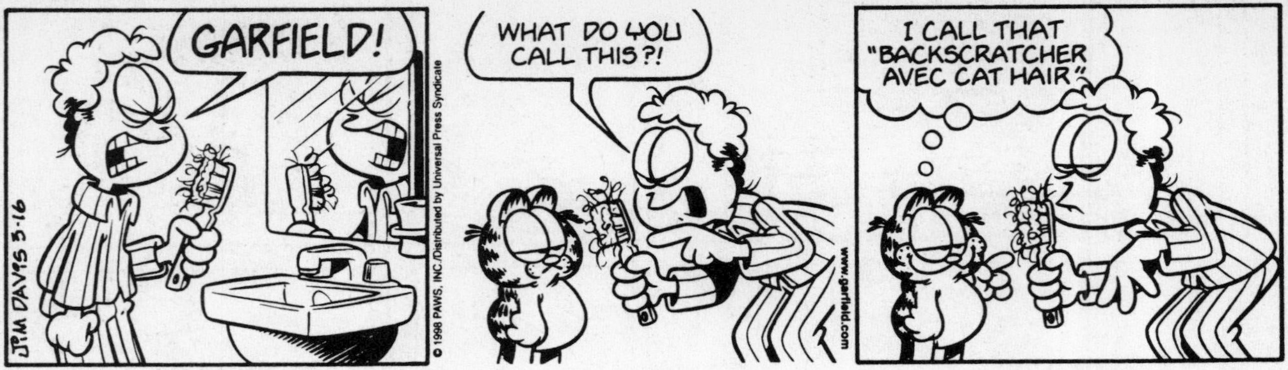
GARFIELD!
WHAT DO YOU CALL THIS?!
I CALL THAT "BACKSCRATCHER AVEC CAT HAIR"
JIM DAVIS 3-16
© 1998 PAWS, INC./Distributed by Universal Press Syndicate
www.garfield.com

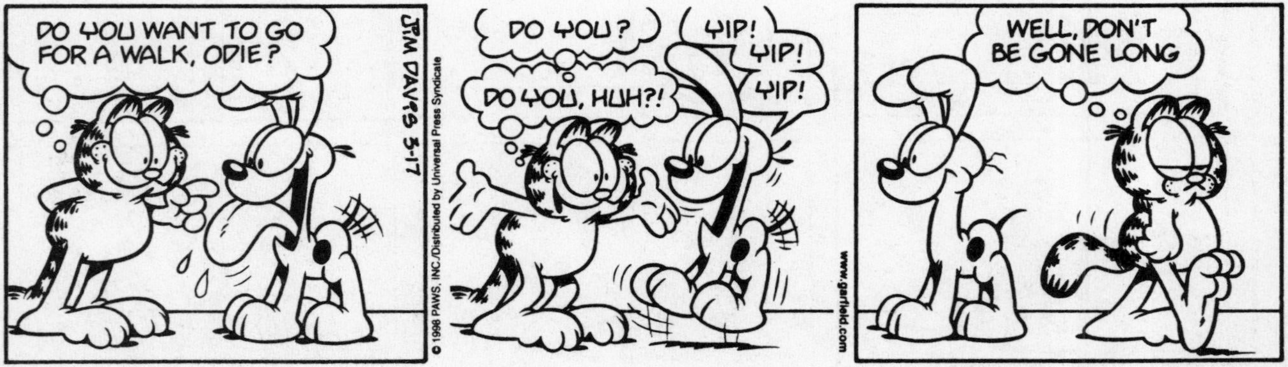
DO YOU WANT TO GO FOR A WALK, ODIE?
DO YOU?
DO YOU, HUH?!
YIP!
YIP!
YIP!
WELL, DON'T BE GONE LONG
JIM DAVIS 3-17
© 1998 PAWS, INC./Distributed by Universal Press Syndicate
www.garfield.com

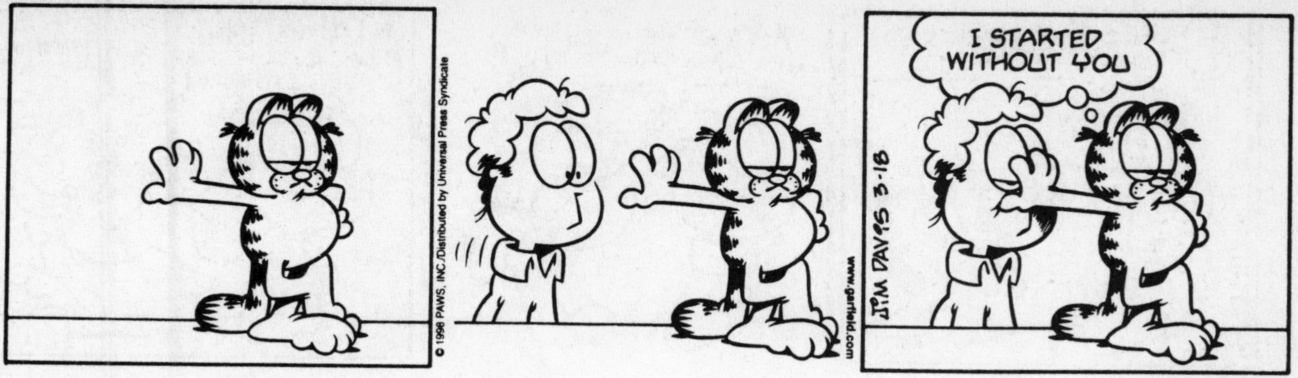
I STARTED WITHOUT YOU
© 1998 PAWS, INC./Distributed by Universal Press Syndicate
JIM DAVIS 3-18
www.garfield.com

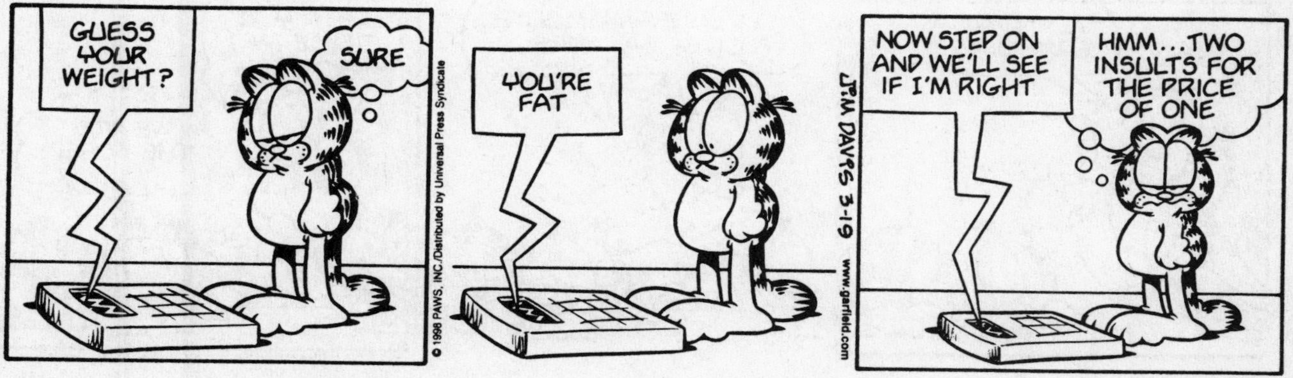
GUESS YOUR WEIGHT?
SURE
YOU'RE FAT
NOW STEP ON AND WE'LL SEE IF I'M RIGHT
HMM...TWO INSULTS FOR THE PRICE OF ONE
© 1998 PAWS, INC./Distributed by Universal Press Syndicate
JIM DAVIS 3-19
www.garfield.com

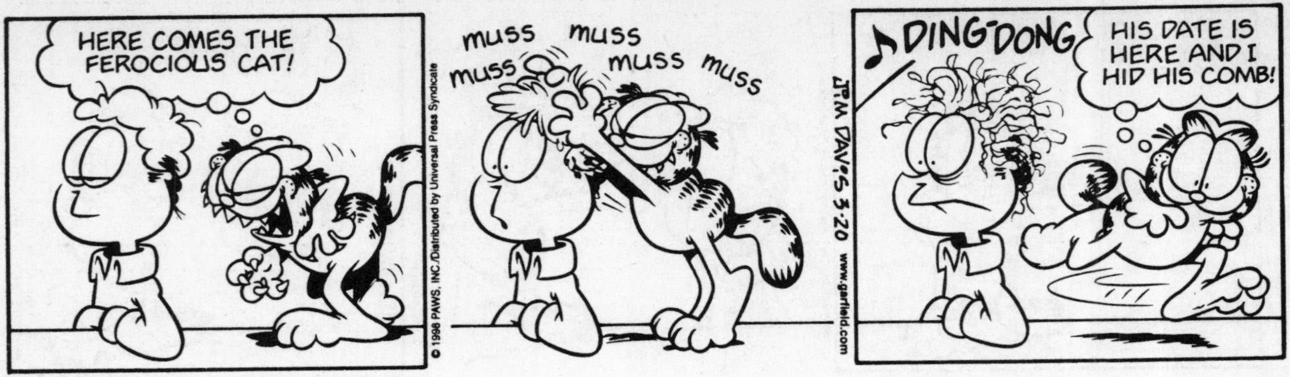
HERE COMES THE FEROCIOUS CAT!
© 1998 PAWS, INC./Distributed by Universal Press Syndicate
muss muss muss muss muss
JIM DAVIS 3-20
www.garfield.com
DING-DONG
HIS DATE IS HERE AND I HID HIS COMB!

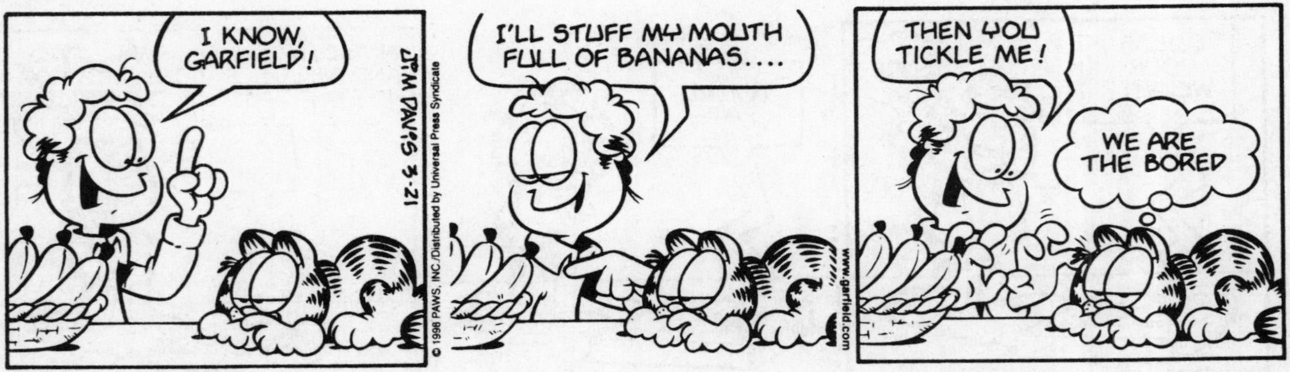
I KNOW, GARFIELD!
JIM DAVIS 3-21
© 1998 PAWS, INC./Distributed by Universal Press Syndicate
I'LL STUFF MY MOUTH FULL OF BANANAS....
www.garfield.com
THEN YOU TICKLE ME!
WE ARE THE BORED

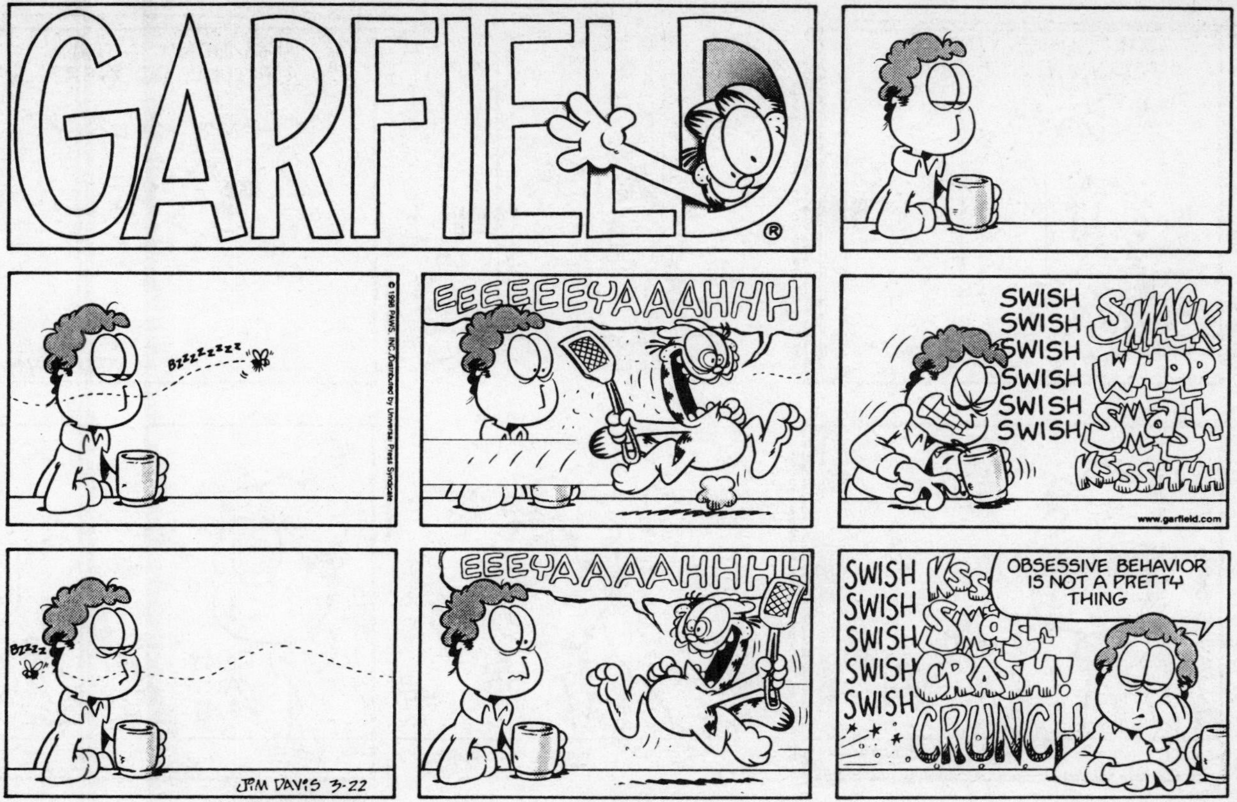
GARFIELD®
© 1998 PAWS, INC./Distributed by Universal Press Syndicate
BZZZZZZZZ
EEEEEEEYAAAHHH
SWISH
SWISH
SWISH
SWISH
SWISH
SWISH
SMACK
WHOP
SMASH
KSSSHHH
www.garfield.com
BZZZZ
JIM DAVIS 3-22
EEEYAAAAHHHH
SWISH
SWISH
SWISH
SWISH
SWISH
SMASH
CRASH!
CRUNCH
OBSESSIVE BEHAVIOR IS NOT A PRETTY THING

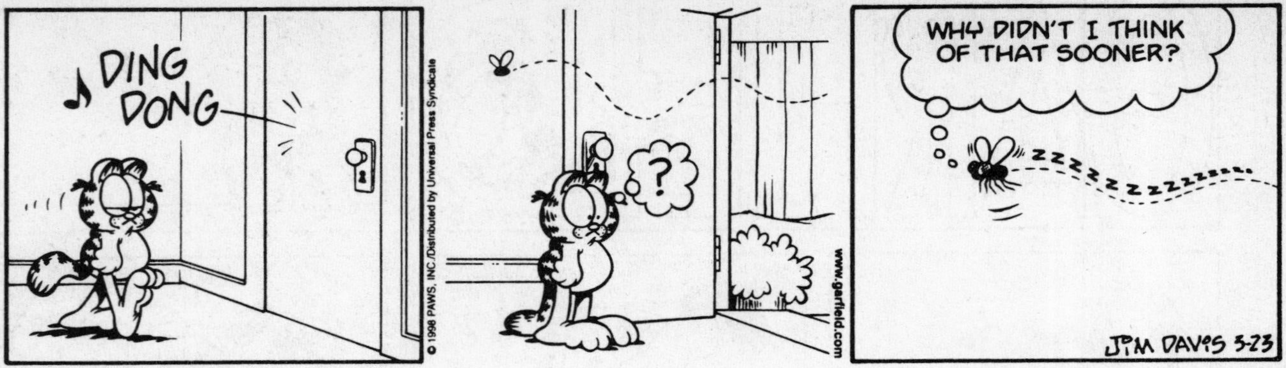
DING DONG
?
© 1998 PAWS, INC./Distributed by Universal Press Syndicate
www.garfield.com
WHY DIDN'T I THINK OF THAT SOONER?
JIM DAVIS 3-23

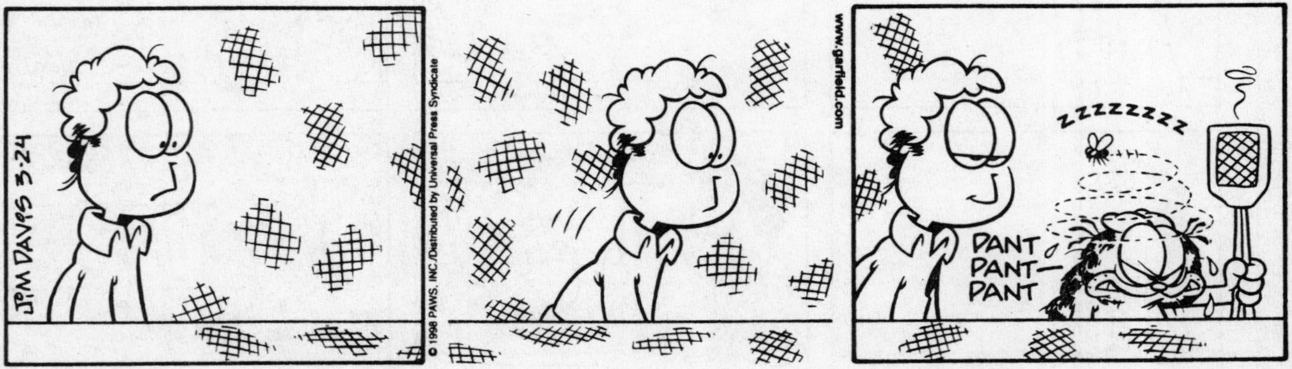
JIM DAVIS 3-24
© 1998 PAWS, INC./Distributed by Universal Press Syndicate
www.garfield.com
ZZZZZZZZ
PANT PANT PANT

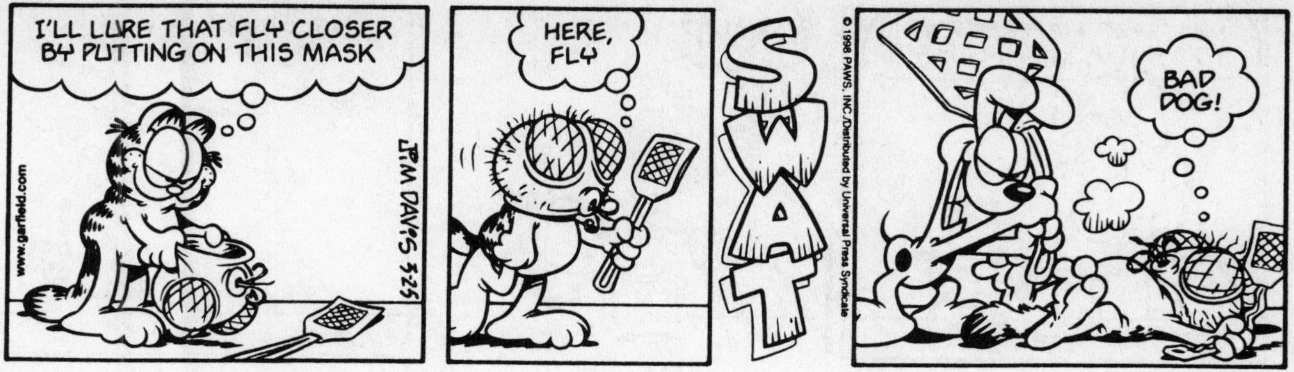
I'LL LURE THAT FLY CLOSER BY PUTTING ON THIS MASK
www.garfield.com
JIM DAVIS 3-25
HERE, FLY
SWAT
© 1998 PAWS, INC./Distributed by Universal Press Syndicate
BAD DOG!

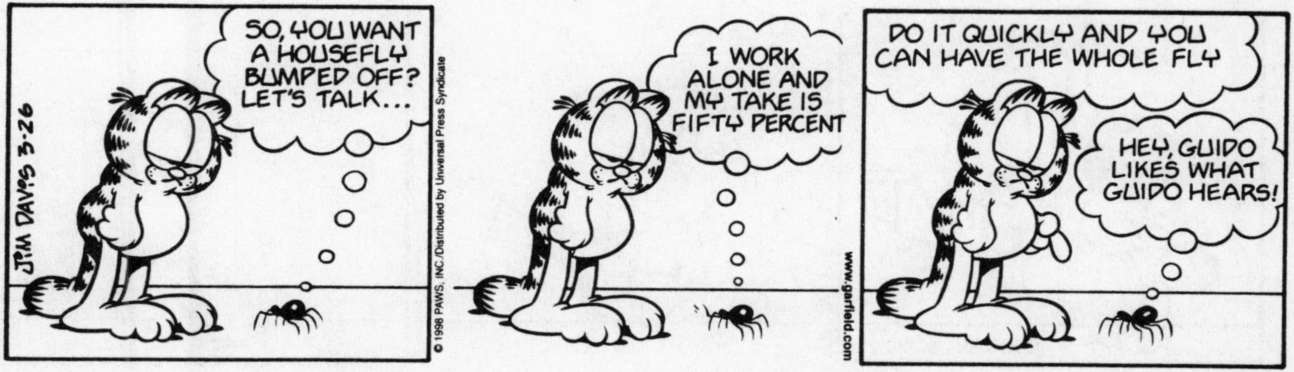
SO, YOU WANT A HOUSEFLY BUMPED OFF? LET'S TALK...
JIM DAVIS 3-26
© 1998 PAWS, INC./Distributed by Universal Press Syndicate
I WORK ALONE AND MY TAKE IS FIFTY PERCENT
www.garfield.com
DO IT QUICKLY AND YOU CAN HAVE THE WHOLE FLY
HEY, GUIDO LIKES WHAT GUIDO HEARS!

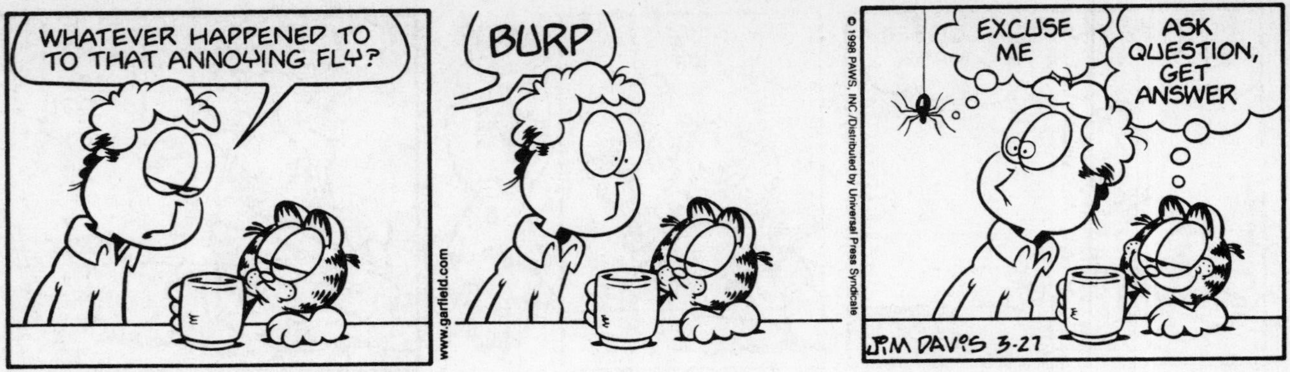
WHATEVER HAPPENED TO
TO THAT ANNOYING FLY?
BURP
EXCUSE ME
ASK QUESTION, GET ANSWER
JIM DAVIS 3-27
www.garfield.com
© 1998 PAWS, INC./Distributed by Universal Press Syndicate

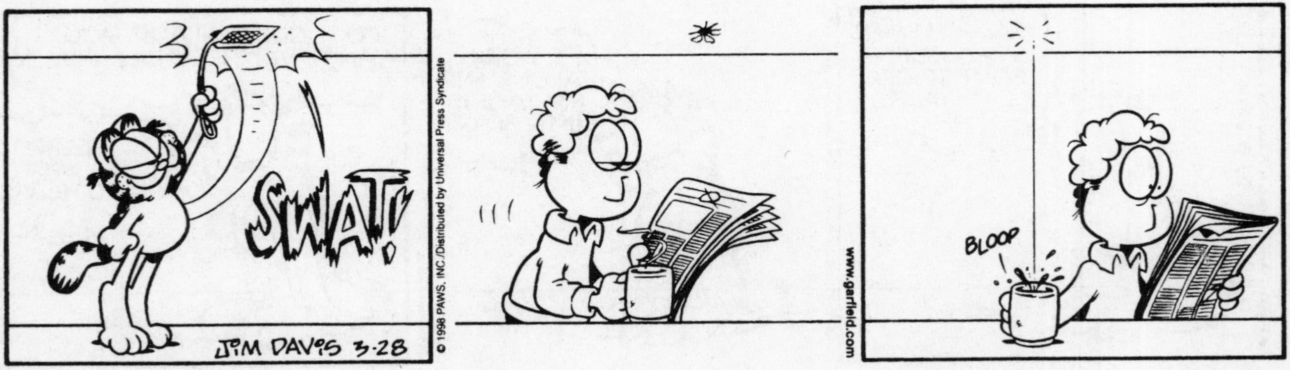
SWAT!
BLOOP
JIM DAVIS 3-28
© 1998 PAWS, INC./Distributed by Universal Press Syndicate
www.garfield.com

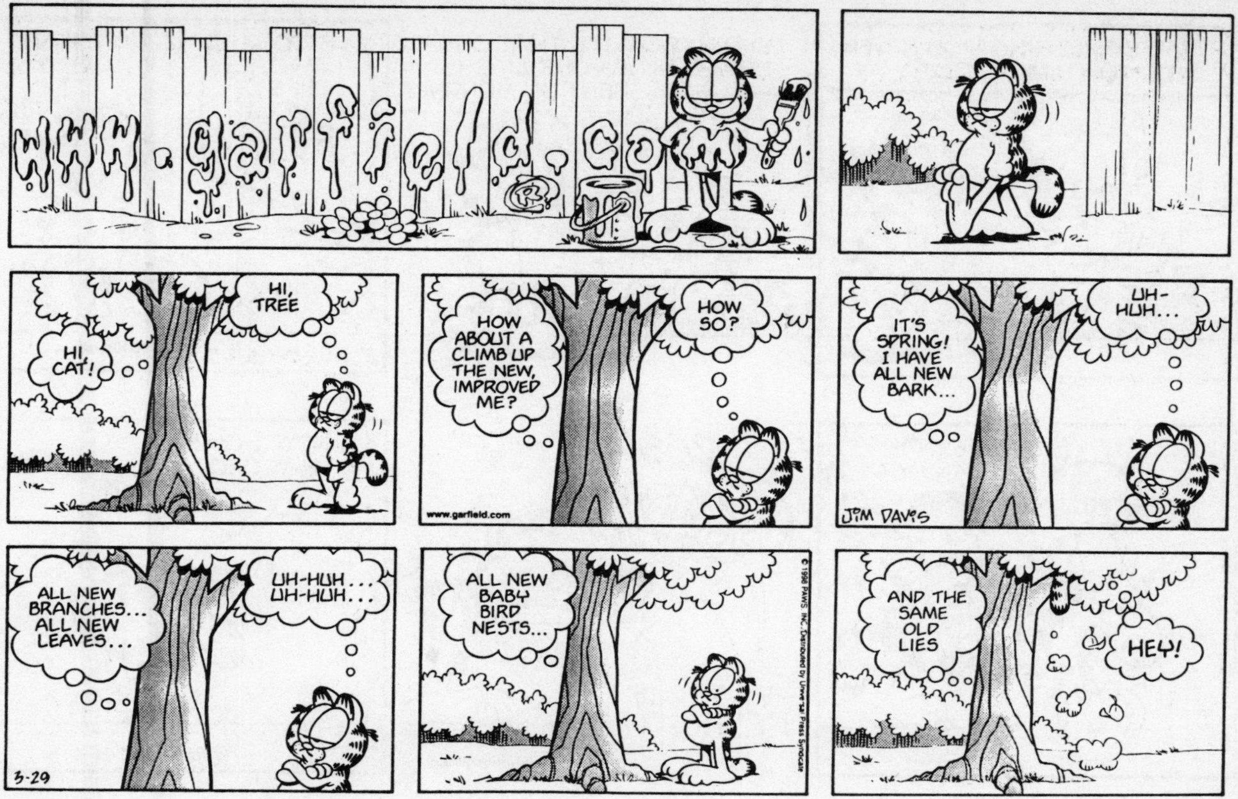
www.garfield.com
HI, TREE
HI CAT!
HOW ABOUT A CLIMB UP THE NEW, IMPROVED ME?
HOW SO?
www.garfield.com
IT'S SPRING! I HAVE ALL NEW BARK...
UH-HUH...
JIM DAVIS
ALL NEW BRANCHES... ALL NEW LEAVES...
UH-HUH... UH-HUH...
3-29
ALL NEW BABY BIRD NESTS...
© 1998 PAWS, INC. Distributed by Universal Press Syndicate
AND THE SAME OLD LIES
HEY!

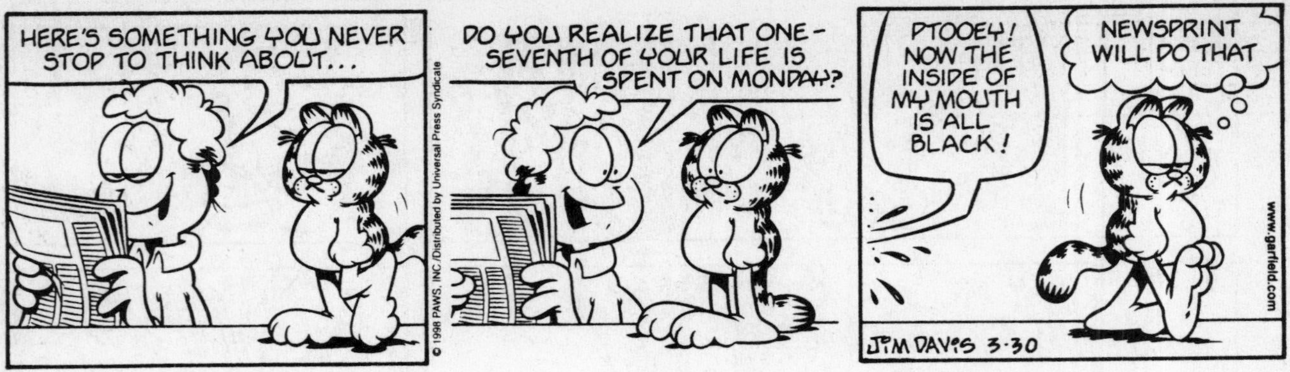
HERE'S SOMETHING YOU NEVER STOP TO THINK ABOUT...
© 1998 PAWS, INC./Distributed by Universal Press Syndicate
DO YOU REALIZE THAT ONE-SEVENTH OF YOUR LIFE IS SPENT ON MONDAY?
PTOOEY! NOW THE INSIDE OF MY MOUTH IS ALL BLACK!
NEWSPRINT WILL DO THAT
JIM DAVIS 3-30
www.garfield.com

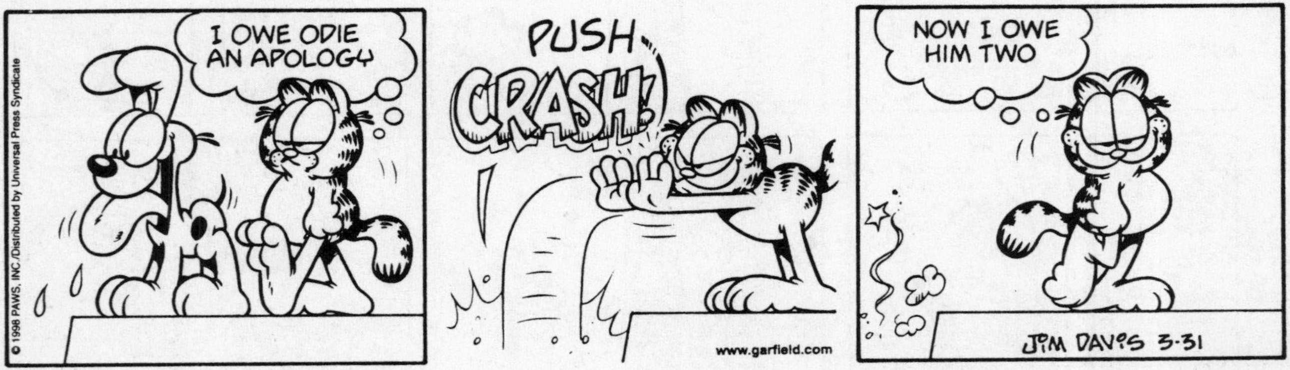
© 1998 PAWS, INC./Distributed by Universal Press Syndicate
I OWE ODIE AN APOLOGY
PUSH
CRASH!
www.garfield.com
NOW I OWE HIM TWO
JIM DAVIS 3-31

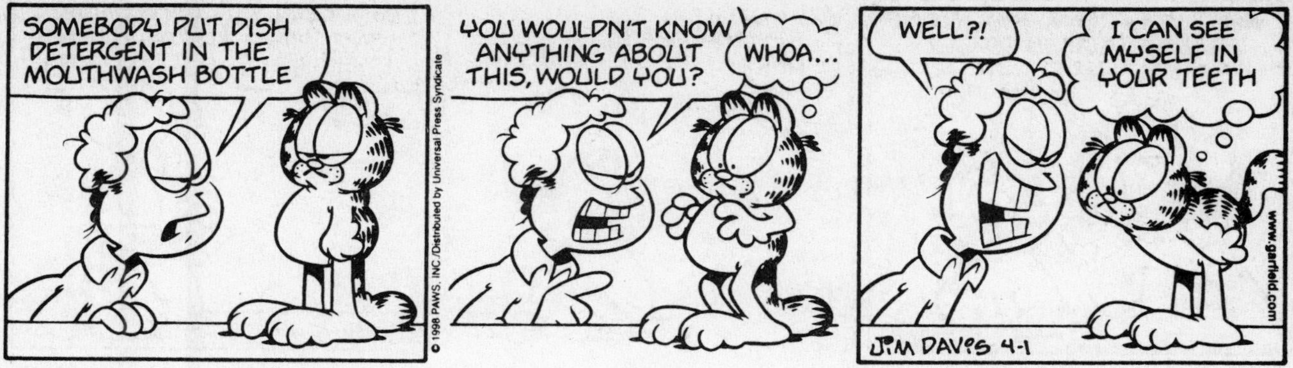
SOMEBODY PUT DISH DETERGENT IN THE MOUTHWASH BOTTLE
YOU WOULDN'T KNOW ANYTHING ABOUT THIS, WOULD YOU?
WHOA...
WELL?!
I CAN SEE MYSELF IN YOUR TEETH
JIM DAVIS 4-1
© 1998 PAWS, INC./Distributed by Universal Press Syndicate
www.garfield.com

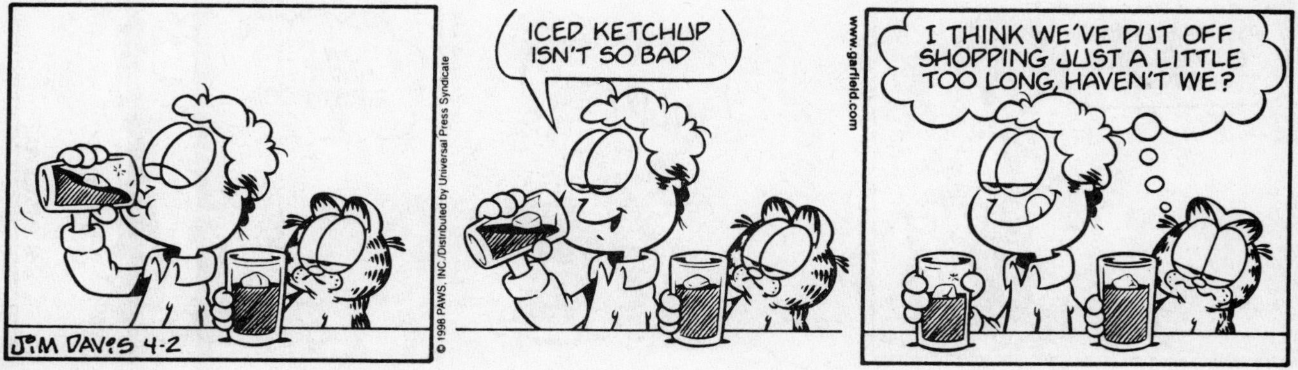
ICED KETCHUP ISN'T SO BAD
I THINK WE'VE PUT OFF SHOPPING JUST A LITTLE TOO LONG, HAVEN'T WE?
JIM DAVIS 4-2
© 1998 PAWS, INC./Distributed by Universal Press Syndicate
www.garfield.com

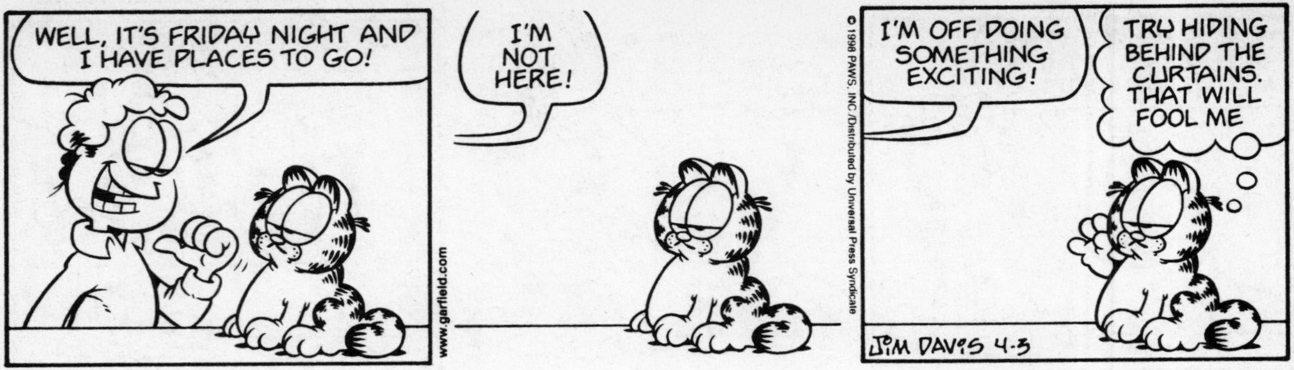
WELL, IT'S FRIDAY NIGHT AND I HAVE PLACES TO GO!
I'M NOT HERE!
I'M OFF DOING SOMETHING EXCITING!
TRY HIDING BEHIND THE CURTAINS. THAT WILL FOOL ME
JIM DAVIS 4-3

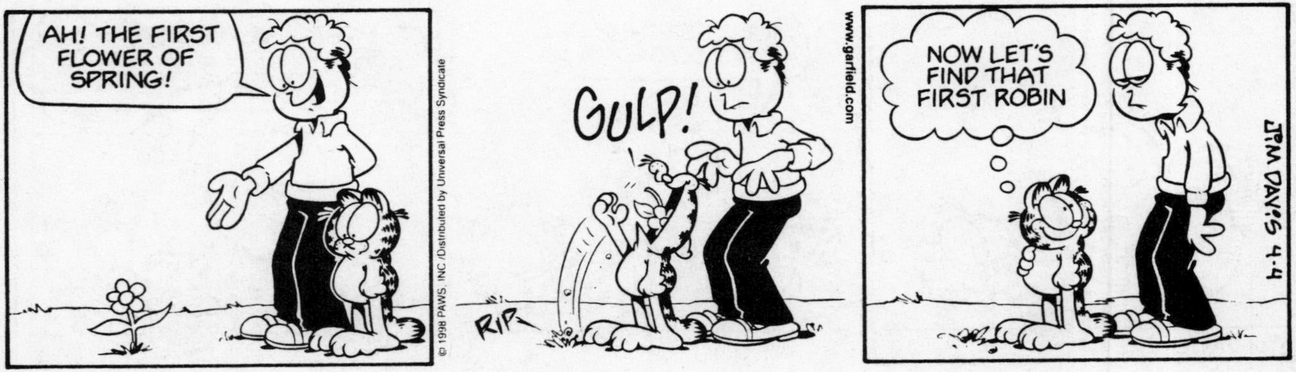
AH! THE FIRST FLOWER OF SPRING!
RIP
GULP!
NOW LET'S FIND THAT FIRST ROBIN
JIM DAVIS 4-4

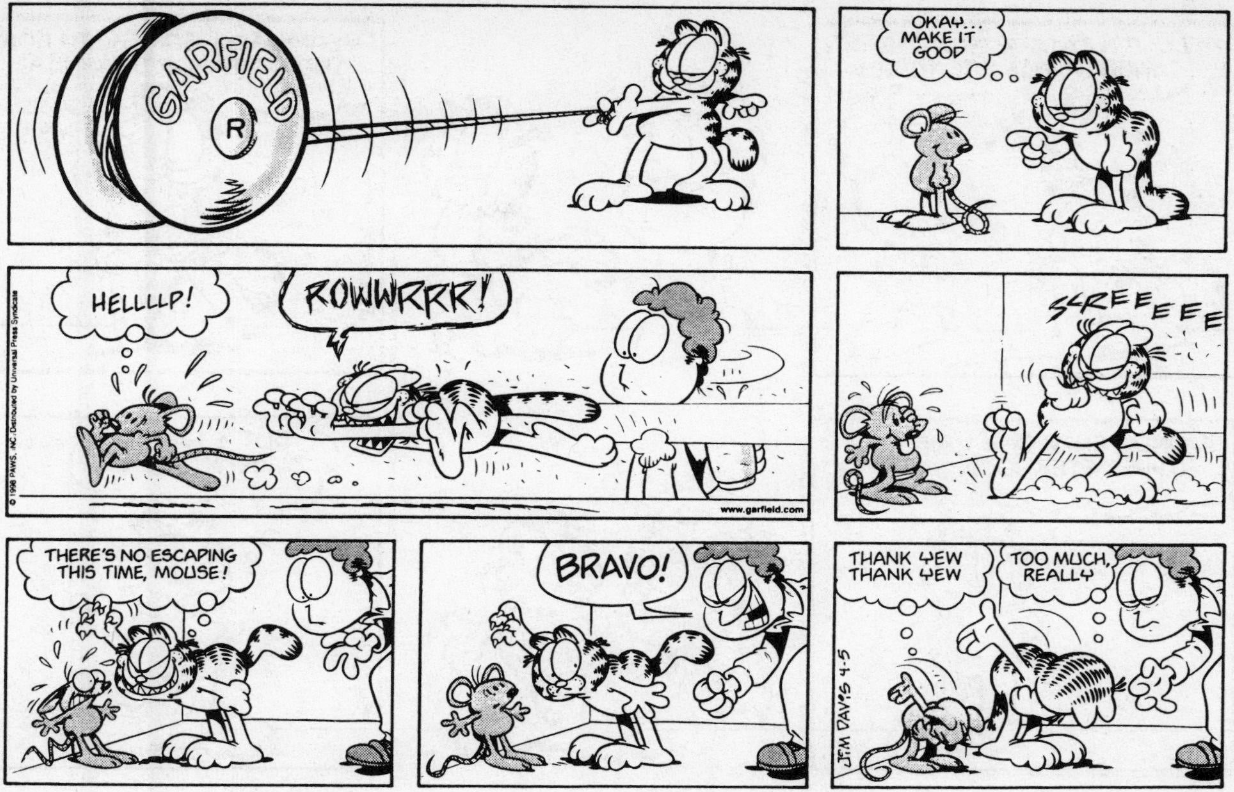
GARFIELD
R
OKAY... MAKE IT GOOD
HELLLLP!
ROWWRRR!
© 1998 PAWS, INC. Distributed by Universal Press Syndicate
www.garfield.com
SCREEEEEE
THERE'S NO ESCAPING THIS TIME, MOUSE!
BRAVO!
JIM DAVIS 4-5
THANK YEW THANK YEW
TOO MUCH, REALLY

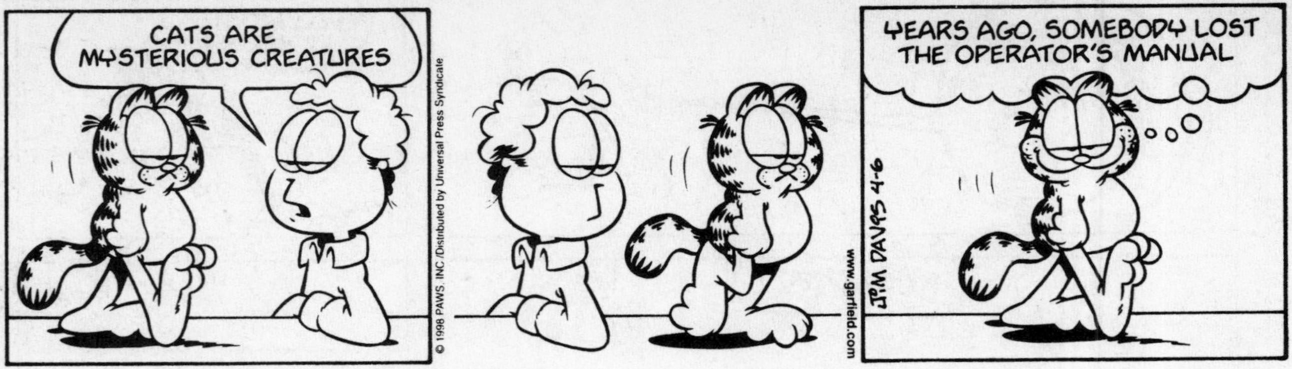
CATS ARE MYSTERIOUS CREATURES
© 1998 PAWS, INC./Distributed by Universal Press Syndicate
YEARS AGO, SOMEBODY LOST THE OPERATOR'S MANUAL
JIM DAVIS 4-6
www.garfield.com

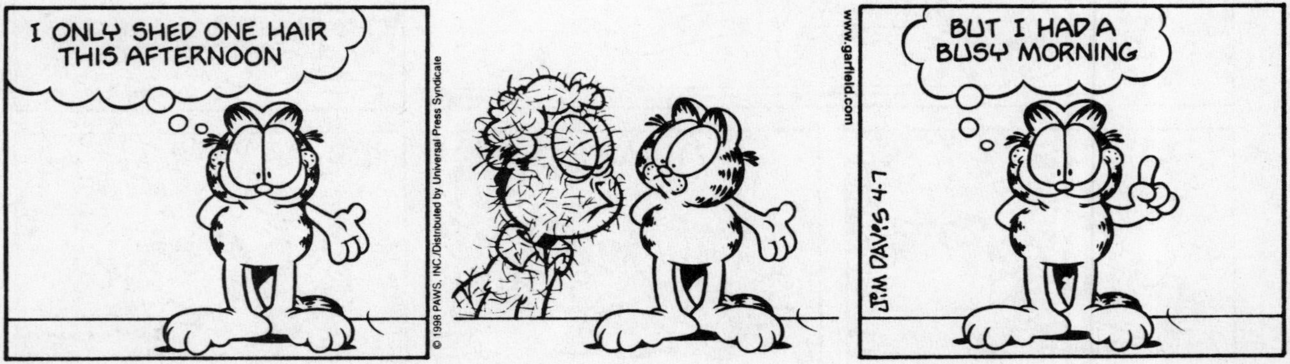
I ONLY SHED ONE HAIR THIS AFTERNOON
© 1998 PAWS, INC./Distributed by Universal Press Syndicate
BUT I HAD A BUSY MORNING
JIM DAVIS 4-7
www.garfield.com

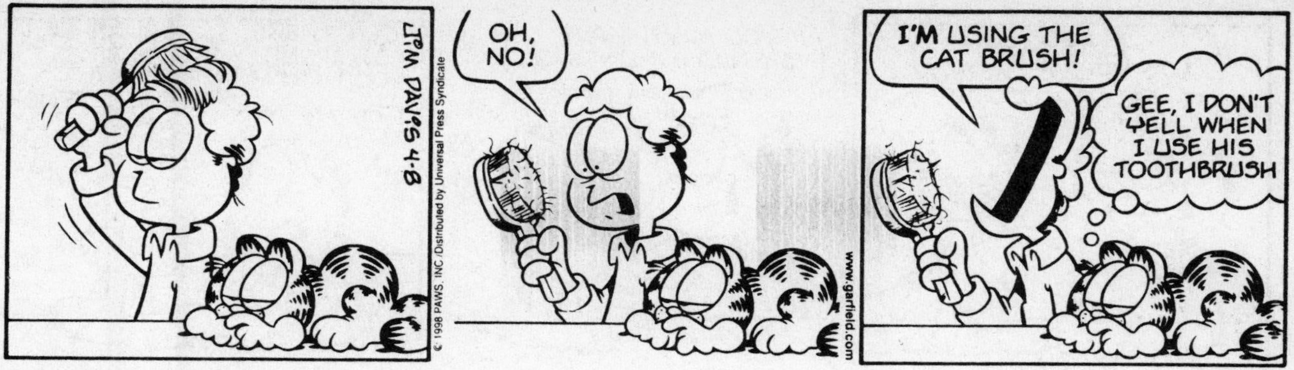
JIM DAVIS 4-8
OH, NO!
© 1998 PAWS, INC./Distributed by Universal Press Syndicate
I'M USING THE CAT BRUSH!
GEE, I DON'T YELL WHEN I USE HIS TOOTHBRUSH
www.garfield.com

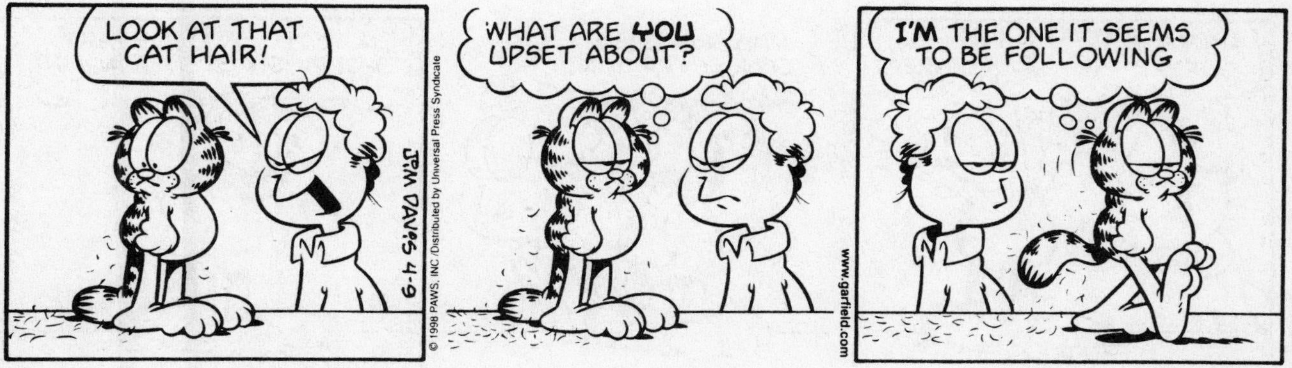
LOOK AT THAT CAT HAIR!
JIM DAVIS 4-9
© 1998 PAWS, INC./Distributed by Universal Press Syndicate
WHAT ARE YOU UPSET ABOUT?
I'M THE ONE IT SEEMS TO BE FOLLOWING
www.garfield.com

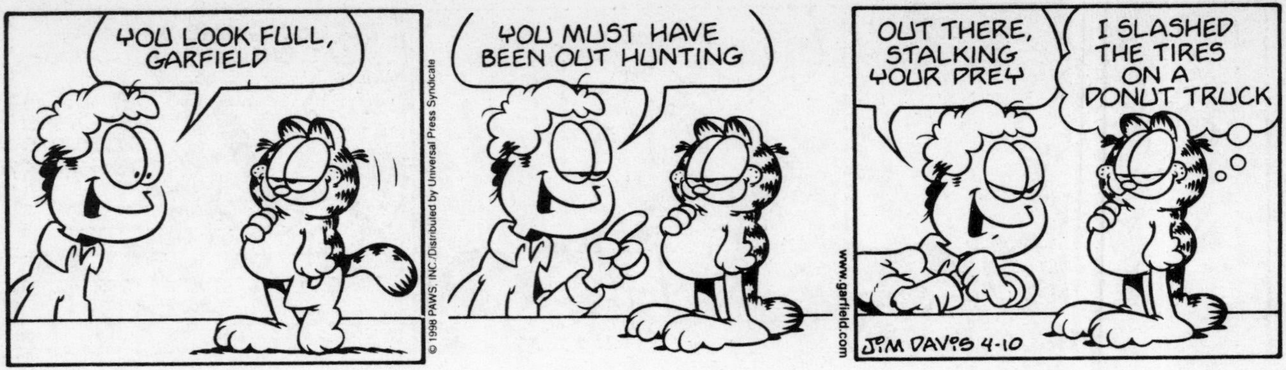
YOU LOOK FULL, GARFIELD
YOU MUST HAVE BEEN OUT HUNTING
OUT THERE, STALKING YOUR PREY
I SLASHED THE TIRES ON A DONUT TRUCK
JIM DAVIS 4-10

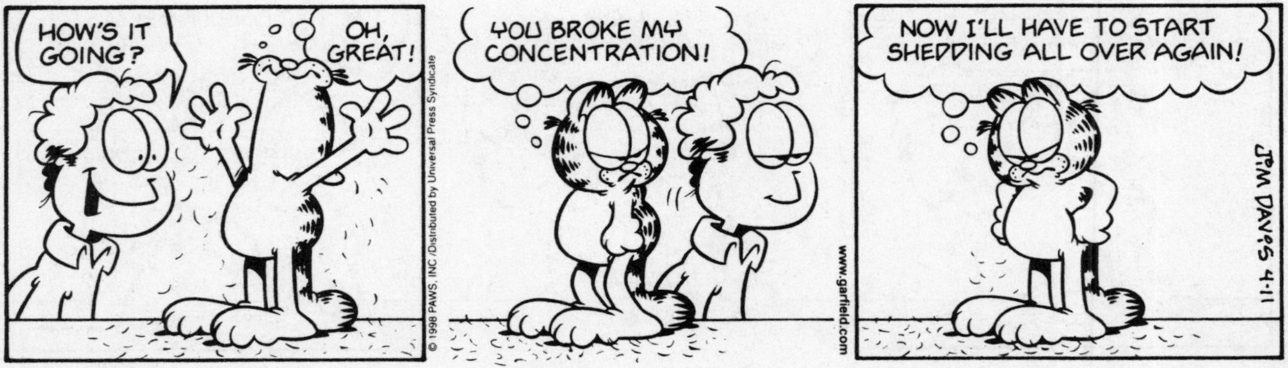
HOW'S IT GOING?
OH, GREAT!
YOU BROKE MY CONCENTRATION!
NOW I'LL HAVE TO START SHEDDING ALL OVER AGAIN!
JIM DAVIS 4-11

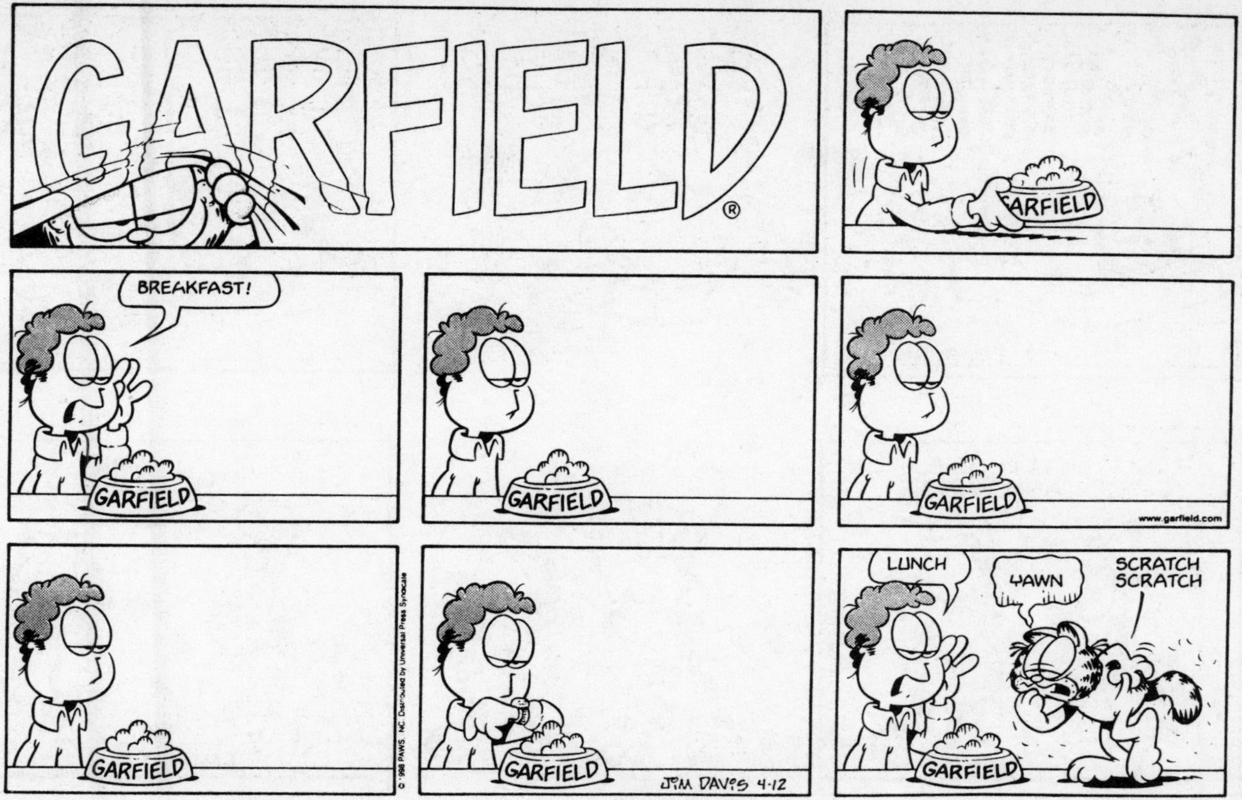
GARFIELD®
GARFIELD
BREAKFAST!
GARFIELD
GARFIELD
GARFIELD
www.garfield.com
GARFIELD
© 1998 PAWS, INC. Distributed by Universal Press Syndicate
GARFIELD
JIM DAVIS 4-12
LUNCH
YAWN
SCRATCH SCRATCH
GARFIELD

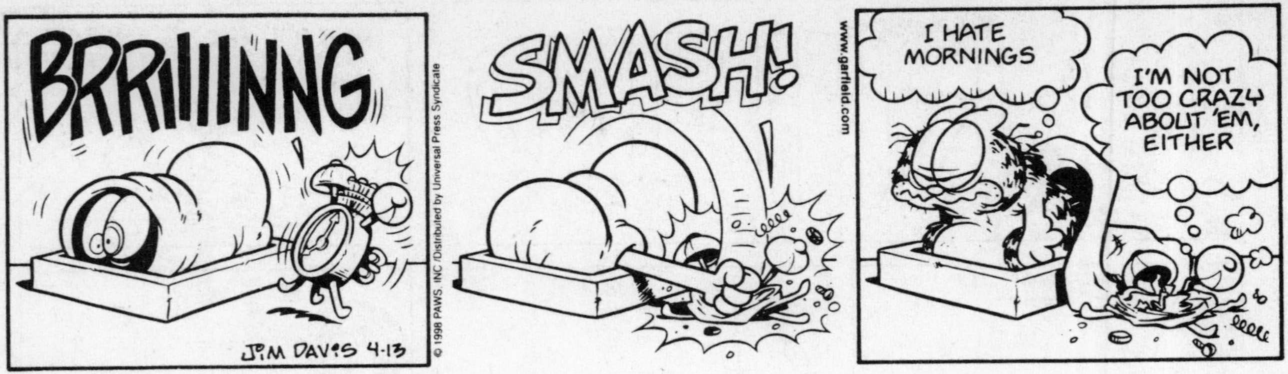
BRRIIIINNG
JIM DAVIS 4-13
© 1998 PAWS, INC /Distributed by Universal Press Syndicate
SMASH!
www.garfield.com
I HATE MORNINGS
I'M NOT TOO CRAZY ABOUT 'EM, EITHER

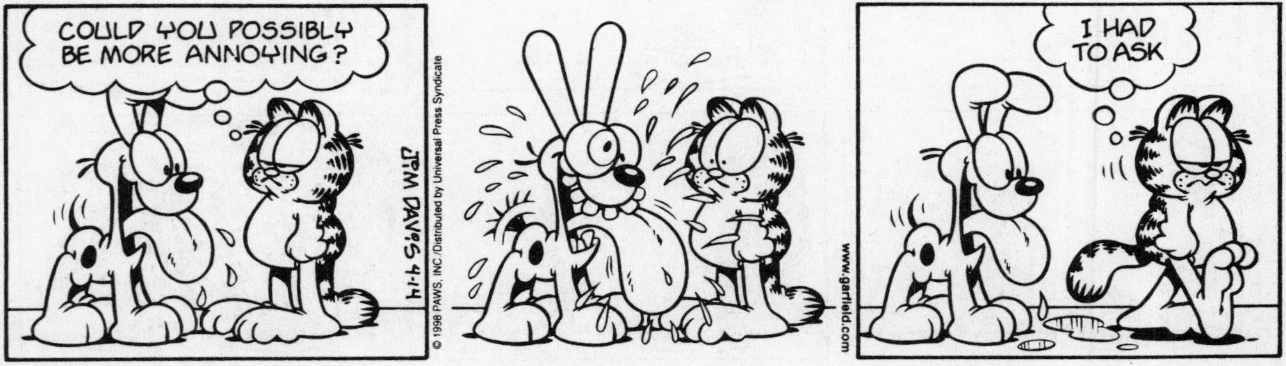
COULD YOU POSSIBLY BE MORE ANNOYING?
JIM DAVIS 4-14
© 1998 PAWS, INC /Distributed by Universal Press Syndicate
www.garfield.com
I HAD TO ASK

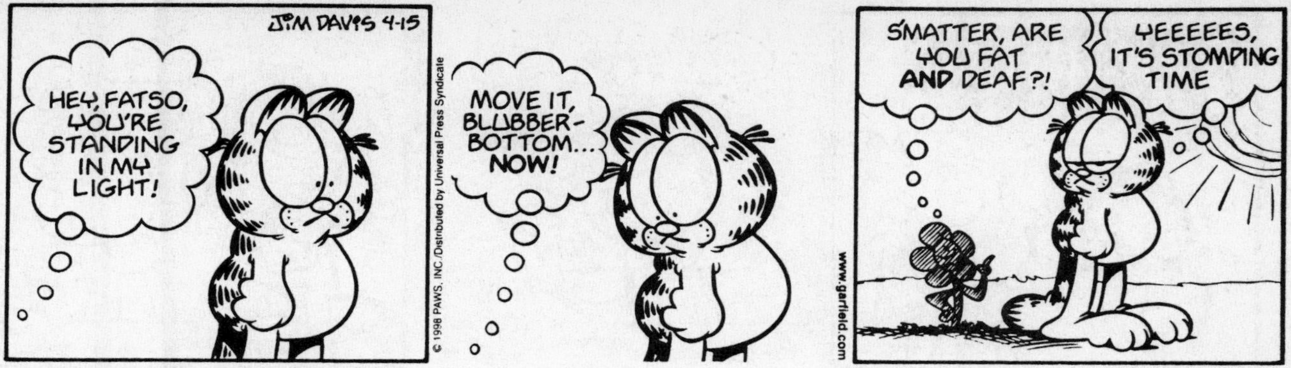
JIM DAVIS 4-15
HEY, FATSO, YOU'RE STANDING IN MY LIGHT!
MOVE IT, BLUBBER-BOTTOM... NOW!
'SMATTER, ARE YOU FAT AND DEAF?!
YEEEEES, IT'S STOMPING TIME

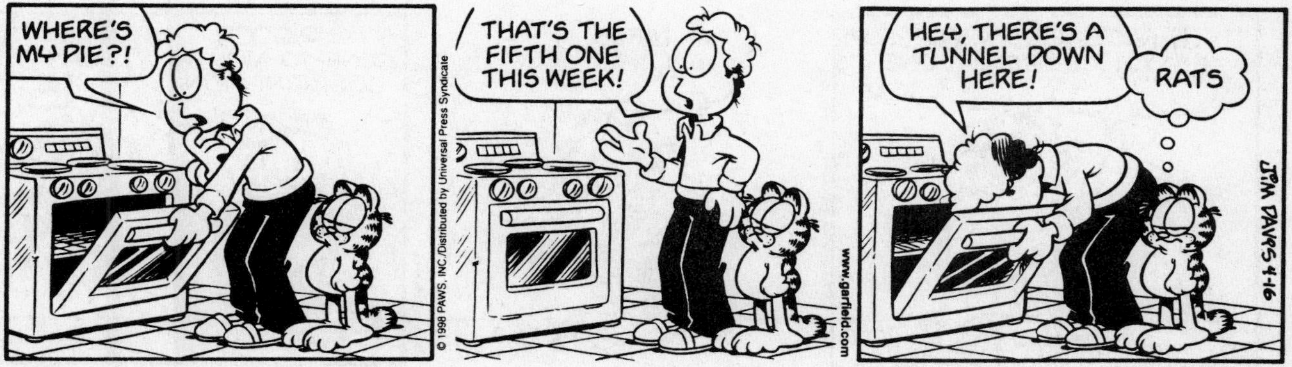
WHERE'S MY PIE?!
THAT'S THE FIFTH ONE THIS WEEK!
HEY, THERE'S A TUNNEL DOWN HERE!
RATS
JIM DAVIS 4-16

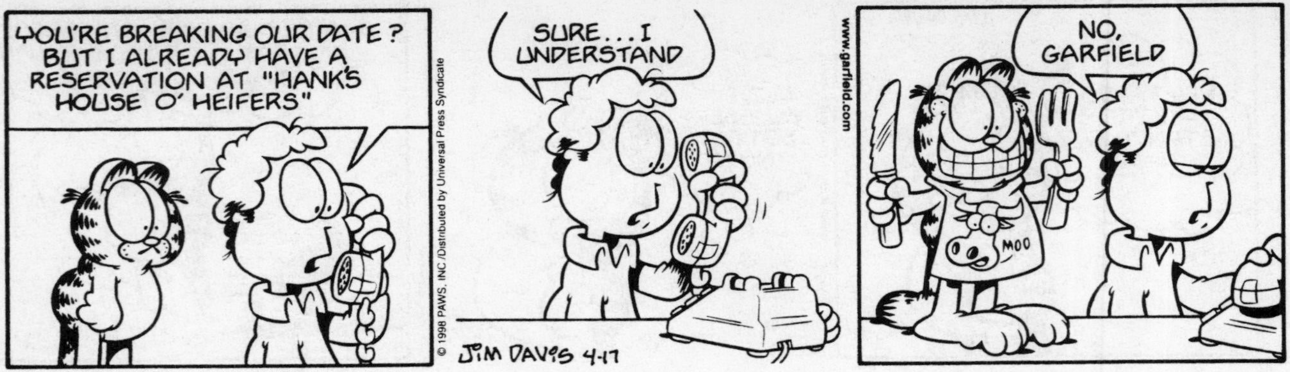
YOU'RE BREAKING OUR DATE? BUT I ALREADY HAVE A RESERVATION AT "HANK'S HOUSE O' HEIFERS"
SURE... I UNDERSTAND
NO, GARFIELD
MOO
JIM DAVIS 4-17
© 1998 PAWS, INC./Distributed by Universal Press Syndicate
www.garfield.com

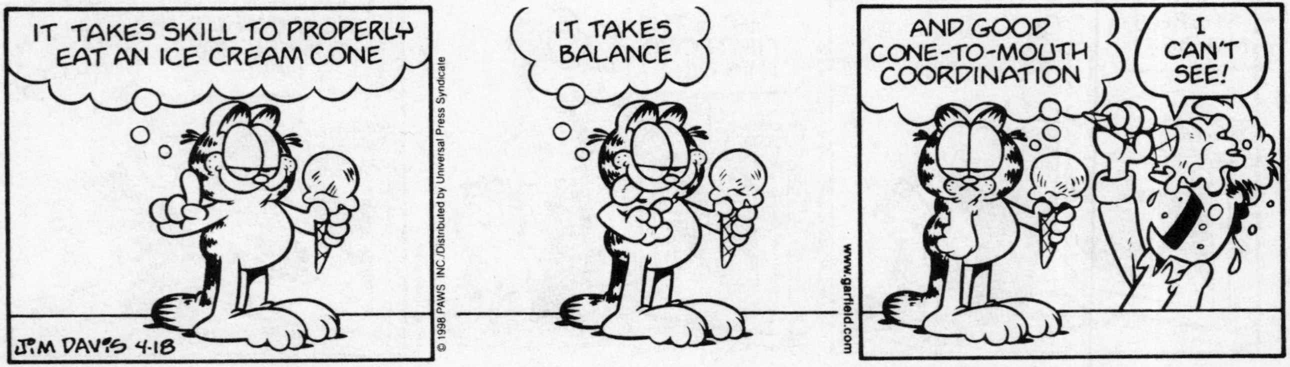
IT TAKES SKILL TO PROPERLY EAT AN ICE CREAM CONE
IT TAKES BALANCE
AND GOOD CONE-TO-MOUTH COORDINATION
I CAN'T SEE!
JIM DAVIS 4-18
© 1998 PAWS, INC./Distributed by Universal Press Syndicate
www.garfield.com

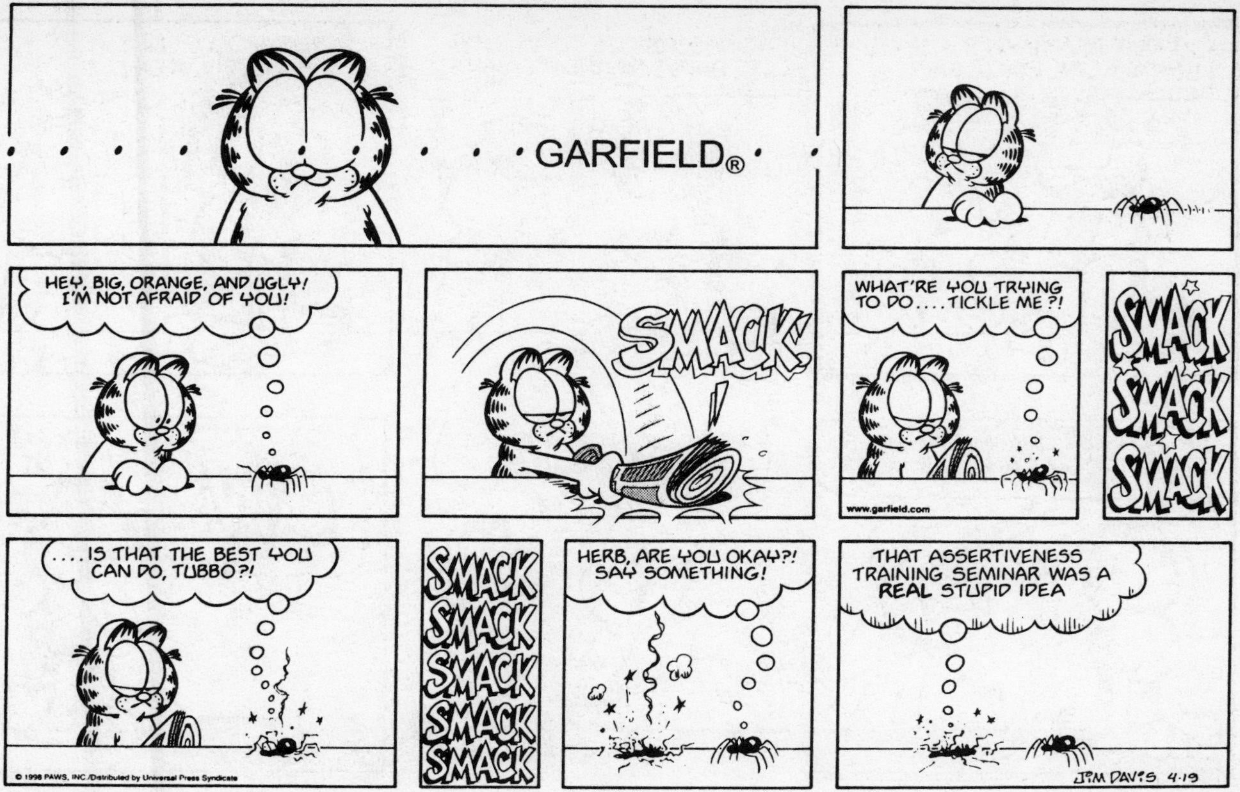
GARFIELD®
HEY, BIG, ORANGE, AND UGLY! I'M NOT AFRAID OF YOU!
SMACK!
WHAT'RE YOU TRYING TO DO.... TICKLE ME?!
www.garfield.com
SMACK SMACK SMACK
....IS THAT THE BEST YOU CAN DO, TUBBO?!
SMACK SMACK SMACK SMACK SMACK
HERB, ARE YOU OKAY?! SAY SOMETHING!
THAT ASSERTIVENESS TRAINING SEMINAR WAS A REAL STUPID IDEA
JIM DAVIS 4-19

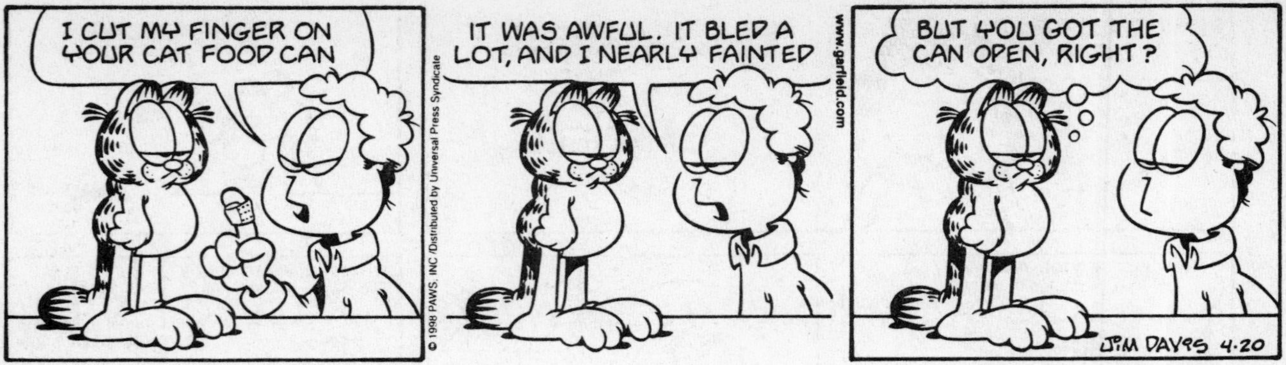

I CUT MY FINGER ON YOUR CAT FOOD CAN
© 1998 PAWS, INC /Distributed by Universal Press Syndicate
IT WAS AWFUL. IT BLED A LOT, AND I NEARLY FAINTED
www.garfield.com
BUT YOU GOT THE CAN OPEN, RIGHT?
JIM DAVIS 4-20

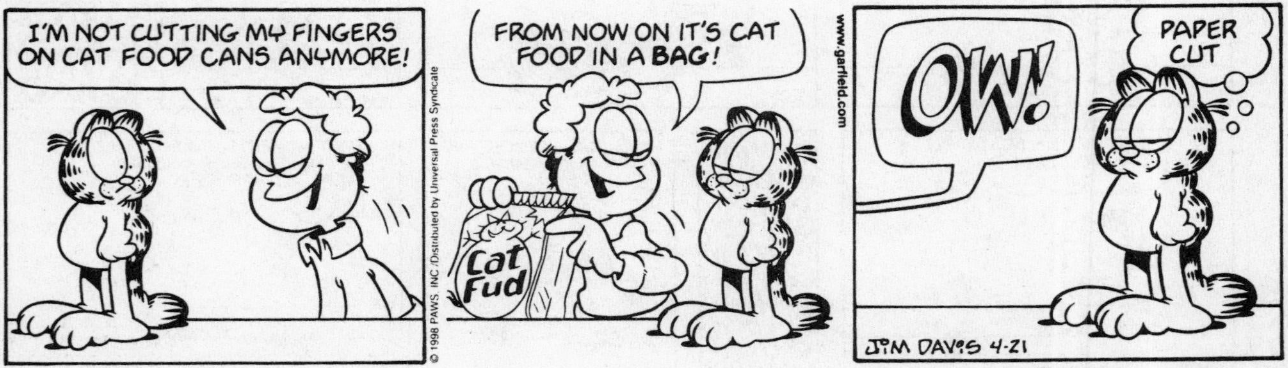

I'M NOT CUTTING MY FINGERS ON CAT FOOD CANS ANYMORE!
© 1998 PAWS, INC /Distributed by Universal Press Syndicate
FROM NOW ON IT'S CAT FOOD IN A BAG!
Cat Fud
www.garfield.com
OW!
PAPER CUT
JIM DAVIS 4-21

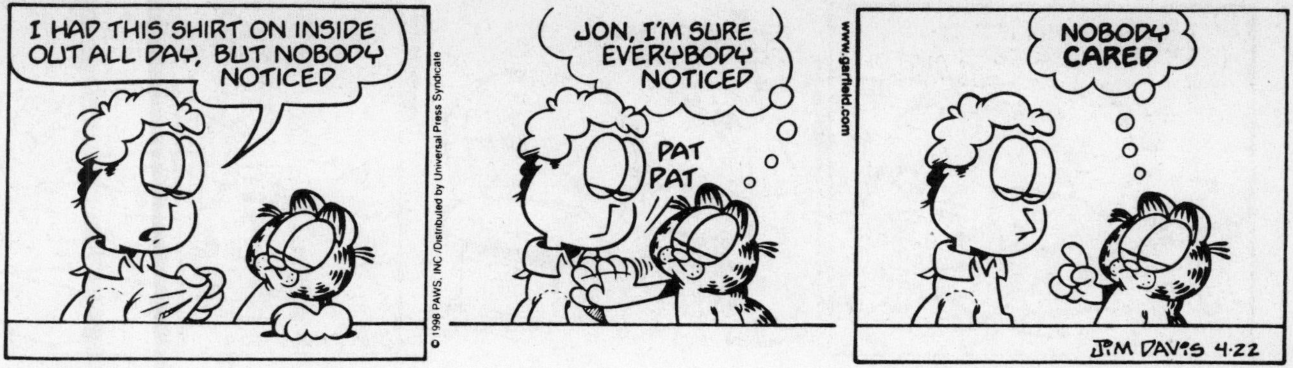
I HAD THIS SHIRT ON INSIDE OUT ALL DAY, BUT NOBODY NOTICED
© 1998 PAWS, INC./Distributed by Universal Press Syndicate
JON, I'M SURE EVERYBODY NOTICED
PAT PAT
www.garfield.com
NOBODY CARED
JIM DAVIS 4-22

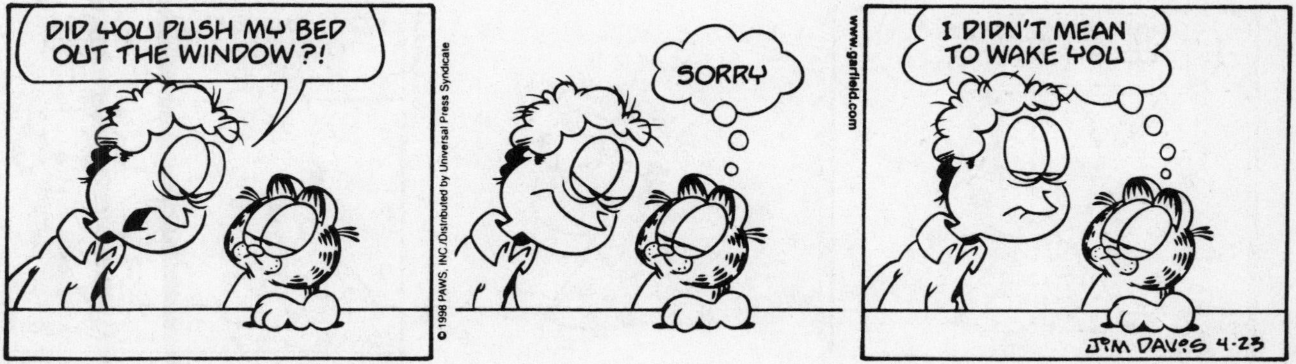
DID YOU PUSH MY BED OUT THE WINDOW?!
© 1998 PAWS, INC./Distributed by Universal Press Syndicate
SORRY
www.garfield.com
I DIDN'T MEAN TO WAKE YOU
JIM DAVIS 4-23

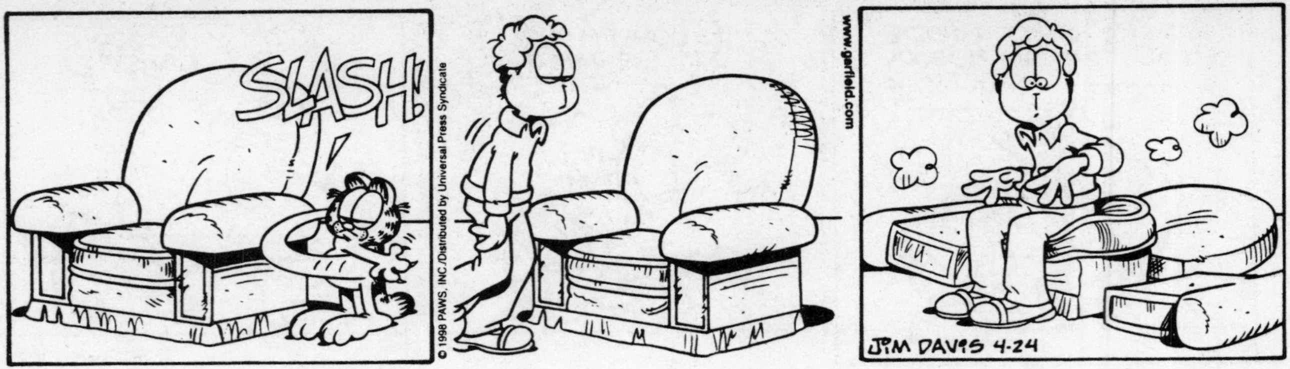
SLASH!
© 1998 PAWS, INC /Distributed by Universal Press Syndicate
www.garfield.com
JIM DAVIS 4-24

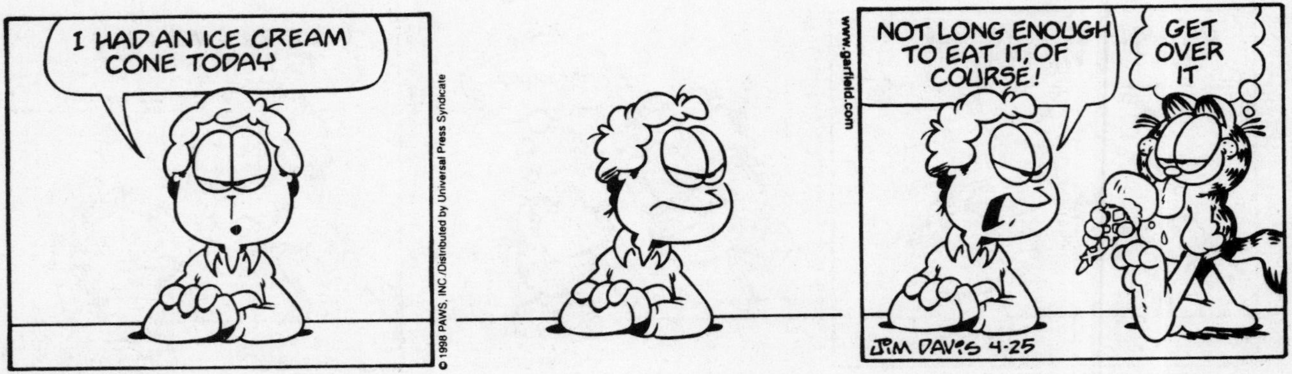
I HAD AN ICE CREAM CONE TODAY
© 1998 PAWS, INC /Distributed by Universal Press Syndicate
www.garfield.com
NOT LONG ENOUGH TO EAT IT, OF COURSE!
GET OVER IT
JIM DAVIS 4-25

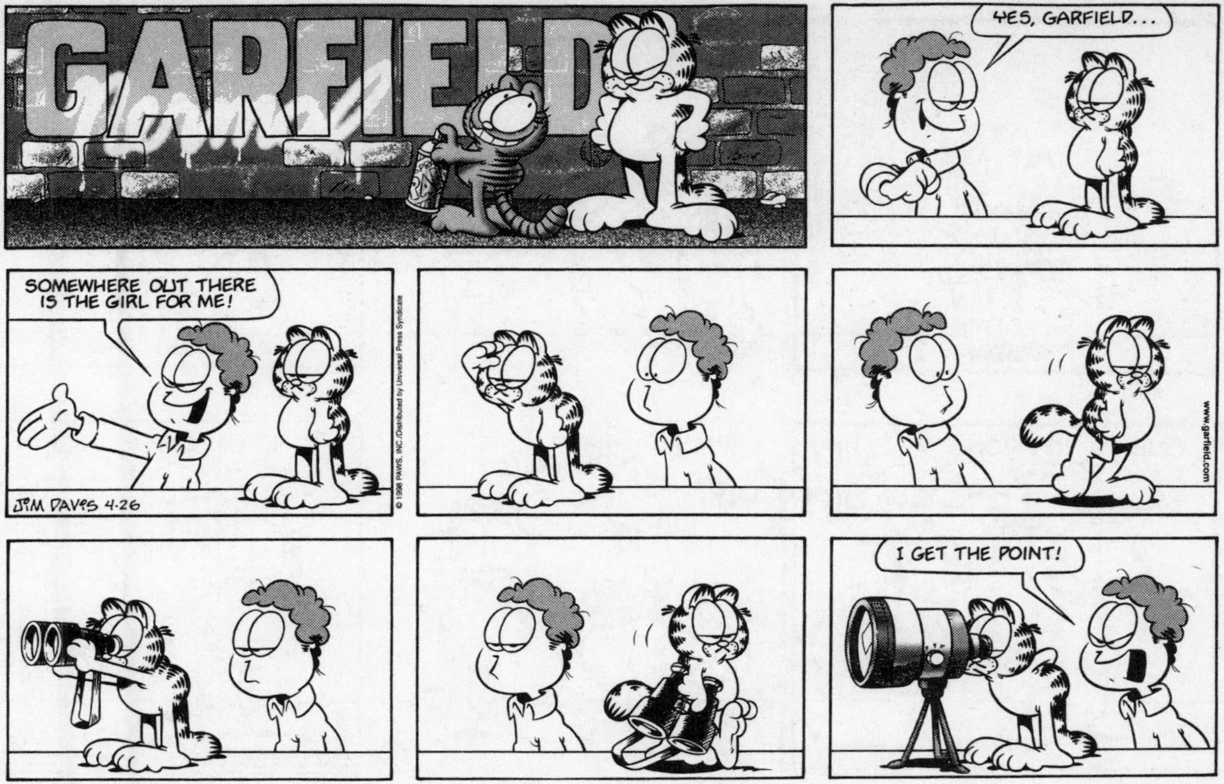
GARFIELD
YES, GARFIELD...
SOMEWHERE OUT THERE IS THE GIRL FOR ME!
JIM DAVIS 4-26
© 1998 PAWS, INC./Distributed by Universal Press Syndicate
www.garfield.com
I GET THE POINT!

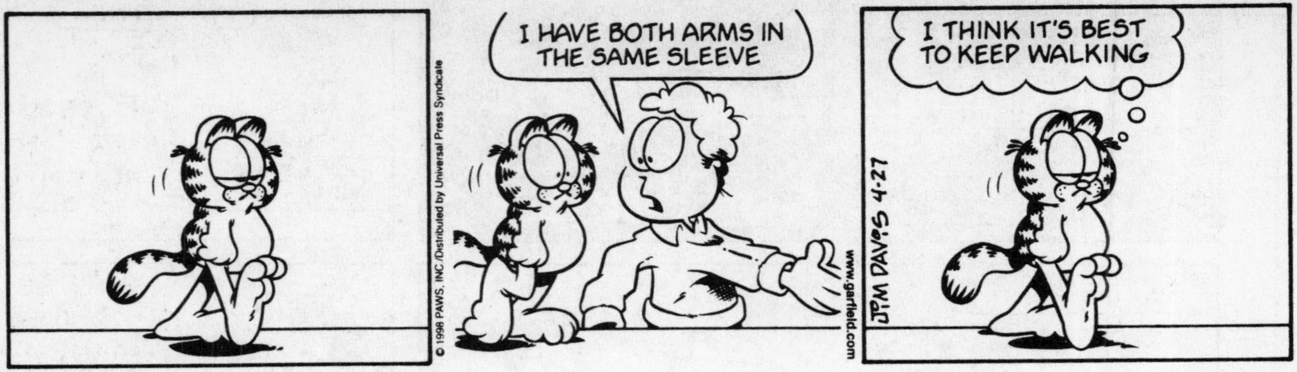
I HAVE BOTH ARMS IN THE SAME SLEEVE
© 1998 PAWS, INC./Distributed by Universal Press Syndicate
www.garfield.com
JIM DAVIS 4-27
I THINK IT'S BEST TO KEEP WALKING

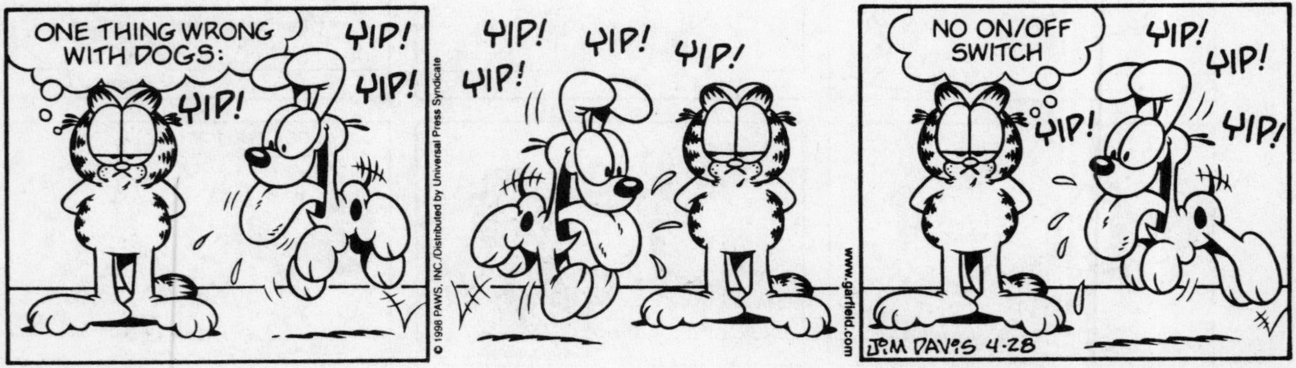
ONE THING WRONG WITH DOGS:
YIP!
YIP!
YIP!
© 1998 PAWS, INC./Distributed by Universal Press Syndicate
YIP!
YIP!
YIP!
YIP!
www.garfield.com
NO ON/OFF SWITCH
YIP!
YIP!
YIP!
YIP!
JIM DAVIS 4-28

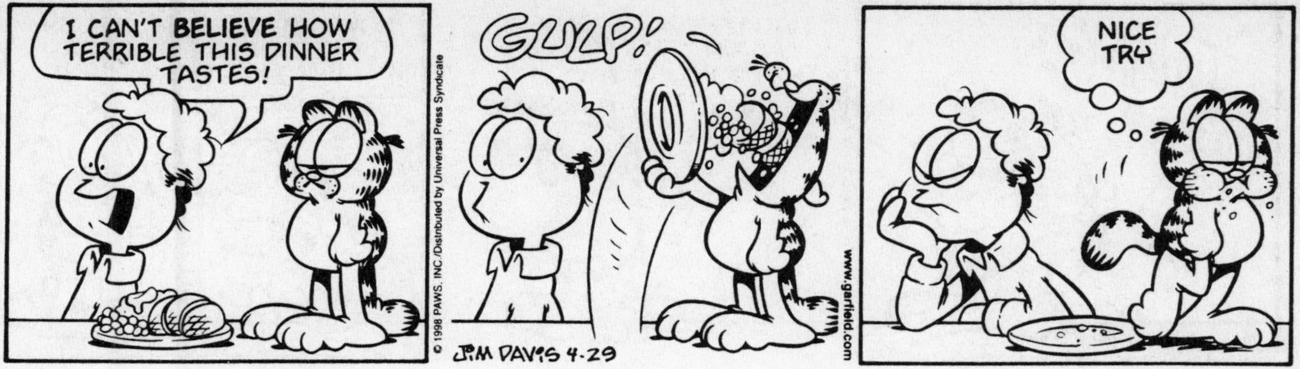
I CAN'T BELIEVE HOW TERRIBLE THIS DINNER TASTES!
© 1998 PAWS, INC./Distributed by Universal Press Syndicate
GULP!
JIM DAVIS 4-29
www.garfield.com
NICE TRY

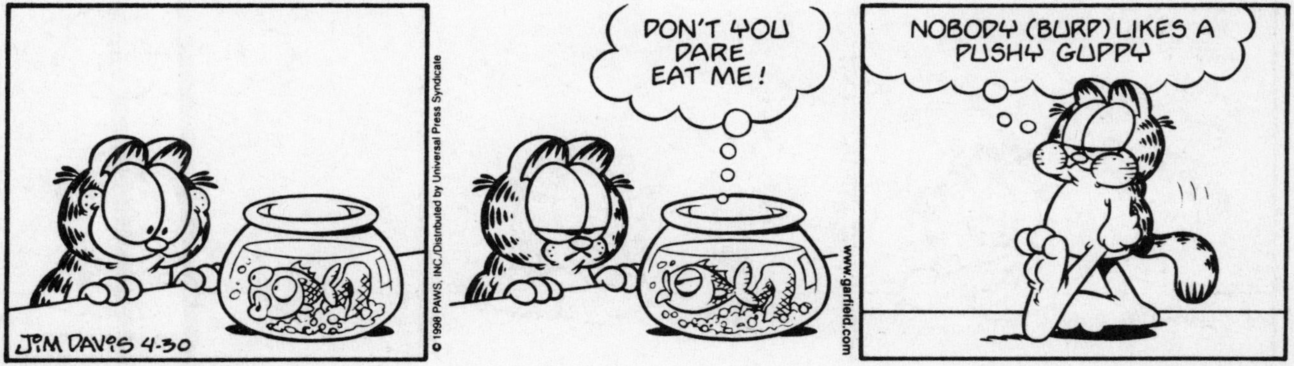
JIM DAVIS 4-30
© 1998 PAWS, INC./Distributed by Universal Press Syndicate
DON'T YOU DARE EAT ME!
www.garfield.com
NOBODY (BURP) LIKES A PUSHY GUPPY

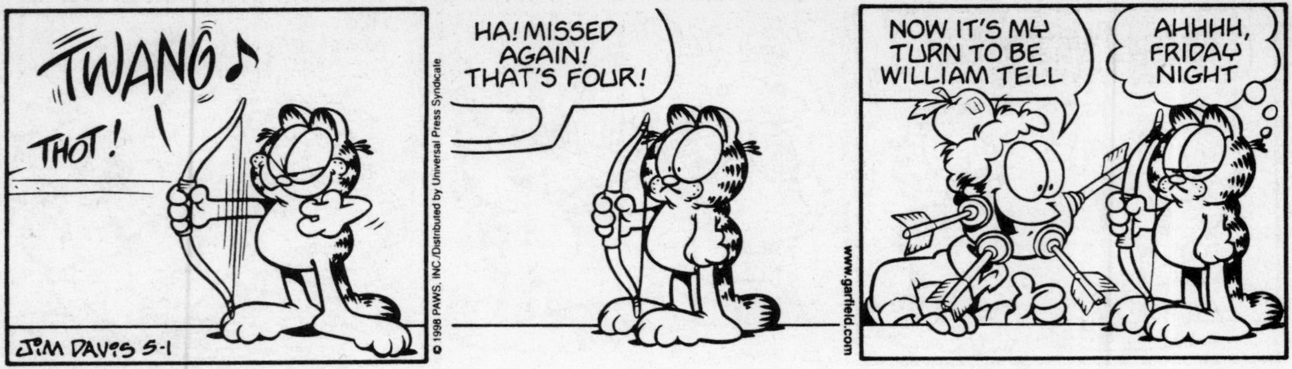
TWANG ♪
THOT!
JIM DAVIS 5-1
© 1998 PAWS, INC./Distributed by Universal Press Syndicate
HA! MISSED AGAIN! THAT'S FOUR!
www.garfield.com
NOW IT'S MY TURN TO BE WILLIAM TELL
AHHHH, FRIDAY NIGHT

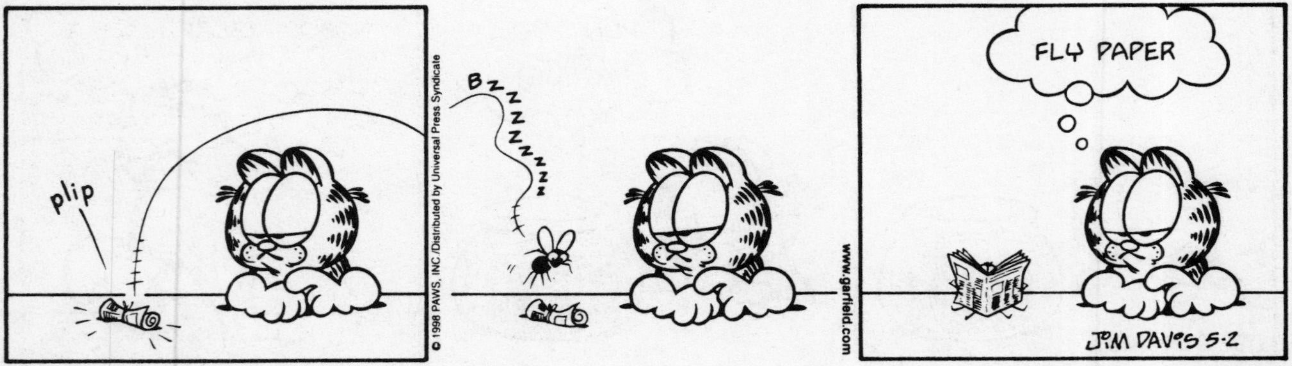
plip
© 1998 PAWS, INC./Distributed by Universal Press Syndicate
BZZZZZZZZ
www.garfield.com
FLY PAPER
JIM DAVIS 5-2

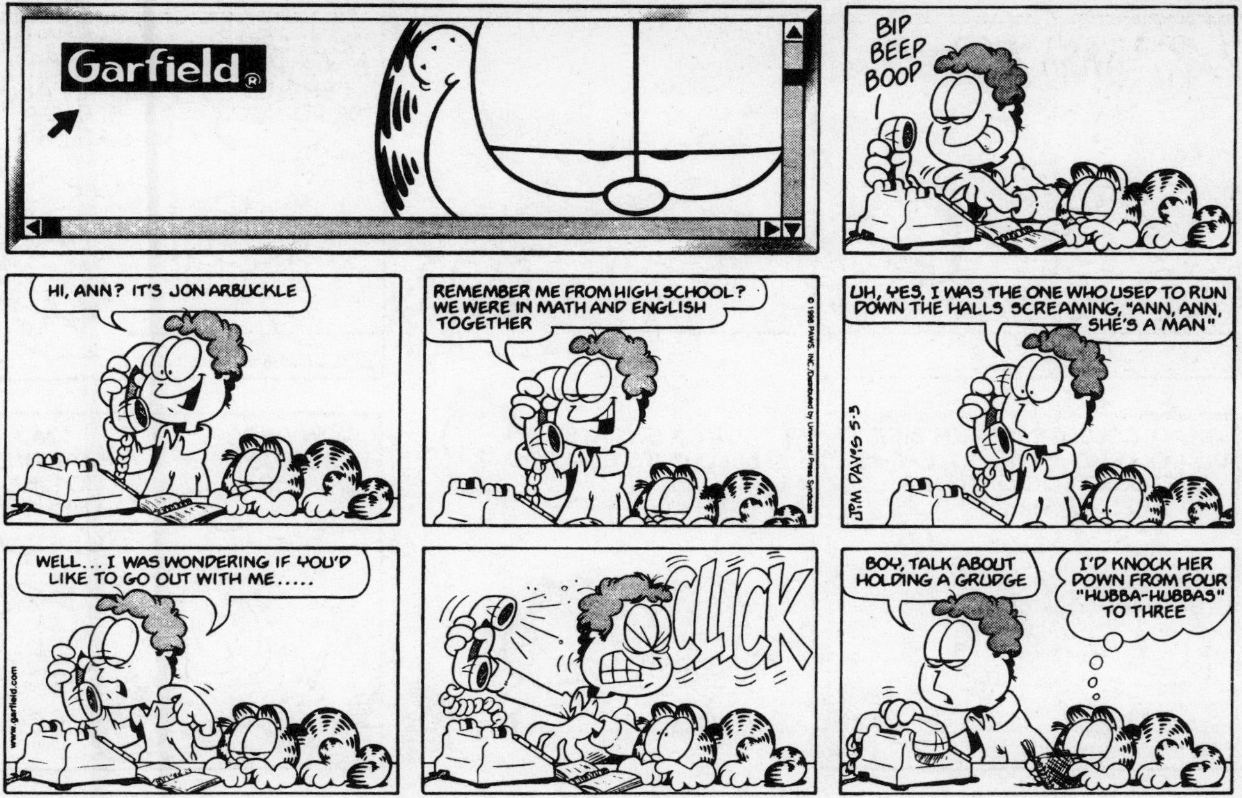
Garfield®
BIP BEEP BOOP
HI, ANN? IT'S JON ARBUCKLE
REMEMBER ME FROM HIGH SCHOOL? WE WERE IN MATH AND ENGLISH TOGETHER
UH, YES, I WAS THE ONE WHO USED TO RUN DOWN THE HALLS SCREAMING, "ANN, ANN, SHE'S A MAN"
© 1988 PAWS, INC./Distributed by Universal Press Syndicate
JIM DAVIS 5-3
WELL... I WAS WONDERING IF YOU'D LIKE TO GO OUT WITH ME.....
www.garfield.com
CLICK
BOY, TALK ABOUT HOLDING A GRUDGE
I'D KNOCK HER DOWN FROM FOUR "HUBBA-HUBBAS" TO THREE

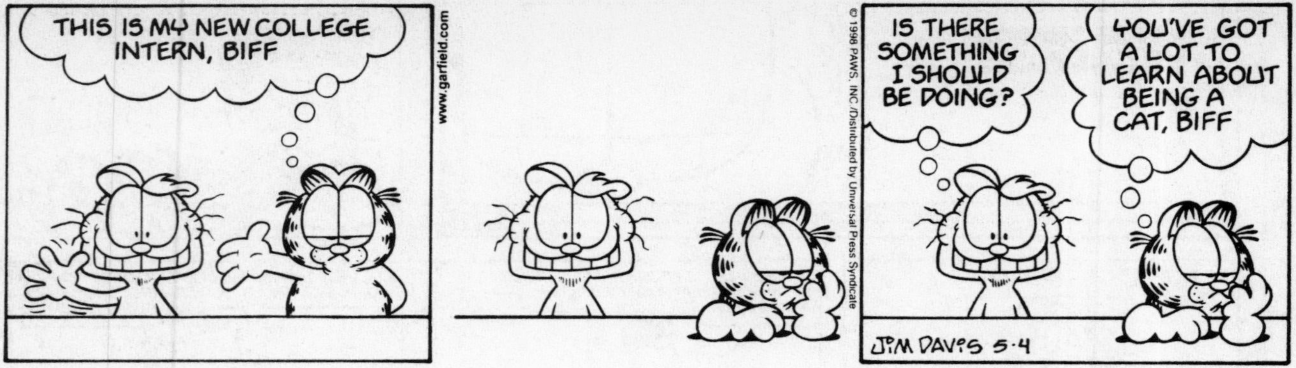
THIS IS MY NEW COLLEGE INTERN, BIFF
www.garfield.com
© 1998 PAWS, INC /Distributed by Universal Press Syndicate
IS THERE SOMETHING I SHOULD BE DOING?
YOU'VE GOT A LOT TO LEARN ABOUT BEING A CAT, BIFF
JIM DAVIS 5-4

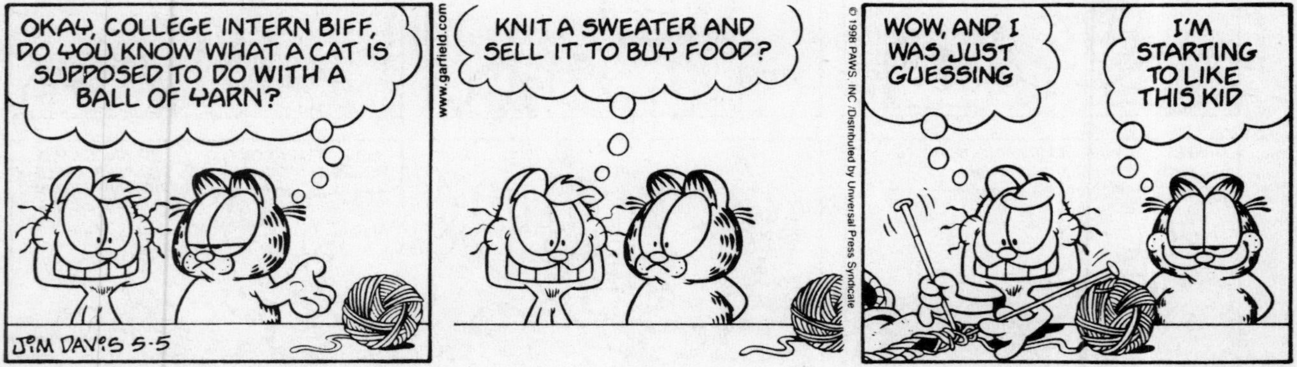
OKAY, COLLEGE INTERN BIFF, DO YOU KNOW WHAT A CAT IS SUPPOSED TO DO WITH A BALL OF YARN?
JIM DAVIS 5-5
www.garfield.com
KNIT A SWEATER AND SELL IT TO BUY FOOD?
© 1998 PAWS, INC /Distributed by Universal Press Syndicate
WOW, AND I WAS JUST GUESSING
I'M STARTING TO LIKE THIS KID

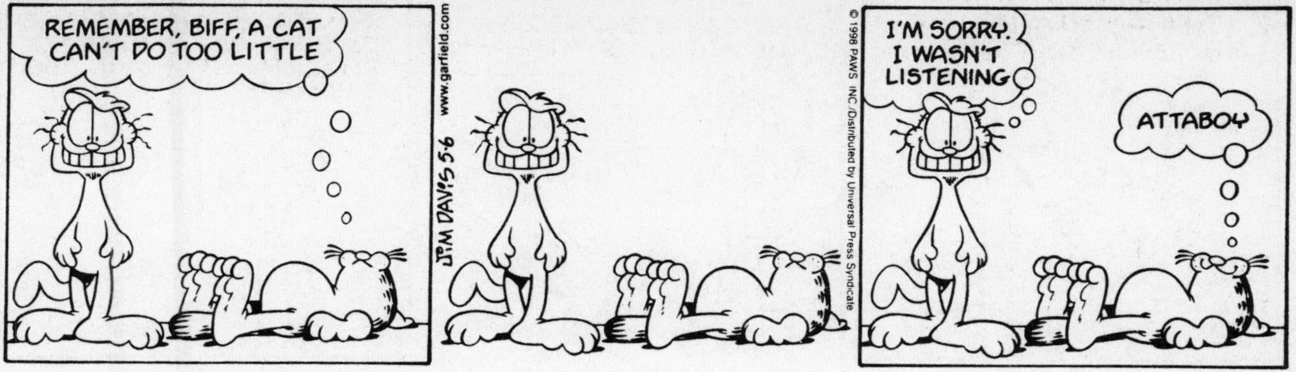

REMEMBER, BIFF, A CAT CAN'T DO TOO LITTLE
JIM DAVIS 5-6
www.garfield.com
I'M SORRY. I WASN'T LISTENING
ATTABOY
© 1998 PAWS INC./Distributed by Universal Press Syndicate

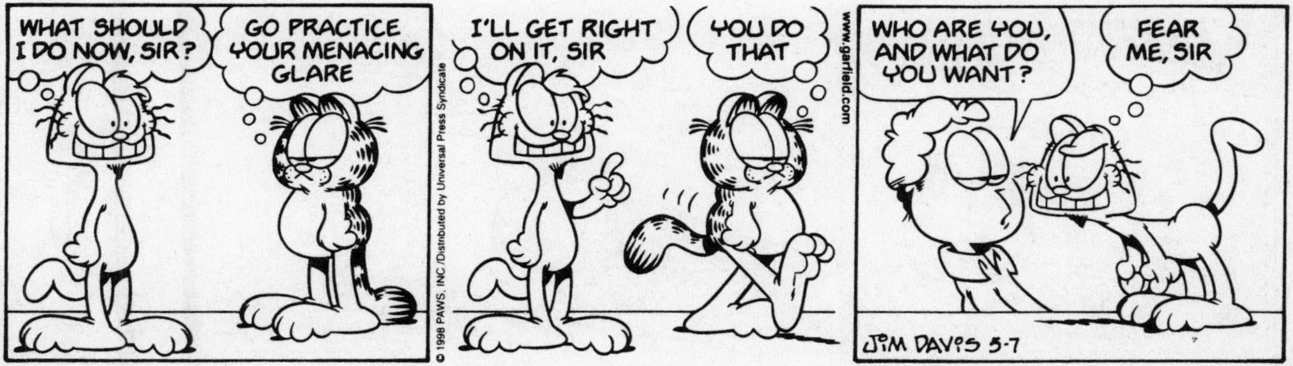

WHAT SHOULD I DO NOW, SIR?
GO PRACTICE YOUR MENACING GLARE
© 1998 PAWS, INC./Distributed by Universal Press Syndicate
I'LL GET RIGHT ON IT, SIR
YOU DO THAT
www.garfield.com
WHO ARE YOU, AND WHAT DO YOU WANT?
FEAR ME, SIR
JIM DAVIS 5-7

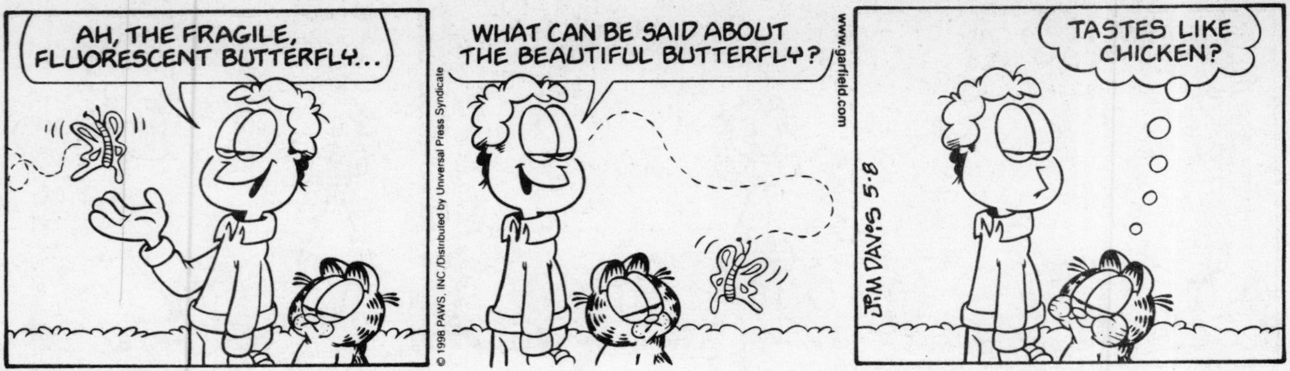
AH, THE FRAGILE, FLUORESCENT BUTTERFLY...
WHAT CAN BE SAID ABOUT THE BEAUTIFUL BUTTERFLY?
TASTES LIKE CHICKEN?
JIM DAVIS 5·8
© 1998 PAWS, INC./Distributed by Universal Press Syndicate
www.garfield.com

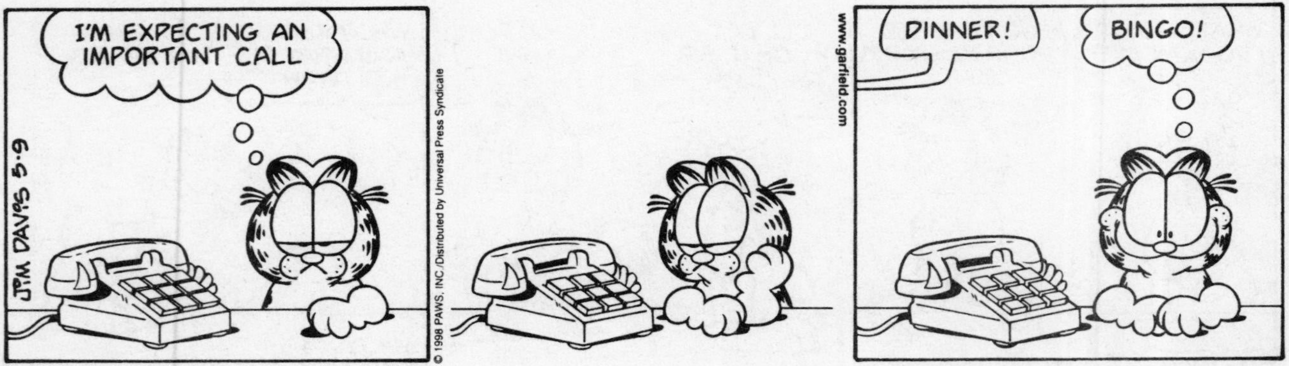
I'M EXPECTING AN IMPORTANT CALL
DINNER!
BINGO!
JIM DAVIS 5·9
© 1998 PAWS, INC./Distributed by Universal Press Syndicate
www.garfield.com

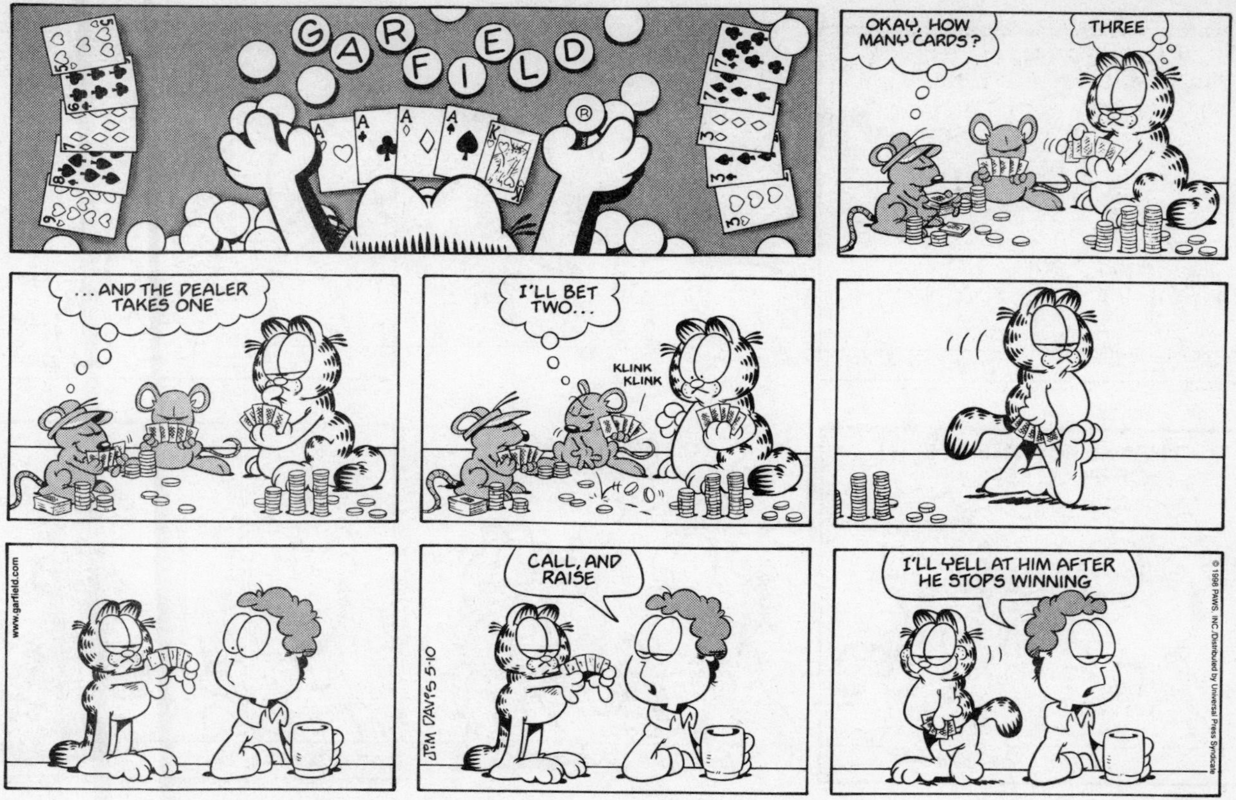
GARFIELD®
OKAY, HOW MANY CARDS?
THREE
...AND THE DEALER TAKES ONE
I'LL BET TWO...
KLINK KLINK
www.garfield.com
JIM DAVIS 5-10
CALL, AND RAISE
I'LL YELL AT HIM AFTER HE STOPS WINNING
© 1998 PAWS, INC./Distributed by Universal Press Syndicate

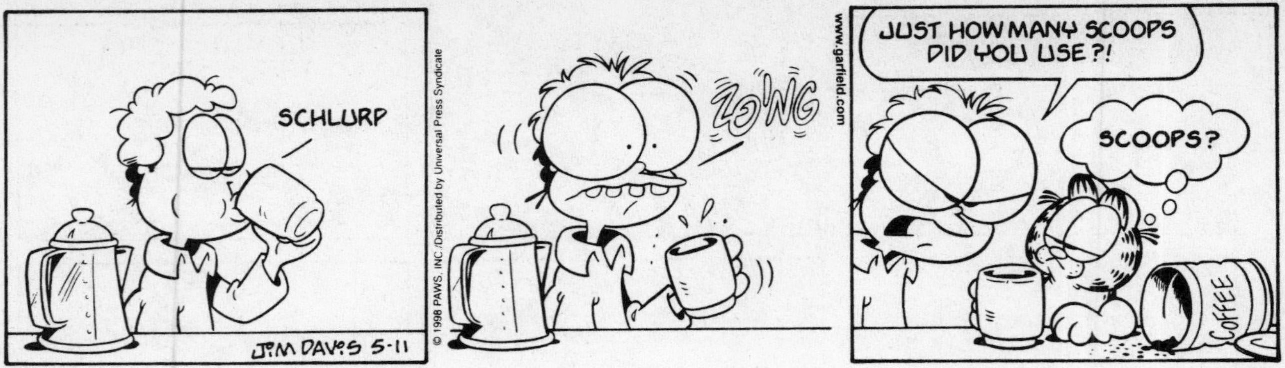
SCHLURP
JIM DAVIS 5-11
© 1998 PAWS, INC./Distributed by Universal Press Syndicate
ZOING
www.garfield.com
JUST HOW MANY SCOOPS DID YOU USE?!
SCOOPS?
COFFEE

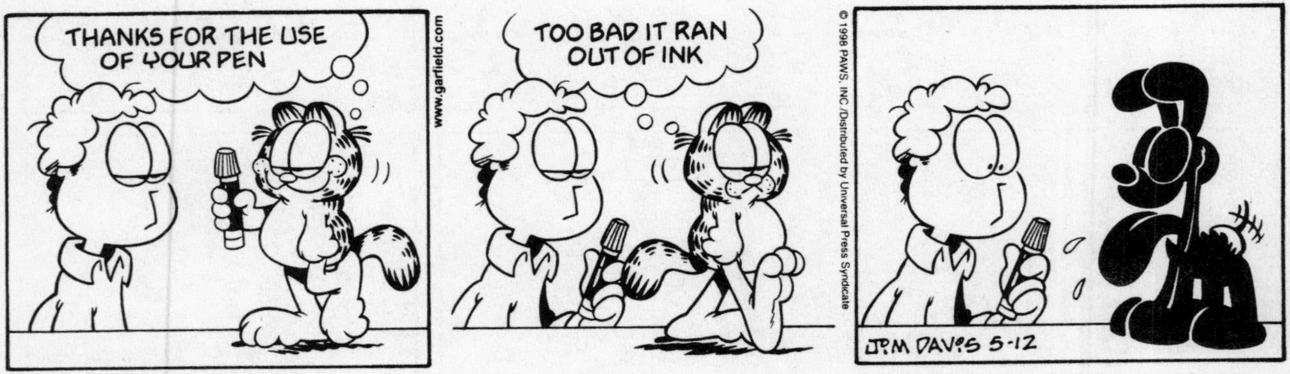
THANKS FOR THE USE OF YOUR PEN
www.garfield.com
TOO BAD IT RAN OUT OF INK
© 1998 PAWS, INC./Distributed by Universal Press Syndicate
JIM DAVIS 5-12

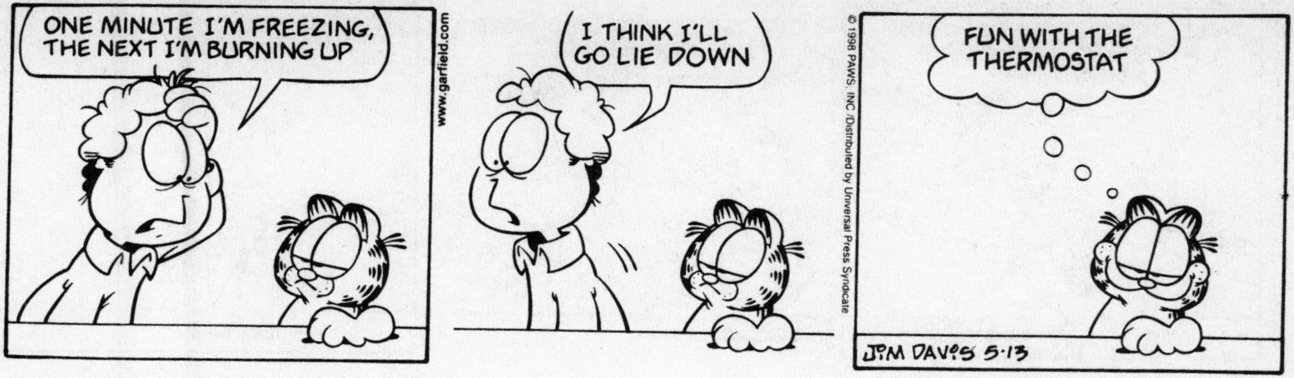
ONE MINUTE I'M FREEZING, THE NEXT I'M BURNING UP
www.garfield.com
I THINK I'LL GO LIE DOWN
© 1998 PAWS, INC./Distributed by Universal Press Syndicate
FUN WITH THE THERMOSTAT
JIM DAVIS 5·13

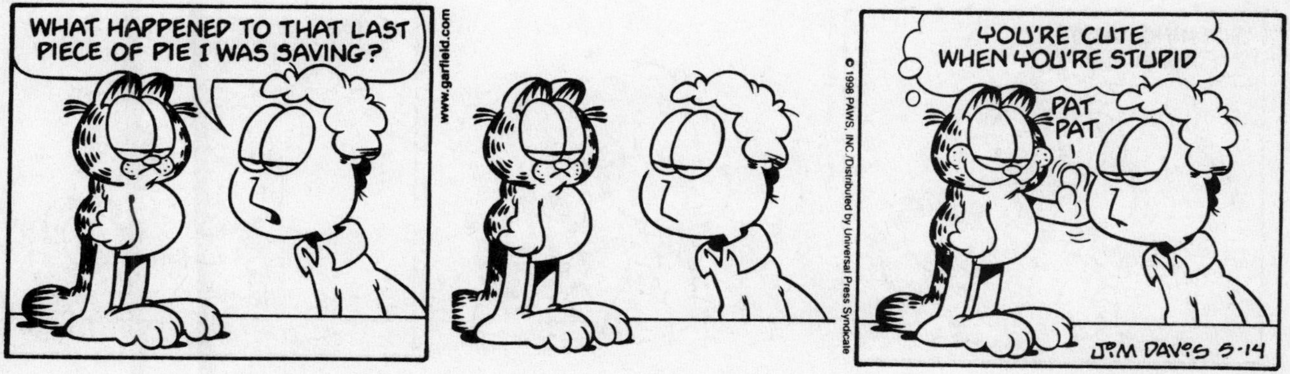
WHAT HAPPENED TO THAT LAST PIECE OF PIE I WAS SAVING?
www.garfield.com
© 1998 PAWS, INC./Distributed by Universal Press Syndicate
YOU'RE CUTE WHEN YOU'RE STUPID
PAT PAT
JIM DAVIS 5·14

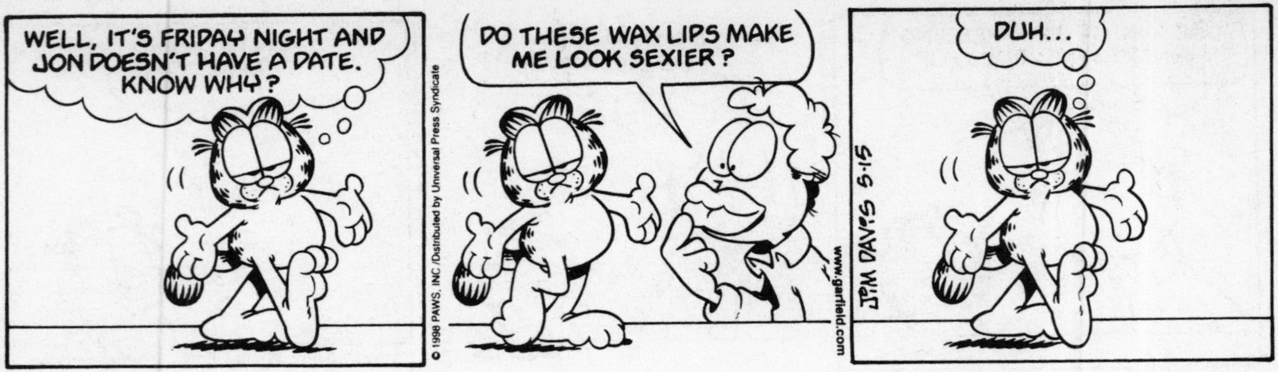
WELL, IT'S FRIDAY NIGHT AND JON DOESN'T HAVE A DATE. KNOW WHY?
DO THESE WAX LIPS MAKE ME LOOK SEXIER?
DUH...
© 1998 PAWS, INC./Distributed by Universal Press Syndicate
JIM DAVIS 5-15
www.garfield.com

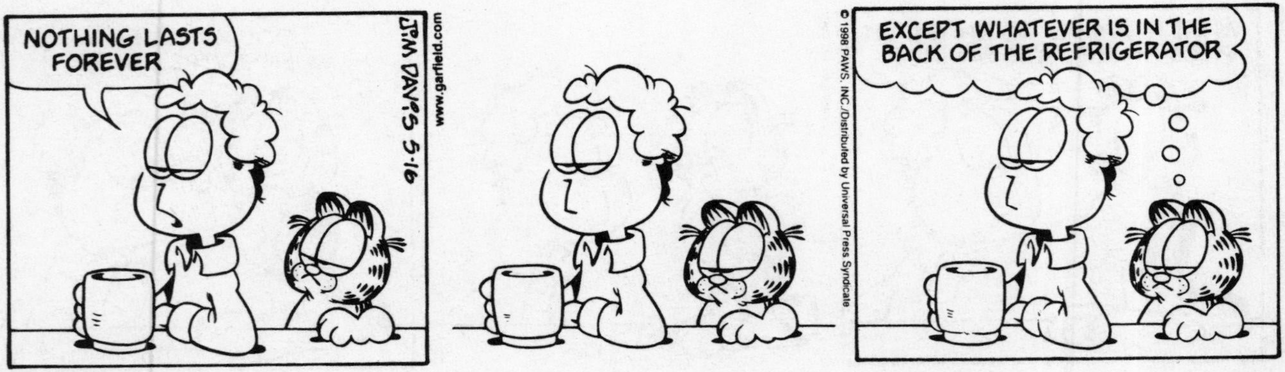
NOTHING LASTS FOREVER
EXCEPT WHATEVER IS IN THE BACK OF THE REFRIGERATOR
JIM DAVIS 5-16
www.garfield.com
© 1998 PAWS, INC./Distributed by Universal Press Syndicate

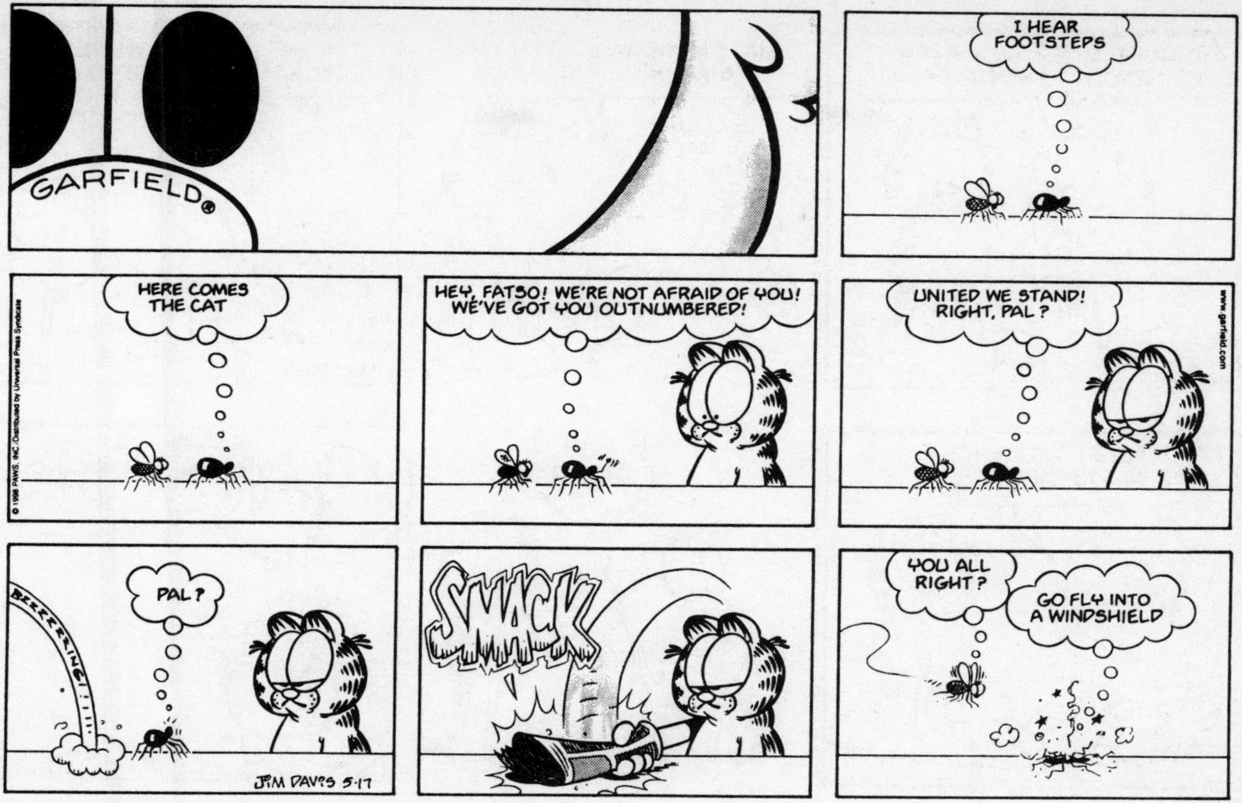
GARFIELD®
I HEAR FOOTSTEPS
HERE COMES THE CAT
HEY, FATSO! WE'RE NOT AFRAID OF YOU! WE'VE GOT YOU OUTNUMBERED!
UNITED WE STAND! RIGHT, PAL?
PAL?
JIM DAVIS 5-17
SMACK
YOU ALL RIGHT?
GO FLY INTO A WINDSHIELD
© 1998 PAWS, INC./Distributed by Universal Press Syndicate
www.garfield.com

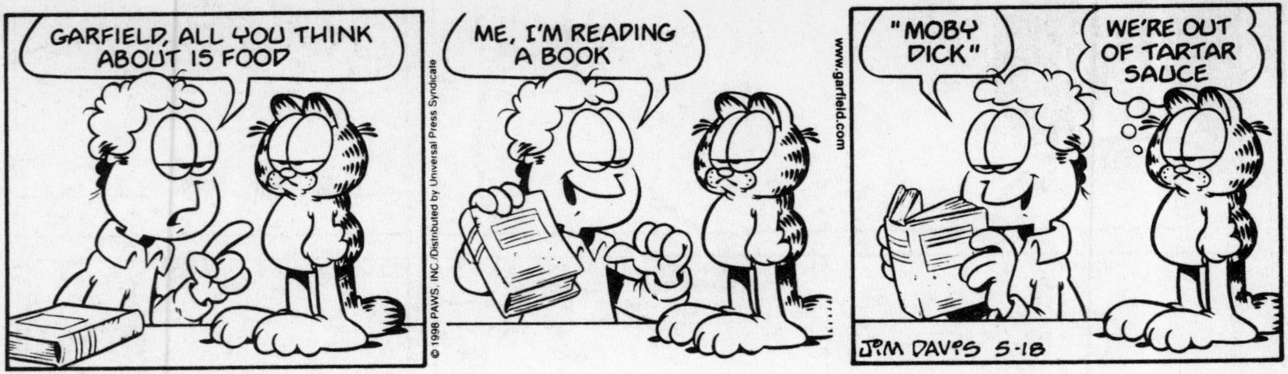
GARFIELD, ALL YOU THINK ABOUT IS FOOD
ME, I'M READING A BOOK
"MOBY DICK"
WE'RE OUT OF TARTAR SAUCE
JIM DAVIS 5-18
© 1998 PAWS, INC./Distributed by Universal Press Syndicate
www.garfield.com

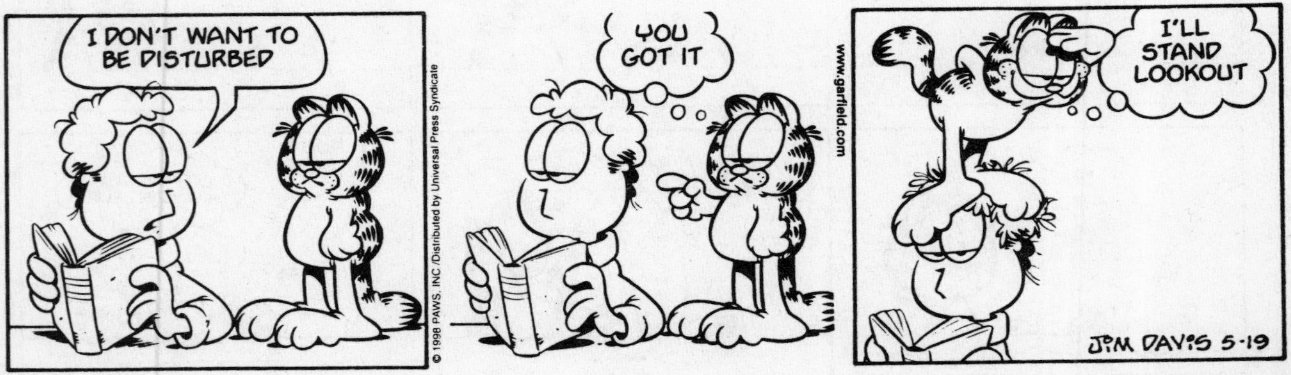
I DON'T WANT TO BE DISTURBED
YOU GOT IT
I'LL STAND LOOKOUT
JIM DAVIS 5-19
© 1998 PAWS, INC./Distributed by Universal Press Syndicate
www.garfield.com

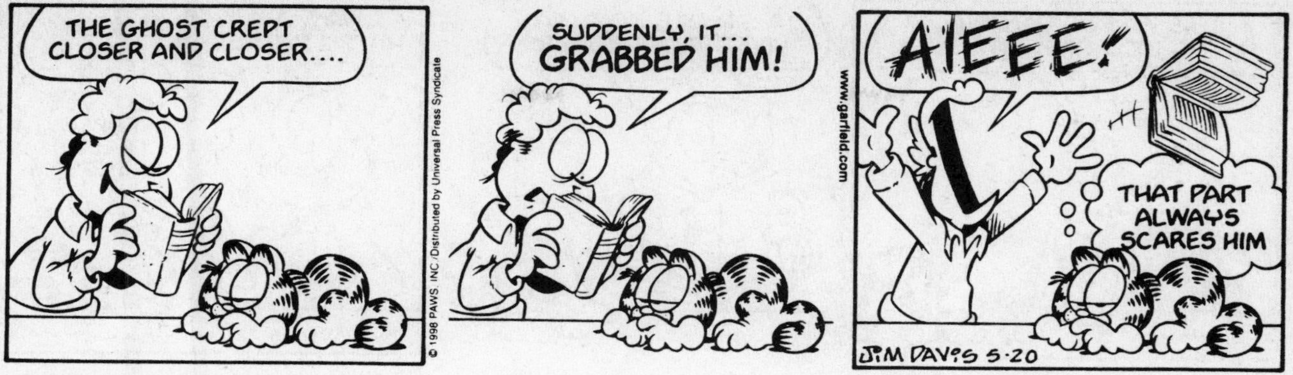
THE GHOST CREPT CLOSER AND CLOSER....
SUDDENLY, IT... GRABBED HIM!
AIEEE!
THAT PART ALWAYS SCARES HIM
JIM DAVIS 5·20
www.garfield.com

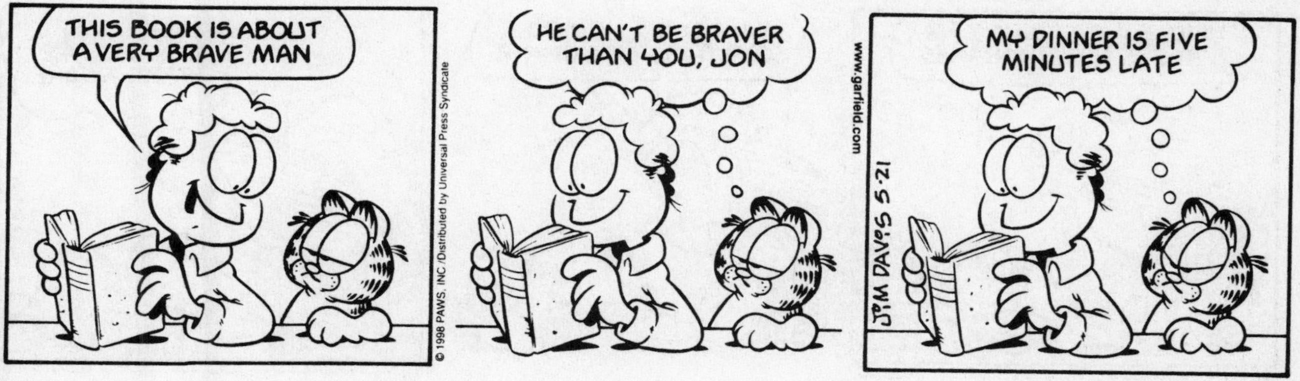
THIS BOOK IS ABOUT A VERY BRAVE MAN
HE CAN'T BE BRAVER THAN YOU, JON
MY DINNER IS FIVE MINUTES LATE
JIM DAVIS 5·21
www.garfield.com

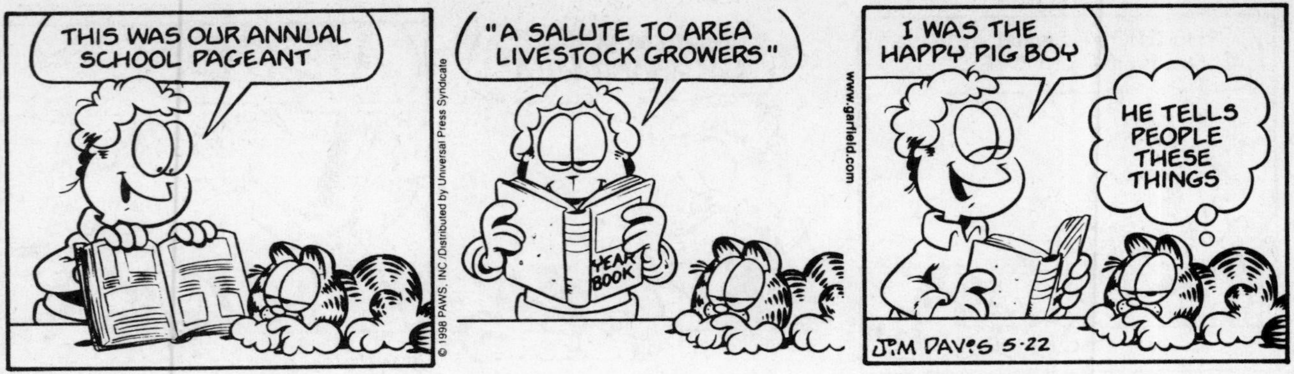
THIS WAS OUR ANNUAL SCHOOL PAGEANT
"A SALUTE TO AREA LIVESTOCK GROWERS"
YEAR BOOK
I WAS THE HAPPY PIG BOY
HE TELLS PEOPLE THESE THINGS
JIM DAVIS 5-22
© 1998 PAWS, INC./Distributed by Universal Press Syndicate
www.garfield.com

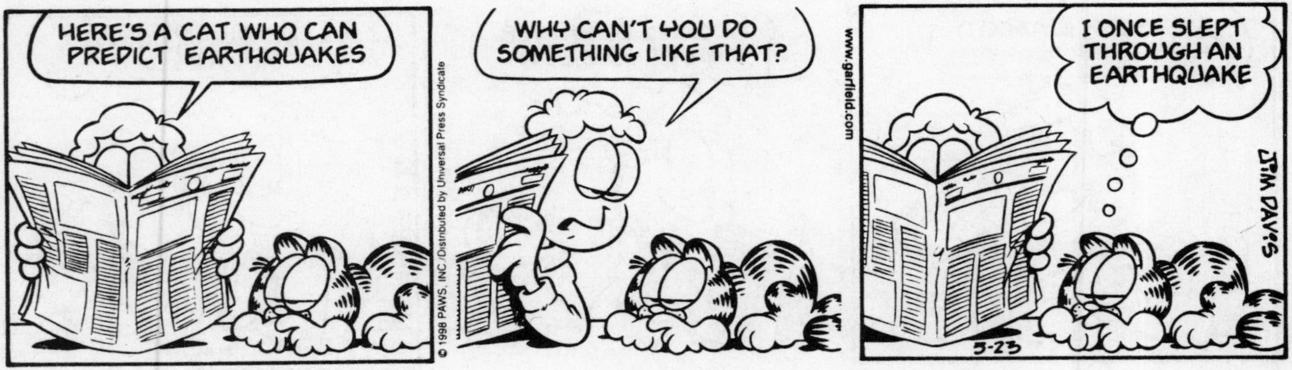
HERE'S A CAT WHO CAN PREDICT EARTHQUAKES
WHY CAN'T YOU DO SOMETHING LIKE THAT?
I ONCE SLEPT THROUGH AN EARTHQUAKE
JIM DAVIS
5-23
© 1998 PAWS, INC./Distributed by Universal Press Syndicate
www.garfield.com

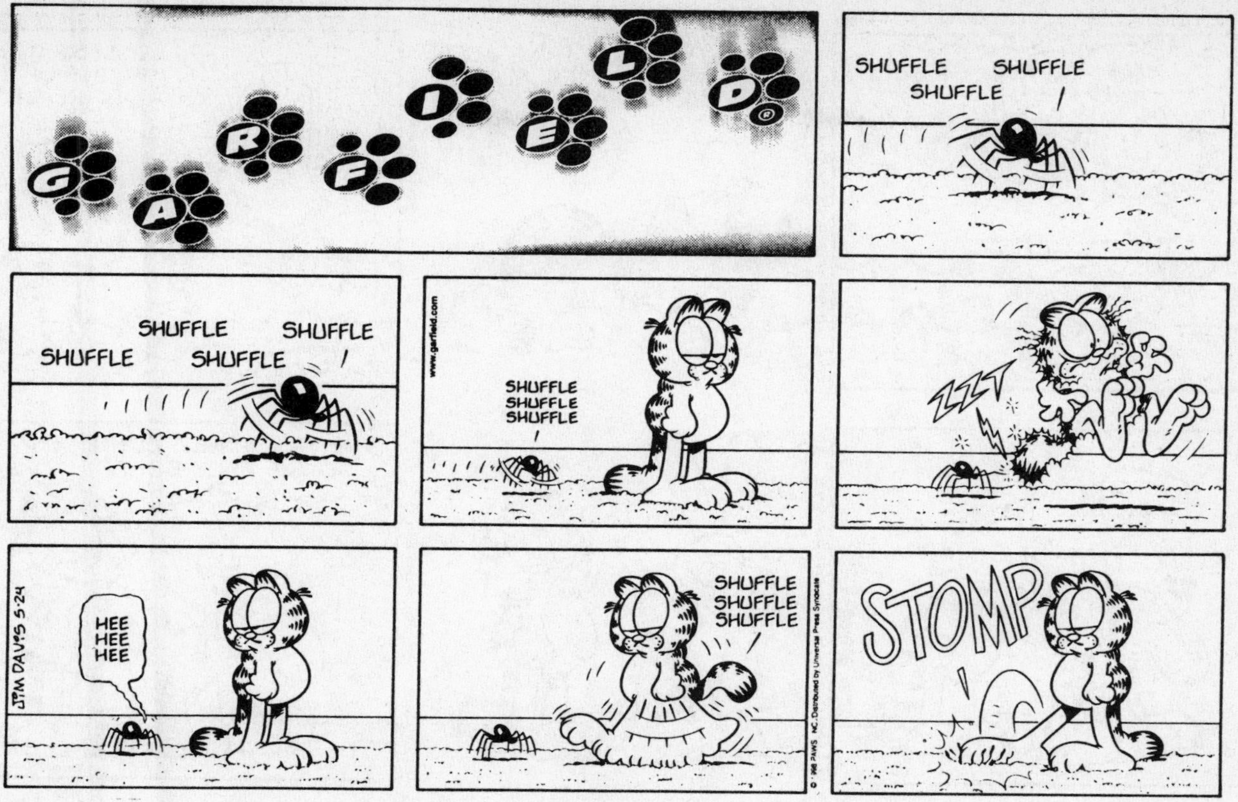
GARFIELD®
SHUFFLE SHUFFLE SHUFFLE
SHUFFLE SHUFFLE SHUFFLE SHUFFLE
www.garfield.com
SHUFFLE SHUFFLE SHUFFLE
ZZZT
JIM DAVIS 5-24
HEE HEE HEE
SHUFFLE SHUFFLE SHUFFLE
PAWS INC. Distributed by Universal Press Syndicate
STOMP

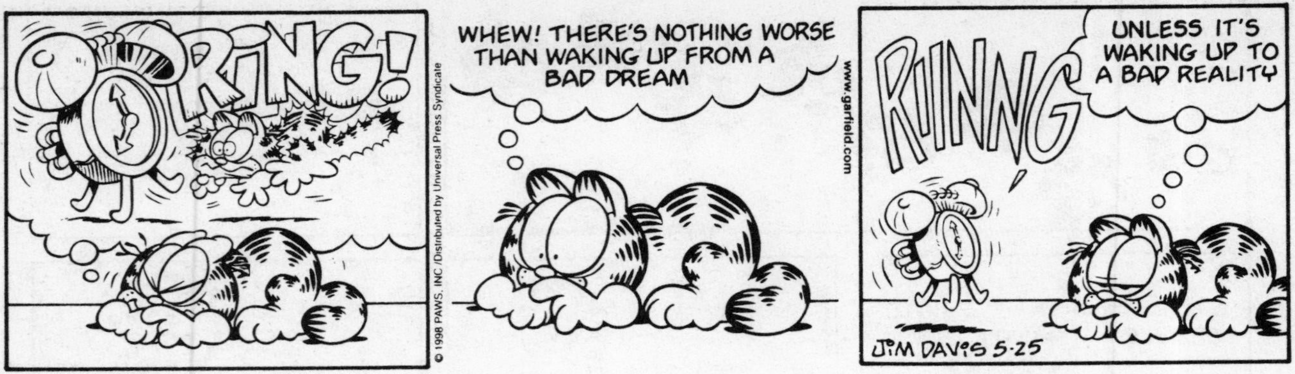
RING!
© 1998 PAWS, INC./Distributed by Universal Press Syndicate
WHEW! THERE'S NOTHING WORSE THAN WAKING UP FROM A BAD DREAM
www.garfield.com
RIINNG
UNLESS IT'S WAKING UP TO A BAD REALITY
JIM DAVIS 5-25

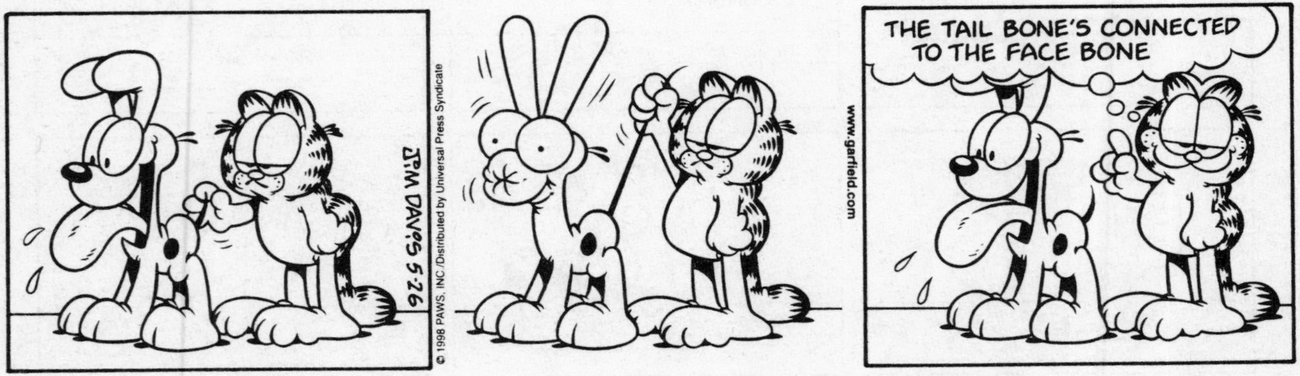
JIM DAVIS 5-26
© 1998 PAWS, INC./Distributed by Universal Press Syndicate
www.garfield.com
THE TAIL BONE'S CONNECTED TO THE FACE BONE

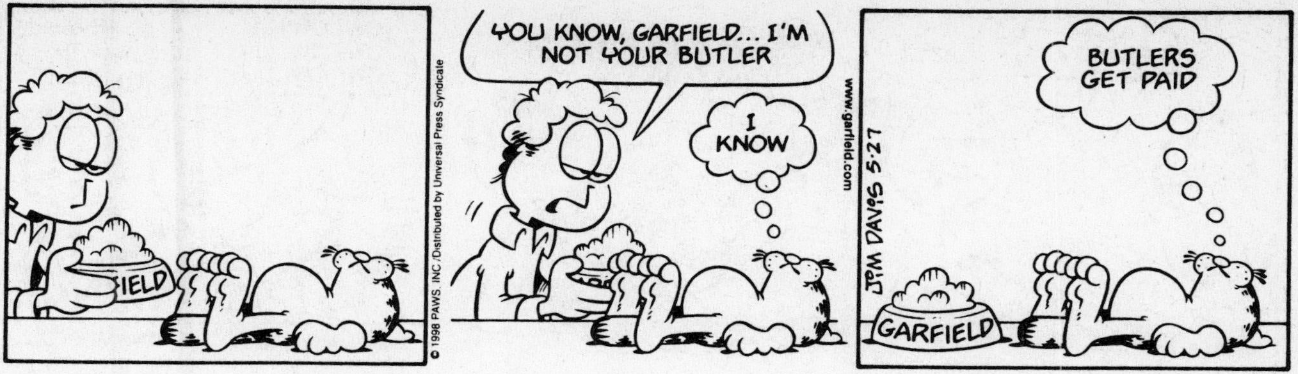

IELD
YOU KNOW, GARFIELD... I'M NOT YOUR BUTLER
I KNOW
BUTLERS GET PAID
GARFIELD
JIM DAVIS 5·27
www.garfield.com
© 1998 PAWS, INC./Distributed by Universal Press Syndicate

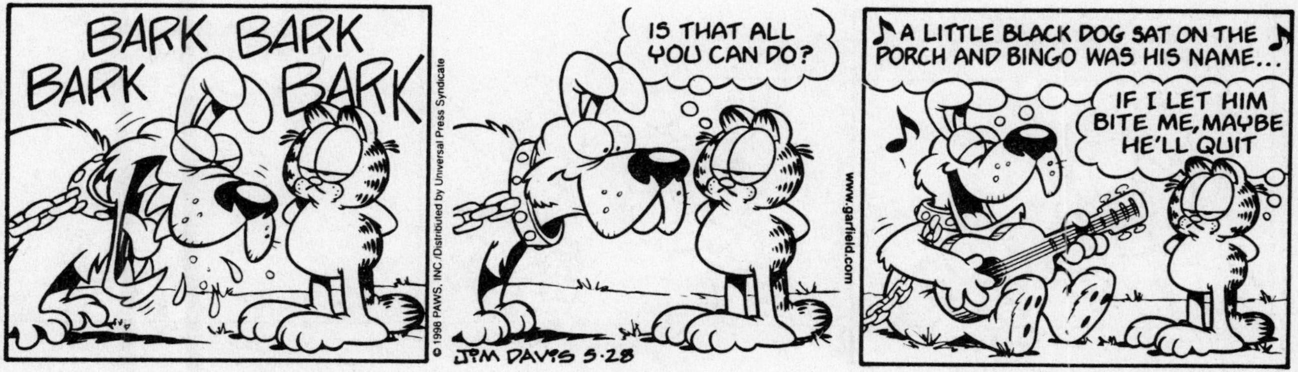

BARK BARK BARK BARK
IS THAT ALL YOU CAN DO?
A LITTLE BLACK DOG SAT ON THE PORCH AND BINGO WAS HIS NAME...
IF I LET HIM BITE ME, MAYBE HE'LL QUIT
JIM DAVIS 5·28
www.garfield.com
© 1998 PAWS, INC./Distributed by Universal Press Syndicate

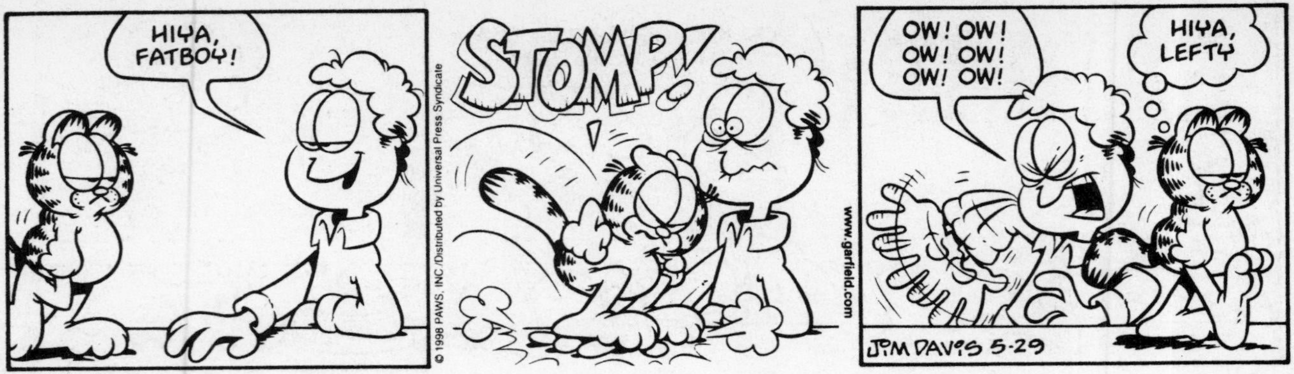
HIYA, FATBOY!
STOMP!
OW! OW! OW! OW! OW! OW!
HIYA, LEFTY
JIM DAVIS 5-29
© 1998 PAWS, INC./Distributed by Universal Press Syndicate
www.garfield.com

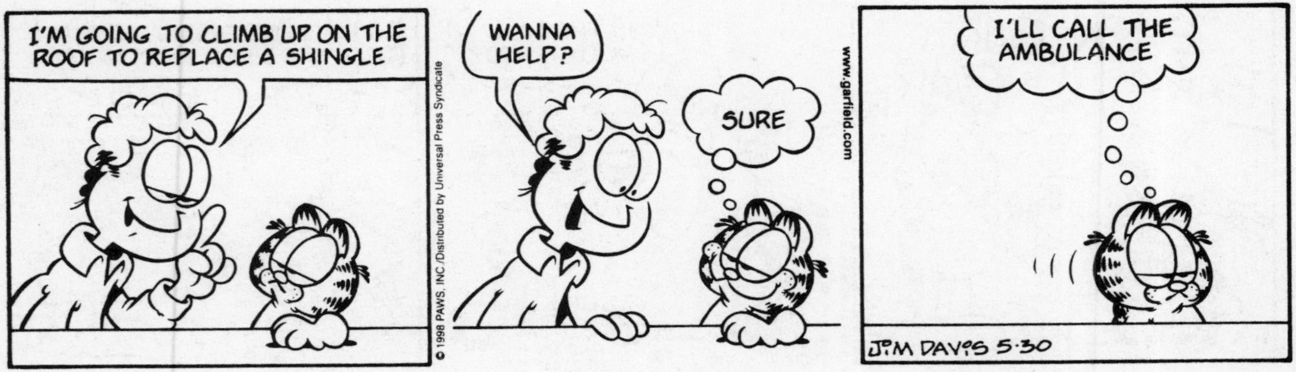
I'M GOING TO CLIMB UP ON THE ROOF TO REPLACE A SHINGLE
WANNA HELP?
SURE
I'LL CALL THE AMBULANCE
JIM DAVIS 5-30
© 1998 PAWS, INC./Distributed by Universal Press Syndicate
www.garfield.com

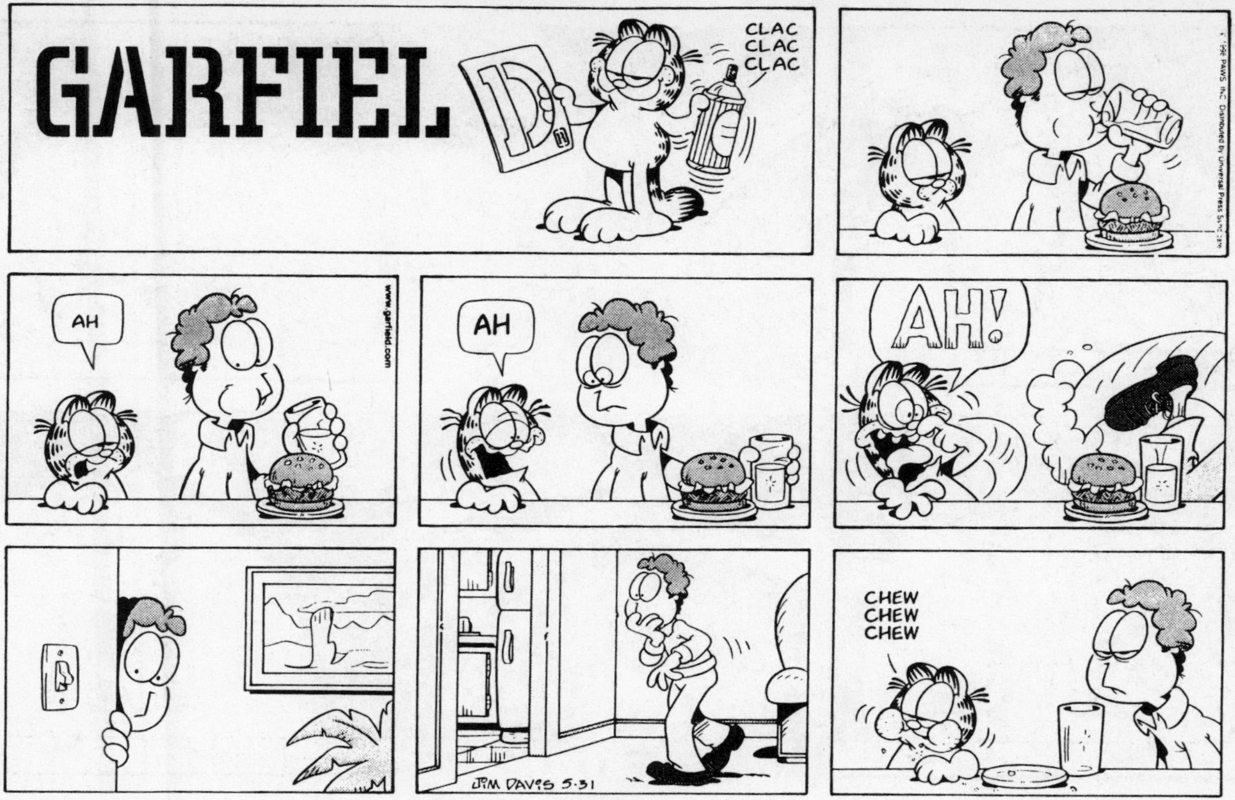

GARFIEL
CLAC CLAC CLAC
PAWS INC Distributed by Universal Press
www.garfield.com
AH
AH
AH!
JIM DAVIS 5-31
CHEW CHEW CHEW

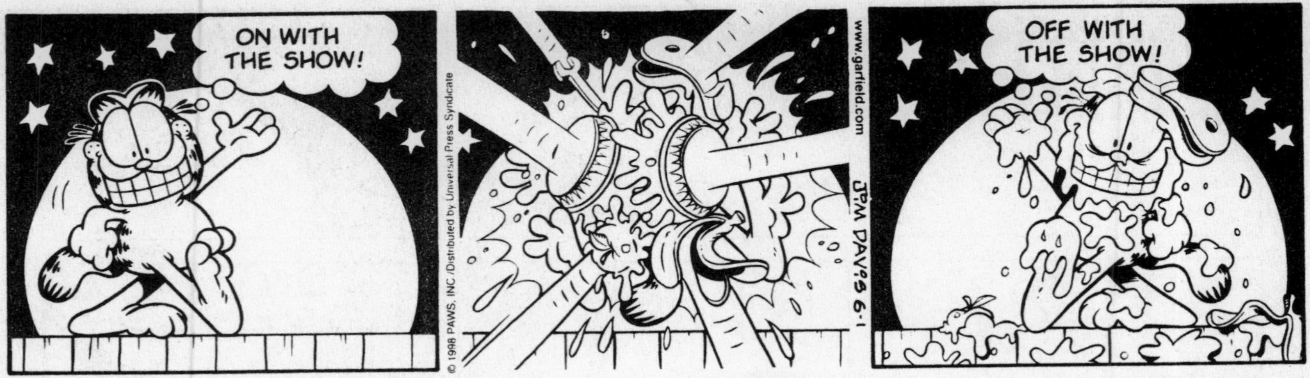
ON WITH THE SHOW!
© 1998 PAWS. INC./Distributed by Universal Press Syndicate
www.garfield.com
JIM DAVIS 6-1
OFF WITH THE SHOW!

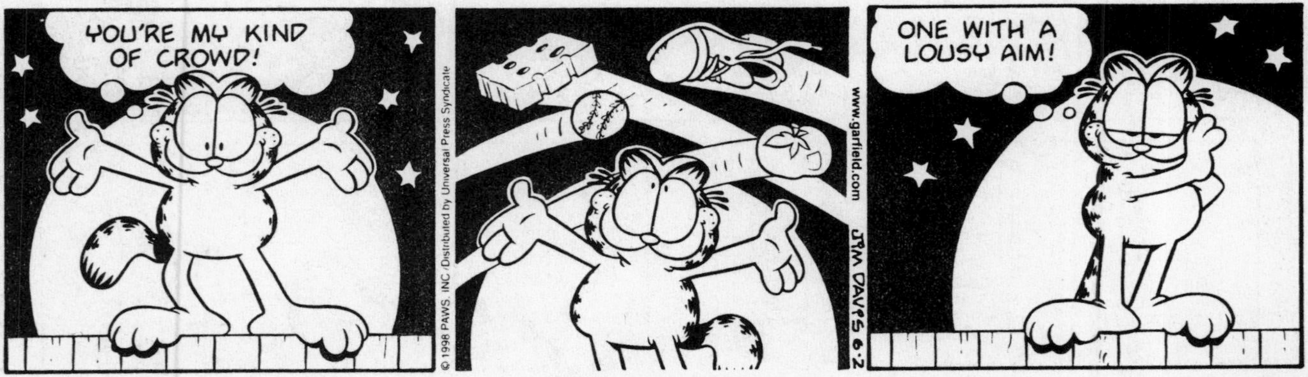
YOU'RE MY KIND OF CROWD!
© 1998 PAWS. INC./Distributed by Universal Press Syndicate
www.garfield.com
JIM DAVIS 6-2
ONE WITH A LOUSY AIM!

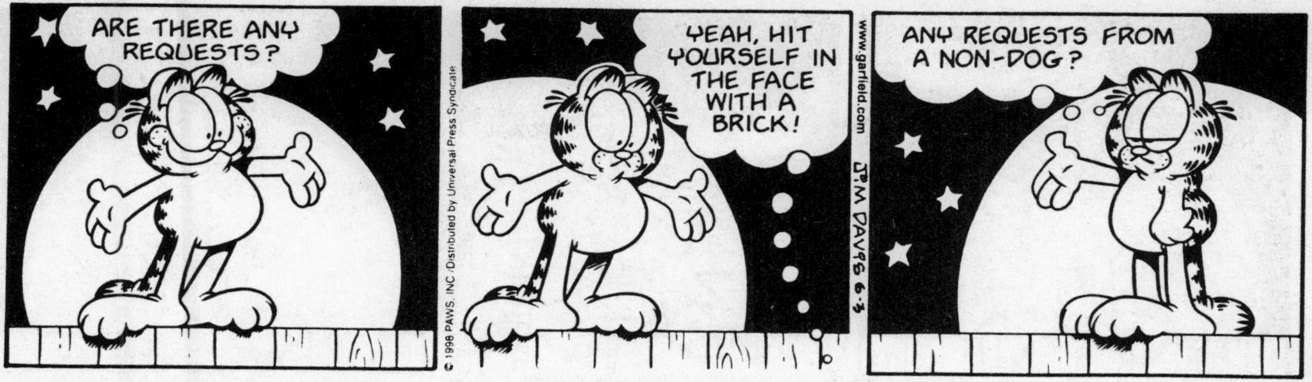
ARE THERE ANY REQUESTS?
YEAH, HIT YOURSELF IN THE FACE WITH A BRICK!
ANY REQUESTS FROM A NON-DOG?
© 1998 PAWS, INC./Distributed by Universal Press Syndicate
www.garfield.com
JIM DAVIS 6-3

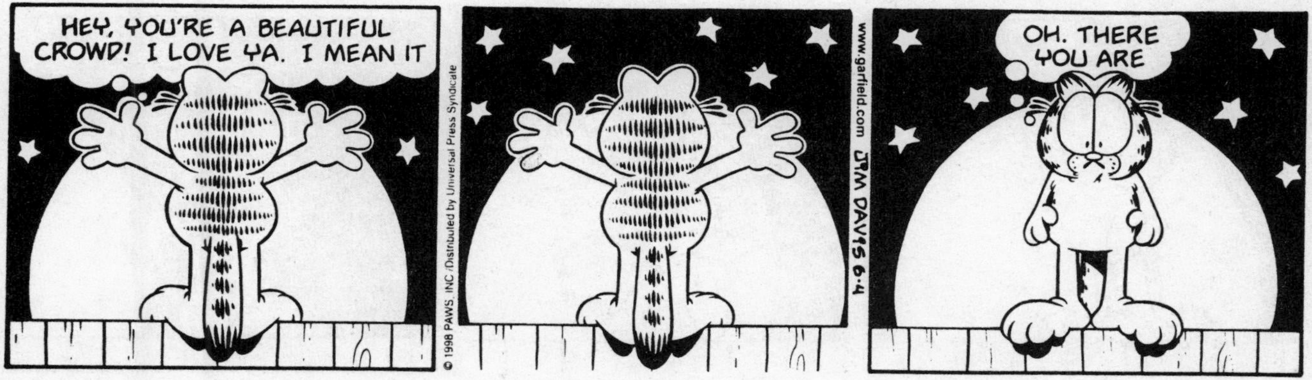
HEY, YOU'RE A BEAUTIFUL CROWD! I LOVE YA. I MEAN IT
OH. THERE YOU ARE
© 1998 PAWS, INC./Distributed by Universal Press Syndicate
www.garfield.com
JIM DAVIS 6-4

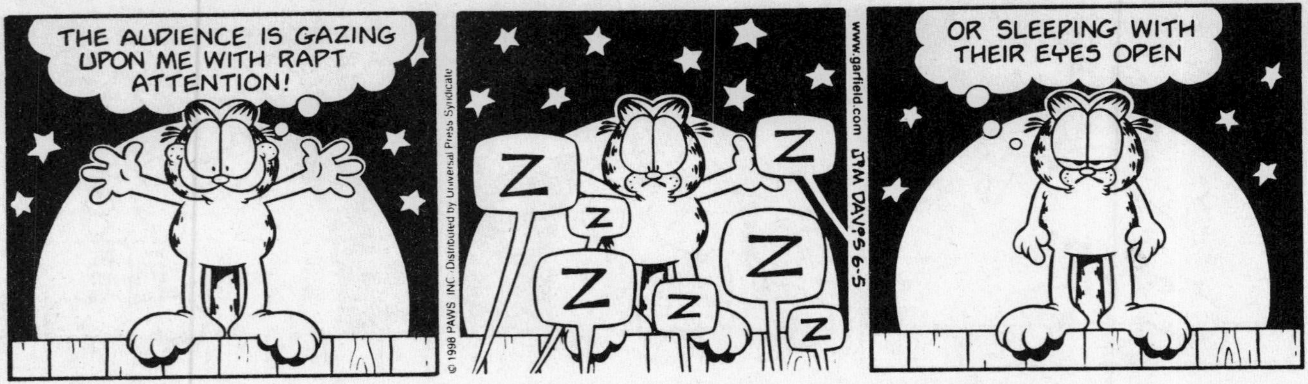
THE AUDIENCE IS GAZING UPON ME WITH RAPT ATTENTION!
Z Z Z Z Z Z Z
OR SLEEPING WITH THEIR EYES OPEN
© 1998 PAWS INC. Distributed by Universal Press Syndicate
www.garfield.com
JIM DAVIS 6-5

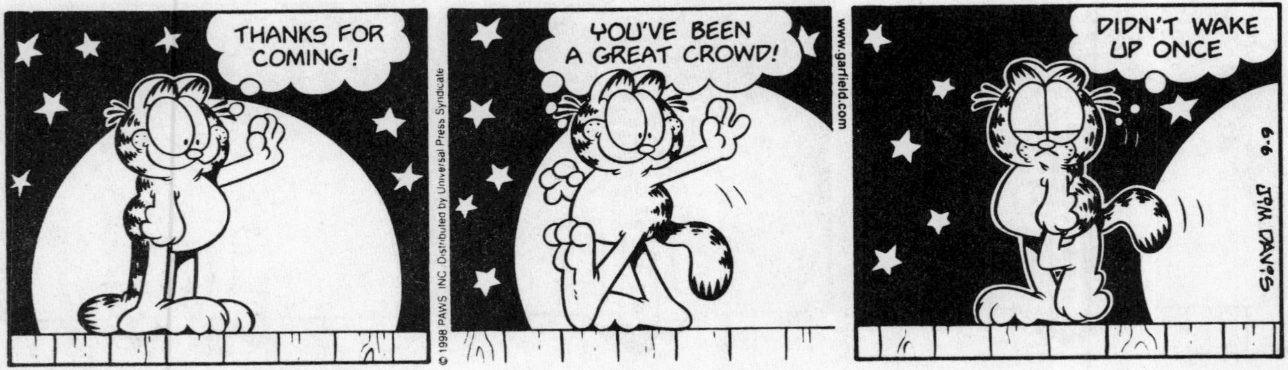
THANKS FOR COMING!
YOU'VE BEEN A GREAT CROWD!
DIDN'T WAKE UP ONCE
© 1998 PAWS INC. Distributed by Universal Press Syndicate
www.garfield.com
JIM DAVIS 6-6

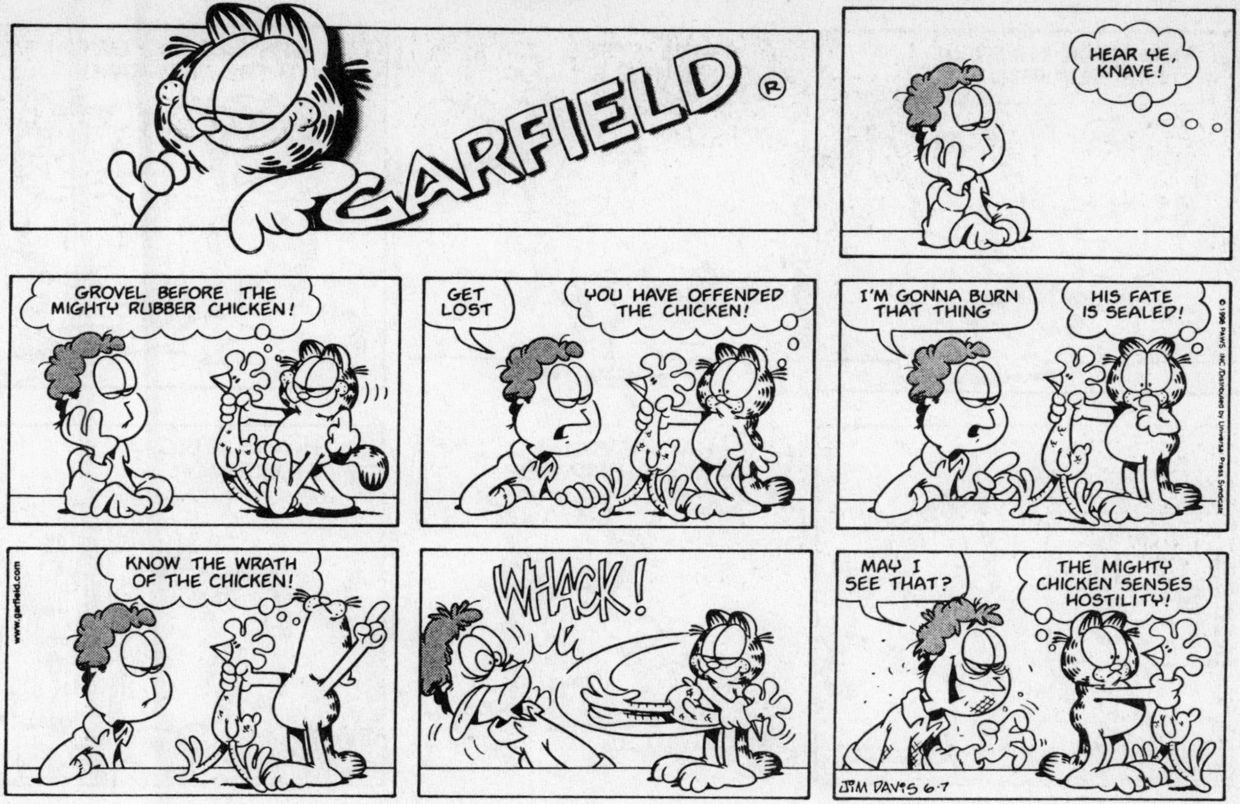
GARFIELD
HEAR YE, KNAVE!
GROVEL BEFORE THE MIGHTY RUBBER CHICKEN!
GET LOST
YOU HAVE OFFENDED THE CHICKEN!
I'M GONNA BURN THAT THING
HIS FATE IS SEALED!
© 1998 PAWS INC./Distributed by Universal Press Syndicate
www.garfield.com
KNOW THE WRATH OF THE CHICKEN!
WHACK!
MAY I SEE THAT?
THE MIGHTY CHICKEN SENSES HOSTILITY!
JIM DAVIS 6-7

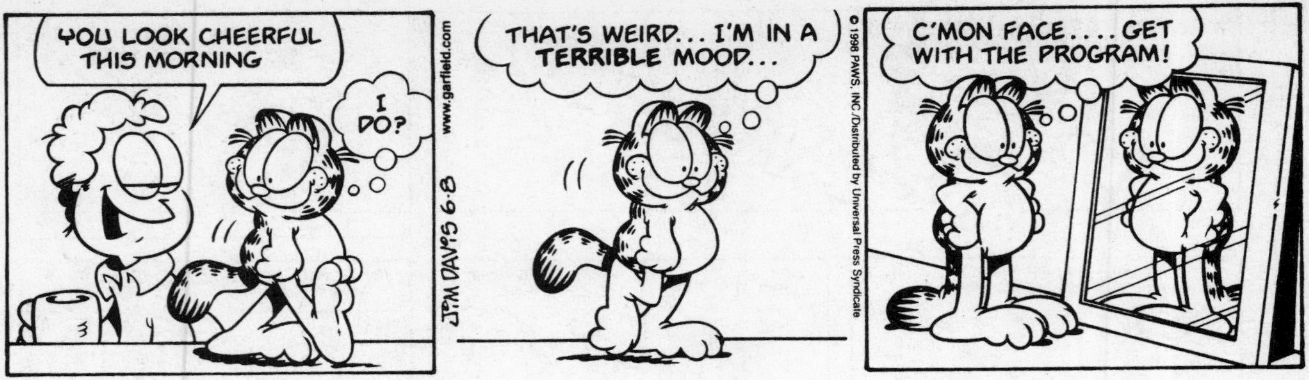
YOU LOOK CHEERFUL THIS MORNING
I DO?
www.garfield.com
JIM DAVIS 6-8
THAT'S WEIRD... I'M IN A TERRIBLE MOOD...
© 1998 PAWS, INC./Distributed by Universal Press Syndicate
C'MON FACE.... GET WITH THE PROGRAM!

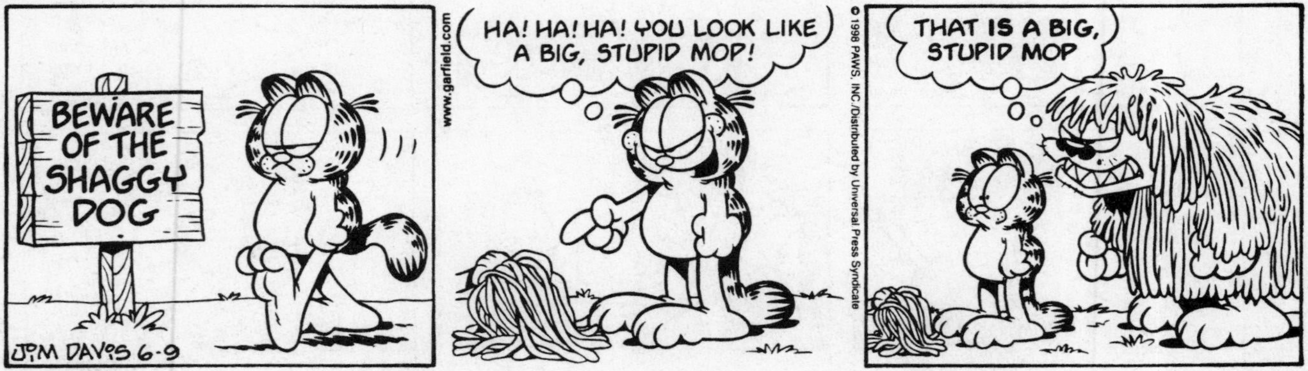
BEWARE OF THE SHAGGY DOG
JIM DAVIS 6-9
www.garfield.com
HA! HA! HA! YOU LOOK LIKE A BIG, STUPID MOP!
© 1998 PAWS, INC./Distributed by Universal Press Syndicate
THAT IS A BIG, STUPID MOP

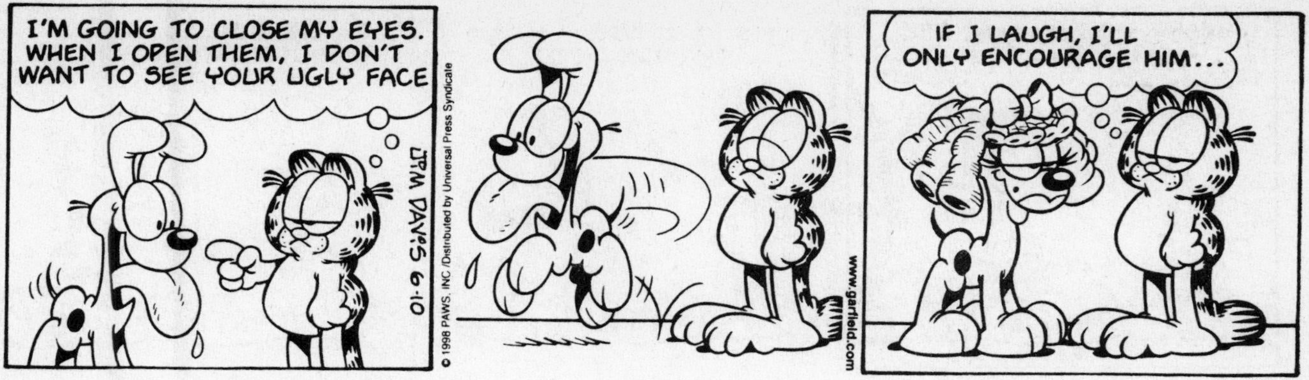
I'M GOING TO CLOSE MY EYES. WHEN I OPEN THEM, I DON'T WANT TO SEE YOUR UGLY FACE
JIM DAVIS 6-10
© 1998 PAWS, INC./Distributed by Universal Press Syndicate
www.garfield.com
IF I LAUGH, I'LL ONLY ENCOURAGE HIM...

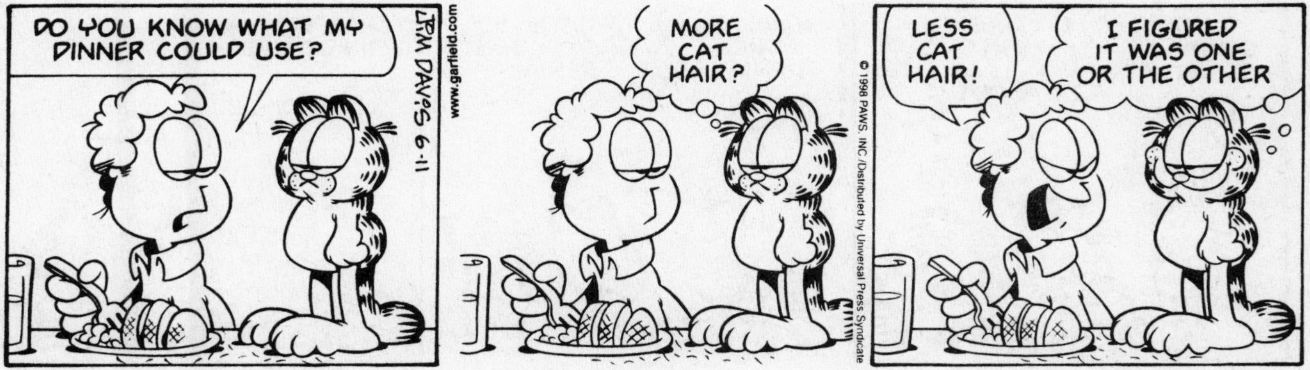
DO YOU KNOW WHAT MY DINNER COULD USE?
JIM DAVIS 6-11
www.garfield.com
MORE CAT HAIR?
© 1998 PAWS, INC./Distributed by Universal Press Syndicate
LESS CAT HAIR!
I FIGURED IT WAS ONE OR THE OTHER

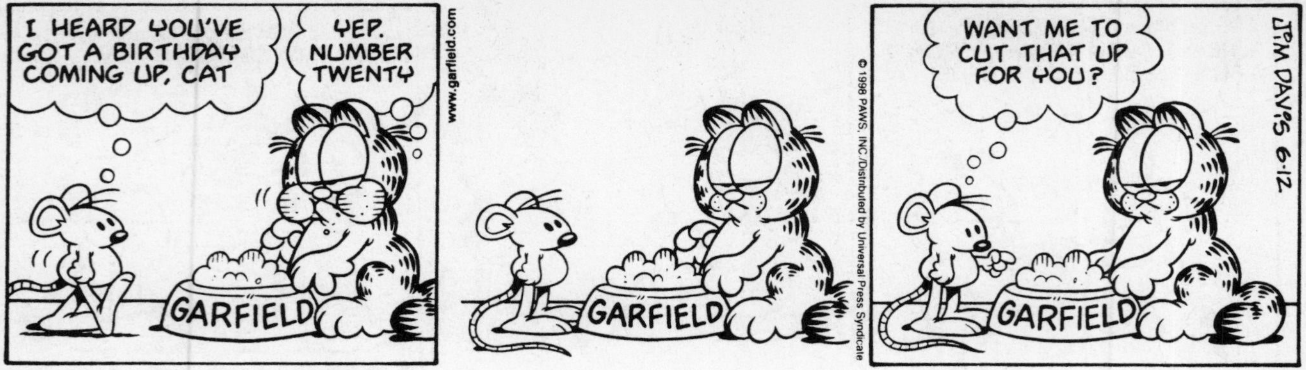
I HEARD YOU'VE GOT A BIRTHDAY COMING UP, CAT
YEP. NUMBER TWENTY
GARFIELD
www.garfield.com
GARFIELD
© 1998 PAWS, INC./Distributed by Universal Press Syndicate
WANT ME TO CUT THAT UP FOR YOU?
GARFIELD
JIM DAVIS 6-12

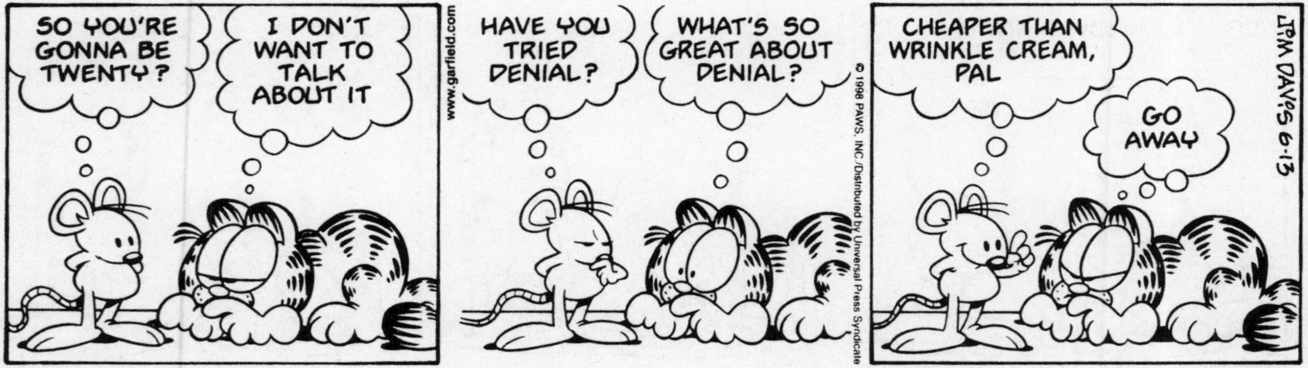
SO YOU'RE GONNA BE TWENTY?
I DON'T WANT TO TALK ABOUT IT
www.garfield.com
HAVE YOU TRIED DENIAL?
WHAT'S SO GREAT ABOUT DENIAL?
© 1998 PAWS, INC./Distributed by Universal Press Syndicate
CHEAPER THAN WRINKLE CREAM, PAL
GO AWAY
JIM DAVIS 6-13

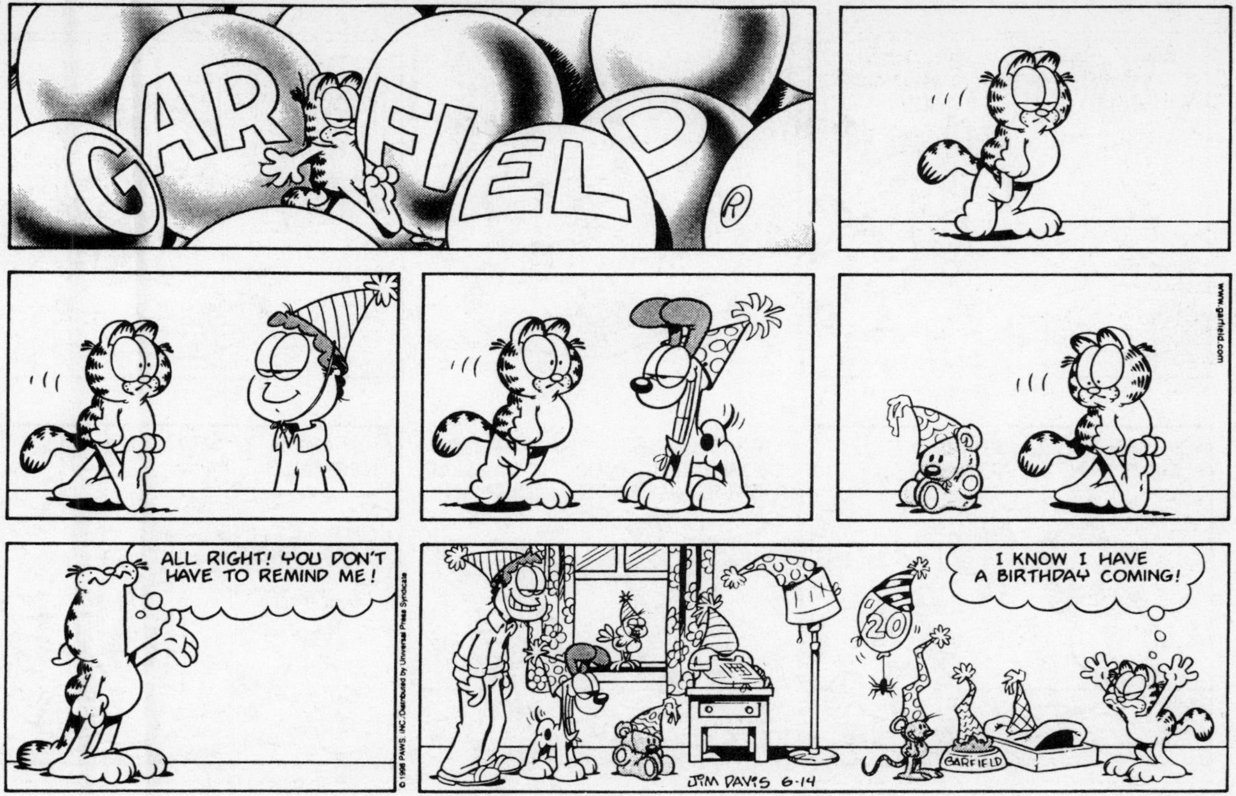
GARFIELD ®
www.garfield.com
ALL RIGHT! YOU DON'T HAVE TO REMIND ME!
© 1998 PAWS, INC./Distributed by Universal Press Syndicate
20
I KNOW I HAVE A BIRTHDAY COMING!
GARFIELD
JIM DAVIS 6-14

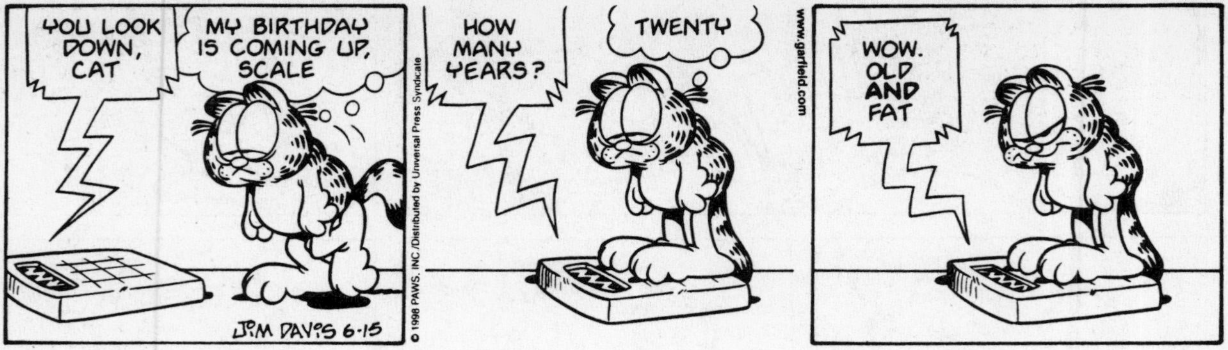
YOU LOOK DOWN, CAT
MY BIRTHDAY IS COMING UP, SCALE
JIM DAVIS 6-15
© 1998 PAWS, INC./Distributed by Universal Press Syndicate
HOW MANY YEARS?
TWENTY
www.garfield.com
WOW. OLD **AND** FAT

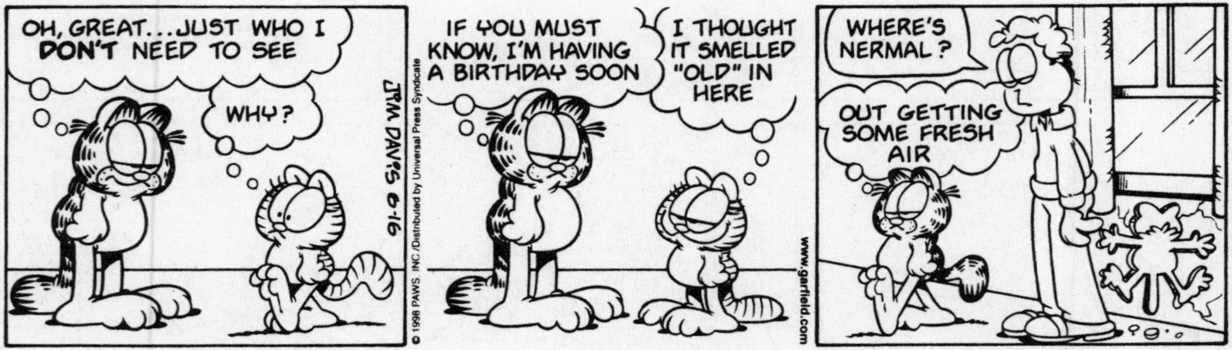
OH, GREAT...JUST WHO I **DON'T** NEED TO SEE
WHY?
JIM DAVIS 6-16
© 1998 PAWS, INC./Distributed by Universal Press Syndicate
IF YOU MUST KNOW, I'M HAVING A BIRTHDAY SOON
I THOUGHT IT SMELLED "OLD" IN HERE
www.garfield.com
WHERE'S NERMAL?
OUT GETTING SOME FRESH AIR

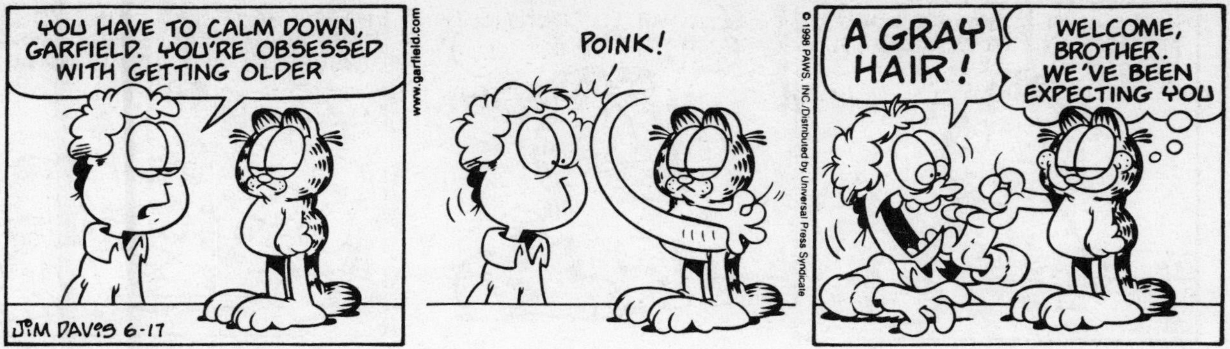
YOU HAVE TO CALM DOWN, GARFIELD. YOU'RE OBSESSED WITH GETTING OLDER
JIM DAVIS 6-17
www.garfield.com
POINK!
© 1998 PAWS, INC./Distributed by Universal Press Syndicate
A GRAY HAIR!
WELCOME, BROTHER. WE'VE BEEN EXPECTING YOU

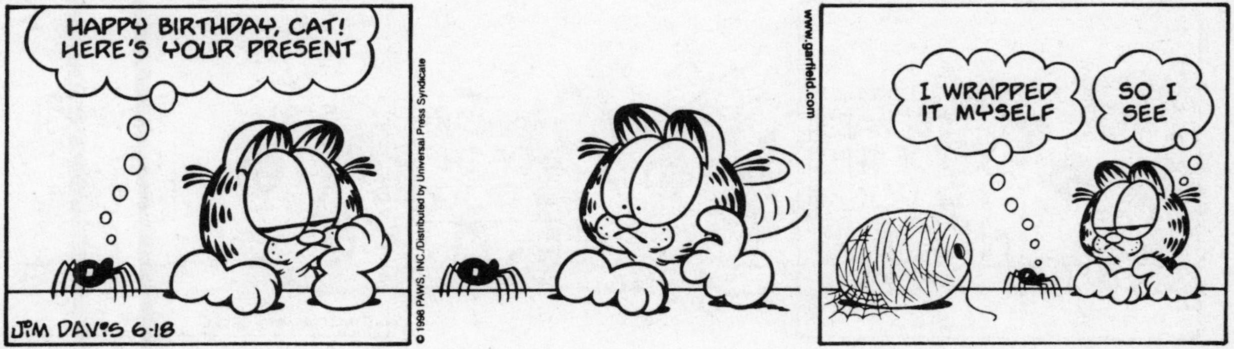
HAPPY BIRTHDAY, CAT! HERE'S YOUR PRESENT
JIM DAVIS 6-18
© 1998 PAWS, INC./Distributed by Universal Press Syndicate
www.garfield.com
I WRAPPED IT MYSELF
SO I SEE

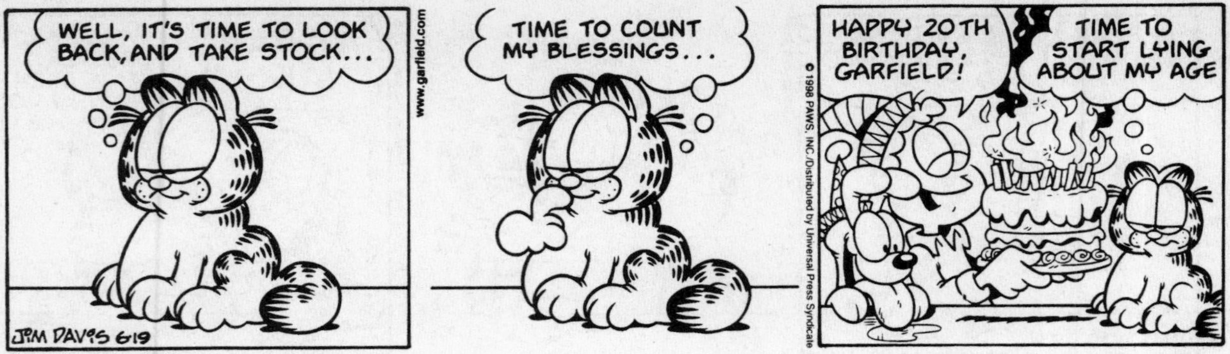

WELL, IT'S TIME TO LOOK BACK, AND TAKE STOCK...
JIM DAVIS 6-19
www.garfield.com
TIME TO COUNT MY BLESSINGS...
© 1998 PAWS, INC./Distributed by Universal Press Syndicate
HAPPY 20TH BIRTHDAY, GARFIELD!
TIME TO START LYING ABOUT MY AGE

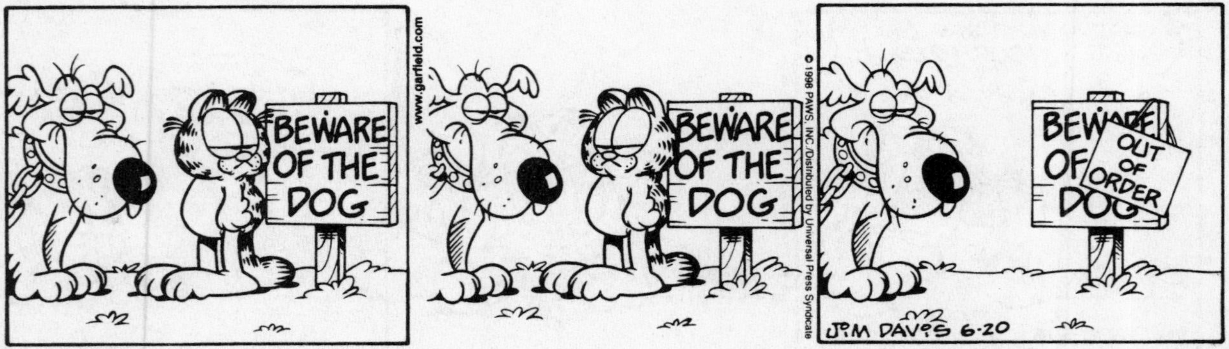

BEWARE OF THE DOG
www.garfield.com
BEWARE OF THE DOG
© 1998 PAWS, INC./Distributed by Universal Press Syndicate
BEWARE OF THE DOG
OUT OF ORDER
JIM DAVIS 6-20

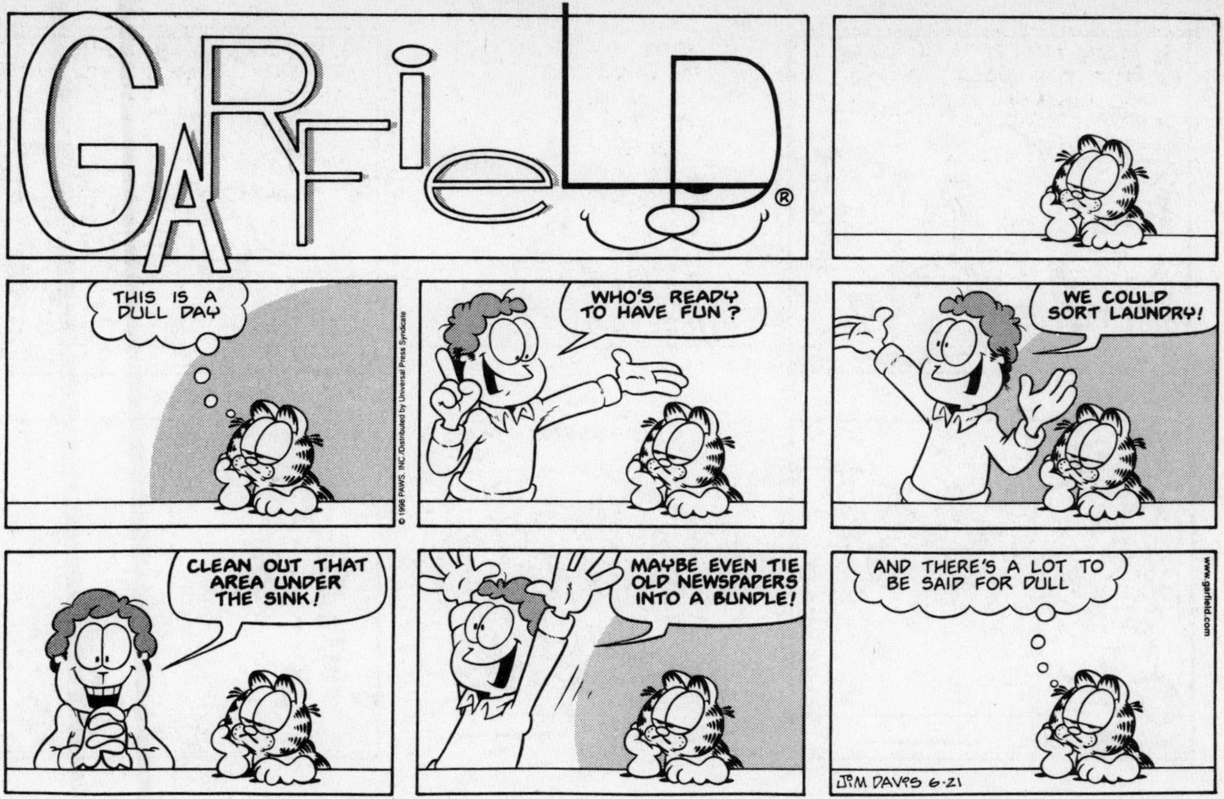
GARFIELD®
THIS IS A DULL DAY
WHO'S READY TO HAVE FUN?
WE COULD SORT LAUNDRY!
CLEAN OUT THAT AREA UNDER THE SINK!
MAYBE EVEN TIE OLD NEWSPAPERS INTO A BUNDLE!
AND THERE'S A LOT TO BE SAID FOR DULL
JIM DAVIS 6-21
© 1998 PAWS, INC./Distributed by Universal Press Syndicate
www.garfield.com

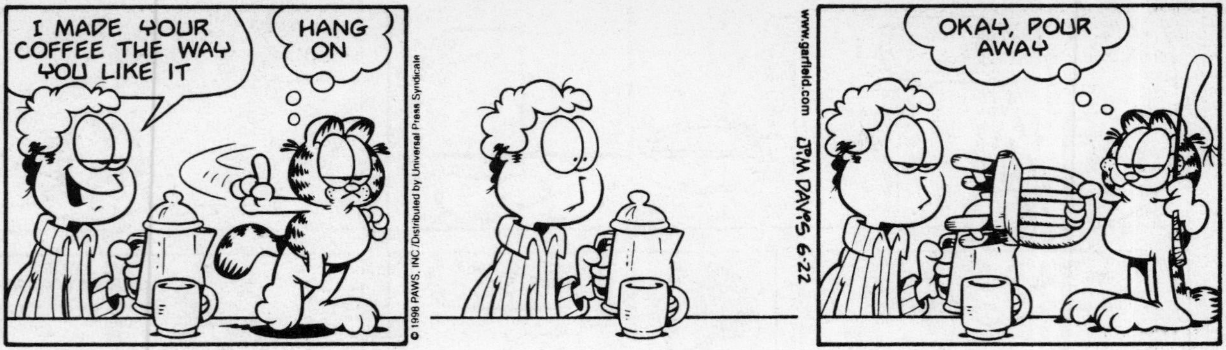
I MADE YOUR COFFEE THE WAY YOU LIKE IT
HANG ON
OKAY, POUR AWAY
© 1998 PAWS, INC./Distributed by Universal Press Syndicate
www.garfield.com
JIM DAVIS 6-22

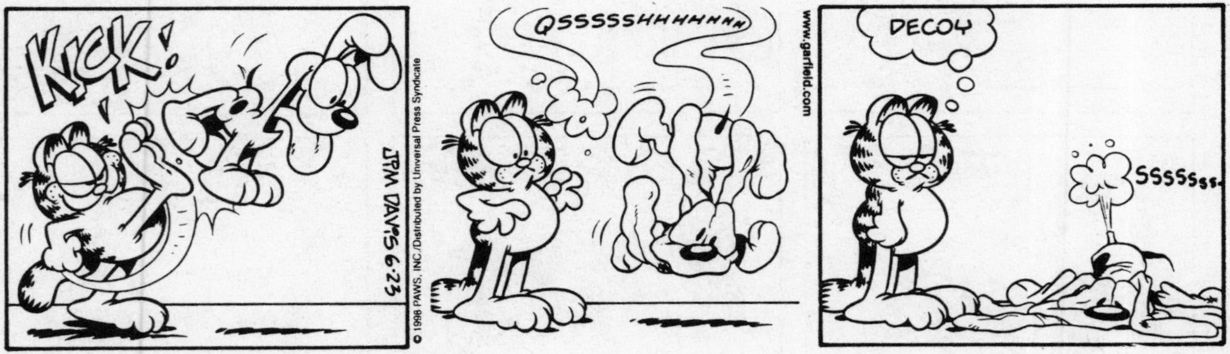
KICK!
QSSSSSHHHHHHH
DECOY
SSSSSss
© 1998 PAWS, INC./Distributed by Universal Press Syndicate
www.garfield.com
JIM DAVIS 6-23

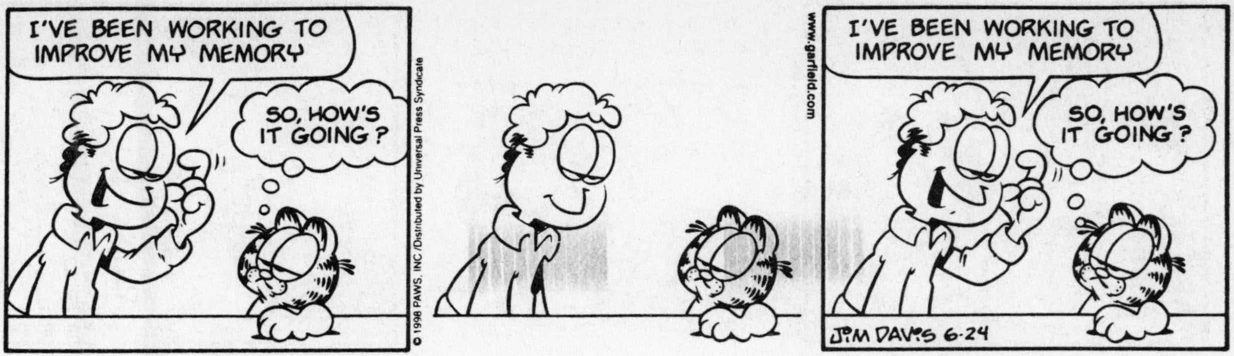
I'VE BEEN WORKING TO IMPROVE MY MEMORY
SO, HOW'S IT GOING?
I'VE BEEN WORKING TO IMPROVE MY MEMORY
SO, HOW'S IT GOING?
JIM DAVIS 6-24
© 1998 PAWS, INC./Distributed by Universal Press Syndicate
www.garfield.com

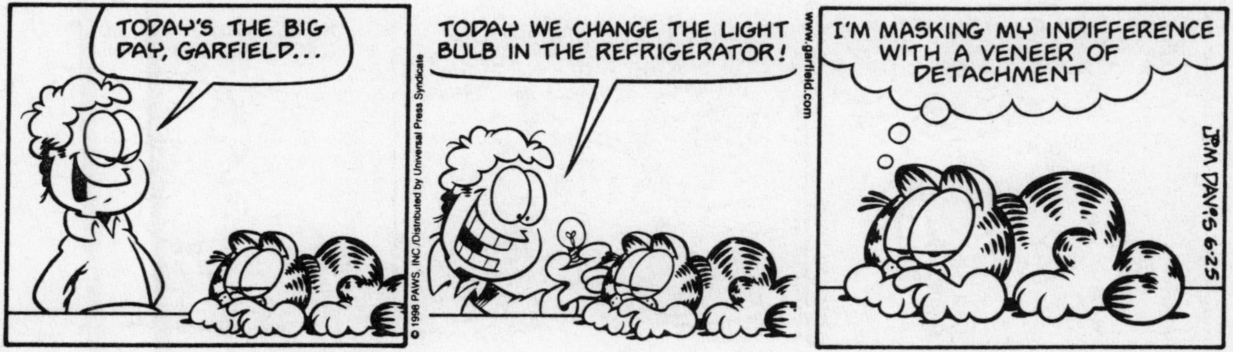
TODAY'S THE BIG DAY, GARFIELD...
TODAY WE CHANGE THE LIGHT BULB IN THE REFRIGERATOR!
I'M MASKING MY INDIFFERENCE WITH A VENEER OF DETACHMENT
JIM DAVIS 6-25
© 1998 PAWS, INC./Distributed by Universal Press Syndicate
www.garfield.com

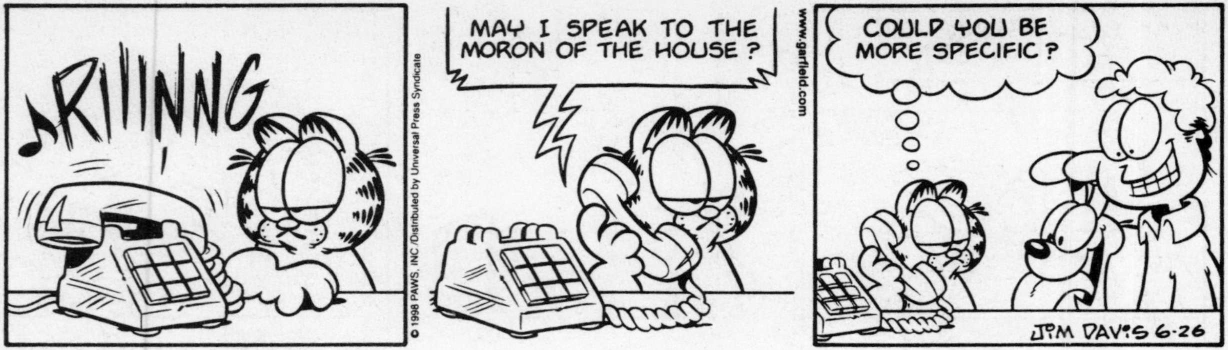
RIIINNG
MAY I SPEAK TO THE MORON OF THE HOUSE ?
COULD YOU BE MORE SPECIFIC ?
JIM DAVIS 6-26
© 1998 PAWS, INC./Distributed by Universal Press Syndicate
www.garfield.com

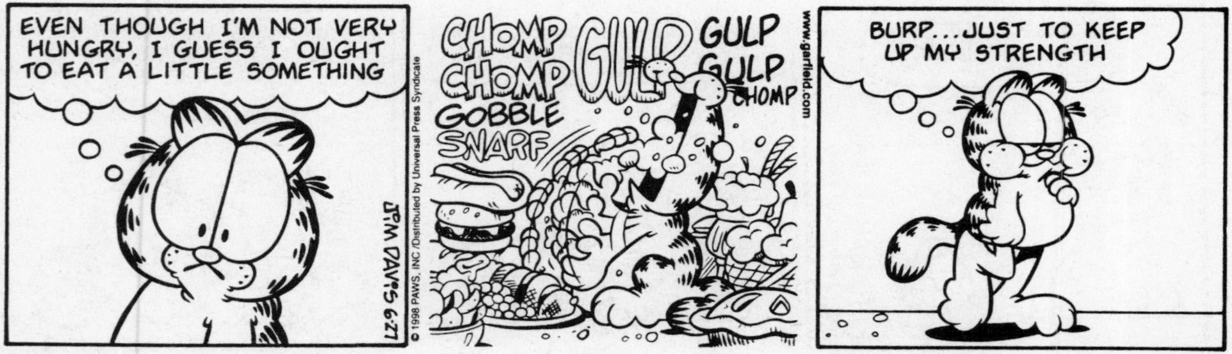
EVEN THOUGH I'M NOT VERY HUNGRY, I GUESS I OUGHT TO EAT A LITTLE SOMETHING
JIM DAVIS 6-27
CHOMP
CHOMP
GOBBLE
SNARF
GULP
GULP
GULP
CHOMP
BURP...JUST TO KEEP UP MY STRENGTH
© 1998 PAWS, INC./Distributed by Universal Press Syndicate
www.garfield.com

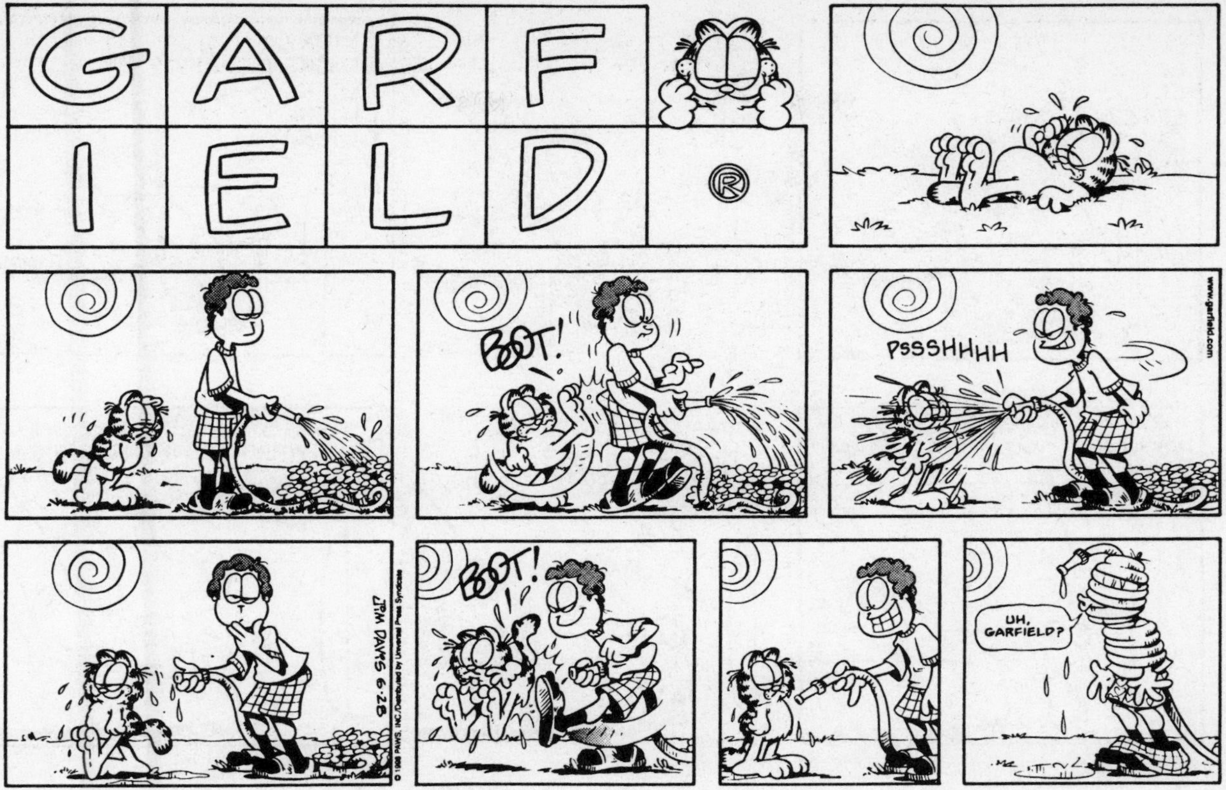
GARFIELD®
BOOT!
www.garfield.com
PSSSHHHH
JPM DAVPS 6·28
© 1998 PAWS, INC./Distributed by Universal Press Syndicate
BOOT!
UH, GARFIELD?

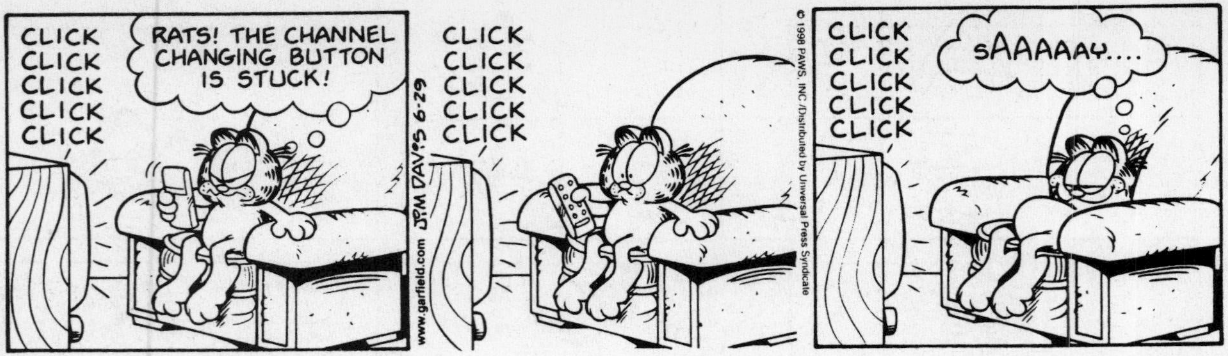
CLICK CLICK CLICK CLICK CLICK
RATS! THE CHANNEL CHANGING BUTTON IS STUCK!
JIM DAVIS 6-29
www.garfield.com
CLICK CLICK CLICK CLICK CLICK
© 1998 PAWS, INC./Distributed by Universal Press Syndicate
CLICK CLICK CLICK CLICK CLICK
sAAAAAY....

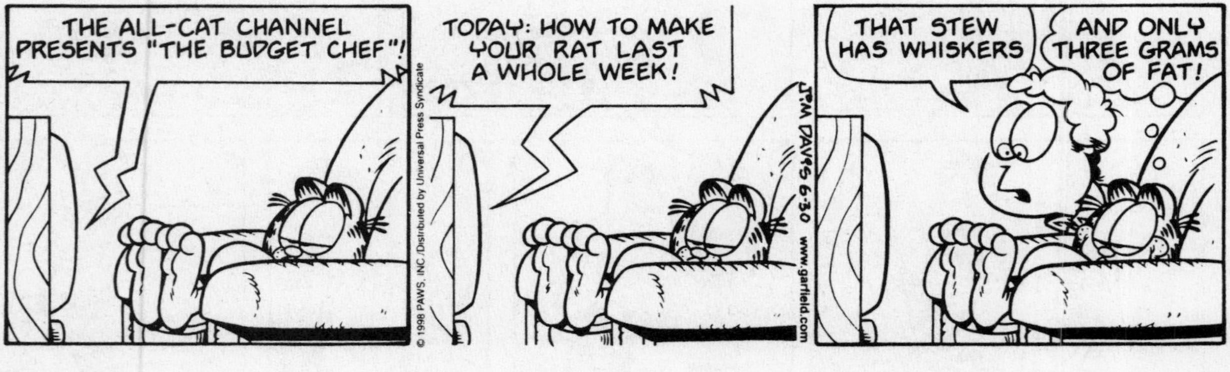
THE ALL-CAT CHANNEL PRESENTS "THE BUDGET CHEF"!
© 1998 PAWS, INC./Distributed by Universal Press Syndicate
TODAY: HOW TO MAKE YOUR RAT LAST A WHOLE WEEK!
JIM DAVIS 6-30
www.garfield.com
THAT STEW HAS WHISKERS
AND ONLY THREE GRAMS OF FAT!

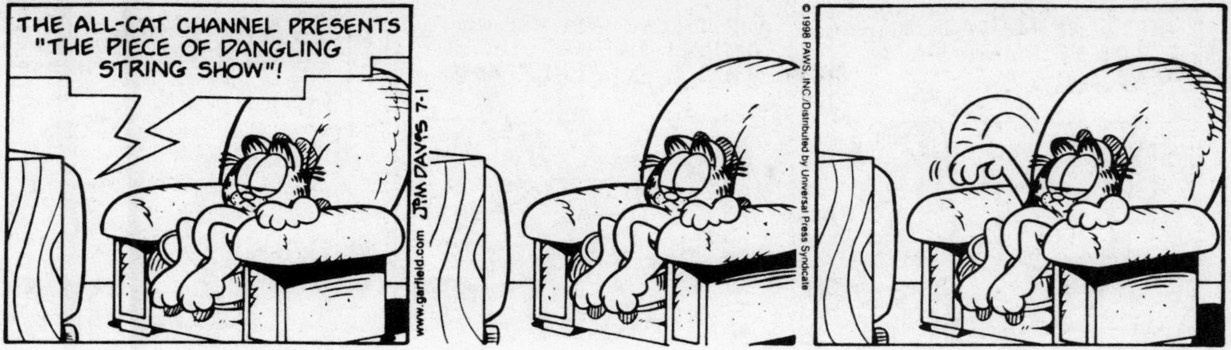
THE ALL-CAT CHANNEL PRESENTS "THE PIECE OF DANGLING STRING SHOW"!
JIM DAVIS 7-1
www.garfield.com
© 1998 PAWS, INC./Distributed by Universal Press Syndicate

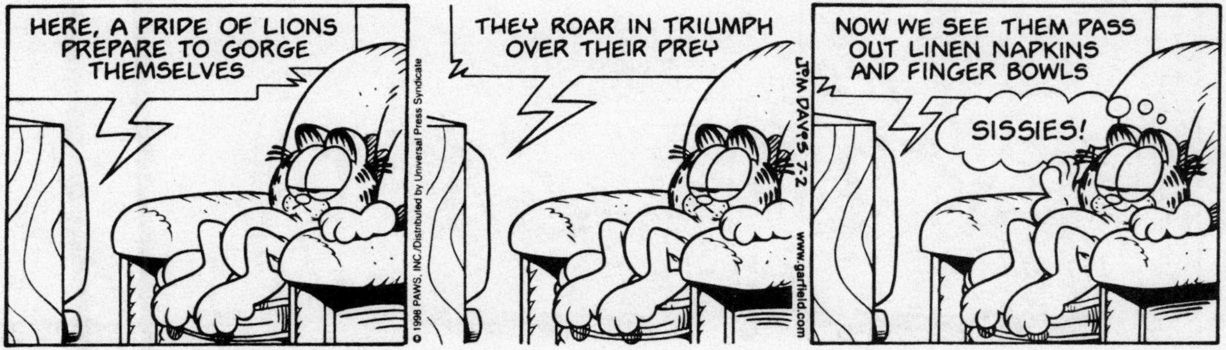
HERE, A PRIDE OF LIONS PREPARE TO GORGE THEMSELVES
© 1998 PAWS, INC./Distributed by Universal Press Syndicate
THEY ROAR IN TRIUMPH OVER THEIR PREY
JIM DAVIS 7-2
www.garfield.com
NOW WE SEE THEM PASS OUT LINEN NAPKINS AND FINGER BOWLS
SISSIES!

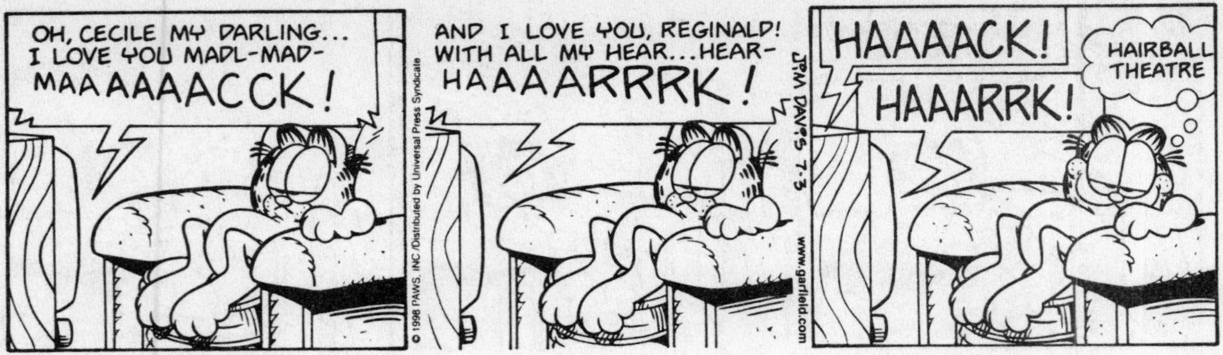
OH, CECILE MY DARLING... I LOVE YOU MADL-MAD-MAAAAAACCK!
© 1998 PAWS, INC./Distributed by Universal Press Syndicate
AND I LOVE YOU, REGINALD! WITH ALL MY HEAR...HEAR-HAAAARRRK!
JPM DAVPS 7-3
www.garfield.com
HAAAACK!
HAAARRK!
HAIRBALL THEATRE

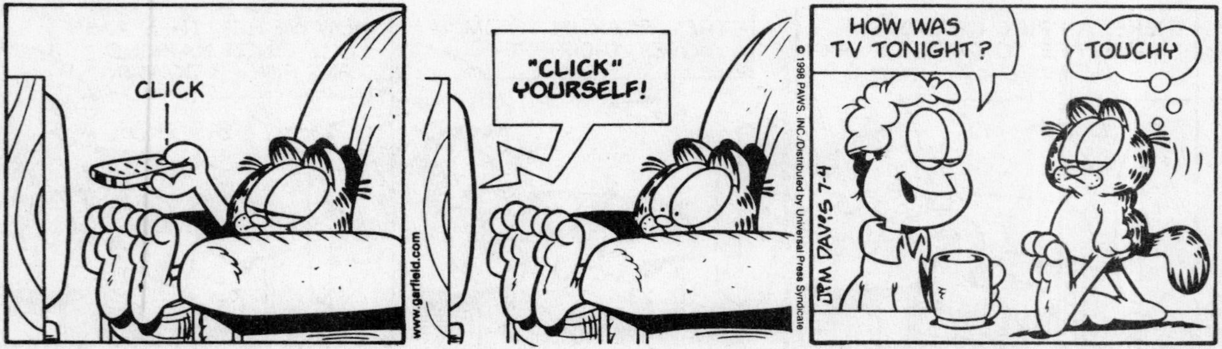
CLICK
www.garfield.com
"CLICK" YOURSELF!
© 1998 PAWS, INC./Distributed by Universal Press Syndicate
JPM DAVPS 7-4
HOW WAS TV TONIGHT?
TOUCHY

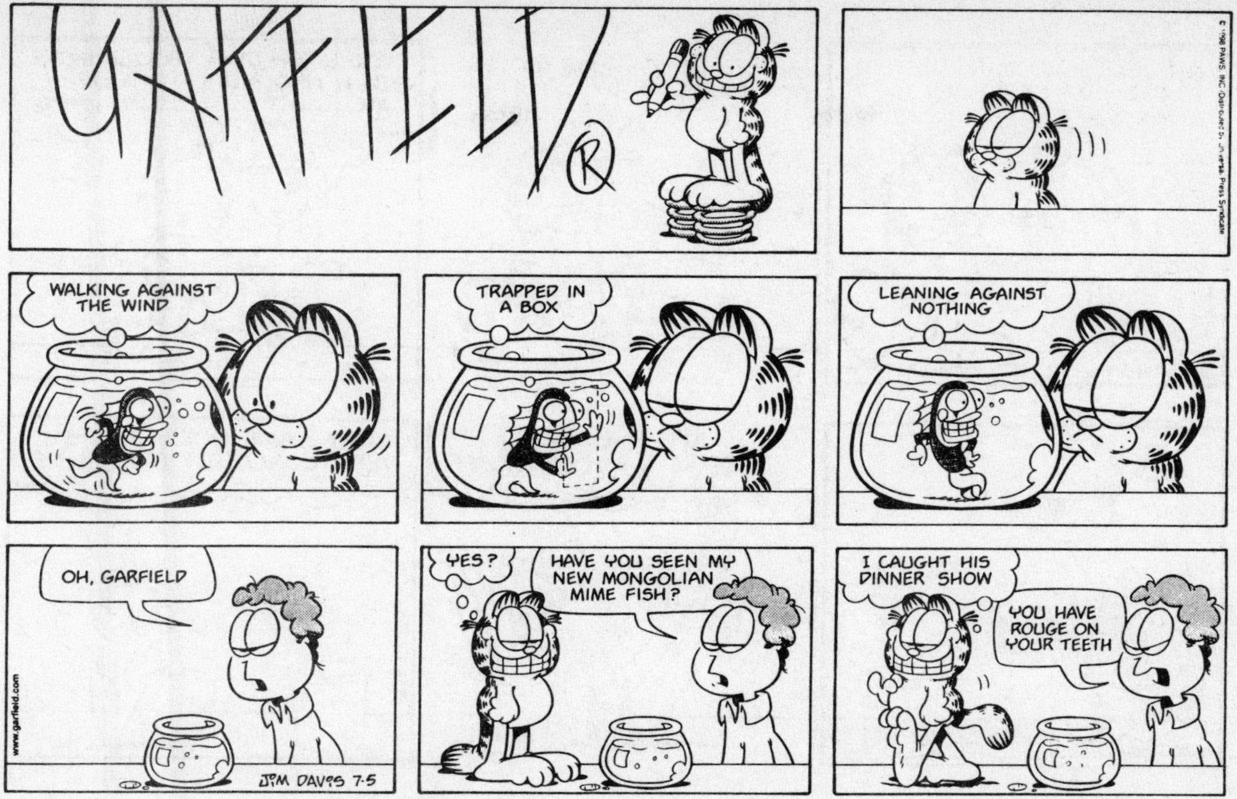
GARFIELD®
WALKING AGAINST THE WIND
TRAPPED IN A BOX
LEANING AGAINST NOTHING
OH, GARFIELD
JIM DAVIS 7-5
www.garfield.com
YES?
HAVE YOU SEEN MY NEW MONGOLIAN MIME FISH?
I CAUGHT HIS DINNER SHOW
YOU HAVE ROUGE ON YOUR TEETH
© 1998 PAWS, INC./Distributed by Universal Press Syndicate

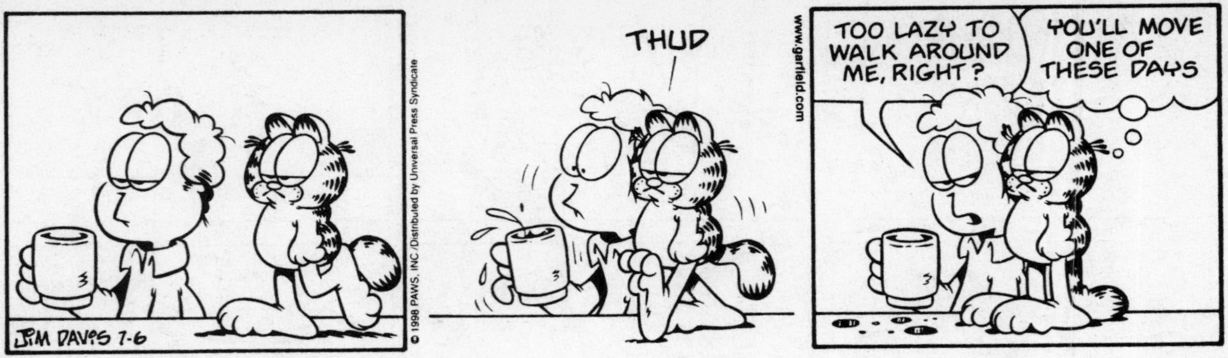
JIM DAVIS 7-6
© 1998 PAWS, INC./Distributed by Universal Press Syndicate
THUD
www.garfield.com
TOO LAZY TO WALK AROUND ME, RIGHT?
YOU'LL MOVE ONE OF THESE DAYS

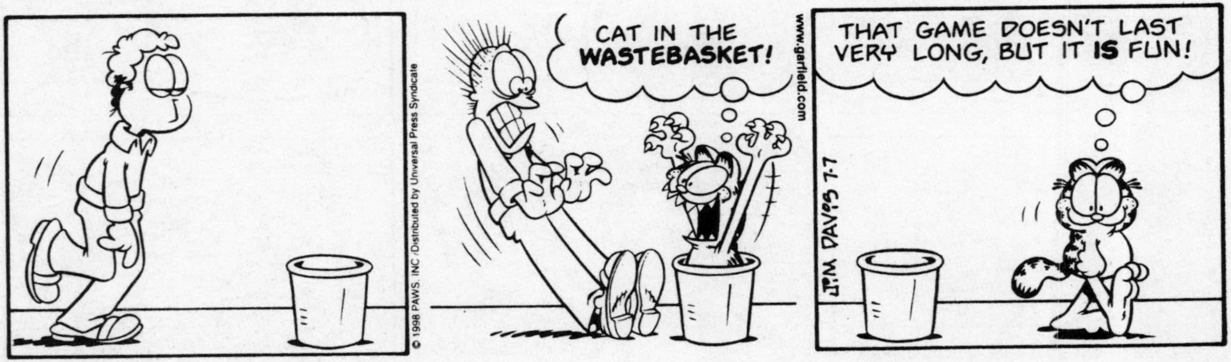
© 1998 PAWS, INC./Distributed by Universal Press Syndicate
CAT IN THE **WASTEBASKET**!
www.garfield.com
THAT GAME DOESN'T LAST VERY LONG, BUT IT **IS** FUN!
JIM DAVIS 7-7

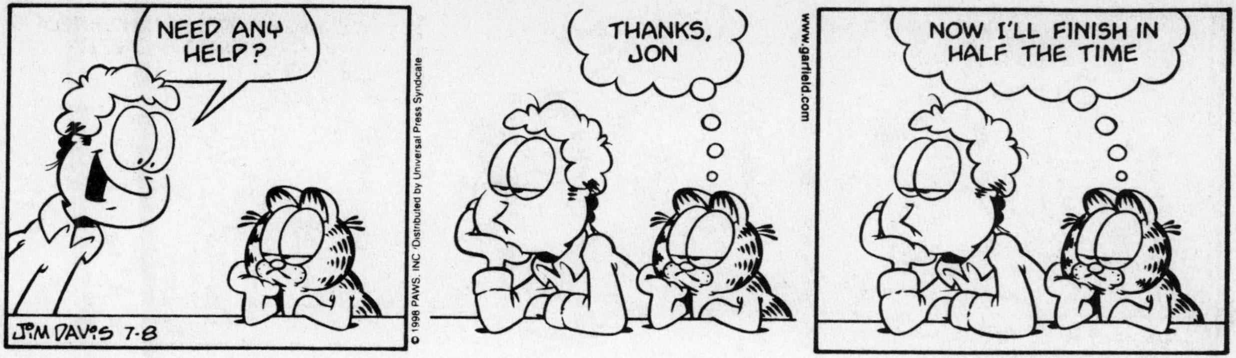
NEED ANY HELP?
THANKS, JON
NOW I'LL FINISH IN HALF THE TIME
JIM DAVIS 7-8
© 1998 PAWS, INC./Distributed by Universal Press Syndicate
www.garfield.com

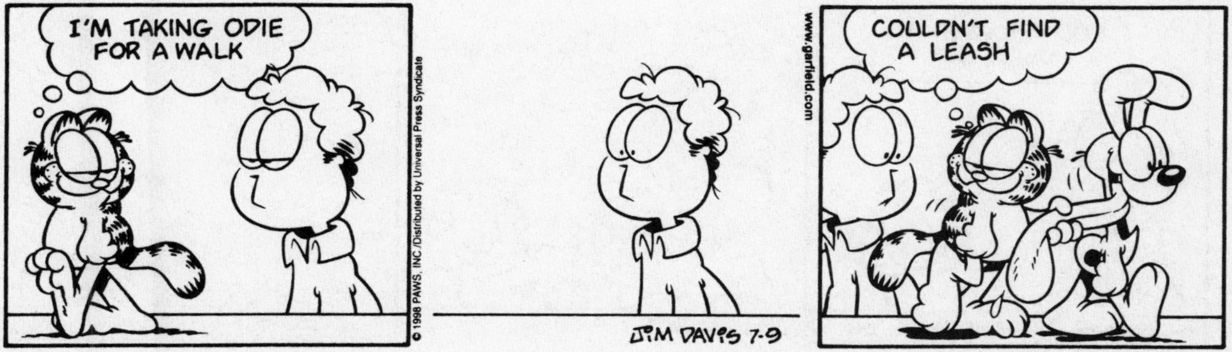
I'M TAKING ODIE FOR A WALK
COULDN'T FIND A LEASH
JIM DAVIS 7-9
© 1998 PAWS, INC./Distributed by Universal Press Syndicate
www.garfield.com

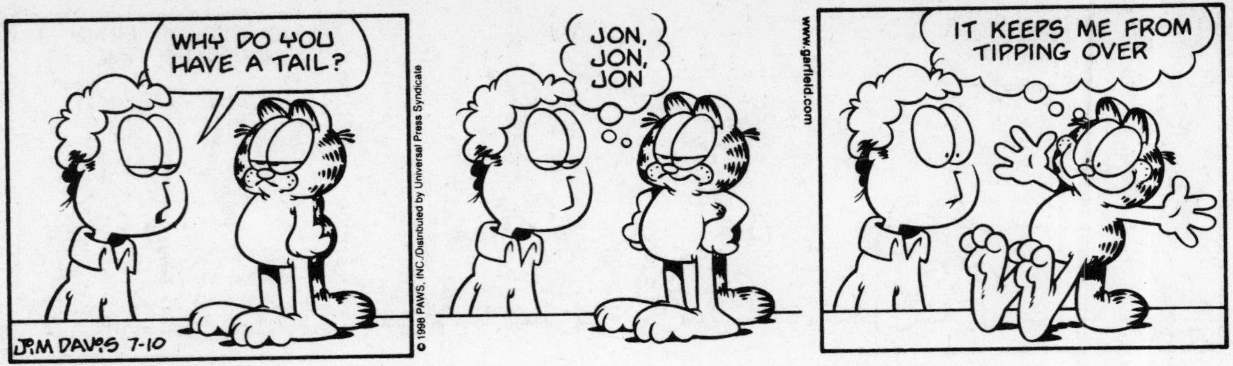
WHY DO YOU HAVE A TAIL?
JIM DAVIS 7-10
© 1998 PAWS, INC./Distributed by Universal Press Syndicate
JON, JON, JON
www.garfield.com
IT KEEPS ME FROM TIPPING OVER

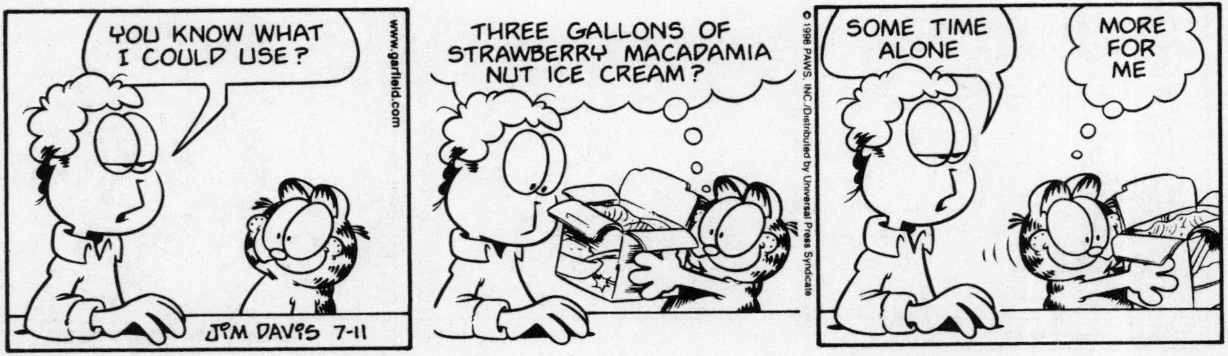
YOU KNOW WHAT I COULD USE?
JIM DAVIS 7-11
www.garfield.com
THREE GALLONS OF STRAWBERRY MACADAMIA NUT ICE CREAM?
© 1998 PAWS, INC./Distributed by Universal Press Syndicate
SOME TIME ALONE
MORE FOR ME

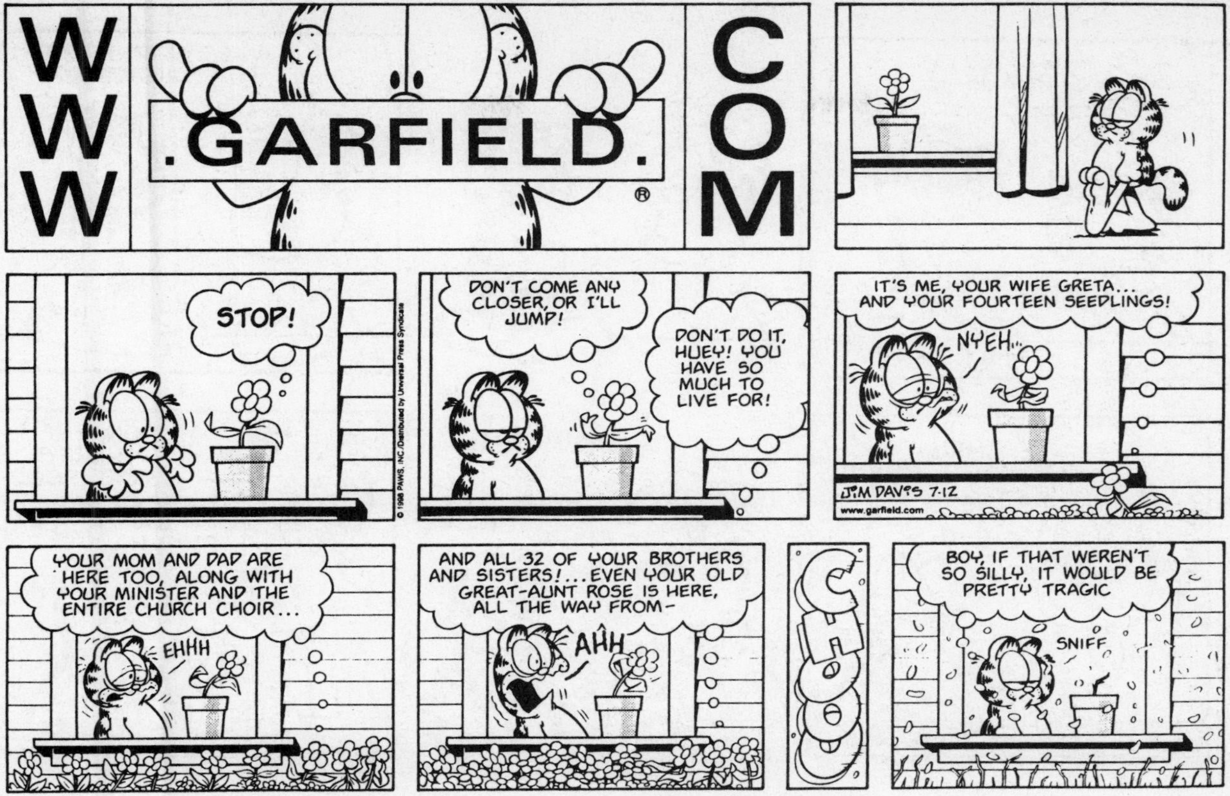

WWW.GARFIELD.COM
STOP!
© 1998 PAWS, INC./Distributed by Universal Press Syndicate
DON'T COME ANY CLOSER, OR I'LL JUMP!
DON'T DO IT, HUEY! YOU HAVE SO MUCH TO LIVE FOR!
IT'S ME, YOUR WIFE GRETA... AND YOUR FOURTEEN SEEDLINGS!
NYEH...
JIM DAVIS 7-12
www.garfield.com
YOUR MOM AND DAD ARE HERE TOO, ALONG WITH YOUR MINISTER AND THE ENTIRE CHURCH CHOIR...
EHHH
AND ALL 32 OF YOUR BROTHERS AND SISTERS!... EVEN YOUR OLD GREAT-AUNT ROSE IS HERE, ALL THE WAY FROM-
AHH
CHOO
BOY, IF THAT WEREN'T SO SILLY, IT WOULD BE PRETTY TRAGIC
SNIFF

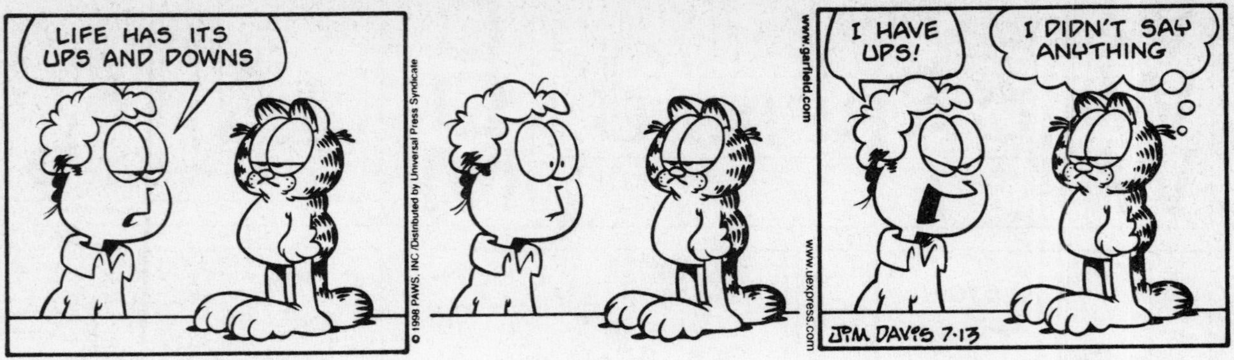
LIFE HAS ITS UPS AND DOWNS
I HAVE UPS!
I DIDN'T SAY ANYTHING
JIM DAVIS 7-13
© 1998 PAWS, INC /Distributed by Universal Press Syndicate
www.garfield.com
www.uexpress.com

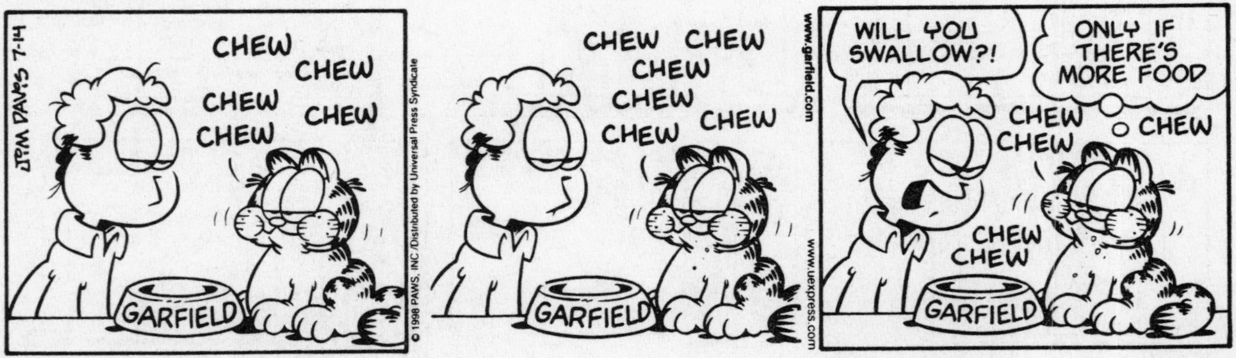
JIM DAVIS 7-14
CHEW
CHEW
CHEW
CHEW
CHEW
GARFIELD
CHEW CHEW
CHEW
CHEW
CHEW CHEW
GARFIELD
WILL YOU SWALLOW?!
ONLY IF THERE'S MORE FOOD
CHEW
CHEW
CHEW
CHEW
CHEW
GARFIELD
© 1998 PAWS, INC /Distributed by Universal Press Syndicate
www.garfield.com
www.uexpress.com

Jon's SCARIEST DATES

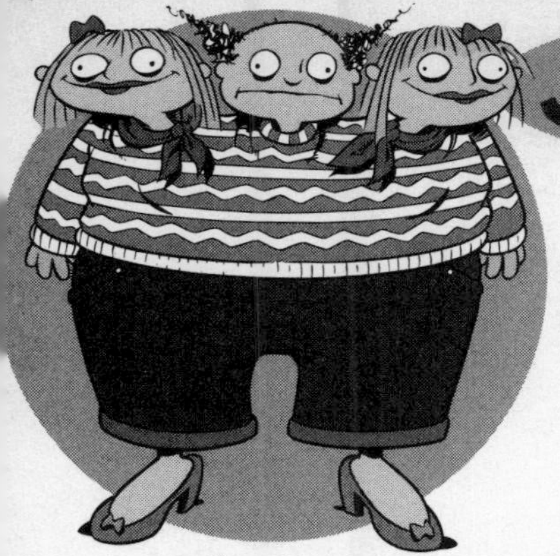

Gertie, Greta,
and Bob, Siamese Triplets

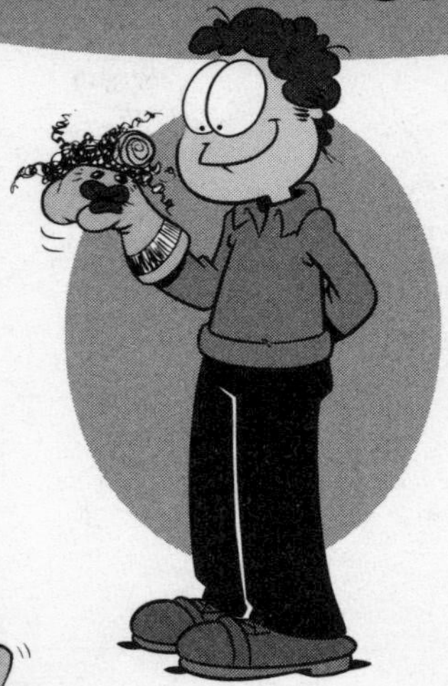

"Señorita
Del Fuego"

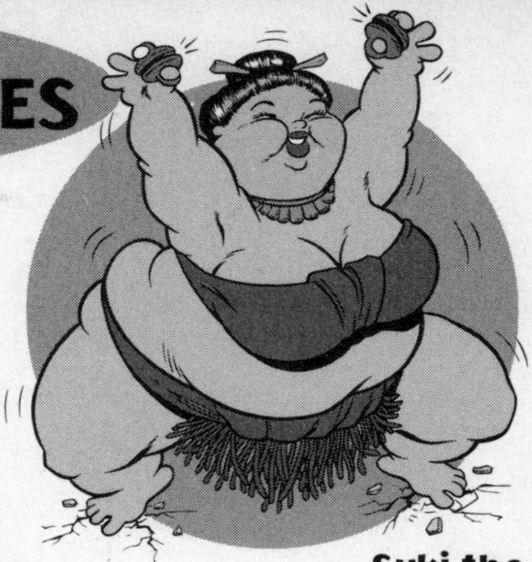

Suki the
Sumo Belly
Dancer

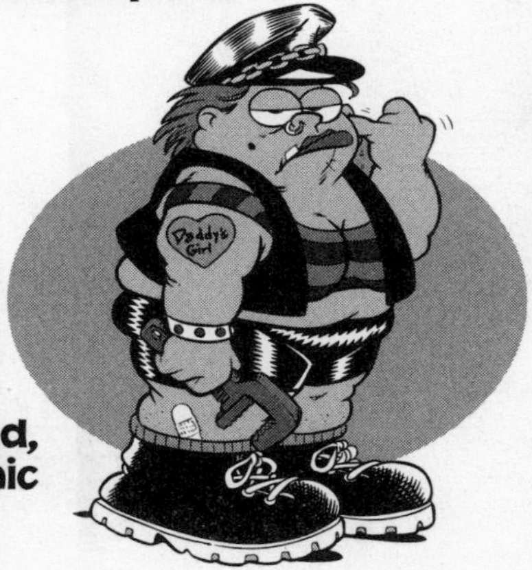

Annie Axelrod,
Harley mechanic

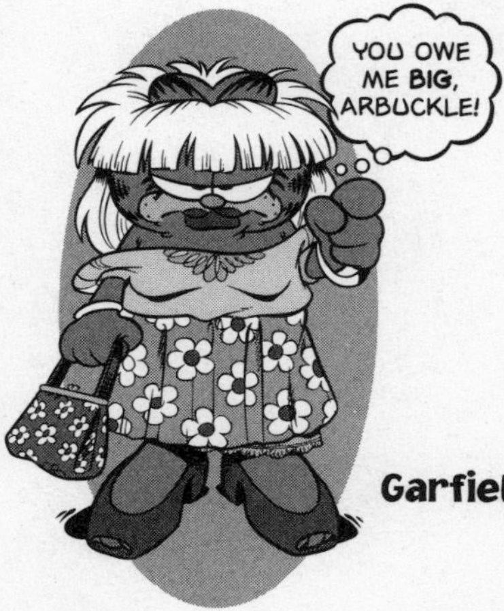
YOU OWE ME BIG, ARBUCKLE!

Garfield

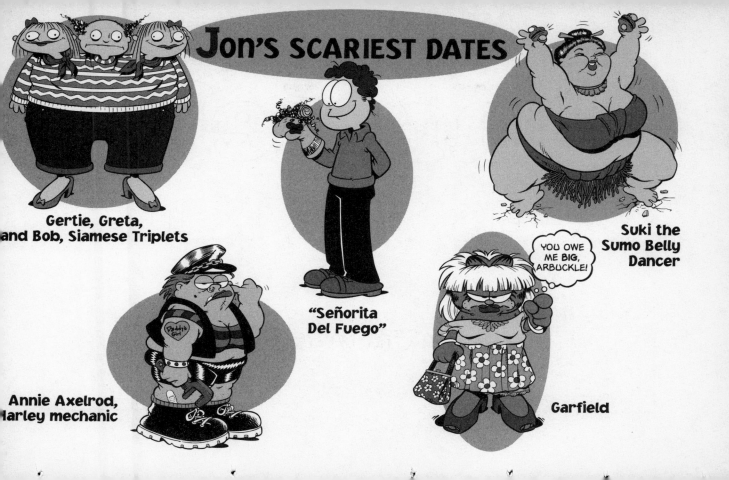

Garfield
feeds the kitty

BY: JIM DAVIS

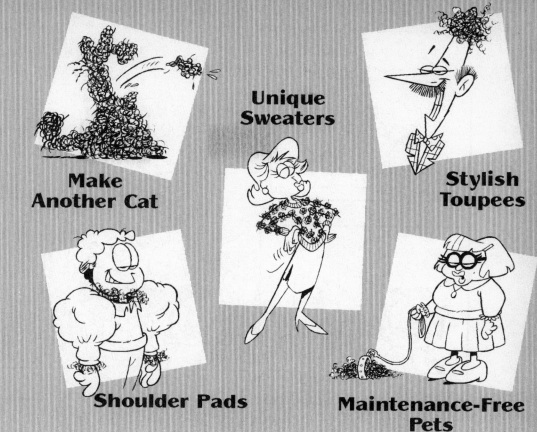

PRACTICAL USES FOR GARFIELD'S HAIRBALLS

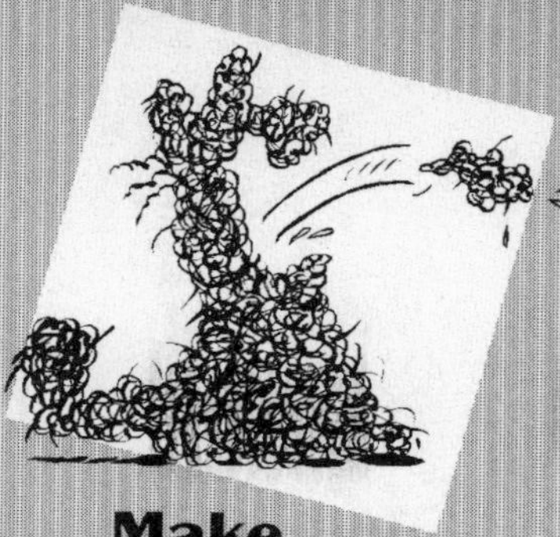

Make Another Cat

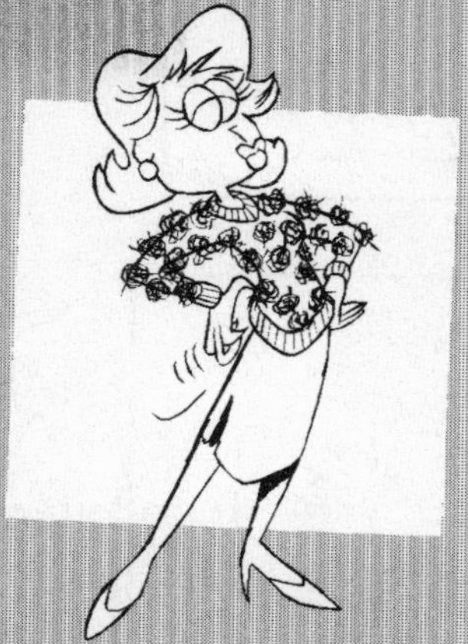

Unique Sweaters

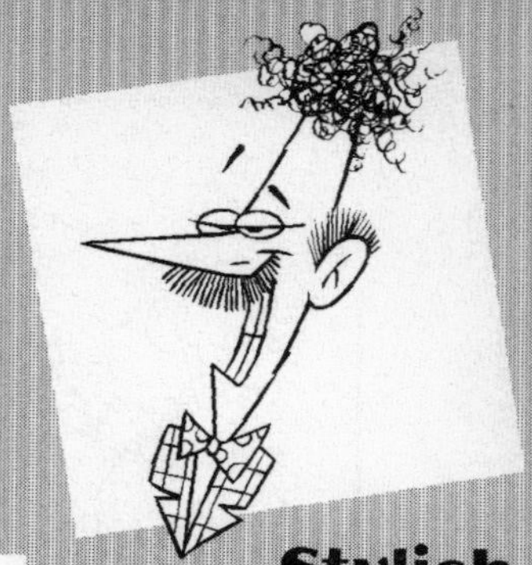

Stylish Toupees

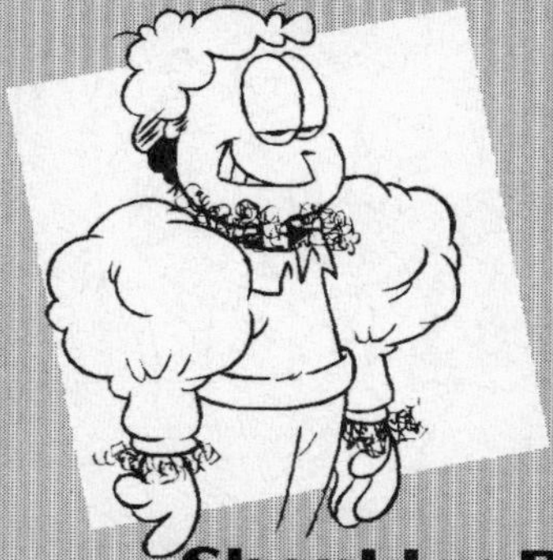

Shoulder Pads

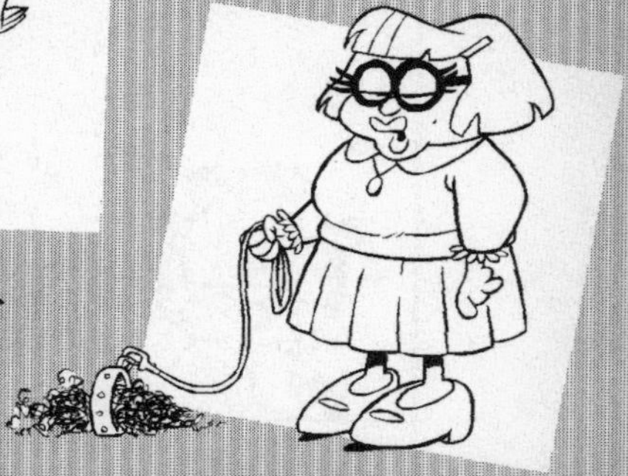

Maintenance-Free Pets

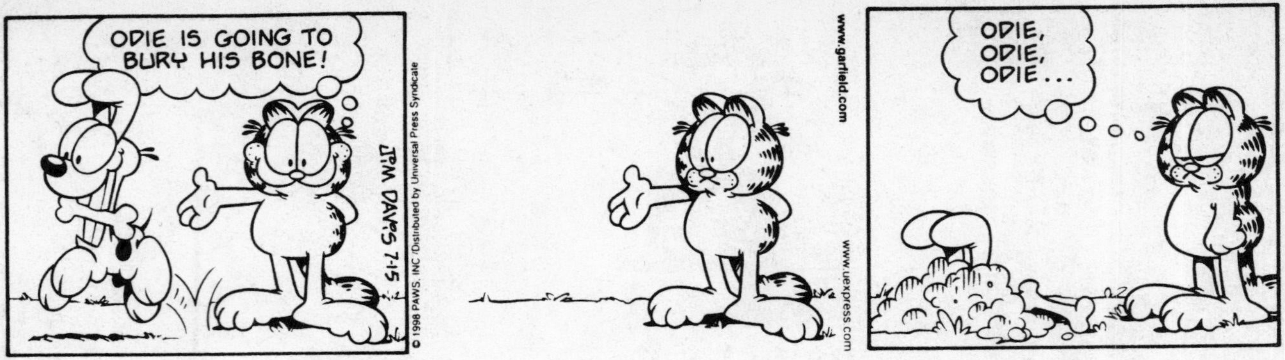
ODIE IS GOING TO BURY HIS BONE!
JIM DAVIS 7-15
ODIE, ODIE, ODIE...

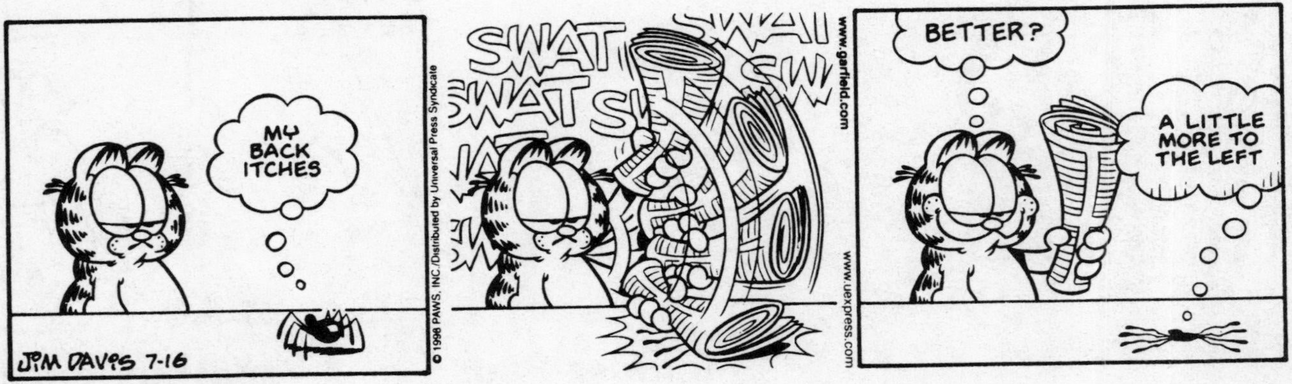
MY BACK ITCHES
JIM DAVIS 7-16
SWAT SWAT SWAT
BETTER?
A LITTLE MORE TO THE LEFT

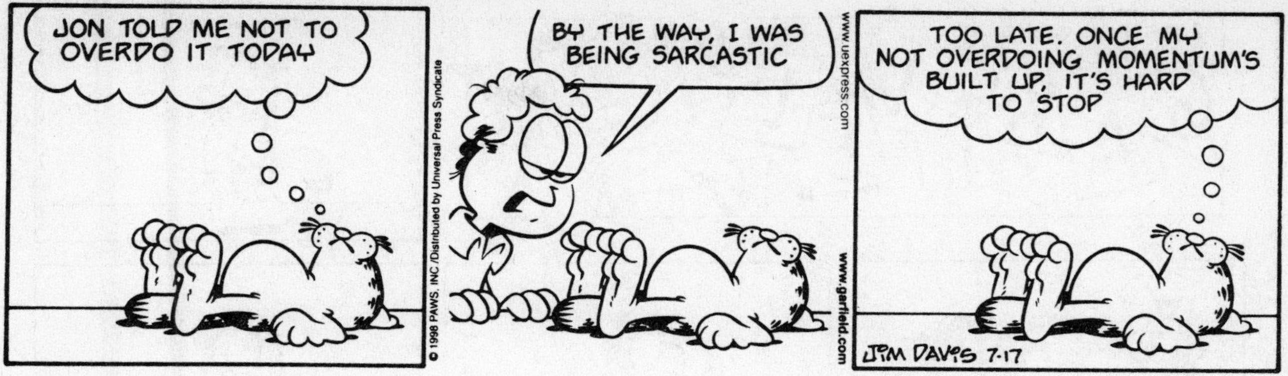
JON TOLD ME NOT TO OVERDO IT TODAY
BY THE WAY, I WAS BEING SARCASTIC
TOO LATE. ONCE MY NOT OVERDOING MOMENTUM'S BUILT UP, IT'S HARD TO STOP
JIM DAVIS 7-17
© 1998 PAWS, INC./Distributed by Universal Press Syndicate
www.uexpress.com
www.garfield.com

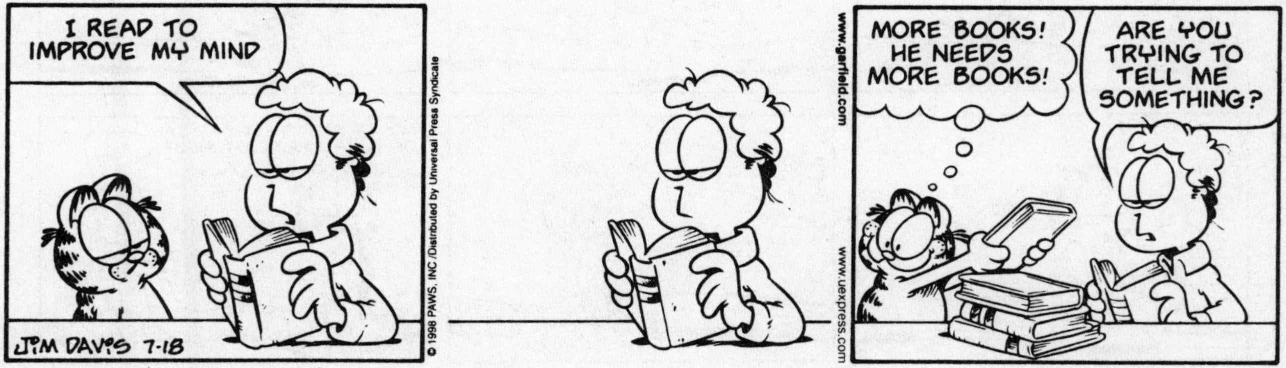
I READ TO IMPROVE MY MIND
MORE BOOKS! HE NEEDS MORE BOOKS!
ARE YOU TRYING TO TELL ME SOMETHING?
JIM DAVIS 7-18
© 1998 PAWS, INC./Distributed by Universal Press Syndicate
www.garfield.com
www.uexpress.com

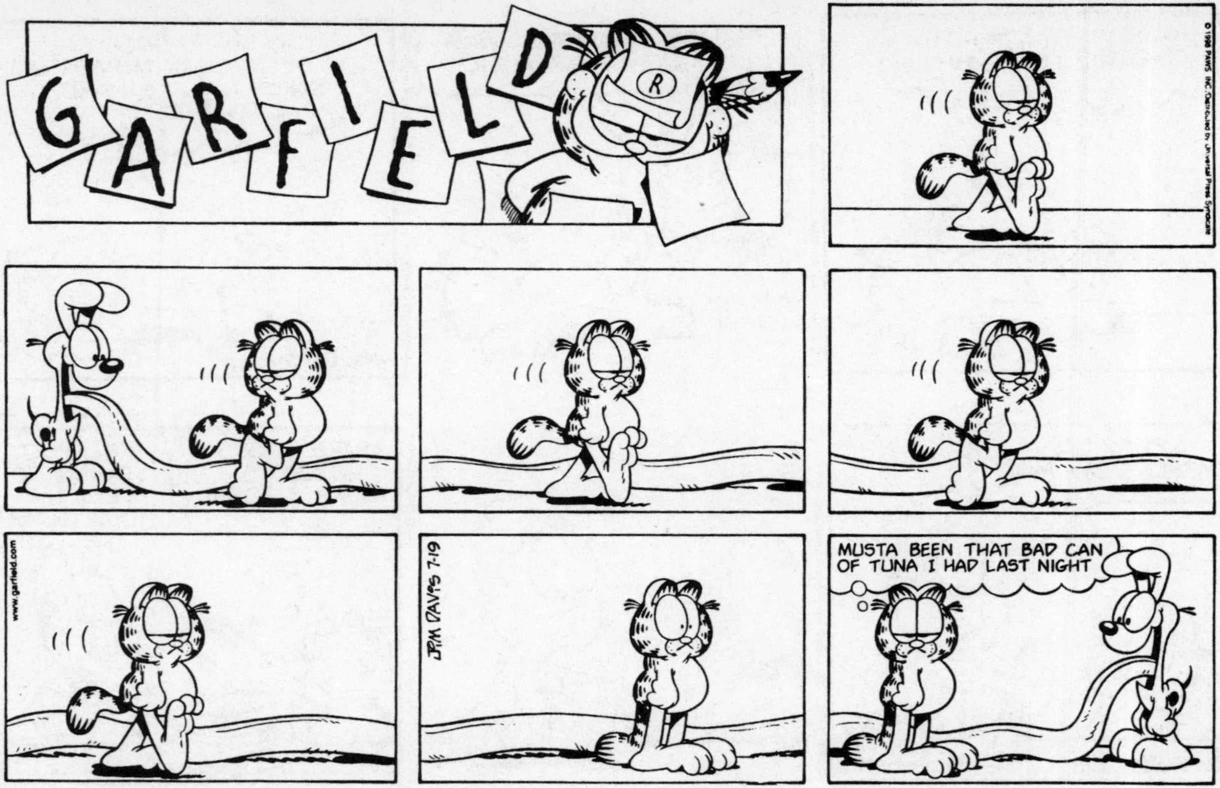
GARFIELD ®
© 1998 PAWS INC./Distributed by Universal Press Syndicate
www.garfield.com
JPM DAVIS 7-19
MUSTA BEEN THAT BAD CAN OF TUNA I HAD LAST NIGHT

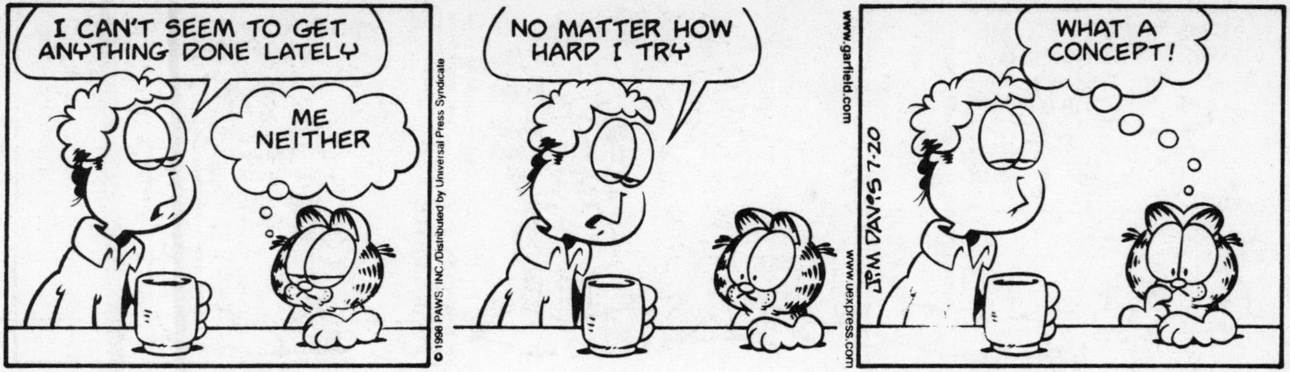
I CAN'T SEEM TO GET ANYTHING DONE LATELY
ME NEITHER
NO MATTER HOW HARD I TRY
WHAT A CONCEPT!
JIM DAVIS 7-20
© 1998 PAWS, INC./Distributed by Universal Press Syndicate
www.garfield.com
www.uexpress.com

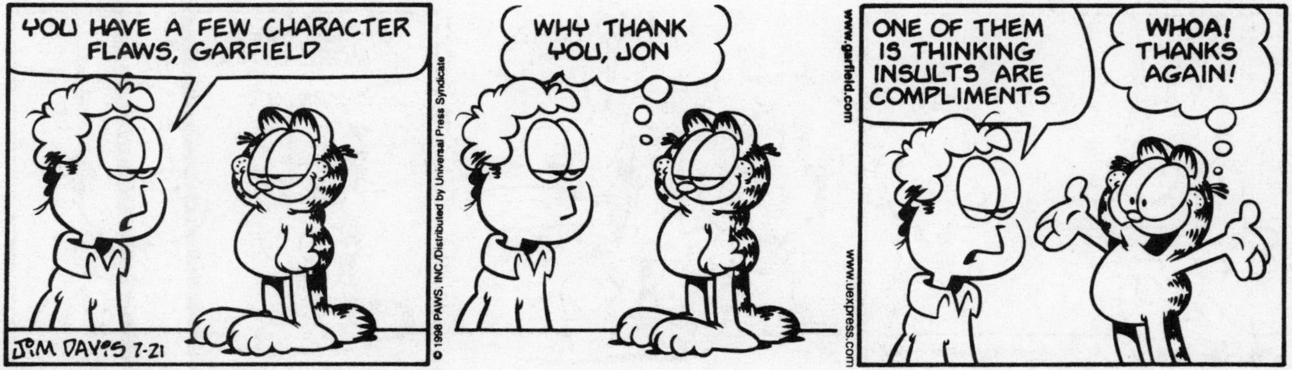
YOU HAVE A FEW CHARACTER FLAWS, GARFIELD
WHY THANK YOU, JON
ONE OF THEM IS THINKING INSULTS ARE COMPLIMENTS
WHOA! THANKS AGAIN!
JIM DAVIS 7-21
© 1998 PAWS, INC./Distributed by Universal Press Syndicate
www.garfield.com
www.uexpress.com

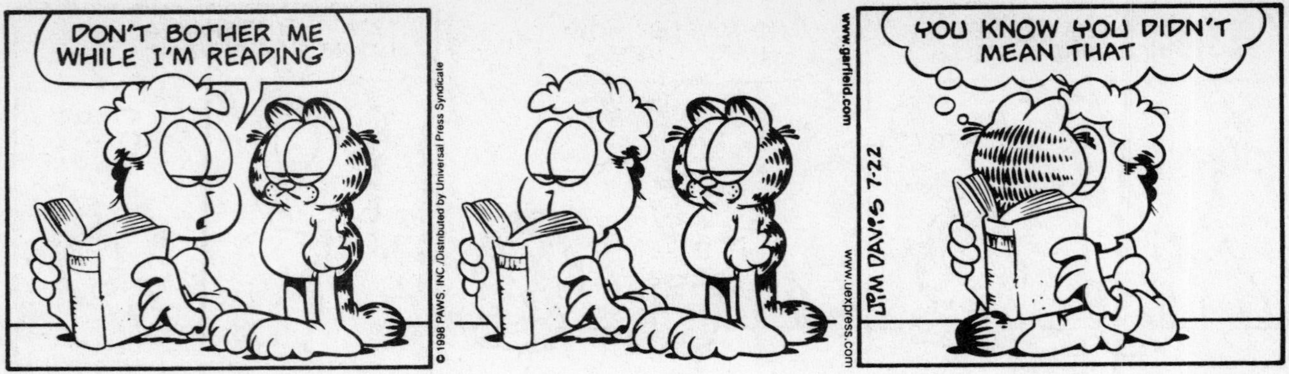
DON'T BOTHER ME WHILE I'M READING
© 1998 PAWS, INC./Distributed by Universal Press Syndicate
YOU KNOW YOU DIDN'T MEAN THAT
www.garfield.com
JIM DAVIS 7-22
www.uexpress.com

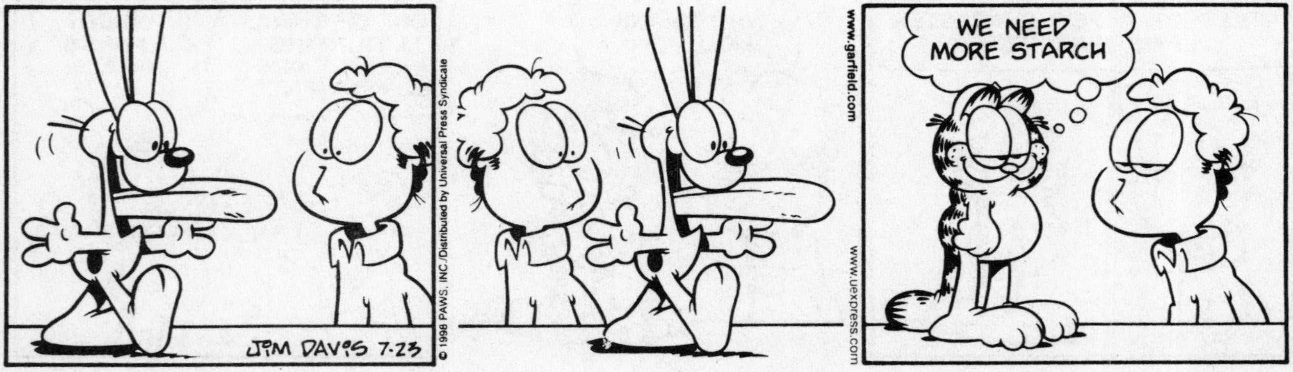
JIM DAVIS 7-23
© 1998 PAWS, INC./Distributed by Universal Press Syndicate
WE NEED MORE STARCH
www.garfield.com
www.uexpress.com

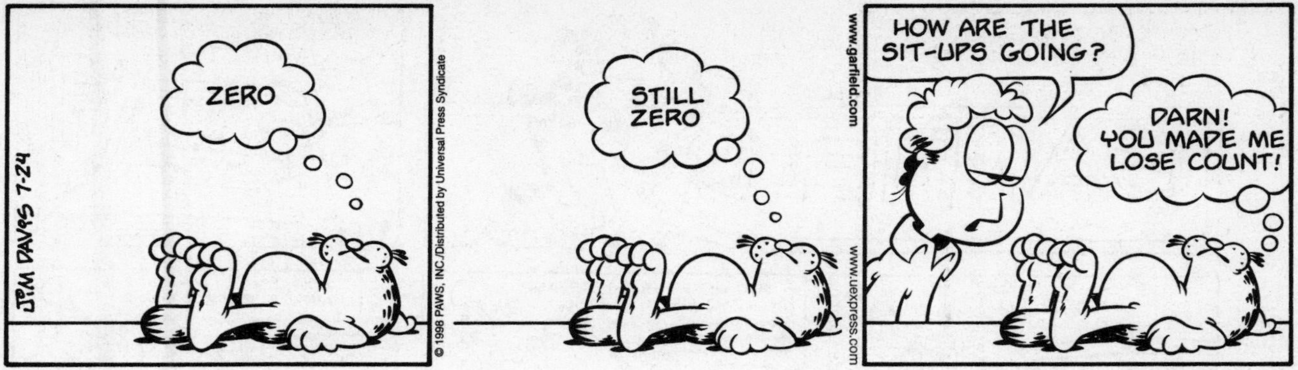
JIM DAVIS 7-24
ZERO
© 1998 PAWS, INC./Distributed by Universal Press Syndicate
STILL ZERO
www.garfield.com
www.uexpress.com
HOW ARE THE SIT-UPS GOING?
DARN! YOU MADE ME LOSE COUNT!

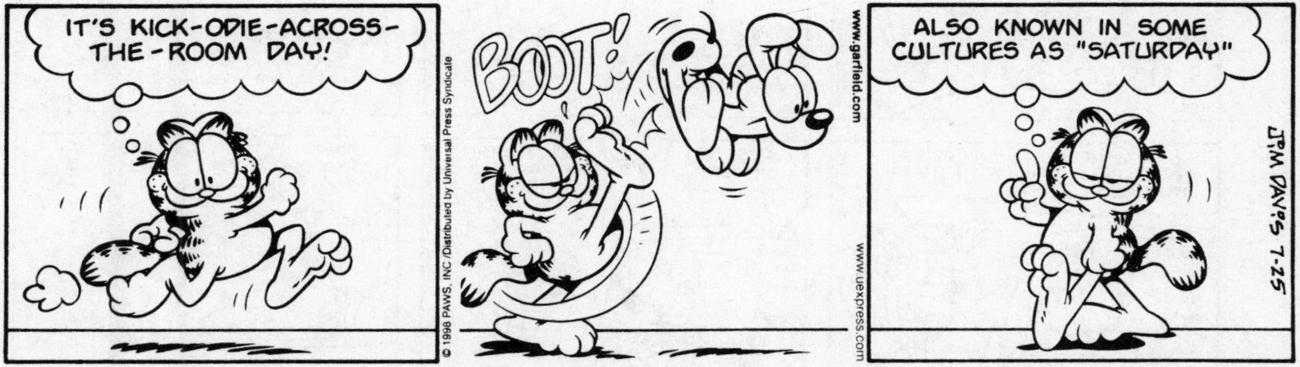
IT'S KICK-ODIE-ACROSS-THE-ROOM DAY!
© 1998 PAWS, INC./Distributed by Universal Press Syndicate
BOOT!
www.garfield.com
www.uexpress.com
ALSO KNOWN IN SOME CULTURES AS "SATURDAY"
JIM DAVIS 7-25

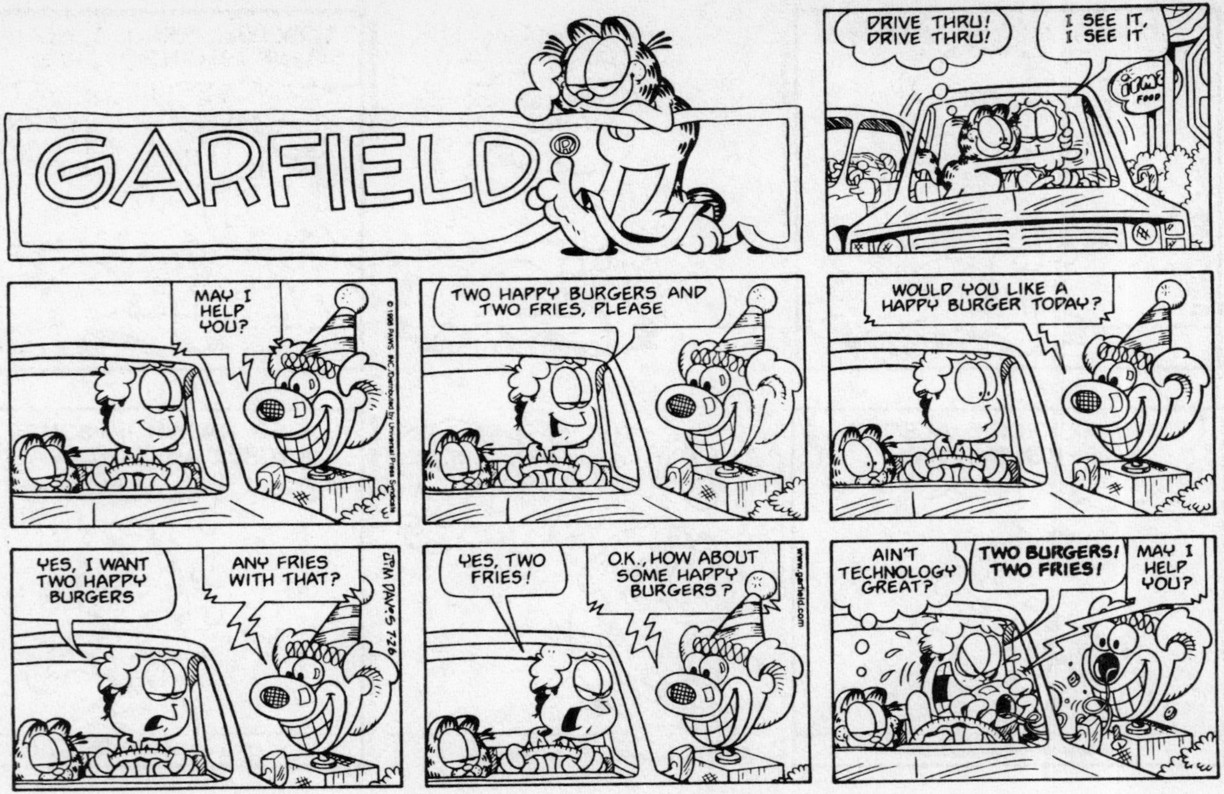
GARFIELD®
DRIVE THRU! DRIVE THRU!
I SEE IT, I SEE IT
MAY I HELP YOU?
© 1986 PAWS INC. Distributed by Universal Press Syndicate
TWO HAPPY BURGERS AND TWO FRIES, PLEASE
WOULD YOU LIKE A HAPPY BURGER TODAY?
YES, I WANT TWO HAPPY BURGERS
ANY FRIES WITH THAT?
JPM DAVIS 7-26
YES, TWO FRIES!
O.K., HOW ABOUT SOME HAPPY BURGERS?
www.garfield.com
AIN'T TECHNOLOGY GREAT?
TWO BURGERS! TWO FRIES!
MAY I HELP YOU?

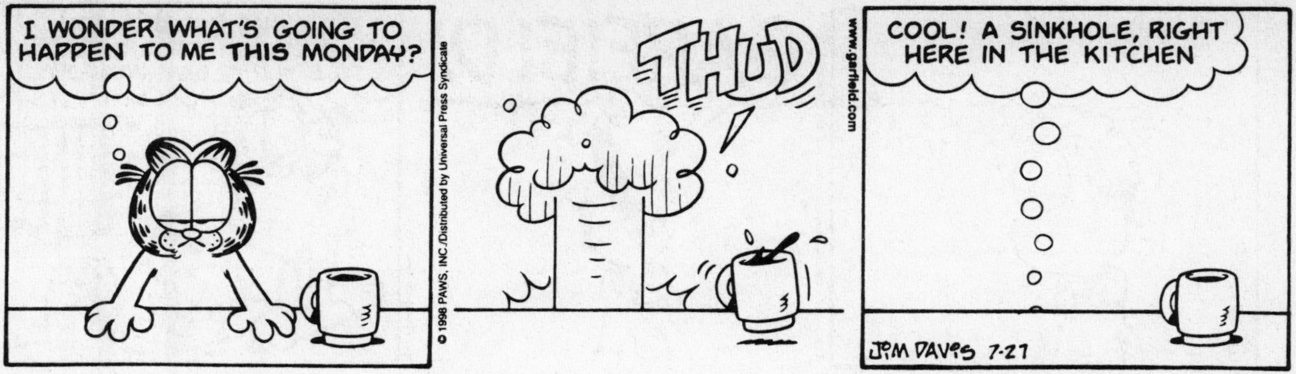
I WONDER WHAT'S GOING TO HAPPEN TO ME THIS MONDAY?
© 1998 PAWS, INC./Distributed by Universal Press Syndicate
THUD
www.garfield.com
COOL! A SINKHOLE, RIGHT HERE IN THE KITCHEN
JIM DAVIS 7-27

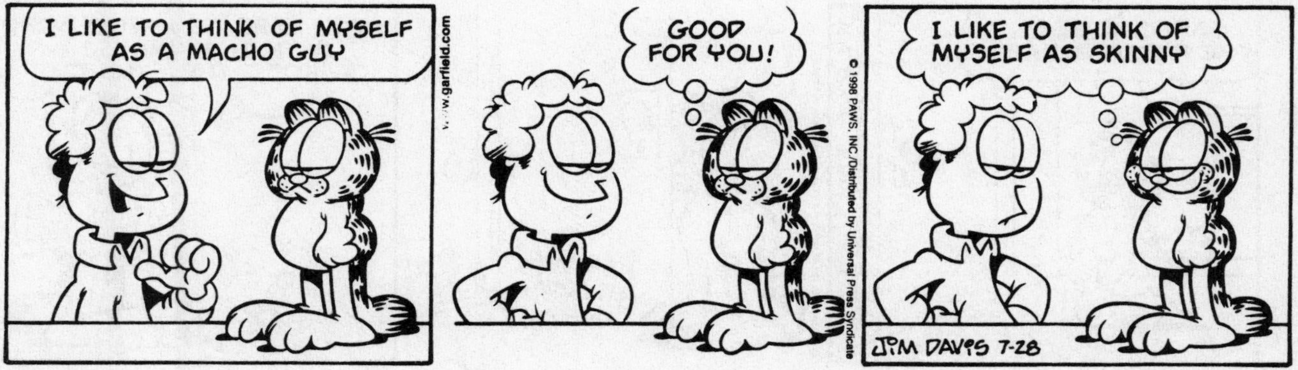
I LIKE TO THINK OF MYSELF AS A MACHO GUY
GOOD FOR YOU!
© 1998 PAWS, INC./Distributed by Universal Press Syndicate
I LIKE TO THINK OF MYSELF AS SKINNY
JIM DAVIS 7-28

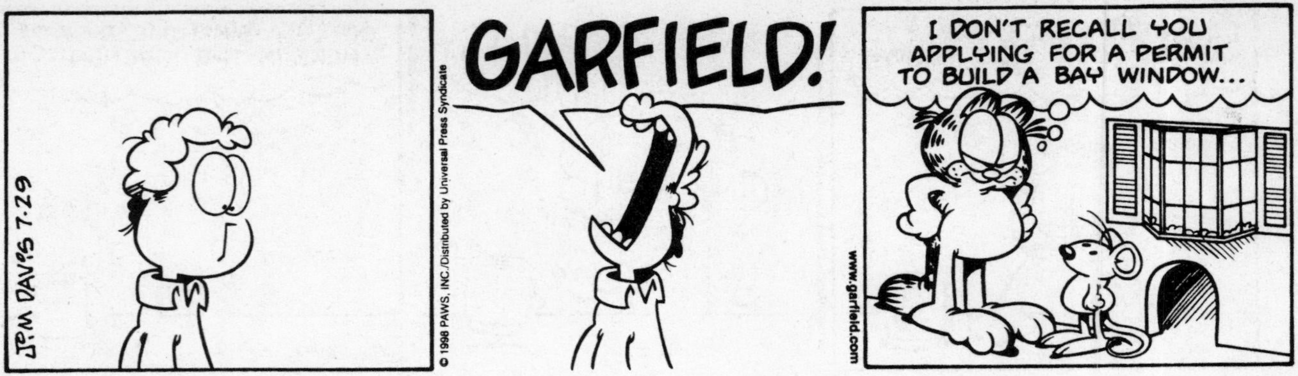
JIM DAVIS 7-29
GARFIELD!
I DON'T RECALL YOU APPLYING FOR A PERMIT TO BUILD A BAY WINDOW...
© 1998 PAWS, INC./Distributed by Universal Press Syndicate
www.garfield.com

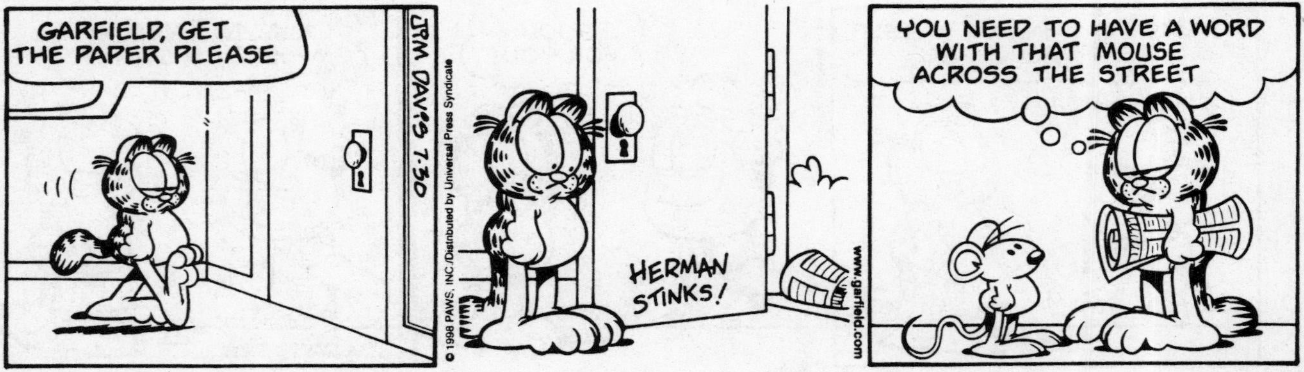
GARFIELD, GET THE PAPER PLEASE
JIM DAVIS 7-30
HERMAN STINKS!
YOU NEED TO HAVE A WORD WITH THAT MOUSE ACROSS THE STREET
© 1998 PAWS, INC./Distributed by Universal Press Syndicate
www.garfield.com

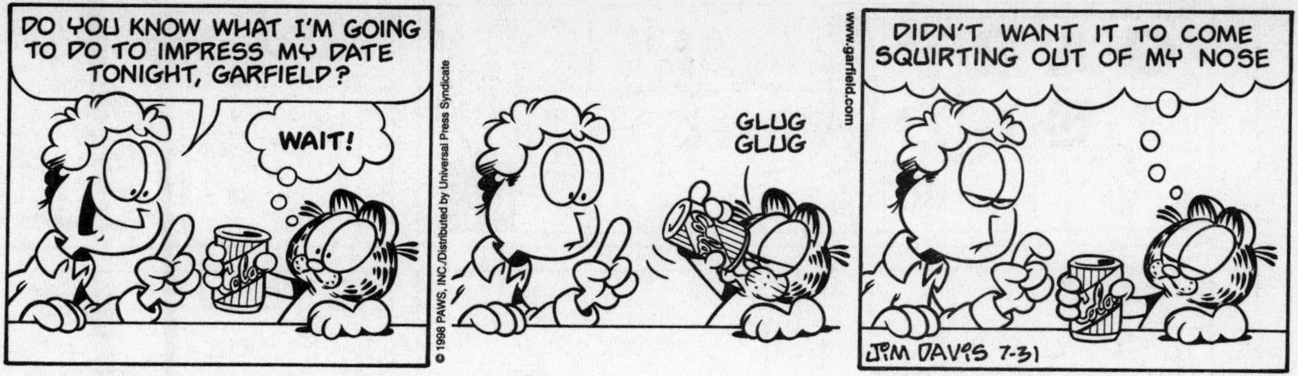
DO YOU KNOW WHAT I'M GOING TO DO TO IMPRESS MY DATE TONIGHT, GARFIELD?
WAIT!
© 1998 PAWS, INC./Distributed by Universal Press Syndicate
GLUG GLUG
www.garfield.com
DIDN'T WANT IT TO COME SQUIRTING OUT OF MY NOSE
JIM DAVIS 7-31

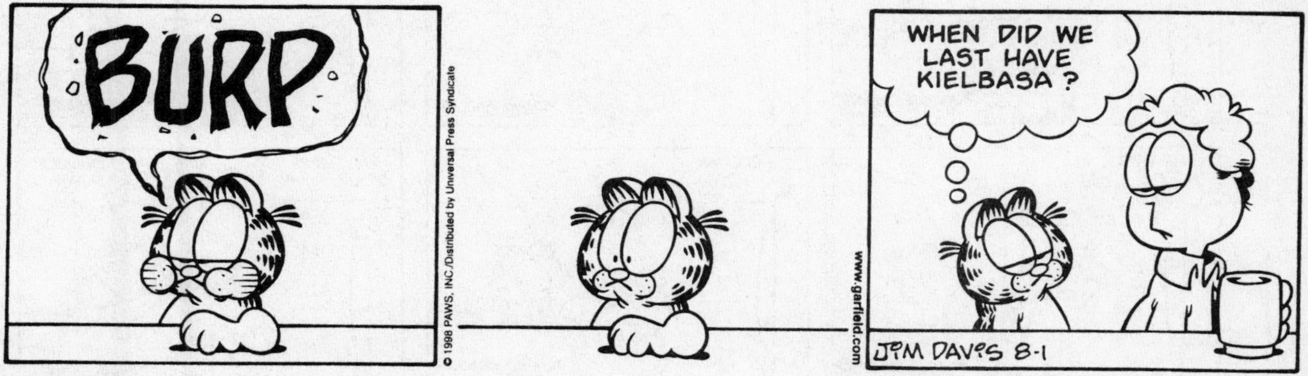
BURP
© 1998 PAWS, INC./Distributed by Universal Press Syndicate
www.garfield.com
WHEN DID WE LAST HAVE KIELBASA ?
JIM DAVIS 8-1

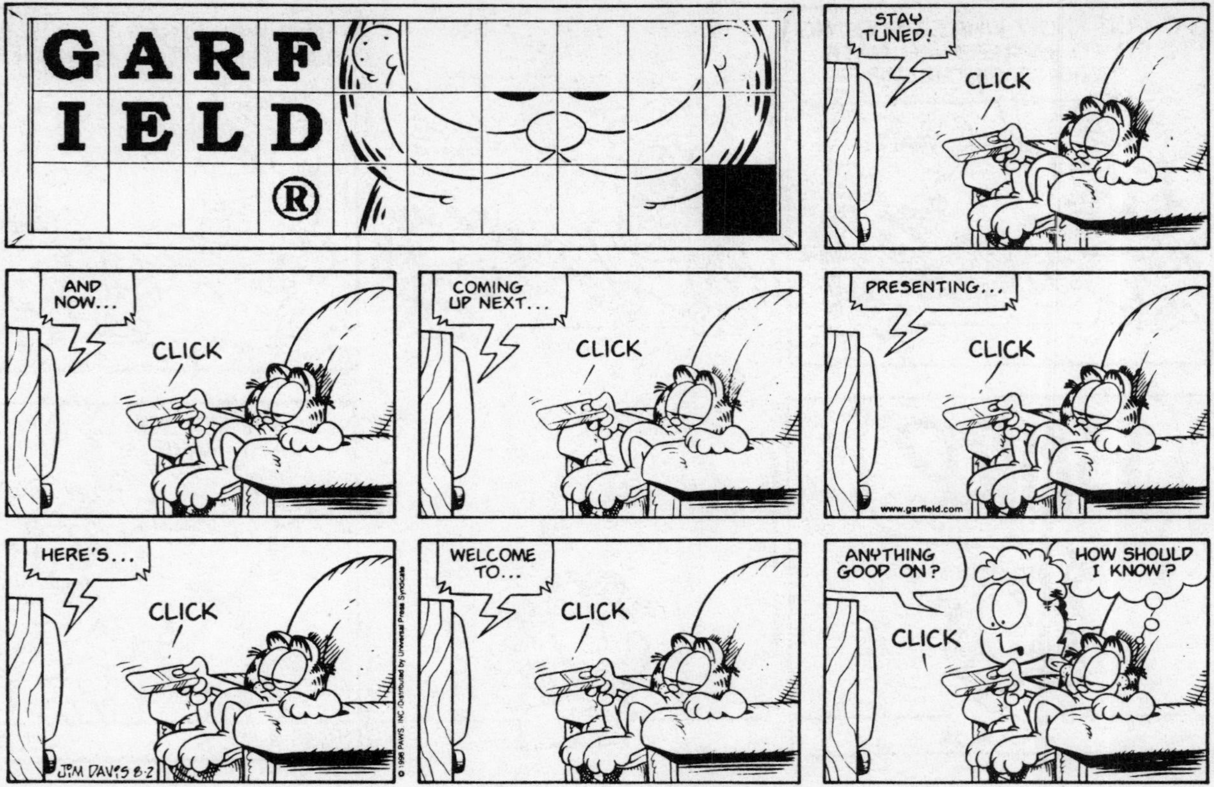
GARFIELD®
STAY TUNED!
CLICK
AND NOW...
CLICK
COMING UP NEXT...
CLICK
PRESENTING...
CLICK
www.garfield.com
HERE'S...
CLICK
JIM DAVIS 8-2
© 1998 PAWS, INC./Distributed by Universal Press Syndicate
WELCOME TO...
CLICK
ANYTHING GOOD ON?
HOW SHOULD I KNOW?
CLICK

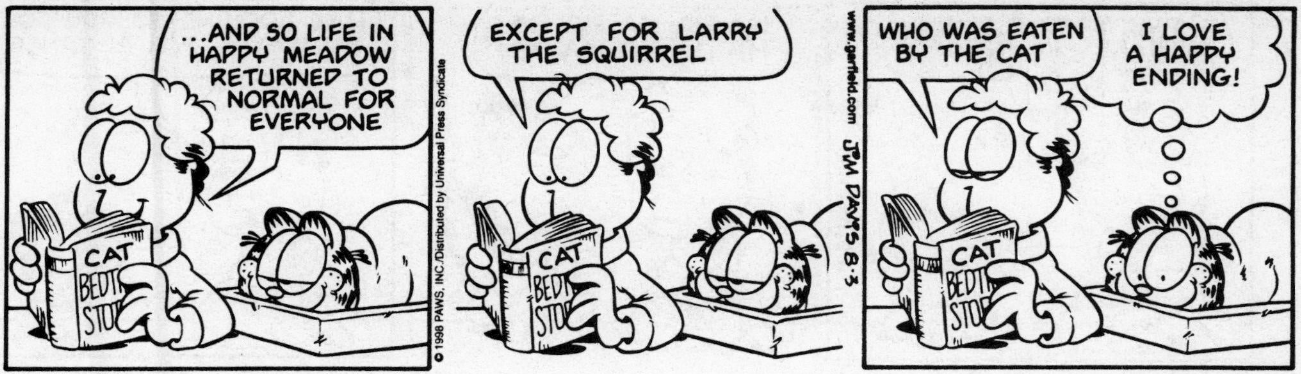
...AND SO LIFE IN HAPPY MEADOW RETURNED TO NORMAL FOR EVERYONE
CAT BEDT STO
© 1998 PAWS, INC./Distributed by Universal Press Syndicate
EXCEPT FOR LARRY THE SQUIRREL
www.garfield.com
JIM DAVIS 8-3
WHO WAS EATEN BY THE CAT
I LOVE A HAPPY ENDING!

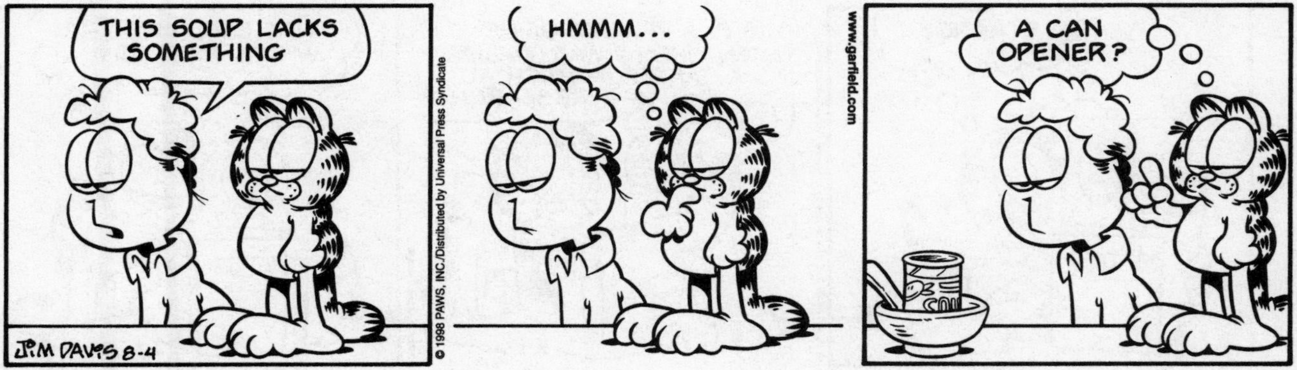
THIS SOUP LACKS SOMETHING
JIM DAVIS 8-4
© 1998 PAWS, INC./Distributed by Universal Press Syndicate
HMMM...
www.garfield.com
A CAN OPENER?

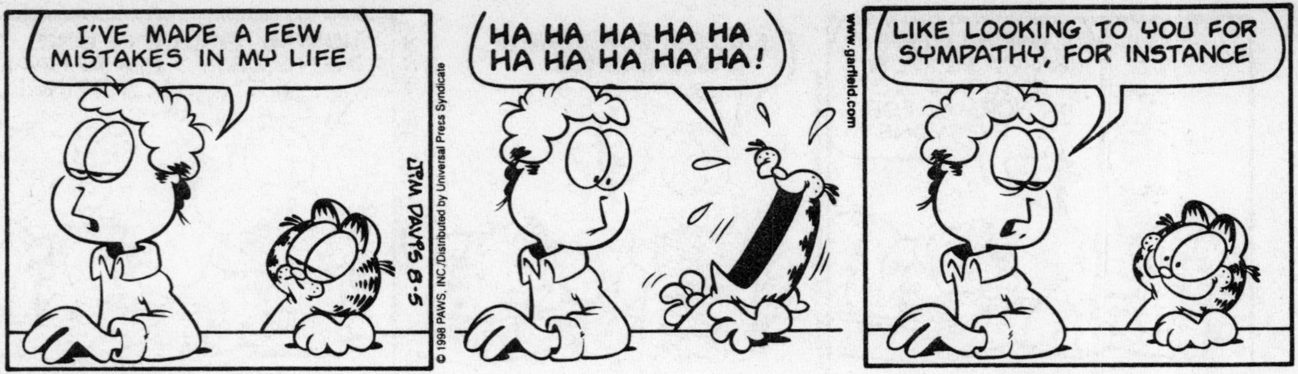
I'VE MADE A FEW MISTAKES IN MY LIFE
HA HA HA HA HA HA HA HA HA HA!
LIKE LOOKING TO YOU FOR SYMPATHY, FOR INSTANCE
JPM DAVPS 8-5
© 1998 PAWS, INC./Distributed by Universal Press Syndicate
www.garfield.com

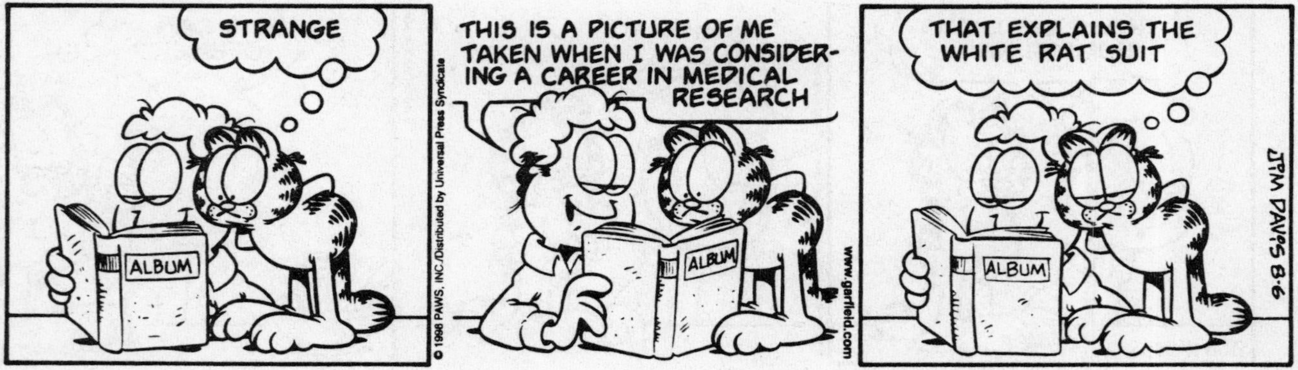
STRANGE
ALBUM
THIS IS A PICTURE OF ME TAKEN WHEN I WAS CONSIDERING A CAREER IN MEDICAL RESEARCH
ALBUM
THAT EXPLAINS THE WHITE RAT SUIT
ALBUM
JPM DAVPS 8-6
© 1998 PAWS, INC./Distributed by Universal Press Syndicate
www.garfield.com

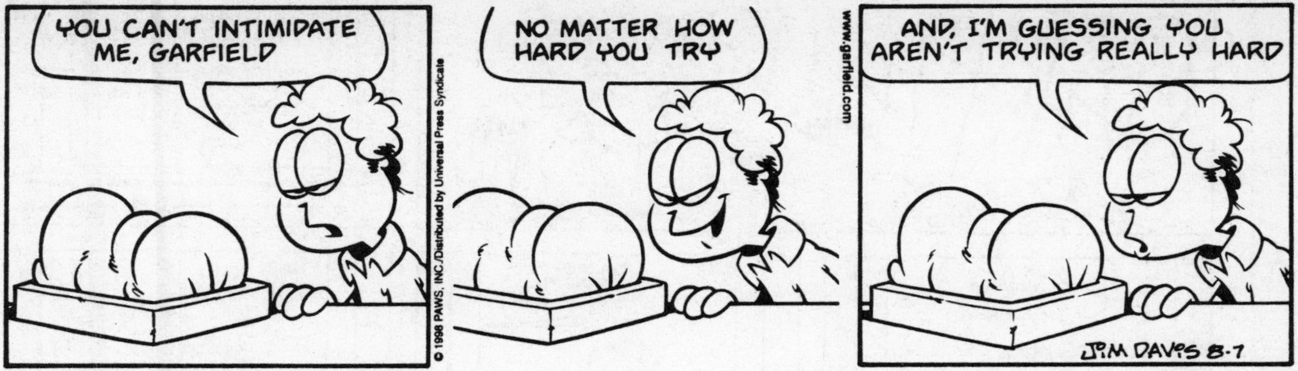
YOU CAN'T INTIMIDATE ME, GARFIELD
NO MATTER HOW HARD YOU TRY
AND, I'M GUESSING YOU AREN'T TRYING REALLY HARD
JIM DAVIS 8-7

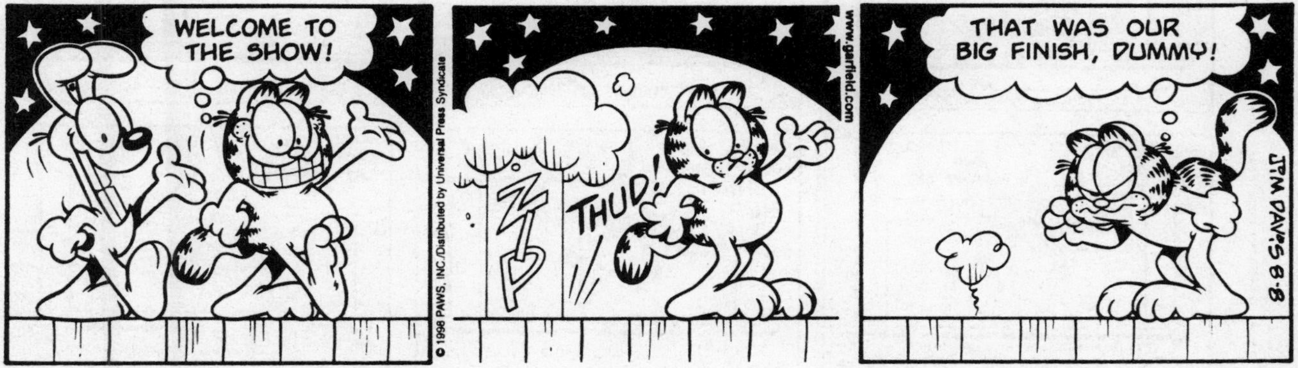
WELCOME TO THE SHOW!
ZIP
THUD!
THAT WAS OUR BIG FINISH, DUMMY!
JIM DAVIS 8-8

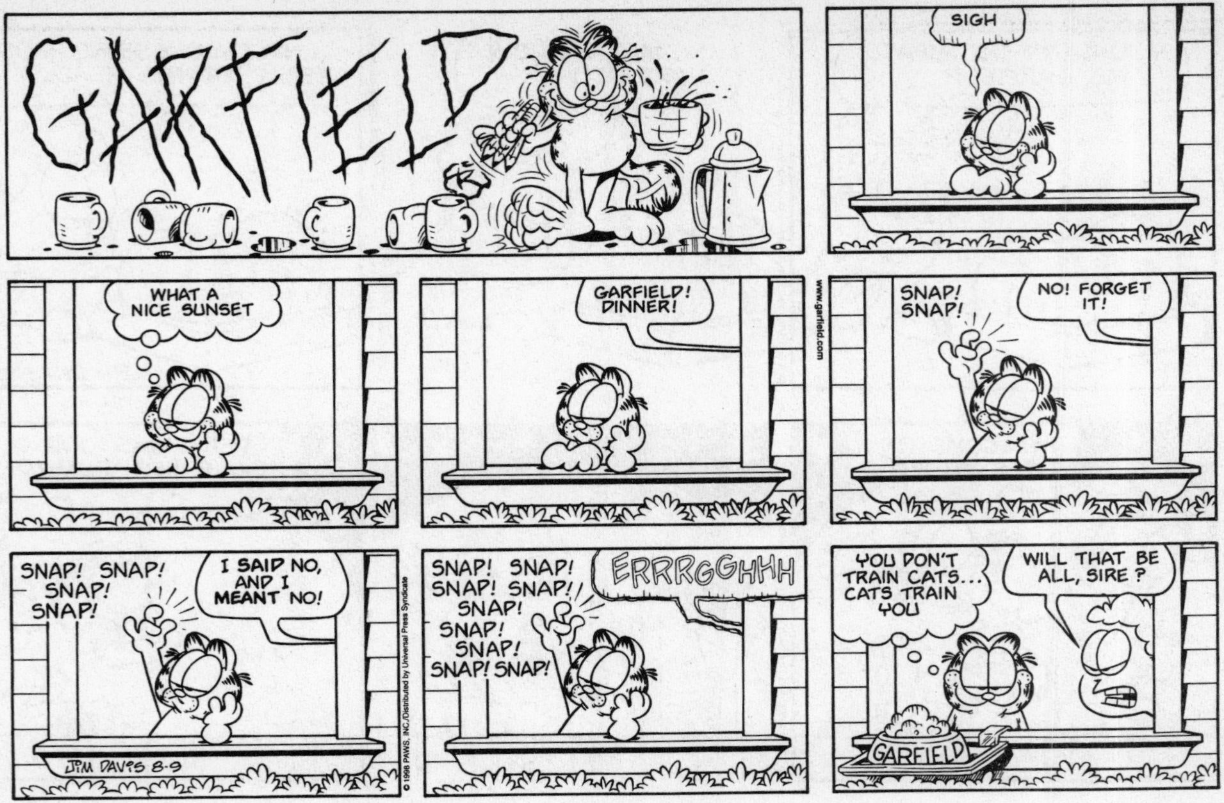
GARFIELD
SIGH
WHAT A NICE SUNSET
GARFIELD! DINNER!
SNAP! SNAP!
NO! FORGET IT!
SNAP! SNAP! SNAP! SNAP!
I SAID NO, AND I MEANT NO!
JIM DAVIS 8-9
© 1998 PAWS, INC./Distributed by Universal Press Syndicate
SNAP! SNAP! SNAP! SNAP! SNAP! SNAP! SNAP! SNAP! SNAP!
ERRRGGHHH
YOU DON'T TRAIN CATS... CATS TRAIN YOU
WILL THAT BE ALL, SIRE ?
GARFIELD
www.garfield.com

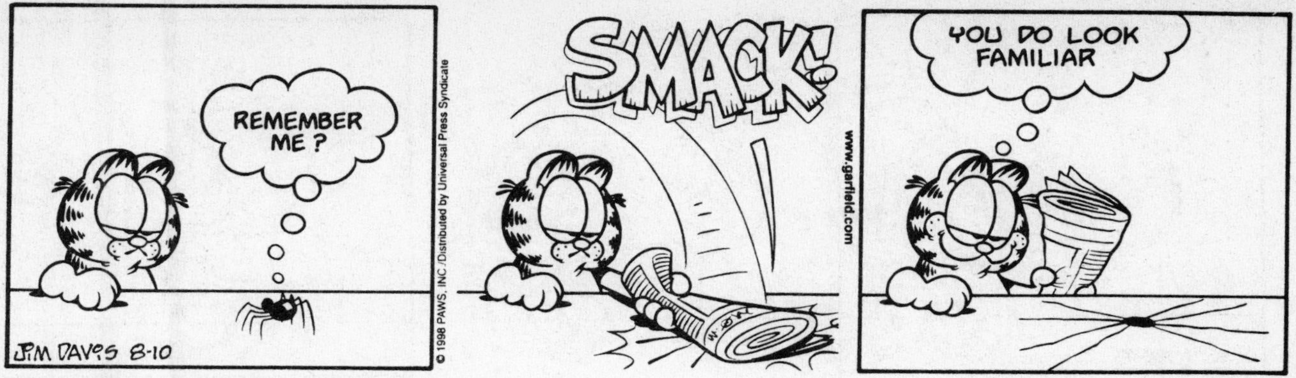
REMEMBER ME?
JIM DAVIS 8-10
© 1998 PAWS, INC./Distributed by Universal Press Syndicate
SMACK!
www.garfield.com
YOU DO LOOK FAMILIAR

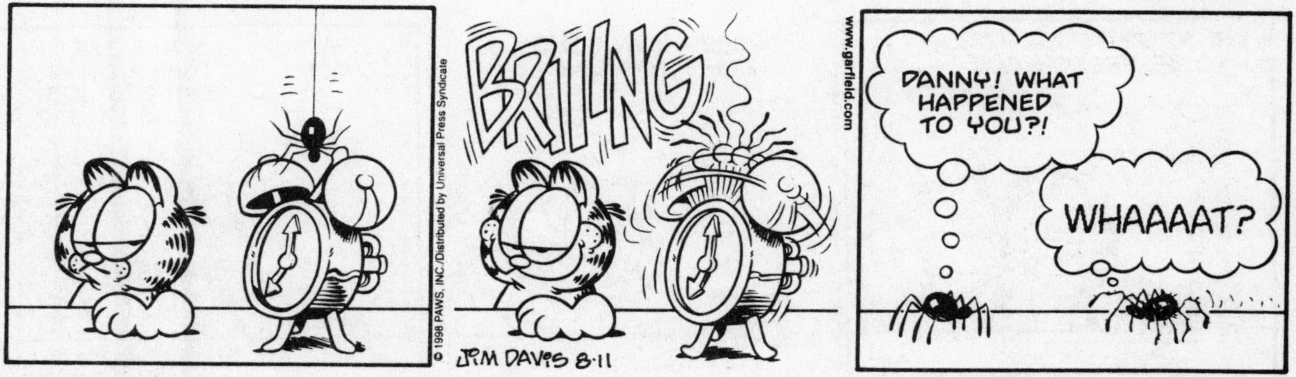
© 1998 PAWS, INC./Distributed by Universal Press Syndicate
BRIIING
JIM DAVIS 8-11
www.garfield.com
DANNY! WHAT HAPPENED TO YOU?!
WHAAAAT?

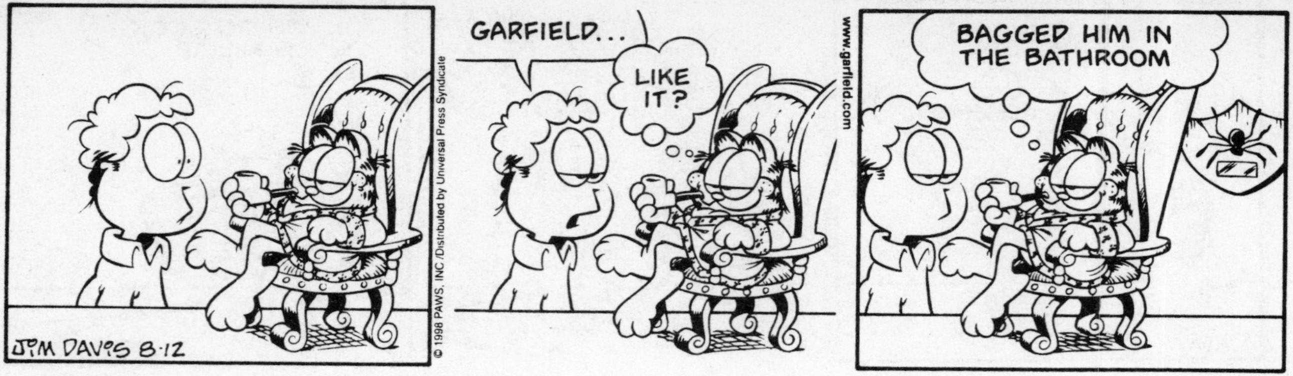
GARFIELD...
LIKE IT?
BAGGED HIM IN THE BATHROOM
JIM DAVIS 8-12
© 1998 PAWS, INC./Distributed by Universal Press Syndicate
www.garfield.com

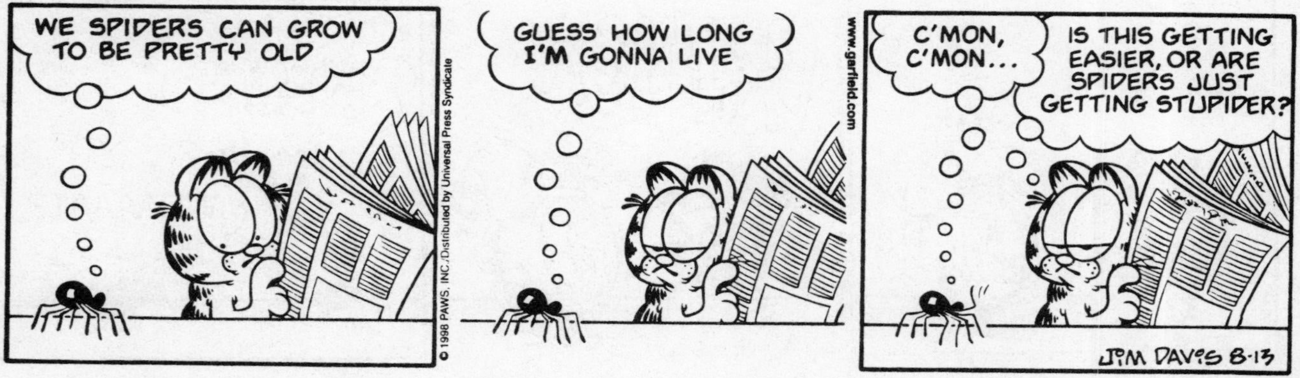
WE SPIDERS CAN GROW TO BE PRETTY OLD
GUESS HOW LONG I'M GONNA LIVE
C'MON, C'MON...
IS THIS GETTING EASIER, OR ARE SPIDERS JUST GETTING STUPIDER?
JIM DAVIS 8-13
© 1998 PAWS, INC./Distributed by Universal Press Syndicate
www.garfield.com

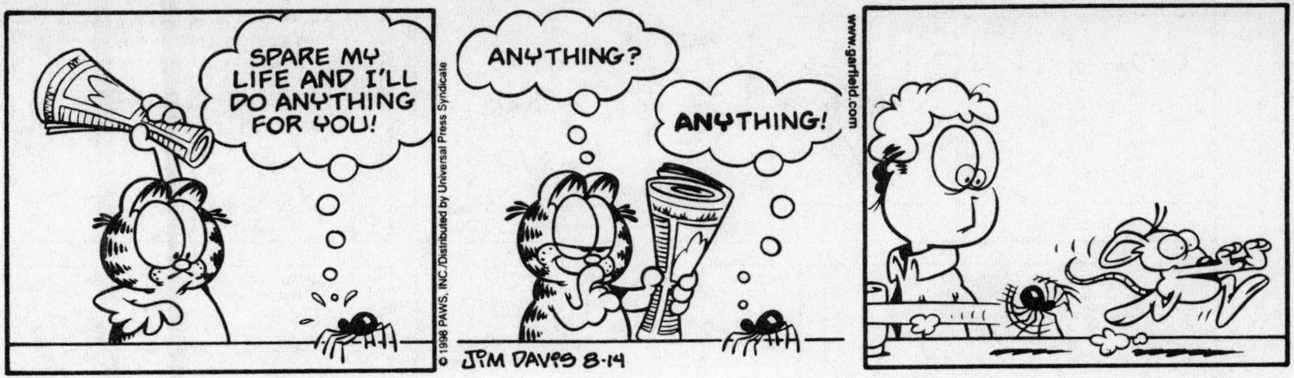
SPARE MY LIFE AND I'LL DO ANYTHING FOR YOU!
ANYTHING?
ANYTHING!
© 1998 PAWS, INC./Distributed by Universal Press Syndicate
JIM DAVIS 8-14
www.garfield.com

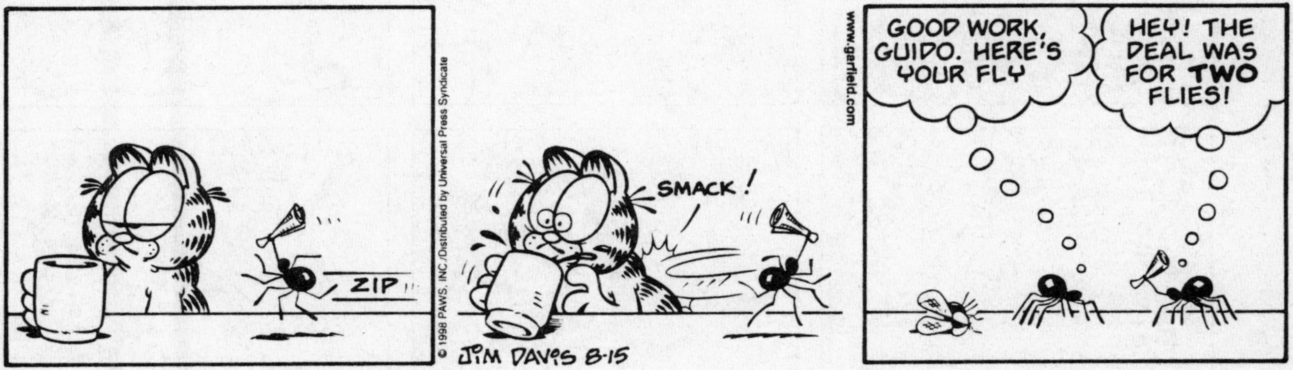
ZIP
SMACK!
© 1998 PAWS, INC./Distributed by Universal Press Syndicate
JIM DAVIS 8-15
www.garfield.com
GOOD WORK, GUIDO. HERE'S YOUR FLY
HEY! THE DEAL WAS FOR **TWO** FLIES!

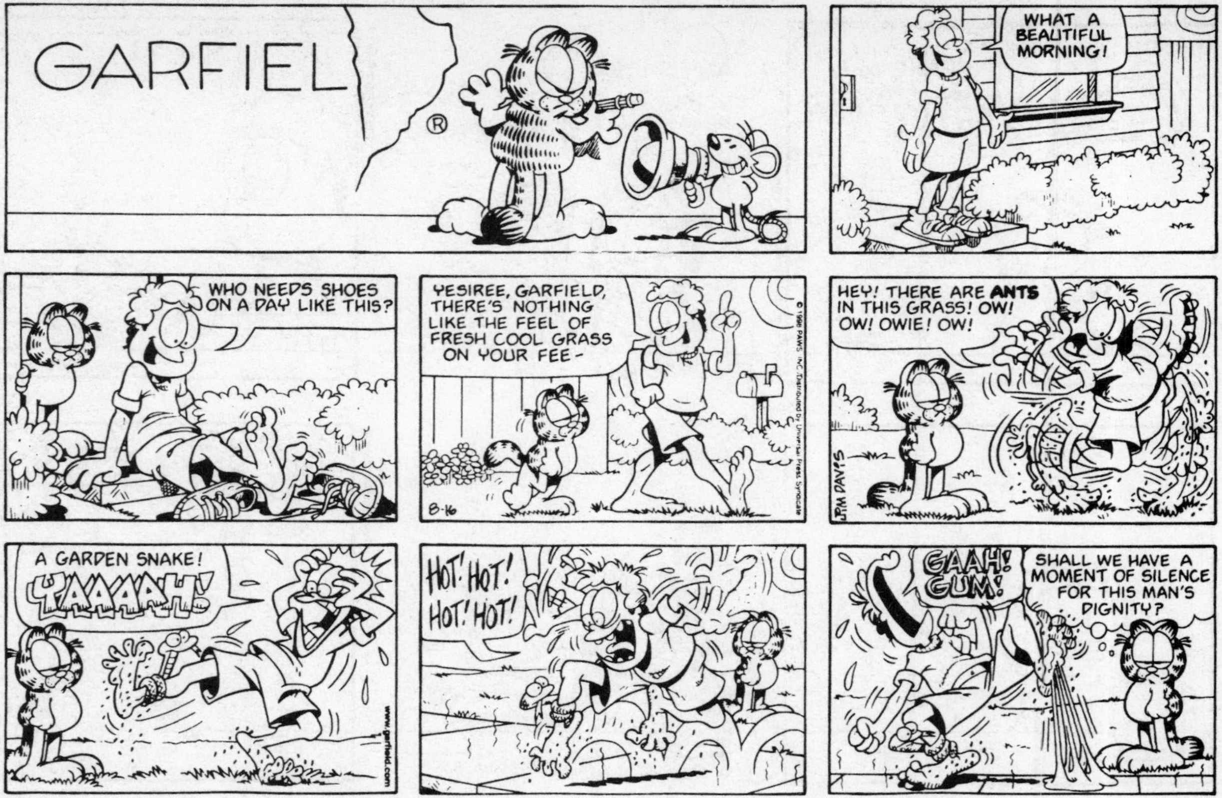
GARFIEL
®
WHAT A BEAUTIFUL MORNING!
WHO NEEDS SHOES ON A DAY LIKE THIS?
YESIREE, GARFIELD, THERE'S NOTHING LIKE THE FEEL OF FRESH COOL GRASS ON YOUR FEE-
8-16
© 1998 PAWS, INC./Distributed by Universal Press Syndicate
HEY! THERE ARE **ANTS** IN THIS GRASS! OW! OW! OWIE! OW!
JPM DAVIS
A GARDEN SNAKE!
YAAAAH!
www.garfield.com
HOT! HOT! HOT! HOT!
GAAH! GUM!
SHALL WE HAVE A MOMENT OF SILENCE FOR THIS MAN'S DIGNITY?

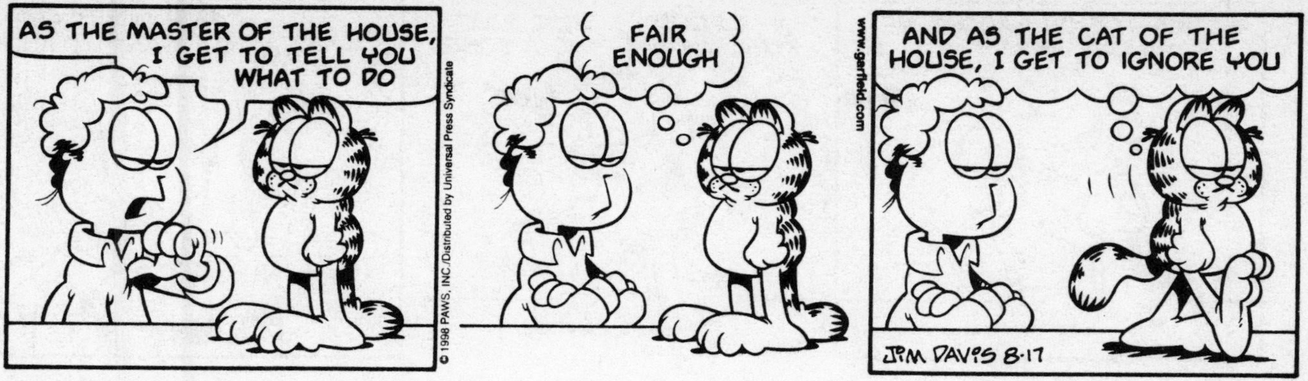
AS THE MASTER OF THE HOUSE, I GET TO TELL YOU WHAT TO DO
FAIR ENOUGH
AND AS THE CAT OF THE HOUSE, I GET TO IGNORE YOU
JIM DAVIS 8-17
© 1998 PAWS, INC./Distributed by Universal Press Syndicate
www.garfield.com

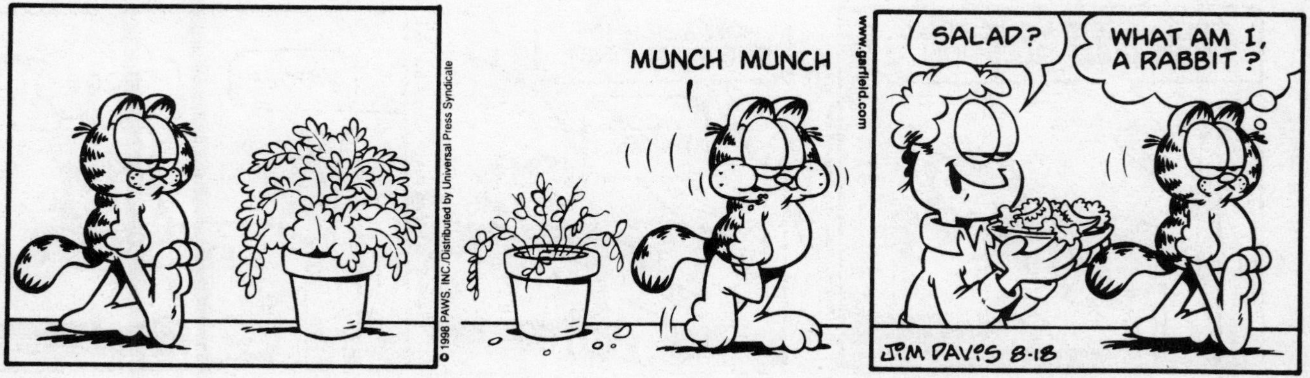
MUNCH MUNCH
SALAD?
WHAT AM I, A RABBIT?
JIM DAVIS 8-18
© 1998 PAWS, INC./Distributed by Universal Press Syndicate
www.garfield.com

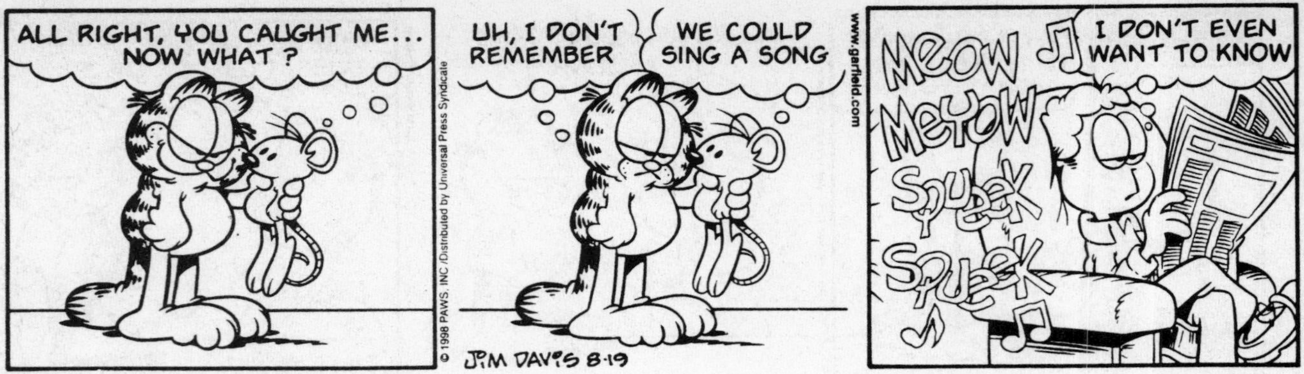
ALL RIGHT, YOU CAUGHT ME... NOW WHAT ?
UH, I DON'T REMEMBER
WE COULD SING A SONG
© 1998 PAWS, INC./Distributed by Universal Press Syndicate
JIM DAVIS 8-19
www.garfield.com
MEOW
MEYOW
SQUEEK
SQUEEK
I DON'T EVEN WANT TO KNOW

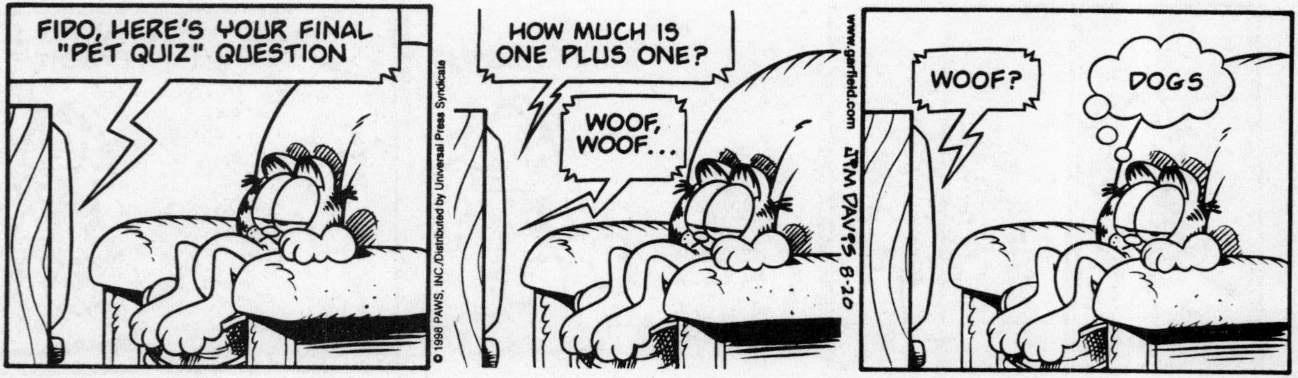
FIDO, HERE'S YOUR FINAL "PET QUIZ" QUESTION
© 1998 PAWS, INC./Distributed by Universal Press Syndicate
HOW MUCH IS ONE PLUS ONE?
WOOF, WOOF...
www.garfield.com
JIM DAVIS 8-20
WOOF?
DOGS

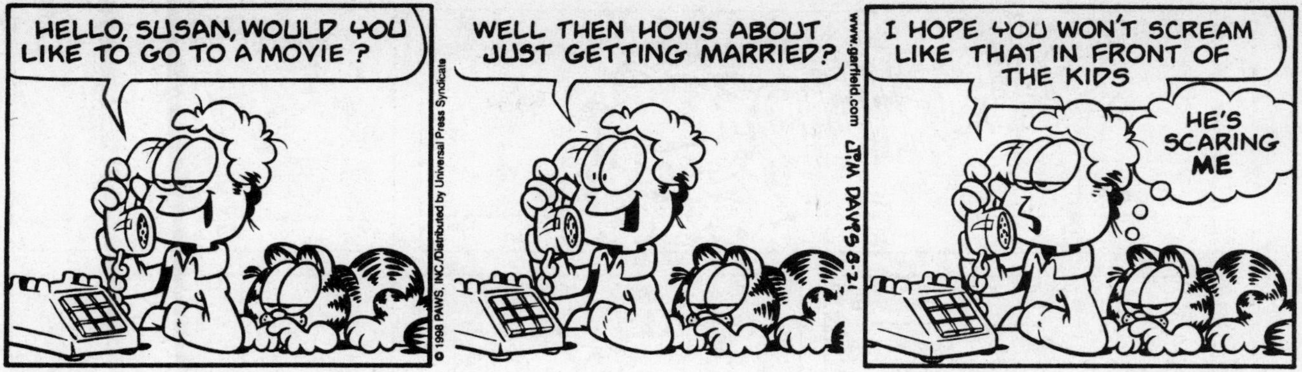
HELLO, SUSAN, WOULD YOU LIKE TO GO TO A MOVIE?
© 1998 PAWS, INC./Distributed by Universal Press Syndicate
WELL THEN HOWS ABOUT JUST GETTING MARRIED?
www.garfield.com JIM DAVIS 8-21
I HOPE YOU WON'T SCREAM LIKE THAT IN FRONT OF THE KIDS
HE'S SCARING ME

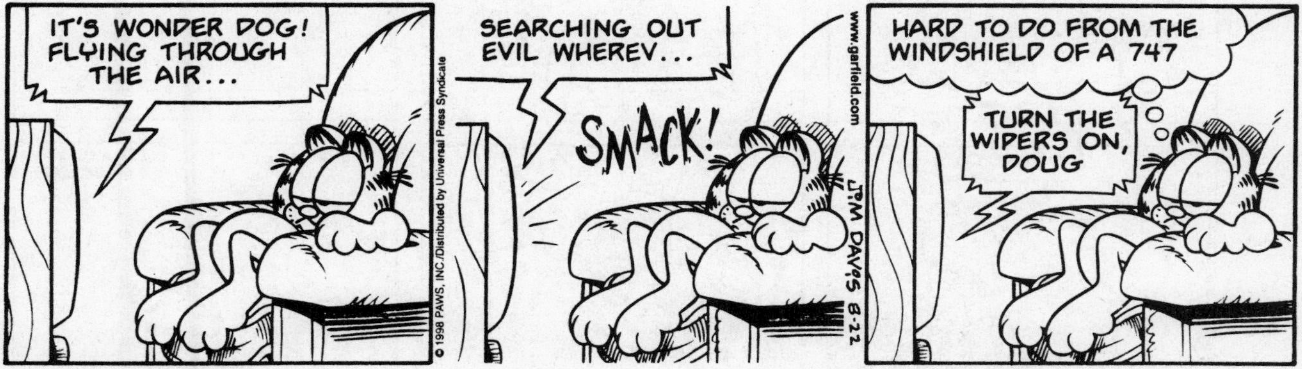
IT'S WONDER DOG! FLYING THROUGH THE AIR...
© 1998 PAWS, INC./Distributed by Universal Press Syndicate
SEARCHING OUT EVIL WHEREV...
SMACK!
www.garfield.com JIM DAVIS 8-22
HARD TO DO FROM THE WINDSHIELD OF A 747
TURN THE WIPERS ON, DOUG

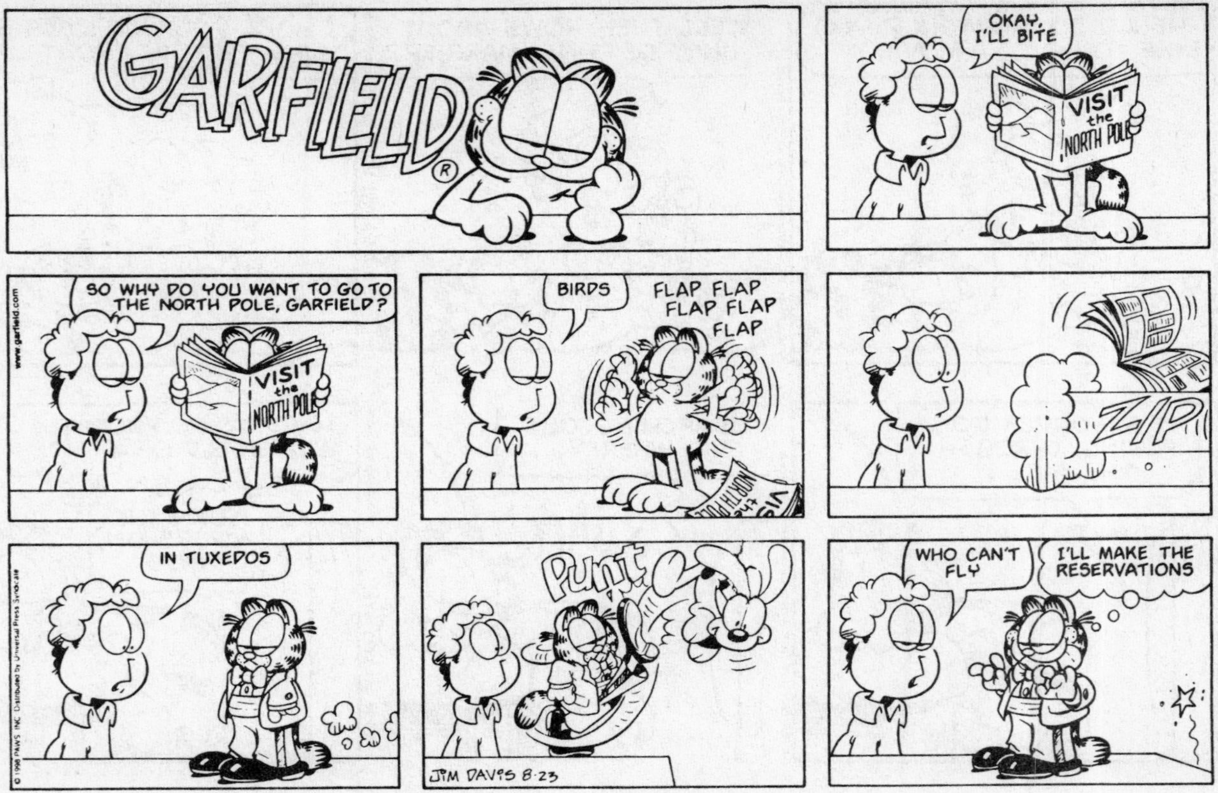
GARFIELD®
OKAY, I'LL BITE
VISIT the NORTH POLE
www.garfield.com
SO WHY DO YOU WANT TO GO TO THE NORTH POLE, GARFIELD?
VISIT the NORTH POLE
BIRDS
FLAP FLAP FLAP FLAP FLAP
ZIP
© 1998 PAWS, INC. Distributed by Universal Press Syndicate
IN TUXEDOS
PUNT
JIM DAVIS 8-23
WHO CAN'T FLY
I'LL MAKE THE RESERVATIONS

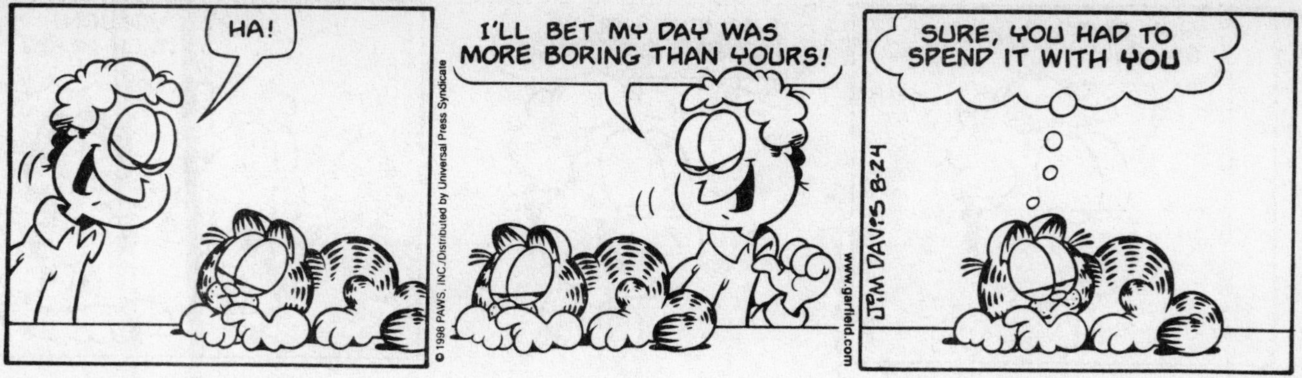
HA!
I'LL BET MY DAY WAS MORE BORING THAN YOURS!
SURE, YOU HAD TO SPEND IT WITH YOU
JIM DAVIS 8-24
© 1998 PAWS, INC./Distributed by Universal Press Syndicate
www.garfield.com

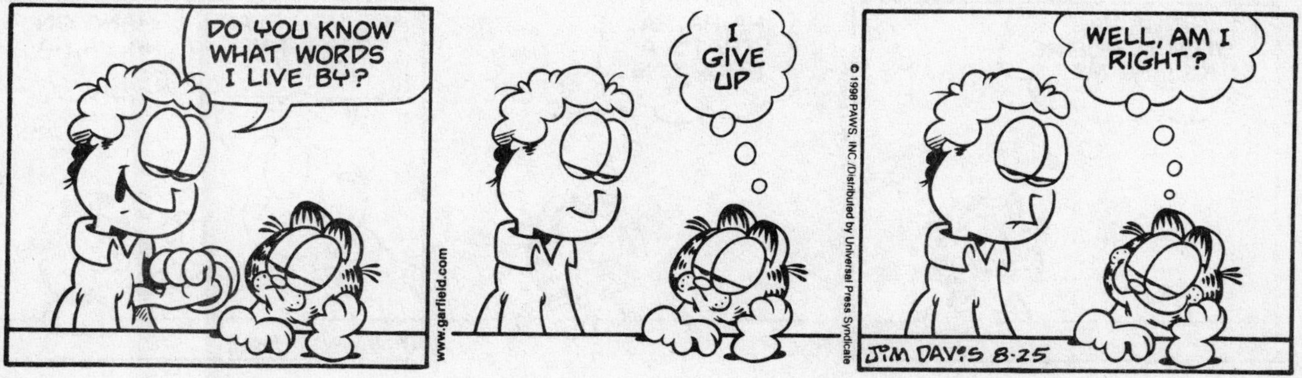
DO YOU KNOW WHAT WORDS I LIVE BY?
I GIVE UP
WELL, AM I RIGHT?
JIM DAVIS 8-25
© 1998 PAWS, INC./Distributed by Universal Press Syndicate
www.garfield.com

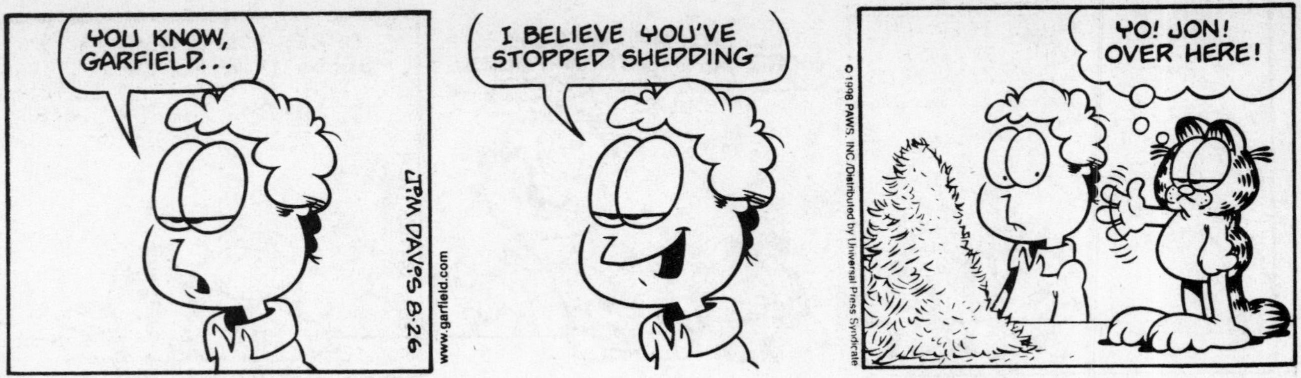
YOU KNOW, GARFIELD...
JIM DAVIS 8-26
www.garfield.com
I BELIEVE YOU'VE STOPPED SHEDDING
© 1998 PAWS, INC./Distributed by Universal Press Syndicate
YO! JON! OVER HERE!

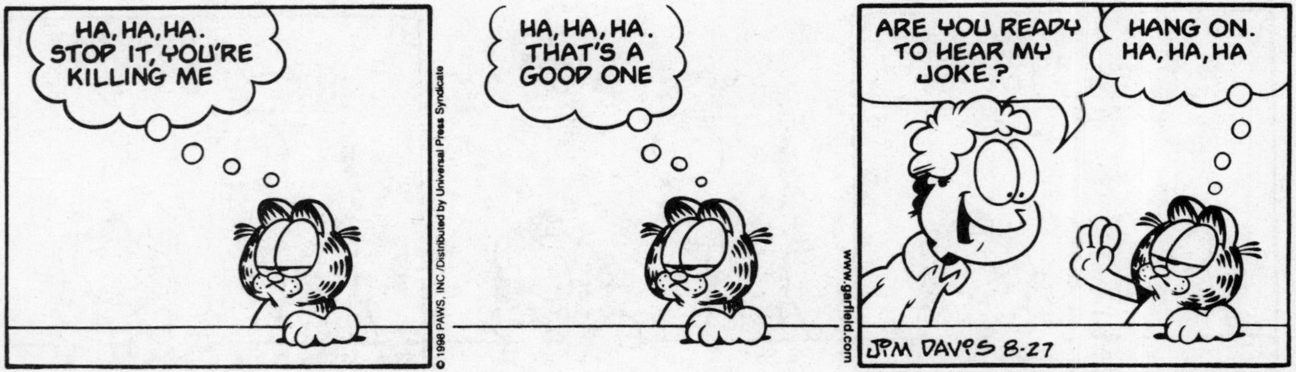
HA, HA, HA. STOP IT, YOU'RE KILLING ME
© 1998 PAWS, INC /Distributed by Universal Press Syndicate
HA, HA, HA. THAT'S A GOOD ONE
www.garfield.com
ARE YOU READY TO HEAR MY JOKE?
HANG ON. HA, HA, HA
JIM DAVIS 8-27

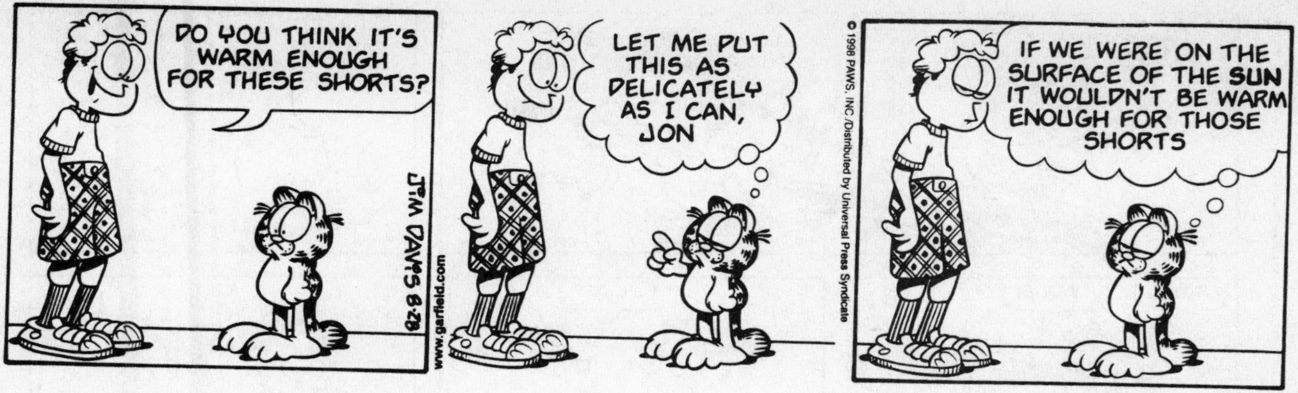
DO YOU THINK IT'S WARM ENOUGH FOR THESE SHORTS?
JIM DAVIS 8-28
www.garfield.com
LET ME PUT THIS AS DELICATELY AS I CAN, JON
© 1998 PAWS, INC./Distributed by Universal Press Syndicate
IF WE WERE ON THE SURFACE OF THE SUN IT WOULDN'T BE WARM ENOUGH FOR THOSE SHORTS

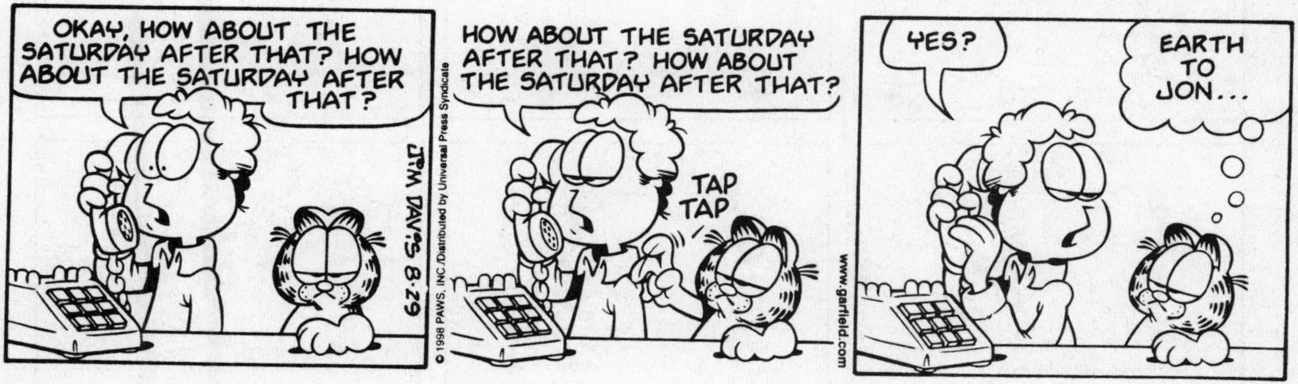
OKAY, HOW ABOUT THE SATURDAY AFTER THAT? HOW ABOUT THE SATURDAY AFTER THAT?
JIM DAVIS 8-29
© 1998 PAWS, INC./Distributed by Universal Press Syndicate
HOW ABOUT THE SATURDAY AFTER THAT? HOW ABOUT THE SATURDAY AFTER THAT?
TAP
TAP
www.garfield.com
YES?
EARTH TO JON...

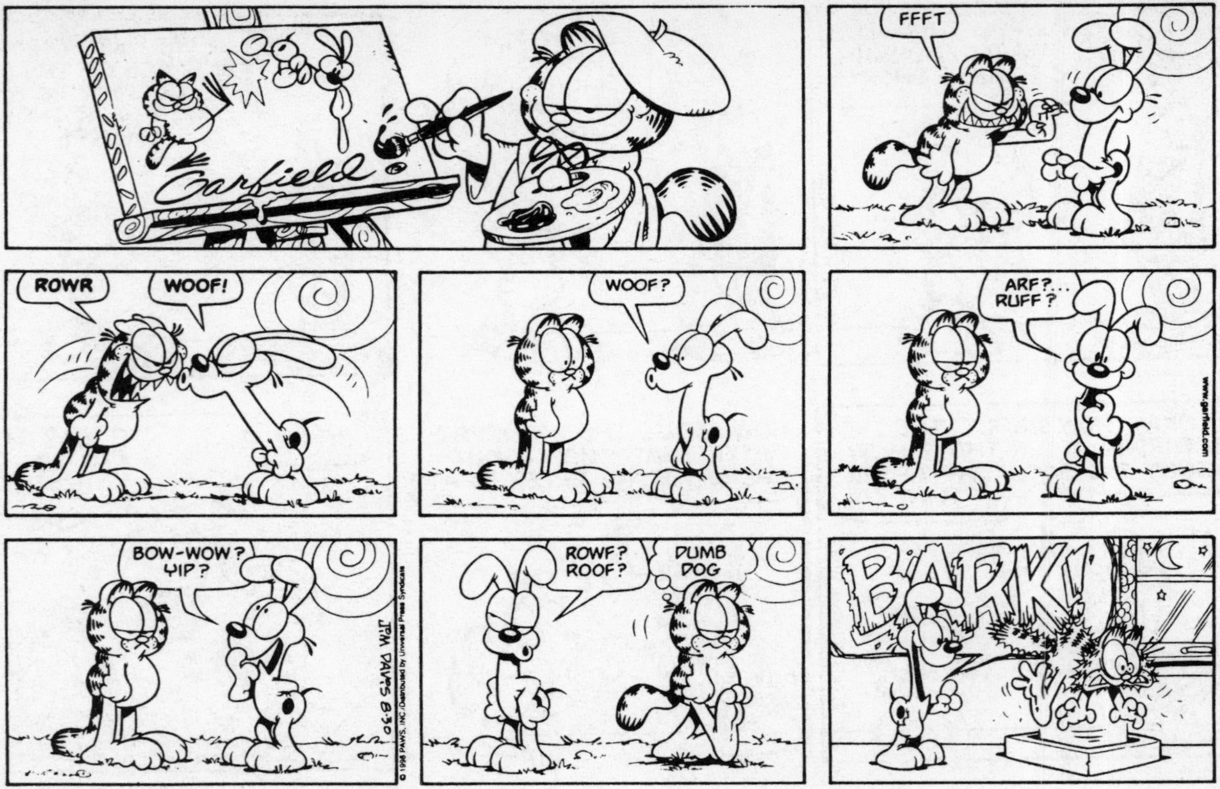

Garfield
FFFT
ROWR
WOOF!
WOOF?
ARF?... RUFF?
www.garfield.com
BOW-WOW? YIP?
JPM DAVIS 8-30
© 1998 PAWS, INC./Distributed by Universal Press Syndicate
ROWF? ROOF?
DUMB DOG
BARK!

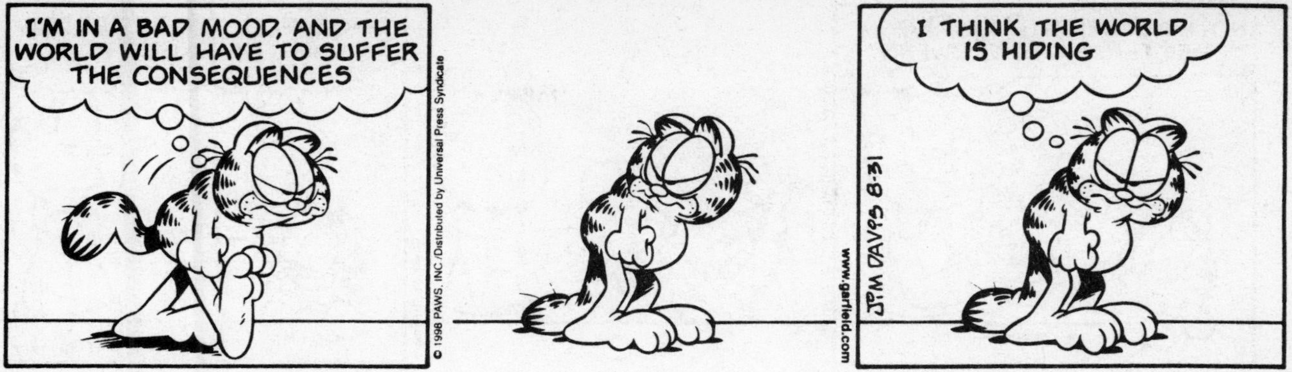
I'M IN A BAD MOOD, AND THE WORLD WILL HAVE TO SUFFER THE CONSEQUENCES
© 1998 PAWS, INC /Distributed by Universal Press Syndicate
JIM DAVIS 8-31
www.garfield.com
I THINK THE WORLD IS HIDING

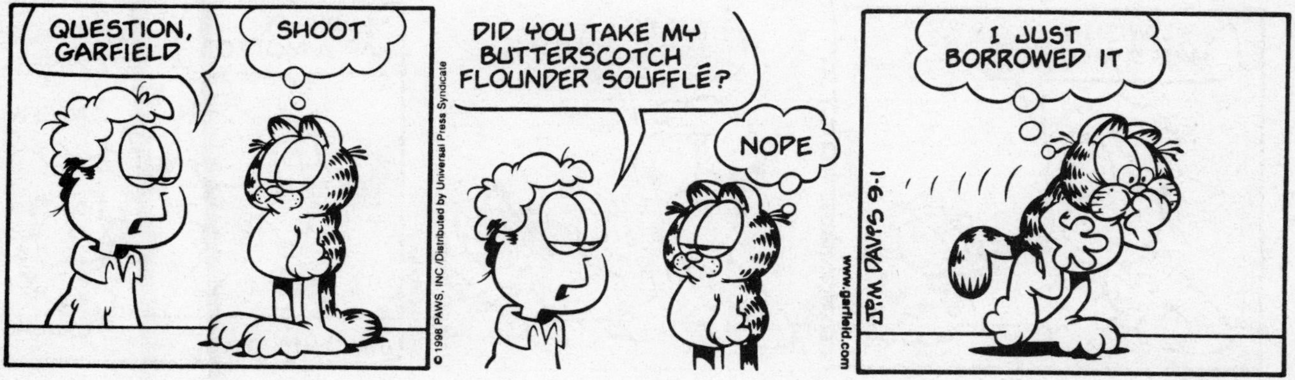
QUESTION, GARFIELD
SHOOT
© 1998 PAWS, INC /Distributed by Universal Press Syndicate
DID YOU TAKE MY BUTTERSCOTCH FLOUNDER SOUFFLÉ?
NOPE
JIM DAVIS 9-1
www.garfield.com
I JUST BORROWED IT

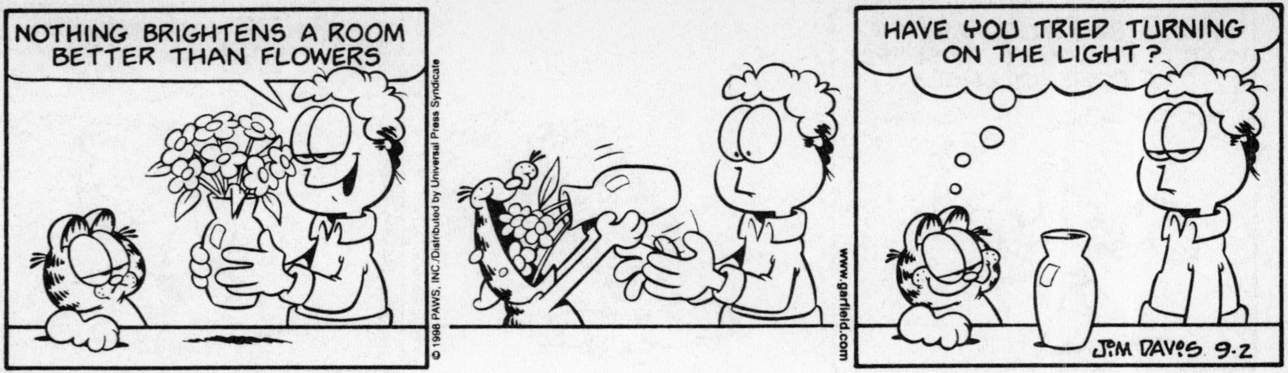
NOTHING BRIGHTENS A ROOM BETTER THAN FLOWERS
© 1998 PAWS, INC./Distributed by Universal Press Syndicate
www.garfield.com
HAVE YOU TRIED TURNING ON THE LIGHT?
JIM DAVIS 9·2

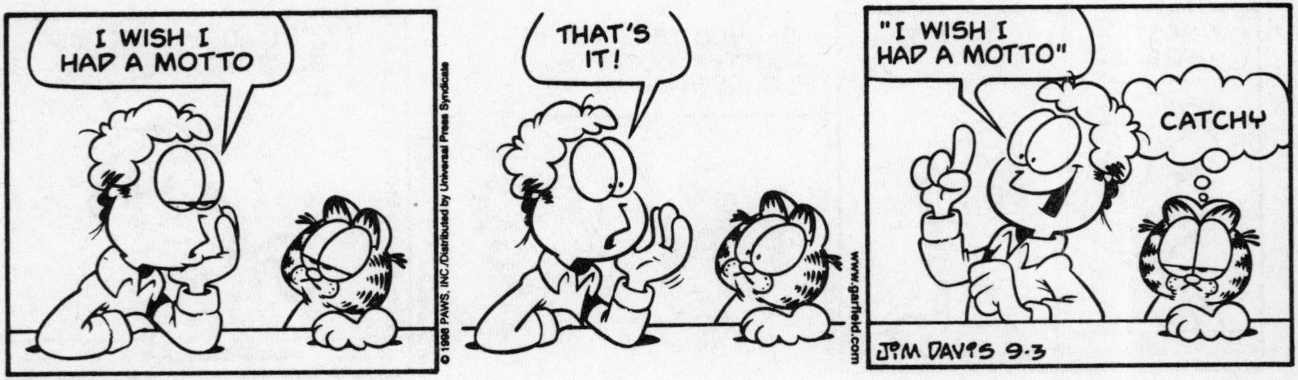
I WISH I HAD A MOTTO
© 1998 PAWS, INC./Distributed by Universal Press Syndicate
THAT'S IT!
www.garfield.com
"I WISH I HAD A MOTTO"
CATCHY
JIM DAVIS 9·3

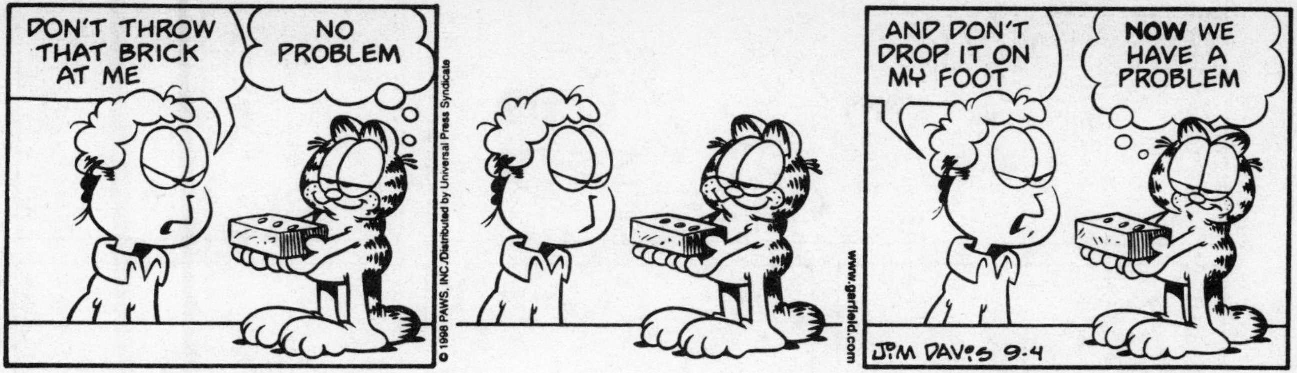
DON'T THROW THAT BRICK AT ME
NO PROBLEM
AND DON'T DROP IT ON MY FOOT
NOW WE HAVE A PROBLEM
JIM DAVIS 9-4
© 1998 PAWS, INC./Distributed by Universal Press Syndicate
www.garfield.com

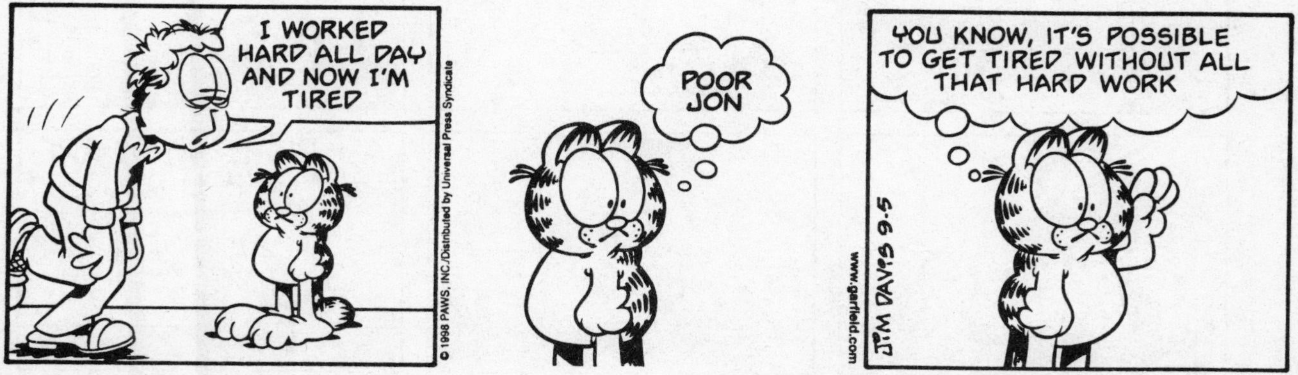
I WORKED HARD ALL DAY AND NOW I'M TIRED
POOR JON
YOU KNOW, IT'S POSSIBLE TO GET TIRED WITHOUT ALL THAT HARD WORK
JIM DAVIS 9-5
© 1998 PAWS, INC./Distributed by Universal Press Syndicate
www.garfield.com

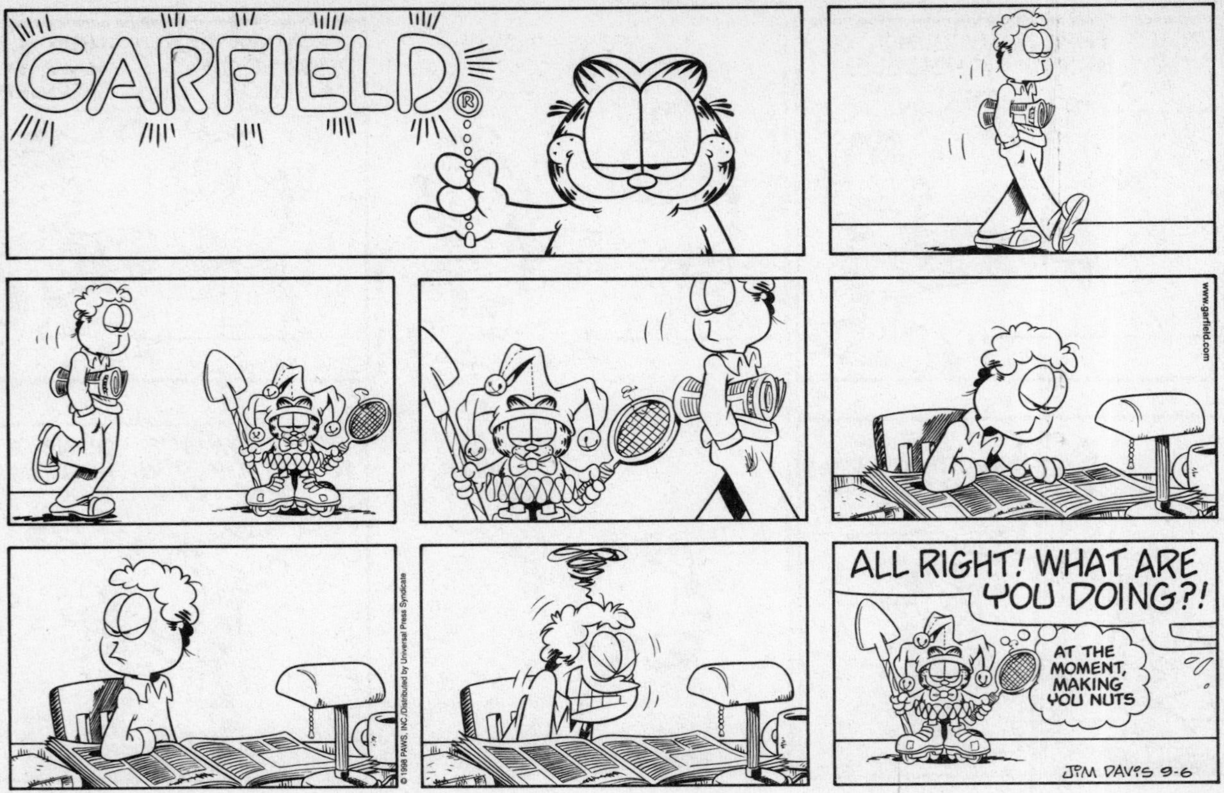
GARFIELD®
www.garfield.com
© 1998 PAWS, INC./Distributed by Universal Press Syndicate
ALL RIGHT! WHAT ARE YOU DOING?!
AT THE MOMENT, MAKING YOU NUTS
JIM DAVIS 9-6

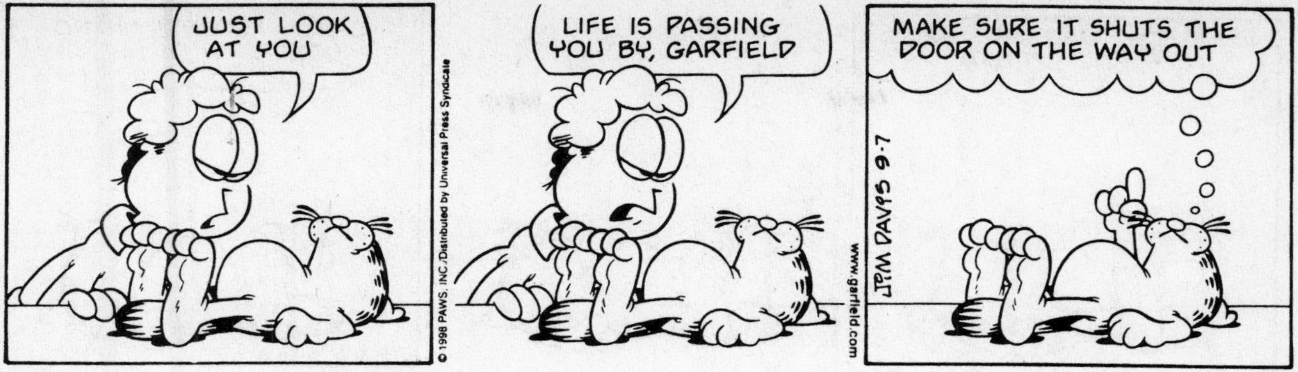
JUST LOOK AT YOU
LIFE IS PASSING YOU BY, GARFIELD
MAKE SURE IT SHUTS THE DOOR ON THE WAY OUT
© 1998 PAWS, INC./Distributed by Universal Press Syndicate
www.garfield.com
JIM DAVIS 9-7

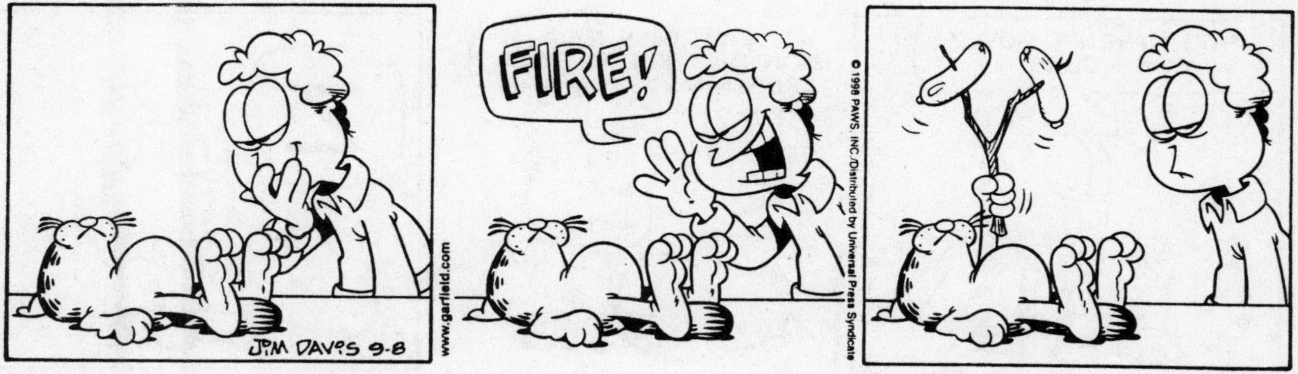
FIRE!
JIM DAVIS 9-8
www.garfield.com
© 1998 PAWS, INC./Distributed by Universal Press Syndicate

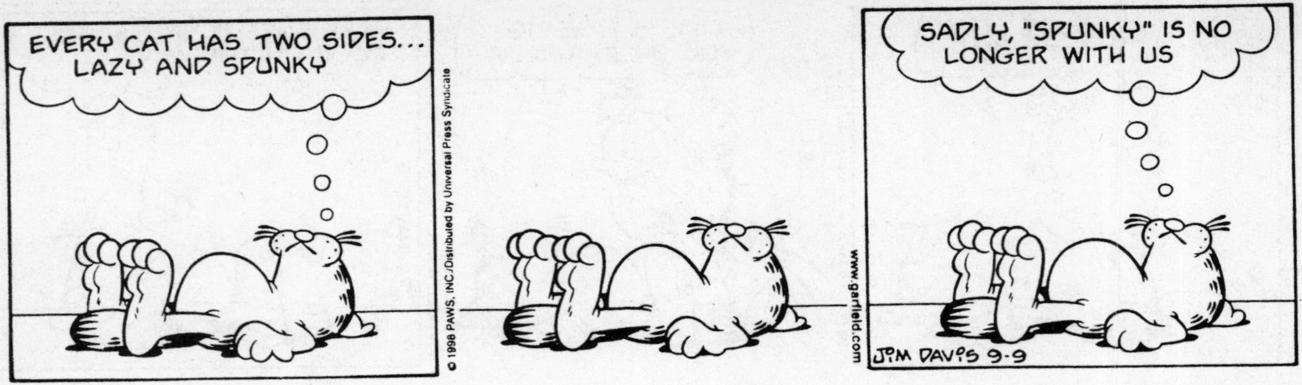
EVERY CAT HAS TWO SIDES... LAZY AND SPUNKY
© 1998 PAWS, INC./Distributed by Universal Press Syndicate
www.garfield.com
SADLY, "SPUNKY" IS NO LONGER WITH US
JIM DAVIS 9-9

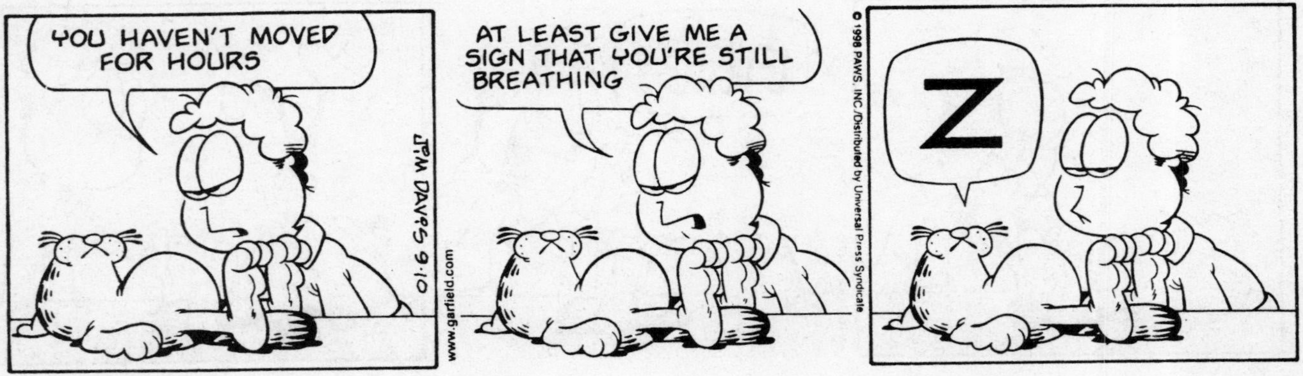
YOU HAVEN'T MOVED FOR HOURS
JIM DAVIS 9-10
www.garfield.com
AT LEAST GIVE ME A SIGN THAT YOU'RE STILL BREATHING
© 1998 PAWS, INC./Distributed by Universal Press Syndicate
Z

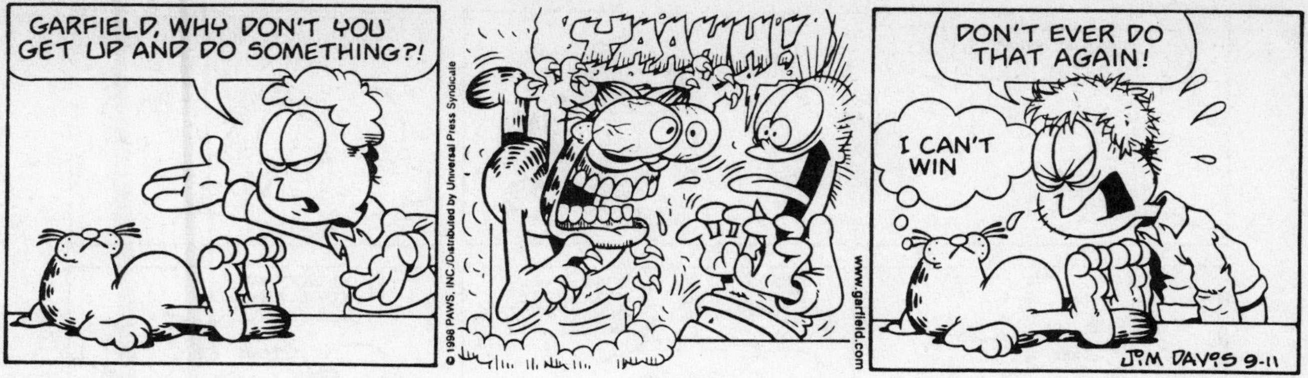
GARFIELD, WHY DON'T YOU GET UP AND DO SOMETHING?!
© 1998 PAWS, INC./Distributed by Universal Press Syndicate
www.garfield.com
DON'T EVER DO THAT AGAIN!
I CAN'T WIN
JIM DAVIS 9-11

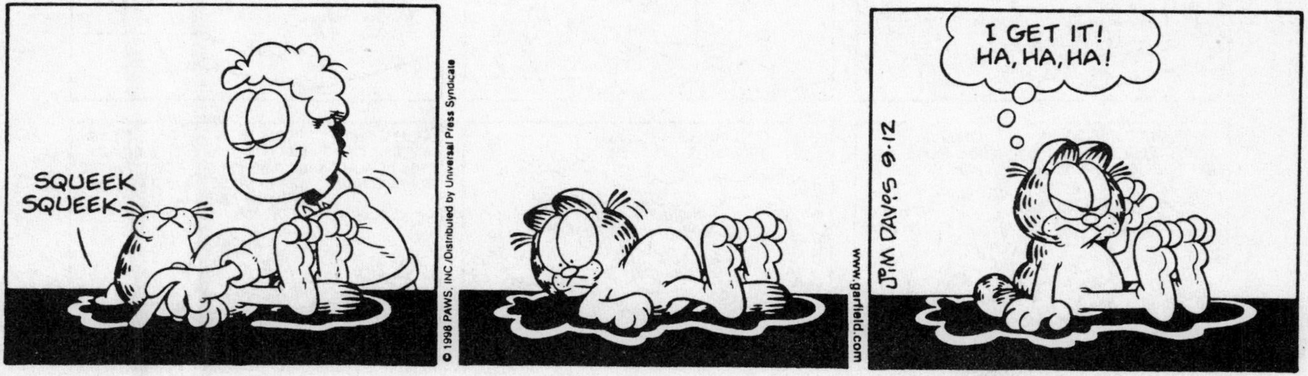
SQUEEK SQUEEK
© 1998 PAWS, INC./Distributed by Universal Press Syndicate
www.garfield.com
JIM DAVIS 9-12
I GET IT! HA, HA, HA!

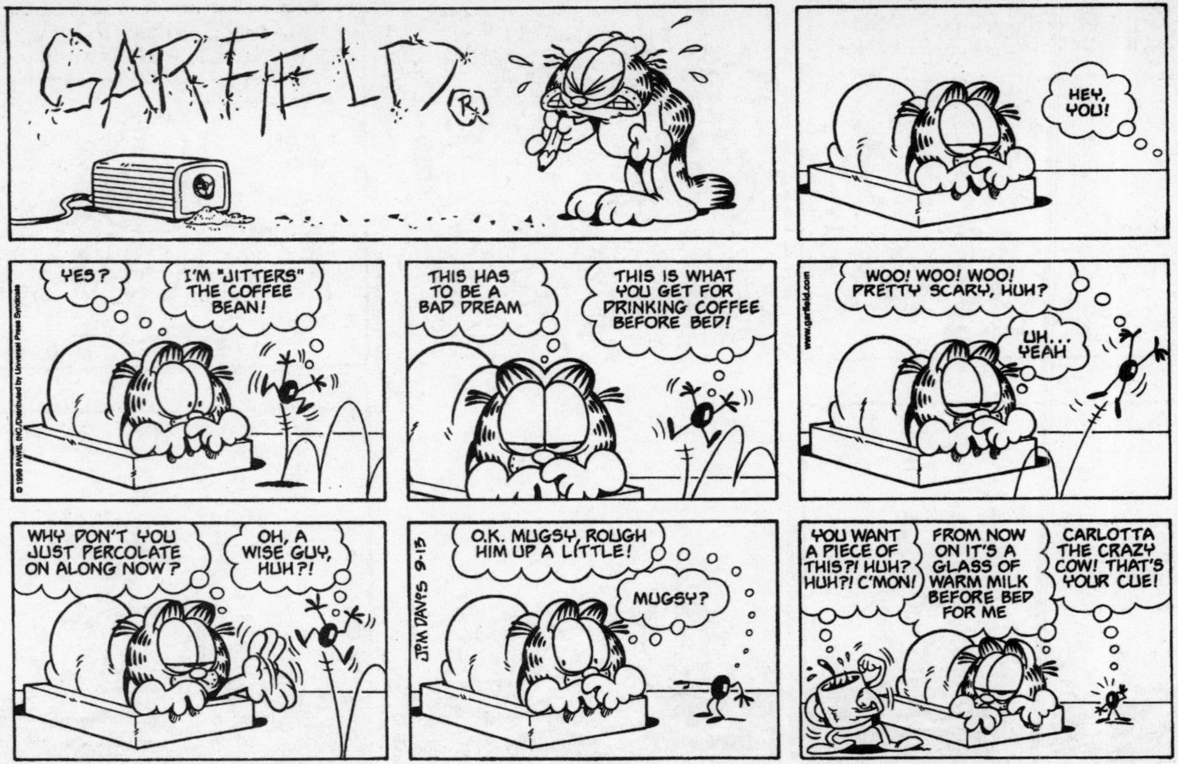
GARFIELD®
HEY, YOU!
YES?
I'M "JITTERS" THE COFFEE BEAN!
© 1998 PAWS, INC./Distributed by Universal Press Syndicate
THIS HAS TO BE A BAD DREAM
THIS IS WHAT YOU GET FOR DRINKING COFFEE BEFORE BED!
www.garfield.com
WOO! WOO! WOO! PRETTY SCARY, HUH?
UH... YEAH
WHY DON'T YOU JUST PERCOLATE ON ALONG NOW?
OH, A WISE GUY, HUH?!
JIM DAVIS 9-13
O.K. MUGSY, ROUGH HIM UP A LITTLE!
MUGSY?
YOU WANT A PIECE OF THIS?! HUH? HUH?! C'MON!
FROM NOW ON IT'S A GLASS OF WARM MILK BEFORE BED FOR ME
CARLOTTA THE CRAZY COW! THAT'S YOUR CUE!

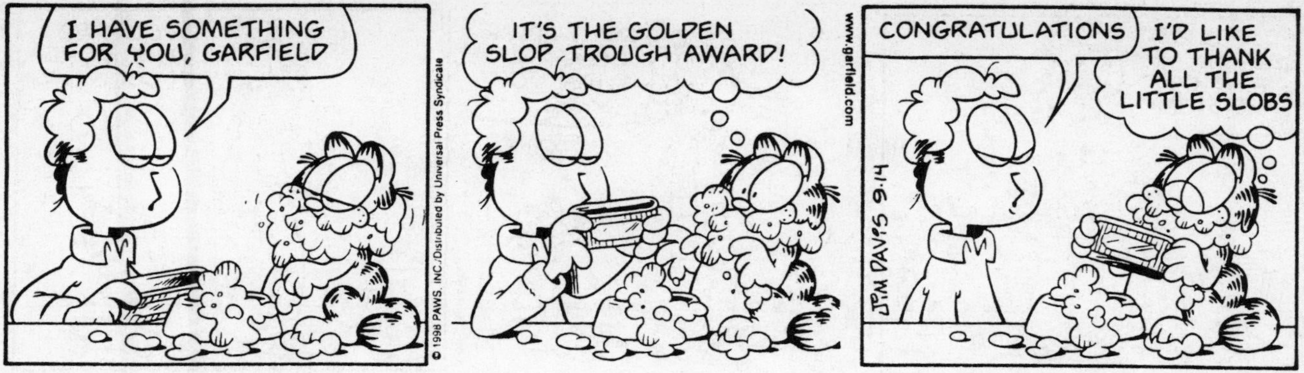
I HAVE SOMETHING FOR YOU, GARFIELD
© 1998 PAWS, INC./Distributed by Universal Press Syndicate
IT'S THE GOLDEN SLOP TROUGH AWARD!
www.garfield.com
JIM DAVIS 9-14
CONGRATULATIONS
I'D LIKE TO THANK ALL THE LITTLE SLOBS

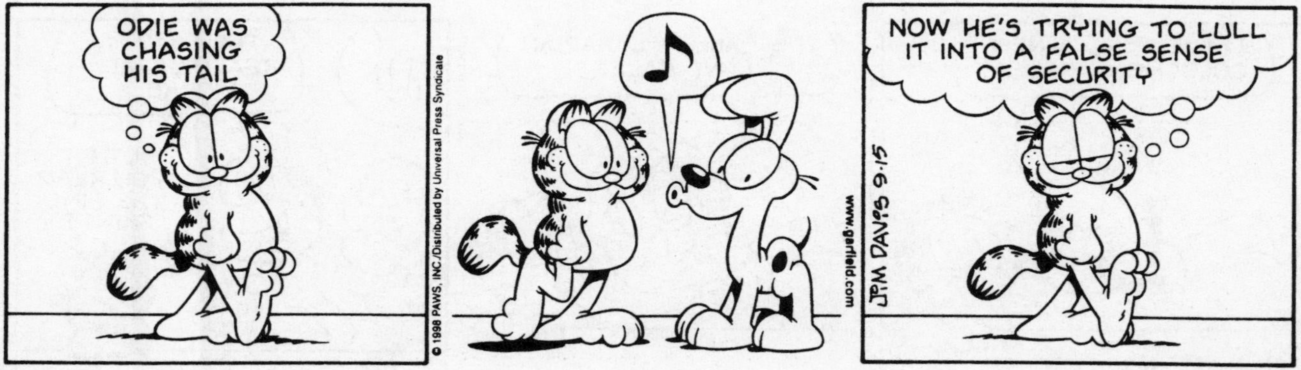
ODIE WAS CHASING HIS TAIL
© 1998 PAWS, INC./Distributed by Universal Press Syndicate
www.garfield.com
JIM DAVIS 9-15
NOW HE'S TRYING TO LULL IT INTO A FALSE SENSE OF SECURITY

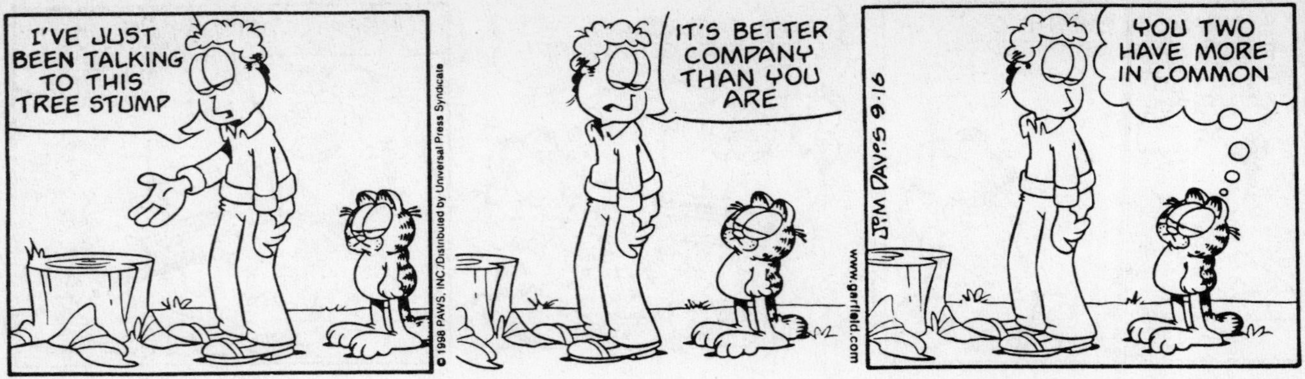
I'VE JUST BEEN TALKING TO THIS TREE STUMP
© 1998 PAWS, INC./Distributed by Universal Press Syndicate
IT'S BETTER COMPANY THAN YOU ARE
JIM DAVIS 9-16
www.garfield.com
YOU TWO HAVE MORE IN COMMON

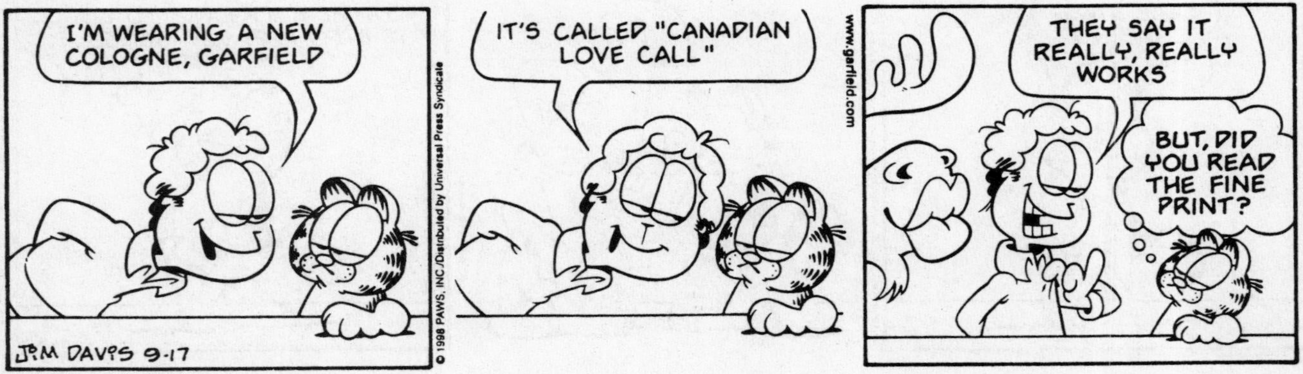
I'M WEARING A NEW COLOGNE, GARFIELD
JIM DAVIS 9-17
© 1998 PAWS, INC./Distributed by Universal Press Syndicate
IT'S CALLED "CANADIAN LOVE CALL"
www.garfield.com
THEY SAY IT REALLY, REALLY WORKS
BUT, DID YOU READ THE FINE PRINT?

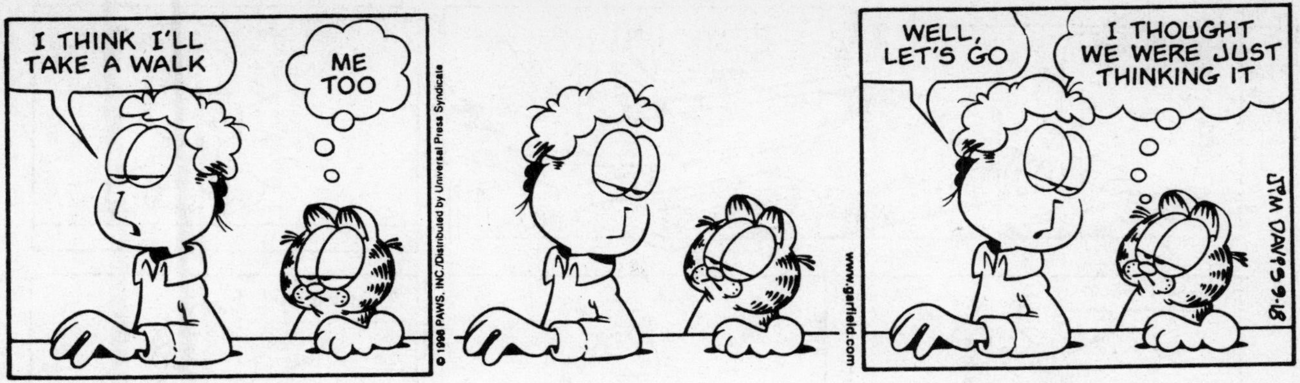
I THINK I'LL TAKE A WALK
ME TOO
WELL, LET'S GO
I THOUGHT WE WERE JUST THINKING IT
JIM DAVIS 9-18

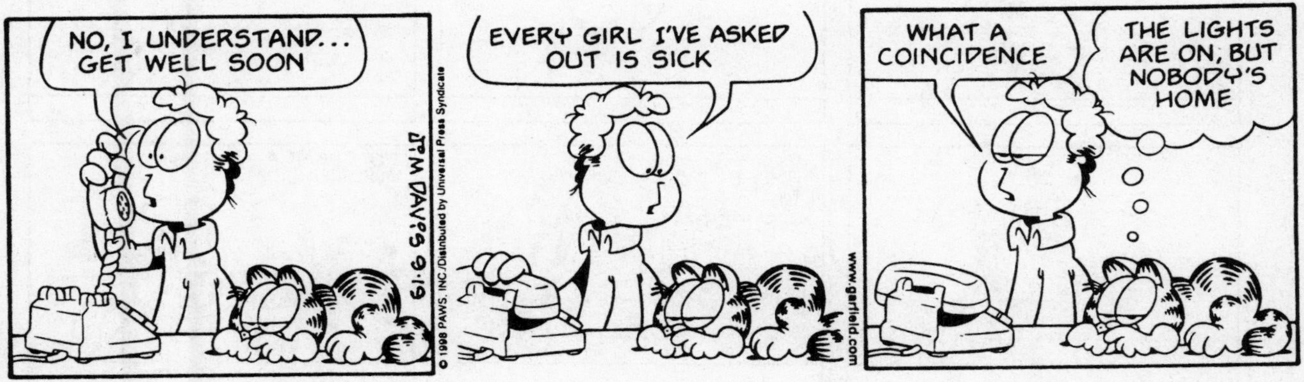
NO, I UNDERSTAND... GET WELL SOON
EVERY GIRL I'VE ASKED OUT IS SICK
WHAT A COINCIDENCE
THE LIGHTS ARE ON, BUT NOBODY'S HOME
JIM DAVIS 9-19

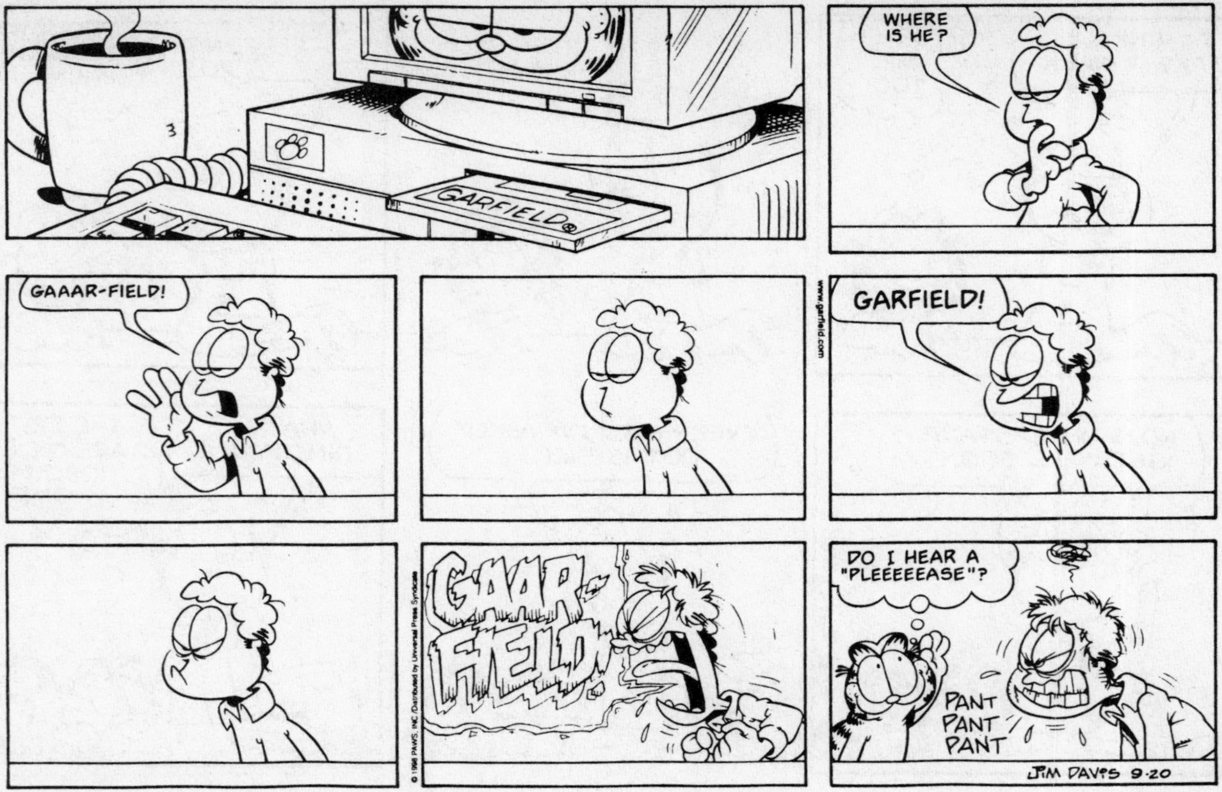
GARFIELD®
WHERE IS HE?
GAAAR-FIELD!
GARFIELD!
GAAR-FIELD!
DO I HEAR A "PLEEEEEASE"?
PANT PANT PANT
JIM DAVIS 9·20
www.garfield.com
© 1998 PAWS, INC./Distributed by Universal Press Syndicate

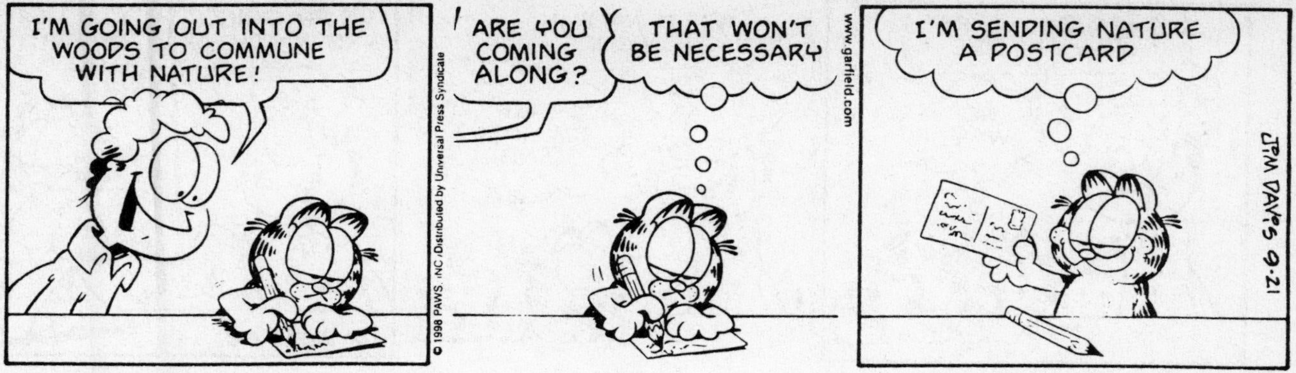
I'M GOING OUT INTO THE WOODS TO COMMUNE WITH NATURE!
ARE YOU COMING ALONG?
THAT WON'T BE NECESSARY
I'M SENDING NATURE A POSTCARD
© 1998 PAWS, INC./Distributed by Universal Press Syndicate
www.garfield.com
JIM DAVIS 9-21

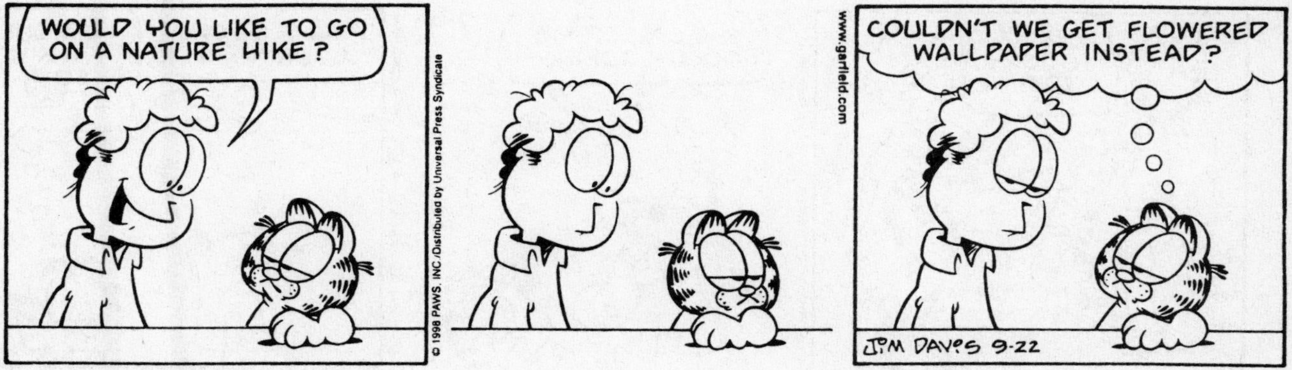
WOULD YOU LIKE TO GO ON A NATURE HIKE?
COULDN'T WE GET FLOWERED WALLPAPER INSTEAD?
© 1998 PAWS, INC./Distributed by Universal Press Syndicate
www.garfield.com
JIM DAVIS 9-22

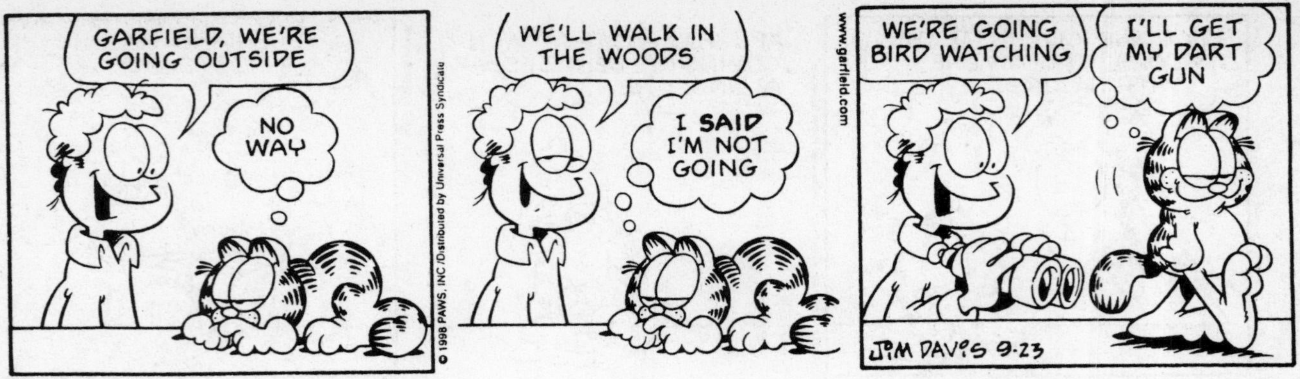
GARFIELD, WE'RE GOING OUTSIDE
NO WAY
WE'LL WALK IN THE WOODS
I SAID I'M NOT GOING
WE'RE GOING BIRD WATCHING
I'LL GET MY DART GUN
© 1998 PAWS, INC./Distributed by Universal Press Syndicate
www.garfield.com
JIM DAVIS 9-23

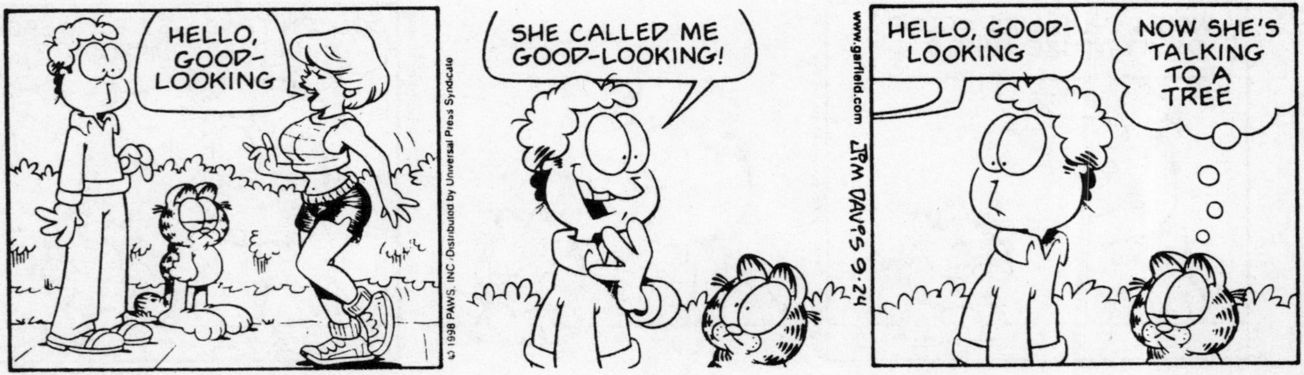
HELLO, GOOD-LOOKING
SHE CALLED ME GOOD-LOOKING!
HELLO, GOOD-LOOKING
NOW SHE'S TALKING TO A TREE
© 1998 PAWS, INC./Distributed by Universal Press Syndicate
www.garfield.com
JIM DAVIS 9-24

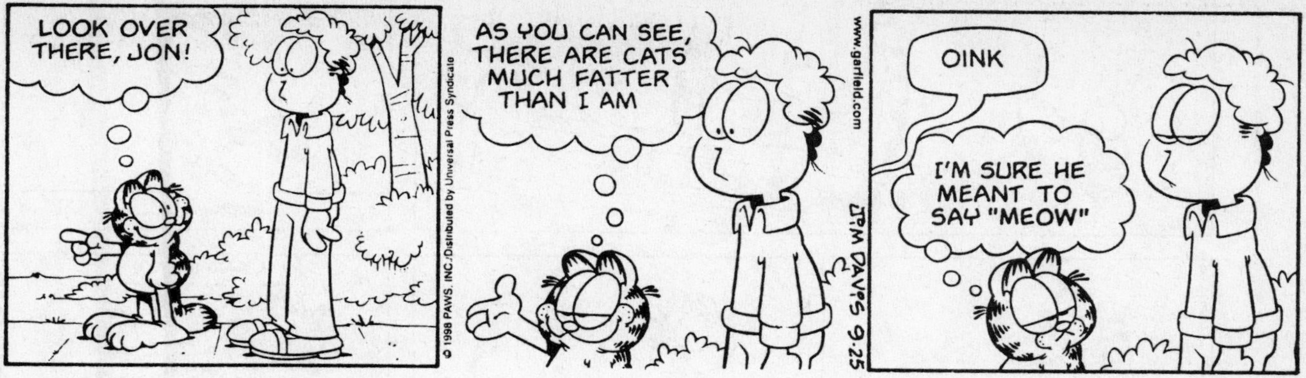
LOOK OVER THERE, JON!
AS YOU CAN SEE, THERE ARE CATS MUCH FATTER THAN I AM
OINK
I'M SURE HE MEANT TO SAY "MEOW"
© 1998 PAWS, INC./Distributed by Universal Press Syndicate
www.garfield.com
JIM DAVIS 9.25

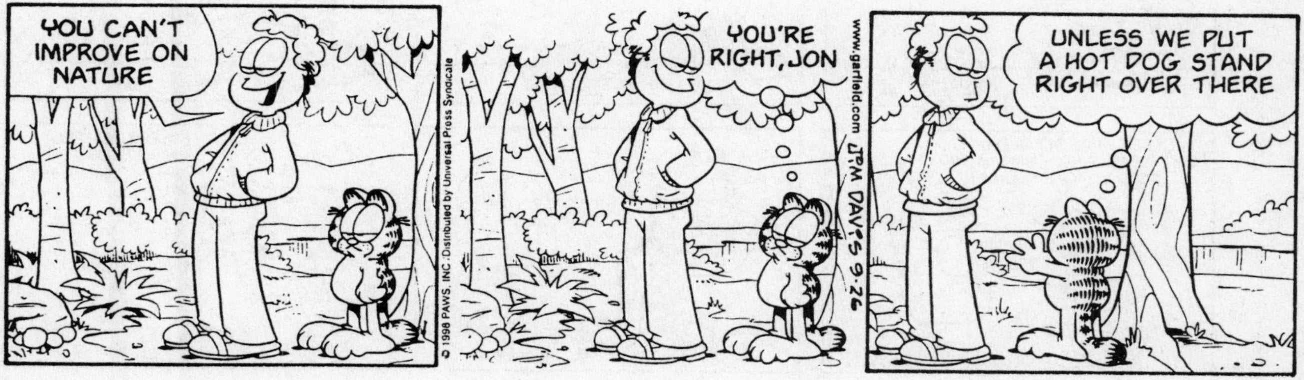
YOU CAN'T IMPROVE ON NATURE
YOU'RE RIGHT, JON
UNLESS WE PUT A HOT DOG STAND RIGHT OVER THERE
© 1998 PAWS, INC./Distributed by Universal Press Syndicate
www.garfield.com
JIM DAVIS 9.26

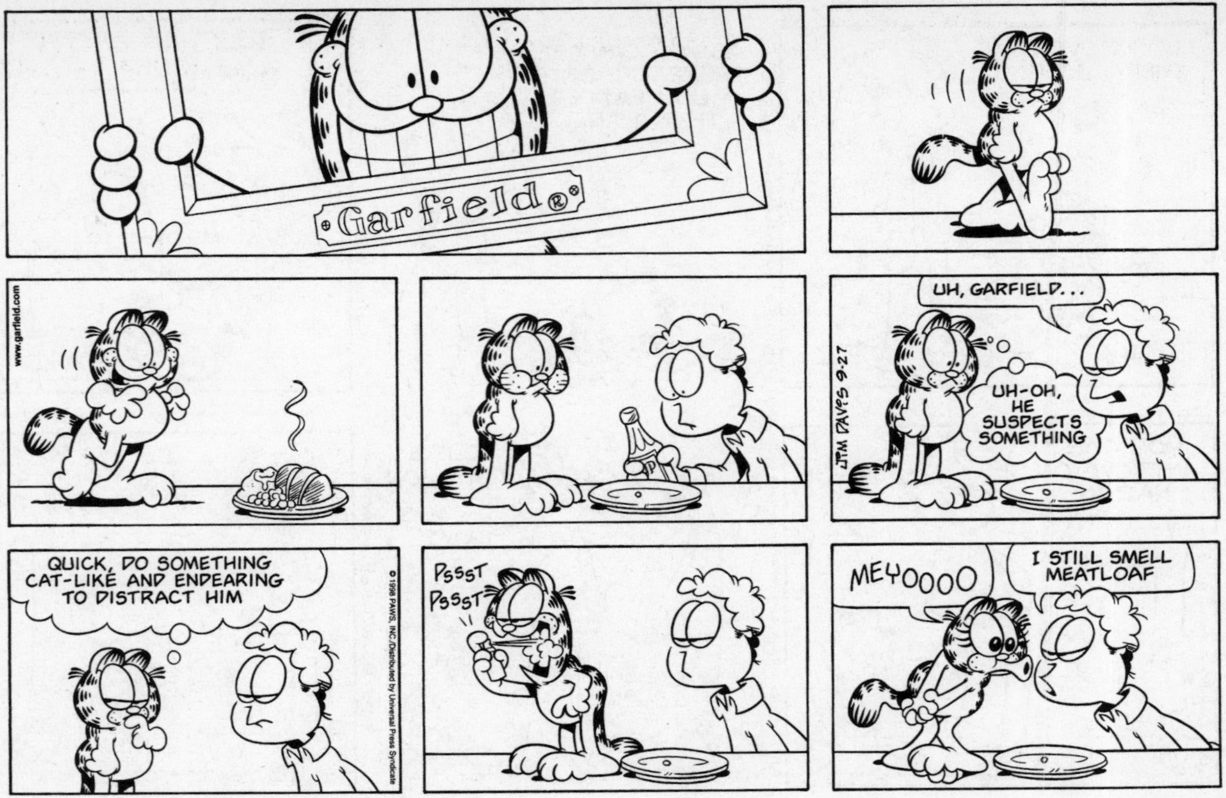
Garfield®
www.garfield.com
UH, GARFIELD...
UH-OH, HE SUSPECTS SOMETHING
JIM DAVIS 9-27
QUICK, DO SOMETHING CAT-LIKE AND ENDEARING TO DISTRACT HIM
© 1998 PAWS, INC./Distributed by Universal Press Syndicate
PSSST
PSSST
MEYOOOO
I STILL SMELL MEATLOAF

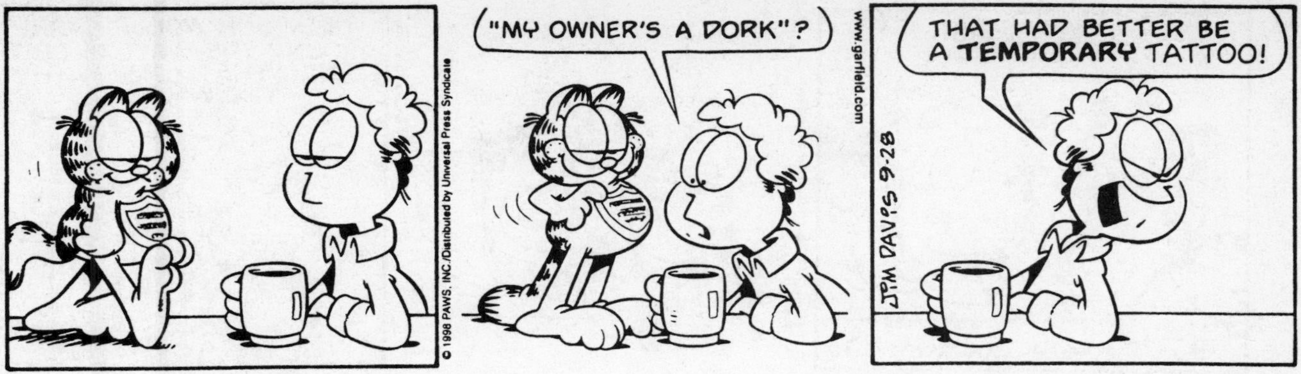
"MY OWNER'S A DORK"?
THAT HAD BETTER BE A **TEMPORARY** TATTOO!
JIM DAVIS 9·28
© 1998 PAWS, INC./Distributed by Universal Press Syndicate
www.garfield.com

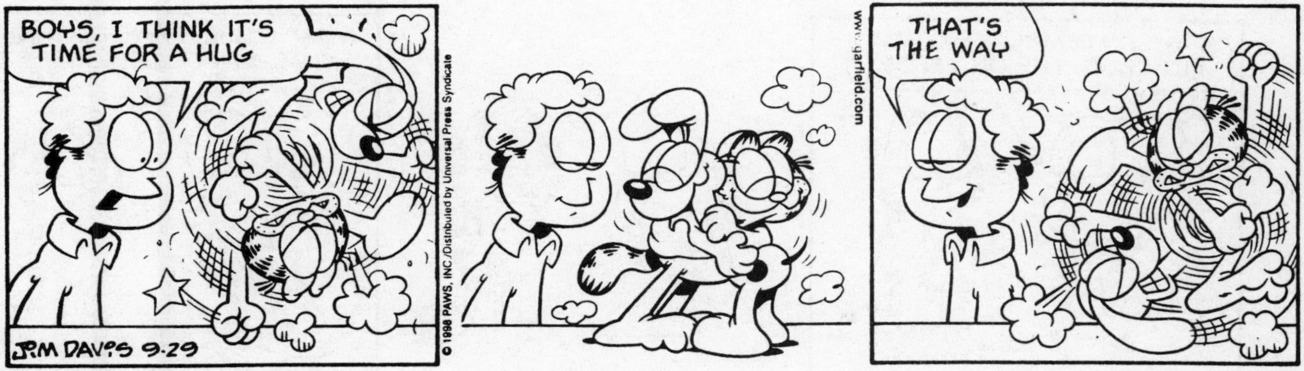
BOYS, I THINK IT'S TIME FOR A HUG
THAT'S THE WAY
JIM DAVIS 9·29
© 1998 PAWS, INC./Distributed by Universal Press Syndicate
www.garfield.com

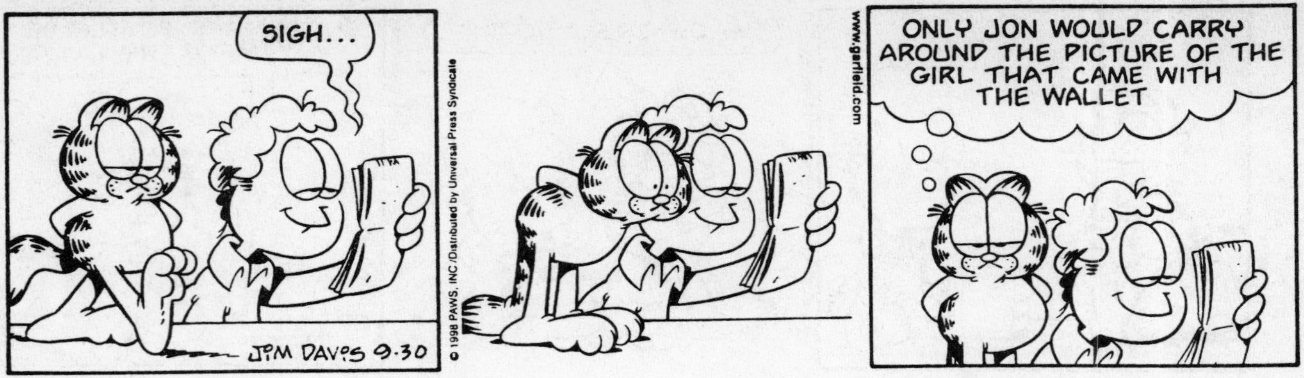
SIGH...
JIM DAVIS 9-30
© 1998 PAWS, INC./Distributed by Universal Press Syndicate
www.garfield.com
ONLY JON WOULD CARRY AROUND THE PICTURE OF THE GIRL THAT CAME WITH THE WALLET

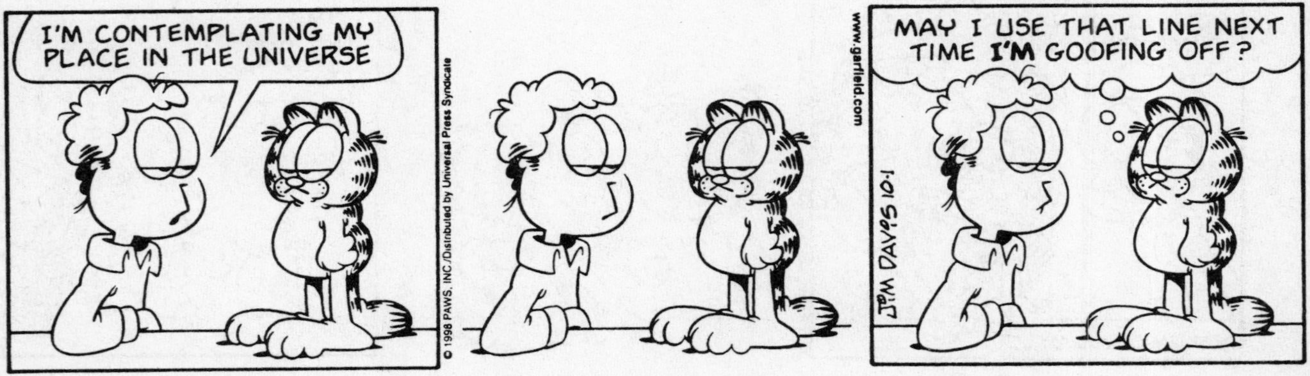
I'M CONTEMPLATING MY PLACE IN THE UNIVERSE
© 1998 PAWS, INC./Distributed by Universal Press Syndicate
www.garfield.com
JIM DAVIS 10-1
MAY I USE THAT LINE NEXT TIME I'M GOOFING OFF?

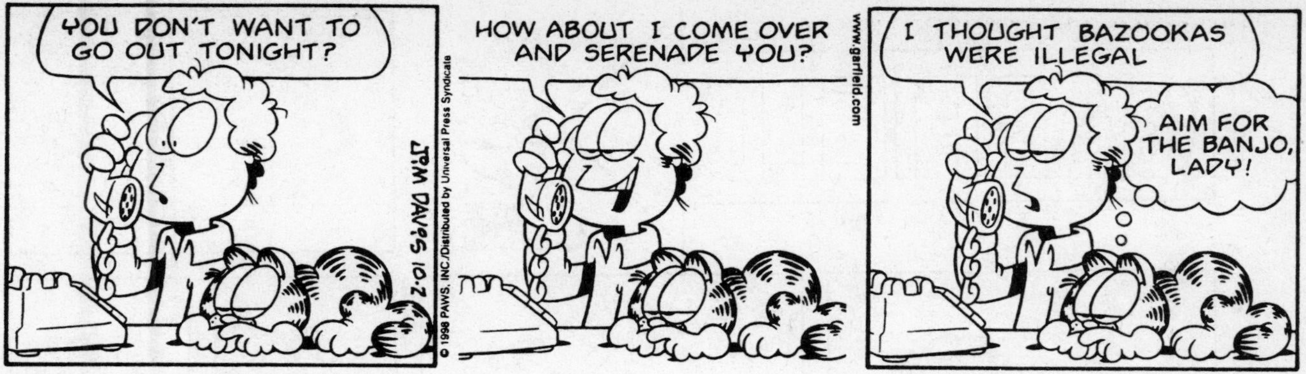
YOU DON'T WANT TO GO OUT TONIGHT?
JIM DAVIS 10·2
© 1998 PAWS, INC/Distributed by Universal Press Syndicate
HOW ABOUT I COME OVER AND SERENADE YOU?
www.garfield.com
I THOUGHT BAZOOKAS WERE ILLEGAL
AIM FOR THE BANJO, LADY!

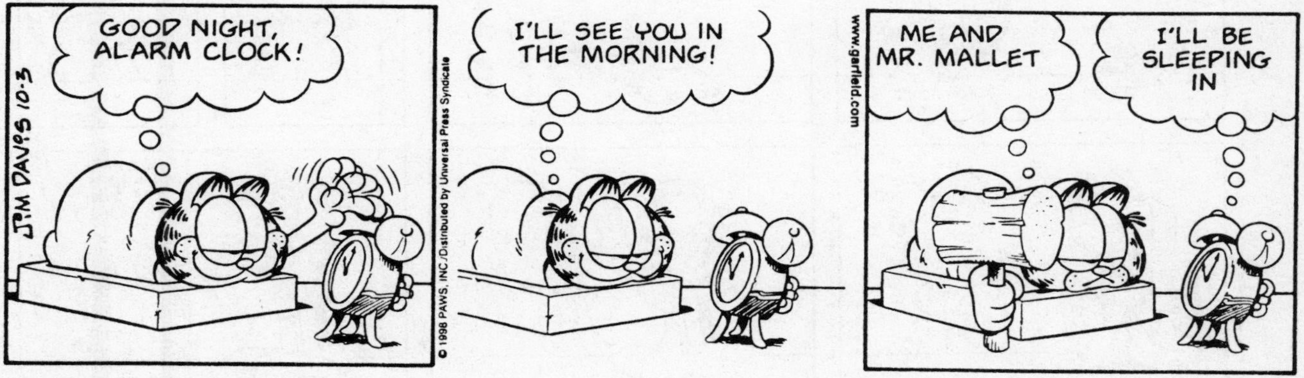
GOOD NIGHT, ALARM CLOCK!
JIM DAVIS 10·3
© 1998 PAWS, INC/Distributed by Universal Press Syndicate
I'LL SEE YOU IN THE MORNING!
www.garfield.com
ME AND MR. MALLET
I'LL BE SLEEPING IN

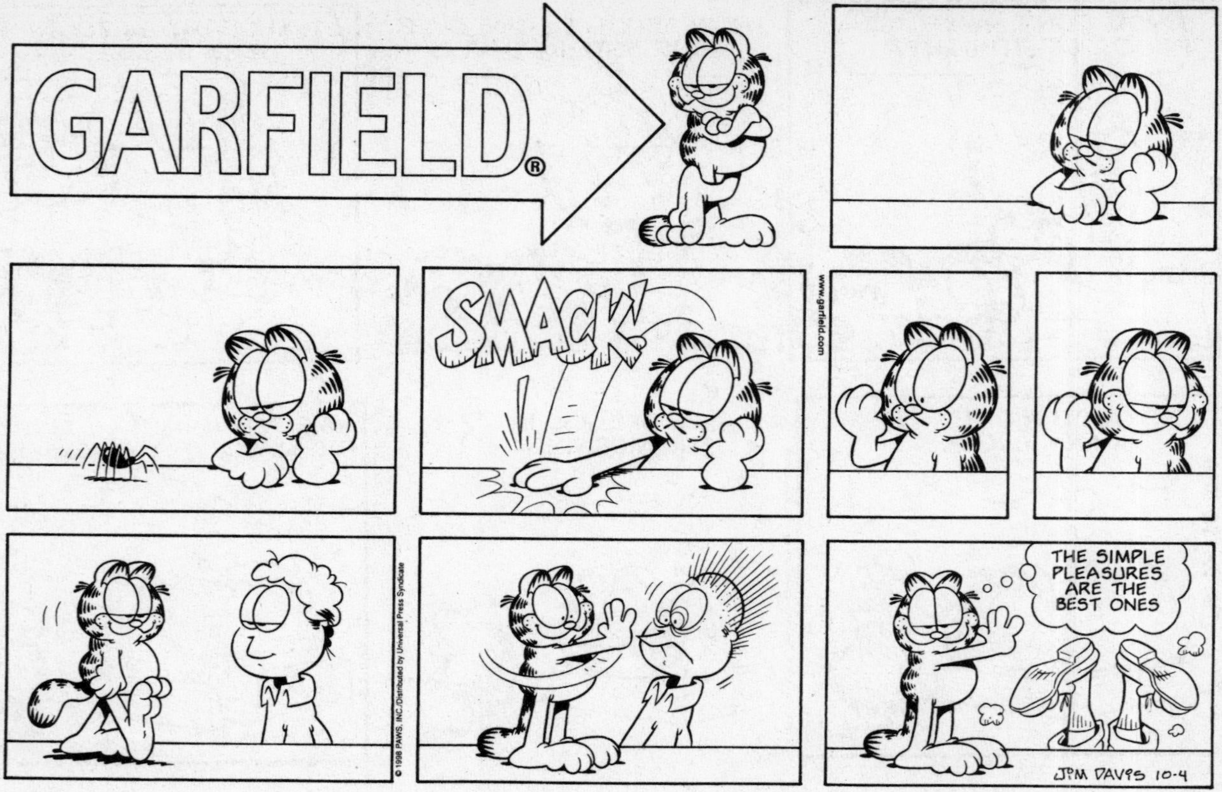
GARFIELD®
SMACK!
www.garfield.com
© 1998 PAWS, INC./Distributed by Universal Press Syndicate
THE SIMPLE PLEASURES ARE THE BEST ONES
JIM DAVIS 10-4

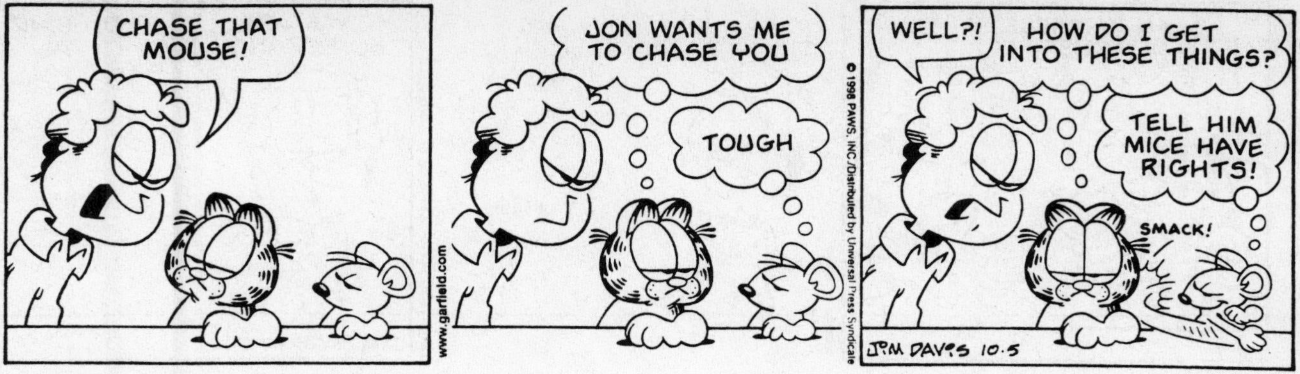
CHASE THAT MOUSE!
www.garfield.com
JON WANTS ME TO CHASE YOU
TOUGH
© 1998 PAWS, INC./Distributed by Universal Press Syndicate
WELL?!
HOW DO I GET INTO THESE THINGS?
TELL HIM MICE HAVE RIGHTS!
SMACK!
JIM DAVIS 10-5

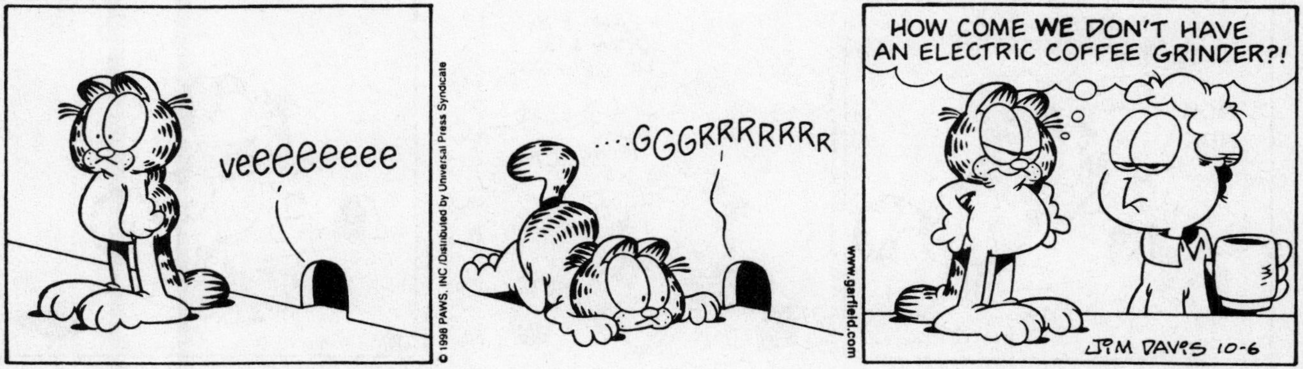
veeeeeeee
© 1998 PAWS, INC./Distributed by Universal Press Syndicate
....GGGRRRRRRR
www.garfield.com
HOW COME WE DON'T HAVE AN ELECTRIC COFFEE GRINDER?!
JIM DAVIS 10-6

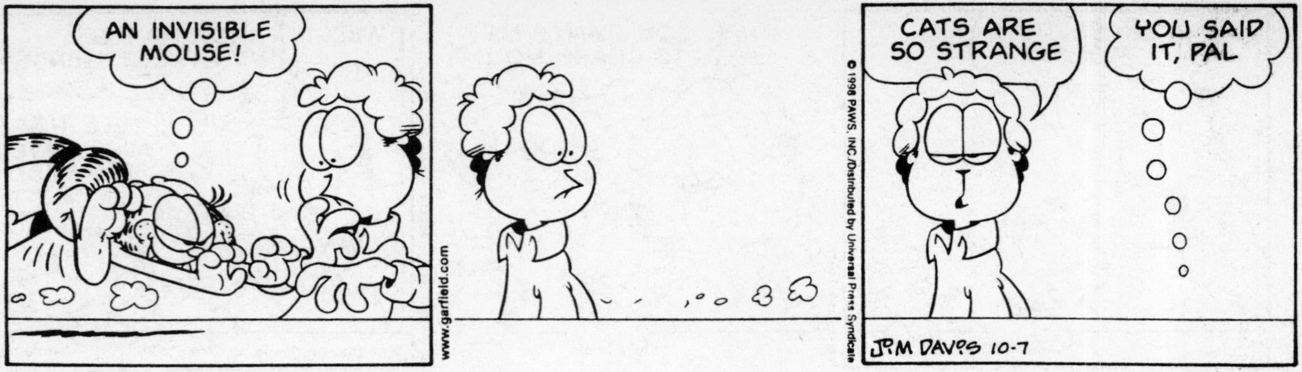
AN INVISIBLE MOUSE!
www.garfield.com
CATS ARE SO STRANGE
YOU SAID IT, PAL
© 1998 PAWS, INC./Distributed by Universal Press Syndicate
JIM DAVIS 10-7

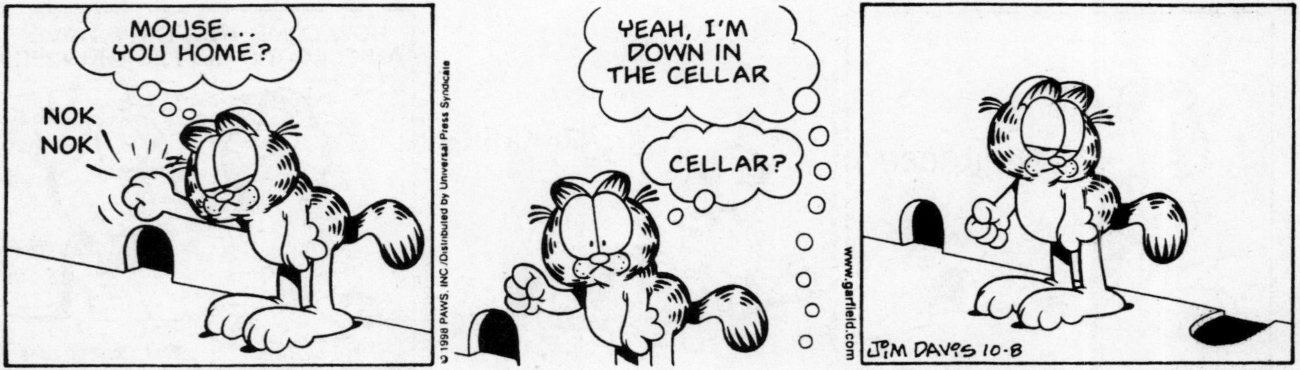
MOUSE... YOU HOME?
NOK NOK
© 1998 PAWS, INC./Distributed by Universal Press Syndicate
YEAH, I'M DOWN IN THE CELLAR
CELLAR?
www.garfield.com
JIM DAVIS 10-8

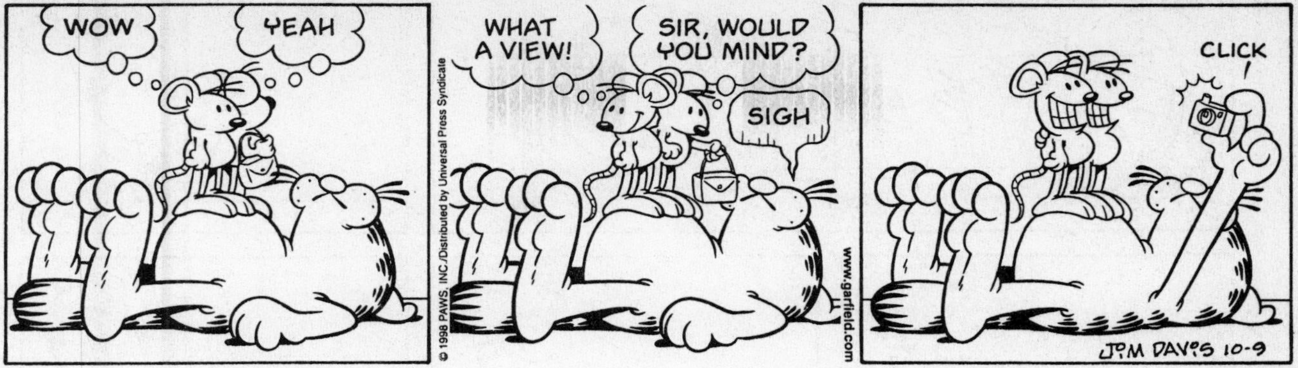
WOW
YEAH
WHAT A VIEW!
SIR, WOULD YOU MIND?
SIGH
CLICK
JIM DAVIS 10-9
© 1998 PAWS, INC./Distributed by Universal Press Syndicate
www.garfield.com

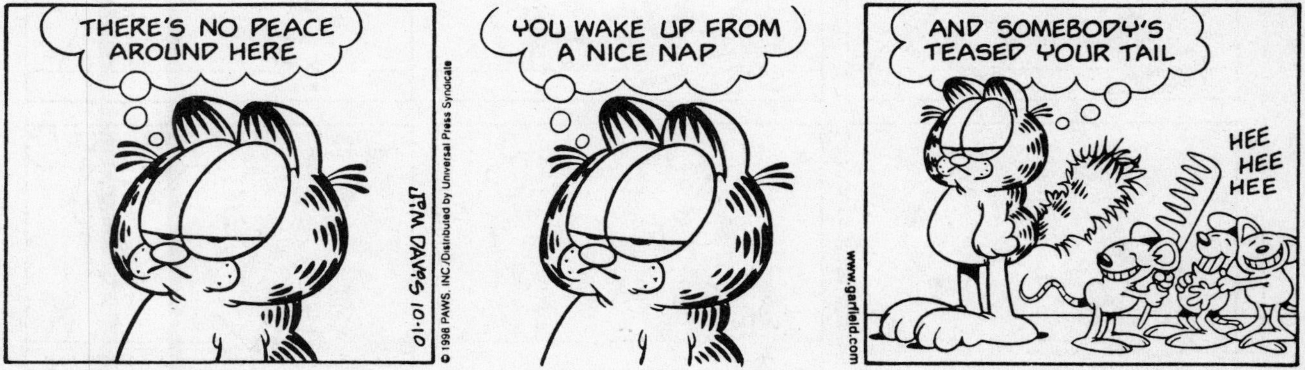
THERE'S NO PEACE AROUND HERE
JIM DAVIS 10-10
© 1998 PAWS, INC./Distributed by Universal Press Syndicate
YOU WAKE UP FROM A NICE NAP
www.garfield.com
AND SOMEBODY'S TEASED YOUR TAIL
HEE HEE HEE

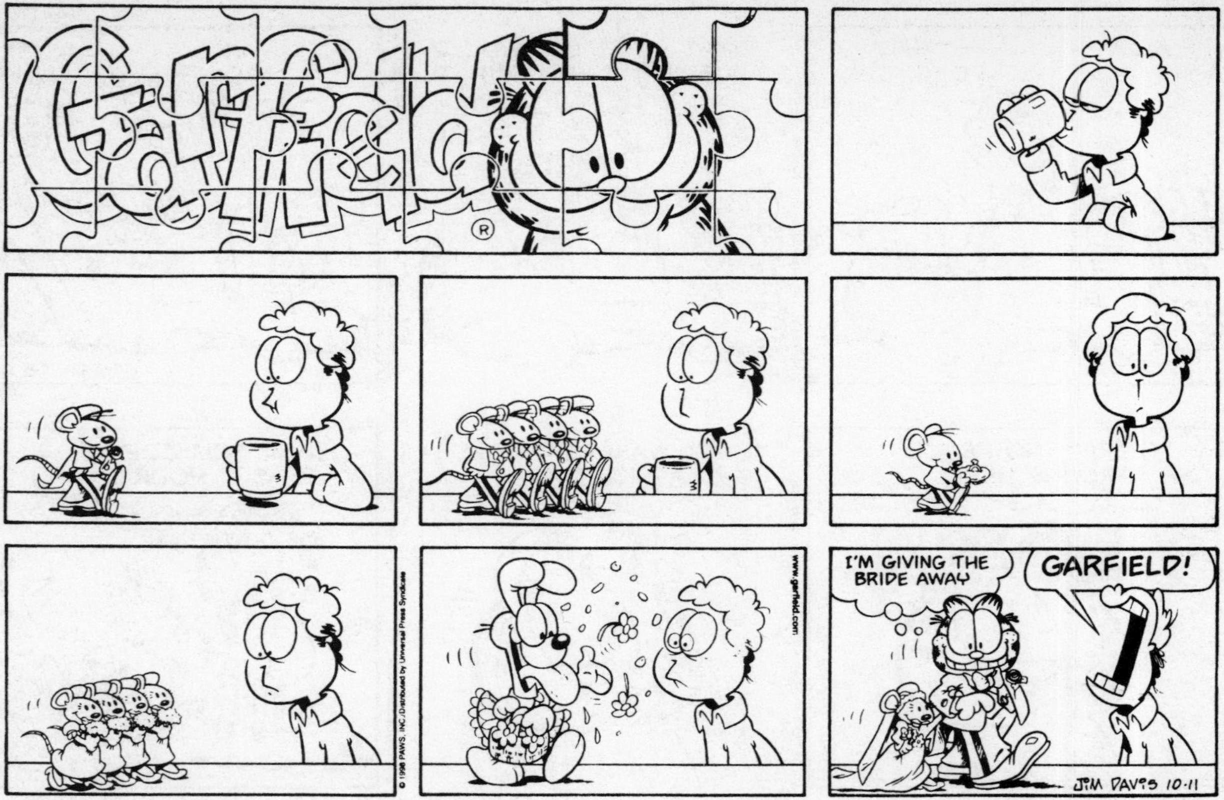
Garfield®
© 1998 PAWS, INC./Distributed by Universal Press Syndicate
www.garfield.com
I'M GIVING THE BRIDE AWAY
GARFIELD!
JIM DAVIS 10-11

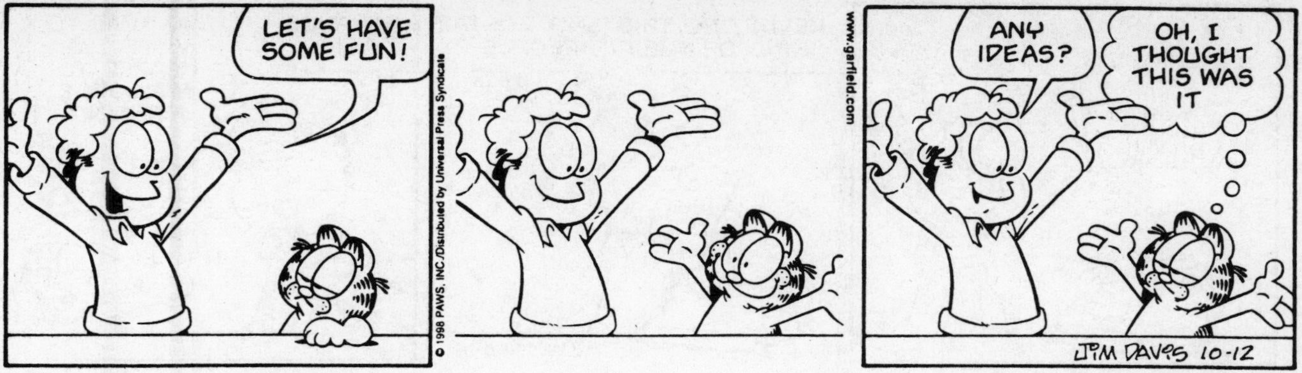
LET'S HAVE SOME FUN!
© 1998 PAWS, INC./Distributed by Universal Press Syndicate
www.garfield.com
ANY IDEAS?
OH, I THOUGHT THIS WAS IT
JIM DAVIS 10-12

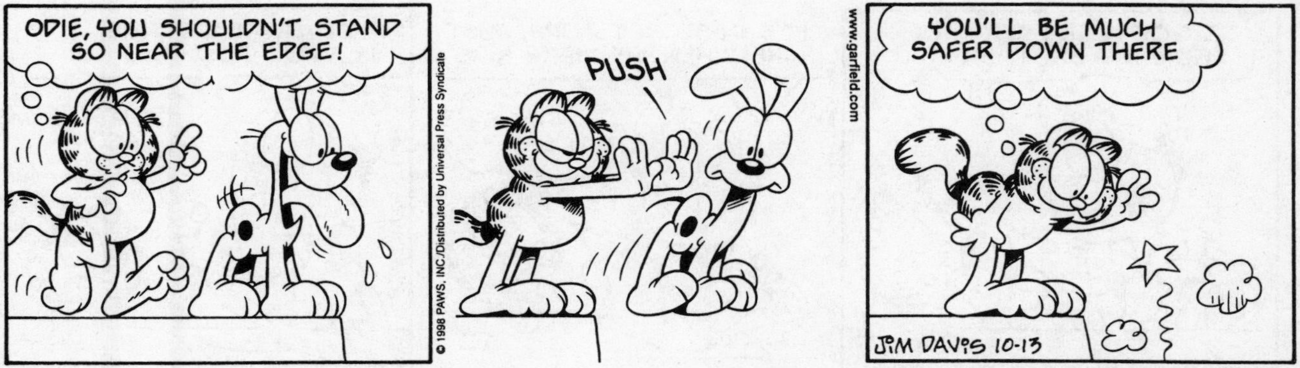
ODIE, YOU SHOULDN'T STAND SO NEAR THE EDGE!
© 1998 PAWS, INC./Distributed by Universal Press Syndicate
PUSH
www.garfield.com
YOU'LL BE MUCH SAFER DOWN THERE
JIM DAVIS 10-13

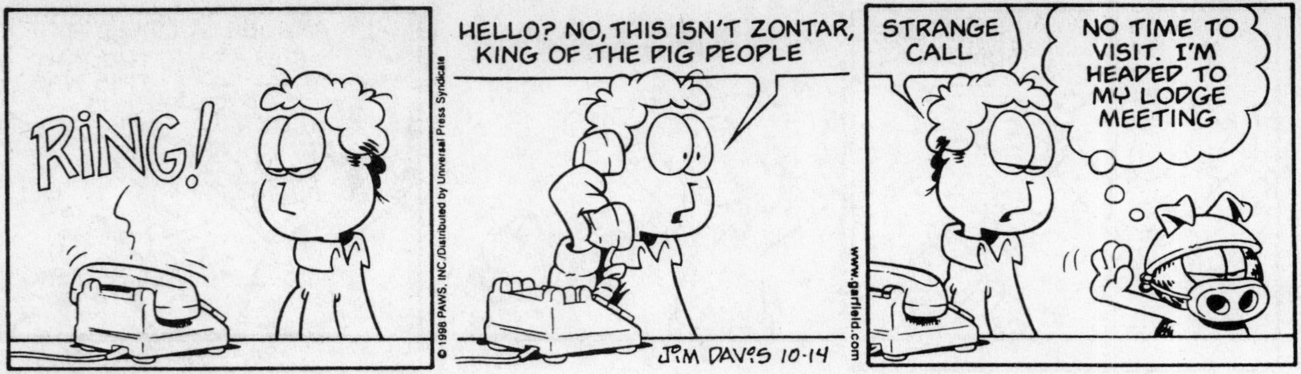
RING!
HELLO? NO, THIS ISN'T ZONTAR, KING OF THE PIG PEOPLE
STRANGE CALL
NO TIME TO VISIT. I'M HEADED TO MY LODGE MEETING
JIM DAVIS 10-14
© 1998 PAWS, INC./Distributed by Universal Press Syndicate
www.garfield.com

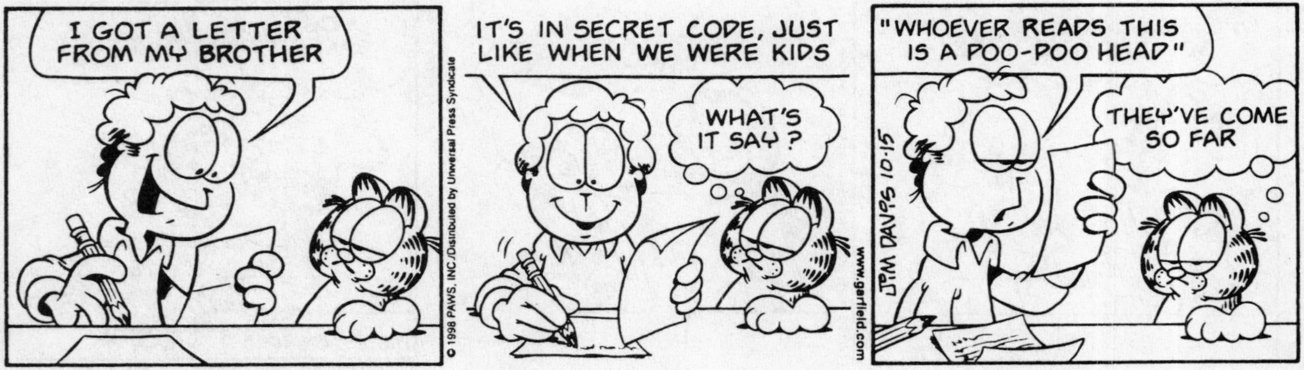
I GOT A LETTER FROM MY BROTHER
IT'S IN SECRET CODE, JUST LIKE WHEN WE WERE KIDS
WHAT'S IT SAY?
"WHOEVER READS THIS IS A POO-POO HEAD"
THEY'VE COME SO FAR
JIM DAVIS 10-15
© 1998 PAWS, INC./Distributed by Universal Press Syndicate
www.garfield.com

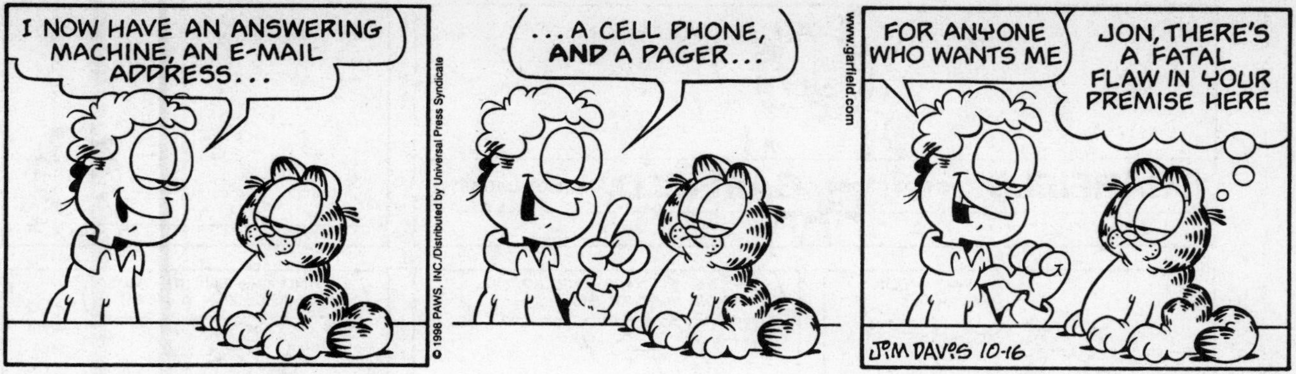
I NOW HAVE AN ANSWERING MACHINE, AN E-MAIL ADDRESS...
...A CELL PHONE, AND A PAGER...
FOR ANYONE WHO WANTS ME
JON, THERE'S A FATAL FLAW IN YOUR PREMISE HERE
JIM DAVIS 10-16
© 1998 PAWS, INC./Distributed by Universal Press Syndicate
www.garfield.com

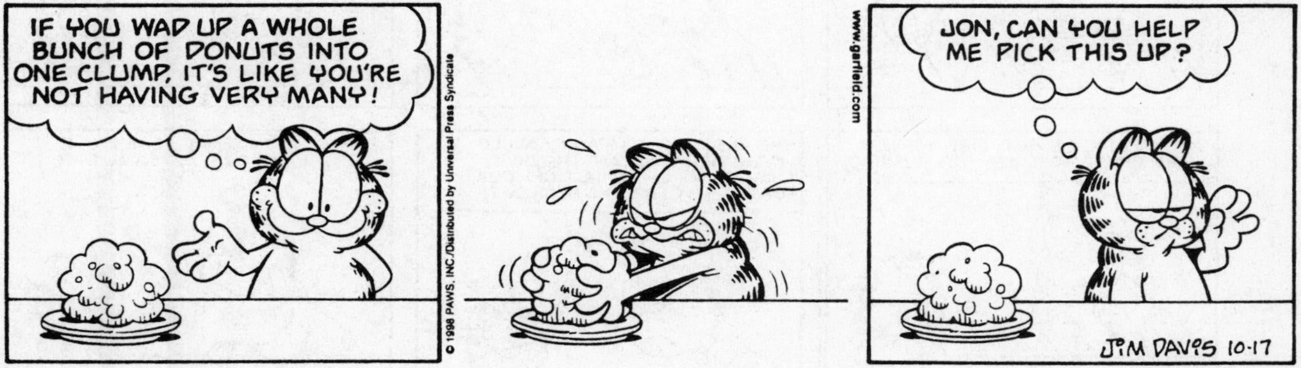
IF YOU WAD UP A WHOLE BUNCH OF DONUTS INTO ONE CLUMP, IT'S LIKE YOU'RE NOT HAVING VERY MANY!
JON, CAN YOU HELP ME PICK THIS UP?
JIM DAVIS 10-17
© 1998 PAWS, INC./Distributed by Universal Press Syndicate
www.garfield.com

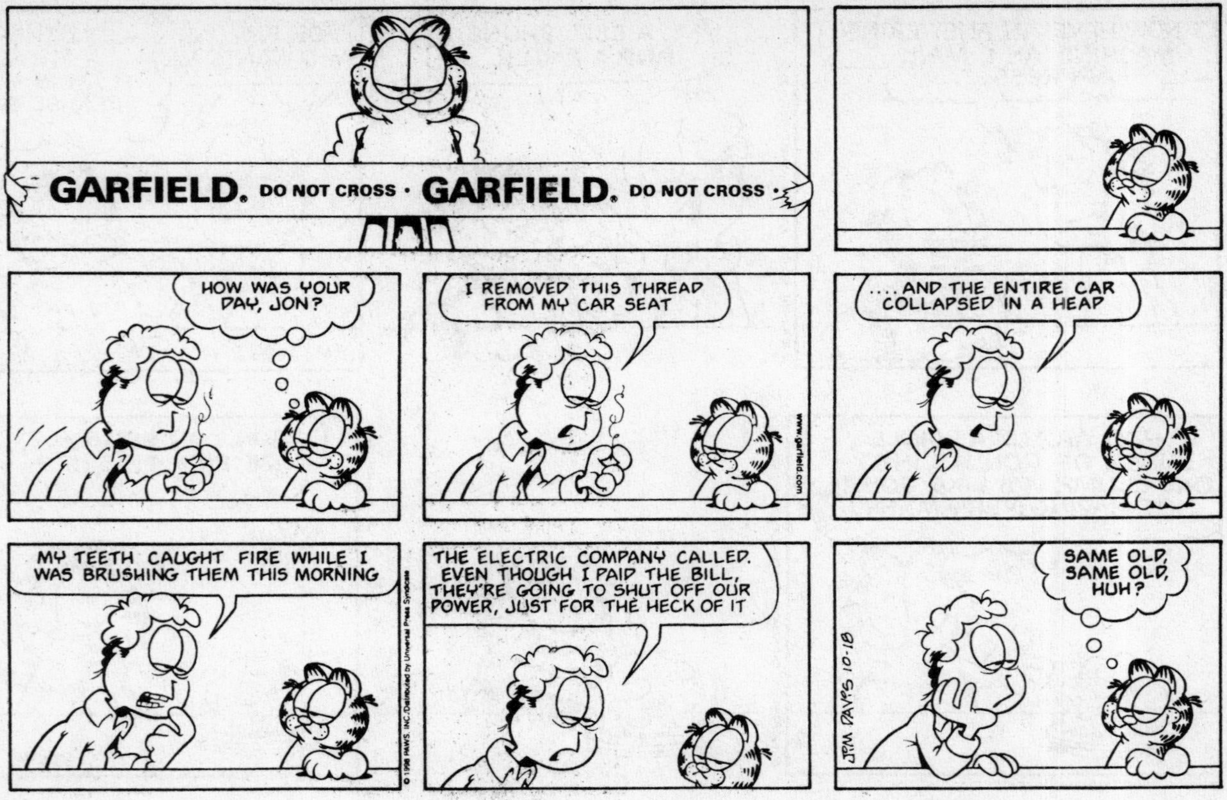
GARFIELD® DO NOT CROSS • GARFIELD® DO NOT CROSS •
HOW WAS YOUR DAY, JON?
I REMOVED THIS THREAD FROM MY CAR SEAT
....AND THE ENTIRE CAR COLLAPSED IN A HEAP
MY TEETH CAUGHT FIRE WHILE I WAS BRUSHING THEM THIS MORNING
THE ELECTRIC COMPANY CALLED. EVEN THOUGH I PAID THE BILL, THEY'RE GOING TO SHUT OFF OUR POWER, JUST FOR THE HECK OF IT
SAME OLD, SAME OLD, HUH?
www.garfield.com
JPM DAVPS 10-18

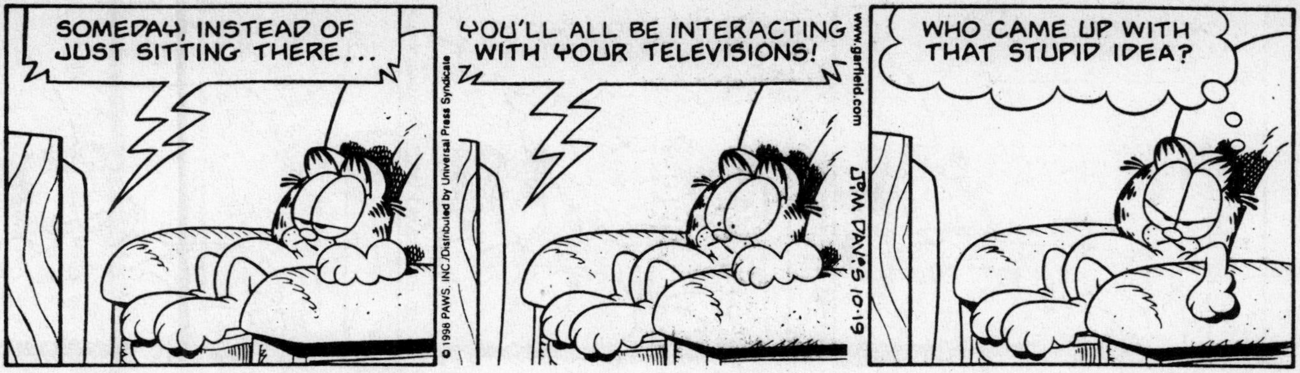
SOMEDAY, INSTEAD OF JUST SITTING THERE...
YOU'LL ALL BE INTERACTING WITH YOUR TELEVISIONS!
WHO CAME UP WITH THAT STUPID IDEA?
© 1998 PAWS, INC./Distributed by Universal Press Syndicate
www.garfield.com
JIM DAVIS 10-19

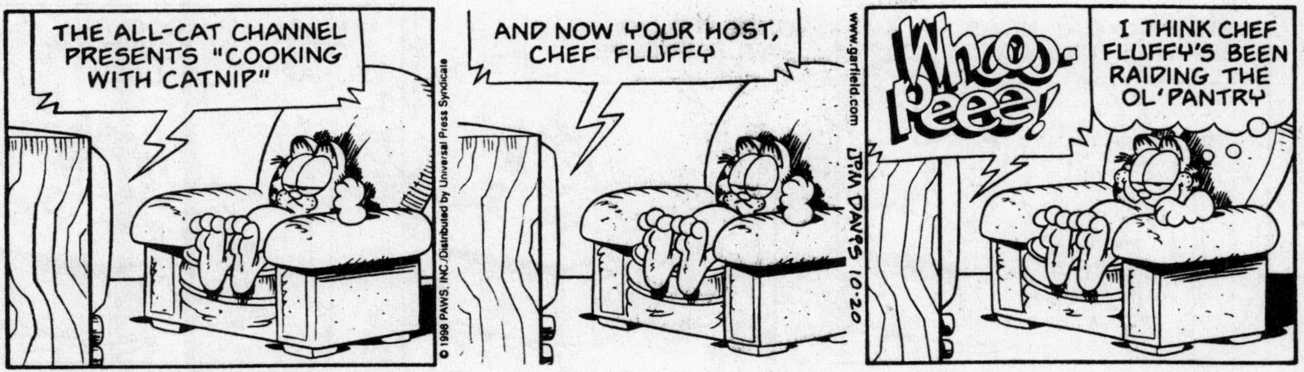
THE ALL-CAT CHANNEL PRESENTS "COOKING WITH CATNIP"
AND NOW YOUR HOST, CHEF FLUFFY
Whoo-peee!
I THINK CHEF FLUFFY'S BEEN RAIDING THE OL' PANTRY
© 1998 PAWS, INC./Distributed by Universal Press Syndicate
www.garfield.com
JIM DAVIS 10-20

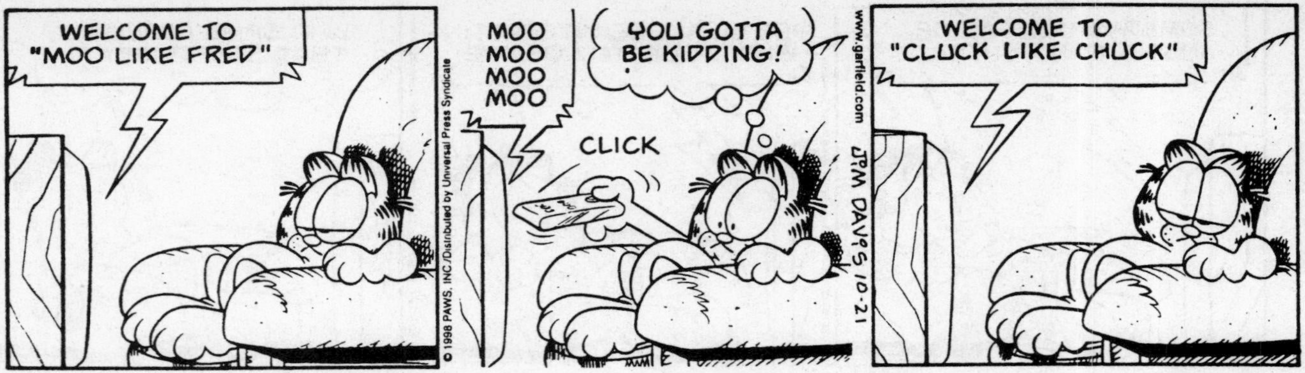
WELCOME TO "MOO LIKE FRED"
MOO MOO MOO MOO
YOU GOTTA BE KIDDING!
CLICK
WELCOME TO "CLUCK LIKE CHUCK"
© 1998 PAWS, INC./Distributed by Universal Press Syndicate
www.garfield.com
JIM DAVIS 10-21

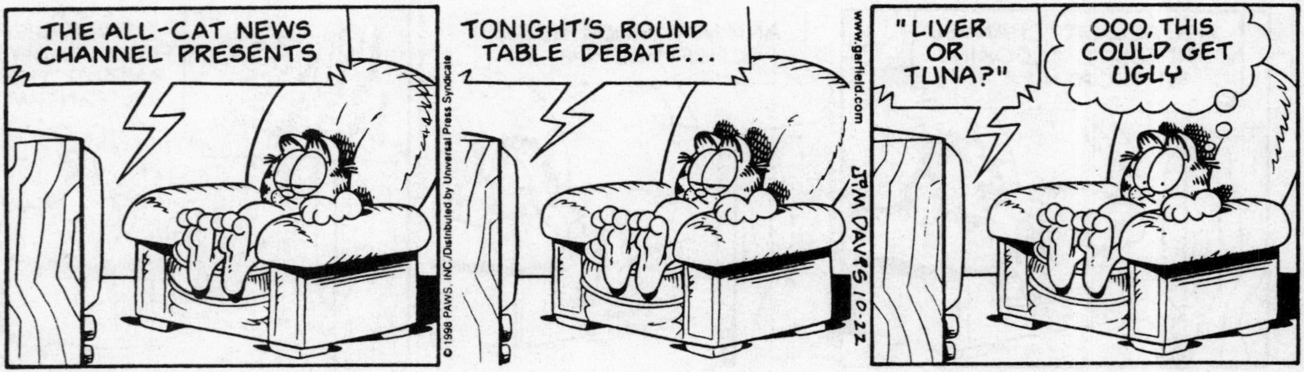
THE ALL-CAT NEWS CHANNEL PRESENTS
TONIGHT'S ROUND TABLE DEBATE...
"LIVER OR TUNA?"
OOO, THIS COULD GET UGLY
© 1998 PAWS, INC./Distributed by Universal Press Syndicate
www.garfield.com
JIM DAVIS 10-22

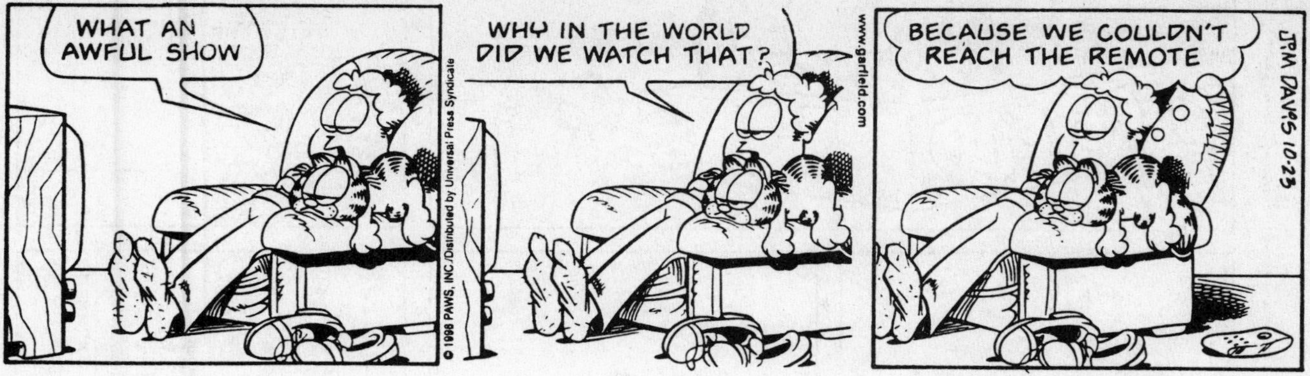
WHAT AN AWFUL SHOW
WHY IN THE WORLD DID WE WATCH THAT?
BECAUSE WE COULDN'T REACH THE REMOTE
© 1998 PAWS, INC/Distributed by Universal Press Syndicate
www.garfield.com
JIM DAVIS 10-23

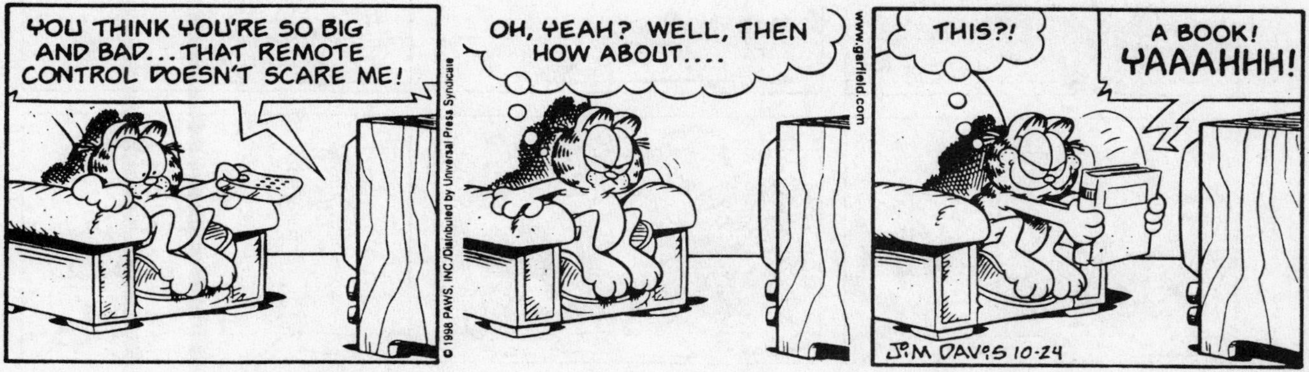
YOU THINK YOU'RE SO BIG AND BAD... THAT REMOTE CONTROL DOESN'T SCARE ME!
OH, YEAH? WELL, THEN HOW ABOUT....
THIS?!
A BOOK! YAAAHHH!
© 1998 PAWS, INC/Distributed by Universal Press Syndicate
www.garfield.com
JIM DAVIS 10-24

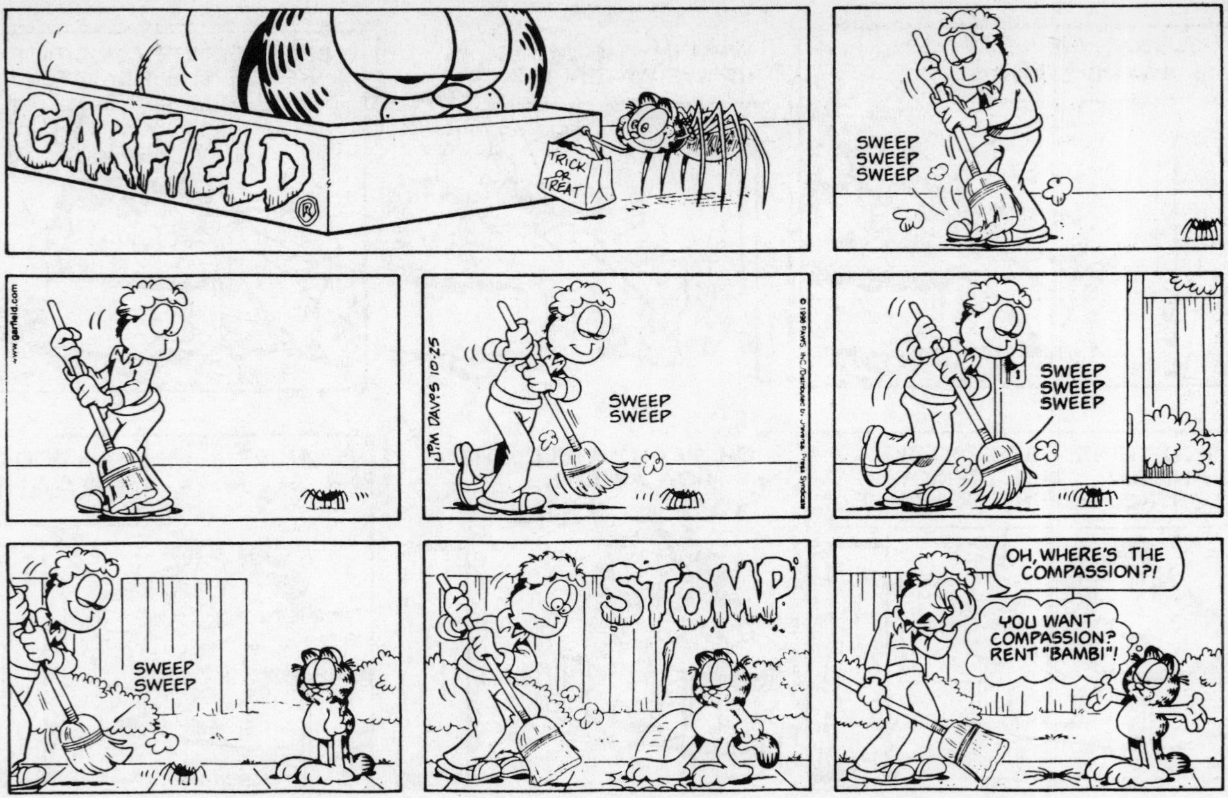
GARFIELD
TRICK OR TREAT
SWEEP SWEEP SWEEP
www.garfield.com
SWEEP SWEEP
SWEEP SWEEP SWEEP
SWEEP SWEEP
STOMP
OH, WHERE'S THE COMPASSION?!
YOU WANT COMPASSION? RENT "BAMBI"!

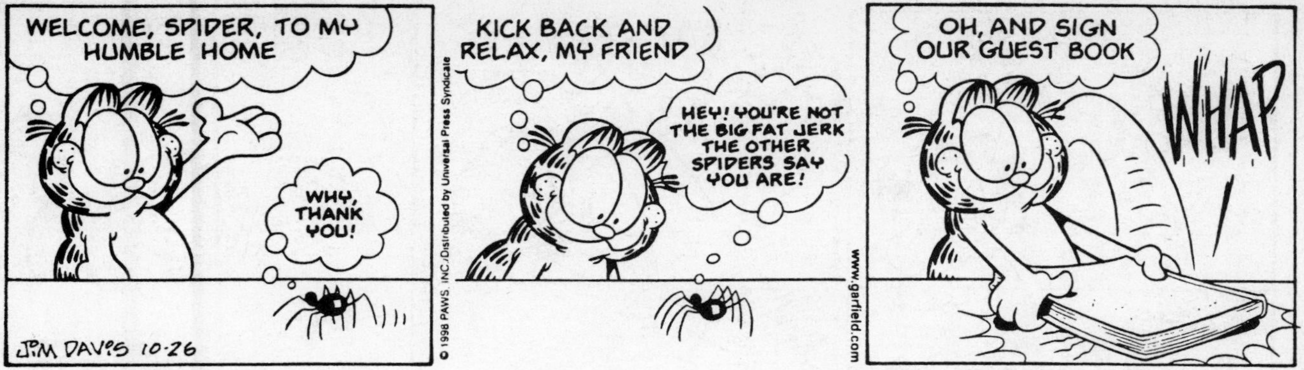
WELCOME, SPIDER, TO MY HUMBLE HOME
WHY, THANK YOU!
JIM DAVIS 10-26
© 1998 PAWS, INC./Distributed by Universal Press Syndicate
KICK BACK AND RELAX, MY FRIEND
HEY! YOU'RE NOT THE BIG FAT JERK THE OTHER SPIDERS SAY YOU ARE!
www.garfield.com
OH, AND SIGN OUR GUEST BOOK
WHAP

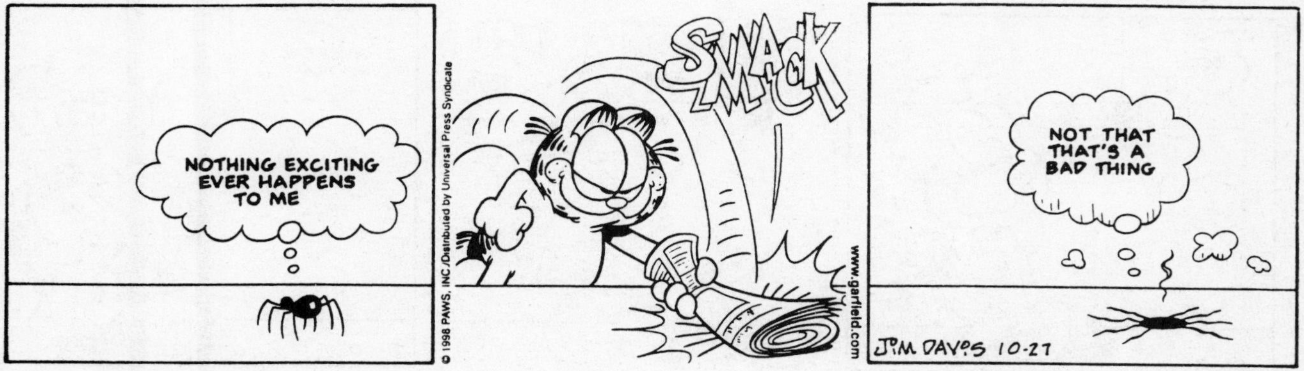
NOTHING EXCITING EVER HAPPENS TO ME
© 1998 PAWS, INC./Distributed by Universal Press Syndicate
SMACK
www.garfield.com
NOT THAT THAT'S A BAD THING
JIM DAVIS 10-27

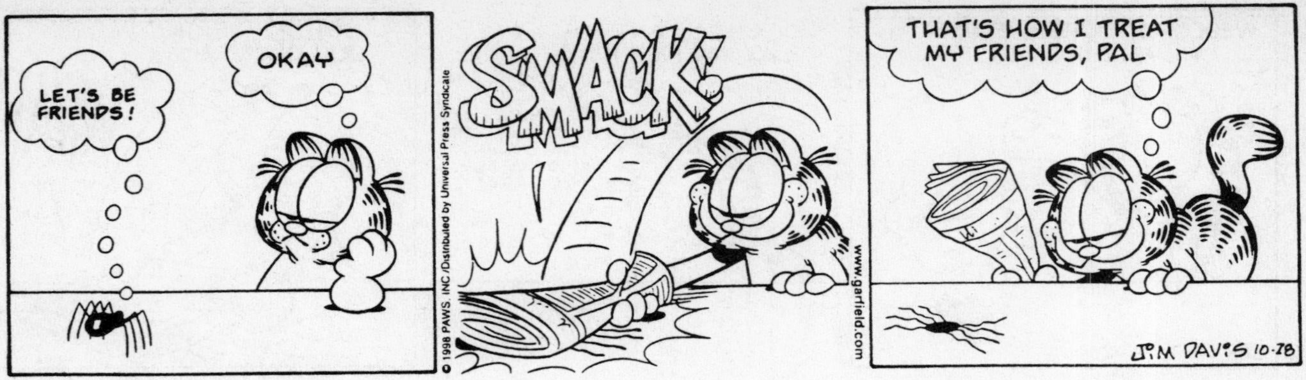
LET'S BE FRIENDS!
OKAY
© 1998 PAWS, INC./Distributed by Universal Press Syndicate
SWACK!
www.garfield.com
THAT'S HOW I TREAT MY FRIENDS, PAL
JIM DAVIS 10-28

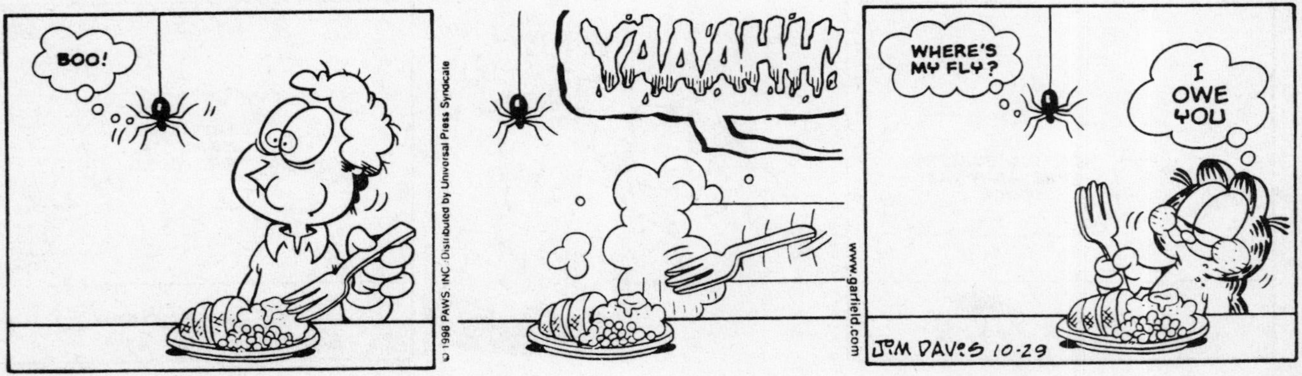
BOO!
© 1998 PAWS, INC./Distributed by Universal Press Syndicate
YAAAHH!
www.garfield.com
WHERE'S MY FLY?
I OWE YOU
JIM DAVIS 10-29

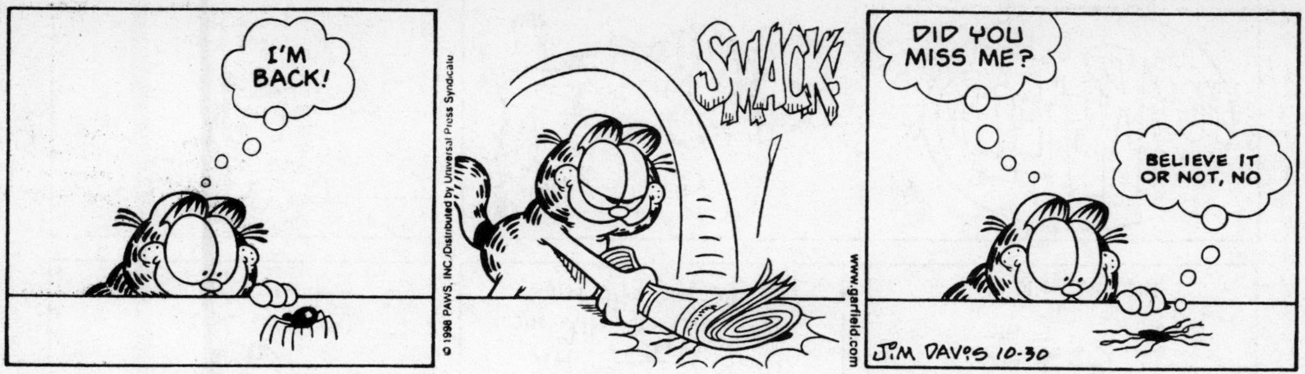
I'M BACK!
© 1998 PAWS, INC./Distributed by Universal Press Syndicate
SMACK!
www.garfield.com
DID YOU MISS ME?
BELIEVE IT OR NOT, NO
JIM DAVIS 10-30

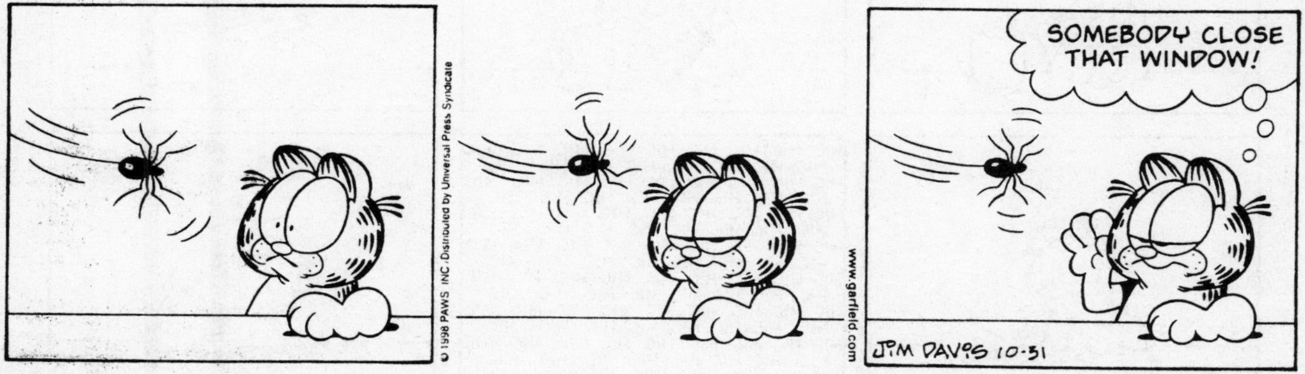
© 1998 PAWS, INC./Distributed by Universal Press Syndicate
www.garfield.com
SOMEBODY CLOSE THAT WINDOW!
JIM DAVIS 10-31

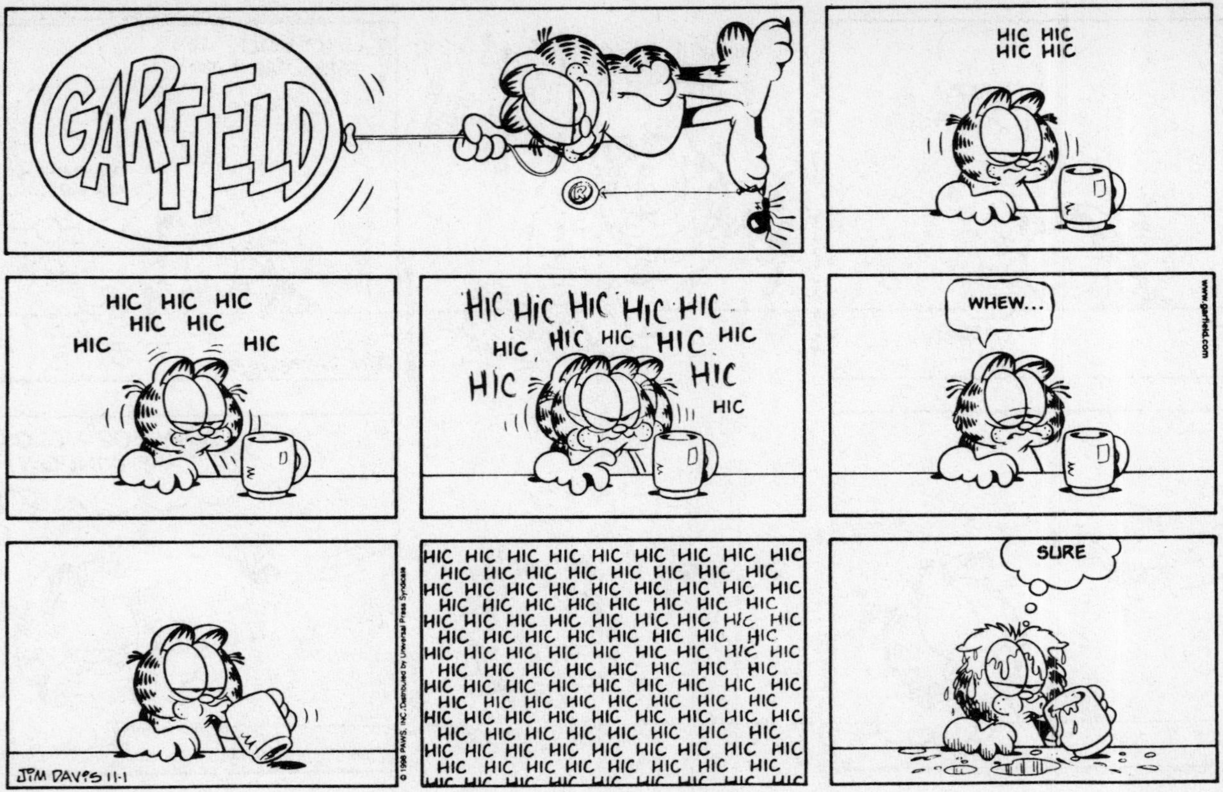
GARFIELD
HIC HIC
HIC HIC
HIC HIC HIC
HIC HIC
HIC
HIC
HIC HIC HIC HIC HIC
HIC HIC HIC HIC HIC
HIC
HIC
HIC
WHEW...
JIM DAVIS 11-1
HIC HIC HIC HIC HIC HIC HIC HIC HIC
HIC HIC HIC HIC HIC HIC HIC HIC
HIC HIC HIC HIC HIC HIC HIC HIC HIC
HIC HIC HIC HIC HIC HIC HIC HIC
HIC HIC HIC HIC HIC HIC HIC HIC HIC
HIC HIC HIC HIC HIC HIC HIC HIC
HIC HIC HIC HIC HIC HIC HIC HIC HIC
HIC HIC HIC HIC HIC HIC HIC HIC
HIC HIC HIC HIC HIC HIC HIC HIC HIC
HIC HIC HIC HIC HIC HIC HIC HIC
HIC HIC HIC HIC HIC HIC HIC HIC HIC
HIC HIC HIC HIC HIC HIC HIC HIC
HIC HIC HIC HIC HIC HIC HIC HIC HIC
HIC HIC HIC HIC HIC HIC HIC HIC
SURE
© 1998 PAWS, INC. Distributed by Universal Press Syndicate
www.garfield.com

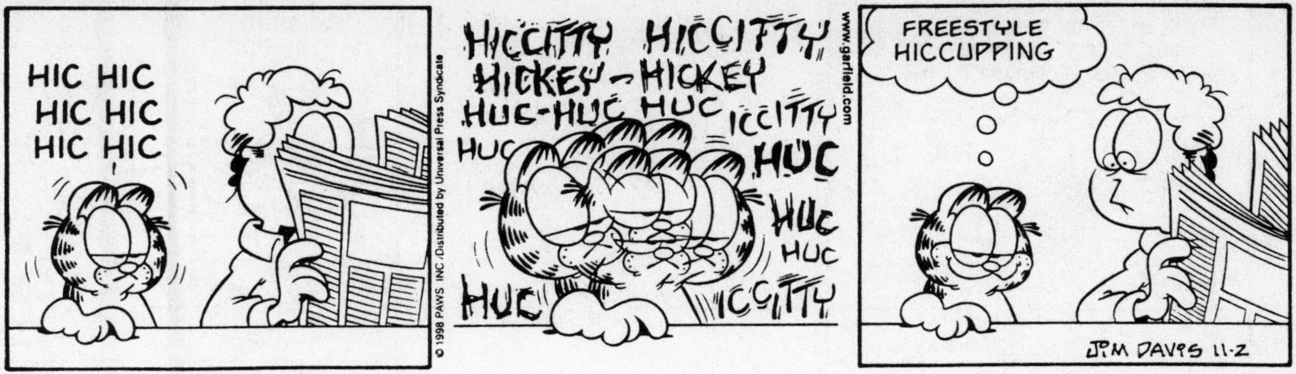
HIC HIC HIC HIC HIC HIC
© 1998 PAWS, INC./Distributed by Universal Press Syndicate
HICCITTY HICCITTY
HICKEY-HICKEY
HUC-HUC HUC ICCITTY
HUC
HUC
HUC
HUC
HUC
ICCITTY
www.garfield.com
FREESTYLE HICCUPPING
JIM DAVIS 11-2

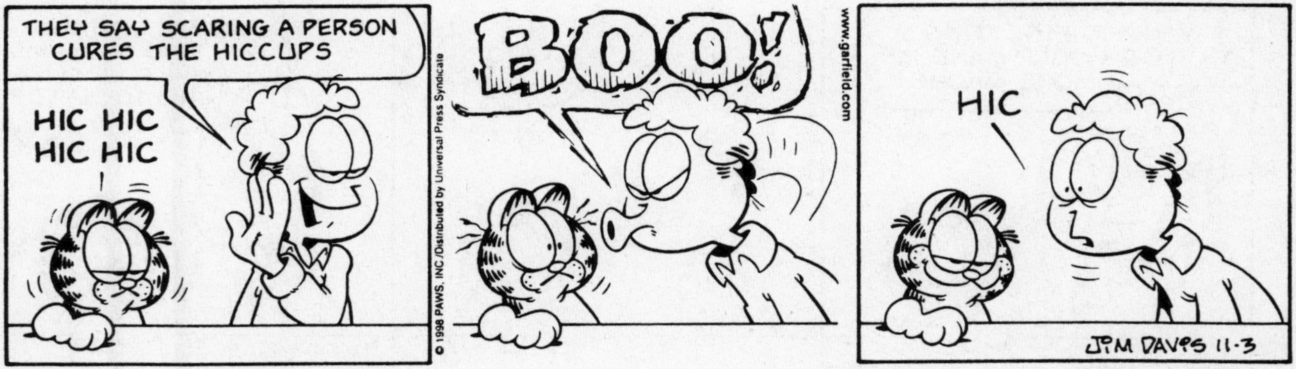
THEY SAY SCARING A PERSON CURES THE HICCUPS
HIC HIC HIC HIC
© 1998 PAWS, INC./Distributed by Universal Press Syndicate
BOO!
www.garfield.com
HIC
JIM DAVIS 11-3

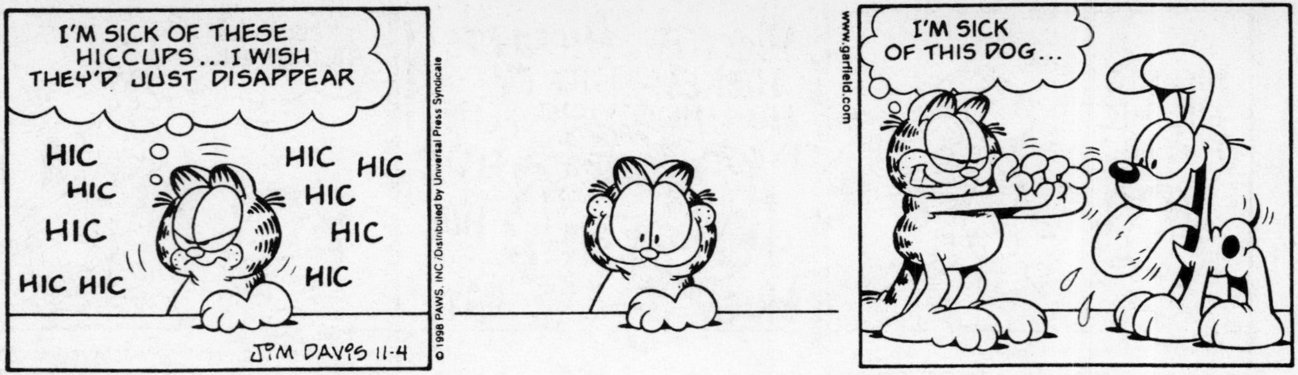
I'M SICK OF THESE HICCUPS... I WISH THEY'D JUST DISAPPEAR
HIC HIC HIC HIC HIC HIC HIC HIC HIC HIC
JIM DAVIS 11-4
© 1998 PAWS, INC./Distributed by Universal Press Syndicate
www.garfield.com
I'M SICK OF THIS DOG...

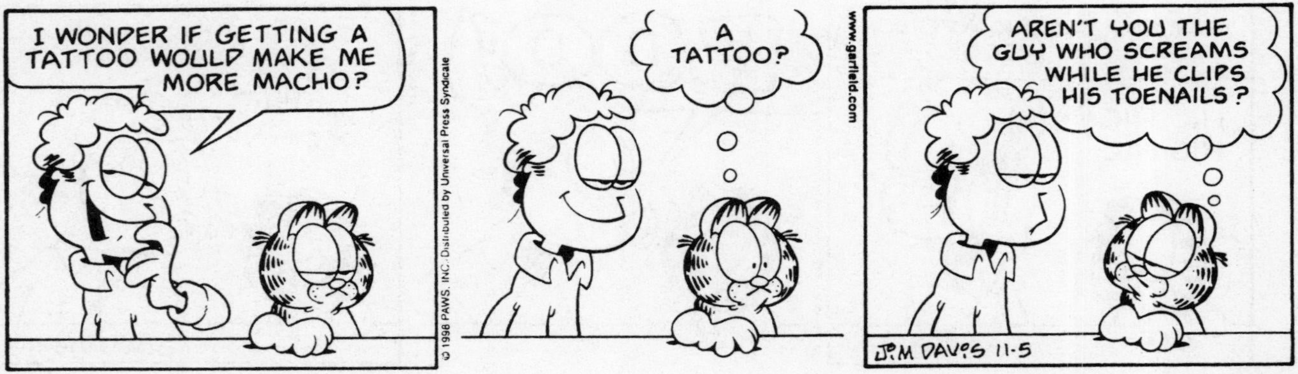
I WONDER IF GETTING A TATTOO WOULD MAKE ME MORE MACHO?
© 1998 PAWS, INC./Distributed by Universal Press Syndicate
A TATTOO?
www.garfield.com
AREN'T YOU THE GUY WHO SCREAMS WHILE HE CLIPS HIS TOENAILS?
JIM DAVIS 11-5

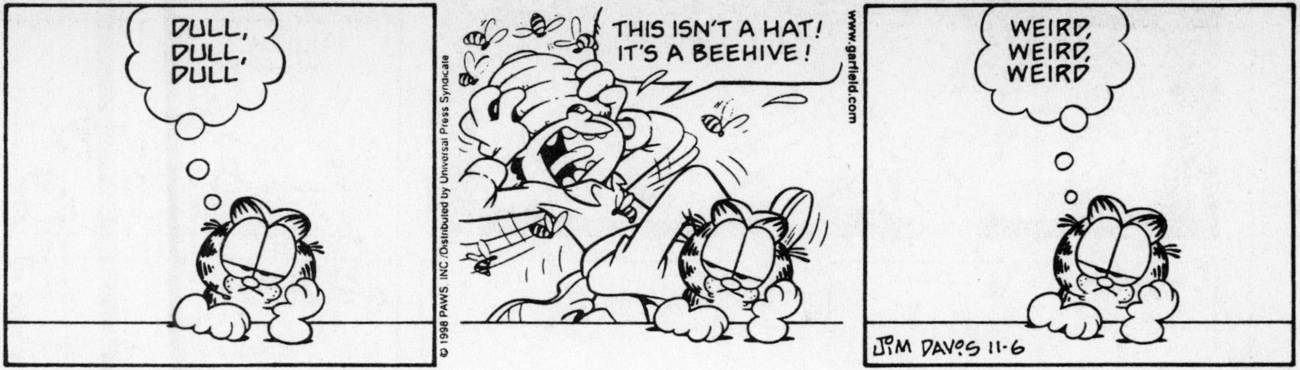
DULL, DULL, DULL
© 1998 PAWS, INC./Distributed by Universal Press Syndicate
THIS ISN'T A HAT! IT'S A BEEHIVE!
www.garfield.com
WEIRD, WEIRD, WEIRD
JIM DAVIS 11-6

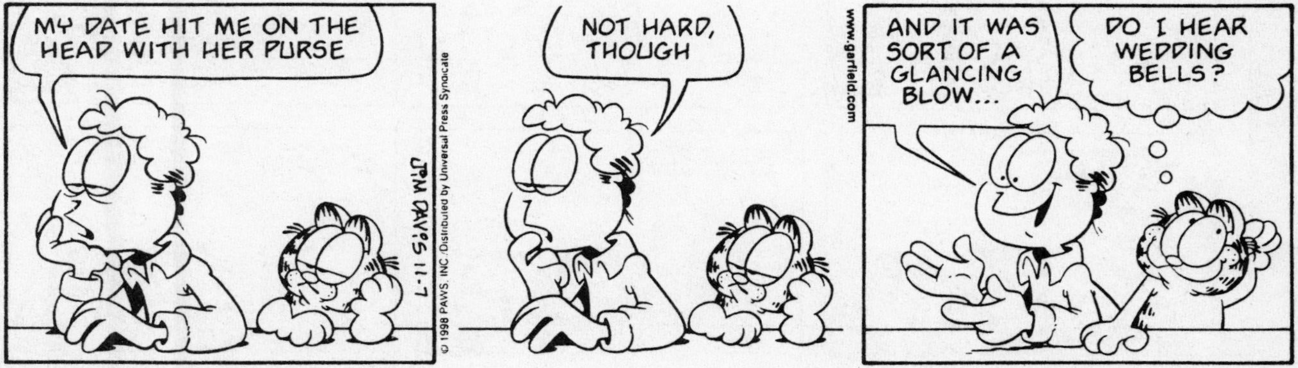
MY DATE HIT ME ON THE HEAD WITH HER PURSE
JIM DAVIS 11-7
© 1998 PAWS, INC./Distributed by Universal Press Syndicate
NOT HARD, THOUGH
www.garfield.com
AND IT WAS SORT OF A GLANCING BLOW...
DO I HEAR WEDDING BELLS?

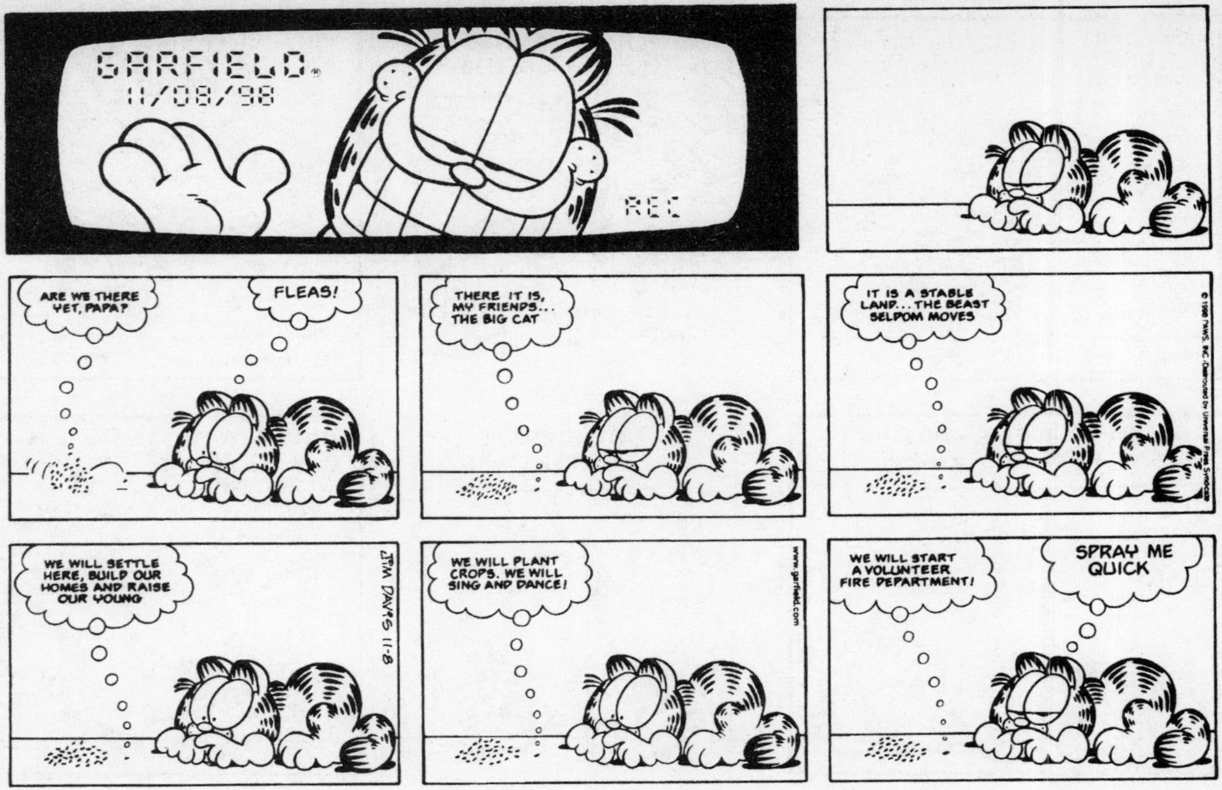
GARFIELD®
11/08/98
REC
ARE WE THERE YET, PAPA?
FLEAS!
THERE IT IS, MY FRIENDS... THE BIG CAT
IT IS A STABLE LAND... THE BEAST SELDOM MOVES
© 1998 PAWS, INC.-Distributed by Universal Press Syndicate
WE WILL SETTLE HERE, BUILD OUR HOMES AND RAISE OUR YOUNG
JIM DAVIS 11-8
WE WILL PLANT CROPS. WE WILL SING AND DANCE!
www.garfield.com
WE WILL START A VOLUNTEER FIRE DEPARTMENT!
SPRAY ME QUICK

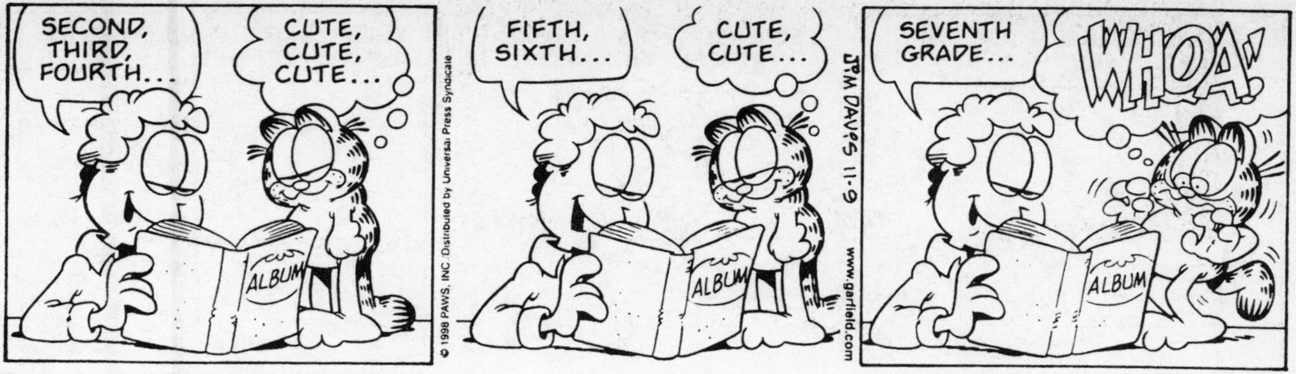
SECOND, THIRD, FOURTH...
CUTE, CUTE, CUTE...
ALBUM
© 1998 PAWS, INC./Distributed by Universal Press Syndicate
FIFTH, SIXTH...
CUTE, CUTE...
ALBUM
JIM DAVIS 11-9
www.garfield.com
SEVENTH GRADE...
WHOA!
ALBUM

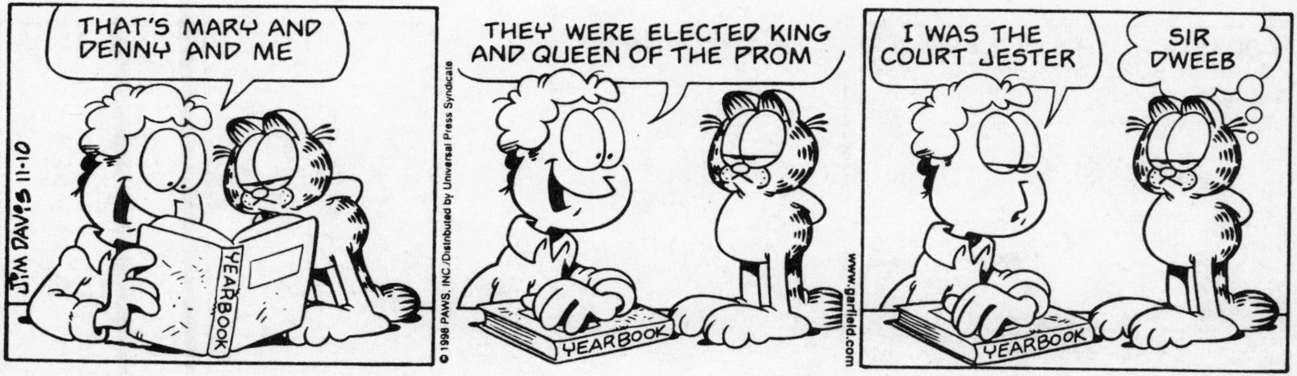
THAT'S MARY AND DENNY AND ME
JIM DAVIS 11-10
YEARBOOK
© 1998 PAWS, INC./Distributed by Universal Press Syndicate
THEY WERE ELECTED KING AND QUEEN OF THE PROM
YEARBOOK
www.garfield.com
I WAS THE COURT JESTER
SIR DWEEB
YEARBOOK

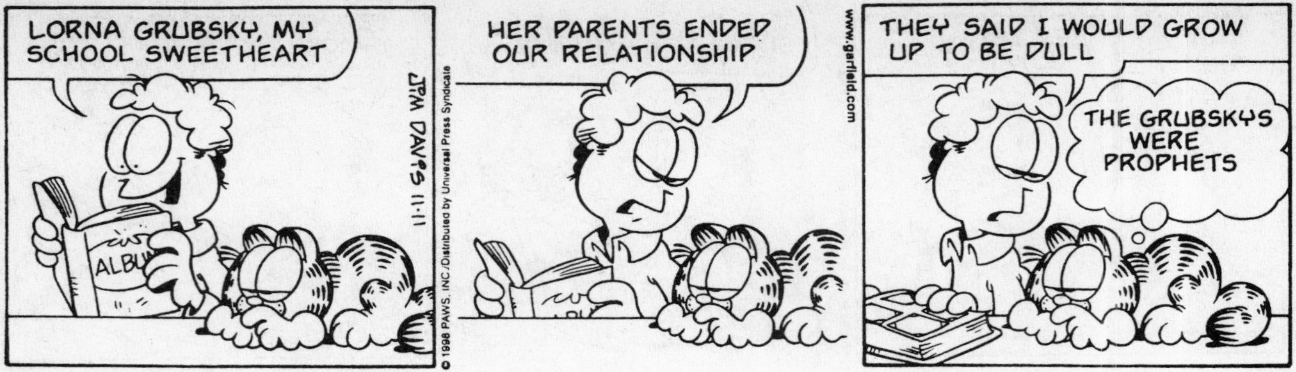
LORNA GRUBSKY, MY SCHOOL SWEETHEART
ALBUM
JIM DAVIS 11-11
© 1998 PAWS, INC./Distributed by Universal Press Syndicate
HER PARENTS ENDED OUR RELATIONSHIP
www.garfield.com
THEY SAID I WOULD GROW UP TO BE DULL
THE GRUBSKYS WERE PROPHETS

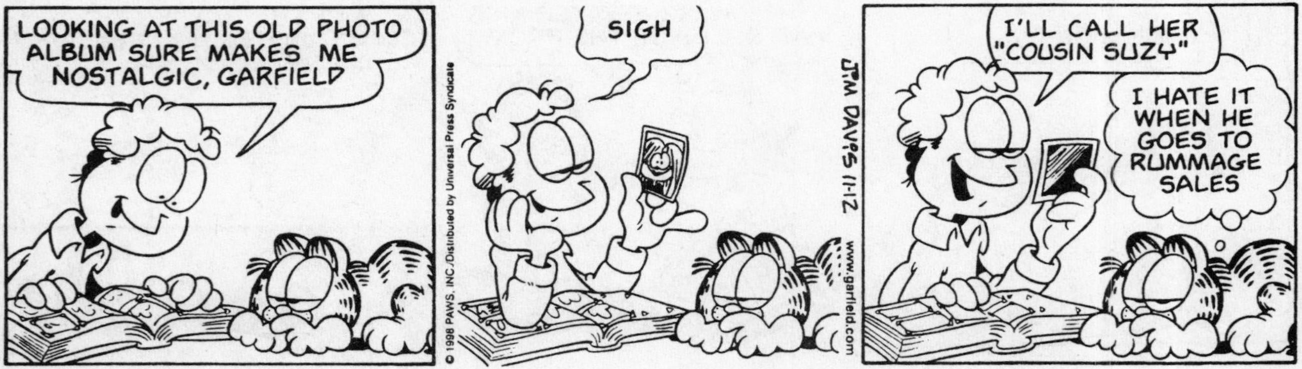
LOOKING AT THIS OLD PHOTO ALBUM SURE MAKES ME NOSTALGIC, GARFIELD
© 1998 PAWS, INC./Distributed by Universal Press Syndicate
SIGH
JIM DAVIS 11-12
www.garfield.com
I'LL CALL HER "COUSIN SUZY"
I HATE IT WHEN HE GOES TO RUMMAGE SALES

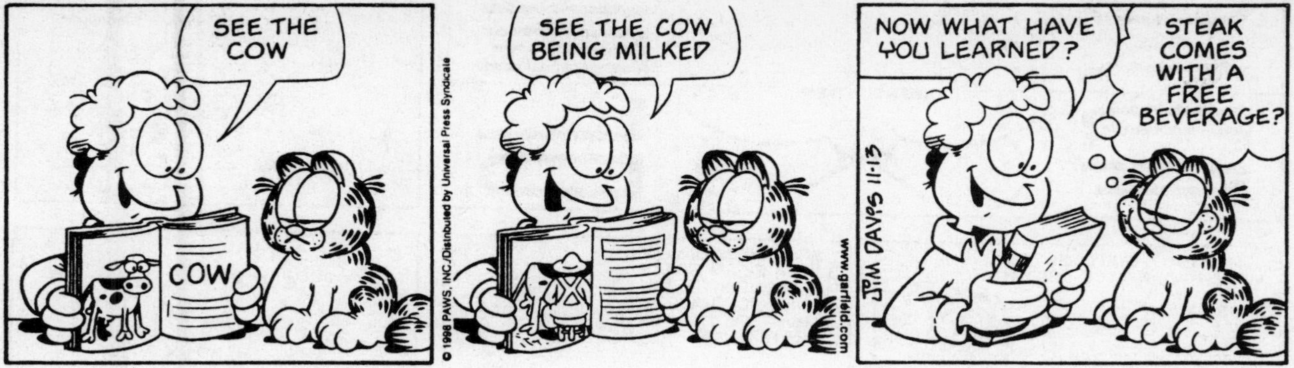
SEE THE COW
COW
SEE THE COW BEING MILKED
© 1998 PAWS, INC./Distributed by Universal Press Syndicate
NOW WHAT HAVE YOU LEARNED?
STEAK COMES WITH A FREE BEVERAGE?
JIM DAVIS 11-13
www.garfield.com

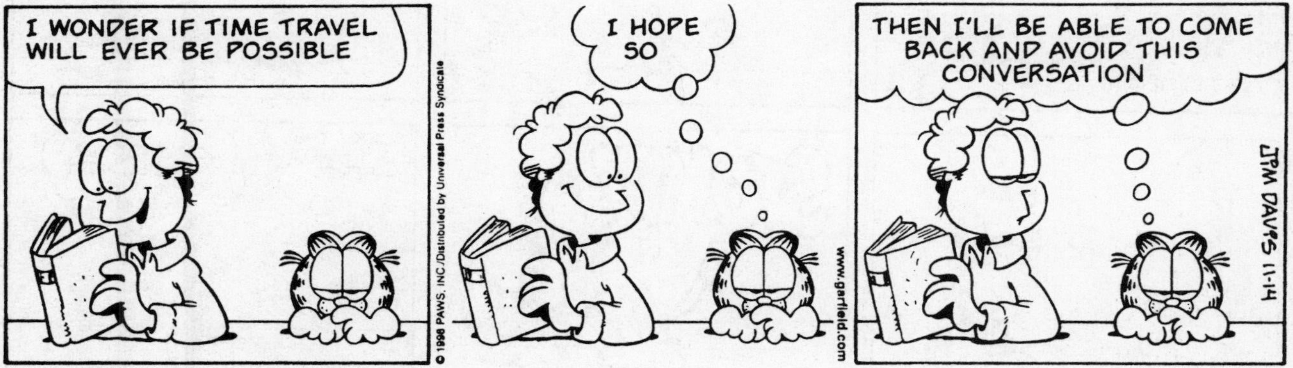
I WONDER IF TIME TRAVEL WILL EVER BE POSSIBLE
© 1998 PAWS, INC./Distributed by Universal Press Syndicate
I HOPE SO
THEN I'LL BE ABLE TO COME BACK AND AVOID THIS CONVERSATION
www.garfield.com
JIM DAVIS 11-14

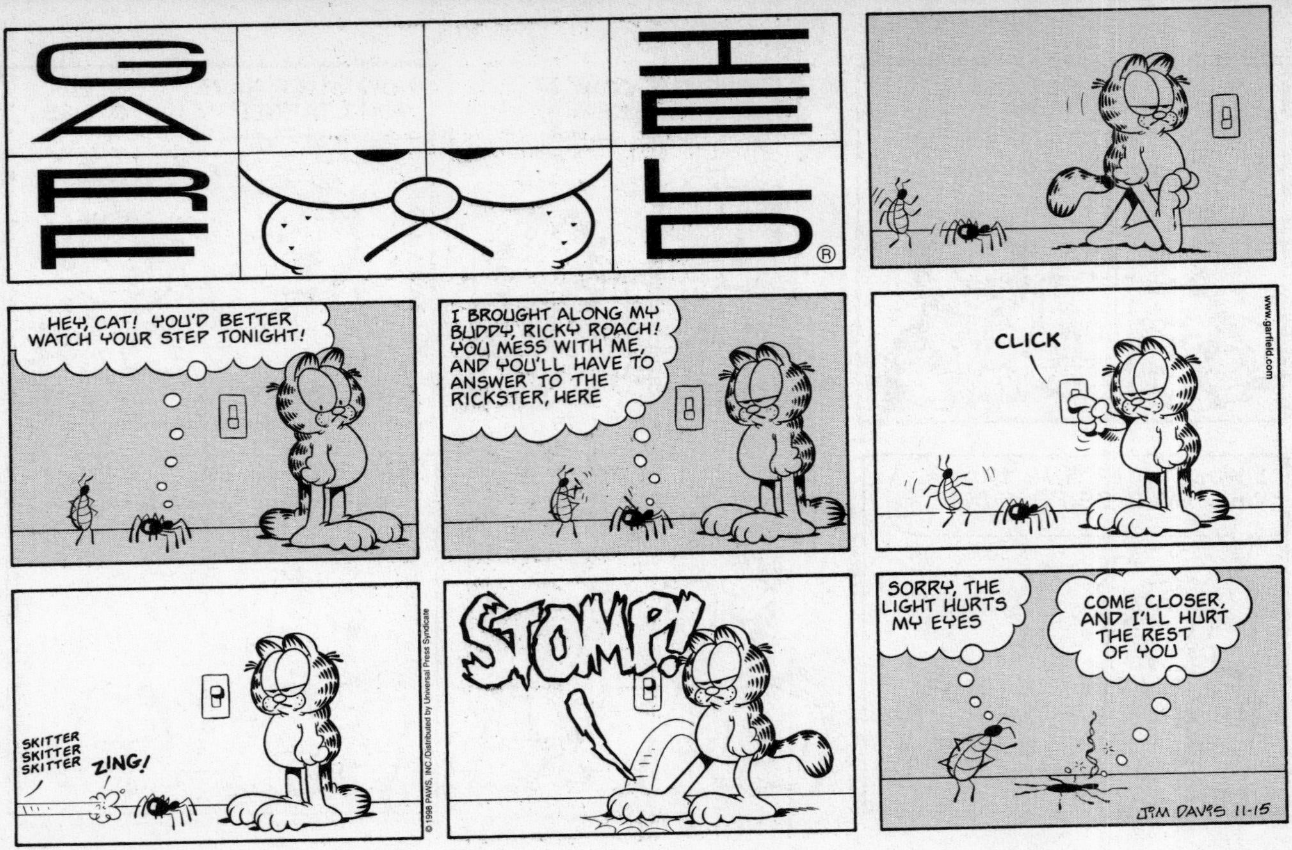
GARFIELD®
HEY, CAT! YOU'D BETTER WATCH YOUR STEP TONIGHT!
I BROUGHT ALONG MY BUDDY, RICKY ROACH! YOU MESS WITH ME, AND YOU'LL HAVE TO ANSWER TO THE RICKSTER, HERE
www.garfield.com
CLICK
SKITTER SKITTER SKITTER
ZING!
© 1998 PAWS, INC./Distributed by Universal Press Syndicate
STOMP!
SORRY, THE LIGHT HURTS MY EYES
COME CLOSER, AND I'LL HURT THE REST OF YOU
JIM DAVIS 11-15

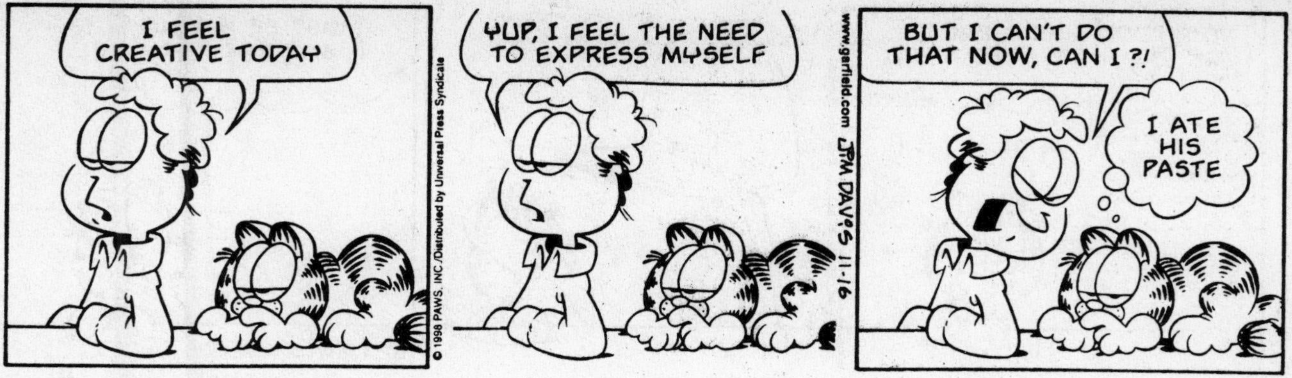
I FEEL CREATIVE TODAY
YUP, I FEEL THE NEED TO EXPRESS MYSELF
BUT I CAN'T DO THAT NOW, CAN I ?!
I ATE HIS PASTE
© 1998 PAWS, INC./Distributed by Universal Press Syndicate
www.garfield.com
JIM DAVIS 11-16

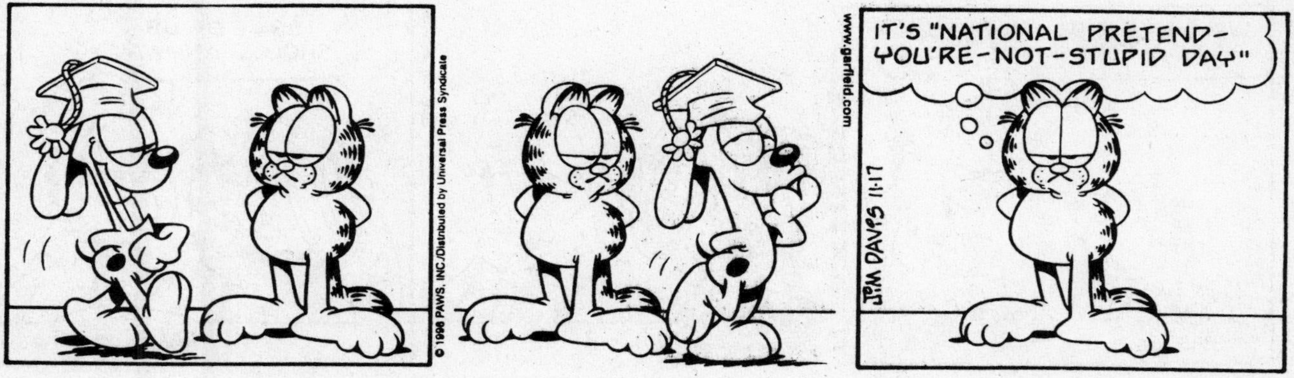
IT'S "NATIONAL PRETEND-YOU'RE-NOT-STUPID DAY"
© 1998 PAWS, INC./Distributed by Universal Press Syndicate
www.garfield.com
JIM DAVIS 11-17

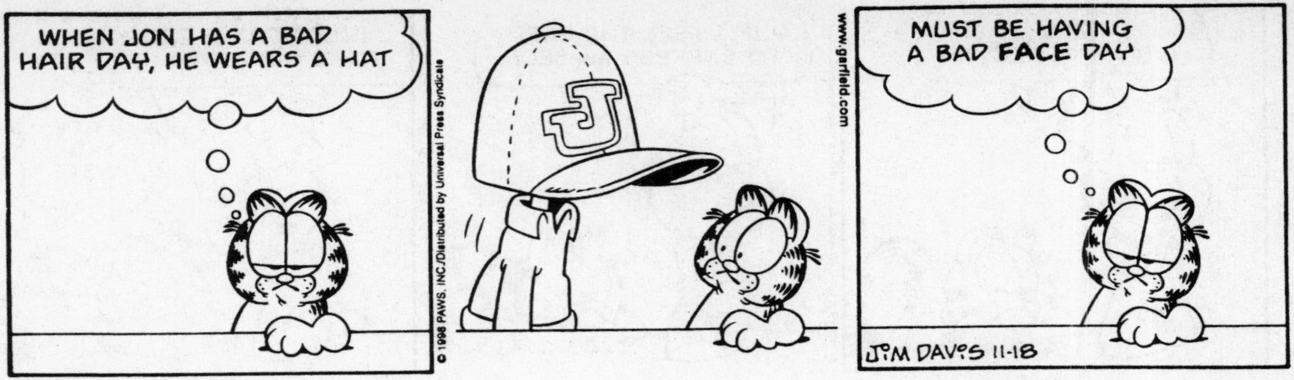
WHEN JON HAS A BAD HAIR DAY, HE WEARS A HAT
MUST BE HAVING A BAD FACE DAY
JIM DAVIS 11-18
© 1998 PAWS, INC./Distributed by Universal Press Syndicate
www.garfield.com

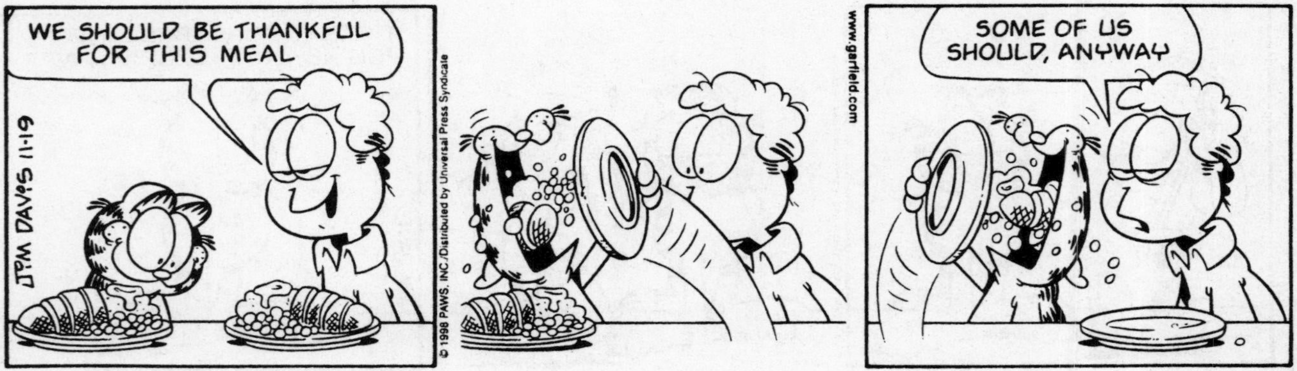
WE SHOULD BE THANKFUL FOR THIS MEAL
SOME OF US SHOULD, ANYWAY
JIM DAVIS 11-19
© 1998 PAWS, INC./Distributed by Universal Press Syndicate
www.garfield.com

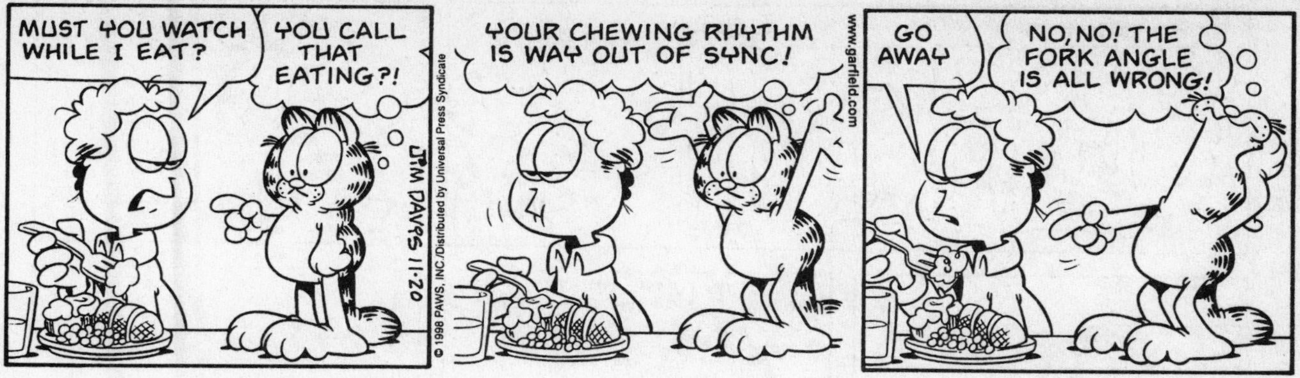
MUST YOU WATCH WHILE I EAT?
YOU CALL THAT EATING?!
JPM DAVPS 11·20
© 1998 PAWS, INC./Distributed by Universal Press Syndicate
YOUR CHEWING RHYTHM IS WAY OUT OF SYNC!
www.garfield.com
GO AWAY
NO, NO! THE FORK ANGLE IS ALL WRONG!

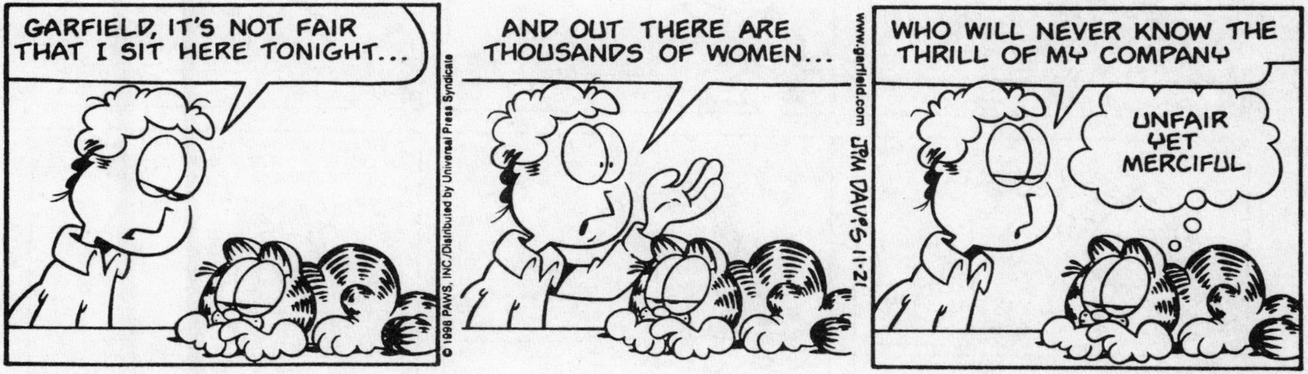
GARFIELD, IT'S NOT FAIR THAT I SIT HERE TONIGHT...
© 1998 PAWS, INC./Distributed by Universal Press Syndicate
AND OUT THERE ARE THOUSANDS OF WOMEN...
www.garfield.com
JPM DAVPS 11·21
WHO WILL NEVER KNOW THE THRILL OF MY COMPANY
UNFAIR YET MERCIFUL

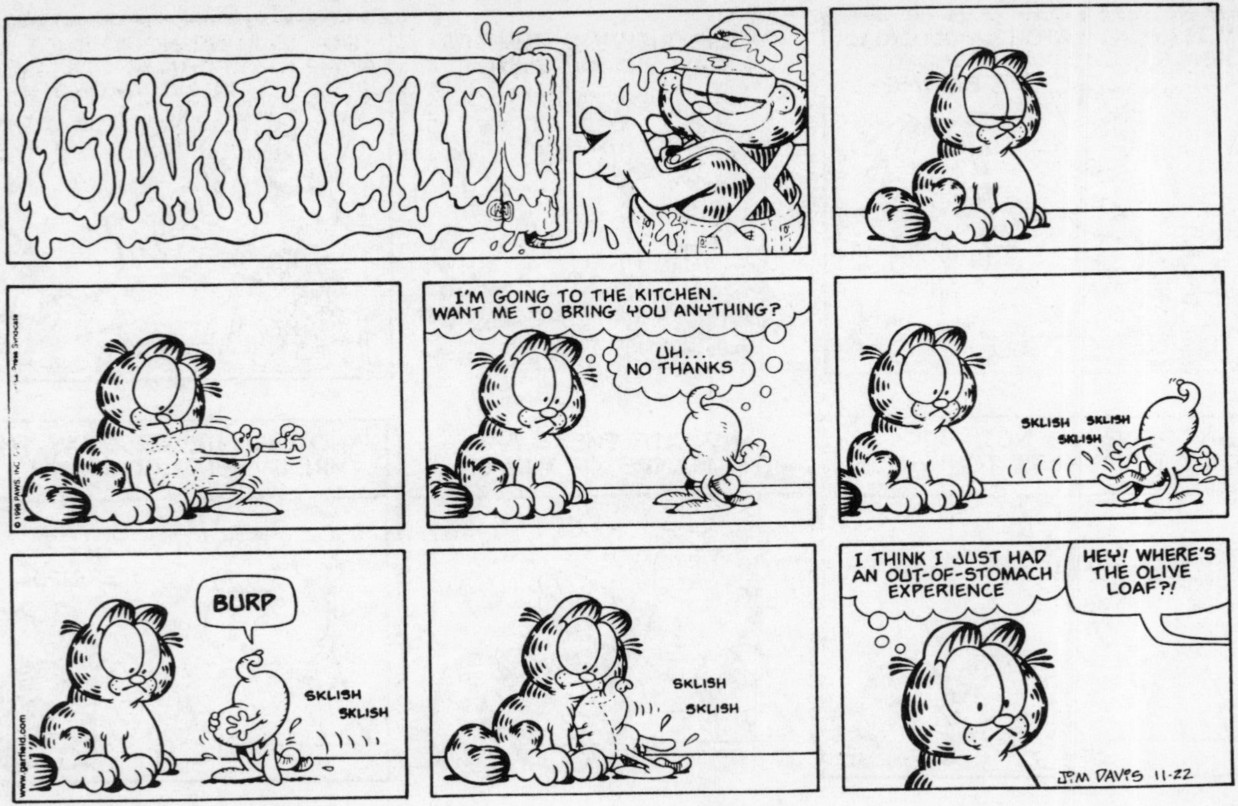
GARFIELD
I'M GOING TO THE KITCHEN. WANT ME TO BRING YOU ANYTHING?
UH... NO THANKS
SKLISH SKLISH
SKLISH
BURP
SKLISH
SKLISH
SKLISH
SKLISH
I THINK I JUST HAD AN OUT-OF-STOMACH EXPERIENCE
HEY! WHERE'S THE OLIVE LOAF?!
JIM DAVIS 11-22

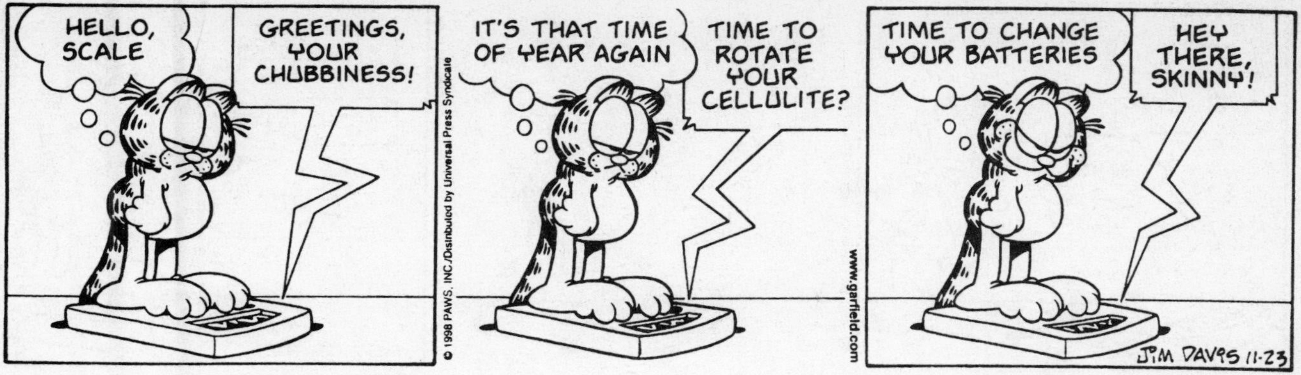
HELLO, SCALE
GREETINGS, YOUR CHUBBINESS!
IT'S THAT TIME OF YEAR AGAIN
TIME TO ROTATE YOUR CELLULITE?
TIME TO CHANGE YOUR BATTERIES
HEY THERE, SKINNY!
JIM DAVIS 11-23
© 1998 PAWS, INC./Distributed by Universal Press Syndicate
www.garfield.com

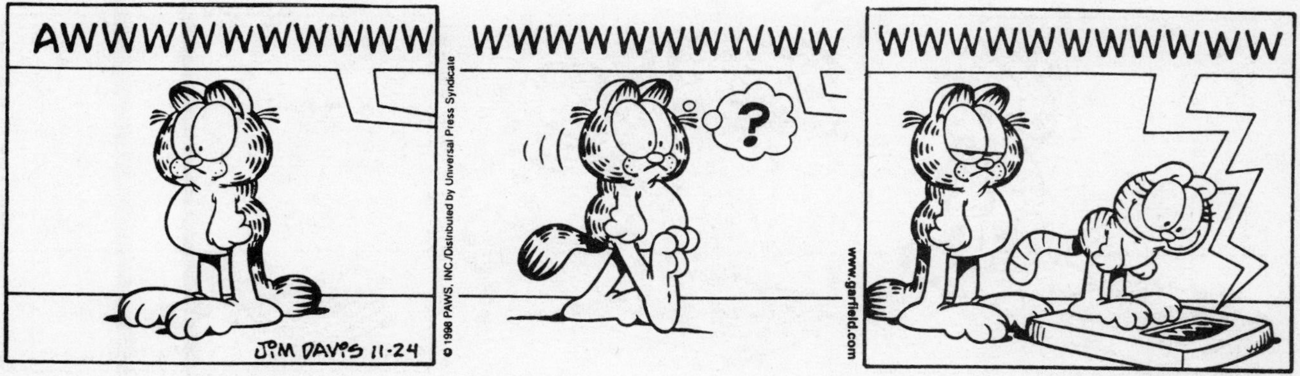
AWWWWWWWWWWW
WWWWWWWWWWWW
WWWWWWWWWWWW
?
JIM DAVIS 11-24
© 1998 PAWS, INC./Distributed by Universal Press Syndicate
www.garfield.com

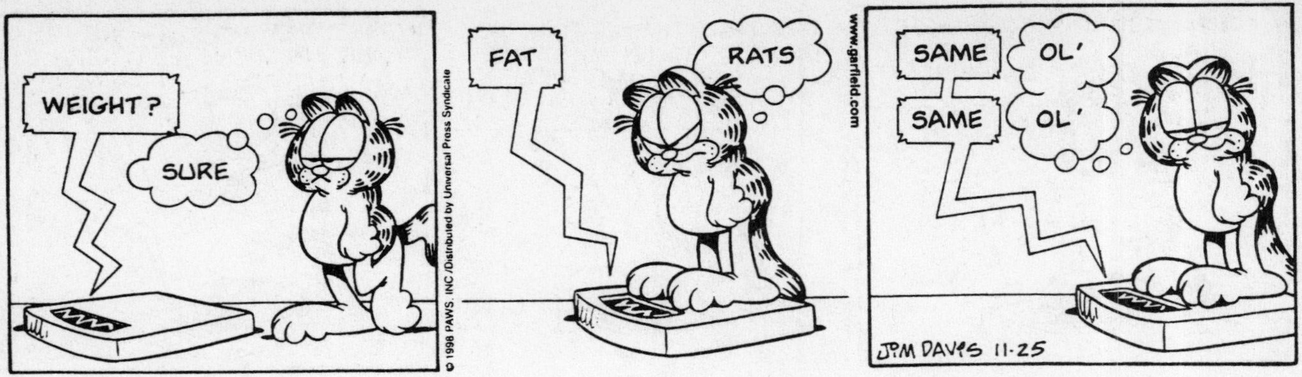
WEIGHT?
SURE
FAT
RATS
SAME
OL'
SAME
OL'
© 1998 PAWS, INC./Distributed by Universal Press Syndicate
www.garfield.com
JIM DAVIS 11-25

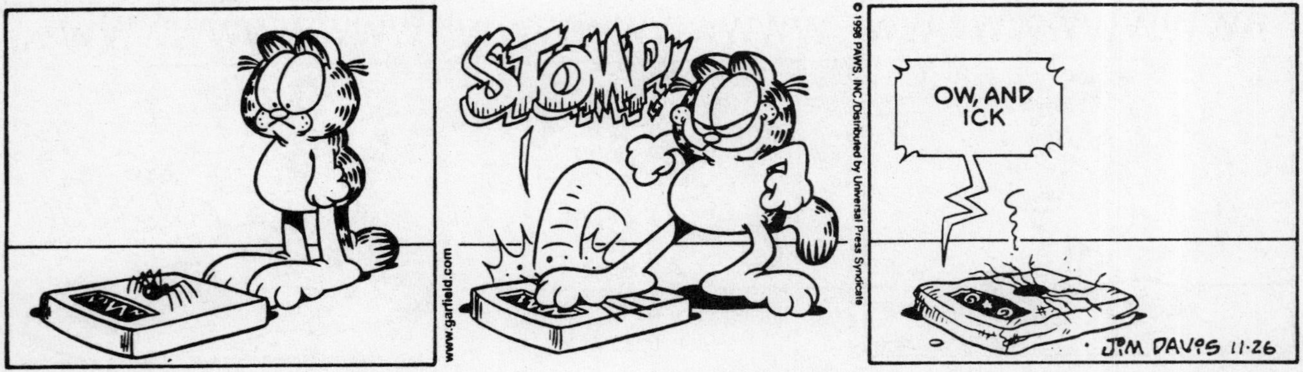
STOMP!
OW, AND ICK
www.garfield.com
© 1998 PAWS, INC./Distributed by Universal Press Syndicate
JIM DAVIS 11-26

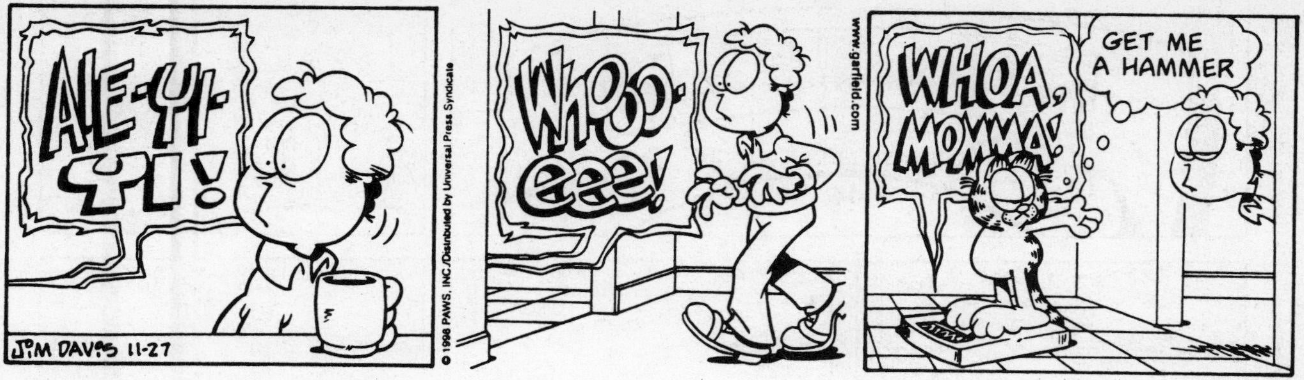
AIE-YI-YI!
JIM DAVIS 11-27
© 1998 PAWS, INC./Distributed by Universal Press Syndicate
WHOOO-eee!
www.garfield.com
WHOA, MOMMA!
GET ME A HAMMER

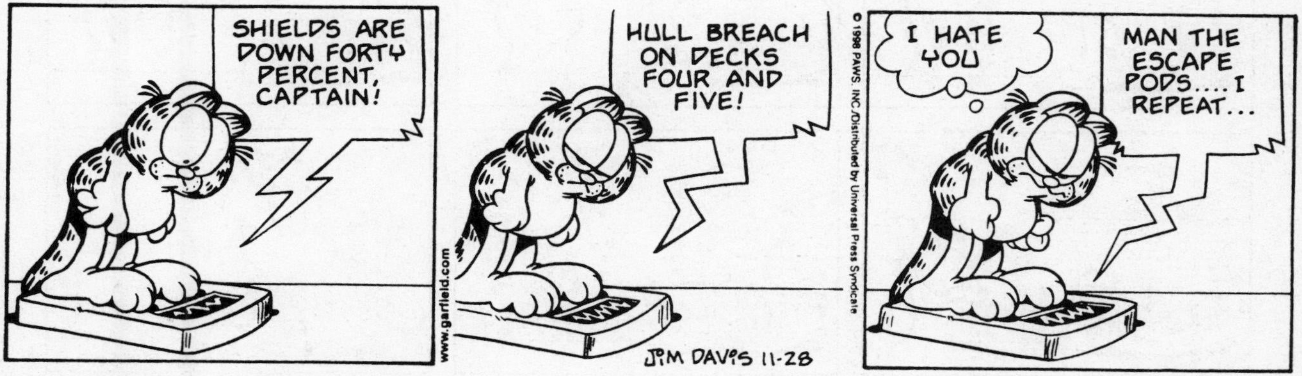
SHIELDS ARE DOWN FORTY PERCENT, CAPTAIN!
www.garfield.com
HULL BREACH ON DECKS FOUR AND FIVE!
JIM DAVIS 11-28
© 1998 PAWS, INC./Distributed by Universal Press Syndicate
I HATE YOU
MAN THE ESCAPE PODS.... I REPEAT...

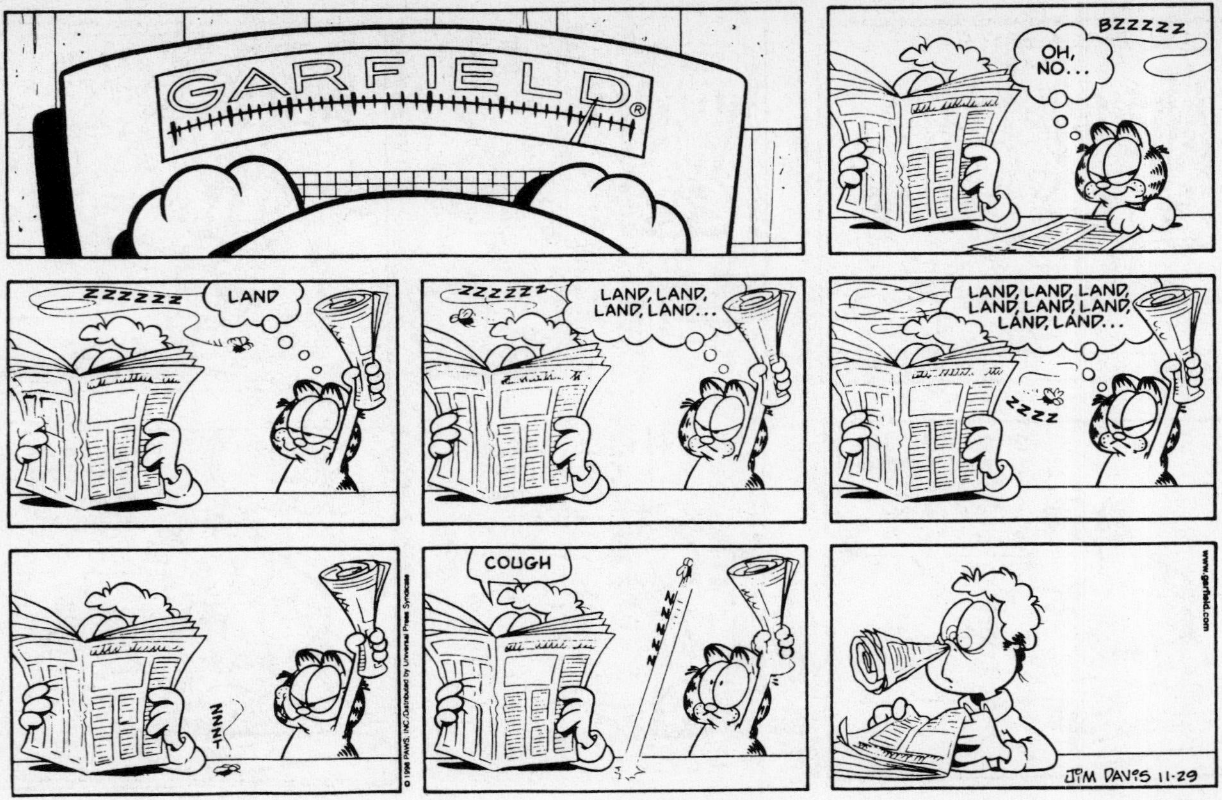
GARFIELD®
OH, NO...
BZZZZZ
ZZZZZZ
LAND
ZZZZZZ
LAND, LAND, LAND, LAND...
LAND, LAND, LAND, LAND, LAND, LAND, LAND, LAND...
ZZZZ
NNNT
COUGH
ZZZZZ
© 1998 PAWS, INC./Distributed by Universal Press Syndicate
www.garfield.com
JIM DAVIS 11-29

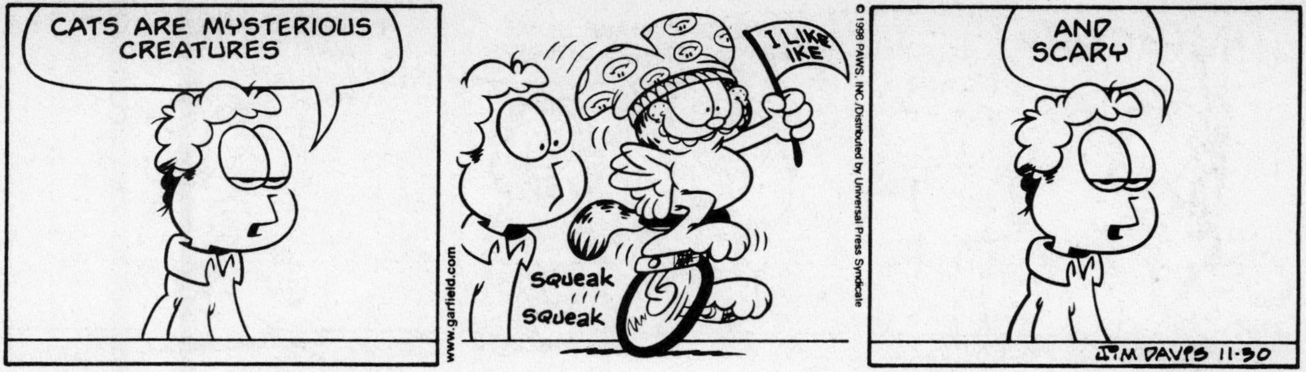
CATS ARE MYSTERIOUS CREATURES
I LIKE IKE
SQUEAK
SQUEAK
AND SCARY
JIM DAVIS 11-30
www.garfield.com
© 1998 PAWS, INC./Distributed by Universal Press Syndicate

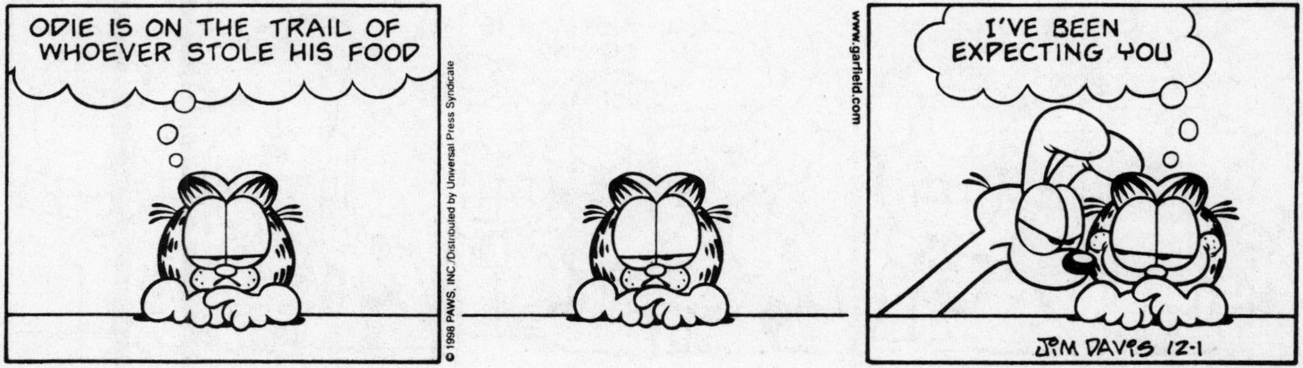
ODIE IS ON THE TRAIL OF WHOEVER STOLE HIS FOOD
I'VE BEEN EXPECTING YOU
JIM DAVIS 12-1
© 1998 PAWS, INC./Distributed by Universal Press Syndicate
www.garfield.com

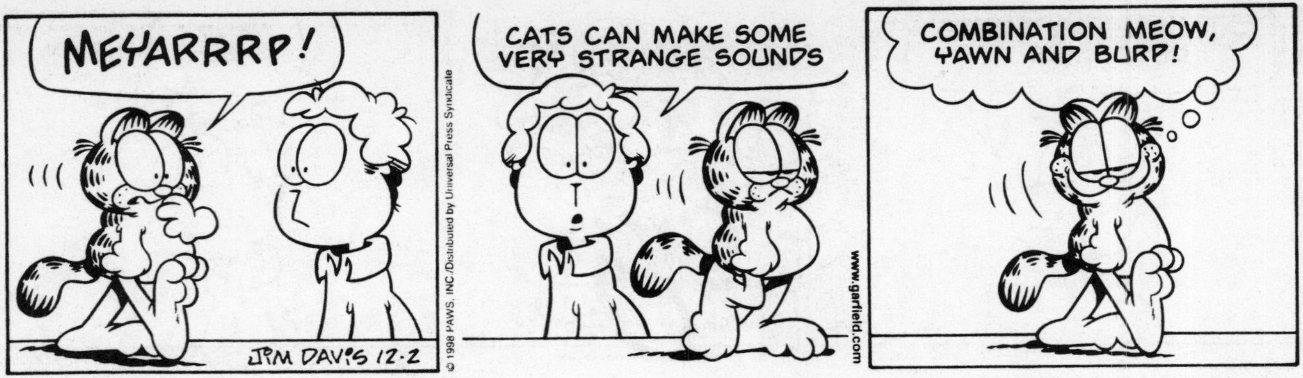
MEYARRRP!
JIM DAVIS 12-2
© 1998 PAWS, INC./Distributed by Universal Press Syndicate
CATS CAN MAKE SOME VERY STRANGE SOUNDS
www.garfield.com
COMBINATION MEOW, YAWN AND BURP!

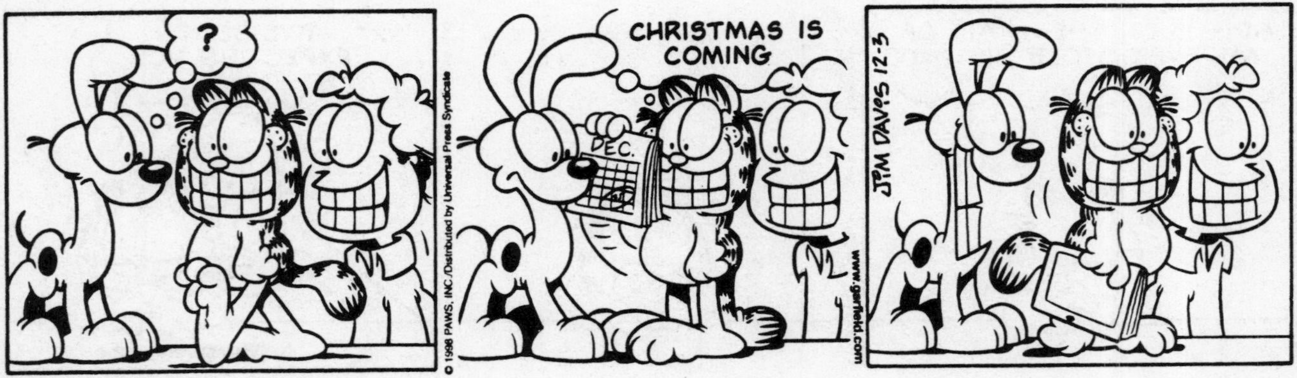
?
© 1998 PAWS, INC./Distributed by Universal Press Syndicate
CHRISTMAS IS COMING
DEC.
www.garfield.com
JIM DAVIS 12-3

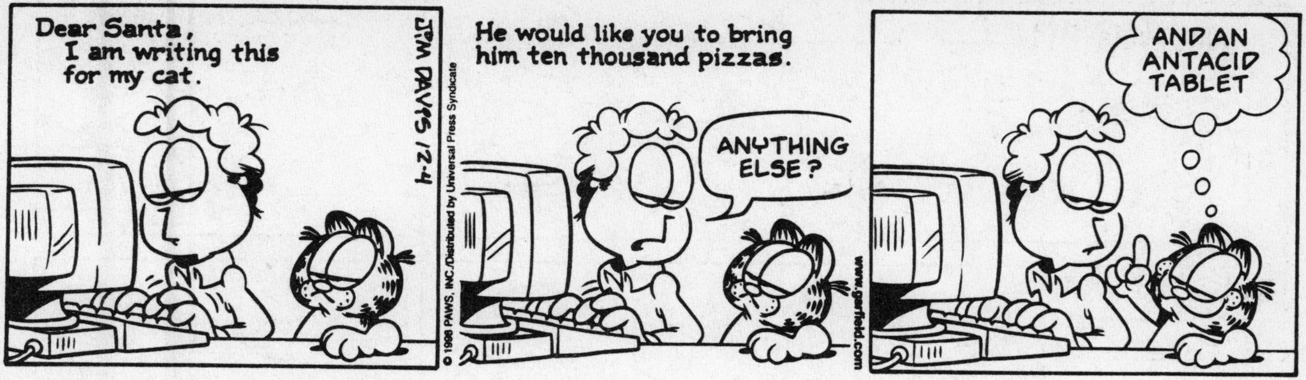
Dear Santa,
I am writing this
for my cat.
JIM DAVIS 12-4
© 1998 PAWS, INC./Distributed by Universal Press Syndicate
He would like you to bring
him ten thousand pizzas.
ANYTHING ELSE?
www.garfield.com
AND AN ANTACID TABLET

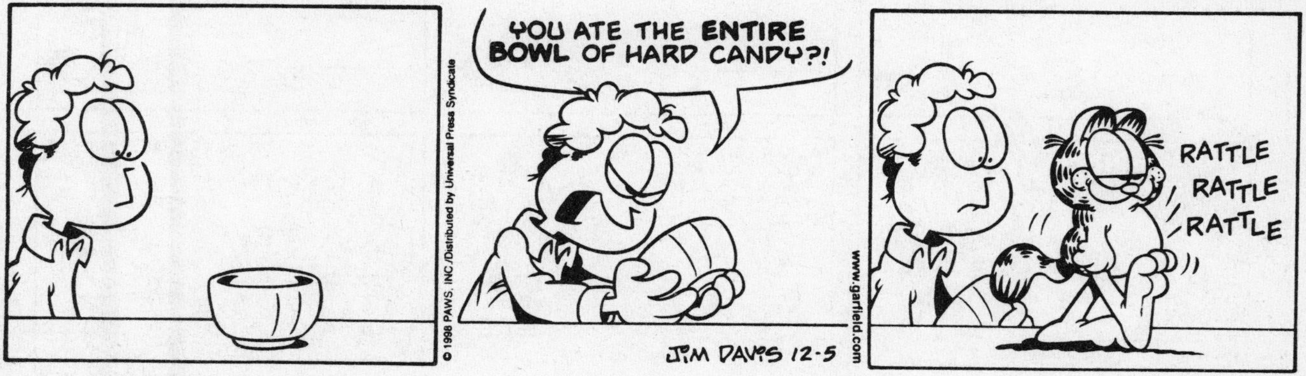
© 1998 PAWS, INC./Distributed by Universal Press Syndicate
YOU ATE THE ENTIRE BOWL OF HARD CANDY?!
JIM DAVIS 12-5
www.garfield.com
RATTLE
RATTLE
RATTLE

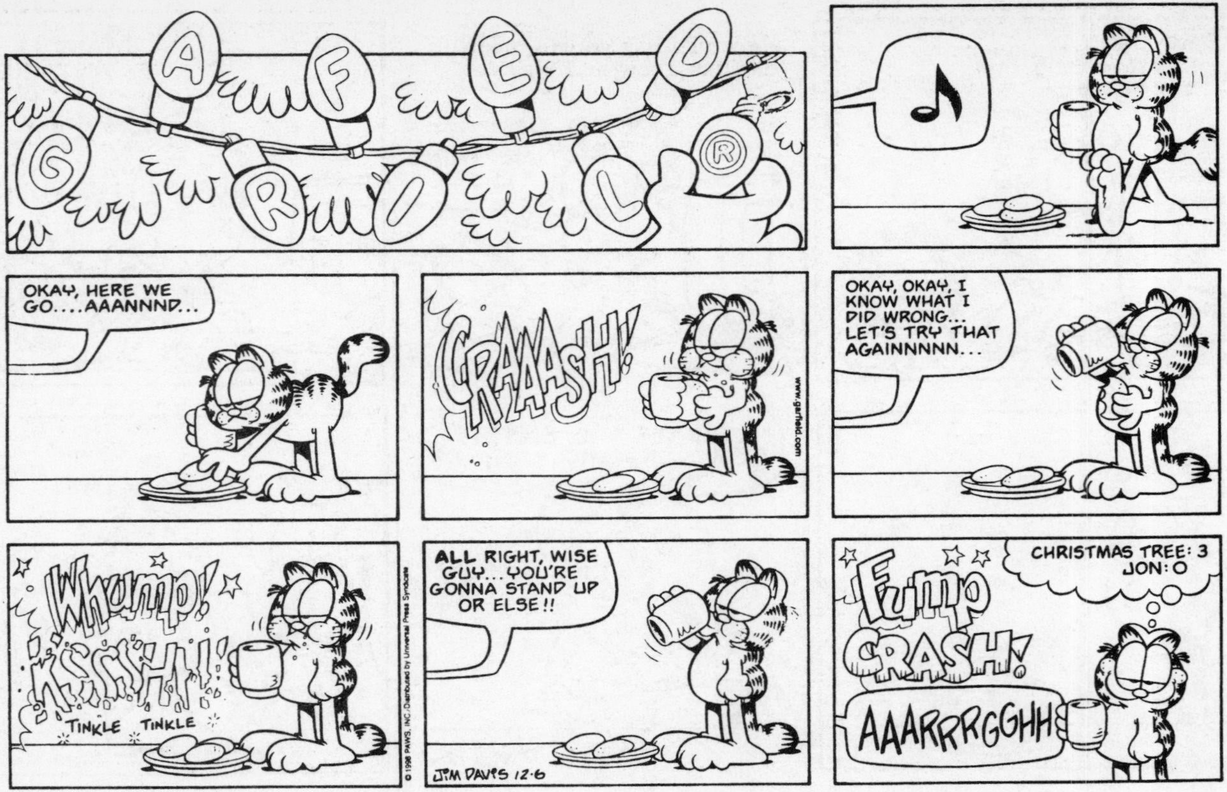
GARFIELD®
♪
OKAY, HERE WE GO....AAANNND...
CRAAASH!
www.garfield.com
OKAY, OKAY, I KNOW WHAT I DID WRONG... LET'S TRY THAT AGAINNNNN...
Whump!
TINKLE TINKLE
© 1998 PAWS, INC./Distributed by Universal Press Syndicate
ALL RIGHT, WISE GUY...YOU'RE GONNA STAND UP OR ELSE!!
JIM DAVIS 12-6
Fump
CRASH!
AAARRRGGHH
CHRISTMAS TREE: 3
JON: 0

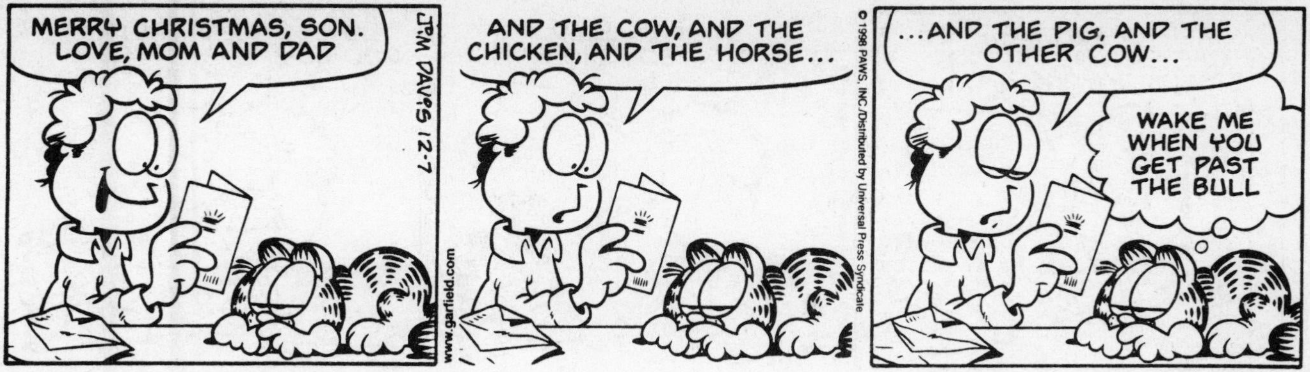
MERRY CHRISTMAS, SON.
LOVE, MOM AND DAD
AND THE COW, AND THE CHICKEN, AND THE HORSE...
...AND THE PIG, AND THE OTHER COW...
WAKE ME WHEN YOU GET PAST THE BULL
JIM DAVIS 12-7
www.garfield.com
© 1998 PAWS, INC./Distributed by Universal Press Syndicate

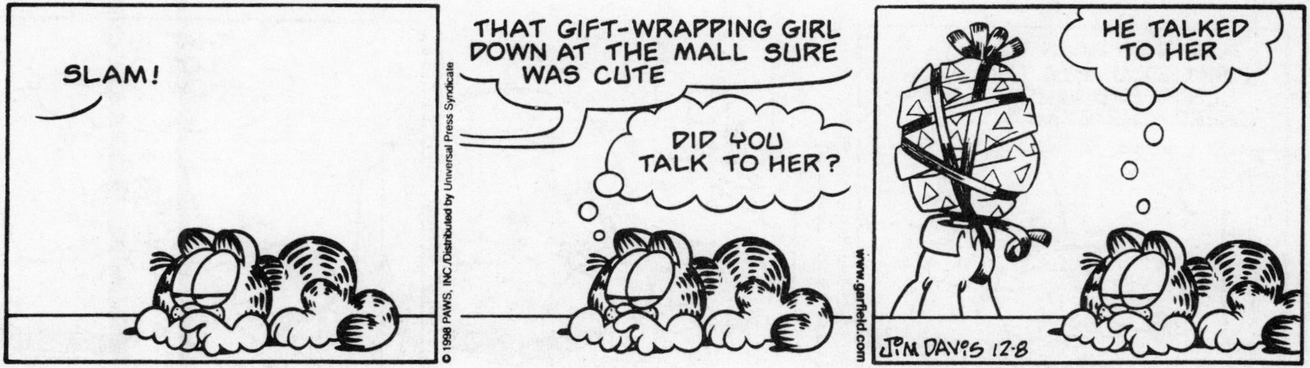
SLAM!
THAT GIFT-WRAPPING GIRL DOWN AT THE MALL SURE WAS CUTE
DID YOU TALK TO HER?
HE TALKED TO HER
© 1998 PAWS, INC./Distributed by Universal Press Syndicate
www.garfield.com
JIM DAVIS 12-8

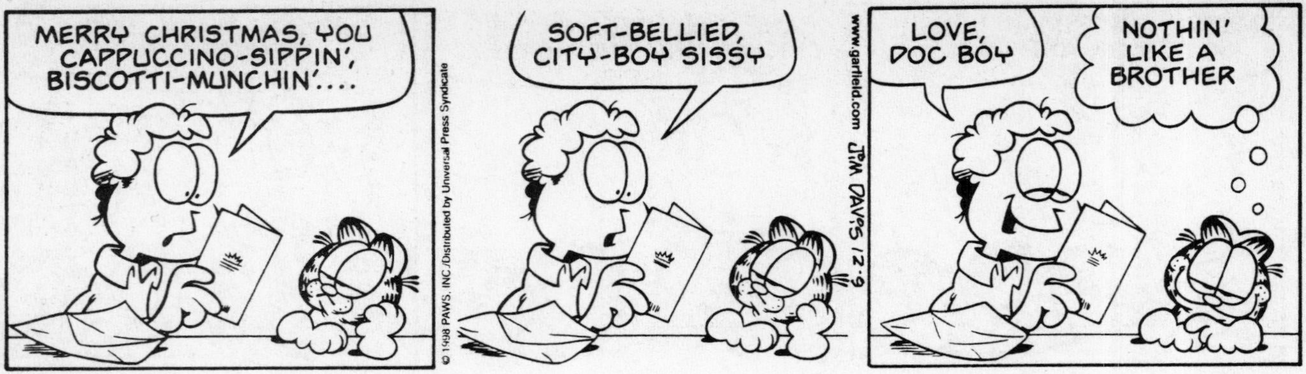
MERRY CHRISTMAS, YOU CAPPUCCINO-SIPPIN', BISCOTTI-MUNCHIN'....
SOFT-BELLIED, CITY-BOY SISSY
LOVE, DOC BOY
NOTHIN' LIKE A BROTHER
JIM DAVIS 12-9

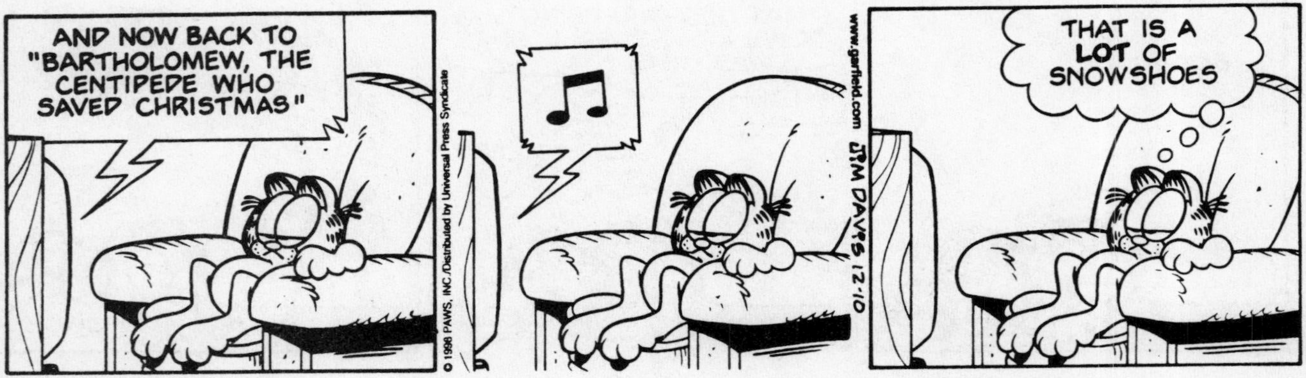
AND NOW BACK TO "BARTHOLOMEW, THE CENTIPEDE WHO SAVED CHRISTMAS"
THAT IS A **LOT** OF SNOWSHOES
JIM DAVIS 12-10

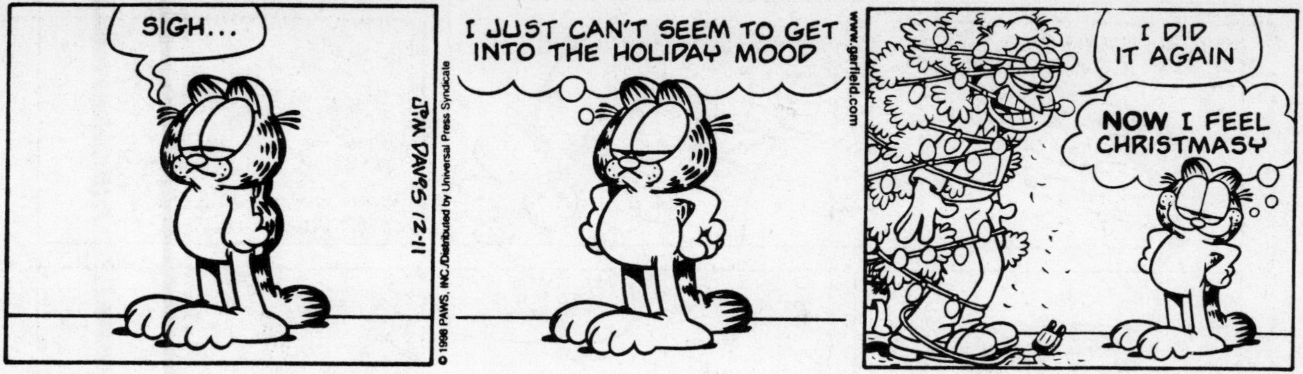
SIGH...
I JUST CAN'T SEEM TO GET INTO THE HOLIDAY MOOD
I DID IT AGAIN
NOW I FEEL CHRISTMASY
JIM DAVIS 12-11
© 1998 PAWS, INC./Distributed by Universal Press Syndicate
www.garfield.com

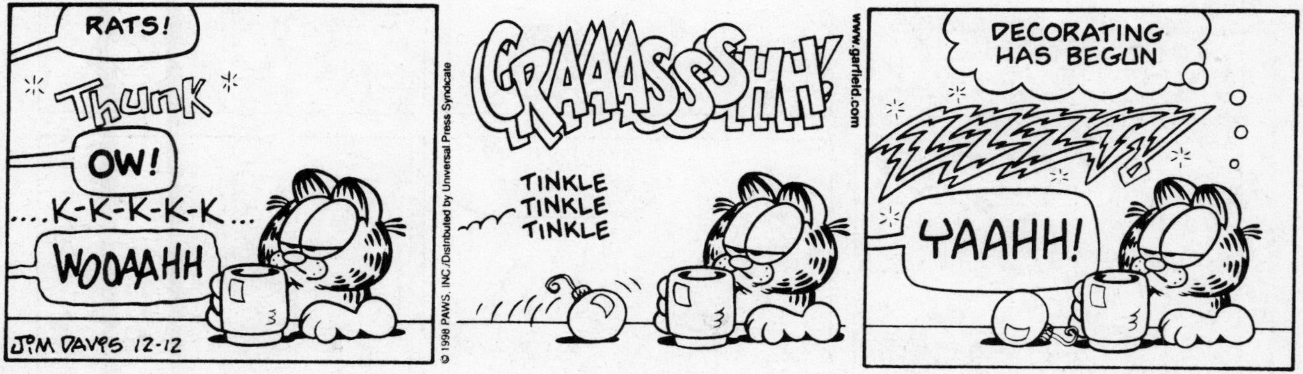
RATS!
Thunk
OW!
....K-K-K-K-K...
WOOAAHH
JIM DAVIS 12-12
© 1998 PAWS, INC./Distributed by Universal Press Syndicate
CRAAASSSHH!
TINKLE
TINKLE
TINKLE
www.garfield.com
DECORATING HAS BEGUN
YAAHH!

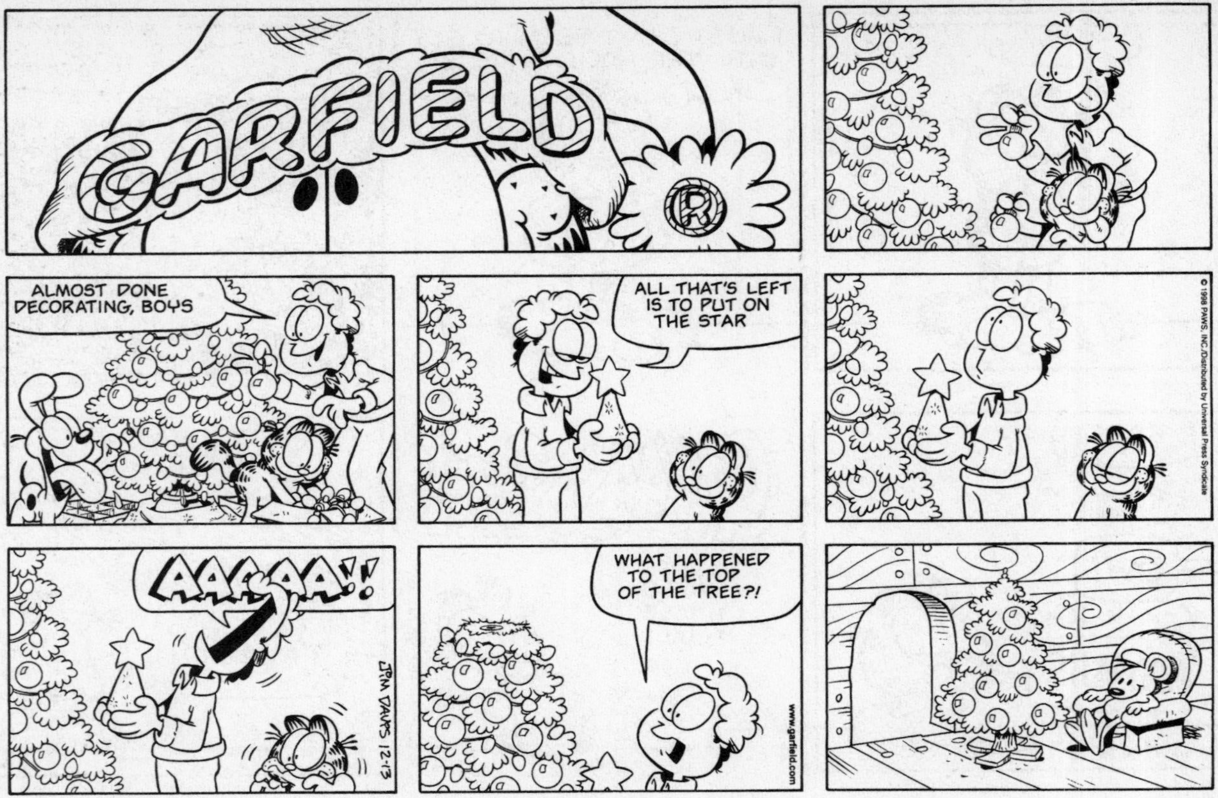
GARFIELD®
ALMOST DONE DECORATING, BOYS
ALL THAT'S LEFT IS TO PUT ON THE STAR
AAAAA!!
JIM DAVIS 12-13
WHAT HAPPENED TO THE TOP OF THE TREE?!
www.garfield.com
© 1998 PAWS, INC./Distributed by Universal Press Syndicate

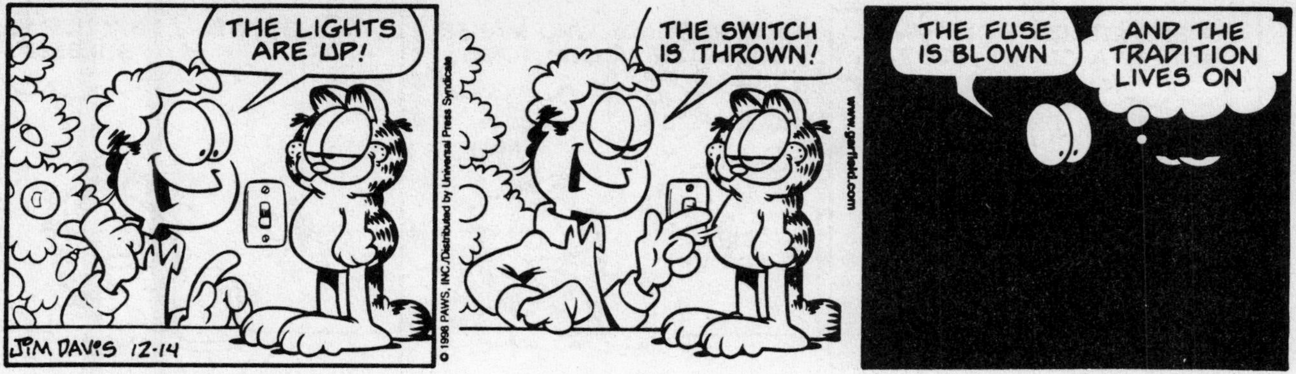
THE LIGHTS ARE UP!
JIM DAVIS 12-14
THE SWITCH IS THROWN!
THE FUSE IS BLOWN
AND THE TRADITION LIVES ON

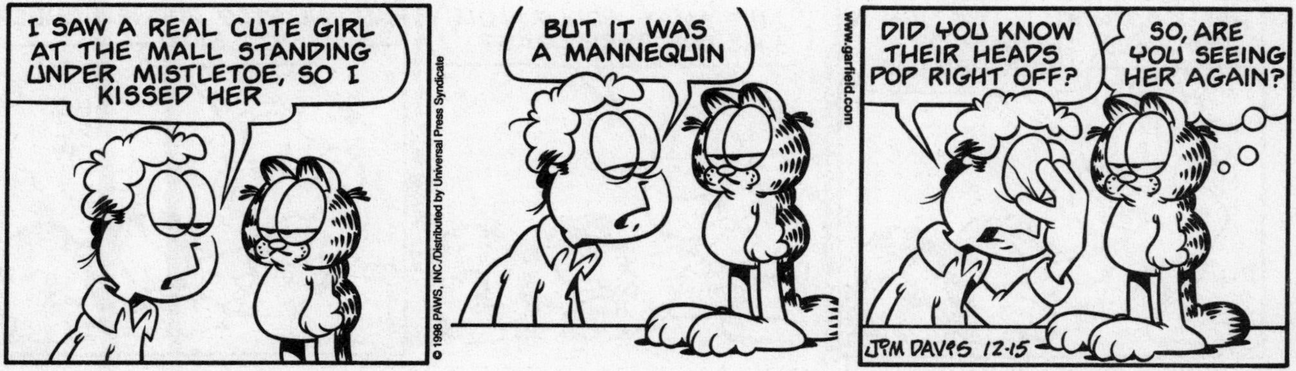
I SAW A REAL CUTE GIRL AT THE MALL STANDING UNDER MISTLETOE, SO I KISSED HER
BUT IT WAS A MANNEQUIN
DID YOU KNOW THEIR HEADS POP RIGHT OFF?
SO, ARE YOU SEEING HER AGAIN?
JIM DAVIS 12-15

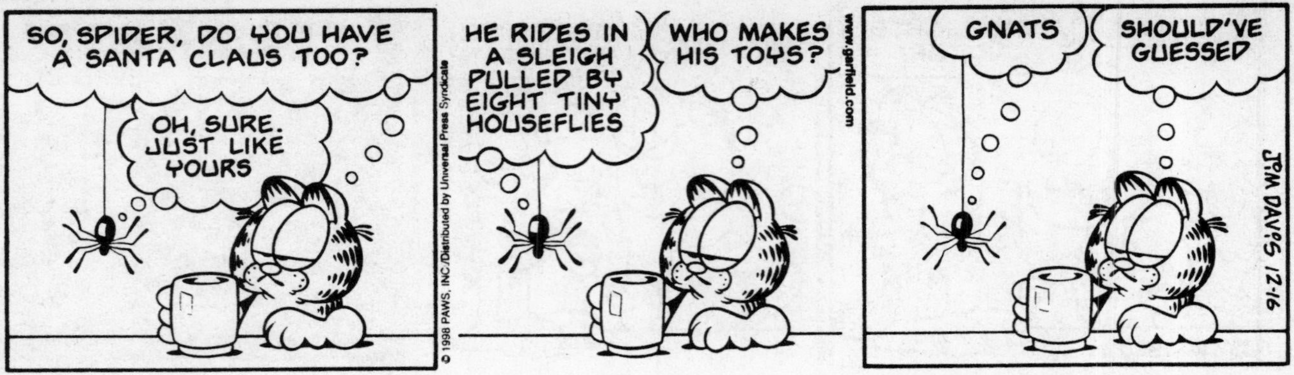
SO, SPIDER, DO YOU HAVE A SANTA CLAUS TOO?
OH, SURE. JUST LIKE YOURS
HE RIDES IN A SLEIGH PULLED BY EIGHT TINY HOUSEFLIES
WHO MAKES HIS TOYS?
GNATS
SHOULD'VE GUESSED
© 1998 PAWS, INC./Distributed by Universal Press Syndicate
www.garfield.com
JIM DAVIS 12-16

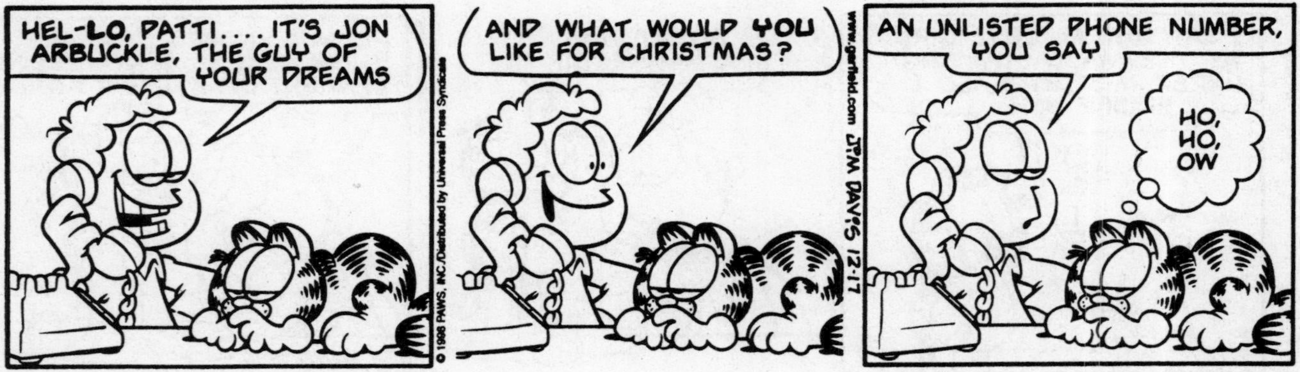
HEL-**LO**, PATTI.... IT'S JON ARBUCKLE, THE GUY OF YOUR DREAMS
AND WHAT WOULD **YOU** LIKE FOR CHRISTMAS?
AN UNLISTED PHONE NUMBER, YOU SAY
HO, HO, OW
© 1998 PAWS, INC./Distributed by Universal Press Syndicate
www.garfield.com
JIM DAVIS 12-17

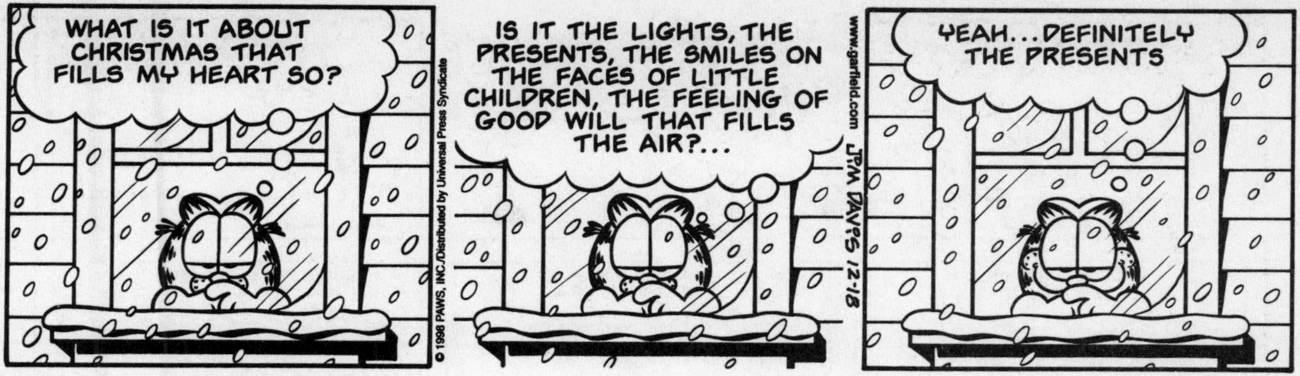
WHAT IS IT ABOUT CHRISTMAS THAT FILLS MY HEART SO?
© 1998 PAWS, INC./Distributed by Universal Press Syndicate
IS IT THE LIGHTS, THE PRESENTS, THE SMILES ON THE FACES OF LITTLE CHILDREN, THE FEELING OF GOOD WILL THAT FILLS THE AIR?...
www.garfield.com
JIM DAVIS 12-18
YEAH... DEFINITELY THE PRESENTS

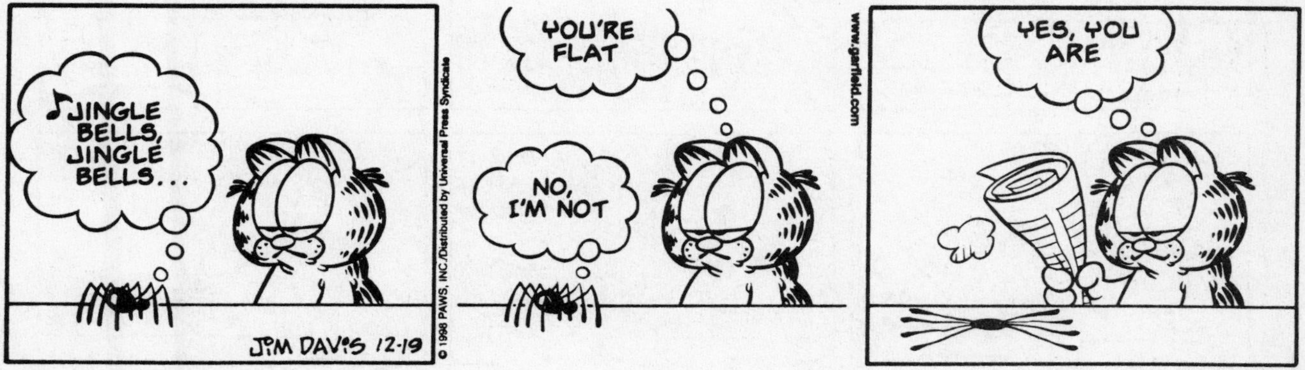
♪JINGLE BELLS, JINGLE BELLS...
JIM DAVIS 12-19
© 1998 PAWS, INC./Distributed by Universal Press Syndicate
YOU'RE FLAT
NO, I'M NOT
www.garfield.com
YES, YOU ARE

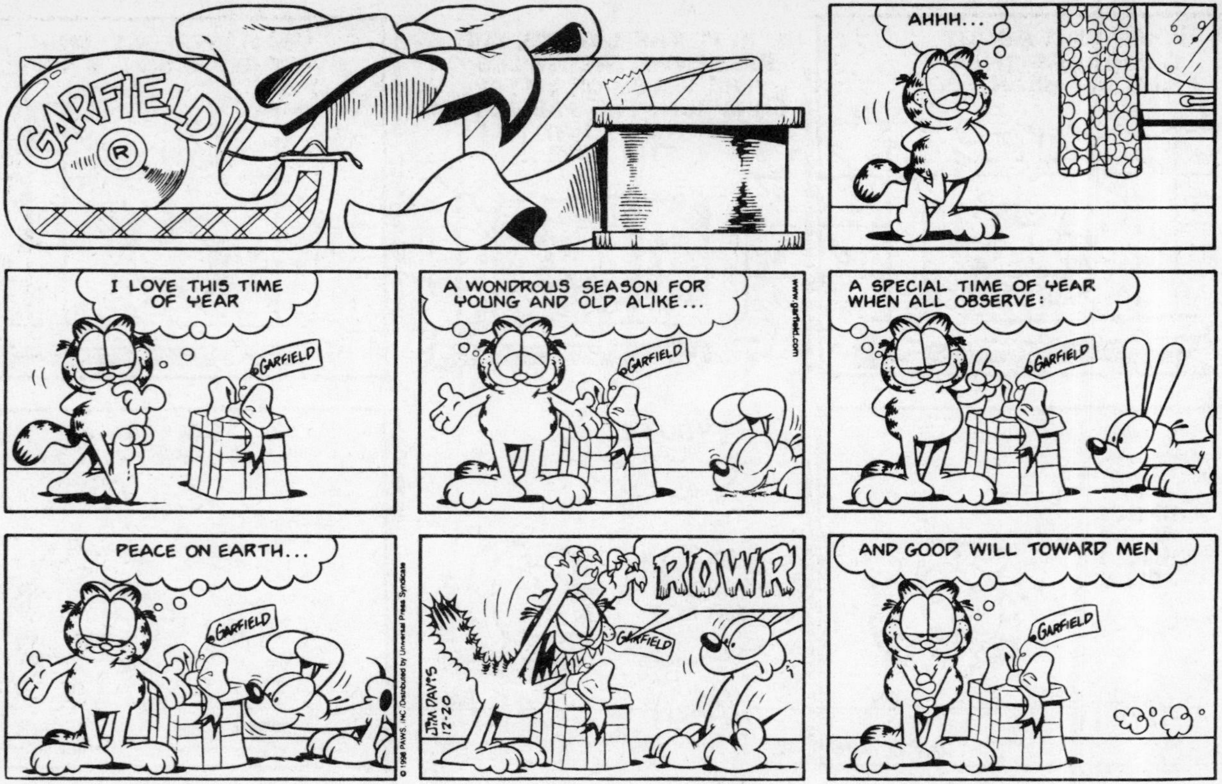
GARFIELD®
AHHH...
I LOVE THIS TIME OF YEAR
GARFIELD
A WONDROUS SEASON FOR YOUNG AND OLD ALIKE...
GARFIELD
www.garfield.com
A SPECIAL TIME OF YEAR WHEN ALL OBSERVE:
GARFIELD
PEACE ON EARTH...
GARFIELD
© 1998 PAWS, INC./Distributed by Universal Press Syndicate
JIM DAVIS 12-20
ROWR
GARFIELD
AND GOOD WILL TOWARD MEN
GARFIELD

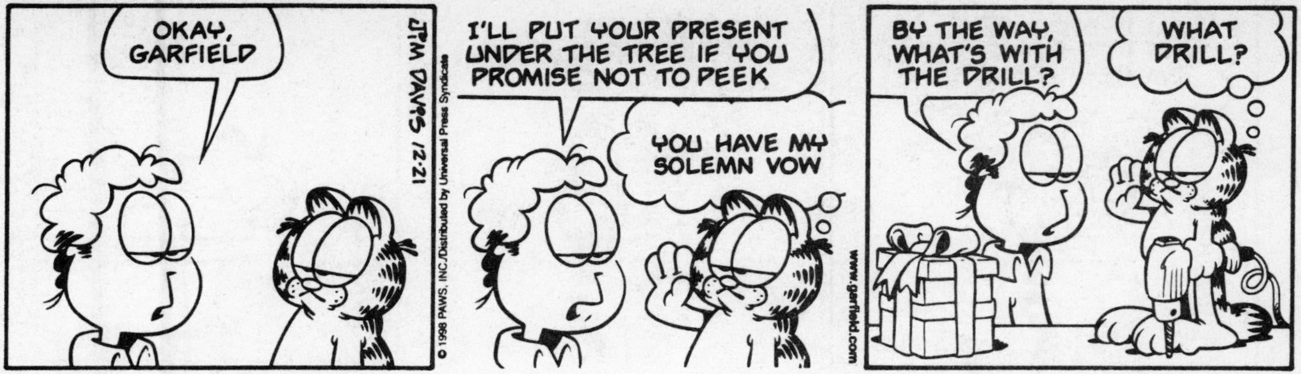
OKAY, GARFIELD
JIM DAVIS 12-21
© 1998 PAWS, INC./Distributed by Universal Press Syndicate
I'LL PUT YOUR PRESENT UNDER THE TREE IF YOU PROMISE NOT TO PEEK
YOU HAVE MY SOLEMN VOW
www.garfield.com
BY THE WAY, WHAT'S WITH THE DRILL?
WHAT DRILL?

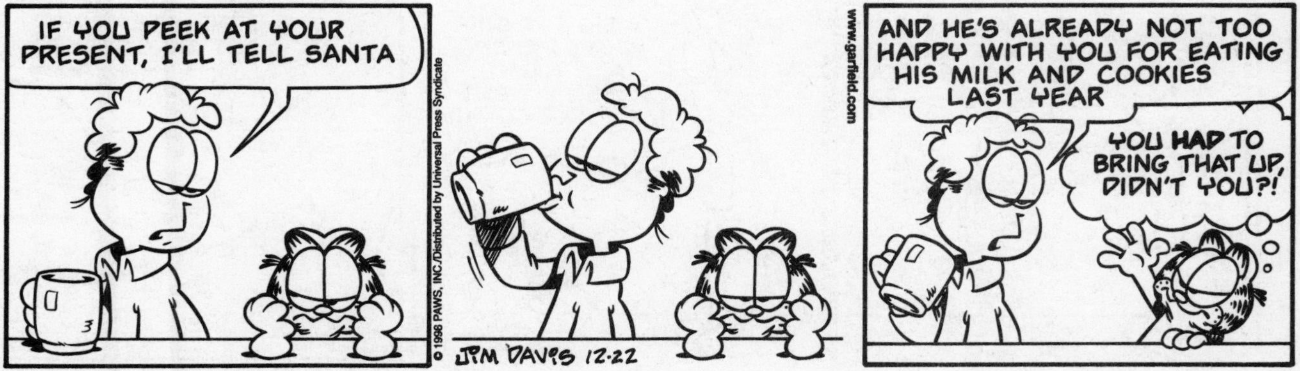
IF YOU PEEK AT YOUR PRESENT, I'LL TELL SANTA
© 1998 PAWS, INC./Distributed by Universal Press Syndicate
JIM DAVIS 12-22
www.garfield.com
AND HE'S ALREADY NOT TOO HAPPY WITH YOU FOR EATING HIS MILK AND COOKIES LAST YEAR
YOU HAD TO BRING THAT UP, DIDN'T YOU?!

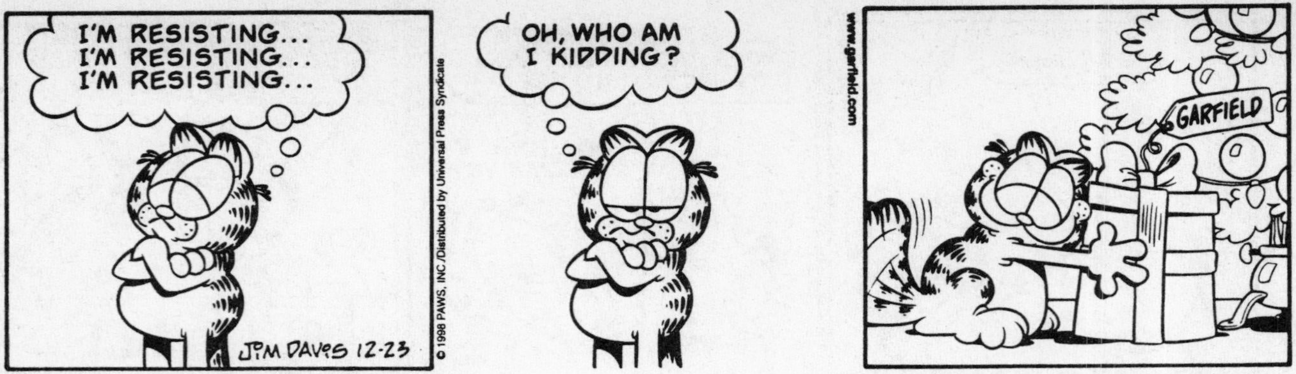
I'M RESISTING...
I'M RESISTING...
I'M RESISTING...
JIM DAVIS 12-23
© 1998 PAWS, INC./Distributed by Universal Press Syndicate
OH, WHO AM I KIDDING?
www.garfield.com
GARFIELD

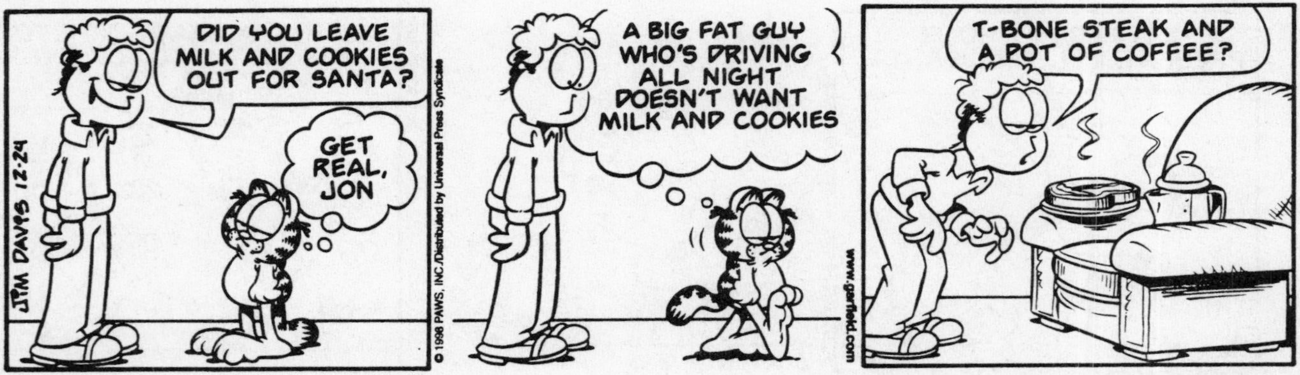
DID YOU LEAVE MILK AND COOKIES OUT FOR SANTA?
GET REAL, JON
JIM DAVIS 12-24
© 1998 PAWS, INC./Distributed by Universal Press Syndicate
A BIG FAT GUY WHO'S DRIVING ALL NIGHT DOESN'T WANT MILK AND COOKIES
www.garfield.com
T-BONE STEAK AND A POT OF COFFEE?

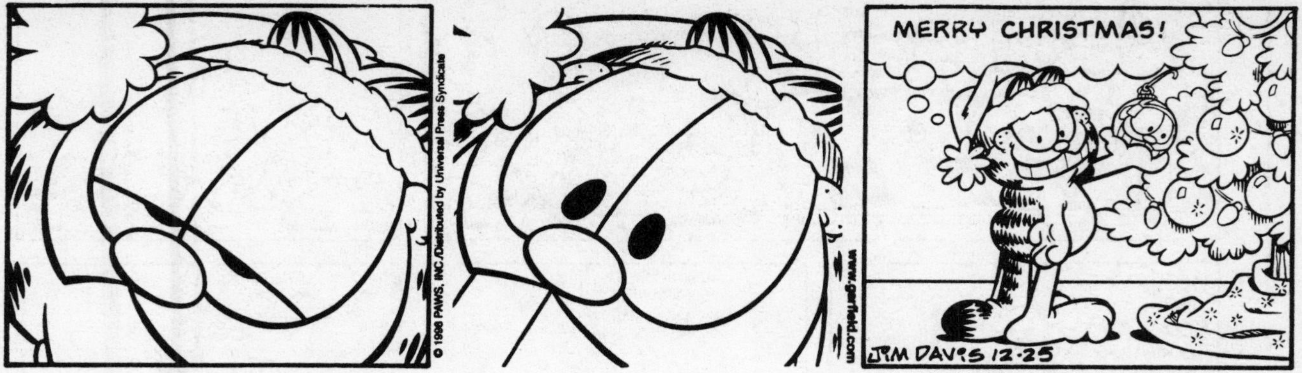
MERRY CHRISTMAS!
JIM DAVIS 12-25
© 1998 PAWS, INC./Distributed by Universal Press Syndicate
www.garfield.com

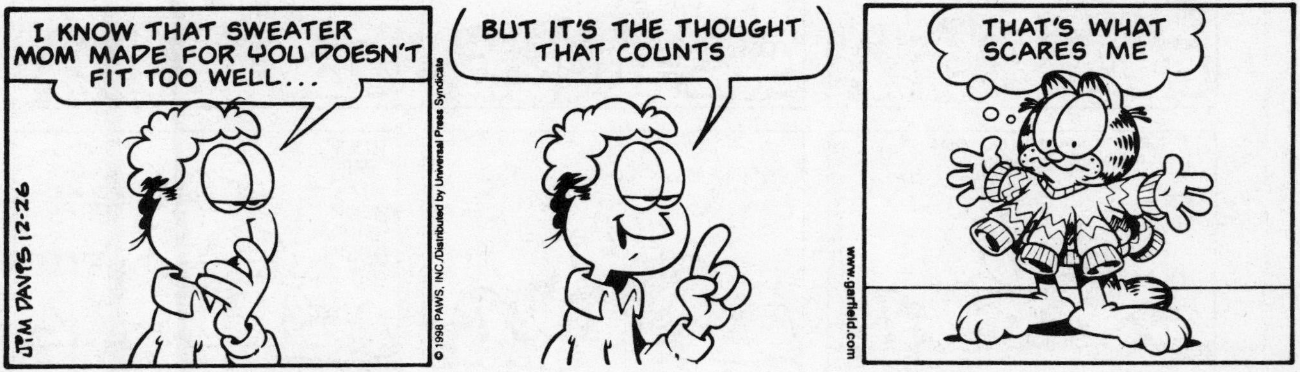
I KNOW THAT SWEATER MOM MADE FOR YOU DOESN'T FIT TOO WELL...
BUT IT'S THE THOUGHT THAT COUNTS
THAT'S WHAT SCARES ME
JIM DAVIS 12-26
© 1998 PAWS, INC./Distributed by Universal Press Syndicate
www.garfield.com

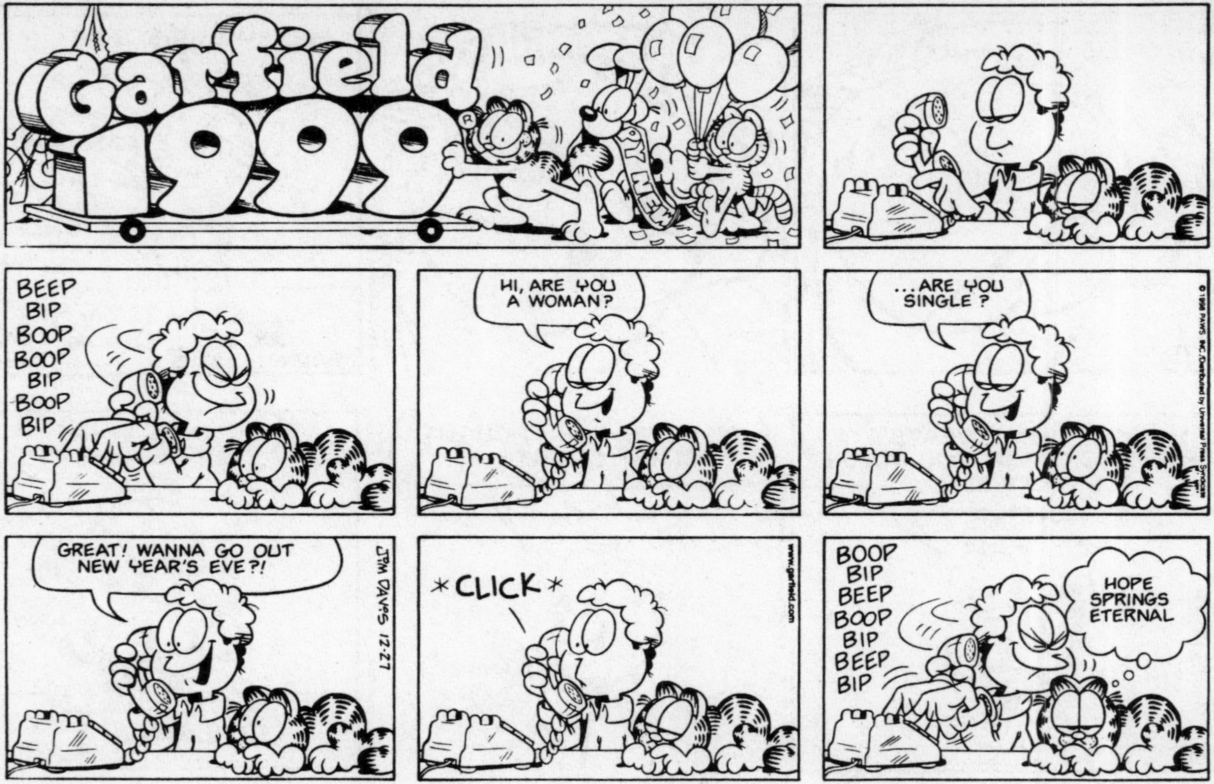
Garfield 1999
BEEP BIP BOOP BOOP BOOP BIP BOOP BIP
HI, ARE YOU A WOMAN?
...ARE YOU SINGLE?
© 1998 PAWS, INC./Distributed by Universal Press Syndicate
GREAT! WANNA GO OUT NEW YEAR'S EVE?!
JIM DAVIS 12-27
CLICK
www.garfield.com
BOOP BIP BEEP BOOP BIP BEEP BIP
HOPE SPRINGS ETERNAL

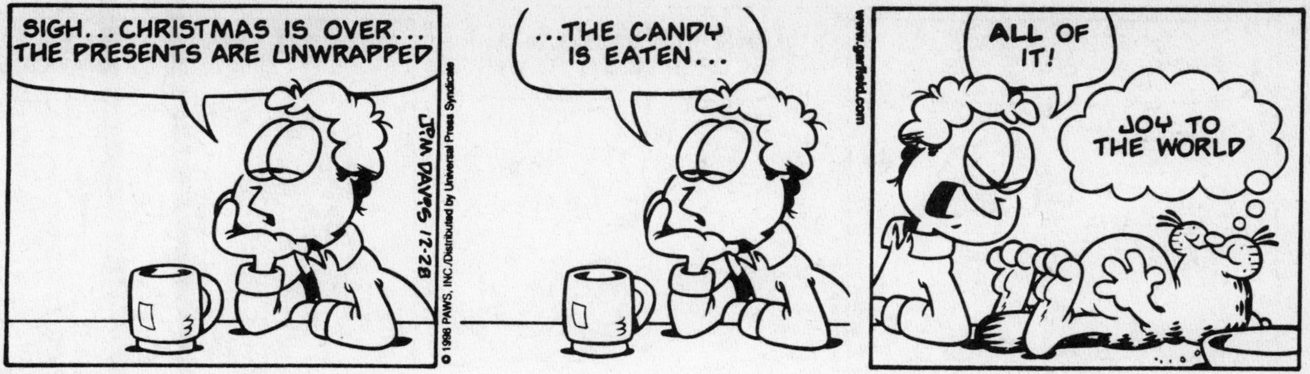
SIGH...CHRISTMAS IS OVER... THE PRESENTS ARE UNWRAPPED
...THE CANDY IS EATEN...
ALL OF IT!
JOY TO THE WORLD
JIM DAVIS 12-28
© 1998 PAWS, INC./Distributed by Universal Press Syndicate
www.garfield.com

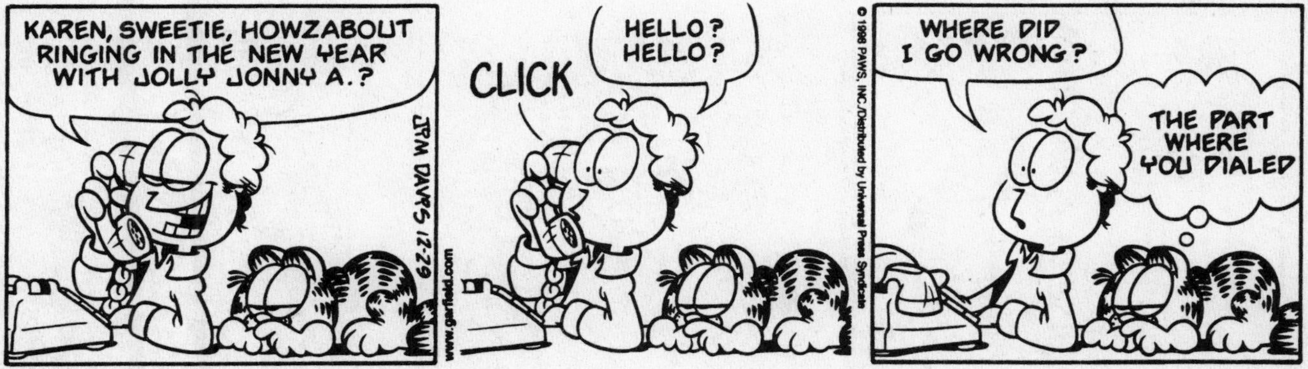
KAREN, SWEETIE, HOWZABOUT RINGING IN THE NEW YEAR WITH JOLLY JONNY A.?
CLICK
HELLO? HELLO?
WHERE DID I GO WRONG?
THE PART WHERE YOU DIALED
JIM DAVIS 12-29
www.garfield.com
© 1998 PAWS, INC./Distributed by Universal Press Syndicate

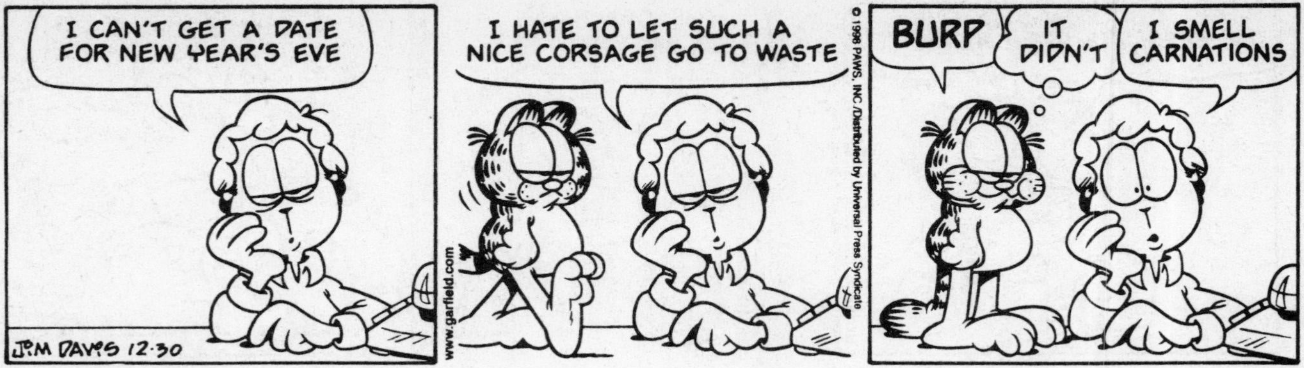
I CAN'T GET A DATE FOR NEW YEAR'S EVE
JIM DAVIS 12-30
www.garfield.com
I HATE TO LET SUCH A NICE CORSAGE GO TO WASTE
© 1998 PAWS, INC./Distributed by Universal Press Syndicate
BURP
IT DIDN'T
I SMELL CARNATIONS

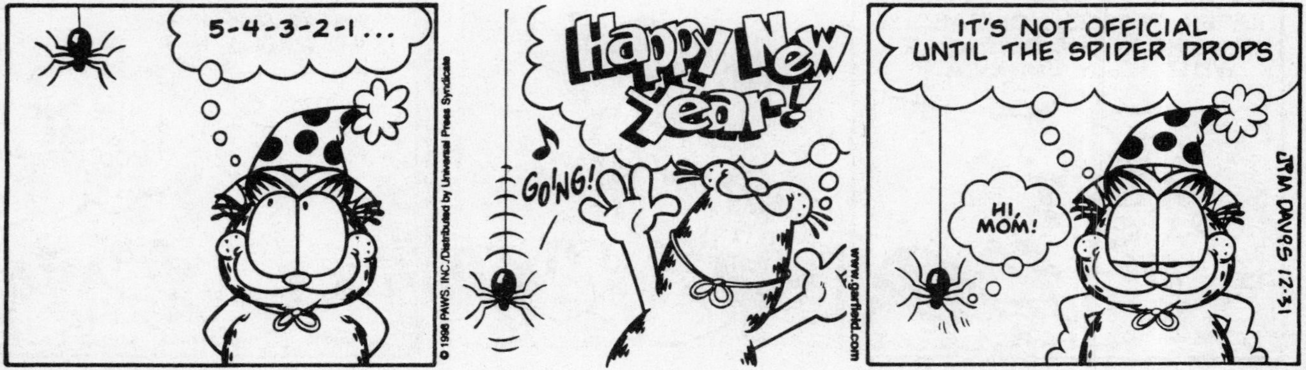
5-4-3-2-1...
© 1998 PAWS, INC./Distributed by Universal Press Syndicate
Happy New Year!
GONG!
www.garfield.com
IT'S NOT OFFICIAL UNTIL THE SPIDER DROPS
HI, MOM!
JIM DAVIS 12-31

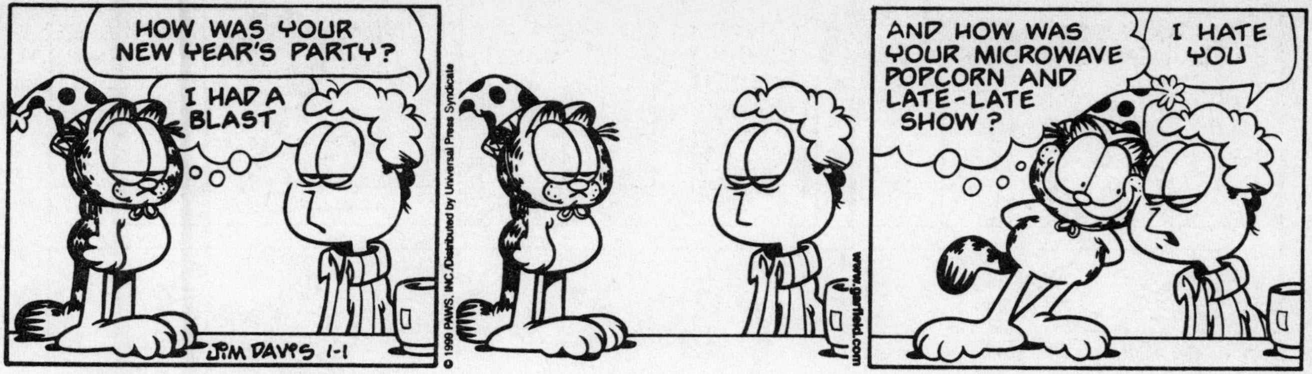
HOW WAS YOUR NEW YEAR'S PARTY?
I HAD A BLAST
JIM DAVIS 1-1
© 1999 PAWS, INC./Distributed by Universal Press Syndicate
www.garfield.com
AND HOW WAS YOUR MICROWAVE POPCORN AND LATE-LATE SHOW?
I HATE YOU

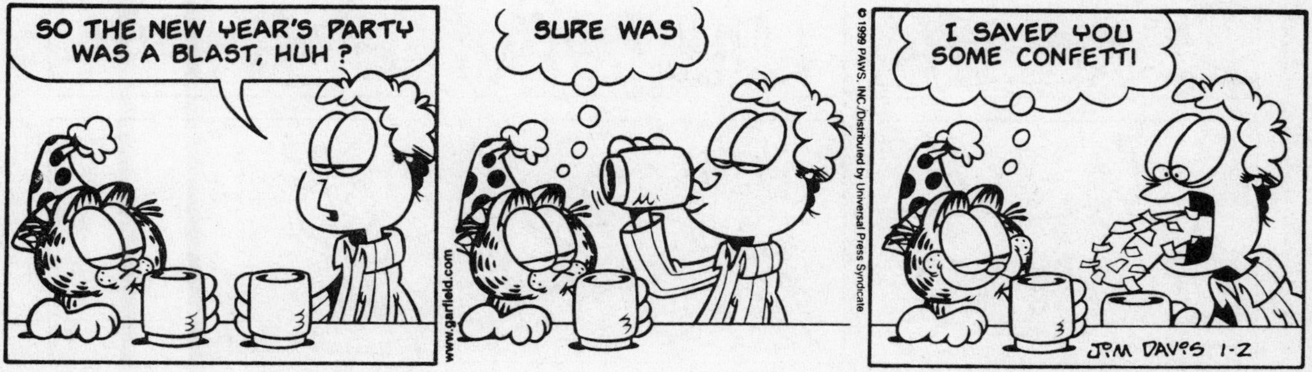
SO THE NEW YEAR'S PARTY WAS A BLAST, HUH?
www.garfield.com
SURE WAS
© 1999 PAWS, INC./Distributed by Universal Press Syndicate
I SAVED YOU SOME CONFETTI
JIM DAVIS 1-2

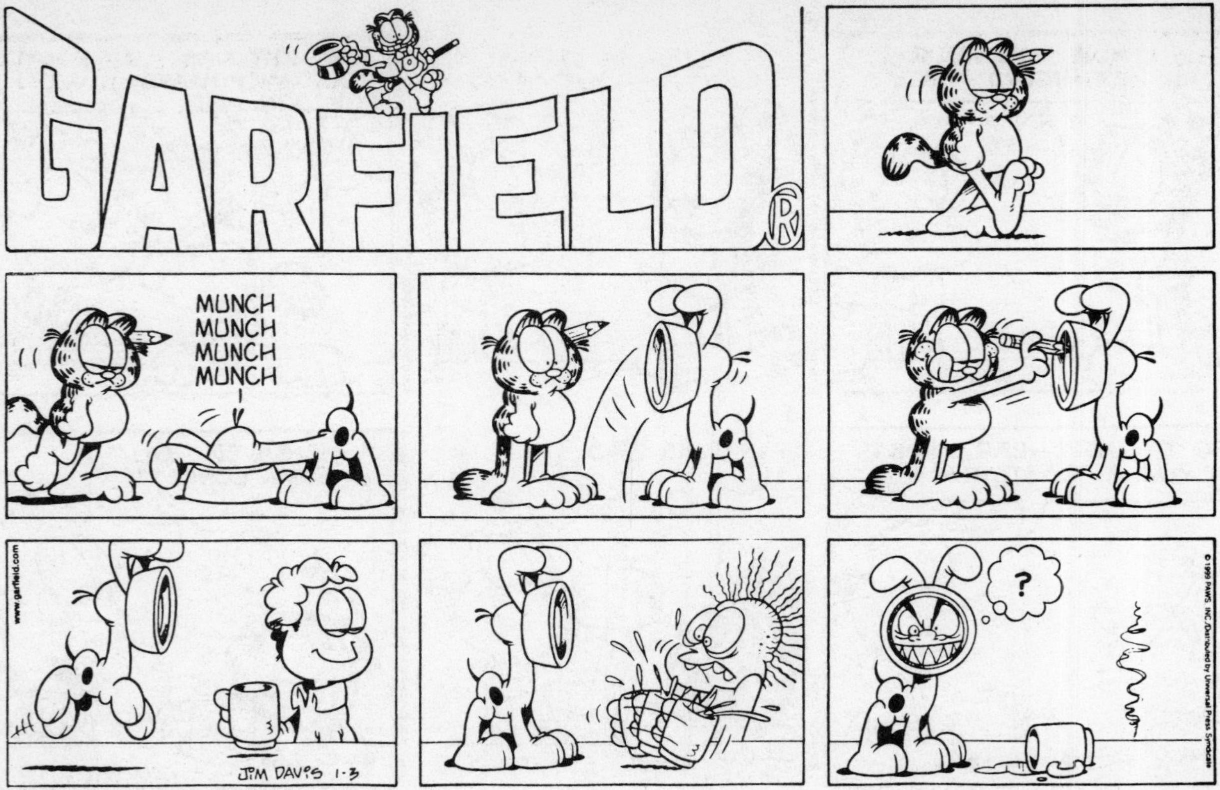
GARFIELD®
MUNCH
MUNCH
MUNCH
MUNCH
www.garfield.com
JIM DAVIS 1-3
?
© 1999 PAWS, INC./Distributed by Universal Press Syndicate

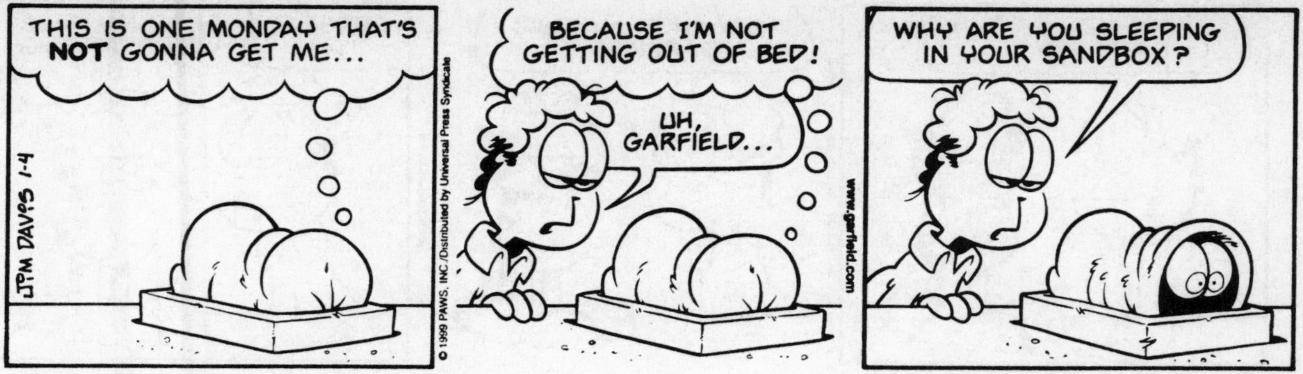
THIS IS ONE MONDAY THAT'S **NOT** GONNA GET ME...
JIM DAVIS 1-4
© 1999 PAWS, INC./Distributed by Universal Press Syndicate
BECAUSE I'M NOT GETTING OUT OF BED!
UH, GARFIELD...
www.garfield.com
WHY ARE YOU SLEEPING IN YOUR SANDBOX?

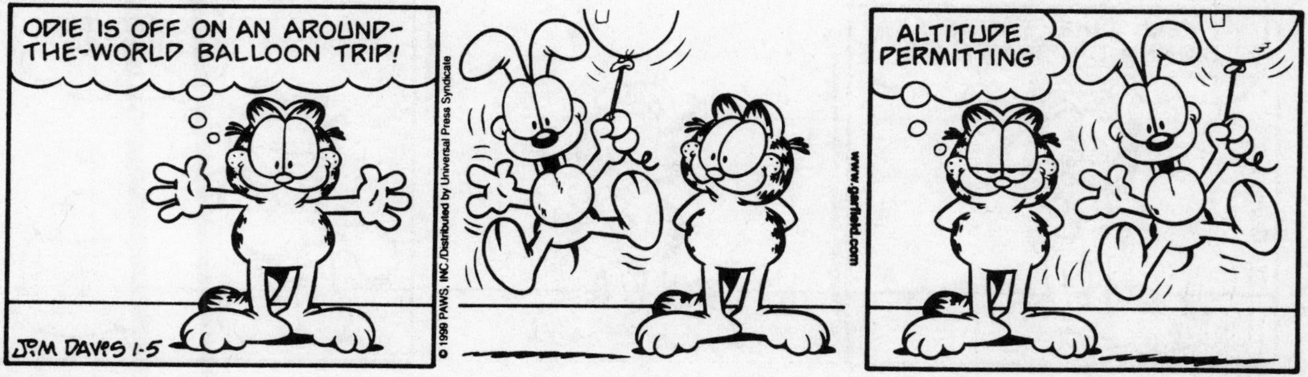
ODIE IS OFF ON AN AROUND-THE-WORLD BALLOON TRIP!
JIM DAVIS 1-5
© 1999 PAWS, INC./Distributed by Universal Press Syndicate
www.garfield.com
ALTITUDE PERMITTING

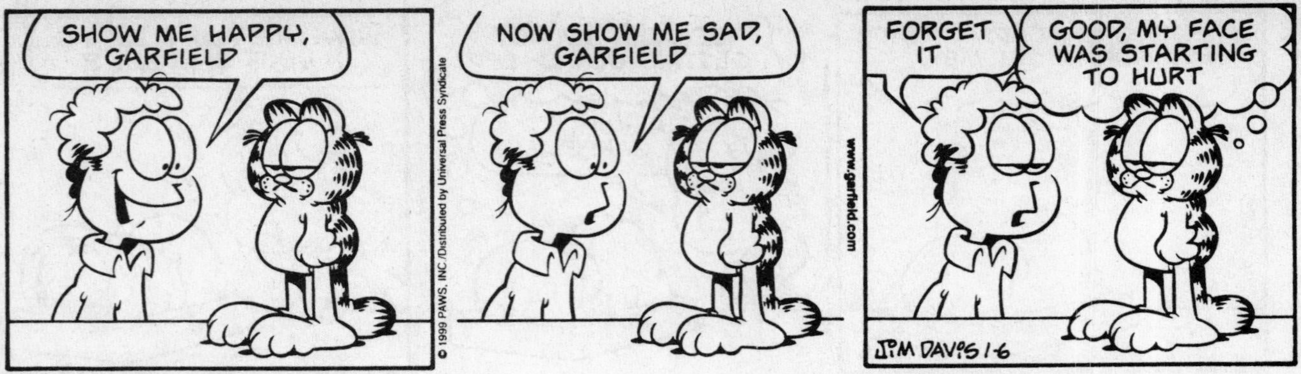
SHOW ME HAPPY, GARFIELD
NOW SHOW ME SAD, GARFIELD
© 1999 PAWS, INC./Distributed by Universal Press Syndicate
FORGET IT
GOOD, MY FACE WAS STARTING TO HURT
www.garfield.com
JIM DAVIS 1-6

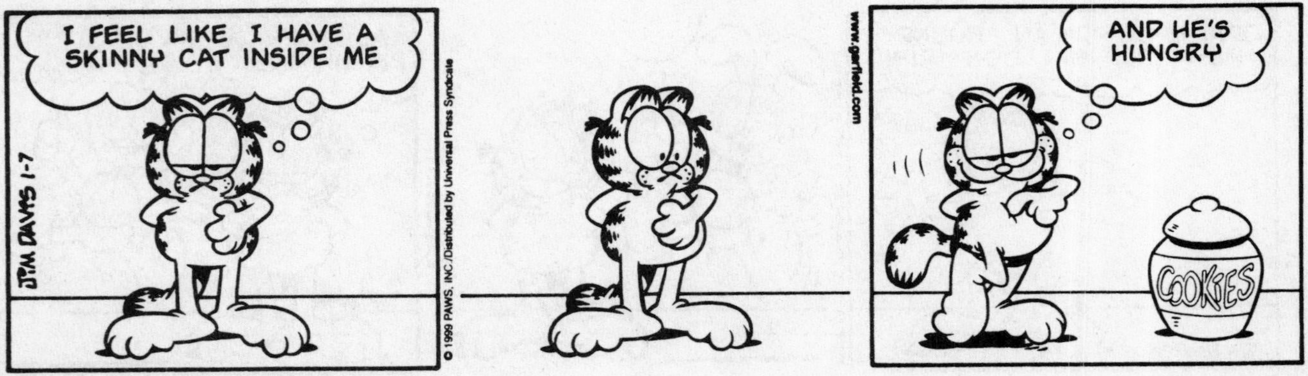
I FEEL LIKE I HAVE A SKINNY CAT INSIDE ME
JIM DAVIS 1-7
© 1999 PAWS, INC./Distributed by Universal Press Syndicate
www.garfield.com
AND HE'S HUNGRY
COOKIES

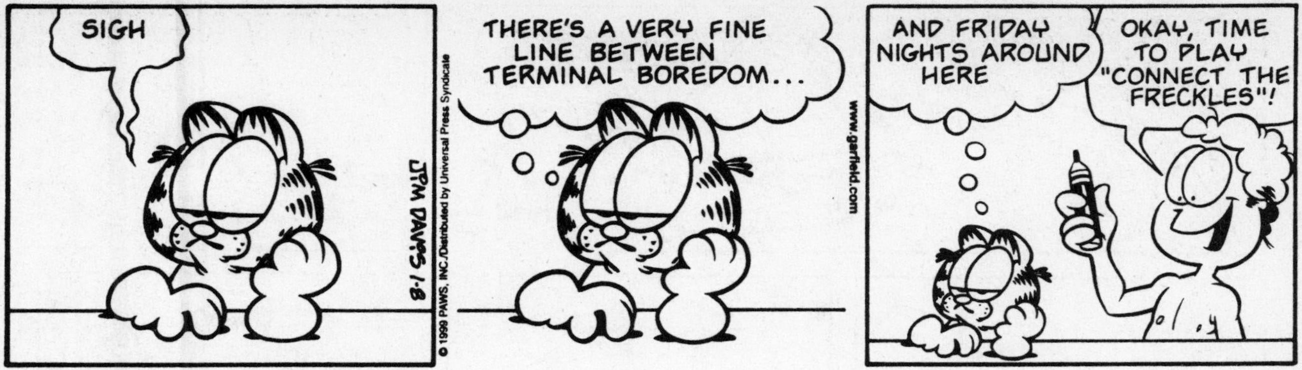
SIGH
JIM DAVIS 1-8
© 1999 PAWS, INC./Distributed by Universal Press Syndicate
THERE'S A VERY FINE LINE BETWEEN TERMINAL BOREDOM...
www.garfield.com
AND FRIDAY NIGHTS AROUND HERE
OKAY, TIME TO PLAY "CONNECT THE FRECKLES"!

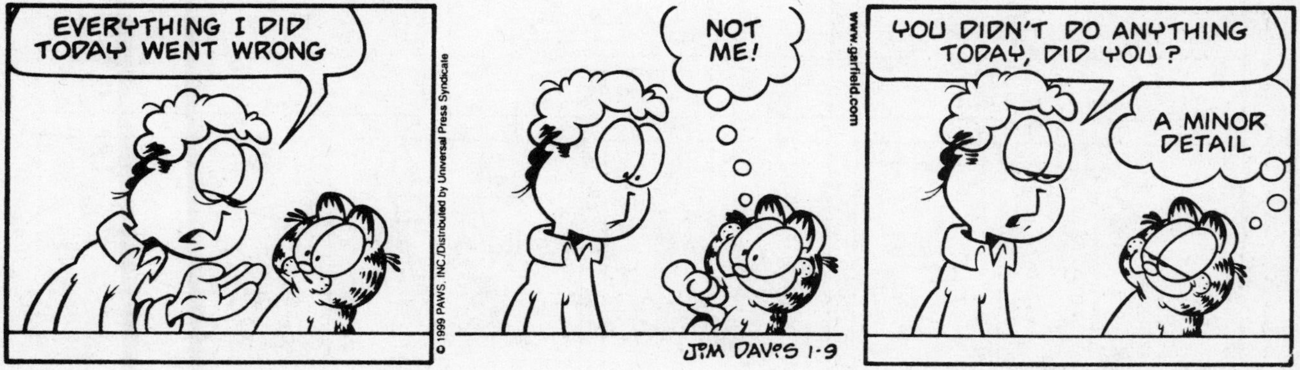
EVERYTHING I DID TODAY WENT WRONG
© 1999 PAWS, INC./Distributed by Universal Press Syndicate
NOT ME!
JIM DAVIS 1-9
www.garfield.com
YOU DIDN'T DO ANYTHING TODAY, DID YOU?
A MINOR DETAIL

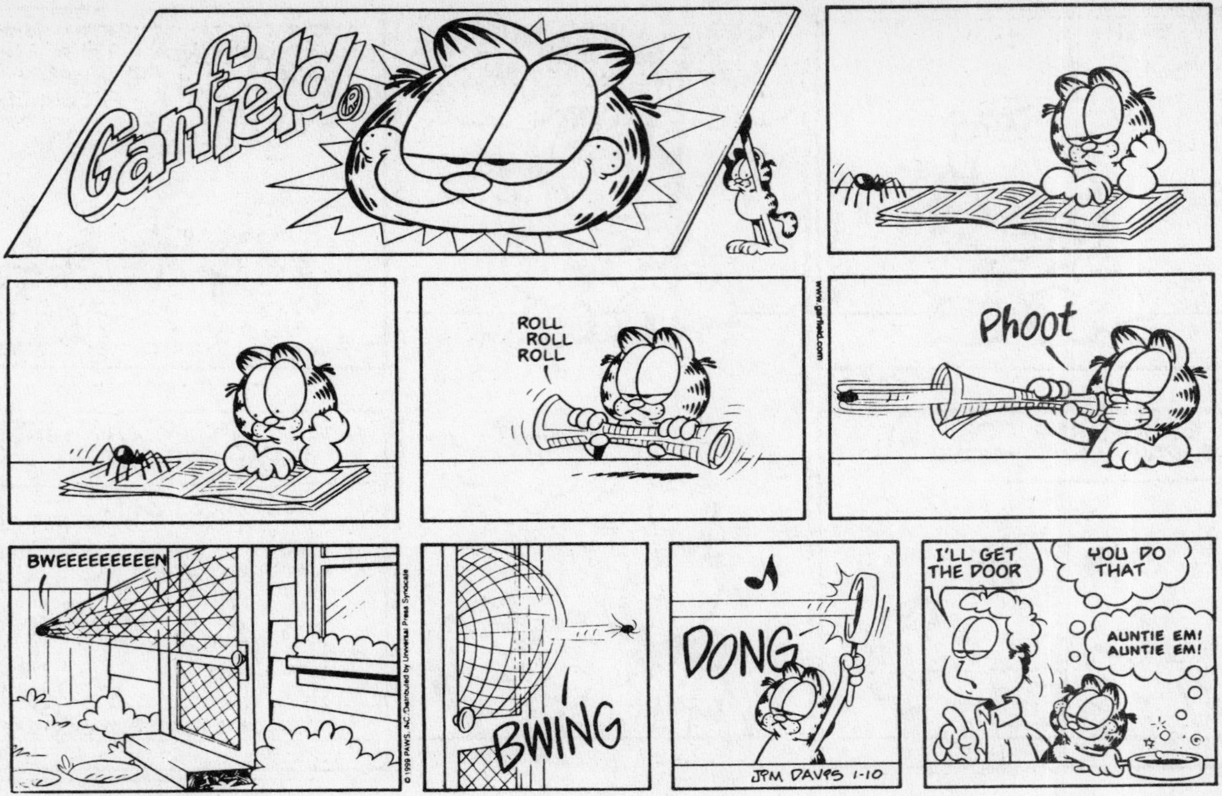
Garfield®
ROLL ROLL ROLL
Phoot
www.garfield.com
BWEEEEEEEEEN
© 1999 PAWS, INC. Distributed by Universal Press Syndicate
BWING
DONG
JIM DAVIS 1-10
I'LL GET THE DOOR
YOU DO THAT
AUNTIE EM! AUNTIE EM!

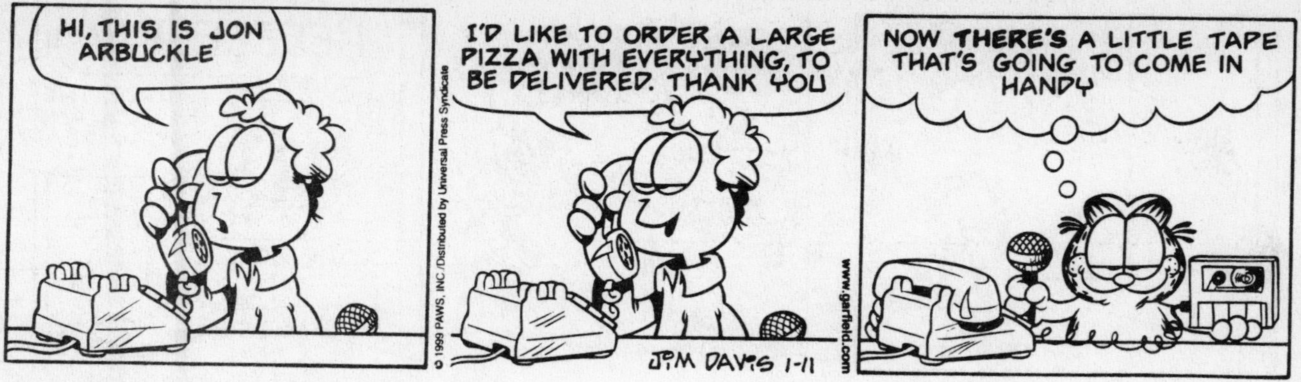
HI, THIS IS JON ARBUCKLE
I'D LIKE TO ORDER A LARGE PIZZA WITH EVERYTHING, TO BE DELIVERED. THANK YOU
NOW **THERE'S** A LITTLE TAPE THAT'S GOING TO COME IN HANDY
JIM DAVIS 1-11
© 1999 PAWS, INC./Distributed by Universal Press Syndicate
www.garfield.com

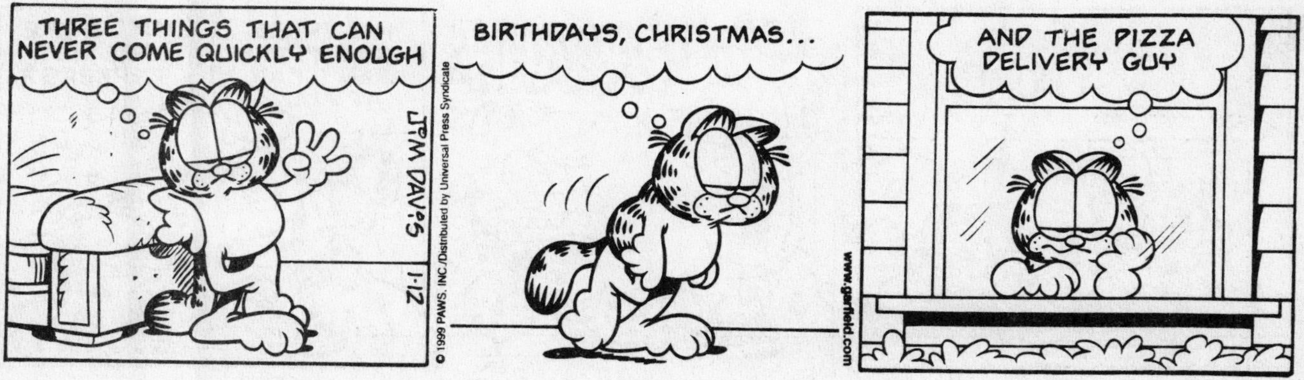
THREE THINGS THAT CAN NEVER COME QUICKLY ENOUGH
BIRTHDAYS, CHRISTMAS...
AND THE PIZZA DELIVERY GUY
JIM DAVIS 1-12
© 1999 PAWS, INC./Distributed by Universal Press Syndicate
www.garfield.com

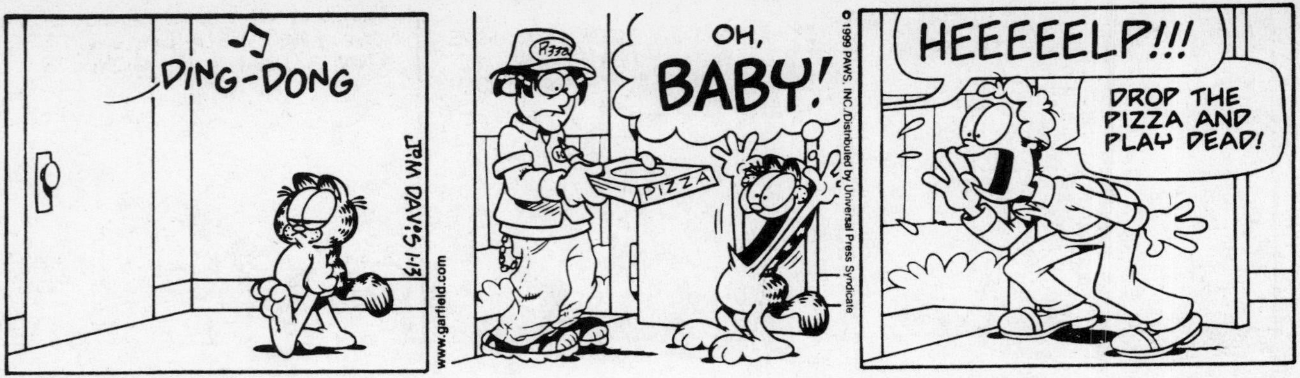
DING-DONG
JIM DAVIS 1-13
www.garfield.com
OH, BABY!
PIZZA
© 1999 PAWS, INC./Distributed by Universal Press Syndicate
HEEEEELP!!!
DROP THE PIZZA AND PLAY DEAD!

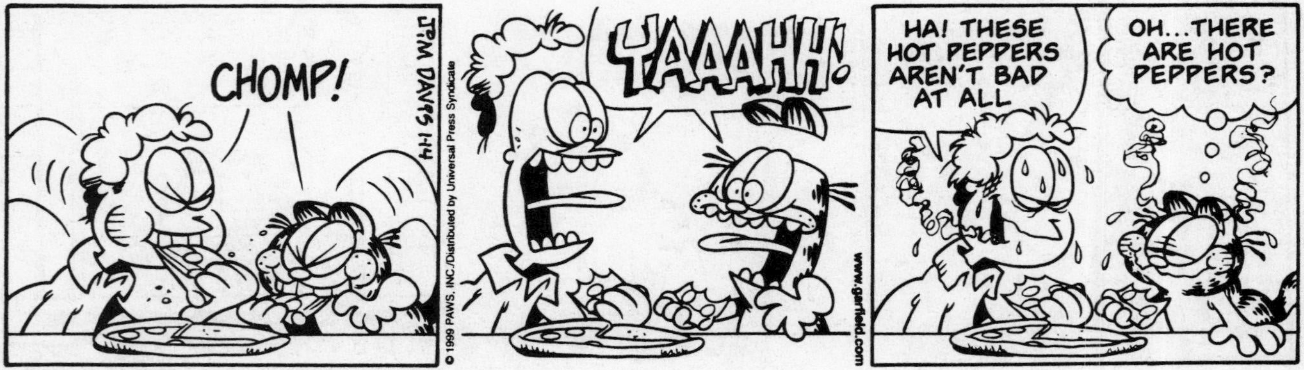
CHOMP!
JIM DAVIS 1-14
© 1999 PAWS, INC./Distributed by Universal Press Syndicate
YAAAHH!
www.garfield.com
HA! THESE HOT PEPPERS AREN'T BAD AT ALL
OH...THERE ARE HOT PEPPERS?

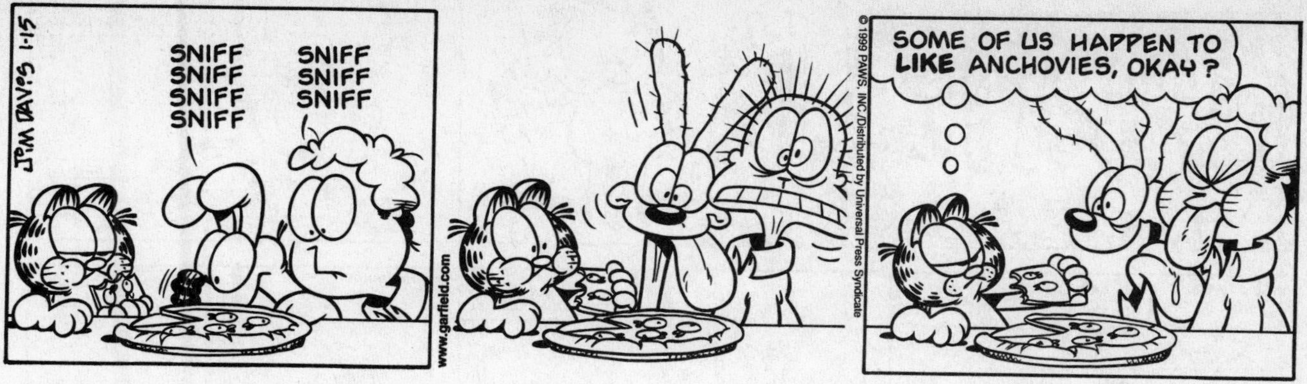
JIM DAVIS 1-15
SNIFF SNIFF SNIFF SNIFF
SNIFF SNIFF SNIFF
www.garfield.com
© 1999 PAWS, INC./Distributed by Universal Press Syndicate
SOME OF US HAPPEN TO LIKE ANCHOVIES, OKAY?

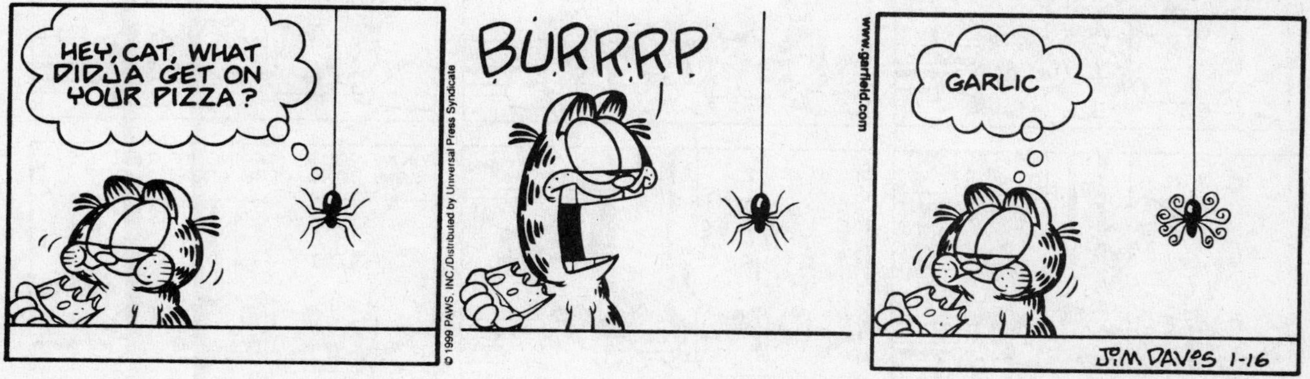
HEY, CAT, WHAT DIDJA GET ON YOUR PIZZA?
© 1999 PAWS, INC./Distributed by Universal Press Syndicate
BURRRP
www.garfield.com
GARLIC
JIM DAVIS 1-16

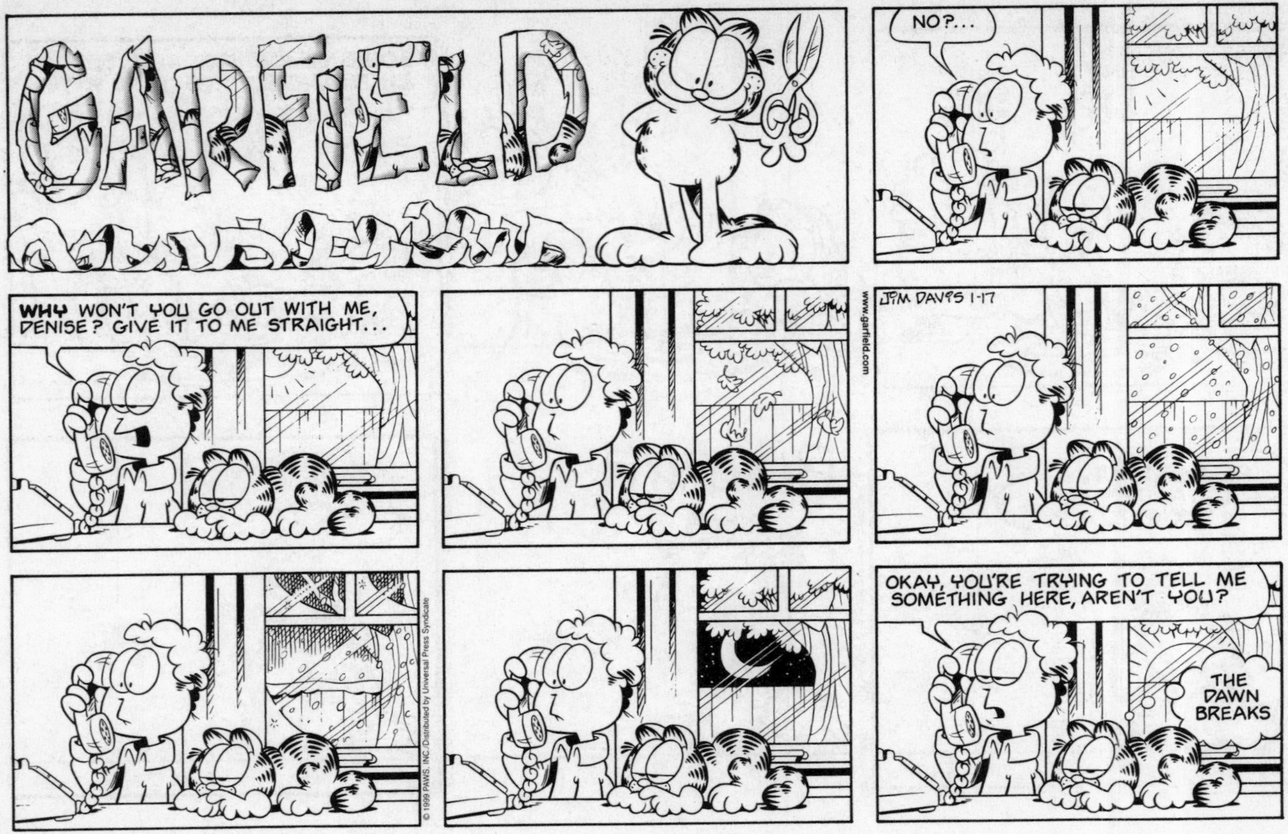
GARFIELD
NO?...
JIM DAVIS 1-17
WHY WON'T YOU GO OUT WITH ME, DENISE? GIVE IT TO ME STRAIGHT...
www.garfield.com
© 1999 PAWS, INC./Distributed by Universal Press Syndicate
OKAY, YOU'RE TRYING TO TELL ME SOMETHING HERE, AREN'T YOU?
THE DAWN BREAKS

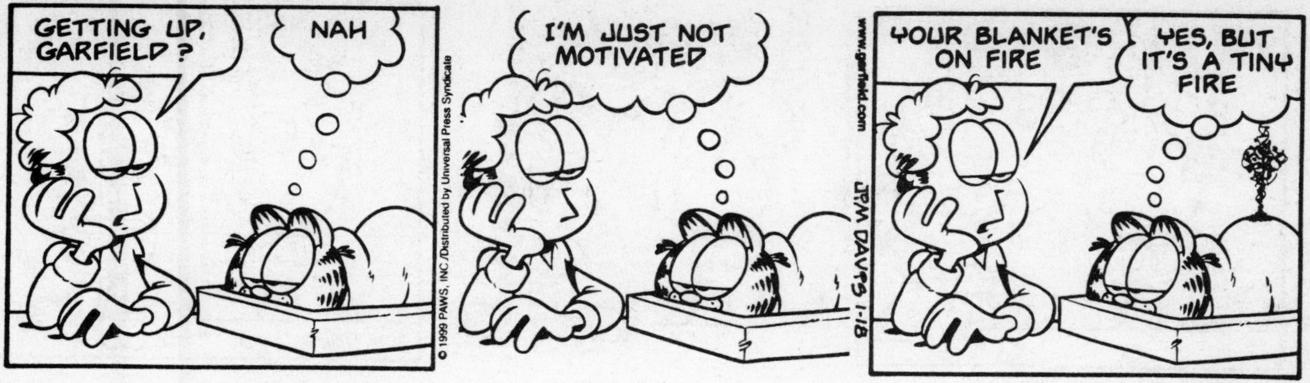
GETTING UP, GARFIELD?
NAH
I'M JUST NOT MOTIVATED
YOUR BLANKET'S ON FIRE
YES, BUT IT'S A TINY FIRE
© 1999 PAWS, INC./Distributed by Universal Press Syndicate
JIM DAVIS 1-18
www.garfield.com

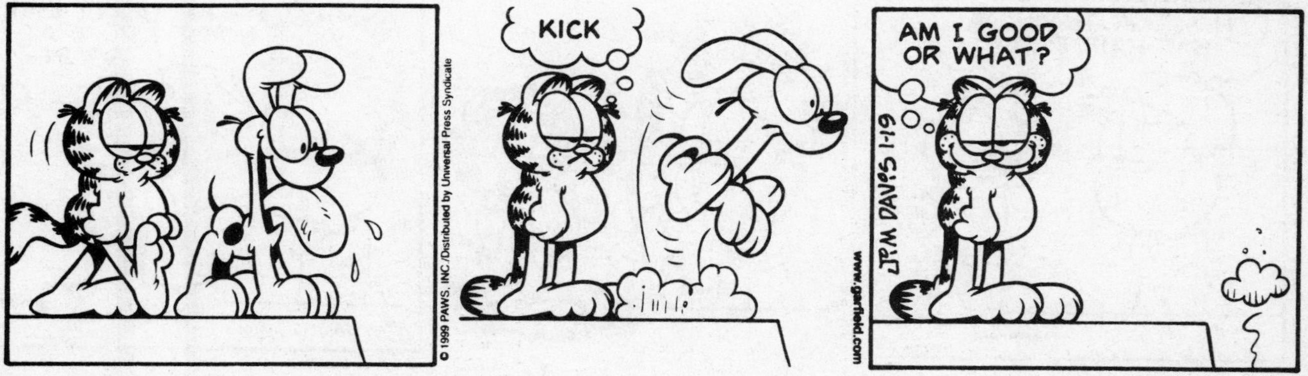
KICK
AM I GOOD OR WHAT?
© 1999 PAWS, INC./Distributed by Universal Press Syndicate
JIM DAVIS 1-19
www.garfield.com

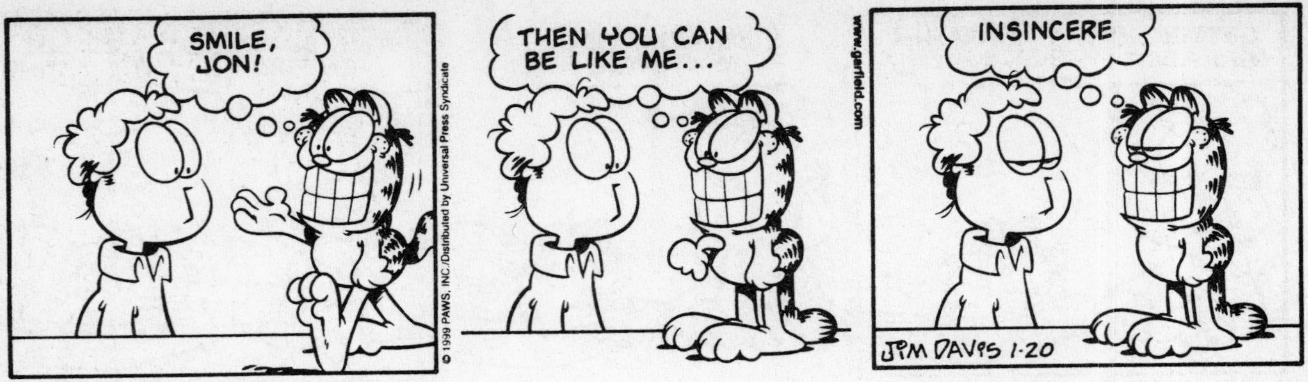
SMILE, JON!
THEN YOU CAN BE LIKE ME...
INSINCERE
JIM DAVIS 1-20
© 1999 PAWS, INC./Distributed by Universal Press Syndicate
www.garfield.com

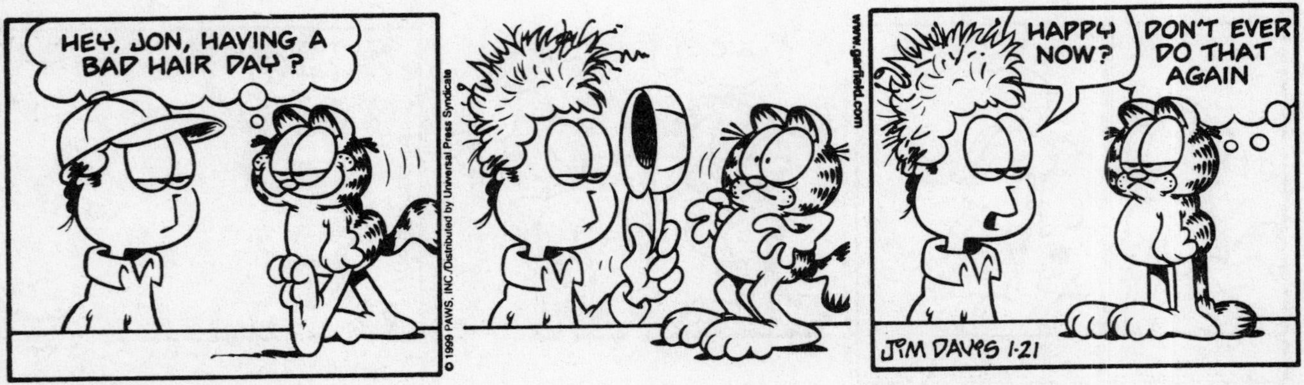
HEY, JON, HAVING A BAD HAIR DAY?
HAPPY NOW?
DON'T EVER DO THAT AGAIN
JIM DAVIS 1-21
© 1999 PAWS, INC./Distributed by Universal Press Syndicate
www.garfield.com

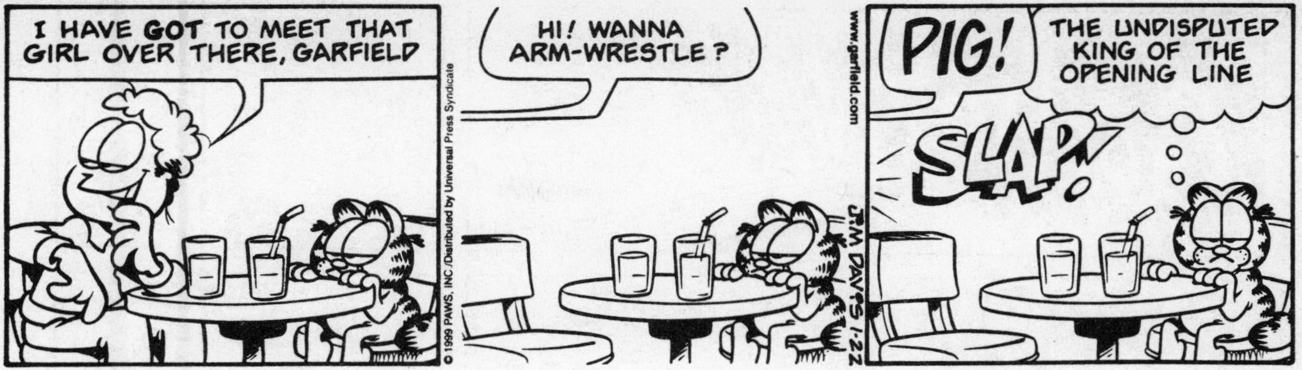
I HAVE GOT TO MEET THAT GIRL OVER THERE, GARFIELD
© 1999 PAWS, INC./Distributed by Universal Press Syndicate
HI! WANNA ARM-WRESTLE?
www.garfield.com
JPM DAVPS 1-22
PIG!
SLAP!
THE UNDISPUTED KING OF THE OPENING LINE

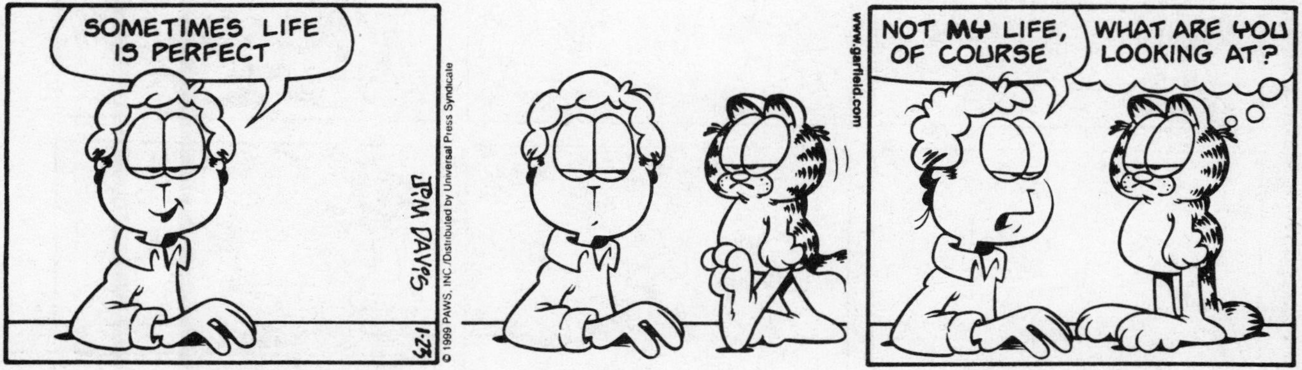
SOMETIMES LIFE IS PERFECT
JPM DAVPS 1-23
© 1999 PAWS, INC./Distributed by Universal Press Syndicate
www.garfield.com
NOT MY LIFE, OF COURSE
WHAT ARE YOU LOOKING AT?

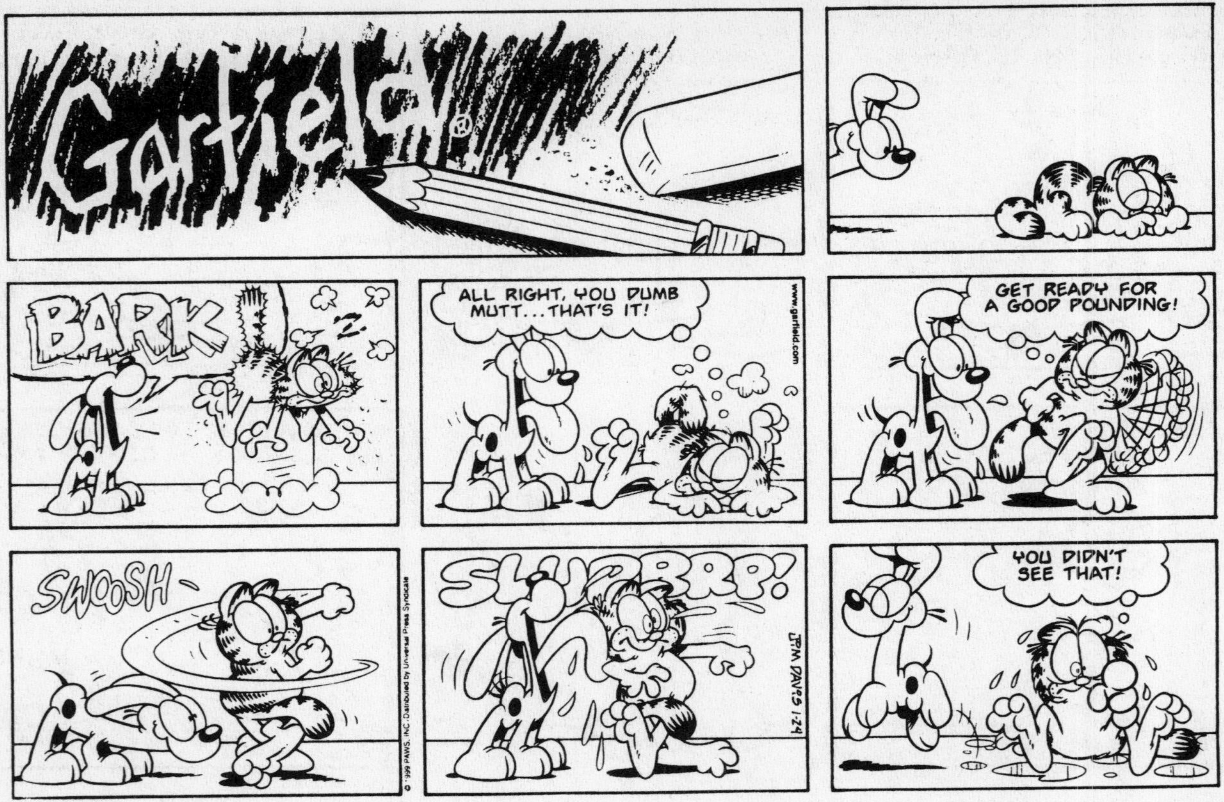
Garfield®
BARK
ALL RIGHT, YOU DUMB MUTT...THAT'S IT!
www.garfield.com
GET READY FOR A GOOD POUNDING!
SWOOSH
SLURRP!
JIM DAVIS 1-24
YOU DIDN'T SEE THAT!
© 1999 PAWS, INC. Distributed by Universal Press Syndicate

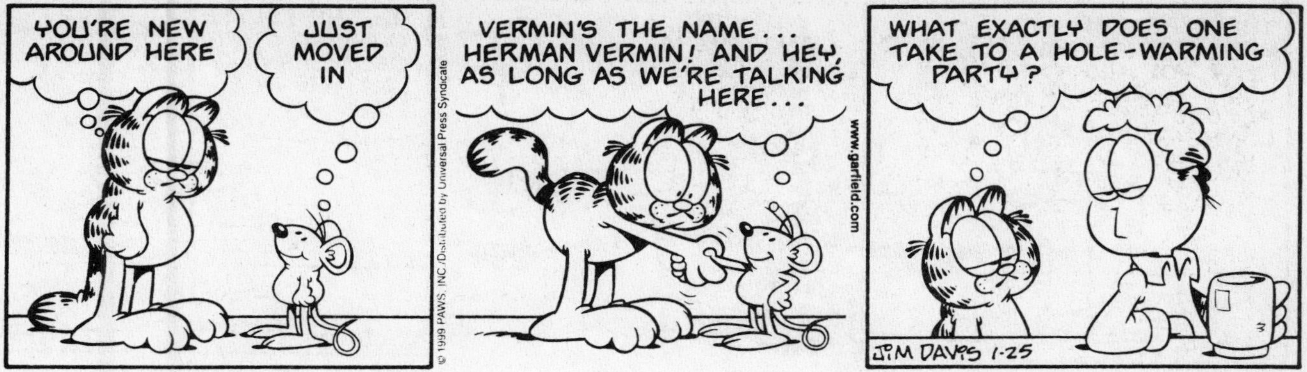
YOU'RE NEW AROUND HERE
JUST MOVED IN
VERMIN'S THE NAME... HERMAN VERMIN! AND HEY, AS LONG AS WE'RE TALKING HERE...
WHAT EXACTLY DOES ONE TAKE TO A HOLE-WARMING PARTY?
JIM DAVIS 1-25
© 1999 PAWS, INC./Distributed by Universal Press Syndicate
www.garfield.com

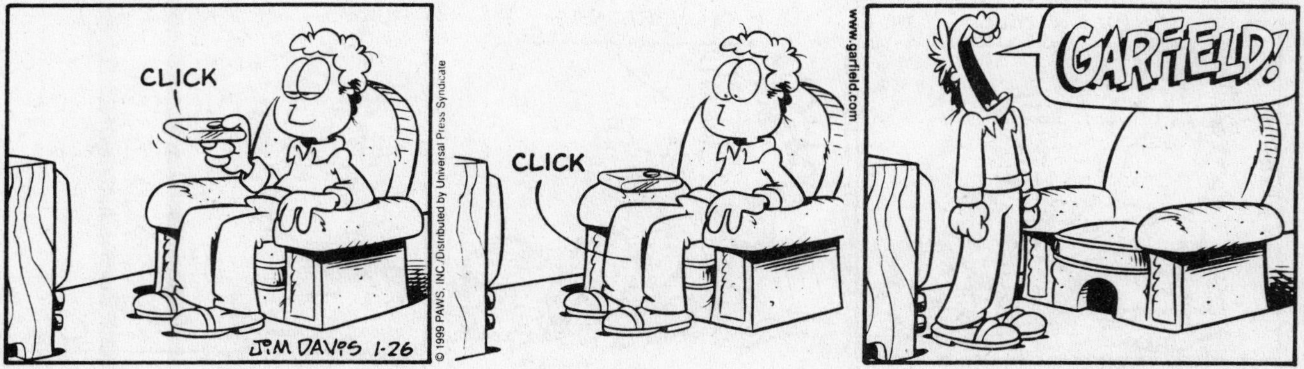
CLICK
JIM DAVIS 1-26
© 1999 PAWS, INC./Distributed by Universal Press Syndicate
CLICK
www.garfield.com
GARFIELD!

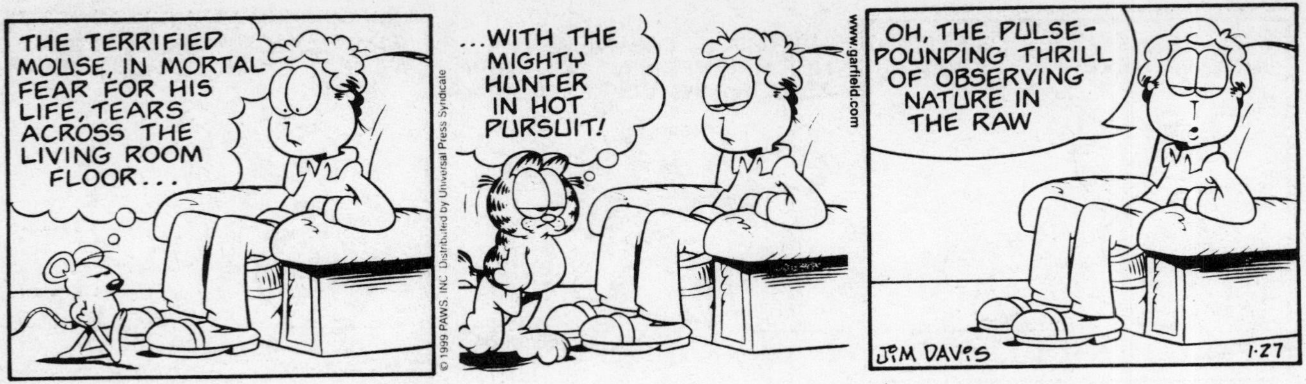
THE TERRIFIED MOUSE, IN MORTAL FEAR FOR HIS LIFE, TEARS ACROSS THE LIVING ROOM FLOOR...
© 1999 PAWS, INC Distributed by Universal Press Syndicate
...WITH THE MIGHTY HUNTER IN HOT PURSUIT!
www.garfield.com
OH, THE PULSE-POUNDING THRILL OF OBSERVING NATURE IN THE RAW
JIM DAVIS 1·27

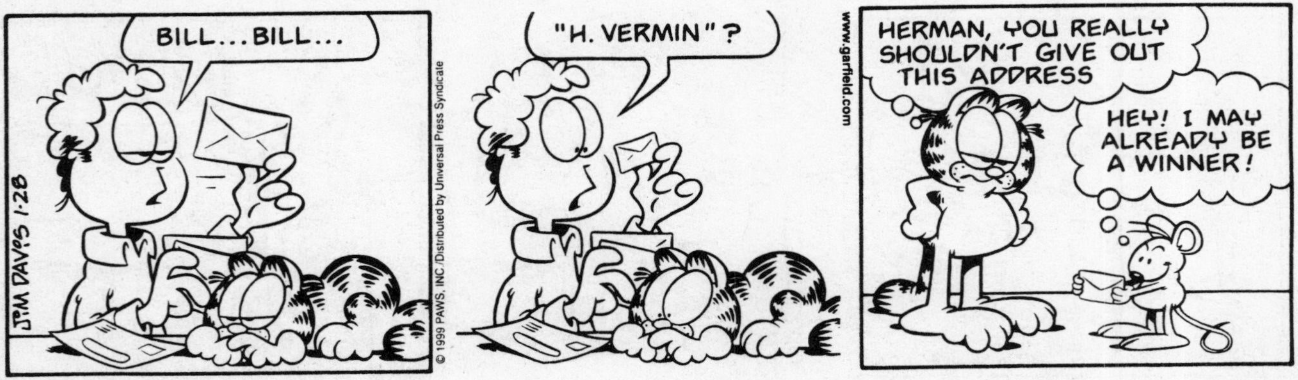
BILL... BILL...
JIM DAVIS 1·28
© 1999 PAWS, INC./Distributed by Universal Press Syndicate
"H. VERMIN"?
www.garfield.com
HERMAN, YOU REALLY SHOULDN'T GIVE OUT THIS ADDRESS
HEY! I MAY ALREADY BE A WINNER!

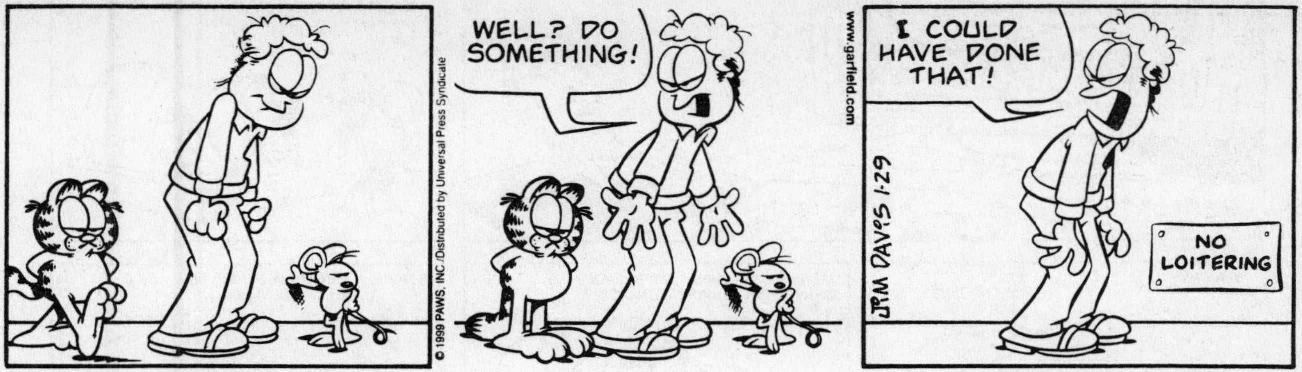
WELL? DO SOMETHING!
© 1999 PAWS, INC./Distributed by Universal Press Syndicate
www.garfield.com
JPM DAVPS 1-29
I COULD HAVE DONE THAT!
NO LOITERING

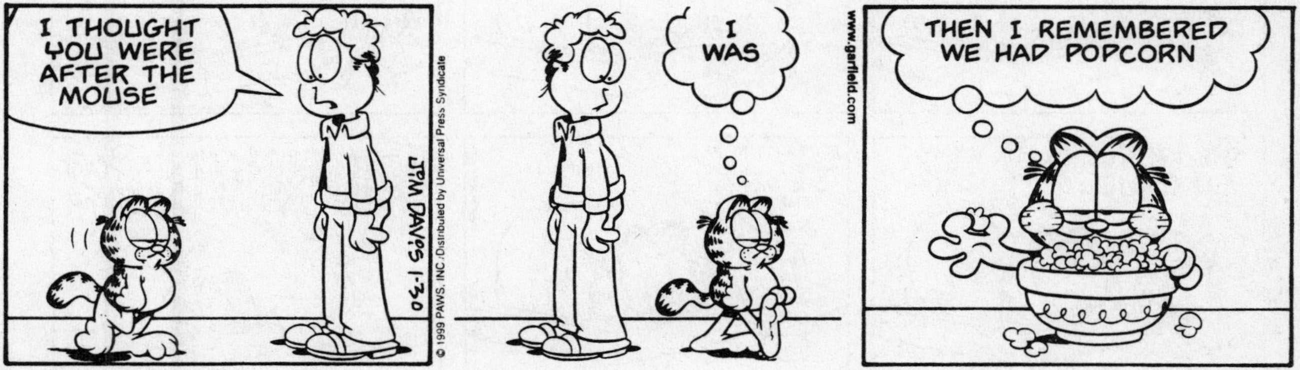
I THOUGHT YOU WERE AFTER THE MOUSE
JPM DAVPS 1-30
© 1999 PAWS, INC./Distributed by Universal Press Syndicate
I WAS
www.garfield.com
THEN I REMEMBERED WE HAD POPCORN

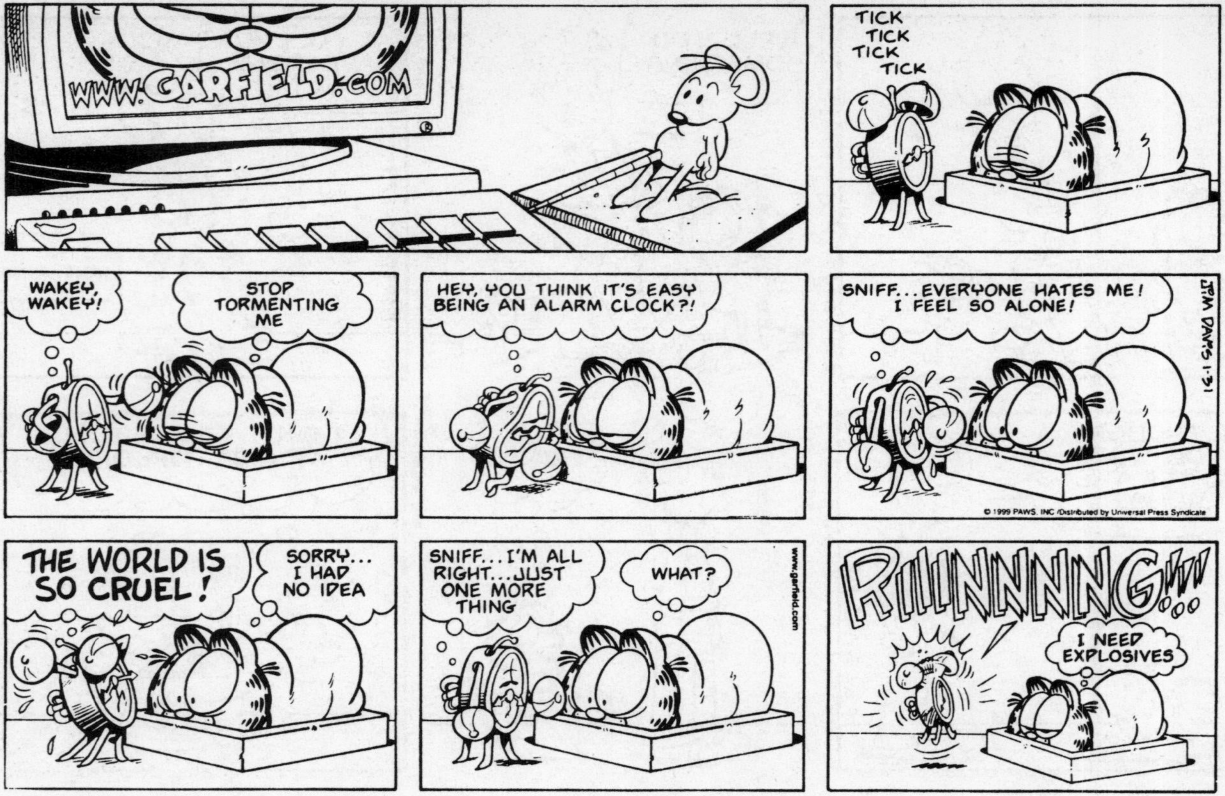
WWW.GARFIELD.COM
TICK
TICK
TICK
TICK
WAKEY, WAKEY!
STOP TORMENTING ME
HEY, YOU THINK IT'S EASY BEING AN ALARM CLOCK?!
SNIFF... EVERYONE HATES ME! I FEEL SO ALONE!
JPM DAVIS 1-31
© 1999 PAWS, INC./Distributed by Universal Press Syndicate
THE WORLD IS SO CRUEL!
SORRY... I HAD NO IDEA
www.garfield.com
SNIFF... I'M ALL RIGHT... JUST ONE MORE THING
WHAT?
RIIINNNNG!!!
I NEED EXPLOSIVES

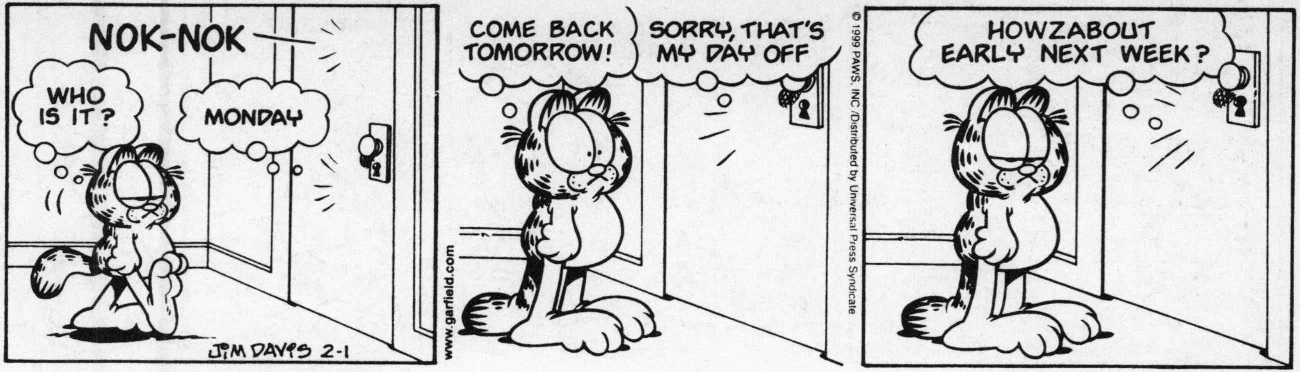
NOK-NOK
WHO IS IT?
MONDAY
JIM DAVIS 2-1
www.garfield.com
COME BACK TOMORROW!
SORRY, THAT'S MY DAY OFF
© 1999 PAWS, INC./Distributed by Universal Press Syndicate
HOWZABOUT EARLY NEXT WEEK?

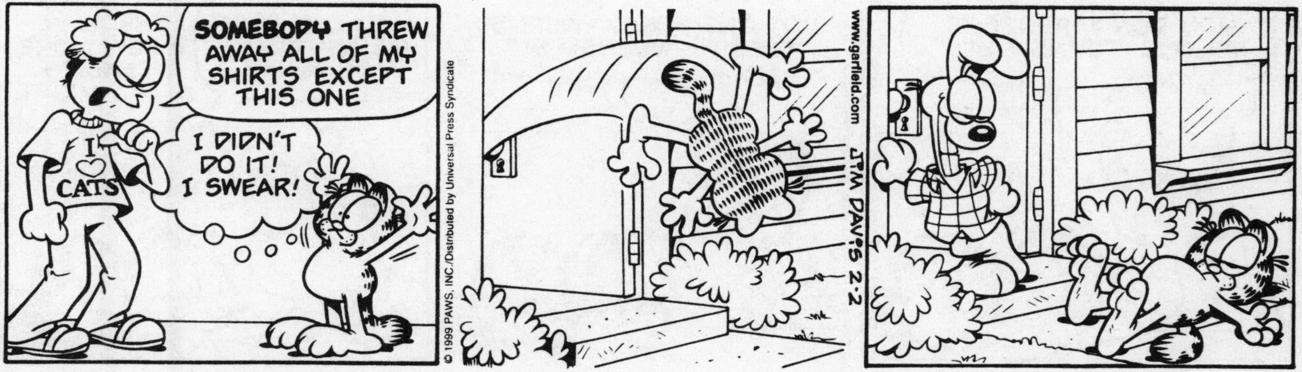
SOMEBODY THREW AWAY ALL OF MY SHIRTS EXCEPT THIS ONE
I ♥ CATS
I DIDN'T DO IT! I SWEAR!
© 1999 PAWS, INC./Distributed by Universal Press Syndicate
www.garfield.com
JIM DAVIS 2-2

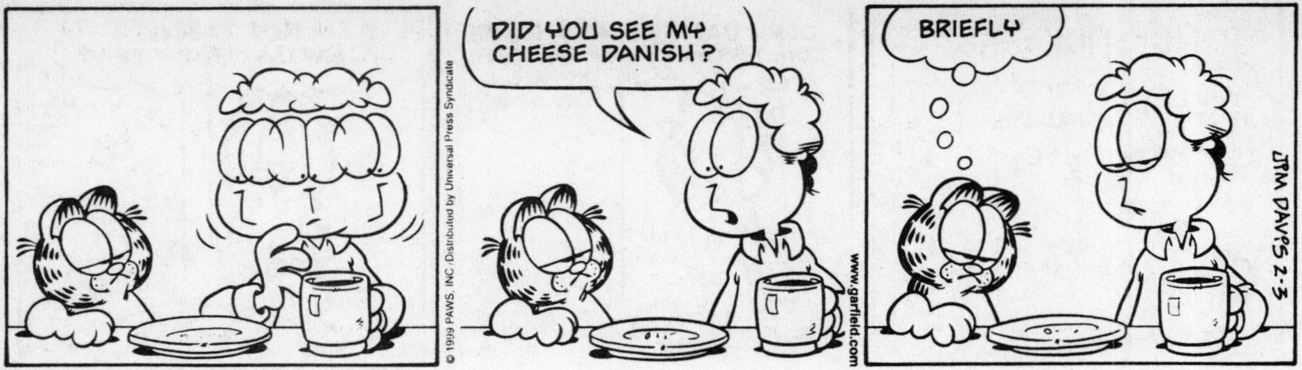
DID YOU SEE MY CHEESE DANISH?
BRIEFLY
JIM DAVIS 2-3
© 1999 PAWS, INC./Distributed by Universal Press Syndicate
www.garfield.com

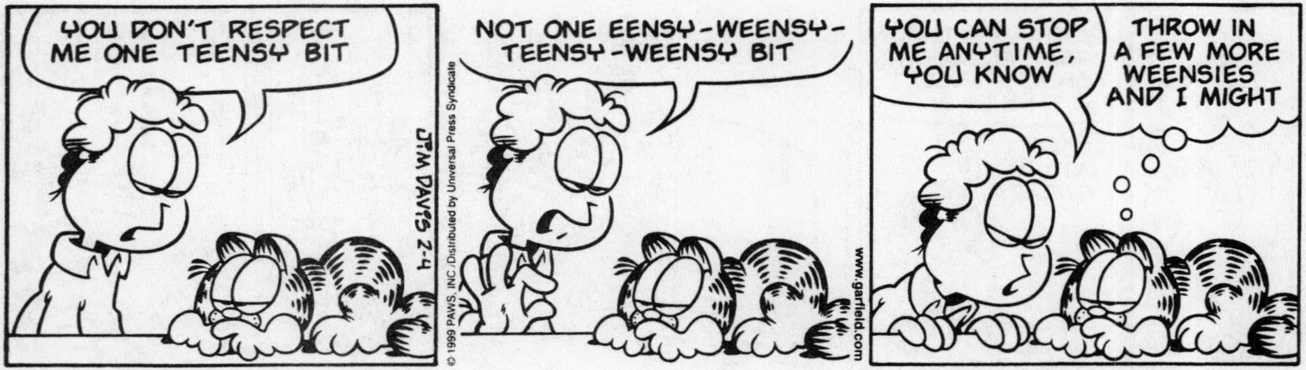
YOU DON'T RESPECT ME ONE TEENSY BIT
NOT ONE EENSY-WEENSY-TEENSY-WEENSY BIT
YOU CAN STOP ME ANYTIME, YOU KNOW
THROW IN A FEW MORE WEENSIES AND I MIGHT
JIM DAVIS 2-4
© 1999 PAWS, INC./Distributed by Universal Press Syndicate
www.garfield.com

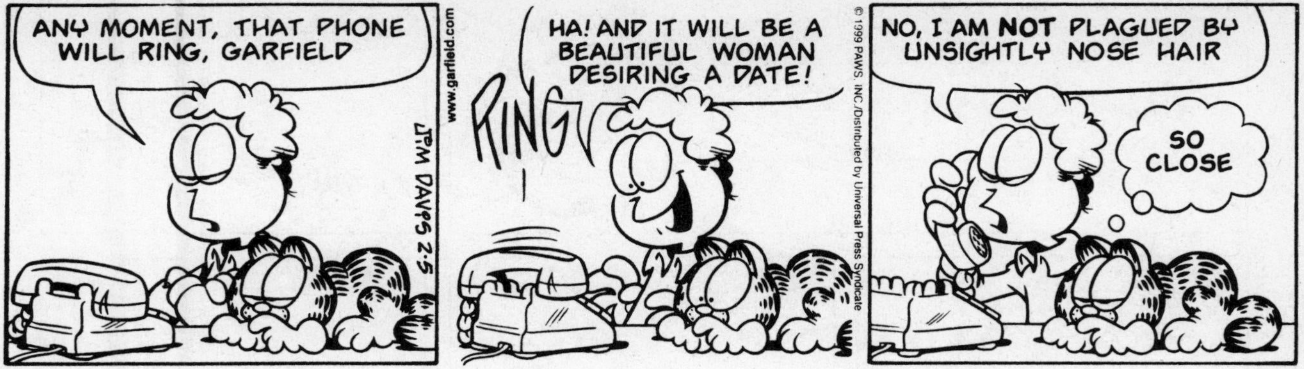
ANY MOMENT, THAT PHONE WILL RING, GARFIELD
JIM DAVIS 2-5
www.garfield.com
RING
HA! AND IT WILL BE A BEAUTIFUL WOMAN DESIRING A DATE!
© 1999 PAWS, INC./Distributed by Universal Press Syndicate
NO, I AM **NOT** PLAGUED BY UNSIGHTLY NOSE HAIR
SO CLOSE

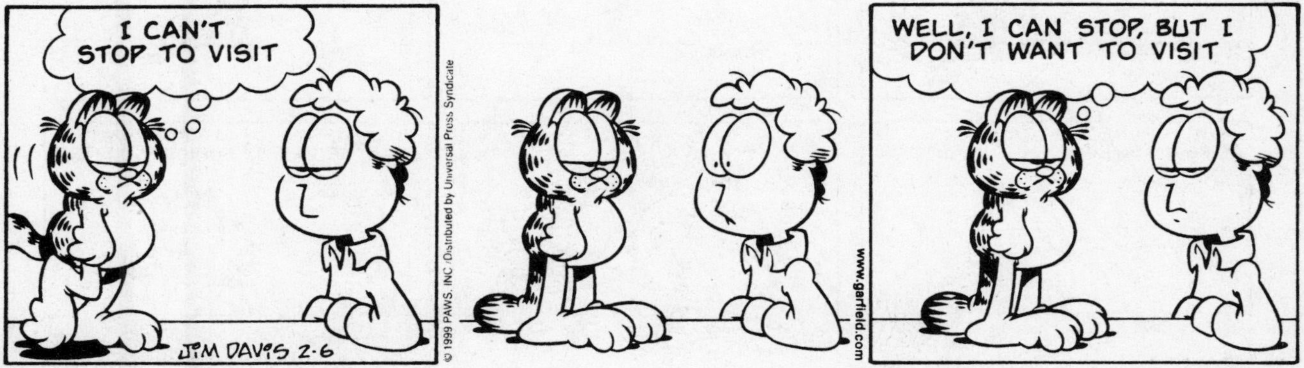
I CAN'T STOP TO VISIT
JIM DAVIS 2-6
© 1999 PAWS, INC./Distributed by Universal Press Syndicate
www.garfield.com
WELL, I CAN STOP, BUT I DON'T WANT TO VISIT

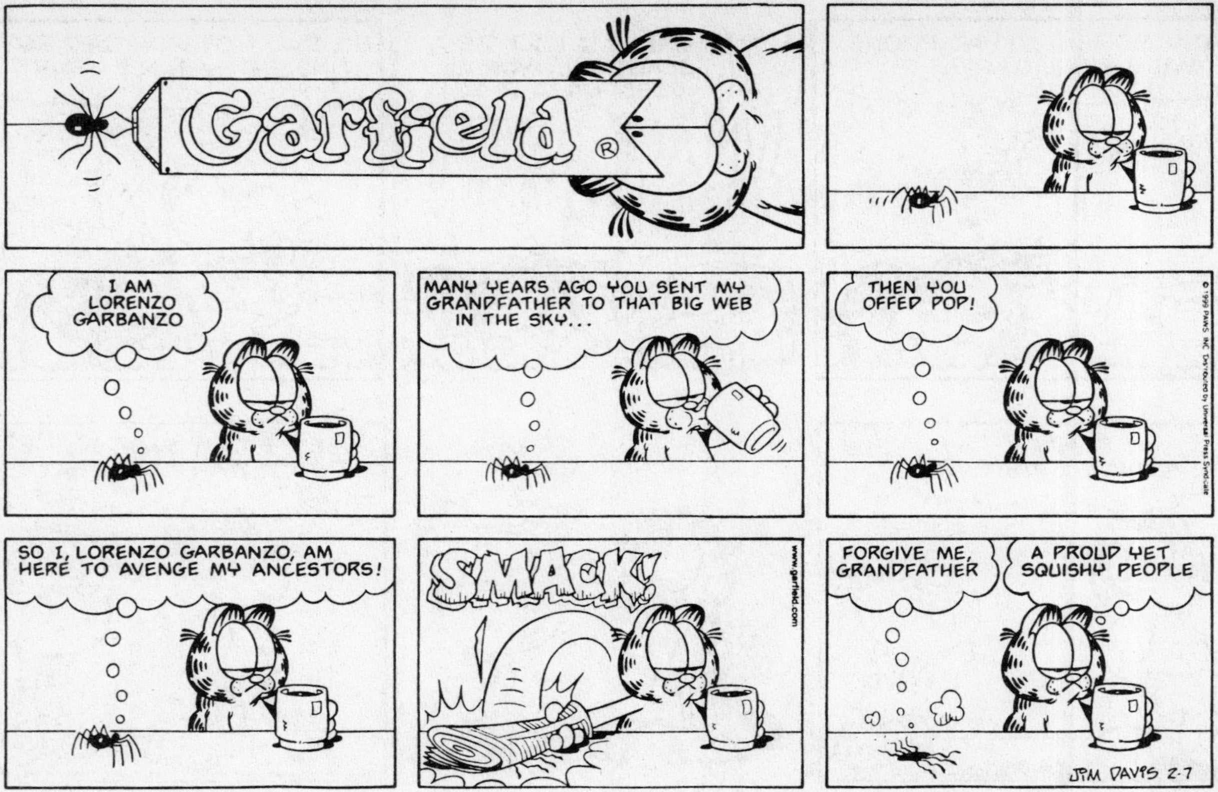
Garfield®
I AM LORENZO GARBANZO
MANY YEARS AGO YOU SENT MY GRANDFATHER TO THAT BIG WEB IN THE SKY...
THEN YOU OFFED POP!
© 1999 PAWS INC. Distributed by Universal Press Syndicate
SO I, LORENZO GARBANZO, AM HERE TO AVENGE MY ANCESTORS!
SMACK!
www.garfield.com
FORGIVE ME, GRANDFATHER
A PROUD YET SQUISHY PEOPLE
JIM DAVIS 2-7

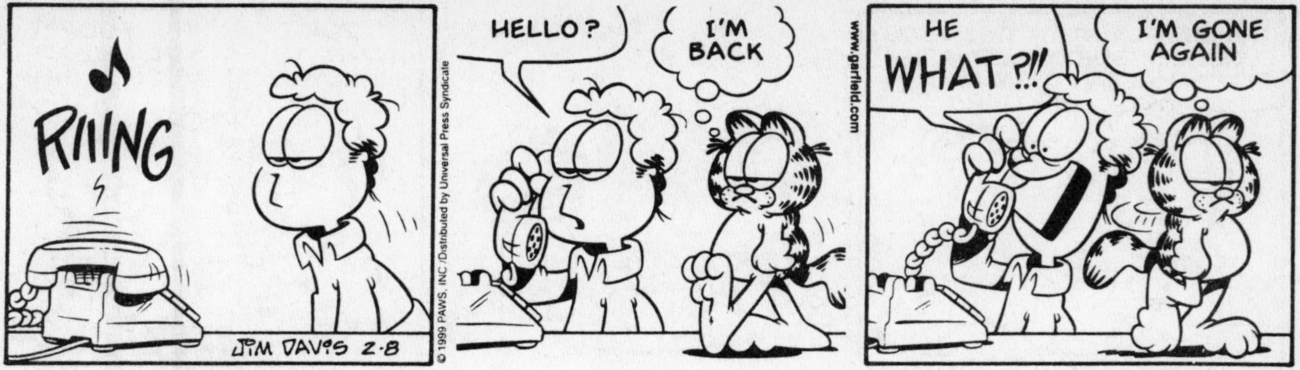
RIIING
JIM DAVIS 2-8
© 1999 PAWS, INC./Distributed by Universal Press Syndicate
HELLO?
I'M BACK
www.garfield.com
HE WHAT?!!
I'M GONE AGAIN

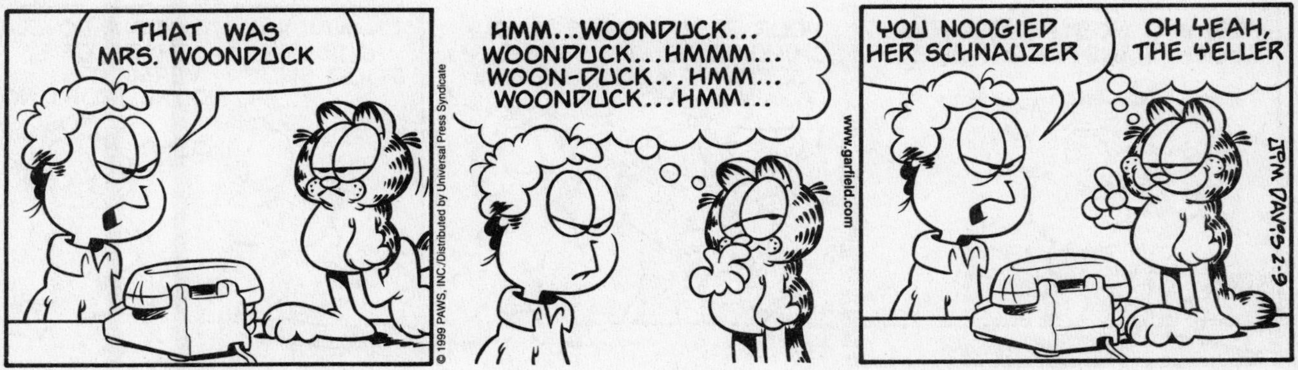
THAT WAS MRS. WOONDUCK
© 1999 PAWS, INC./Distributed by Universal Press Syndicate
HMM...WOONDUCK...
WOONDUCK...HMMM...
WOON-DUCK...HMM...
WOONDUCK...HMM...
www.garfield.com
YOU NOOGIED HER SCHNAUZER
OH YEAH, THE YELLER
JIM DAVIS 2-9

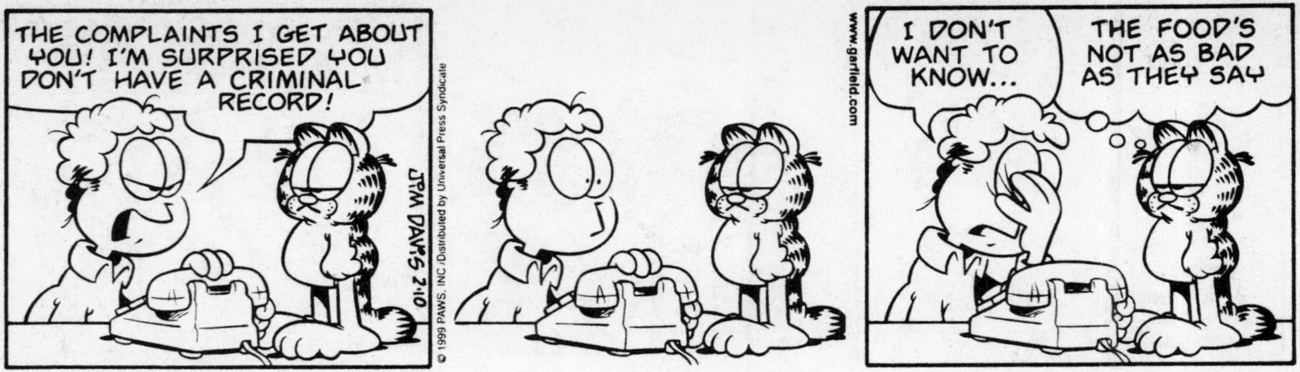
THE COMPLAINTS I GET ABOUT YOU! I'M SURPRISED YOU DON'T HAVE A CRIMINAL RECORD!
JIM DAVIS 2-10
© 1999 PAWS, INC./Distributed by Universal Press Syndicate
www.garfield.com
I DON'T WANT TO KNOW...
THE FOOD'S NOT AS BAD AS THEY SAY

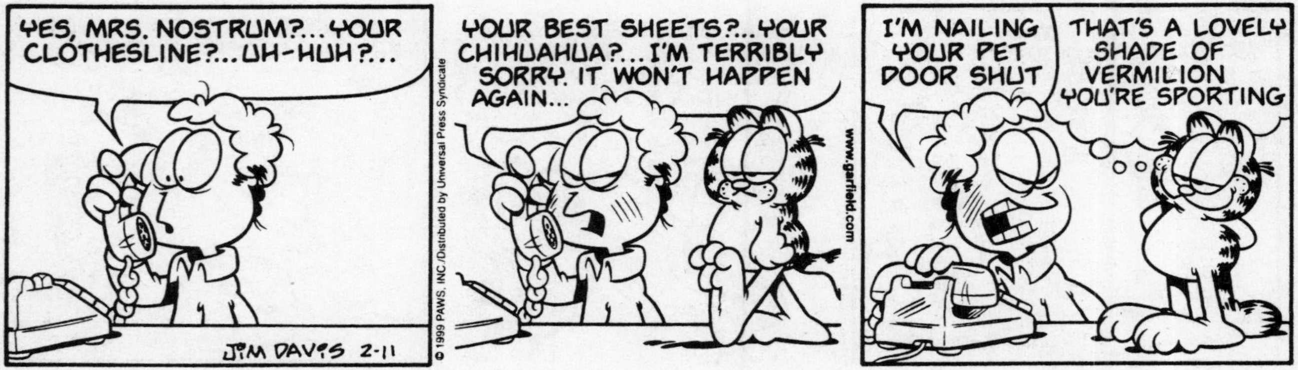
YES, MRS. NOSTRUM?... YOUR CLOTHESLINE?... UH-HUH?...
JIM DAVIS 2-11
© 1999 PAWS, INC./Distributed by Universal Press Syndicate
YOUR BEST SHEETS?... YOUR CHIHUAHUA?... I'M TERRIBLY SORRY. IT WON'T HAPPEN AGAIN...
www.garfield.com
I'M NAILING YOUR PET DOOR SHUT
THAT'S A LOVELY SHADE OF VERMILION YOU'RE SPORTING

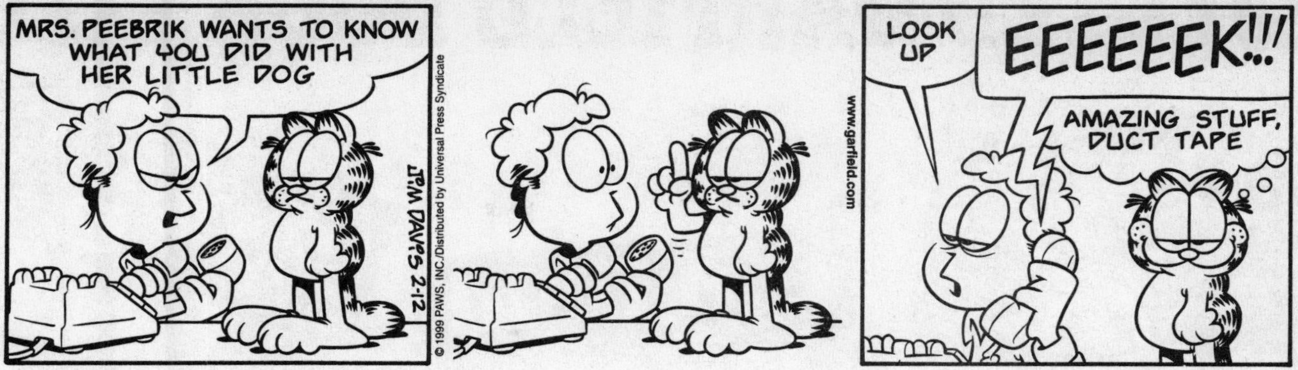
MRS. PEEBRIK WANTS TO KNOW WHAT YOU DID WITH HER LITTLE DOG
JIM DAVIS 2-12
© 1999 PAWS, INC./Distributed by Universal Press Syndicate
www.garfield.com
LOOK UP
EEEEEEK!!!
AMAZING STUFF, DUCT TAPE

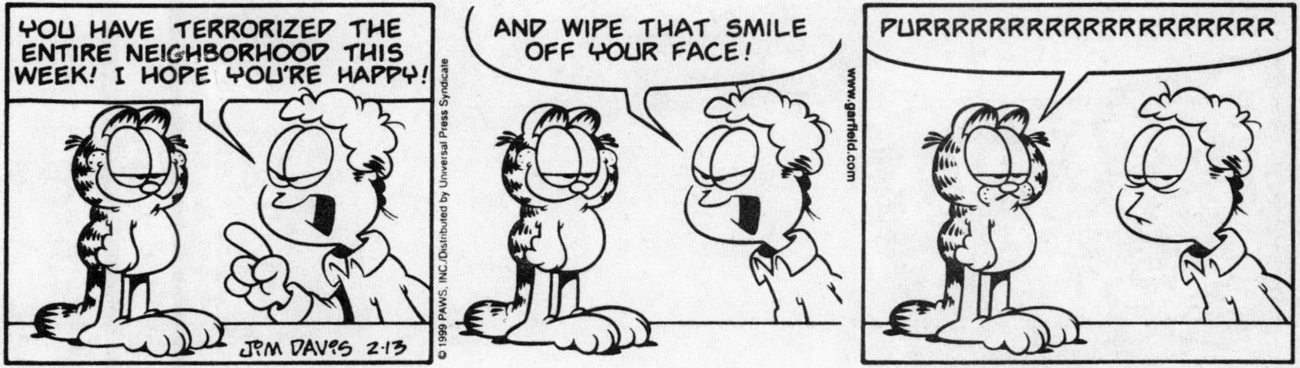
YOU HAVE TERRORIZED THE ENTIRE NEIGHBORHOOD THIS WEEK! I HOPE YOU'RE HAPPY!
JIM DAVIS 2-13
© 1999 PAWS, INC./Distributed by Universal Press Syndicate
AND WIPE THAT SMILE OFF YOUR FACE!
www.garfield.com
PURRRRRRRRRRRRRRRRRRRR

REJECTED GARFIELD BOOK TITLES

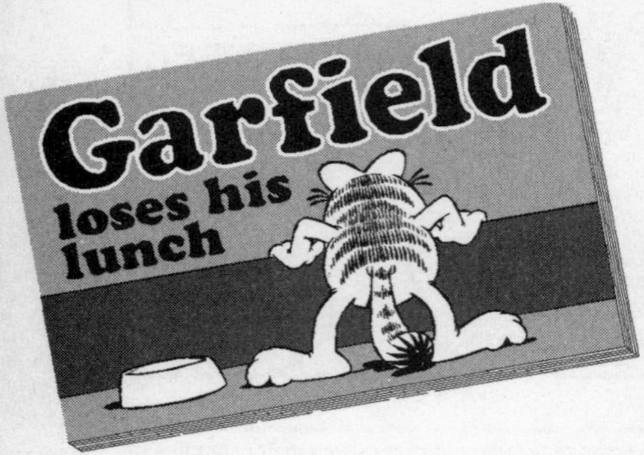
Garfield
loses his lunch

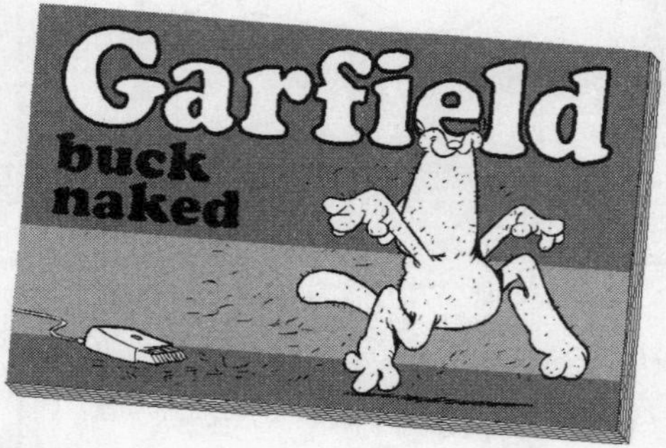
Garfield
buck naked

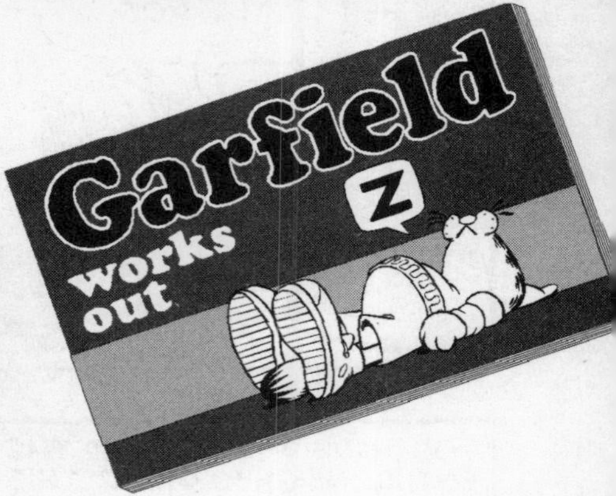
Garfield
works out
Z

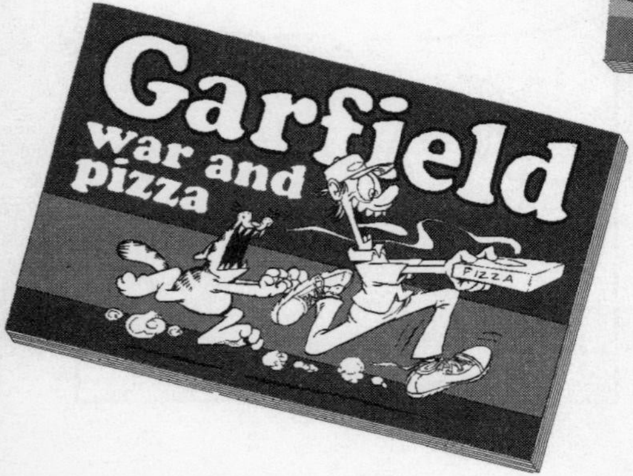
Garfield
war and pizza
PIZZA

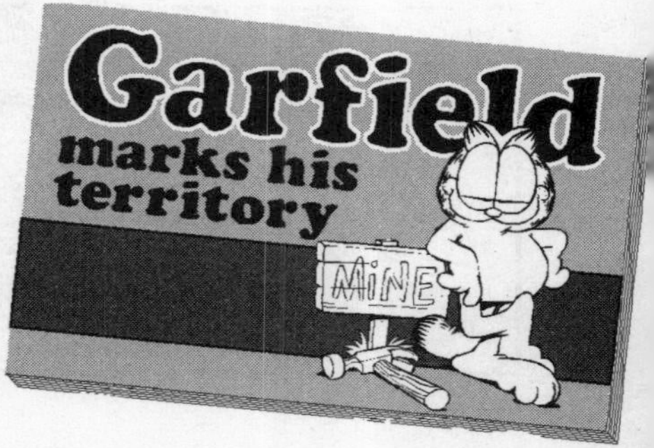
Garfield
marks his territory
MINE

Garfield

hogs the
spotlight

BY: JIM DAVIS

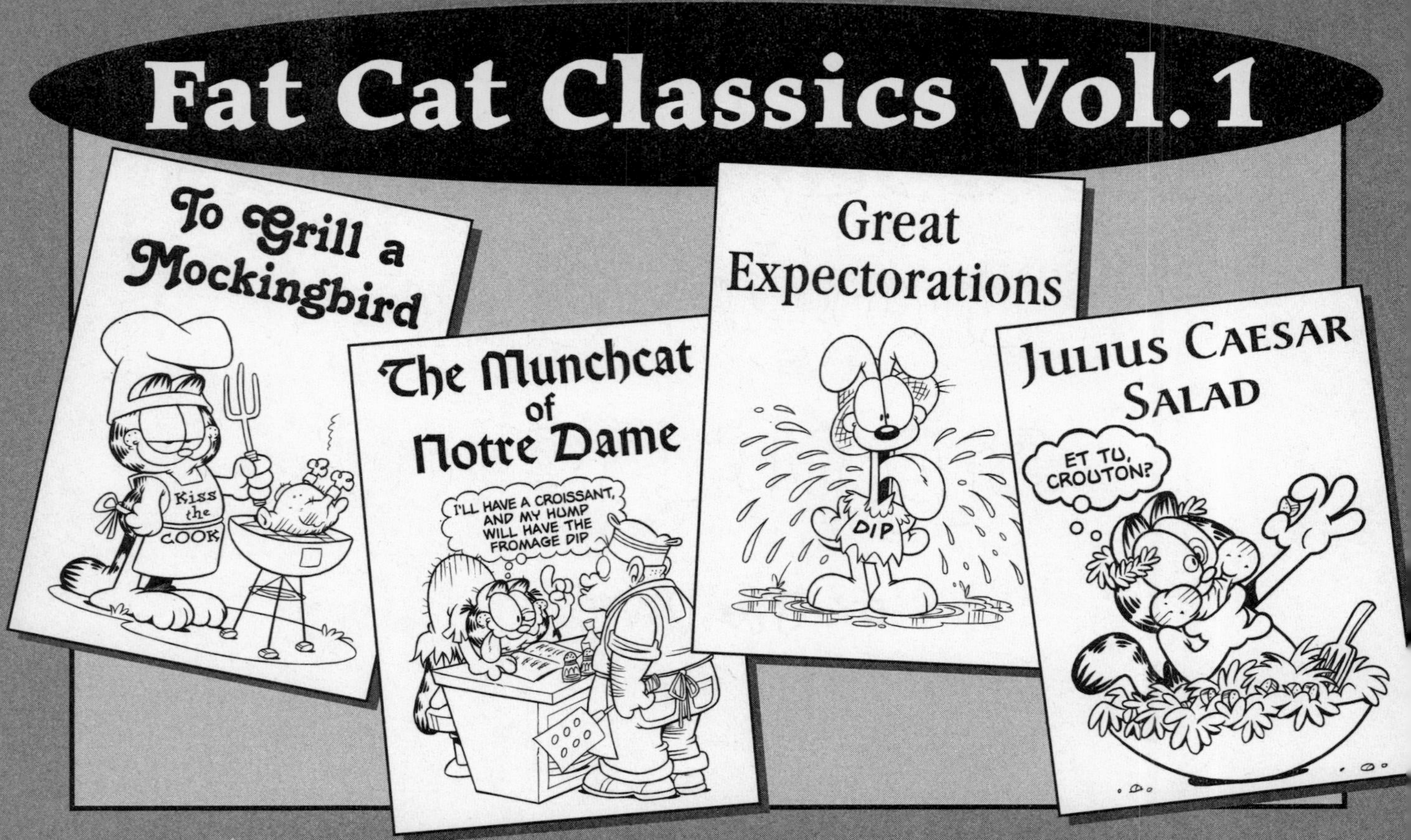

Fat Cat Classics Vol. 1
To Grill a Mockingbird
Kiss the COOK
The Munchcat of Notre Dame
I'LL HAVE A CROISSANT, AND MY HUMP WILL HAVE THE FROMAGE DIP
Great Expectorations
DIP
JULIUS CAESAR SALAD
ET TU, CROUTON?

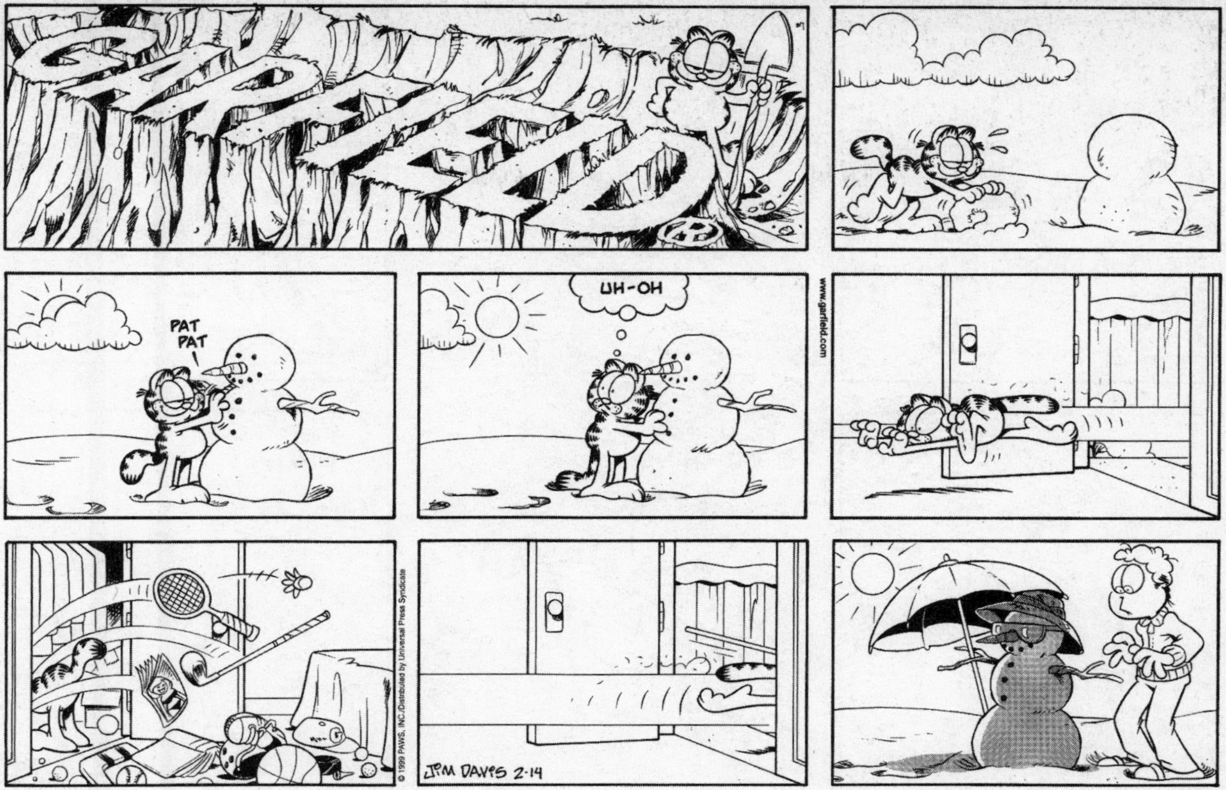
PAT
PAT
UH-OH
www.garfield.com
© 1999 PAWS, INC./Distributed by Universal Press Syndicate
JIM DAVIS 2-14

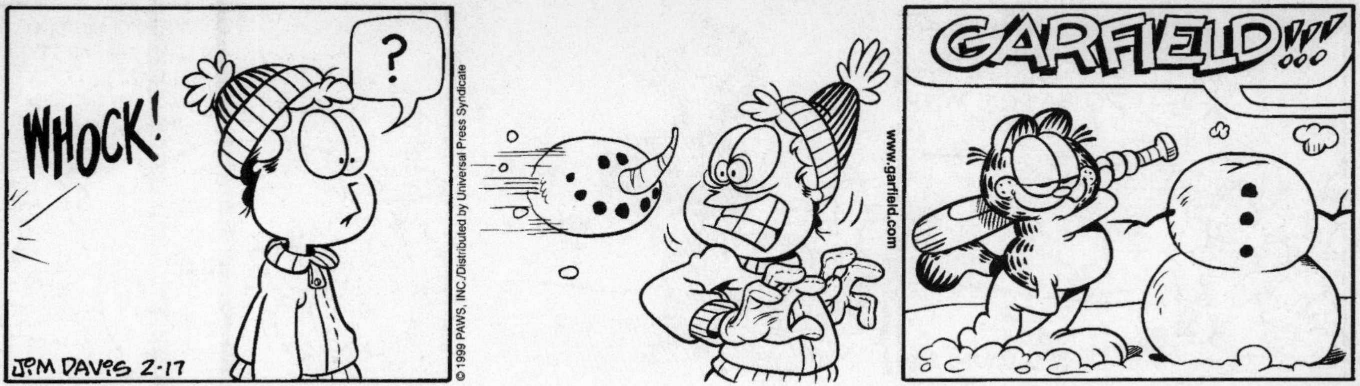
WHOCK!
?
JIM DAVIS 2-17
© 1999 PAWS, INC./Distributed by Universal Press Syndicate
www.garfield.com
GARFIELD!!!

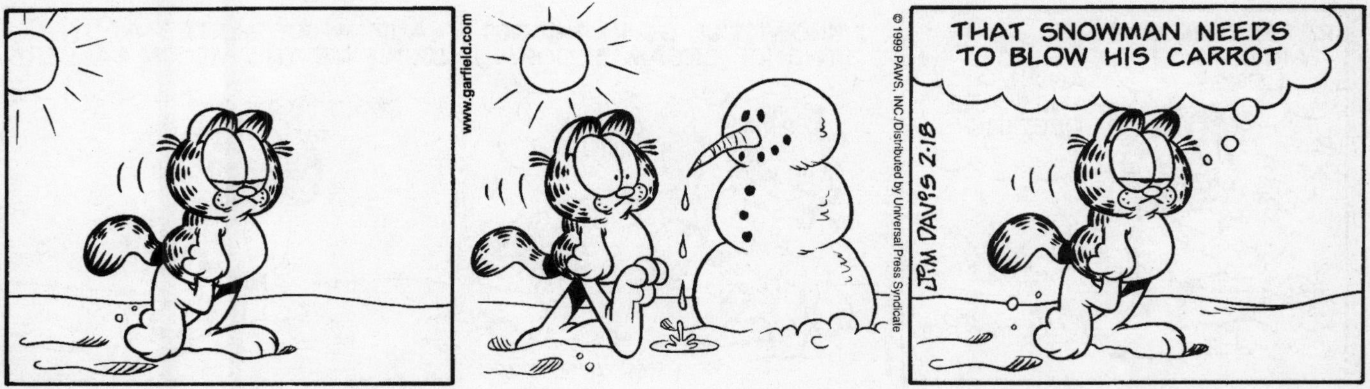
www.garfield.com
© 1999 PAWS, INC./Distributed by Universal Press Syndicate
JIM DAVIS 2-18
THAT SNOWMAN NEEDS TO BLOW HIS CARROT

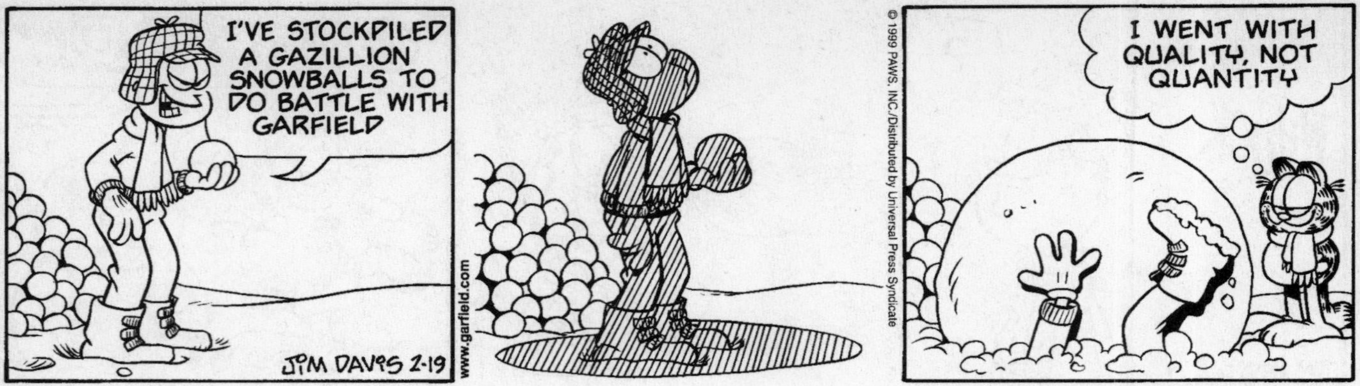
I'VE STOCKPILED A GAZILLION SNOWBALLS TO DO BATTLE WITH GARFIELD
JIM DAVIS 2-19
www.garfield.com
© 1999 PAWS, INC./Distributed by Universal Press Syndicate
I WENT WITH QUALITY, NOT QUANTITY

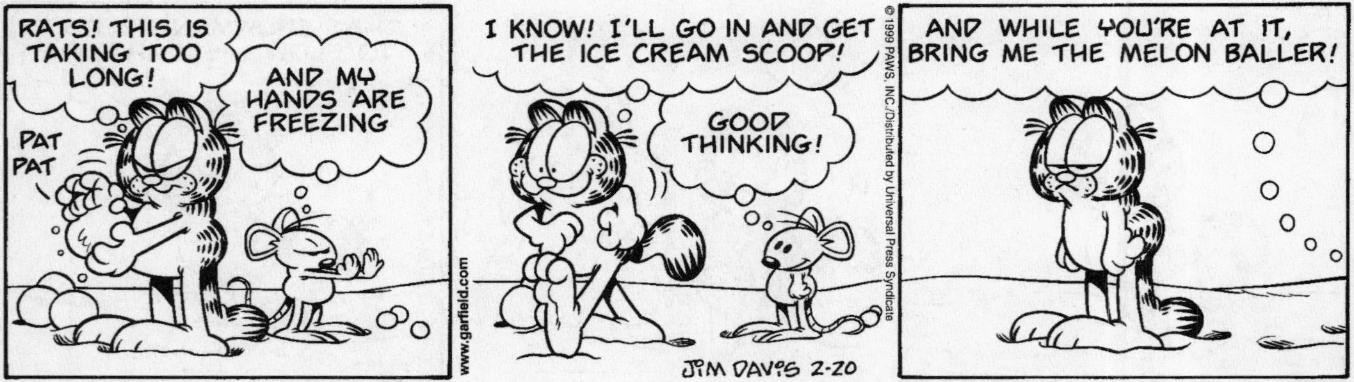
RATS! THIS IS TAKING TOO LONG!
AND MY HANDS ARE FREEZING
PAT PAT
www.garfield.com
I KNOW! I'LL GO IN AND GET THE ICE CREAM SCOOP!
GOOD THINKING!
JIM DAVIS 2-20
© 1999 PAWS, INC./Distributed by Universal Press Syndicate
AND WHILE YOU'RE AT IT, BRING ME THE MELON BALLER!

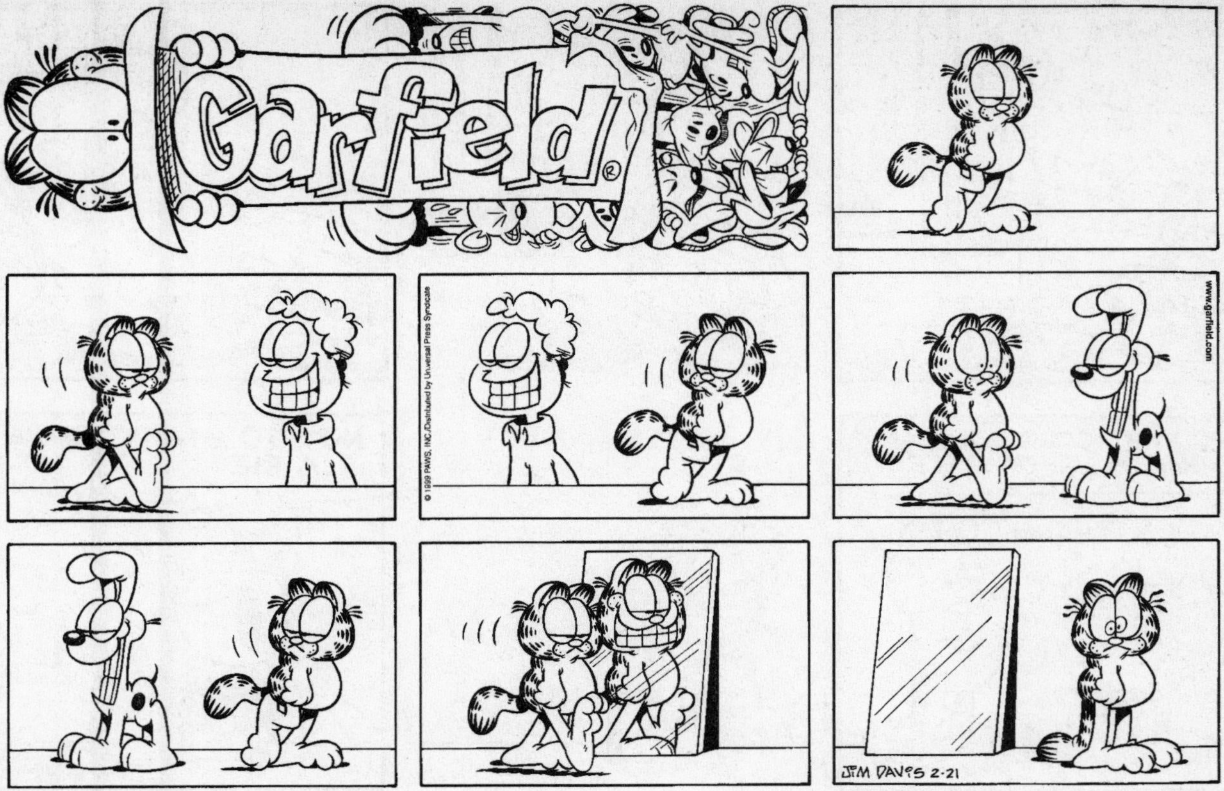
Garfield®
© 1999 PAWS, INC./Distributed by Universal Press Syndicate
www.garfield.com
JIM DAVIS 2-21

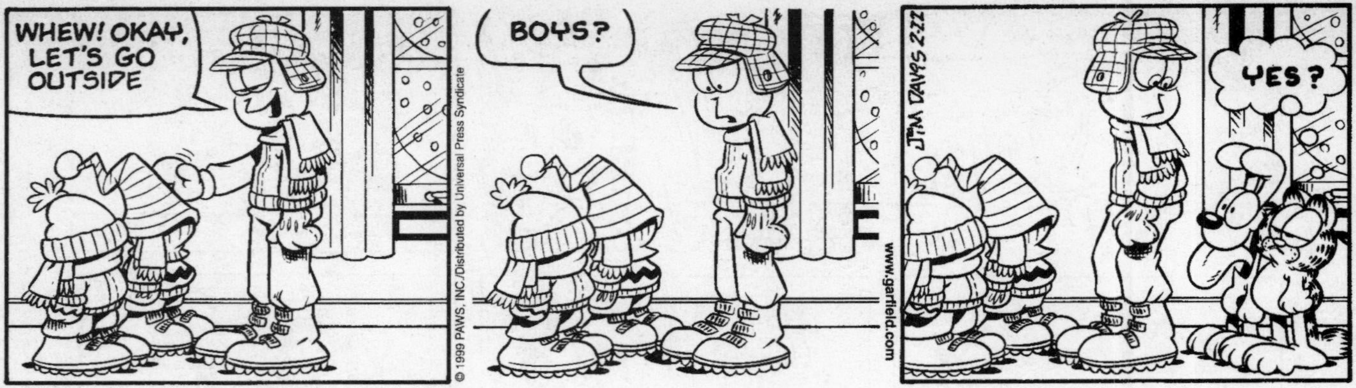
WHEW! OKAY, LET'S GO OUTSIDE
BOYS?
YES?
JIM DAVIS 2-22
© 1999 PAWS, INC./Distributed by Universal Press Syndicate
www.garfield.com

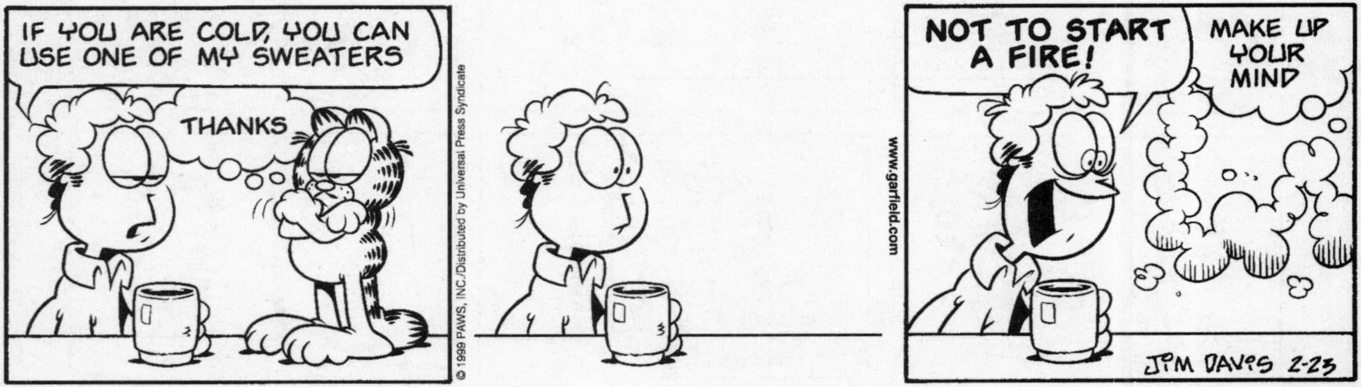
IF YOU ARE COLD, YOU CAN USE ONE OF MY SWEATERS
THANKS
NOT TO START A FIRE!
MAKE UP YOUR MIND
JIM DAVIS 2-23
© 1999 PAWS, INC./Distributed by Universal Press Syndicate
www.garfield.com

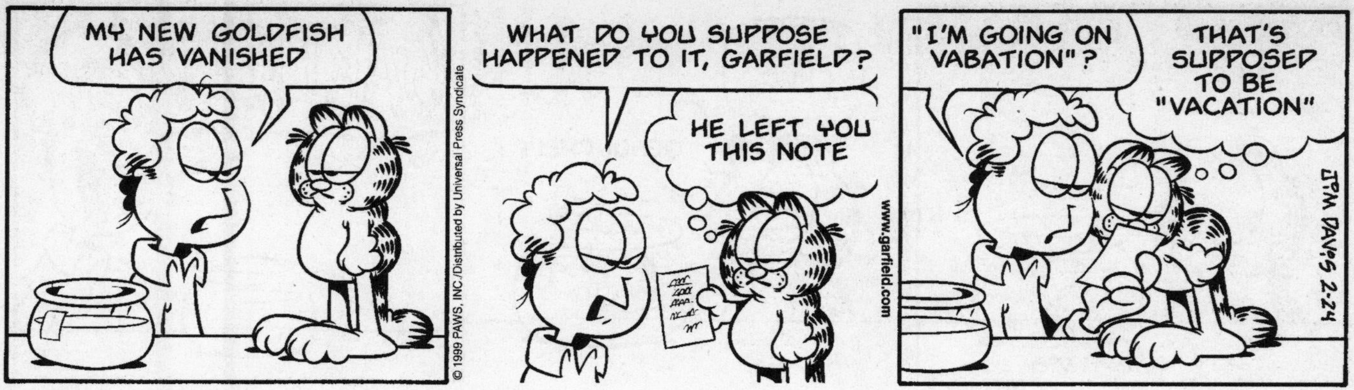
MY NEW GOLDFISH HAS VANISHED
WHAT DO YOU SUPPOSE HAPPENED TO IT, GARFIELD?
HE LEFT YOU THIS NOTE
"I'M GOING ON VABATION"?
THAT'S SUPPOSED TO BE "VACATION"
© 1999 PAWS, INC./Distributed by Universal Press Syndicate
www.garfield.com
JIM DAVIS 2-24

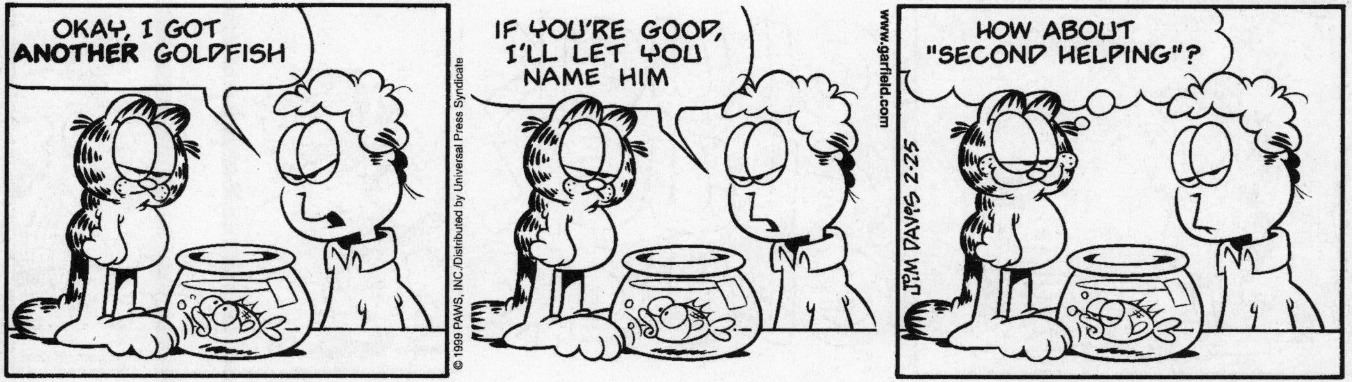
OKAY, I GOT **ANOTHER** GOLDFISH
IF YOU'RE GOOD, I'LL LET YOU NAME HIM
HOW ABOUT "SECOND HELPING"?
© 1999 PAWS, INC./Distributed by Universal Press Syndicate
www.garfield.com
JIM DAVIS 2-25

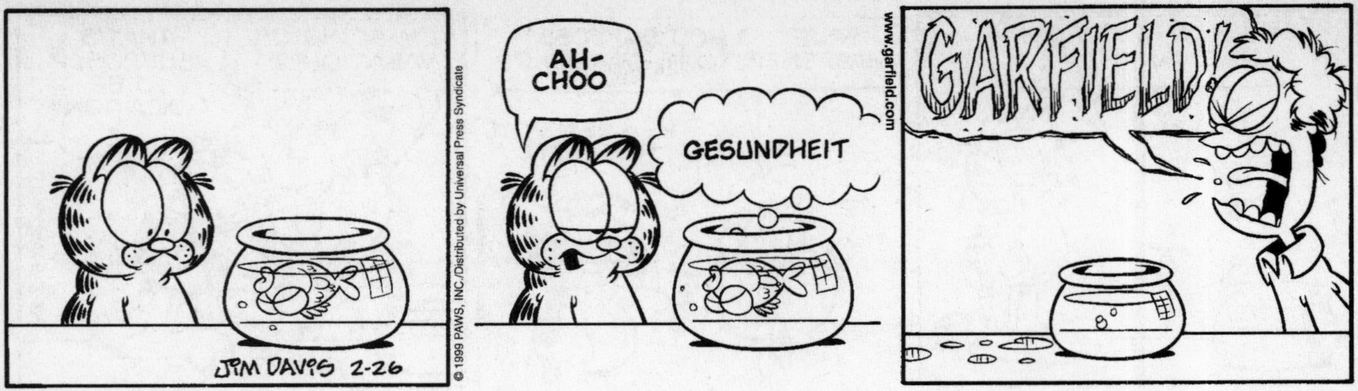
JIM DAVIS 2-26
© 1999 PAWS, INC./Distributed by Universal Press Syndicate
AH-CHOO
GESUNDHEIT
www.garfield.com
GARFIELD!

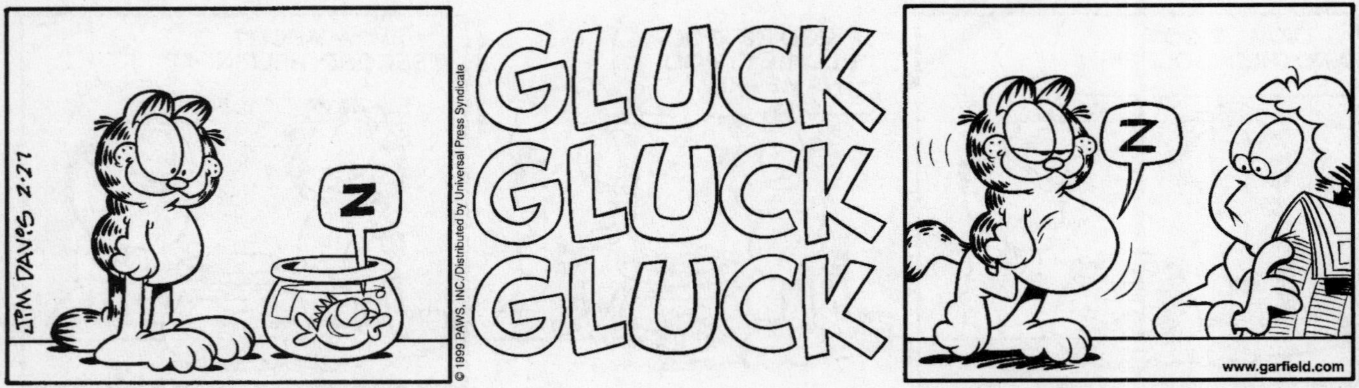
JIM DAVIS 2-27
Z
© 1999 PAWS, INC./Distributed by Universal Press Syndicate
GLUCK
GLUCK
GLUCK
Z
www.garfield.com

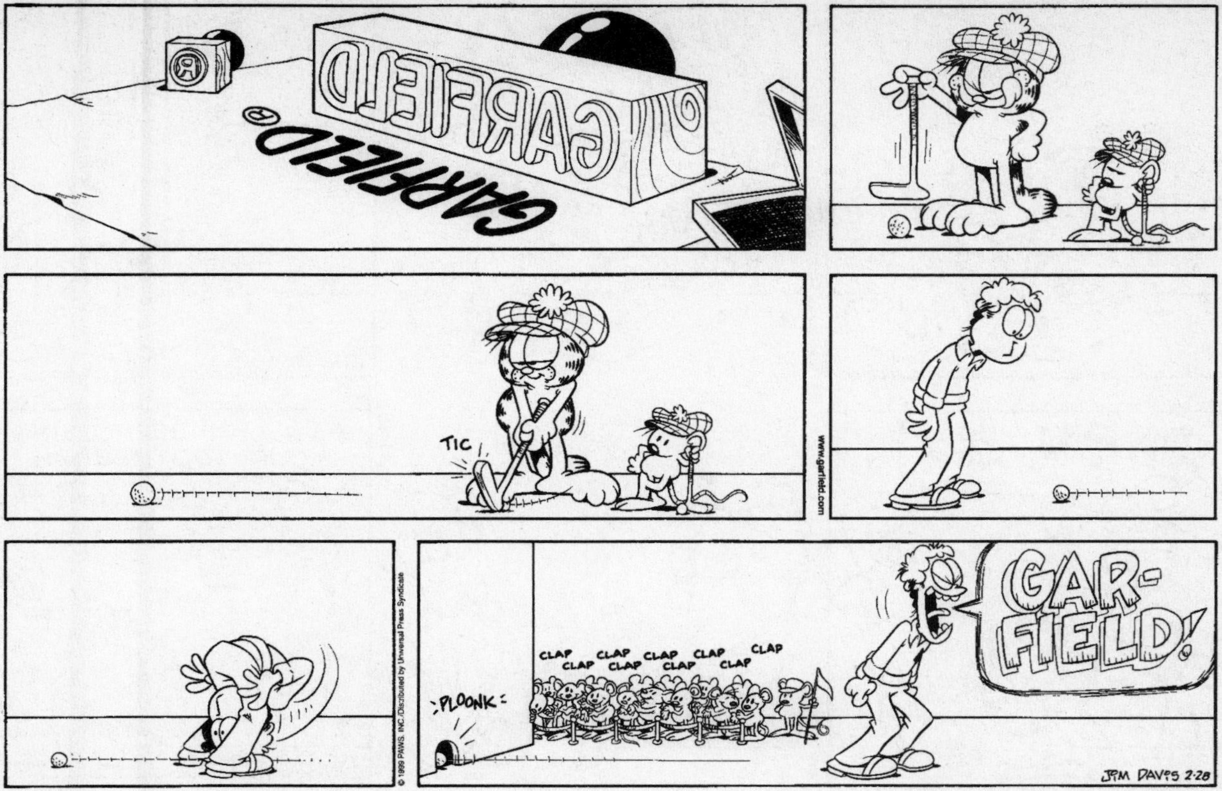
GARFIELD
TIC
www.garfield.com
© 1999 PAWS, INC./Distributed by Universal Press Syndicate
PLOONK
CLAP CLAP CLAP CLAP CLAP CLAP CLAP CLAP CLAP
GAR-FIELD!
JIM DAVIS 2·28

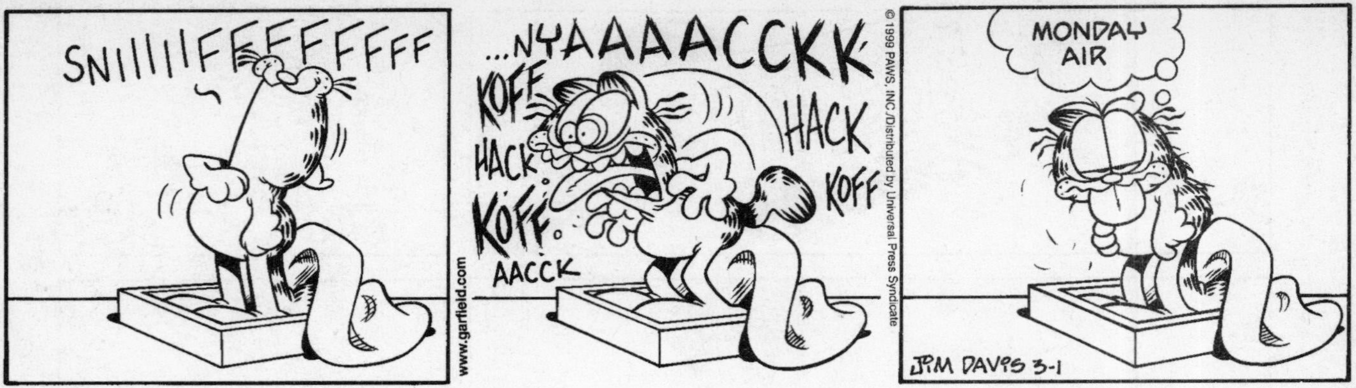
SNIIIIIFFFFFFFFF
www.garfield.com
...NYAAAACCKK
KOFF
HACK
KOFF
AACCK
HACK
KOFF
© 1999 PAWS, INC./Distributed by Universal Press Syndicate
MONDAY AIR
JIM DAVIS 3-1

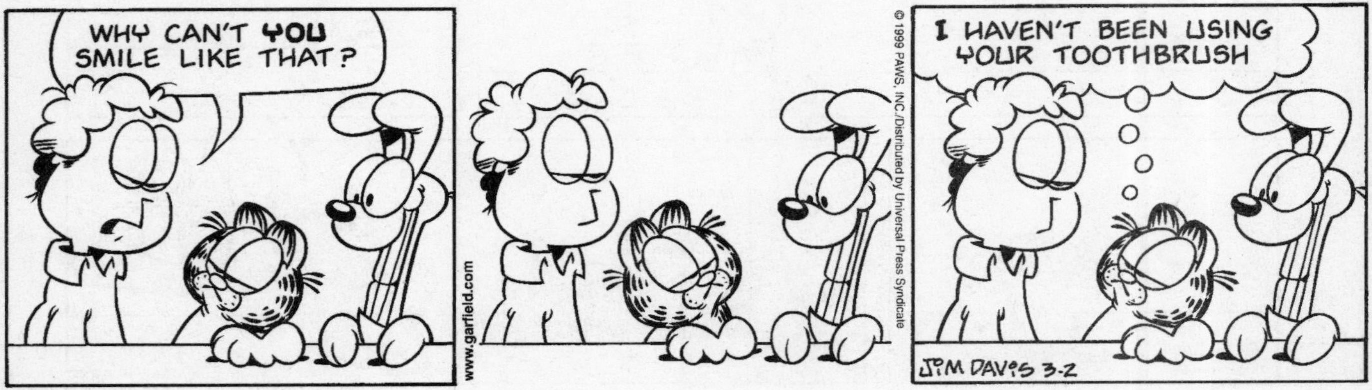
WHY CAN'T **YOU** SMILE LIKE THAT?
www.garfield.com
© 1999 PAWS, INC./Distributed by Universal Press Syndicate
I HAVEN'T BEEN USING YOUR TOOTHBRUSH
JIM DAVIS 3-2

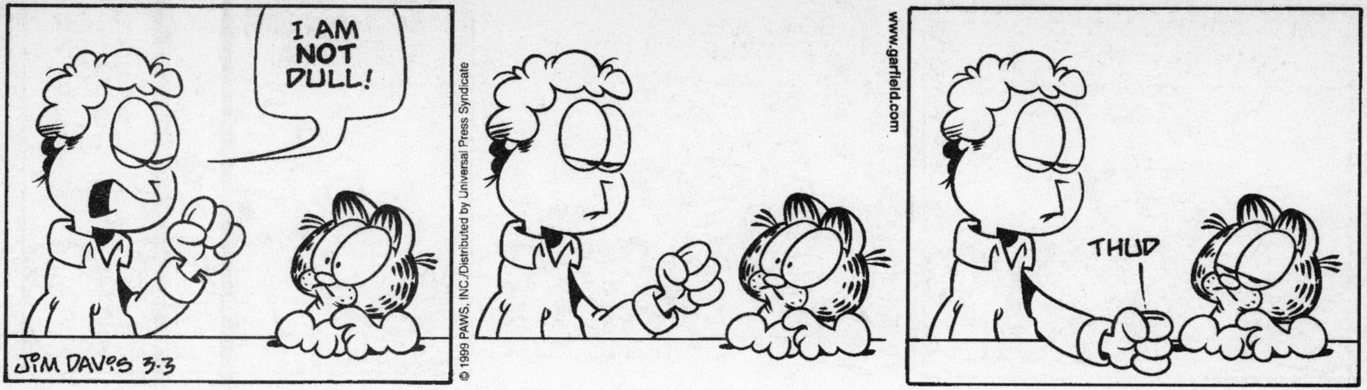
I AM NOT DULL!
JIM DAVIS 3-3
© 1999 PAWS, INC./Distributed by Universal Press Syndicate
www.garfield.com
THUD

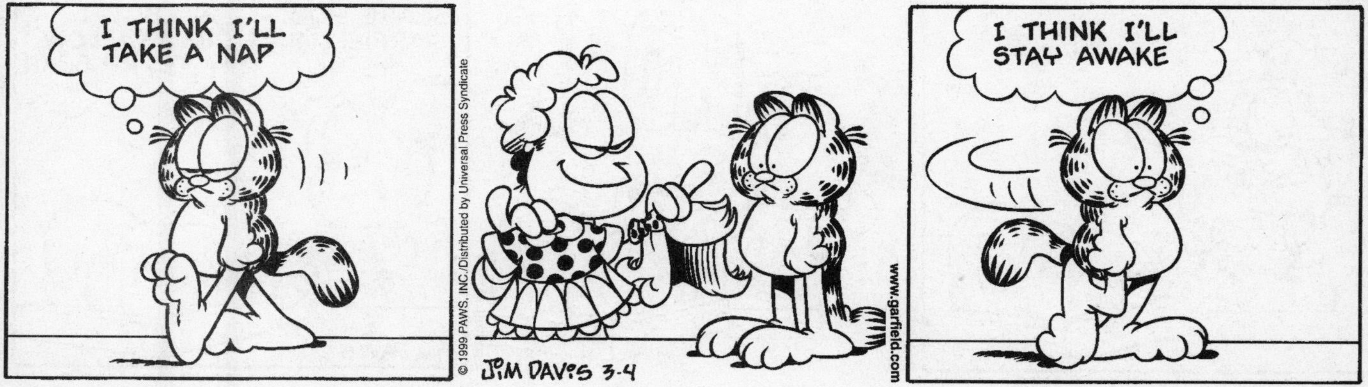
I THINK I'LL TAKE A NAP
© 1999 PAWS, INC./Distributed by Universal Press Syndicate
JIM DAVIS 3-4
www.garfield.com
I THINK I'LL STAY AWAKE

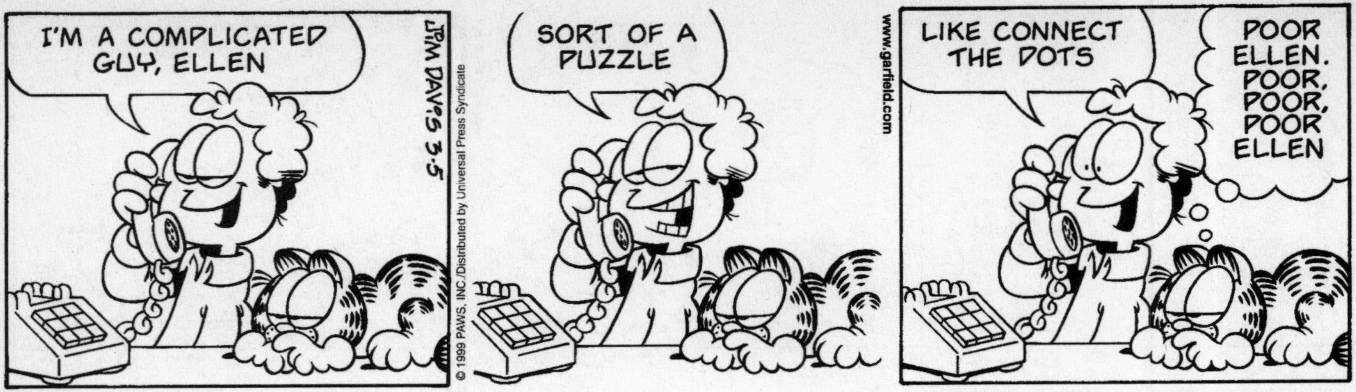
I'M A COMPLICATED GUY, ELLEN
SORT OF A PUZZLE
LIKE CONNECT THE DOTS
POOR ELLEN. POOR, POOR, POOR ELLEN
JIM DAVIS 3-5
© 1999 PAWS, INC./Distributed by Universal Press Syndicate
www.garfield.com

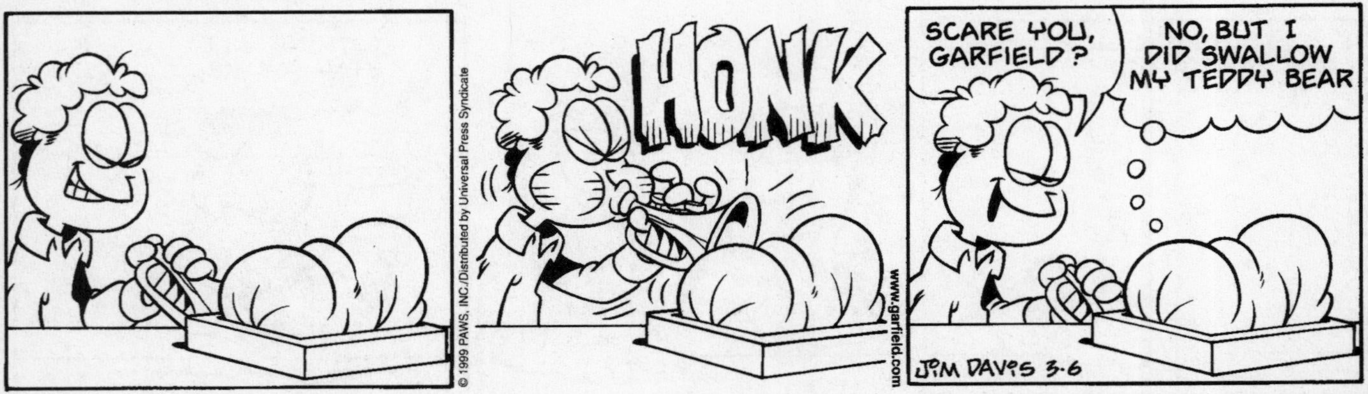
HONK
SCARE YOU, GARFIELD?
NO, BUT I DID SWALLOW MY TEDDY BEAR
JIM DAVIS 3-6
© 1999 PAWS, INC./Distributed by Universal Press Syndicate
www.garfield.com

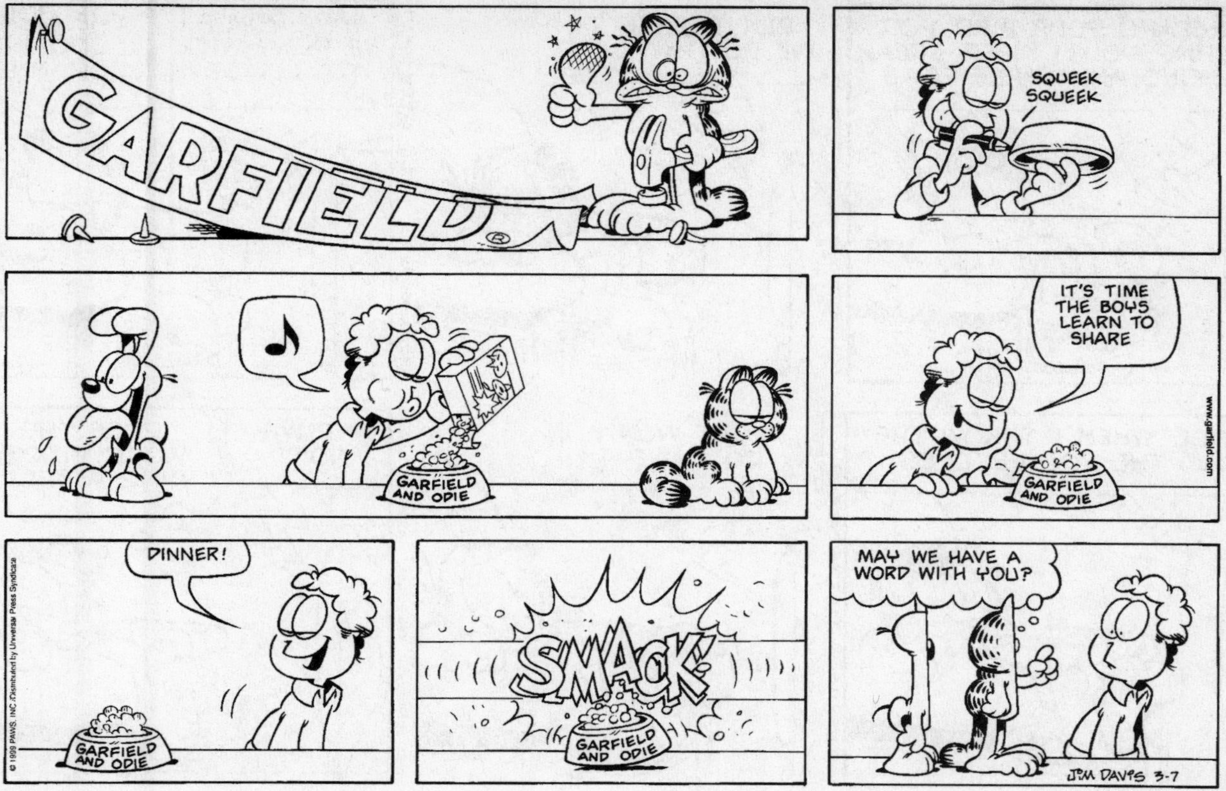
GARFIELD®
SQUEEK SQUEEK
GARFIELD AND ODIE
IT'S TIME THE BOYS LEARN TO SHARE
GARFIELD AND ODIE
www.garfield.com
DINNER!
GARFIELD AND ODIE
© 1999 PAWS, INC./Distributed by Universal Press Syndicate
SMACK
GARFIELD AND ODIE
MAY WE HAVE A WORD WITH YOU?
JIM DAVIS 3-7

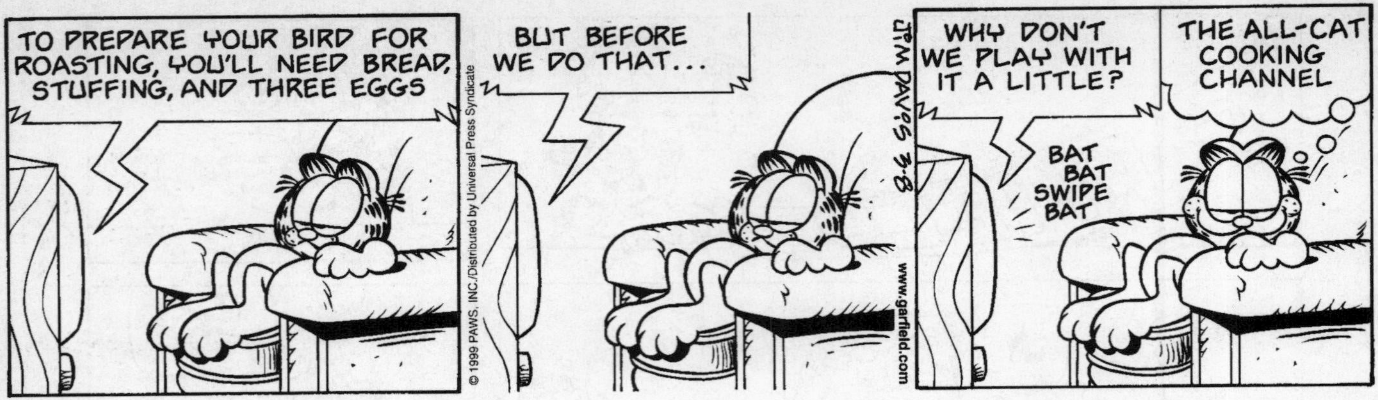
TO PREPARE YOUR BIRD FOR ROASTING, YOU'LL NEED BREAD, STUFFING, AND THREE EGGS
© 1999 PAWS, INC./Distributed by Universal Press Syndicate
BUT BEFORE WE DO THAT...
JIM DAVIS 3-8
www.garfield.com
WHY DON'T WE PLAY WITH IT A LITTLE?
BAT BAT SWIPE BAT
THE ALL-CAT COOKING CHANNEL

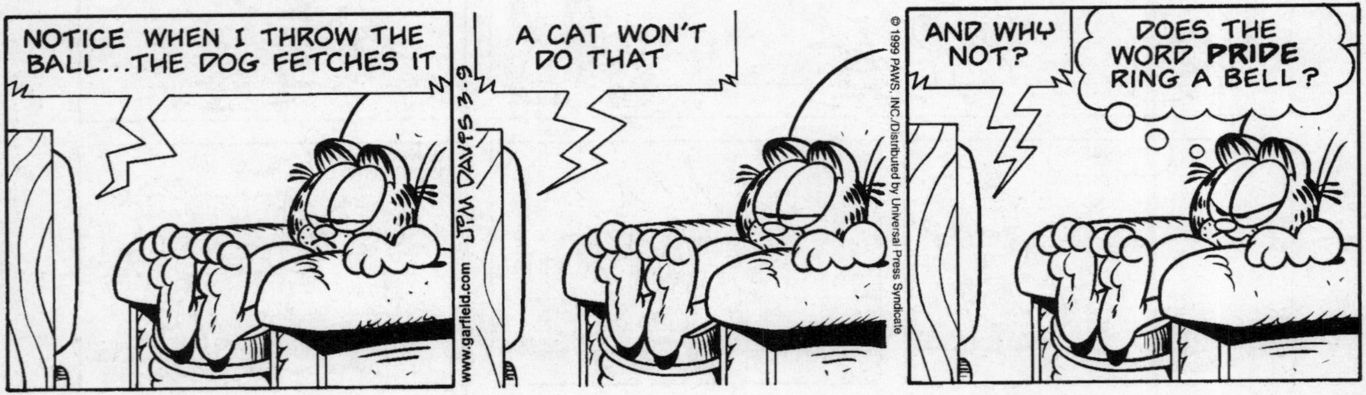
NOTICE WHEN I THROW THE BALL...THE DOG FETCHES IT
JIM DAVIS 3-9
www.garfield.com
A CAT WON'T DO THAT
© 1999 PAWS, INC./Distributed by Universal Press Syndicate
AND WHY NOT?
DOES THE WORD PRIDE RING A BELL?

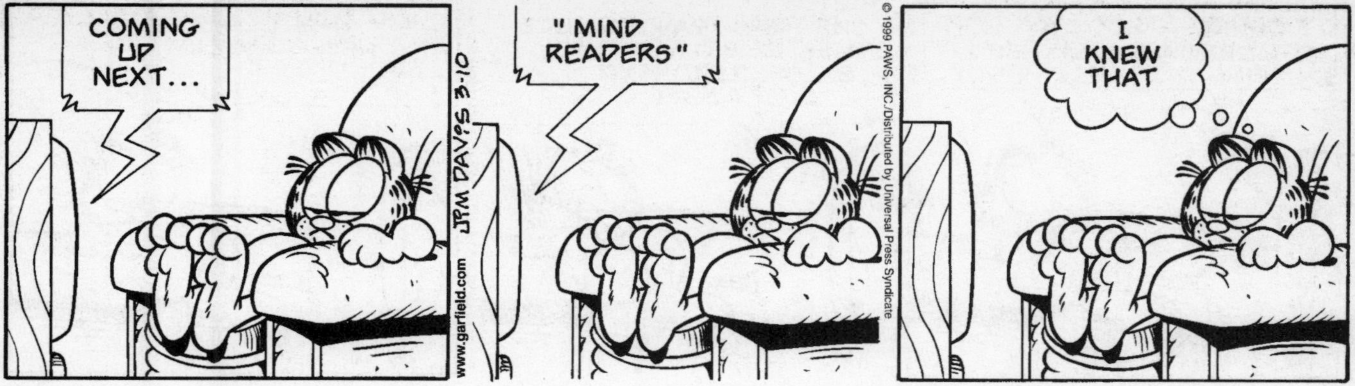
COMING UP NEXT...
"MIND READERS"
I KNEW THAT
JPM DAVIS 3-10
www.garfield.com
© 1999 PAWS, INC./Distributed by Universal Press Syndicate

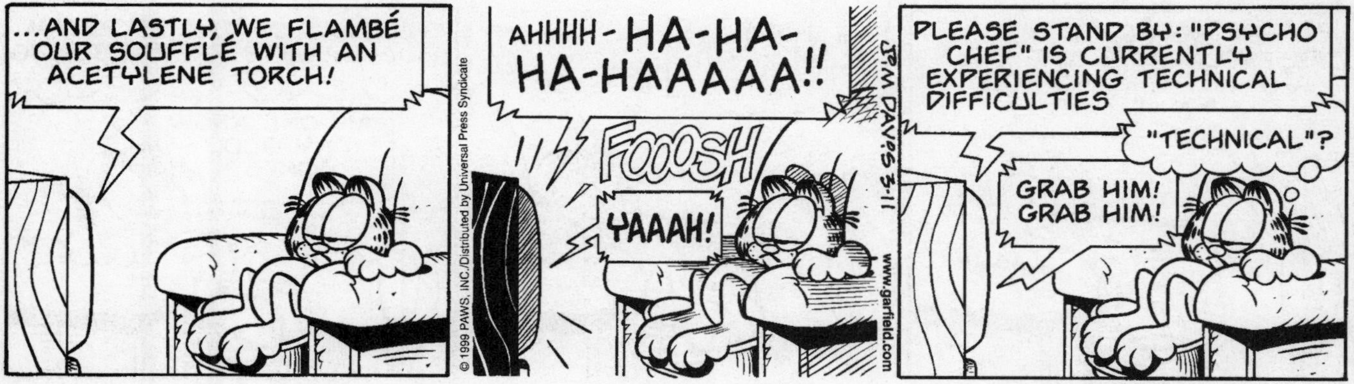
...AND LASTLY, WE FLAMBÉ OUR SOUFFLÉ WITH AN ACETYLENE TORCH!
AHHHH-HA-HA-HA-HAAAAA!!
FOOOSH
YAAAH!
PLEASE STAND BY: "PSYCHO CHEF" IS CURRENTLY EXPERIENCING TECHNICAL DIFFICULTIES
"TECHNICAL"?
GRAB HIM! GRAB HIM!
JPM DAVIS 3-11
www.garfield.com
© 1999 PAWS, INC./Distributed by Universal Press Syndicate

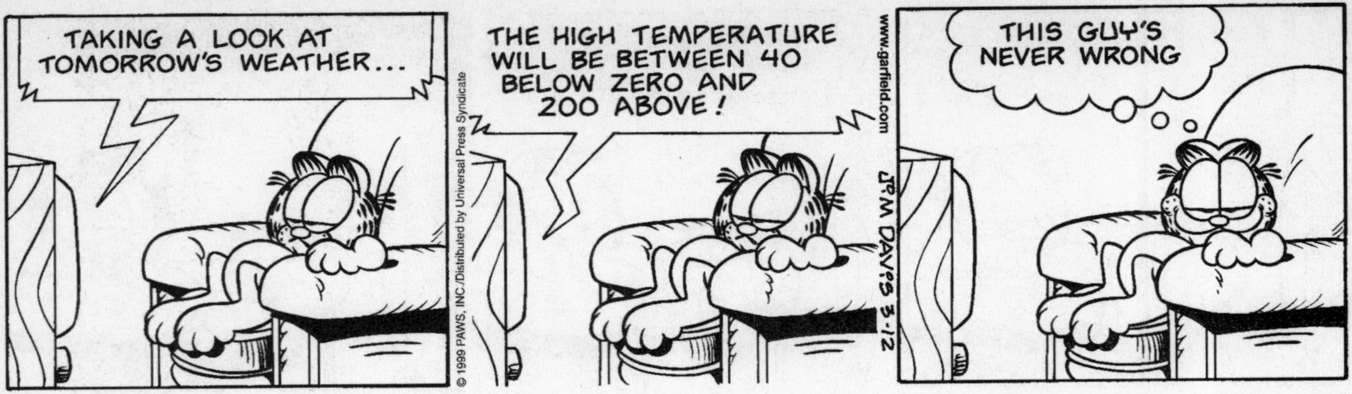
TAKING A LOOK AT TOMORROW'S WEATHER...
THE HIGH TEMPERATURE WILL BE BETWEEN 40 BELOW ZERO AND 200 ABOVE!
THIS GUY'S NEVER WRONG
© 1999 PAWS, INC./Distributed by Universal Press Syndicate
www.garfield.com
JPM DAVPS 3-12

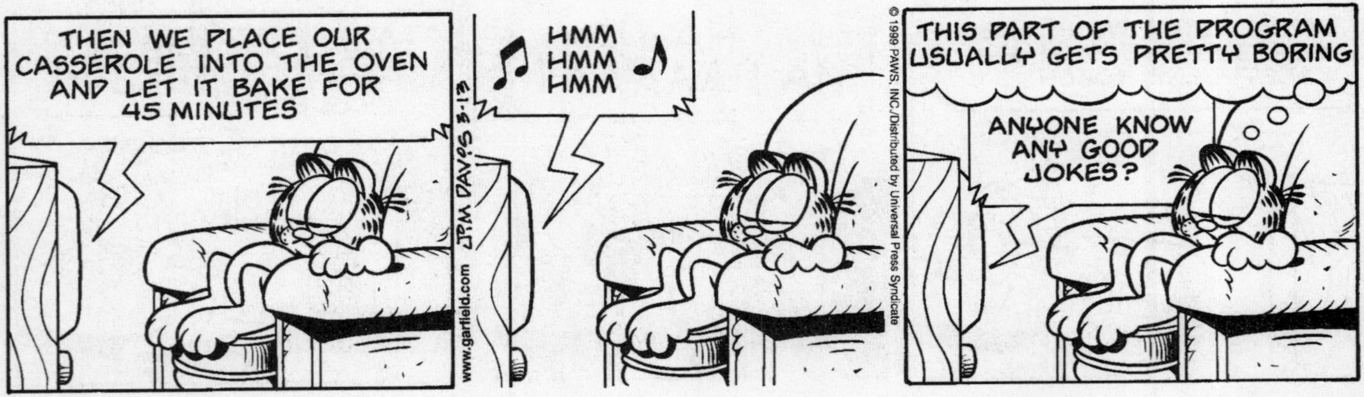
THEN WE PLACE OUR CASSEROLE INTO THE OVEN AND LET IT BAKE FOR 45 MINUTES
HMM HMM HMM
THIS PART OF THE PROGRAM USUALLY GETS PRETTY BORING
ANYONE KNOW ANY GOOD JOKES?
© 1999 PAWS, INC./Distributed by Universal Press Syndicate
www.garfield.com
JPM DAVPS 3-13

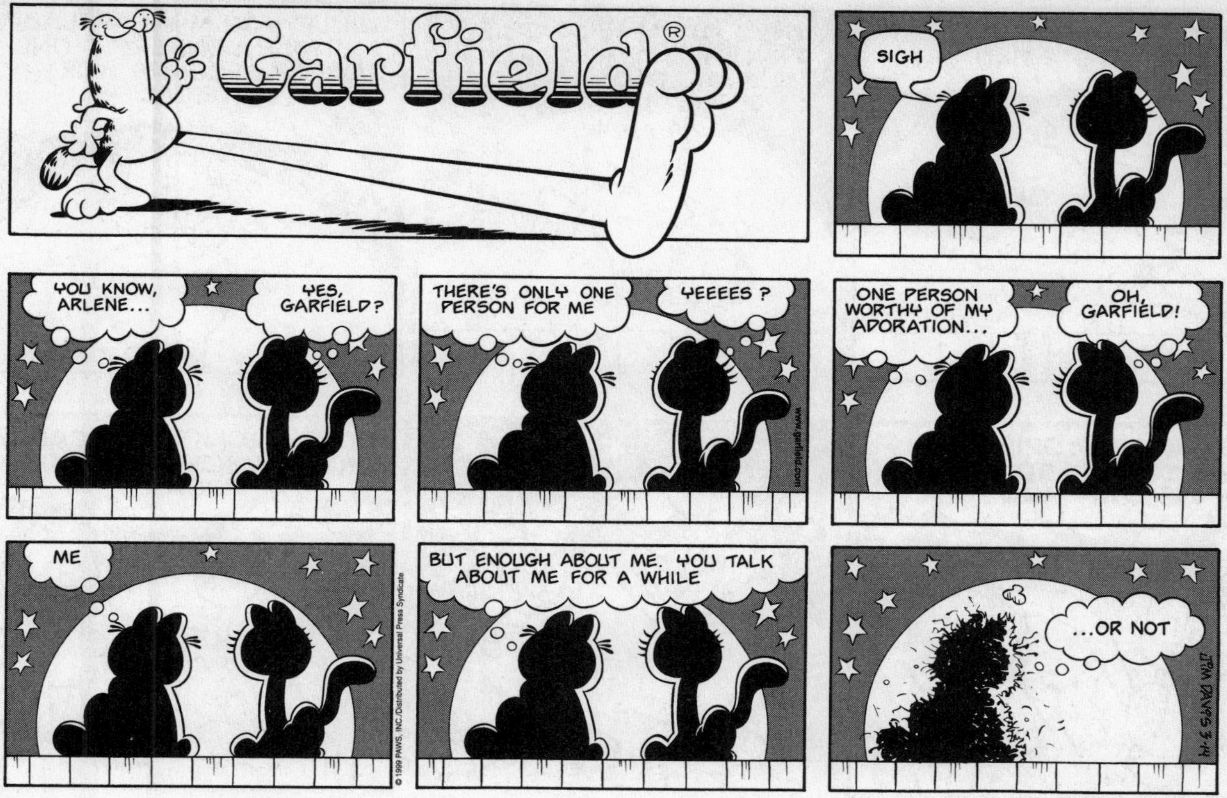
Garfield®
SIGH
YOU KNOW, ARLENE...
YES, GARFIELD?
THERE'S ONLY ONE PERSON FOR ME
YEEEES ?
ONE PERSON WORTHY OF MY ADORATION...
OH, GARFIELD!
ME
BUT ENOUGH ABOUT ME. YOU TALK ABOUT ME FOR A WHILE
...OR NOT
www.garfield.com
© 1999 PAWS, INC./Distributed by Universal Press Syndicate
JPM DAVIS 3-14

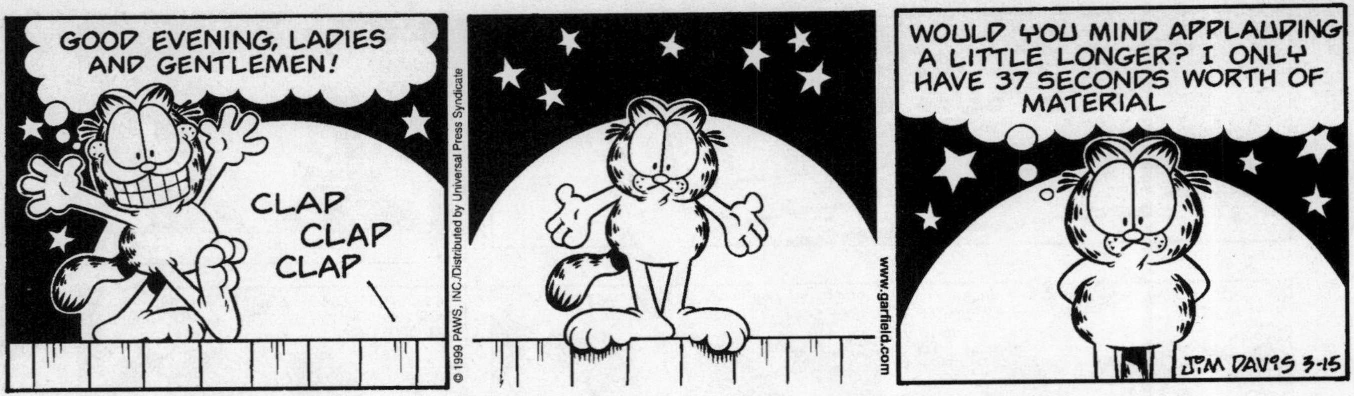
GOOD EVENING, LADIES AND GENTLEMEN!
CLAP CLAP CLAP
© 1999 PAWS, INC./Distributed by Universal Press Syndicate
www.garfield.com
WOULD YOU MIND APPLAUDING A LITTLE LONGER? I ONLY HAVE 37 SECONDS WORTH OF MATERIAL
JIM DAVIS 3-15

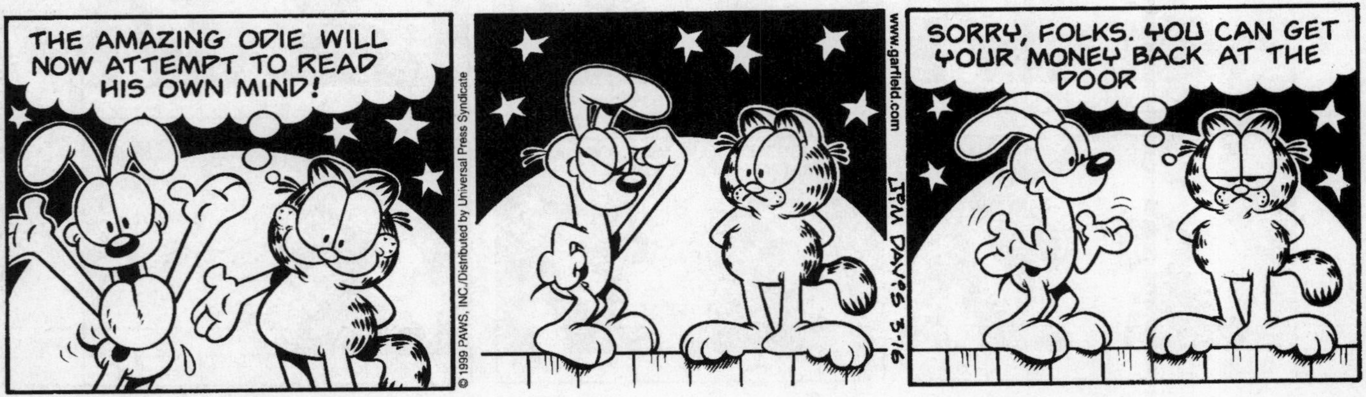
THE AMAZING ODIE WILL NOW ATTEMPT TO READ HIS OWN MIND!
© 1999 PAWS, INC./Distributed by Universal Press Syndicate
www.garfield.com
JIM DAVIS 3-16
SORRY, FOLKS. YOU CAN GET YOUR MONEY BACK AT THE DOOR

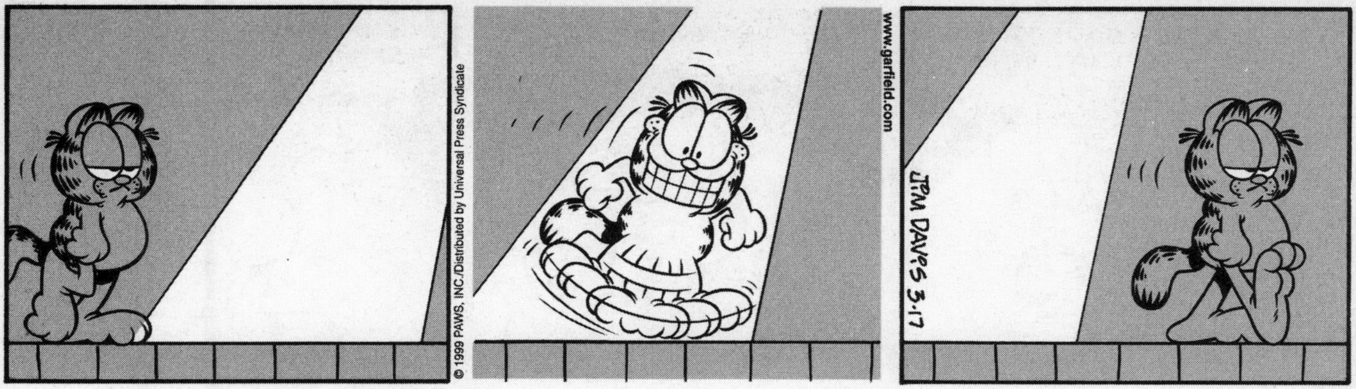
JIM DAVIS 3-17

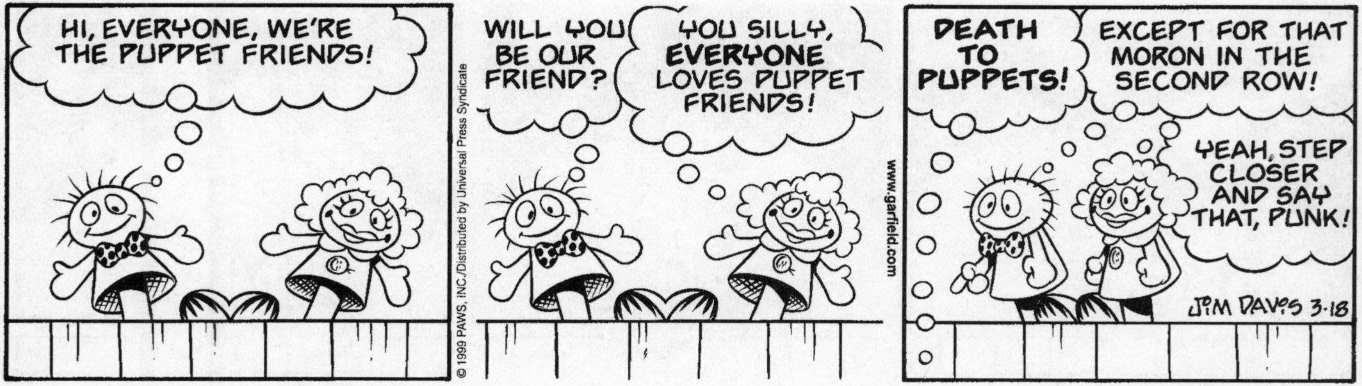
HI, EVERYONE, WE'RE THE PUPPET FRIENDS!
WILL YOU BE OUR FRIEND?
YOU SILLY, EVERYONE LOVES PUPPET FRIENDS!
DEATH TO PUPPETS!
EXCEPT FOR THAT MORON IN THE SECOND ROW!
YEAH, STEP CLOSER AND SAY THAT, PUNK!
JIM DAVIS 3-18

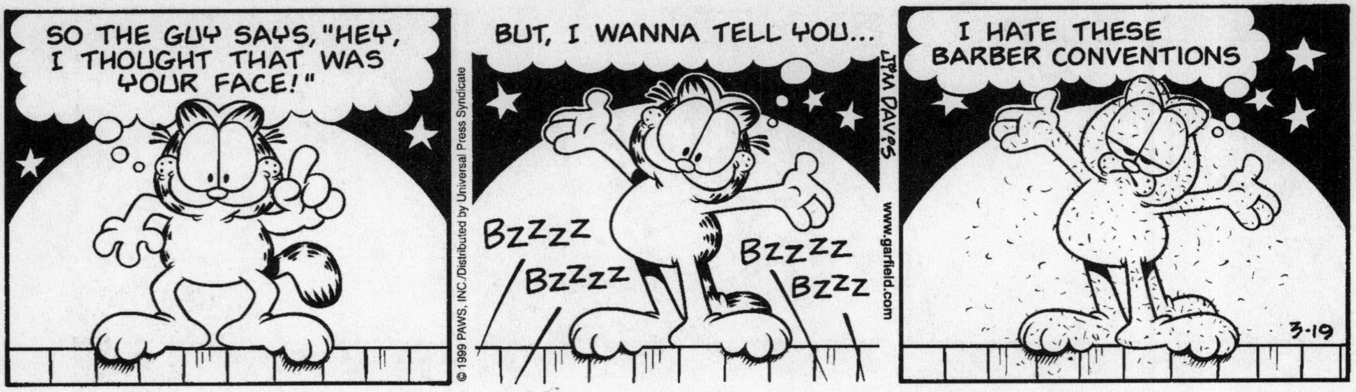
SO THE GUY SAYS, "HEY, I THOUGHT THAT WAS YOUR FACE!"
BUT, I WANNA TELL YOU...
BZZZZ
BZZZZ
BZZZZ
BZZZ
I HATE THESE BARBER CONVENTIONS
3-19
JIM DAVIS
© 1999 PAWS, INC./Distributed by Universal Press Syndicate
www.garfield.com

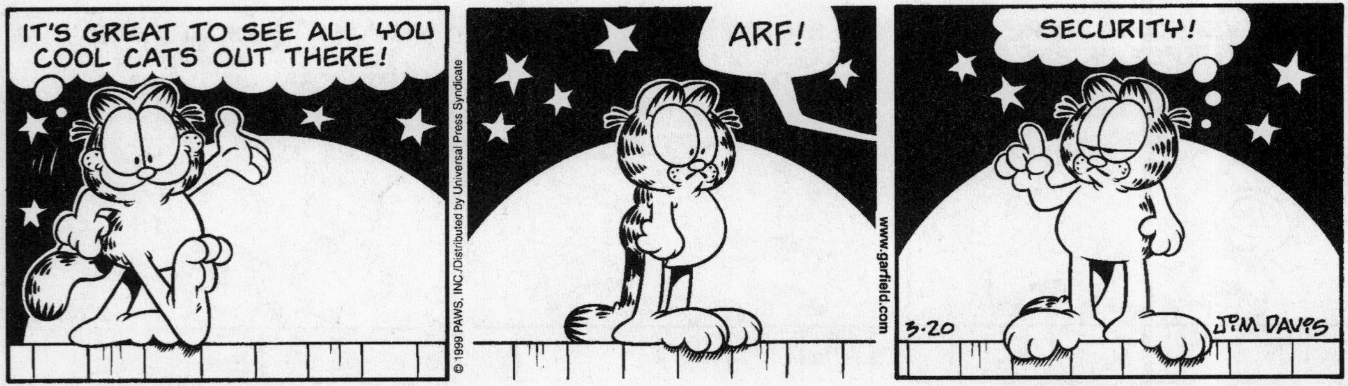
IT'S GREAT TO SEE ALL YOU COOL CATS OUT THERE!
ARF!
SECURITY!
3-20
JIM DAVIS
© 1999 PAWS, INC./Distributed by Universal Press Syndicate
www.garfield.com

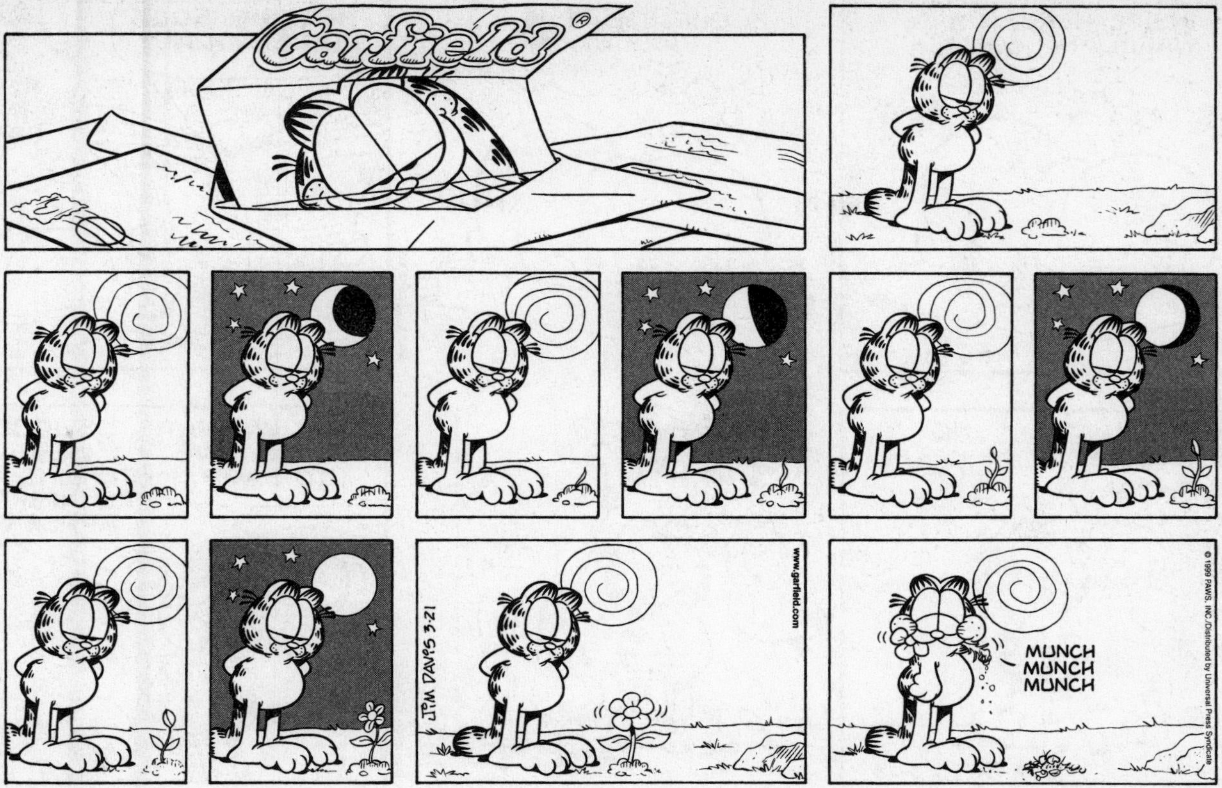
Garfield®
JIM DAVIS 3-21
www.garfield.com
MUNCH
MUNCH
MUNCH
© 1999 PAWS, INC./Distributed by Universal Press Syndicate

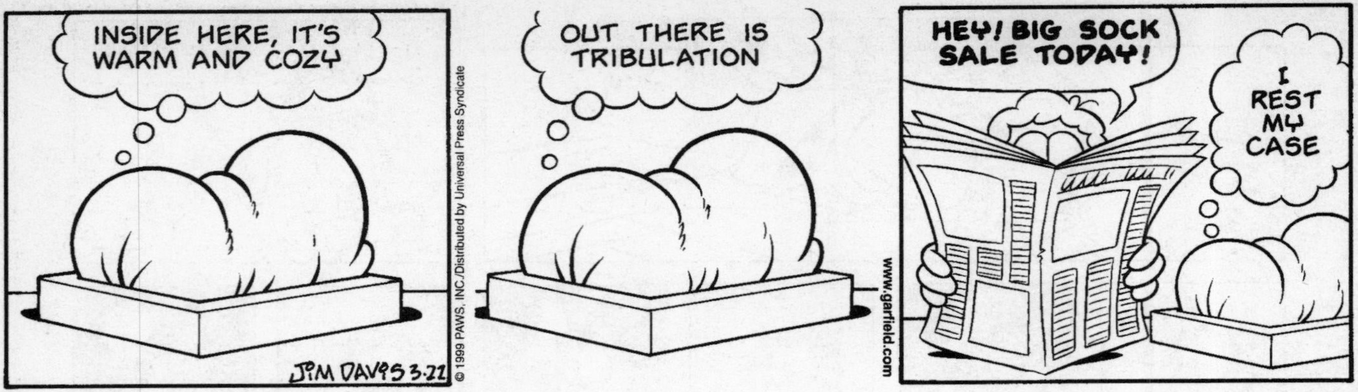
INSIDE HERE, IT'S WARM AND COZY
JIM DAVIS 3-21
© 1999 PAWS, INC./Distributed by Universal Press Syndicate
OUT THERE IS TRIBULATION
www.garfield.com
HEY! BIG SOCK SALE TODAY!
I REST MY CASE

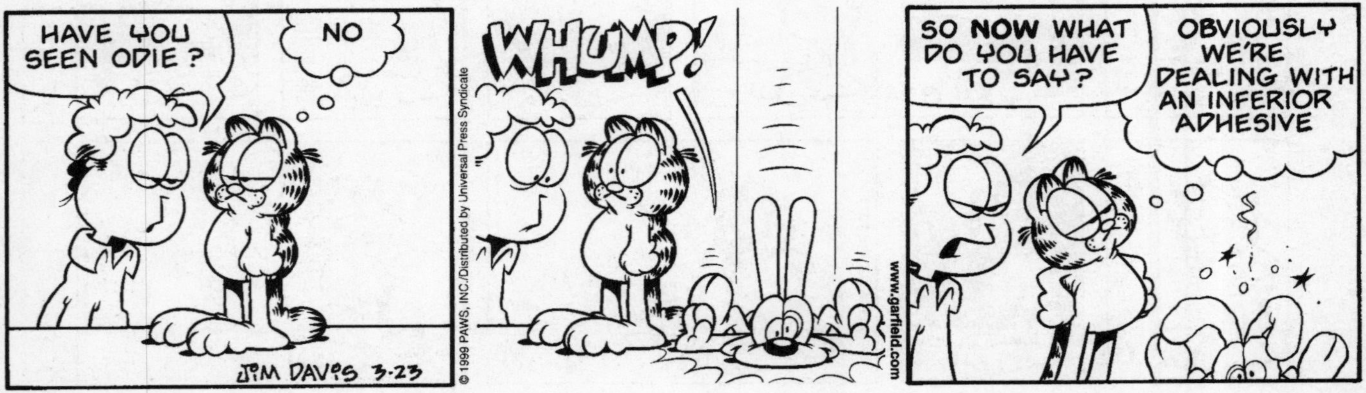
HAVE YOU SEEN ODIE ?
NO
JIM DAVIS 3-23
© 1999 PAWS, INC./Distributed by Universal Press Syndicate
WHUMP!
www.garfield.com
SO NOW WHAT DO YOU HAVE TO SAY?
OBVIOUSLY WE'RE DEALING WITH AN INFERIOR ADHESIVE

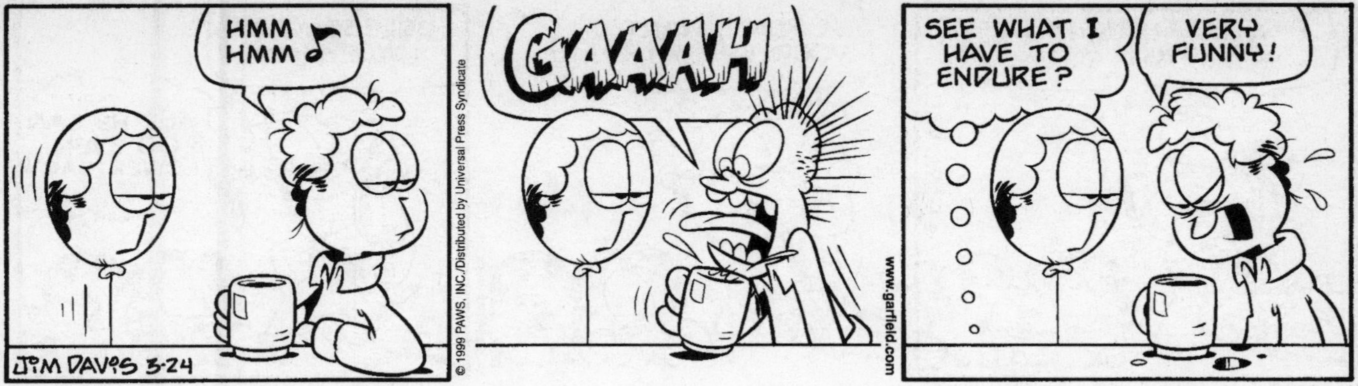
HMM HMM ♪
JIM DAVIS 3-24
© 1999 PAWS, INC./Distributed by Universal Press Syndicate
GAAAH
www.garfield.com
SEE WHAT I HAVE TO ENDURE?
VERY FUNNY!

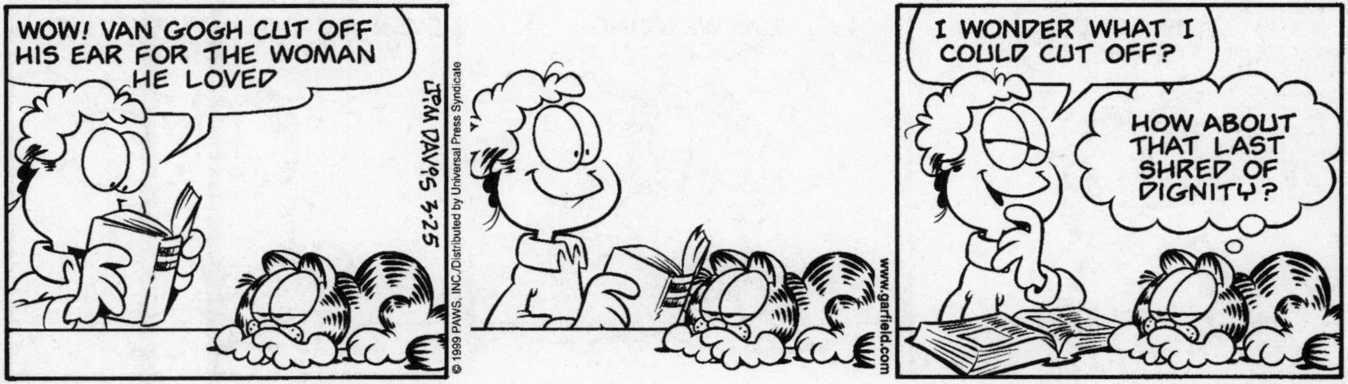
WOW! VAN GOGH CUT OFF HIS EAR FOR THE WOMAN HE LOVED
JIM DAVIS 3-25
© 1999 PAWS, INC./Distributed by Universal Press Syndicate
www.garfield.com
I WONDER WHAT I COULD CUT OFF?
HOW ABOUT THAT LAST SHRED OF DIGNITY?

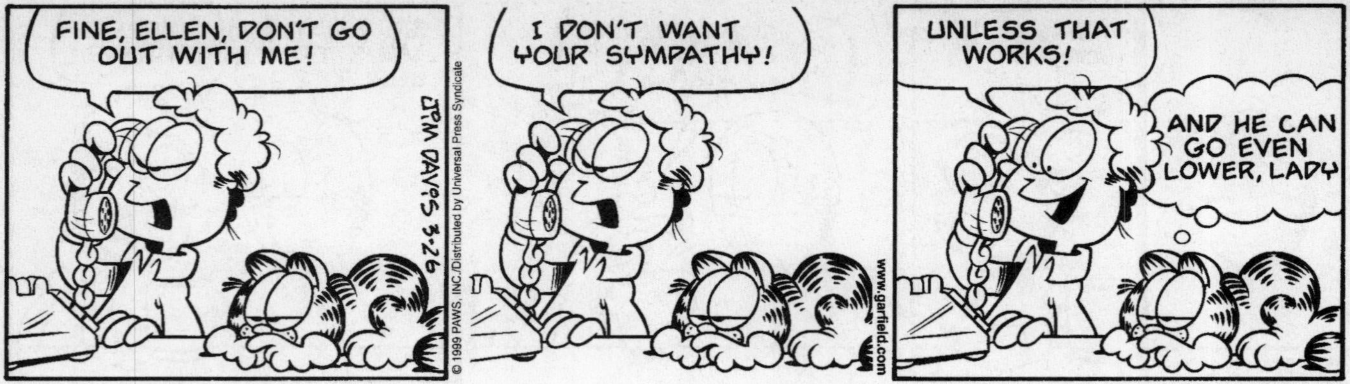
FINE, ELLEN, DON'T GO OUT WITH ME!
JIM DAVIS 3-26
© 1999 PAWS, INC./Distributed by Universal Press Syndicate
I DON'T WANT YOUR SYMPATHY!
www.garfield.com
UNLESS THAT WORKS!
AND HE CAN GO EVEN LOWER, LADY

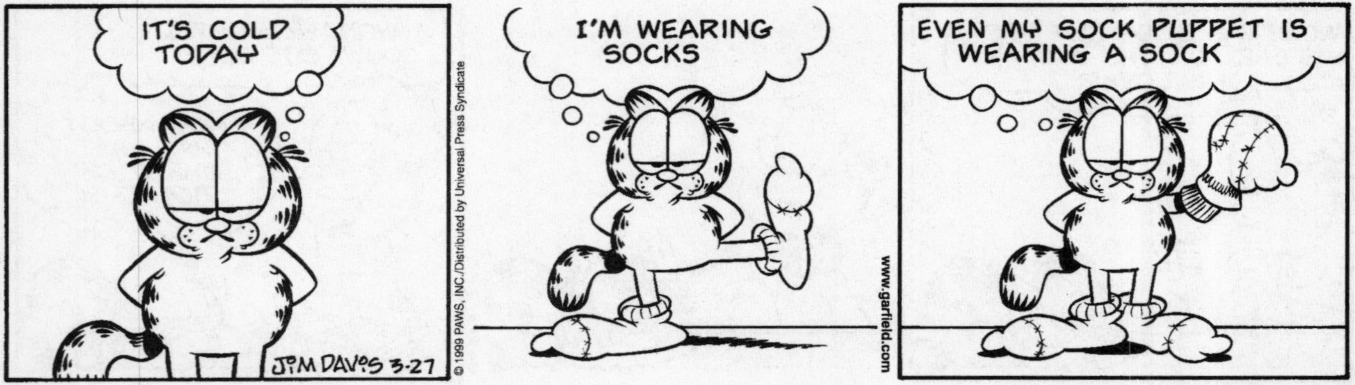
IT'S COLD TODAY
JIM DAVIS 3-27
© 1999 PAWS, INC./Distributed by Universal Press Syndicate
I'M WEARING SOCKS
www.garfield.com
EVEN MY SOCK PUPPET IS WEARING A SOCK

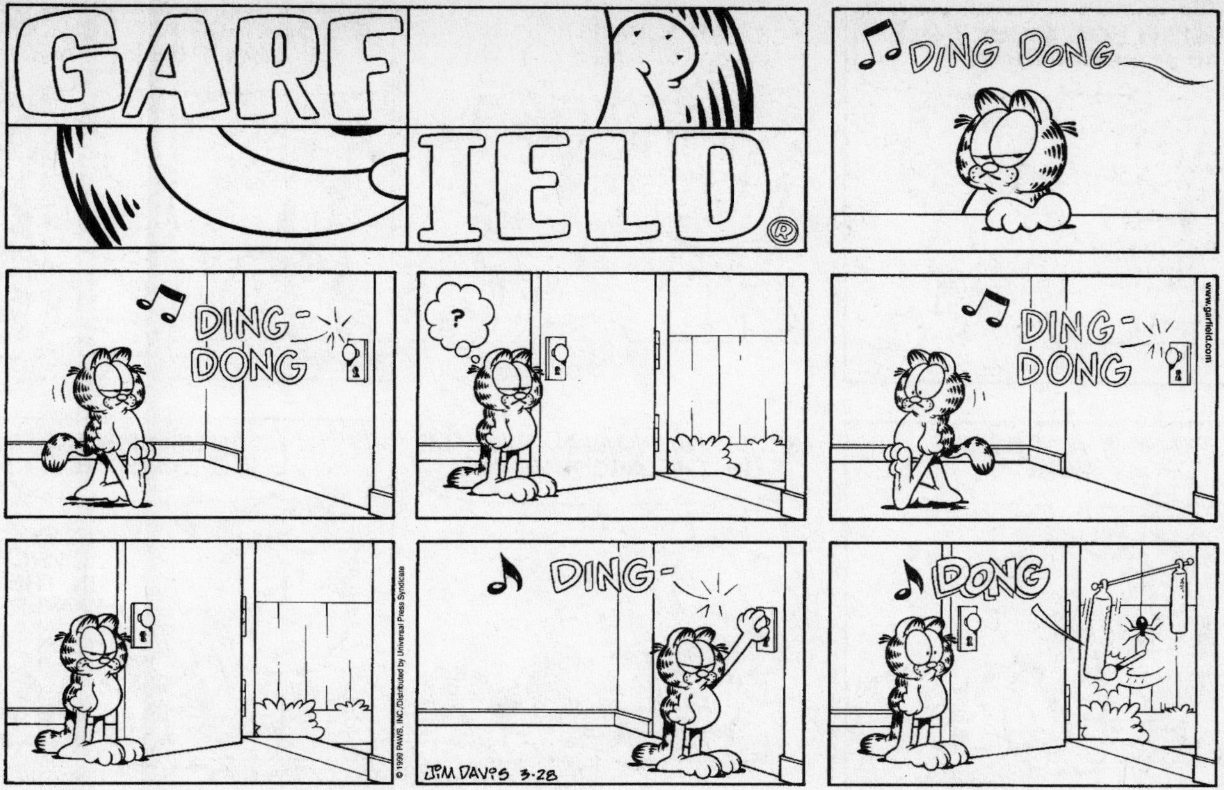
GARFIELD®
DING DONG
DING-DONG
?
DING-DONG
DING-
DONG
www.garfield.com
© 1998 PAWS, INC./Distributed by Universal Press Syndicate
JIM DAVIS 3-28

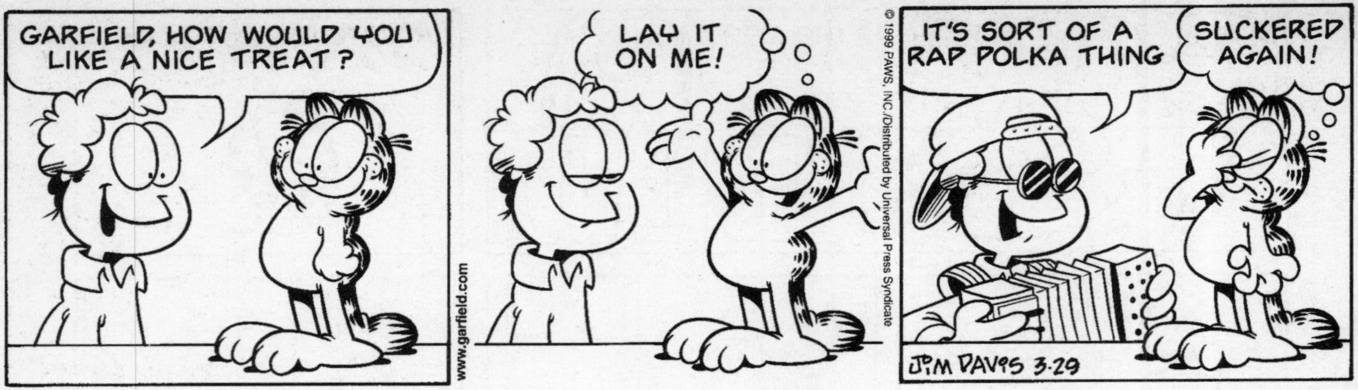
GARFIELD, HOW WOULD YOU LIKE A NICE TREAT?
www.garfield.com
LAY IT ON ME!
© 1999 PAWS, INC./Distributed by Universal Press Syndicate
IT'S SORT OF A RAP POLKA THING
SUCKERED AGAIN!
JIM DAVIS 3-29

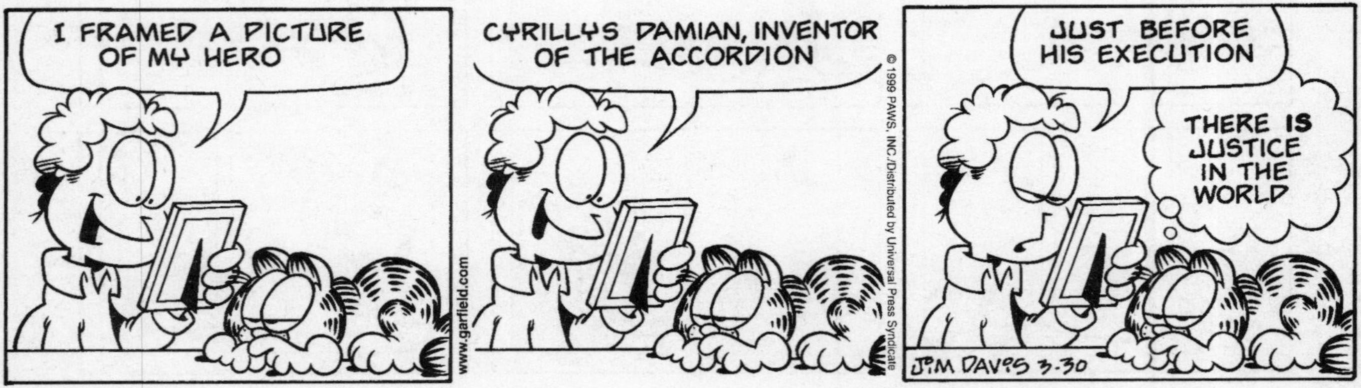
I FRAMED A PICTURE OF MY HERO
www.garfield.com
CYRILLYS DAMIAN, INVENTOR OF THE ACCORDION
© 1999 PAWS, INC./Distributed by Universal Press Syndicate
JUST BEFORE HIS EXECUTION
THERE IS JUSTICE IN THE WORLD
JIM DAVIS 3-30

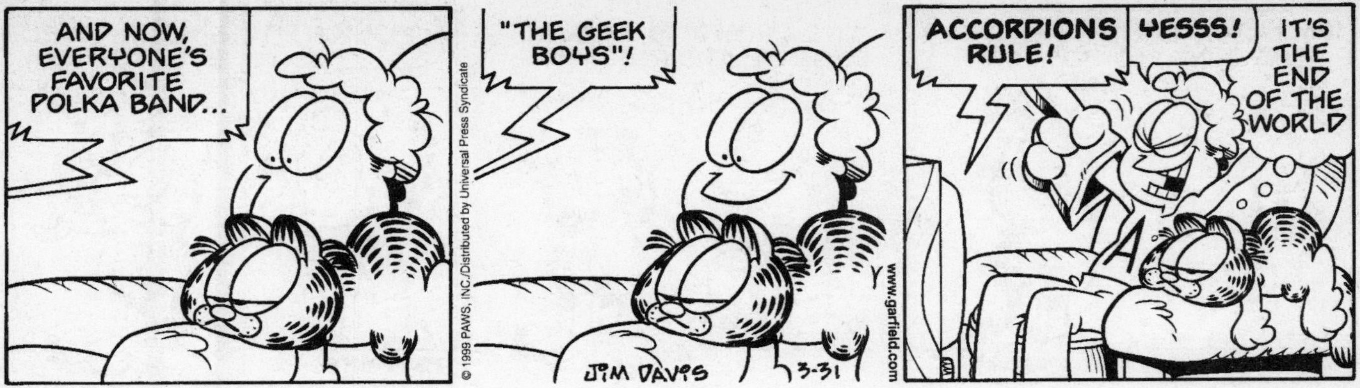

AND NOW, EVERYONE'S FAVORITE POLKA BAND...
"THE GEEK BOYS"!
ACCORDIONS RULE!
YESSS!
IT'S THE END OF THE WORLD
JIM DAVIS 3-31
© 1999 PAWS, INC./Distributed by Universal Press Syndicate
www.garfield.com

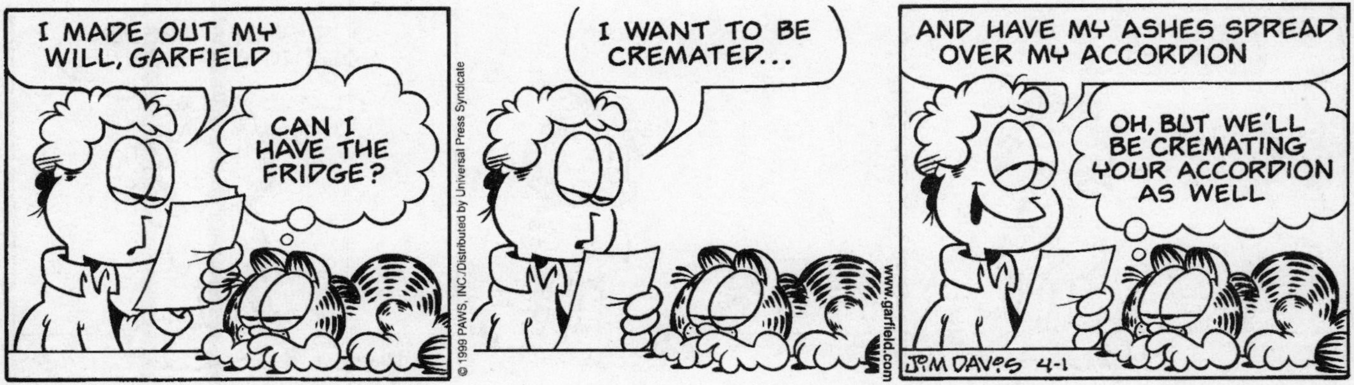

I MADE OUT MY WILL, GARFIELD
CAN I HAVE THE FRIDGE?
I WANT TO BE CREMATED...
AND HAVE MY ASHES SPREAD OVER MY ACCORDION
OH, BUT WE'LL BE CREMATING YOUR ACCORDION AS WELL
JIM DAVIS 4-1
© 1999 PAWS, INC./Distributed by Universal Press Syndicate
www.garfield.com

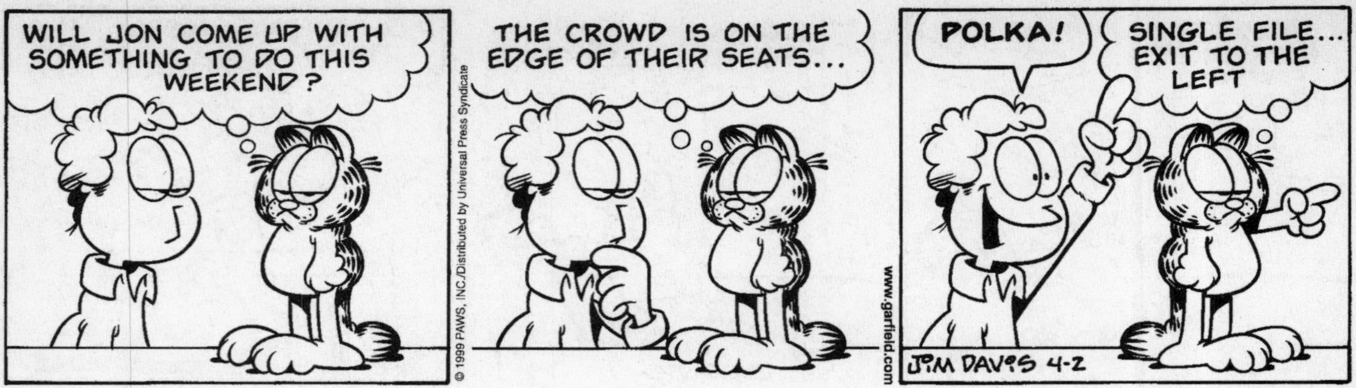
WILL JON COME UP WITH SOMETHING TO DO THIS WEEKEND?
© 1999 PAWS, INC./Distributed by Universal Press Syndicate
THE CROWD IS ON THE EDGE OF THEIR SEATS...
www.garfield.com
POLKA!
SINGLE FILE... EXIT TO THE LEFT
JIM DAVIS 4-2

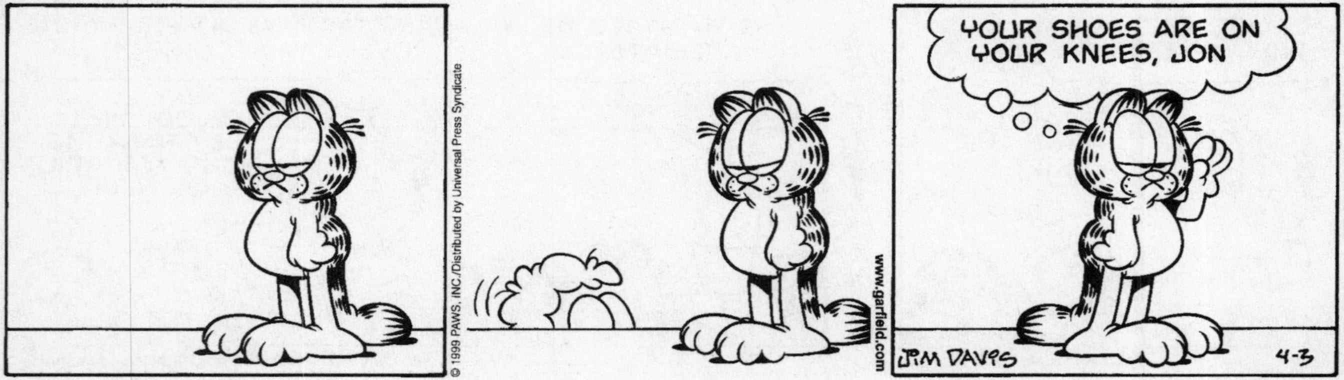
© 1999 PAWS, INC./Distributed by Universal Press Syndicate
www.garfield.com
YOUR SHOES ARE ON YOUR KNEES, JON
JIM DAVIS
4-3

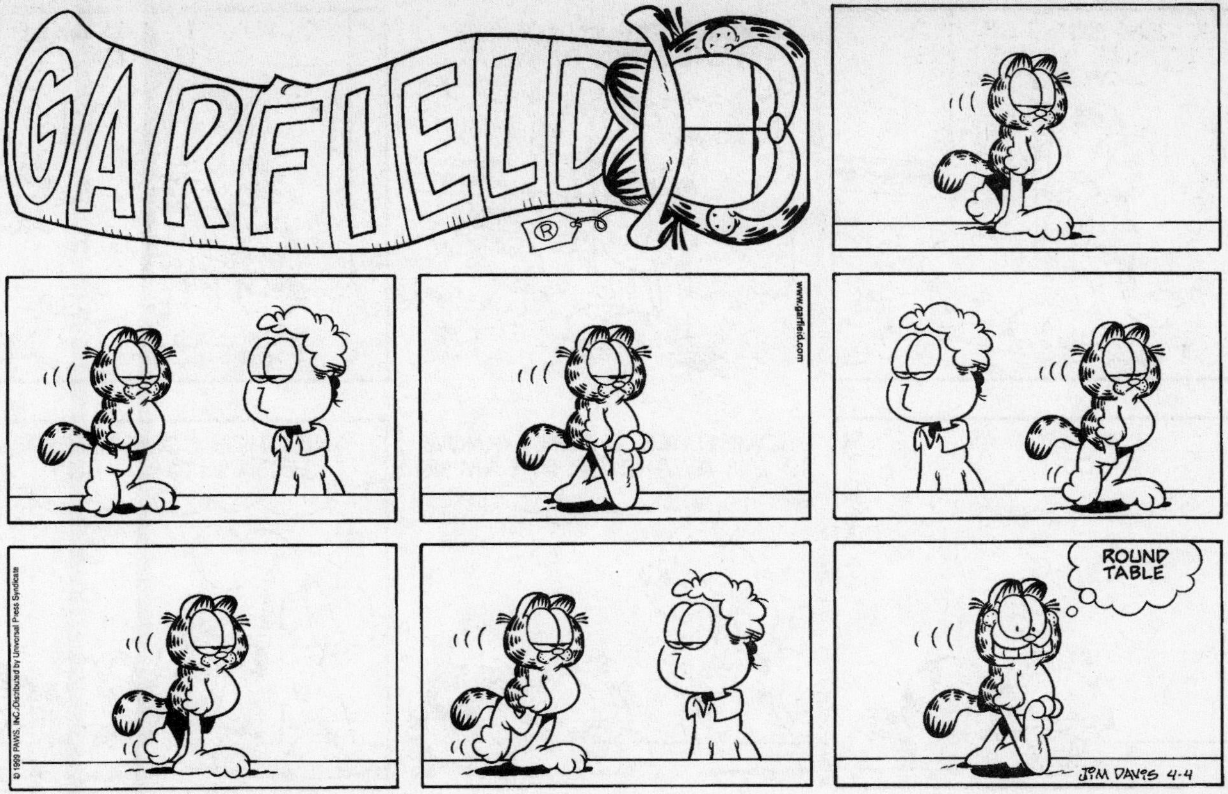
GARFIELD
www.garfield.com
© 1999 PAWS, INC./Distributed by Universal Press Syndicate
ROUND TABLE
JIM DAVIS 4-4

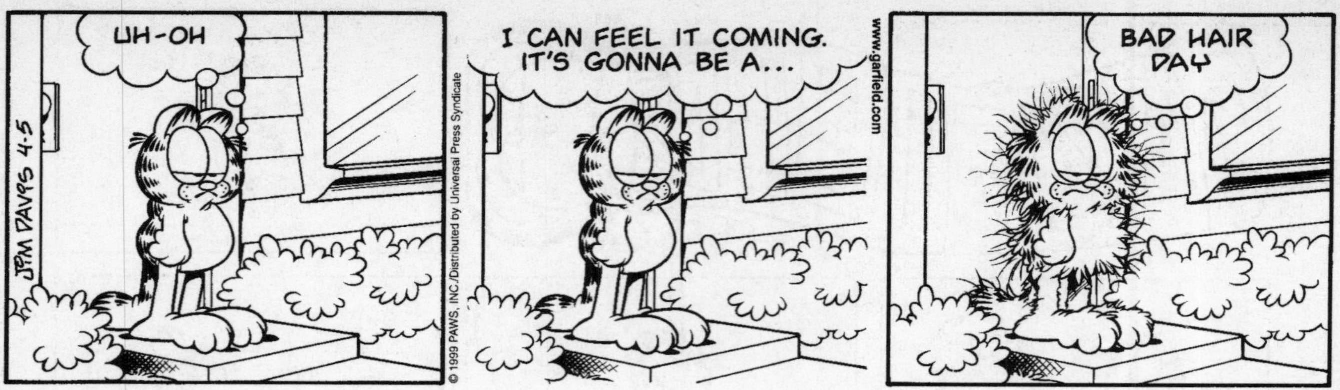
UH-OH
I CAN FEEL IT COMING. IT'S GONNA BE A...
BAD HAIR DAY
JIM DAVIS 4-5
© 1999 PAWS, INC./Distributed by Universal Press Syndicate
www.garfield.com

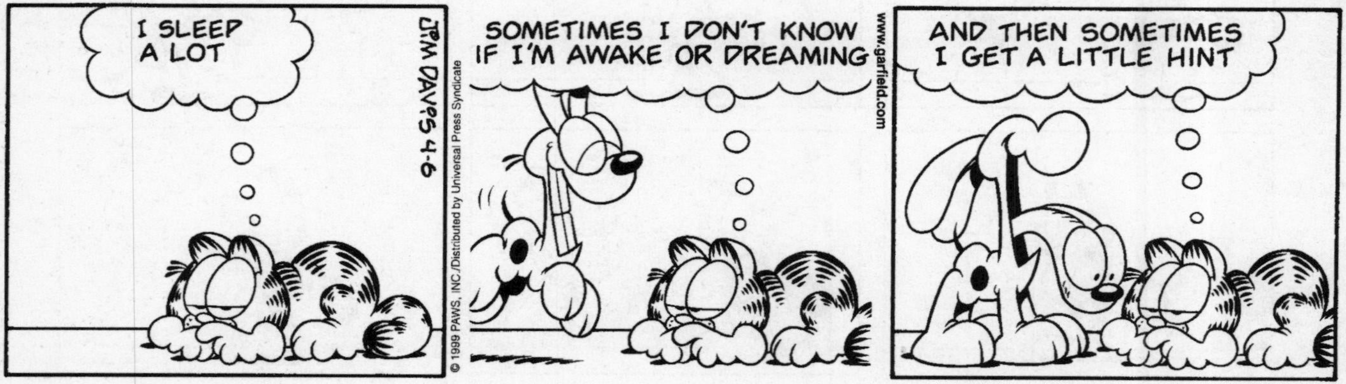
I SLEEP A LOT
SOMETIMES I DON'T KNOW IF I'M AWAKE OR DREAMING
AND THEN SOMETIMES I GET A LITTLE HINT
JIM DAVIS 4-6
© 1999 PAWS, INC./Distributed by Universal Press Syndicate
www.garfield.com

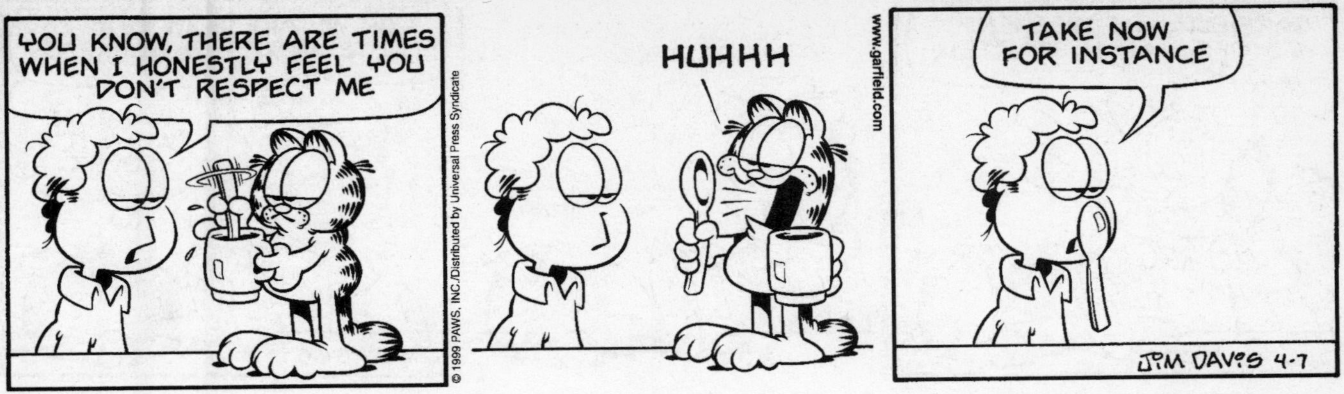
YOU KNOW, THERE ARE TIMES WHEN I HONESTLY FEEL YOU DON'T RESPECT ME
HUHHH
TAKE NOW FOR INSTANCE
JIM DAVIS 4-7
© 1999 PAWS, INC./Distributed by Universal Press Syndicate
www.garfield.com

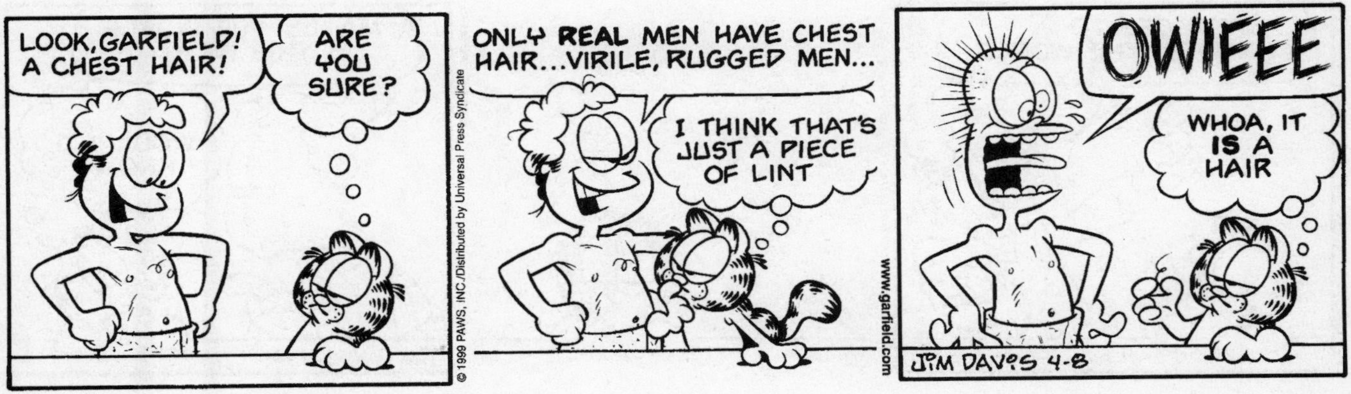
LOOK, GARFIELD! A CHEST HAIR!
ARE YOU SURE?
ONLY REAL MEN HAVE CHEST HAIR... VIRILE, RUGGED MEN...
I THINK THAT'S JUST A PIECE OF LINT
OWIEEE
WHOA, IT IS A HAIR
JIM DAVIS 4-8
© 1999 PAWS, INC./Distributed by Universal Press Syndicate
www.garfield.com

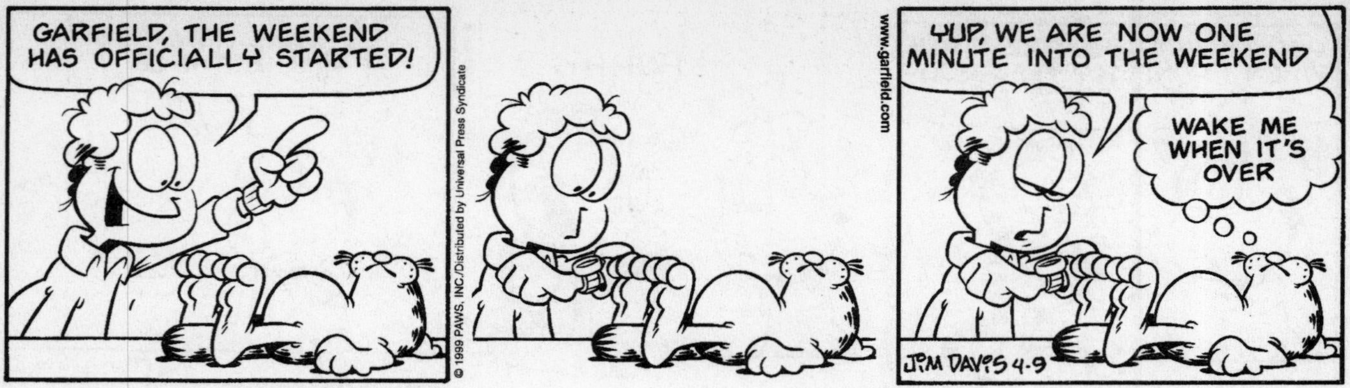
GARFIELD, THE WEEKEND HAS OFFICIALLY STARTED!
YUP, WE ARE NOW ONE MINUTE INTO THE WEEKEND
WAKE ME WHEN IT'S OVER
JIM DAVIS 4-9

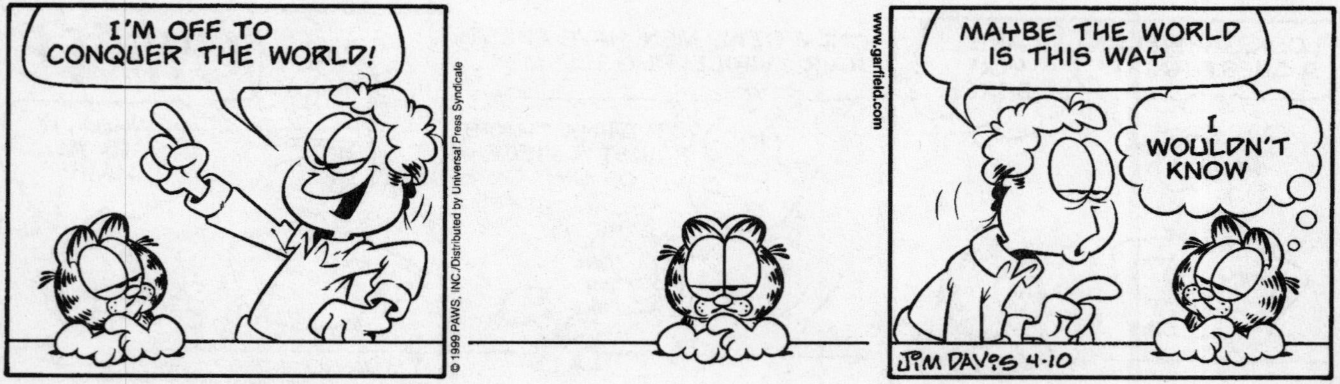
I'M OFF TO CONQUER THE WORLD!
MAYBE THE WORLD IS THIS WAY
I WOULDN'T KNOW
JIM DAVIS 4-10

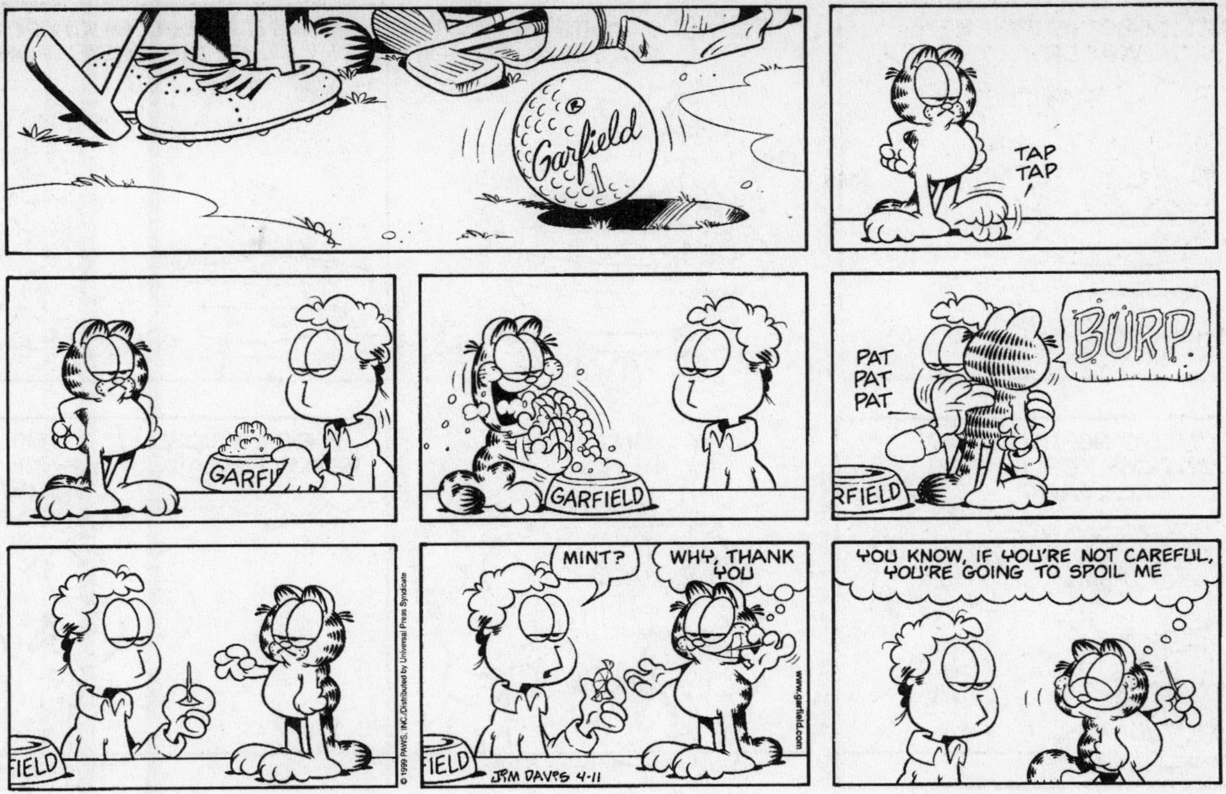
Garfield
TAP TAP
GARFIELD
GARFIELD
PAT PAT PAT
BURP
RFIELD
© 1999 PAWS, INC./Distributed by Universal Press Syndicate
FIELD
MINT?
WHY, THANK YOU
FIELD
JIM DAVIS 4-11
www.garfield.com
YOU KNOW, IF YOU'RE NOT CAREFUL, YOU'RE GOING TO SPOIL ME

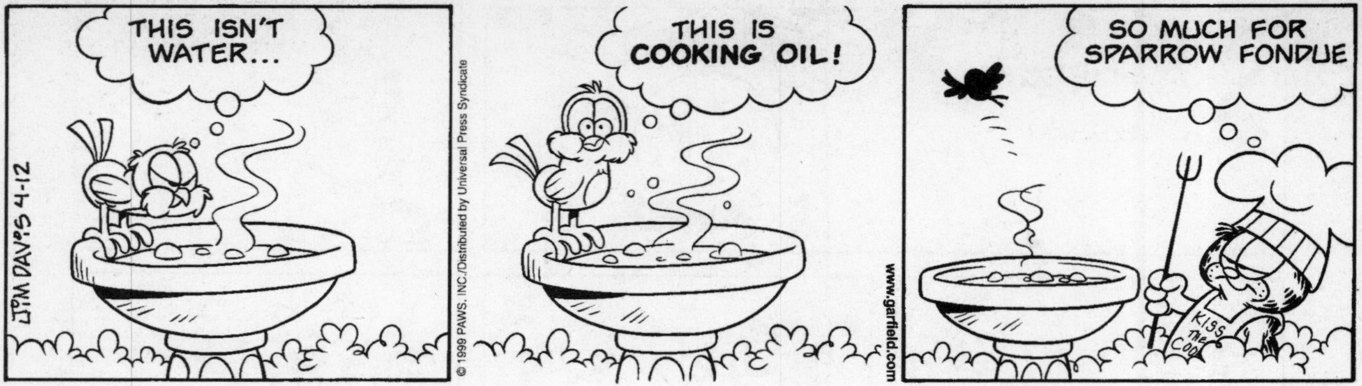
THIS ISN'T WATER...
JIM DAVIS 4-12
© 1999 PAWS, INC./Distributed by Universal Press Syndicate
THIS IS COOKING OIL!
www.garfield.com
SO MUCH FOR SPARROW FONDUE
KISS THE COOK

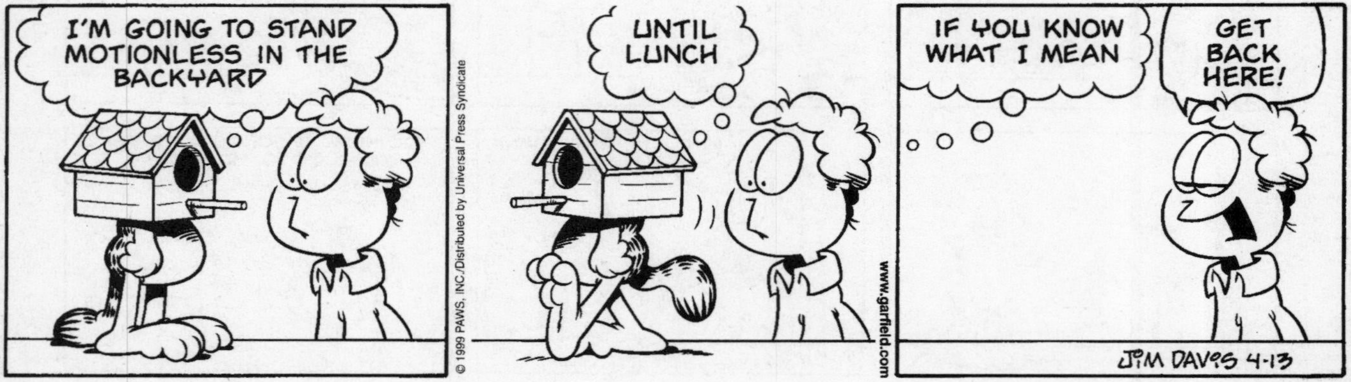
I'M GOING TO STAND MOTIONLESS IN THE BACKYARD
© 1999 PAWS, INC./Distributed by Universal Press Syndicate
UNTIL LUNCH
www.garfield.com
IF YOU KNOW WHAT I MEAN
GET BACK HERE!
JIM DAVIS 4-13

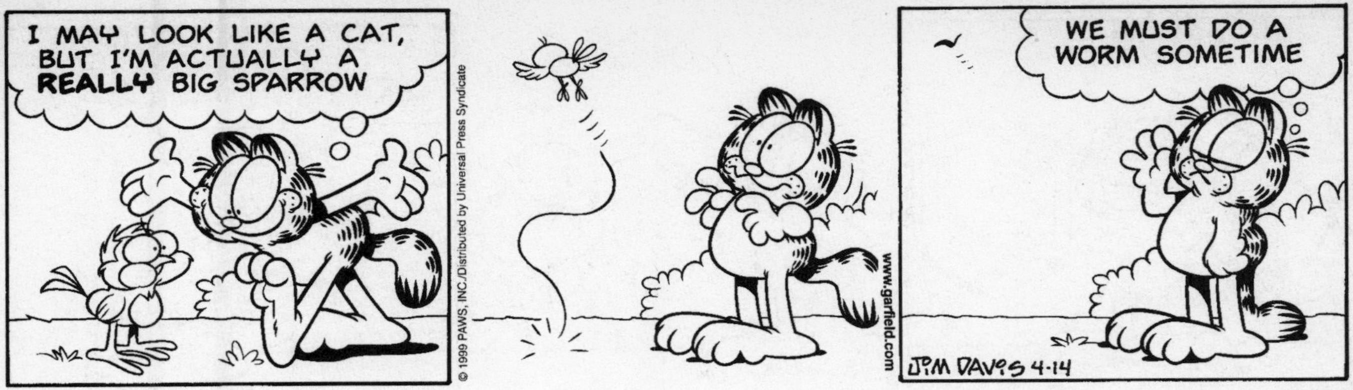
I MAY LOOK LIKE A CAT, BUT I'M ACTUALLY A REALLY BIG SPARROW
© 1999 PAWS, INC./Distributed by Universal Press Syndicate
www.garfield.com
WE MUST DO A WORM SOMETIME
JIM DAVIS 4-14

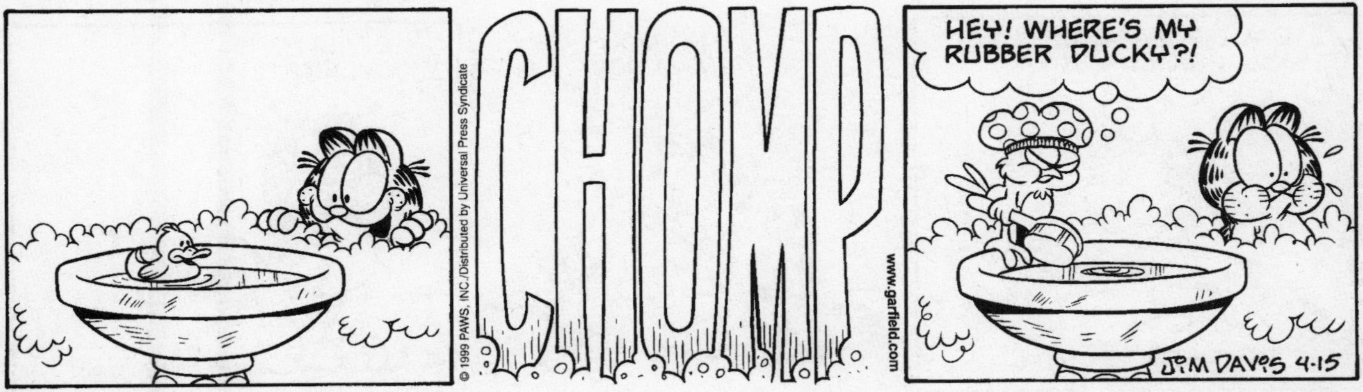
© 1999 PAWS, INC./Distributed by Universal Press Syndicate
CHOMP
www.garfield.com
HEY! WHERE'S MY RUBBER DUCKY?!
JIM DAVIS 4-15

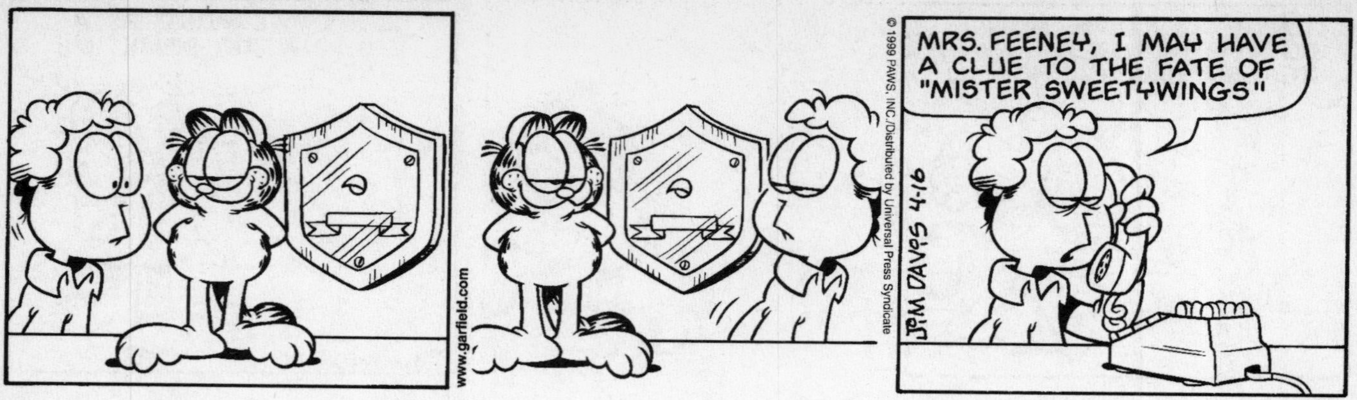
MRS. FEENEY, I MAY HAVE A CLUE TO THE FATE OF "MISTER SWEETYWINGS"
JIM DAVIS 4-16
© 1999 PAWS, INC./Distributed by Universal Press Syndicate
www.garfield.com

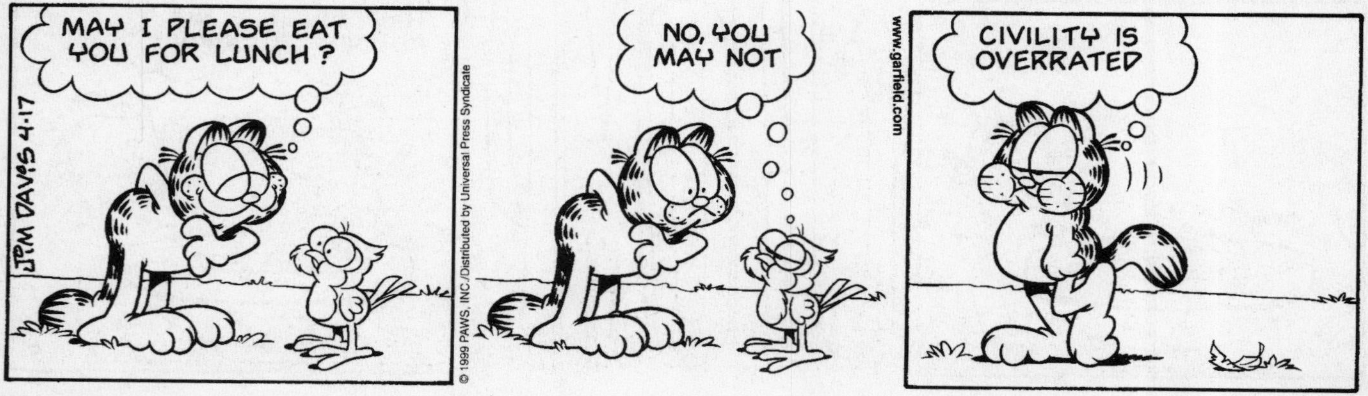
MAY I PLEASE EAT YOU FOR LUNCH?
NO, YOU MAY NOT
CIVILITY IS OVERRATED
JIM DAVIS 4-17
© 1999 PAWS, INC./Distributed by Universal Press Syndicate
www.garfield.com

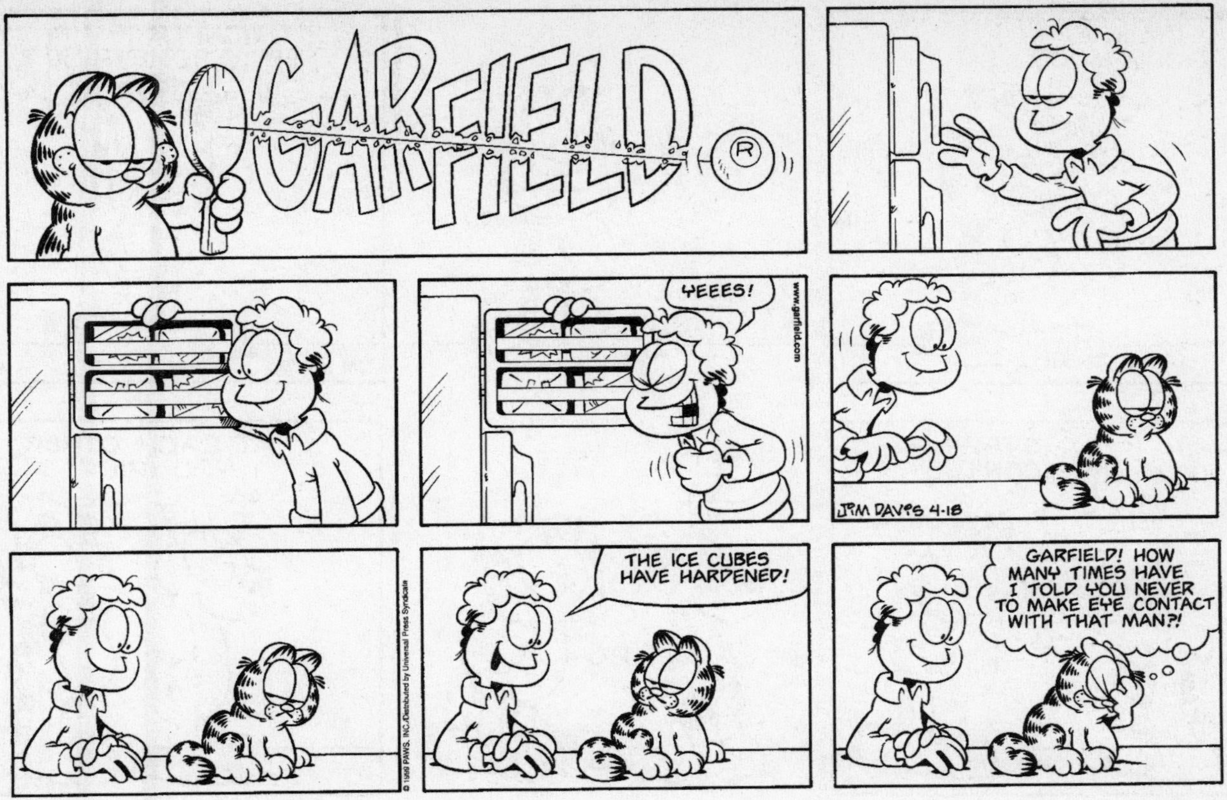
GARFIELD
YEEEES!
www.garfield.com
JIM DAVIS 4-18
© 1999 PAWS, INC./Distributed by Universal Press Syndicate
THE ICE CUBES HAVE HARDENED!
GARFIELD! HOW MANY TIMES HAVE I TOLD YOU NEVER TO MAKE EYE CONTACT WITH THAT MAN?!

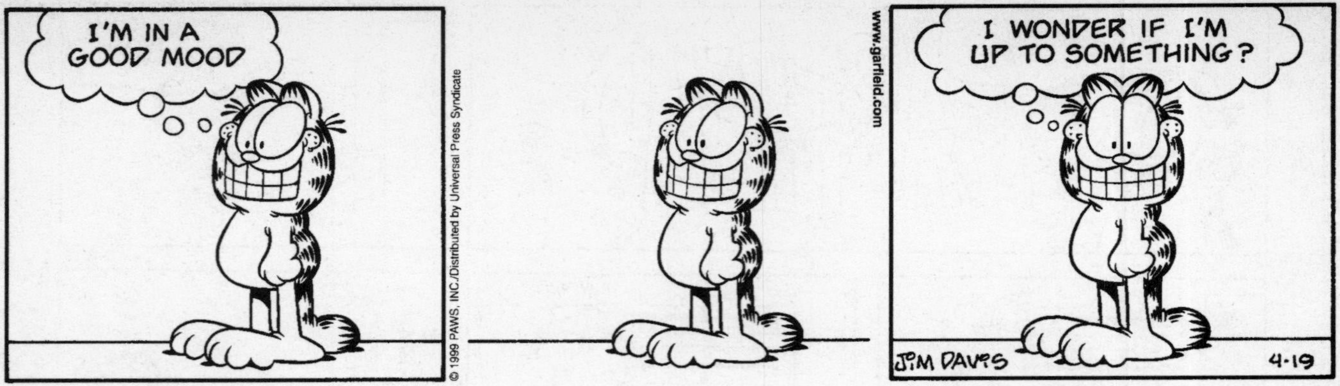
I'M IN A GOOD MOOD
I WONDER IF I'M UP TO SOMETHING?
JIM DAVIS
4-19
© 1999 PAWS, INC./Distributed by Universal Press Syndicate
www.garfield.com

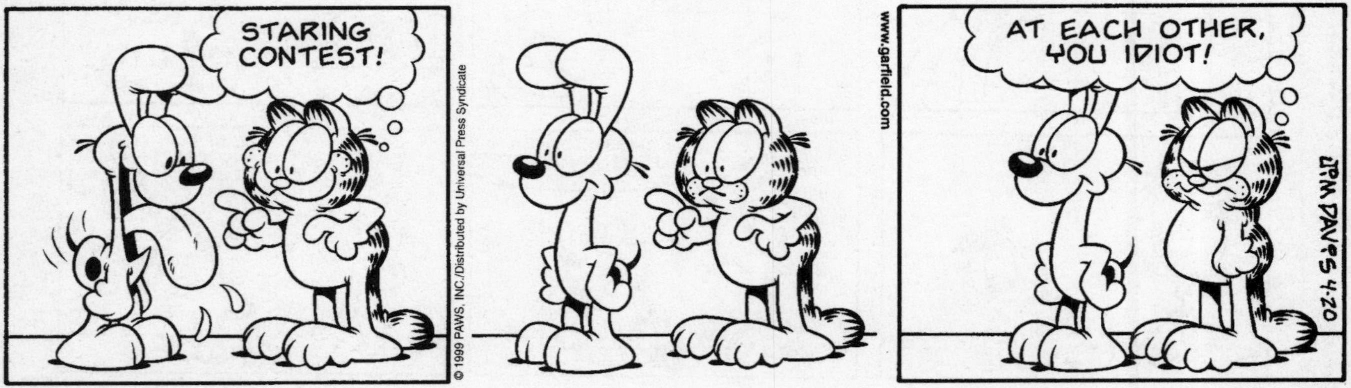
STARING CONTEST!
AT EACH OTHER, YOU IDIOT!
JIM DAVIS 4-20
© 1999 PAWS, INC./Distributed by Universal Press Syndicate
www.garfield.com

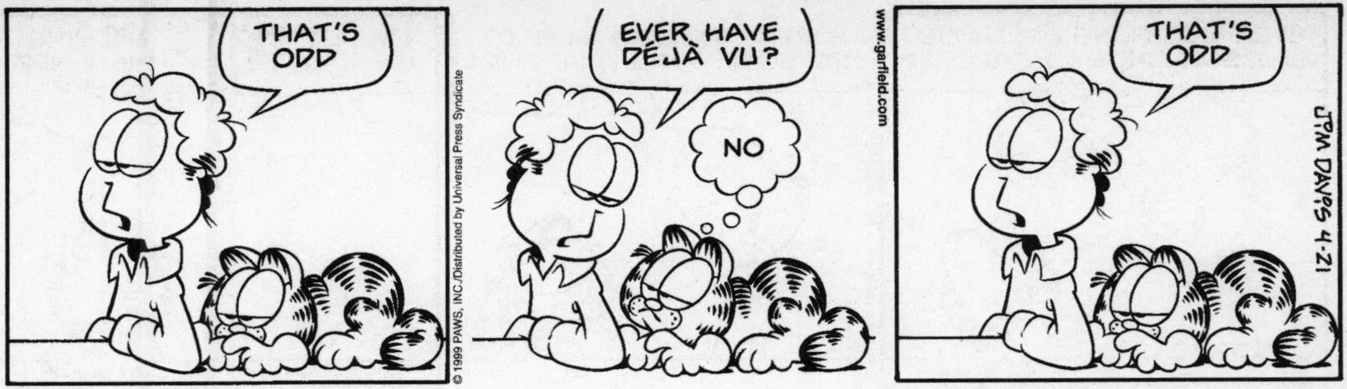
THAT'S ODD
EVER HAVE DÉJÀ VU?
NO
THAT'S ODD
JIM DAVIS 4-21
www.garfield.com

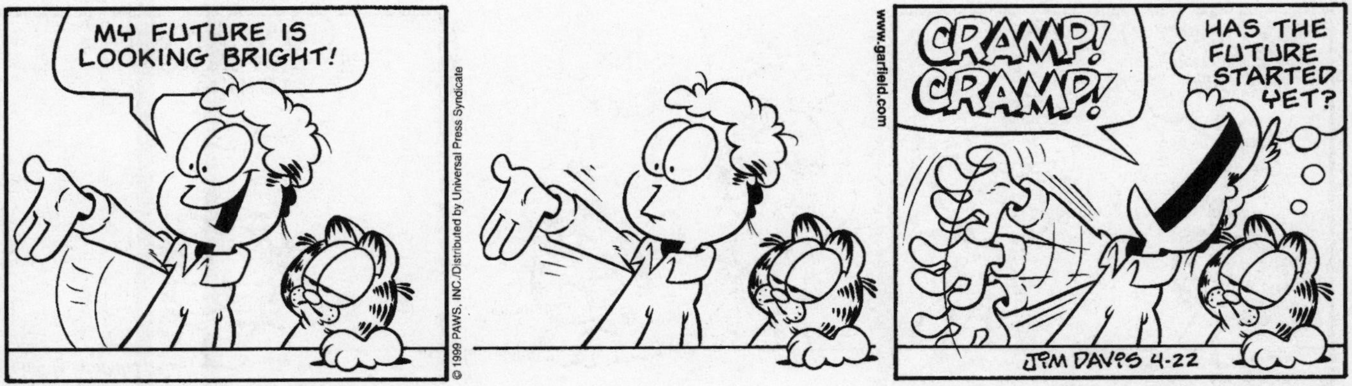
MY FUTURE IS LOOKING BRIGHT!
CRAMP! CRAMP!
HAS THE FUTURE STARTED YET?
JIM DAVIS 4-22
www.garfield.com

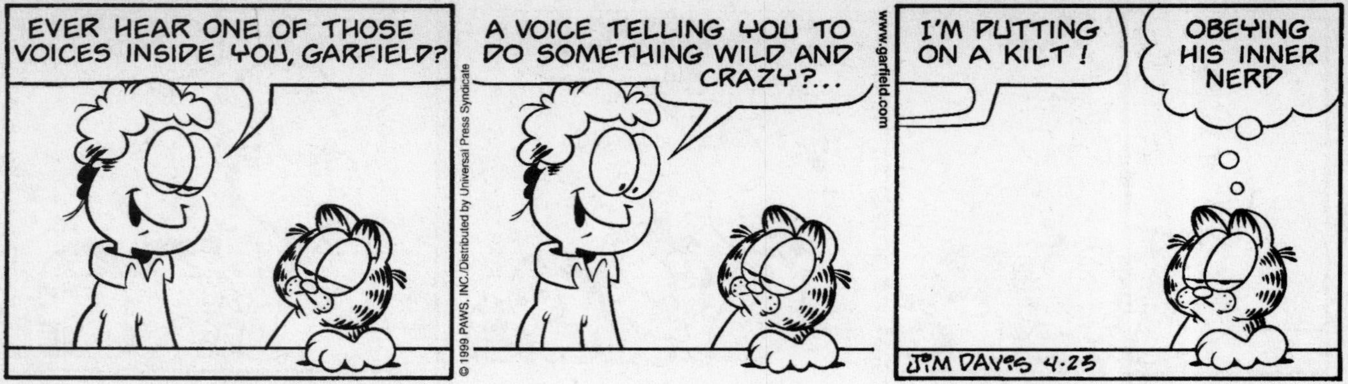
EVER HEAR ONE OF THOSE VOICES INSIDE YOU, GARFIELD?
A VOICE TELLING YOU TO DO SOMETHING WILD AND CRAZY?...
I'M PUTTING ON A KILT!
OBEYING HIS INNER NERD
JIM DAVIS 4-23
© 1999 PAWS, INC./Distributed by Universal Press Syndicate
www.garfield.com

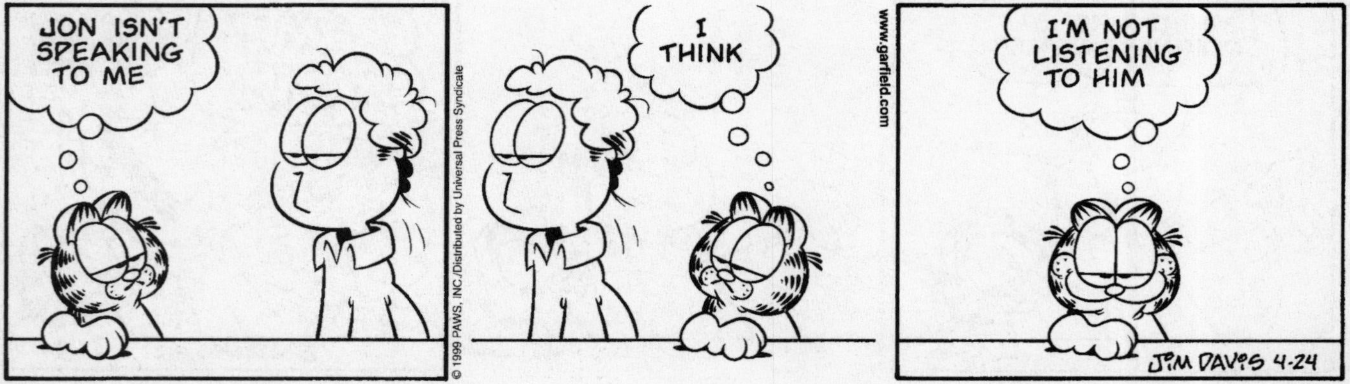
JON ISN'T SPEAKING TO ME
I THINK
I'M NOT LISTENING TO HIM
JIM DAVIS 4-24
© 1999 PAWS, INC./Distributed by Universal Press Syndicate
www.garfield.com

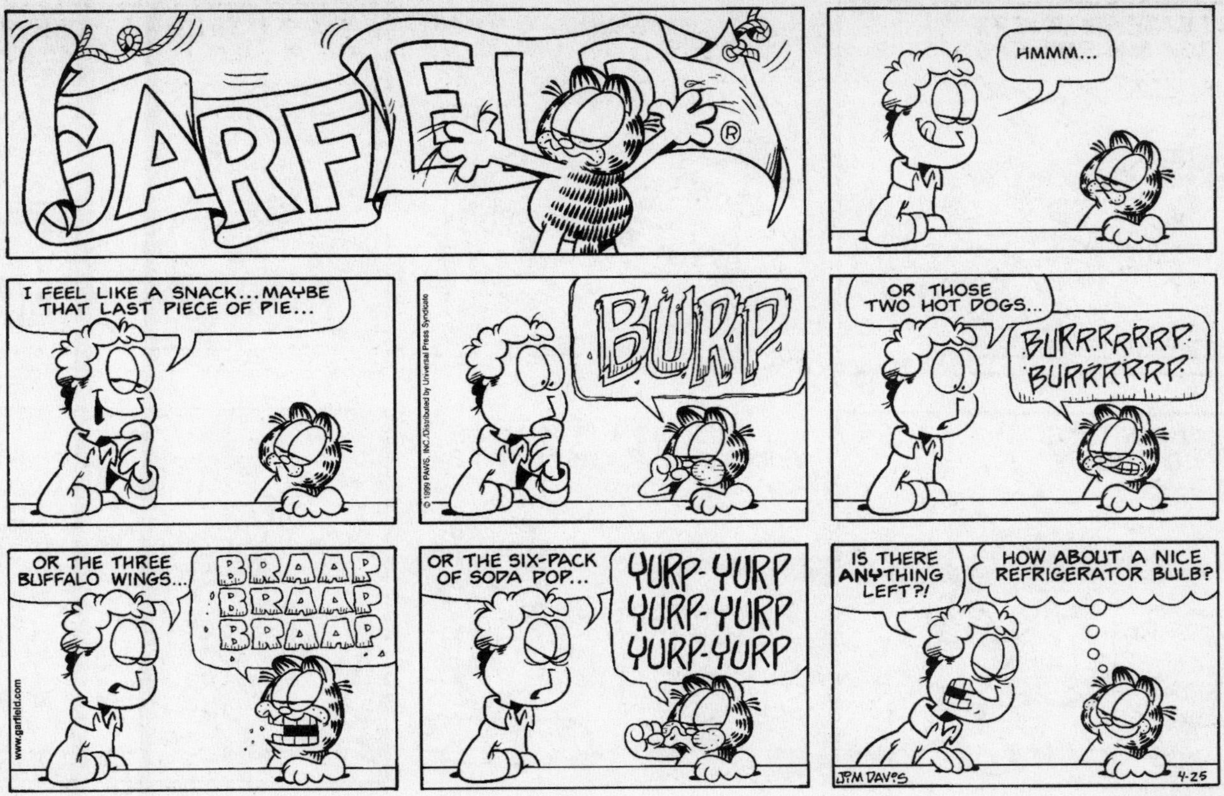
GARFIELD®
HMMM...
I FEEL LIKE A SNACK... MAYBE THAT LAST PIECE OF PIE...
BURP
OR THOSE TWO HOT DOGS...
BURRRRRRP BURRRRRRP
OR THE THREE BUFFALO WINGS...
BRAAP BRAAP BRAAP
OR THE SIX-PACK OF SODA POP...
YURP-YURP YURP-YURP YURP-YURP
IS THERE ANYTHING LEFT?!
HOW ABOUT A NICE REFRIGERATOR BULB?
© 1999 PAWS, INC./Distributed by Universal Press Syndicate
www.garfield.com
JPM DAVPS
4-25

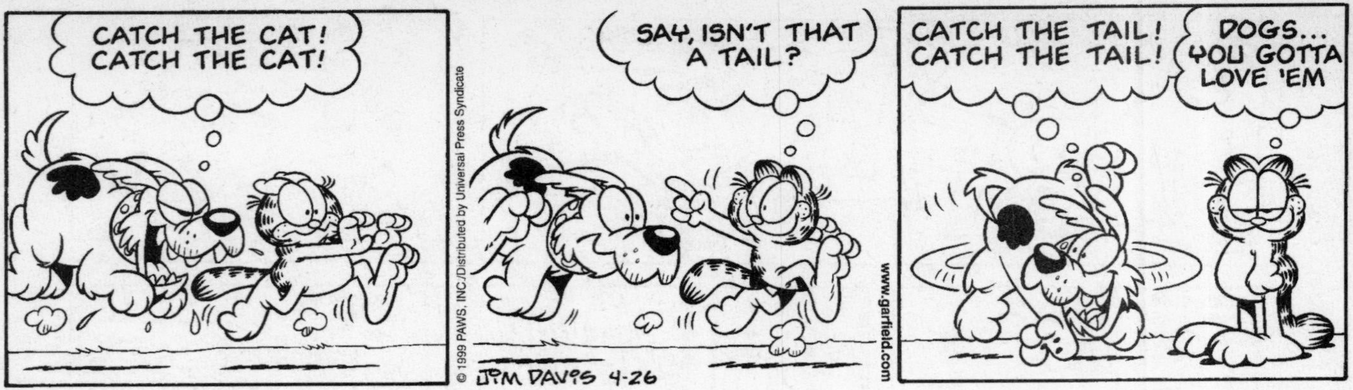
CATCH THE CAT! CATCH THE CAT!
SAY, ISN'T THAT A TAIL?
CATCH THE TAIL! CATCH THE TAIL!
DOGS... YOU GOTTA LOVE 'EM
© 1999 PAWS, INC./Distributed by Universal Press Syndicate
JIM DAVIS 4-26
www.garfield.com

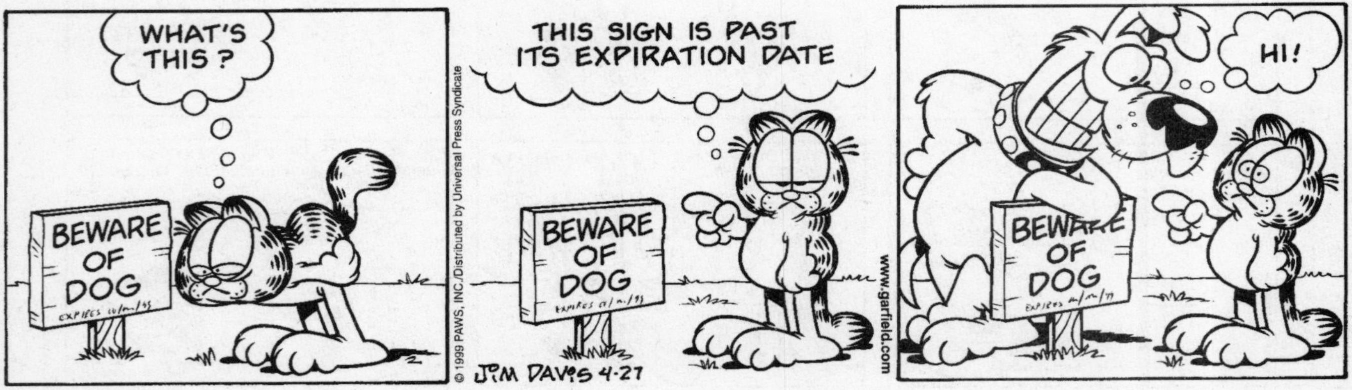
WHAT'S THIS?
BEWARE OF DOG
THIS SIGN IS PAST ITS EXPIRATION DATE
BEWARE OF DOG
HI!
BEWARE OF DOG
© 1999 PAWS, INC./Distributed by Universal Press Syndicate
JIM DAVIS 4-27
www.garfield.com

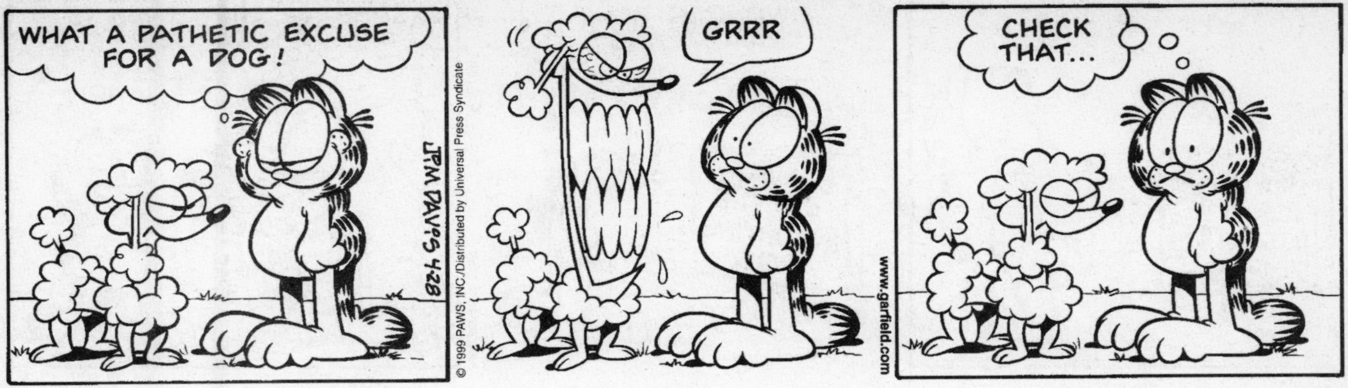
WHAT A PATHETIC EXCUSE FOR A DOG!
JPM DAVPS 4·28
© 1999 PAWS, INC./Distributed by Universal Press Syndicate
GRRR
www.garfield.com
CHECK THAT...

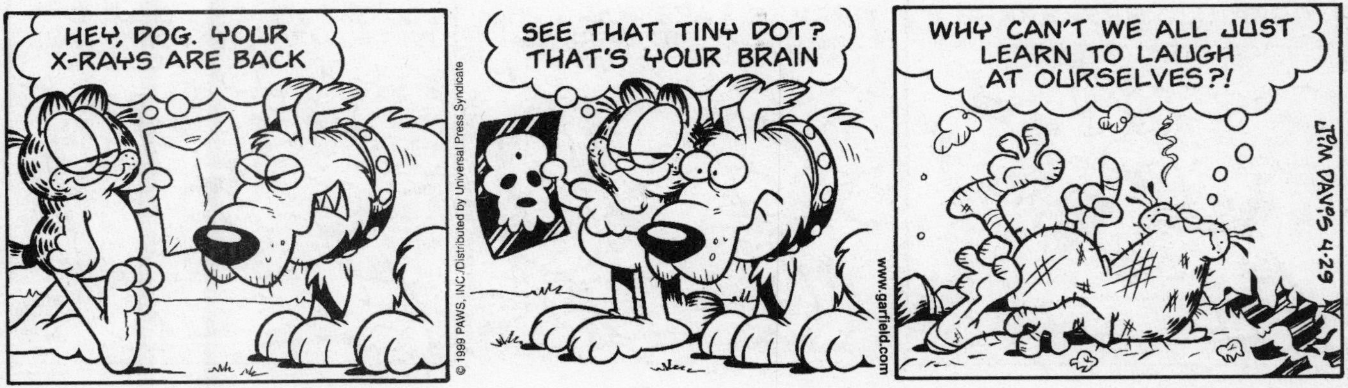
HEY, DOG. YOUR X-RAYS ARE BACK
© 1999 PAWS, INC./Distributed by Universal Press Syndicate
SEE THAT TINY DOT? THAT'S YOUR BRAIN
www.garfield.com
WHY CAN'T WE ALL JUST LEARN TO LAUGH AT OURSELVES?!
JPM DAVPS 4·29

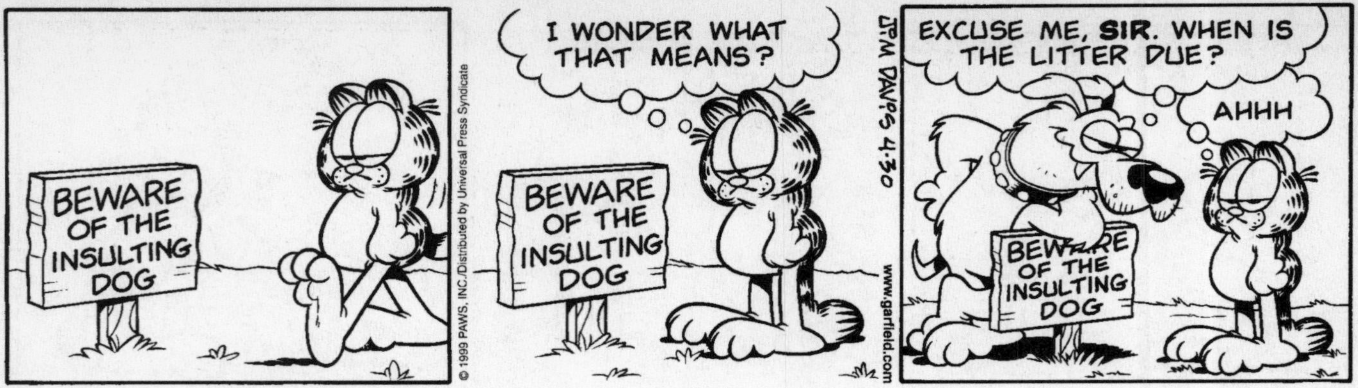
BEWARE OF THE INSULTING DOG
© 1999 PAWS, INC./Distributed by Universal Press Syndicate
I WONDER WHAT THAT MEANS?
BEWARE OF THE INSULTING DOG
JIM DAVIS 4-30
www.garfield.com
EXCUSE ME, **SIR**. WHEN IS THE LITTER DUE?
AHHH
BEWARE OF THE INSULTING DOG

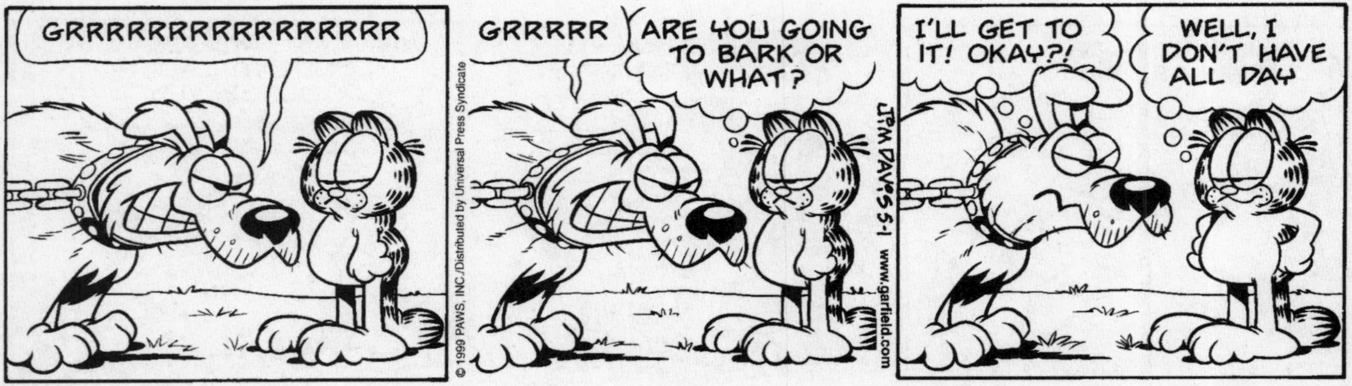
GRRRRRRRRRRRRRRRRR
© 1999 PAWS, INC./Distributed by Universal Press Syndicate
GRRRRR
ARE YOU GOING TO BARK OR WHAT?
JIM DAVIS 5-1
www.garfield.com
I'LL GET TO IT! OKAY?!
WELL, I DON'T HAVE ALL DAY

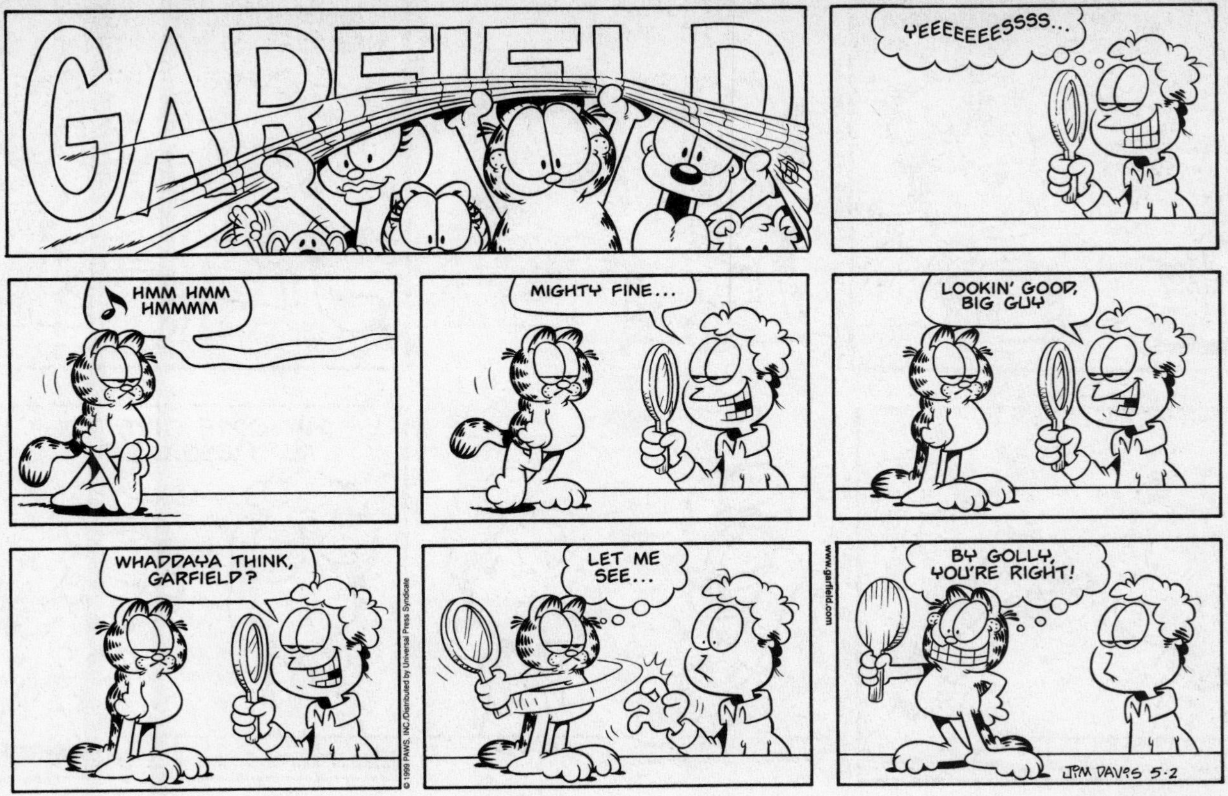
GARFIELD
YEEEEEEESSSS...
HMM HMM HMMMM
MIGHTY FINE...
LOOKIN' GOOD, BIG GUY
WHADDAYA THINK, GARFIELD?
LET ME SEE...
BY GOLLY, YOU'RE RIGHT!
JIM DAVIS 5-2
© 1999 PAWS, INC./Distributed by Universal Press Syndicate
www.garfield.com

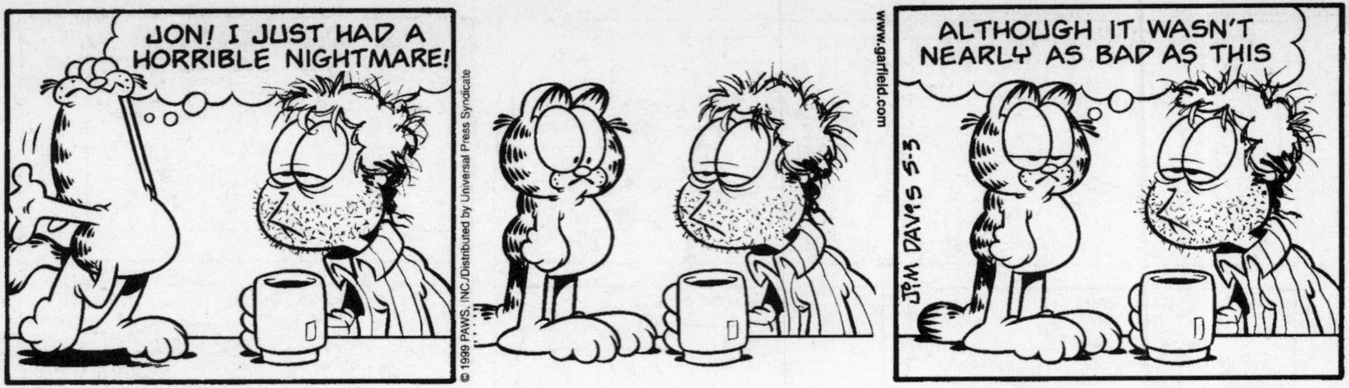
JON! I JUST HAD A HORRIBLE NIGHTMARE!
© 1999 PAWS, INC./Distributed by Universal Press Syndicate
ALTHOUGH IT WASN'T NEARLY AS BAD AS THIS
www.garfield.com
JIM DAVIS 5-3

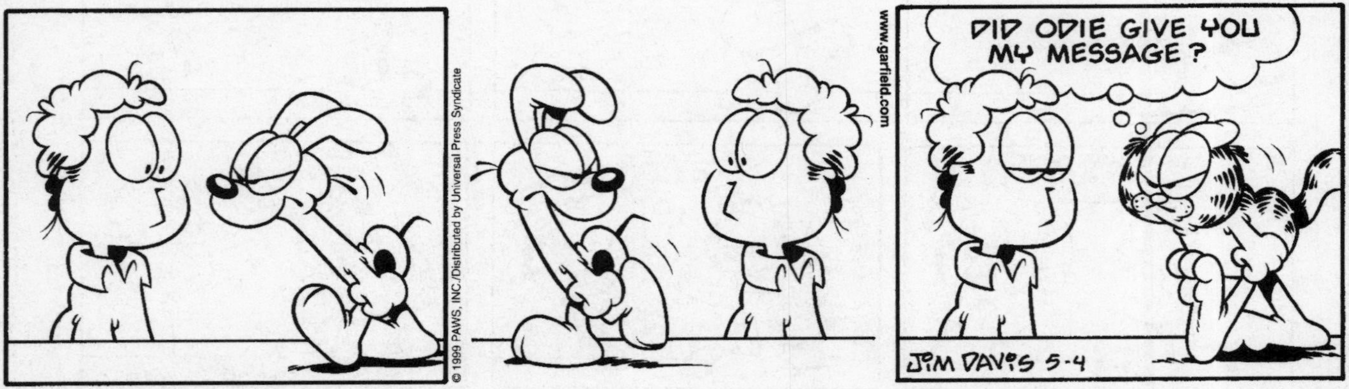
© 1999 PAWS, INC./Distributed by Universal Press Syndicate
www.garfield.com
DID ODIE GIVE YOU MY MESSAGE?
JIM DAVIS 5-4

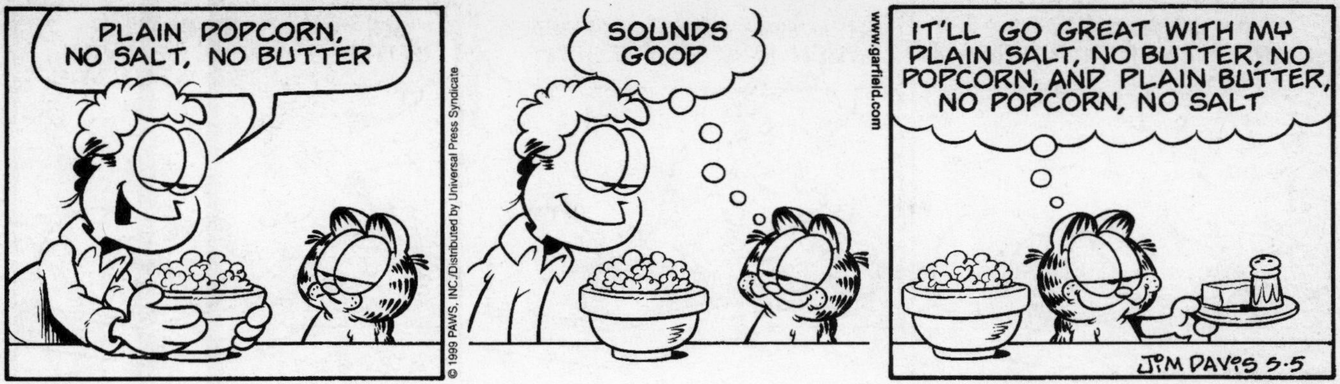
PLAIN POPCORN, NO SALT, NO BUTTER
SOUNDS GOOD
IT'LL GO GREAT WITH MY PLAIN SALT, NO BUTTER, NO POPCORN, AND PLAIN BUTTER, NO POPCORN, NO SALT
© 1999 PAWS, INC./Distributed by Universal Press Syndicate
www.garfield.com
JIM DAVIS 5-5

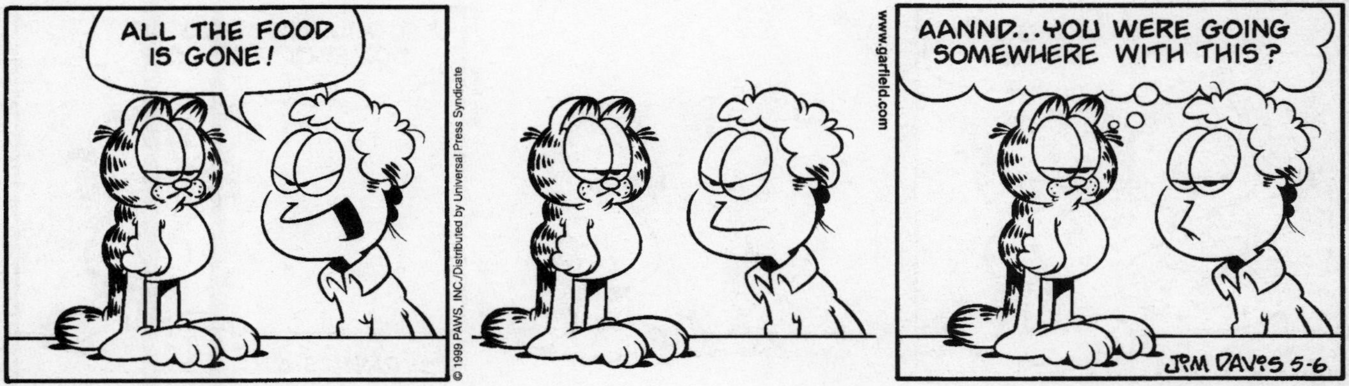
ALL THE FOOD IS GONE!
AANND...YOU WERE GOING SOMEWHERE WITH THIS?
© 1999 PAWS, INC./Distributed by Universal Press Syndicate
www.garfield.com
JIM DAVIS 5-6

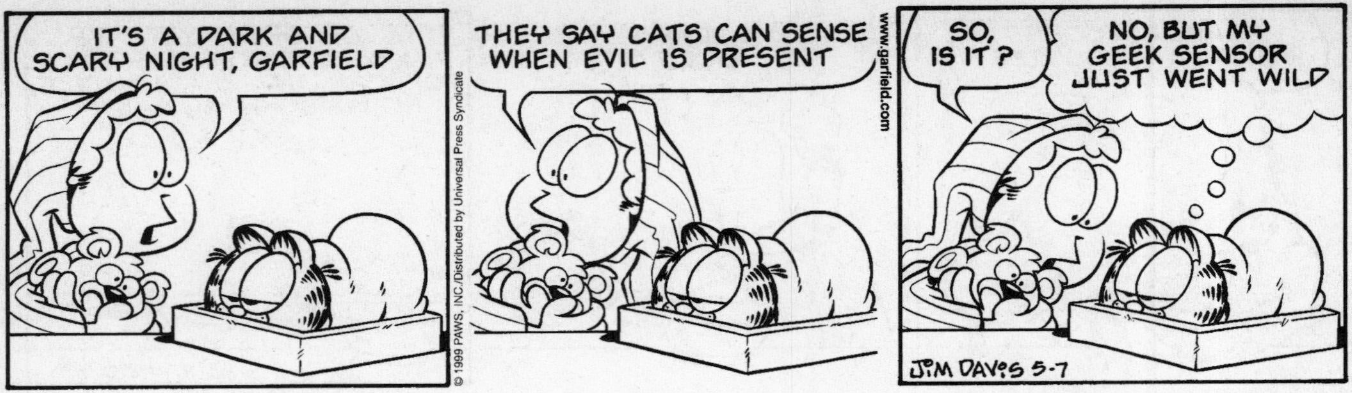
IT'S A DARK AND SCARY NIGHT, GARFIELD
THEY SAY CATS CAN SENSE WHEN EVIL IS PRESENT
SO, IS IT ?
NO, BUT MY GEEK SENSOR JUST WENT WILD
JIM DAVIS 5-7

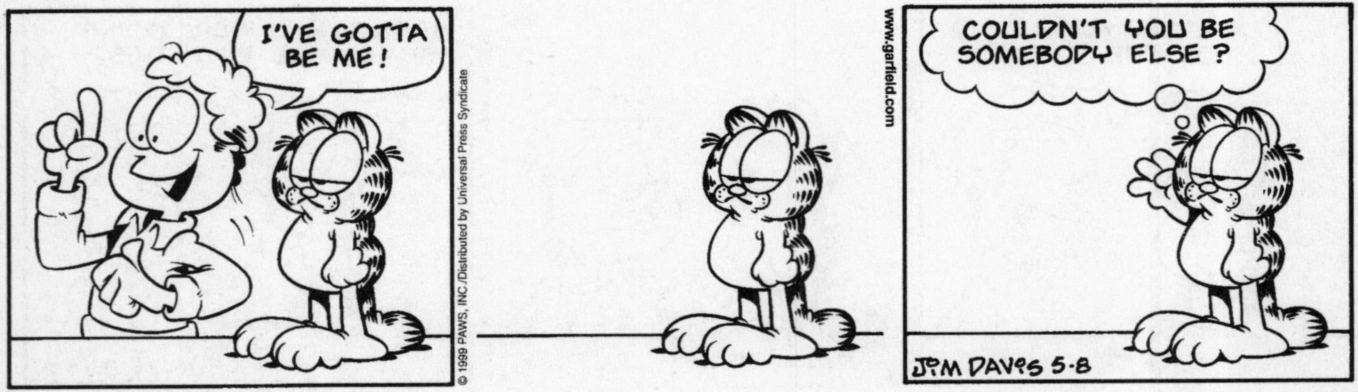
I'VE GOTTA BE ME !
COULDN'T YOU BE SOMEBODY ELSE ?
JIM DAVIS 5-8

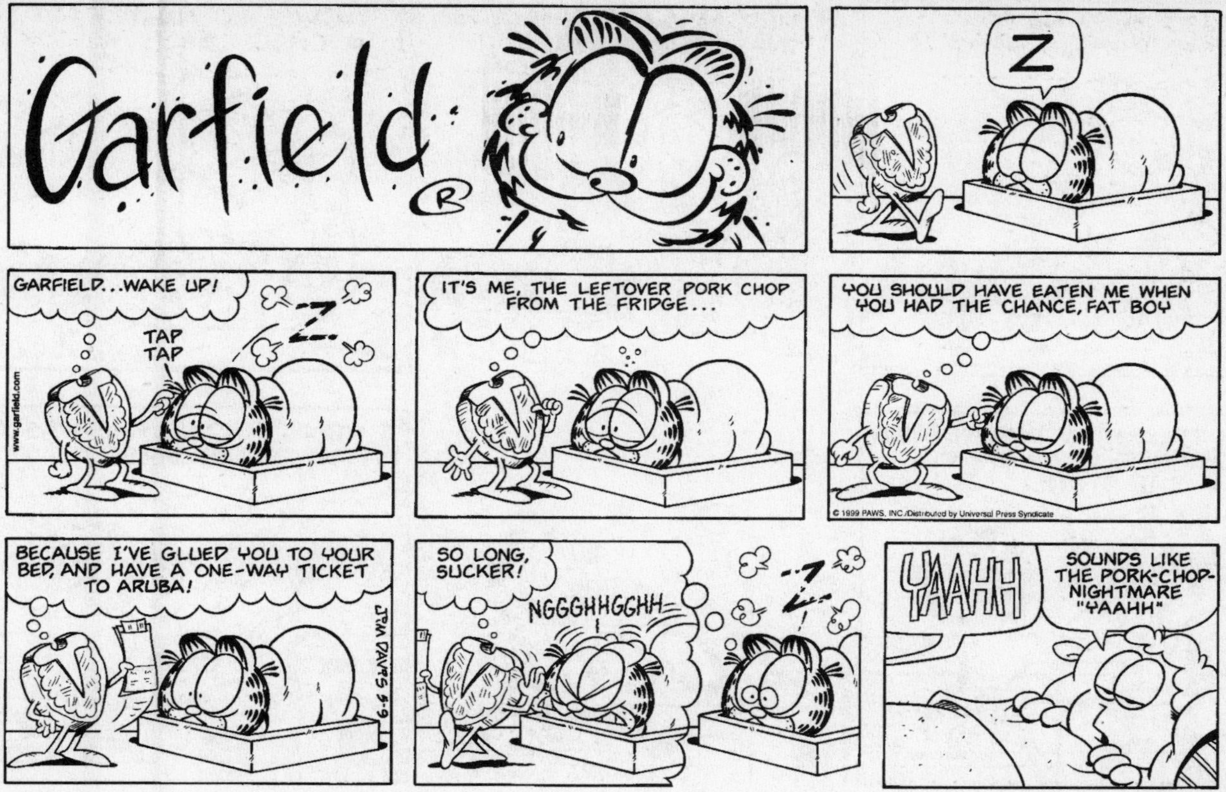
Garfield ®
Z
GARFIELD...WAKE UP!
TAP TAP
www.garfield.com
IT'S ME, THE LEFTOVER PORK CHOP FROM THE FRIDGE...
YOU SHOULD HAVE EATEN ME WHEN YOU HAD THE CHANCE, FAT BOY
© 1999 PAWS, INC./Distributed by Universal Press Syndicate
BECAUSE I'VE GLUED YOU TO YOUR BED, AND HAVE A ONE-WAY TICKET TO ARUBA!
JIM DAVIS 5-9
SO LONG, SUCKER!
NGGGHHGGHH
YAAHH
SOUNDS LIKE THE PORK-CHOP-NIGHTMARE "YAAHH"

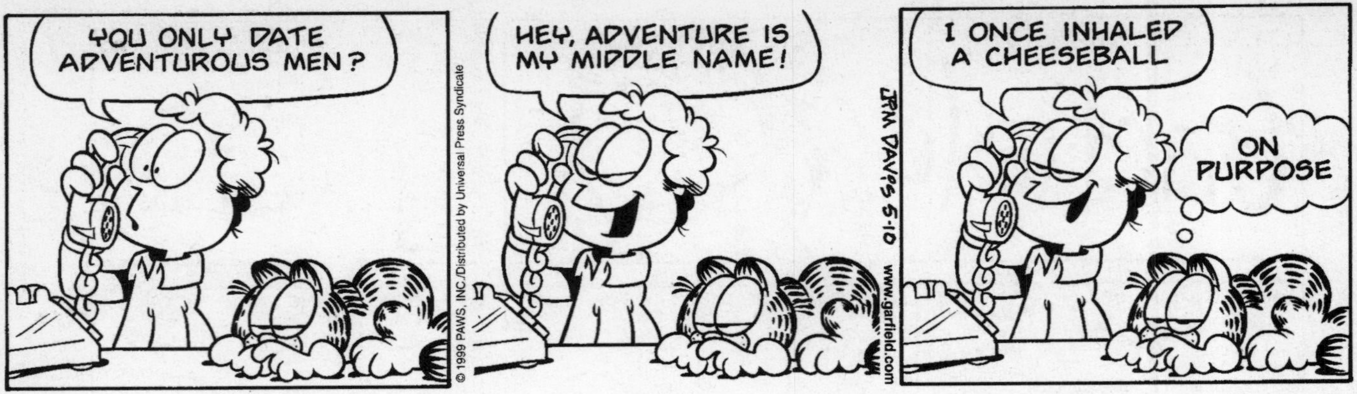
YOU ONLY DATE ADVENTUROUS MEN?
HEY, ADVENTURE IS MY MIDDLE NAME!
I ONCE INHALED A CHEESEBALL
ON PURPOSE
© 1999 PAWS, INC./Distributed by Universal Press Syndicate
JIM DAVIS 5-10
www.garfield.com

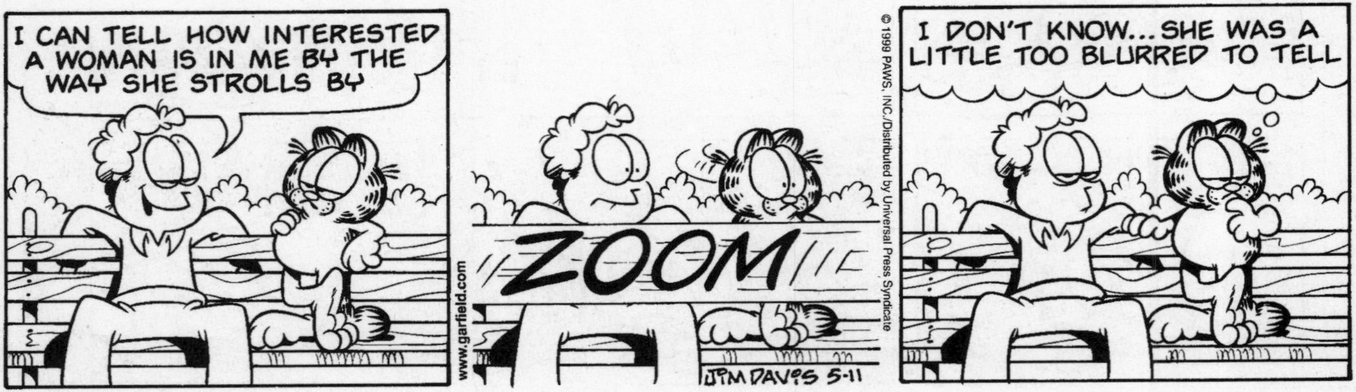
I CAN TELL HOW INTERESTED A WOMAN IS IN ME BY THE WAY SHE STROLLS BY
ZOOM
I DON'T KNOW... SHE WAS A LITTLE TOO BLURRED TO TELL
www.garfield.com
© 1999 PAWS, INC./Distributed by Universal Press Syndicate
JIM DAVIS 5-11

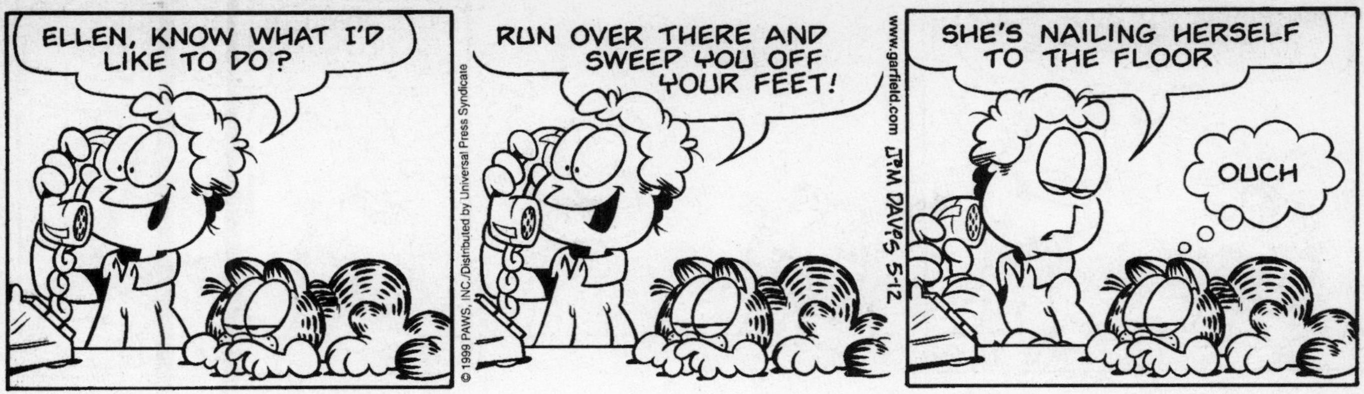
ELLEN, KNOW WHAT I'D LIKE TO DO?
RUN OVER THERE AND SWEEP YOU OFF YOUR FEET!
© 1999 PAWS, INC./Distributed by Universal Press Syndicate
www.garfield.com
JIM DAVIS 5-12
SHE'S NAILING HERSELF TO THE FLOOR
OUCH

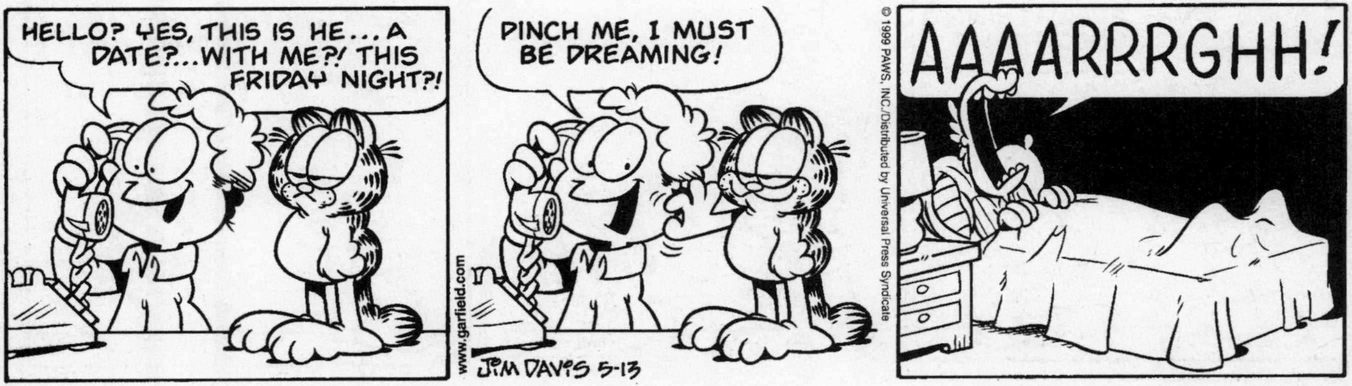
HELLO? YES, THIS IS HE... A DATE?...WITH ME?! THIS FRIDAY NIGHT?!
PINCH ME, I MUST BE DREAMING!
www.garfield.com
JIM DAVIS 5-13
© 1999 PAWS, INC./Distributed by Universal Press Syndicate
AAAARRRGHH!

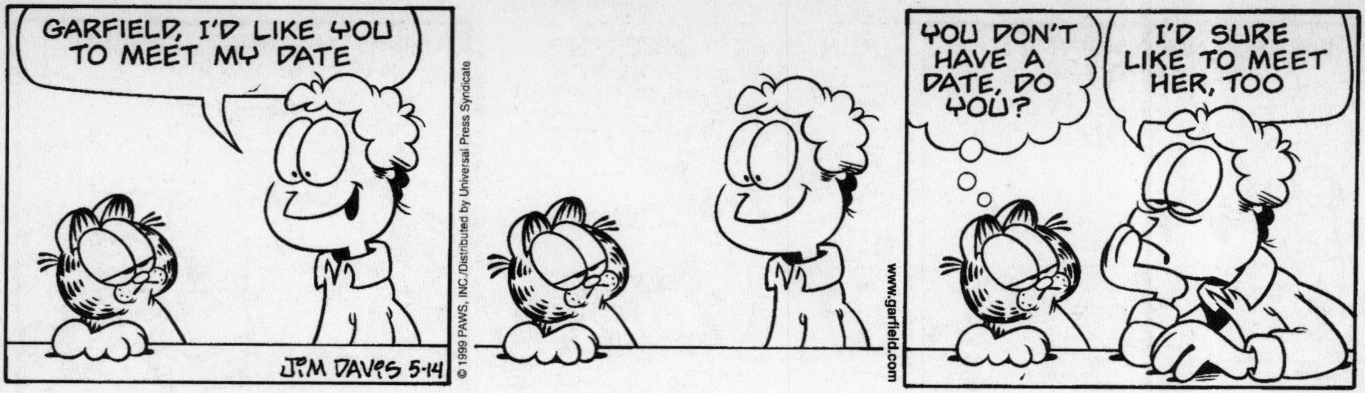
GARFIELD, I'D LIKE YOU TO MEET MY DATE
JIM DAVIS 5-14
YOU DON'T HAVE A DATE, DO YOU?
I'D SURE LIKE TO MEET HER, TOO
© 1999 PAWS, INC./Distributed by Universal Press Syndicate
www.garfield.com

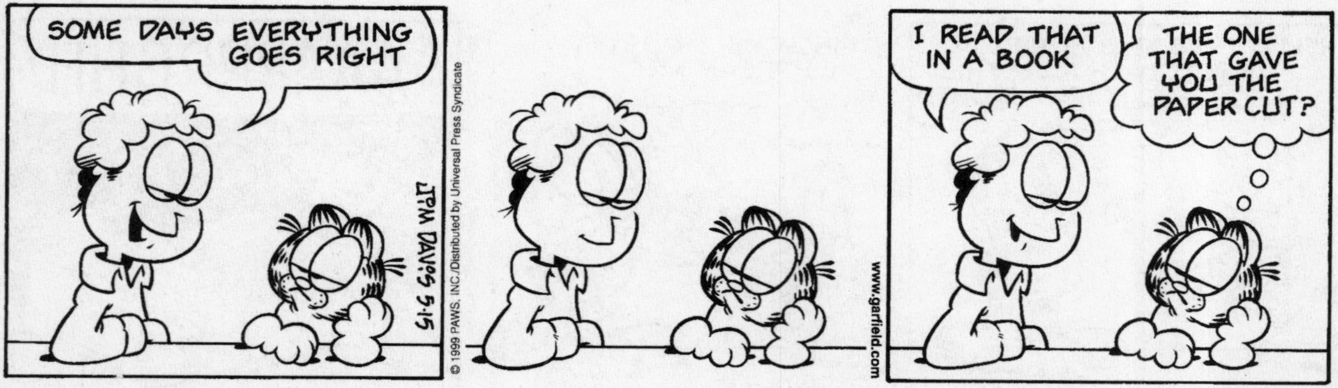
SOME DAYS EVERYTHING GOES RIGHT
JIM DAVIS 5-15
I READ THAT IN A BOOK
THE ONE THAT GAVE YOU THE PAPER CUT?
© 1999 PAWS, INC./Distributed by Universal Press Syndicate
www.garfield.com

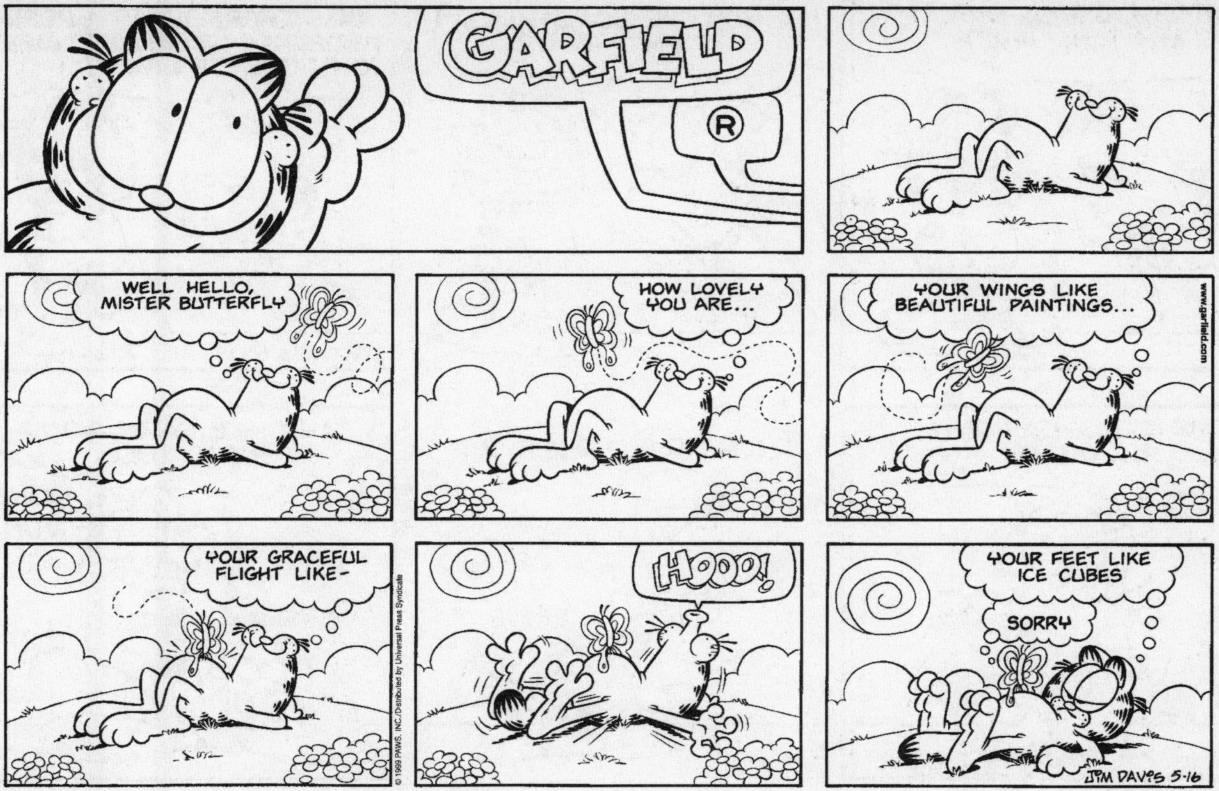
GARFIELD®
WELL HELLO, MISTER BUTTERFLY
HOW LOVELY YOU ARE...
YOUR WINGS LIKE BEAUTIFUL PAINTINGS...
www.garfield.com
YOUR GRACEFUL FLIGHT LIKE-
© 1999 PAWS. INC./Distributed by Universal Press Syndicate
HOOO!
YOUR FEET LIKE ICE CUBES
SORRY
JIM DAVIS 5-16

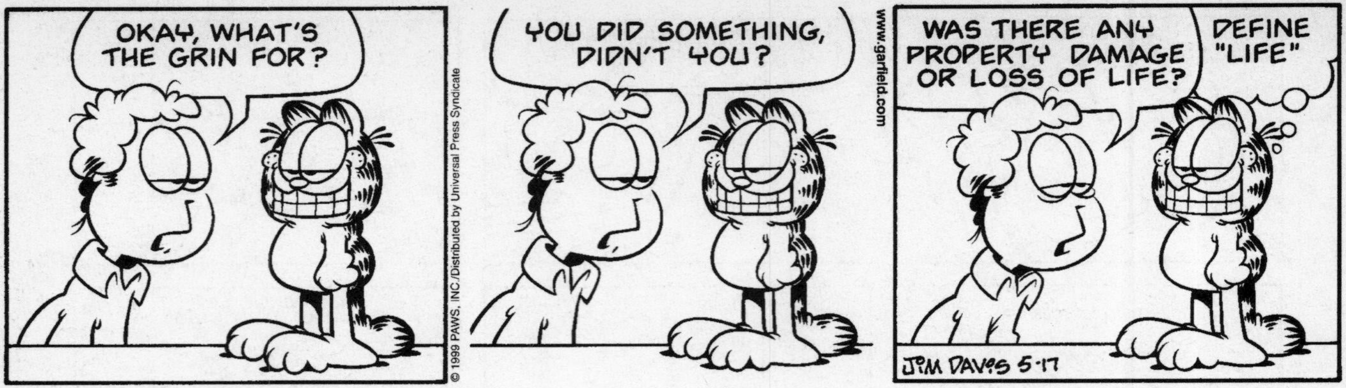
OKAY, WHAT'S THE GRIN FOR?
YOU DID SOMETHING, DIDN'T YOU?
WAS THERE ANY PROPERTY DAMAGE OR LOSS OF LIFE?
DEFINE "LIFE"
JIM DAVIS 5-17
© 1999 PAWS, INC./Distributed by Universal Press Syndicate
www.garfield.com

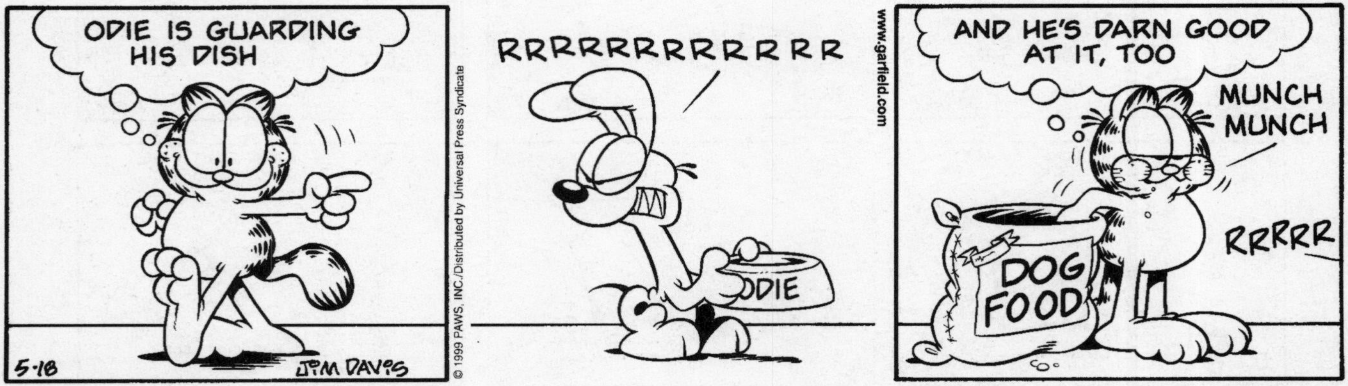
ODIE IS GUARDING HIS DISH
5-18
JIM DAVIS
RRRRRRRRRRRR
DIE
AND HE'S DARN GOOD AT IT, TOO
MUNCH MUNCH
DOG FOOD
RRRRR
© 1999 PAWS, INC./Distributed by Universal Press Syndicate
www.garfield.com

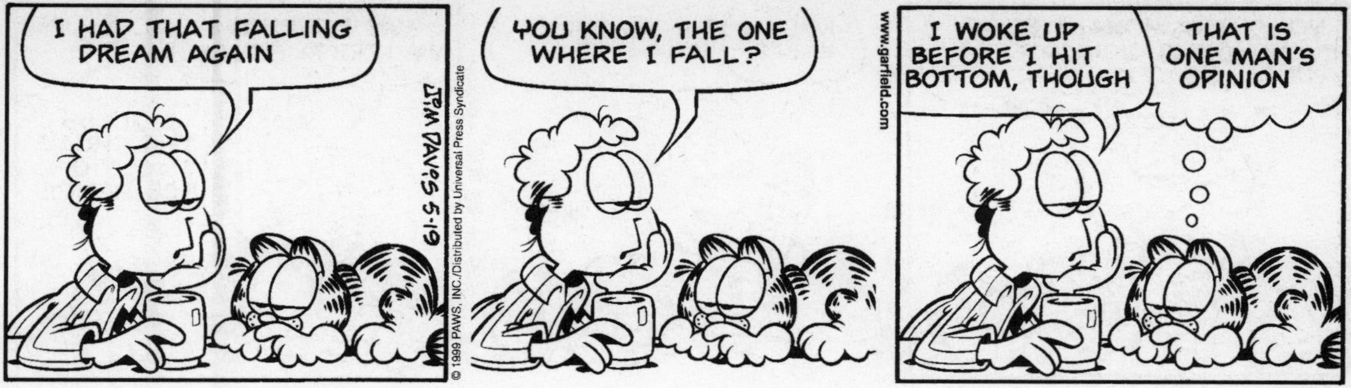
I HAD THAT FALLING DREAM AGAIN
JIM DAVIS 5-19
© 1999 PAWS, INC./Distributed by Universal Press Syndicate
YOU KNOW, THE ONE WHERE I FALL?
www.garfield.com
I WOKE UP BEFORE I HIT BOTTOM, THOUGH
THAT IS ONE MAN'S OPINION

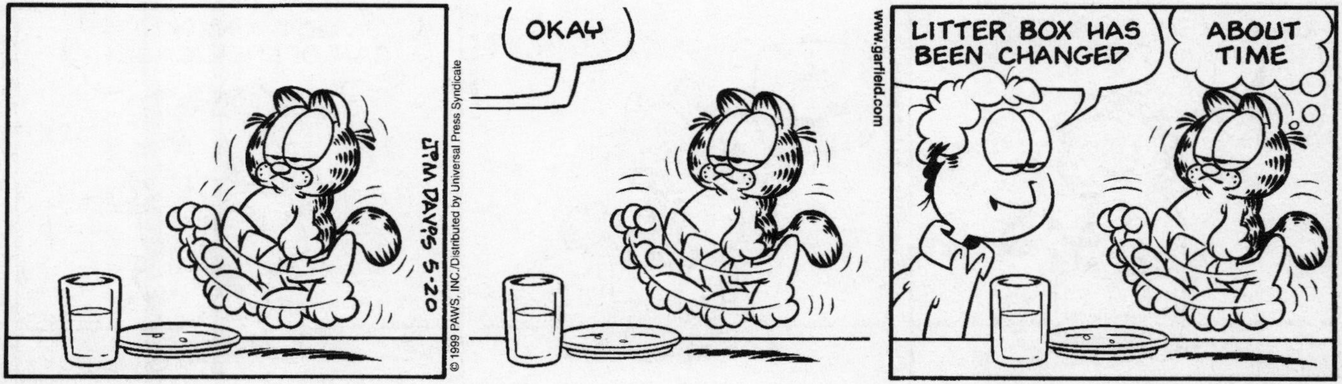
JIM DAVIS 5-20
© 1999 PAWS, INC./Distributed by Universal Press Syndicate
OKAY
www.garfield.com
LITTER BOX HAS BEEN CHANGED
ABOUT TIME

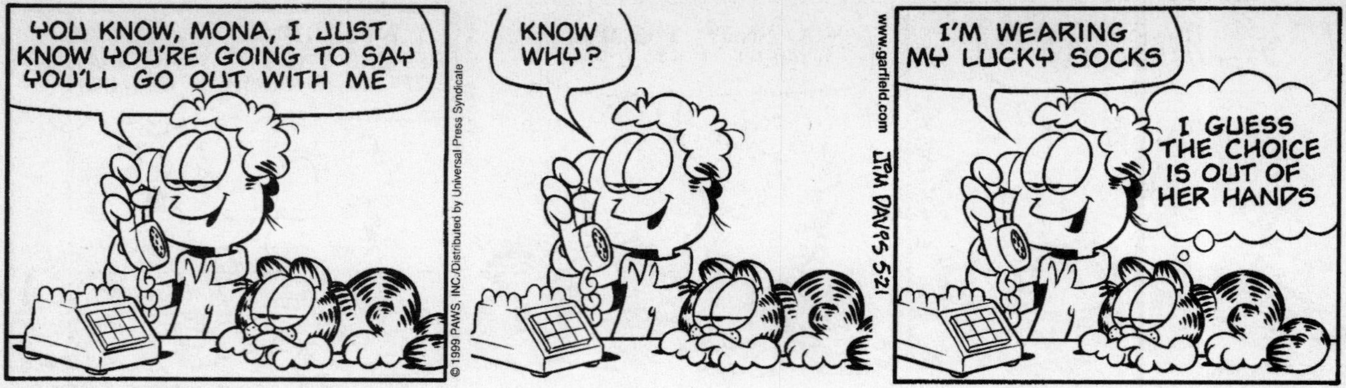
YOU KNOW, MONA, I JUST KNOW YOU'RE GOING TO SAY YOU'LL GO OUT WITH ME
KNOW WHY?
I'M WEARING MY LUCKY SOCKS
I GUESS THE CHOICE IS OUT OF HER HANDS
JIM DAVIS 5-21

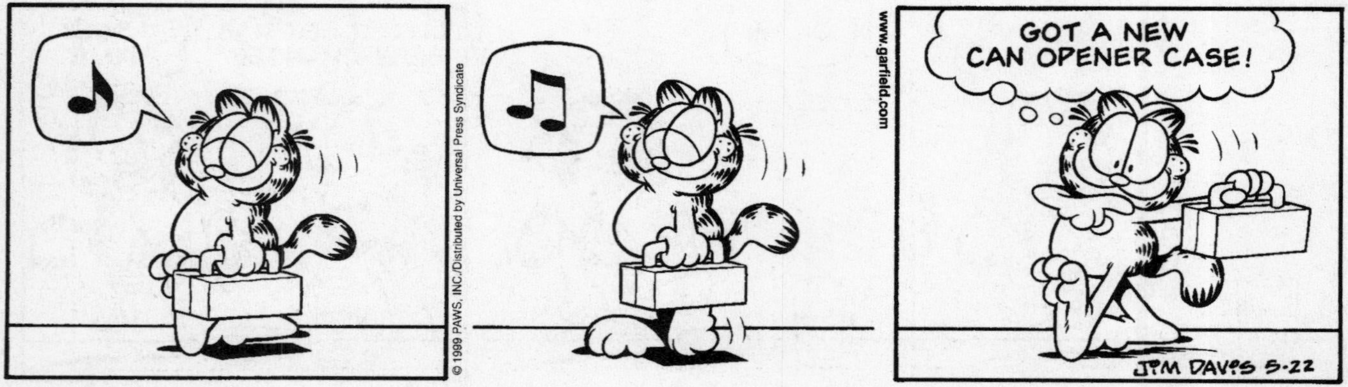
GOT A NEW CAN OPENER CASE!
JIM DAVIS 5-22

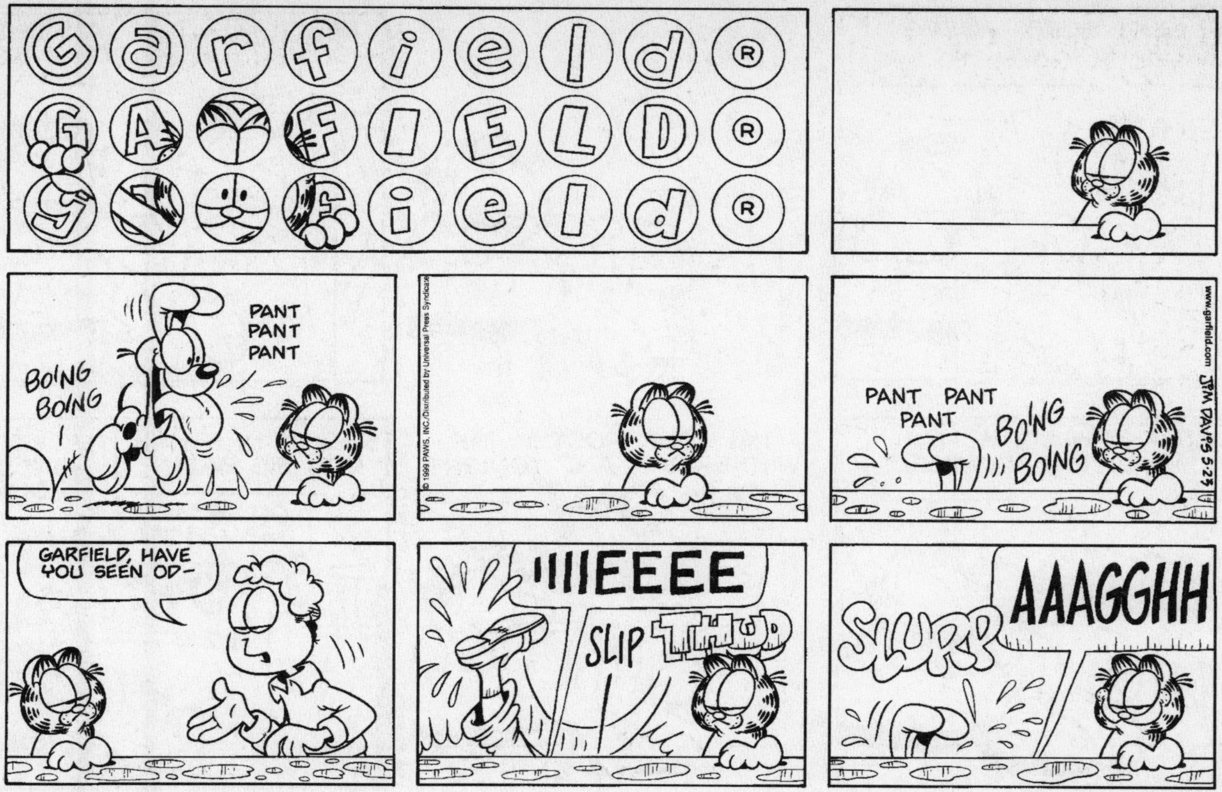
Garfield®
GARFIELD®
garfield®
BOING BOING
PANT PANT PANT
© 1999 PAWS, INC./Distributed by Universal Press Syndicate
PANT PANT PANT
BOING BOING
www.garfield.com
JIM DAVIS 5-23
GARFIELD, HAVE YOU SEEN OD-
IIIEEEE
SLIP THUD
SLURP
AAAGGHH

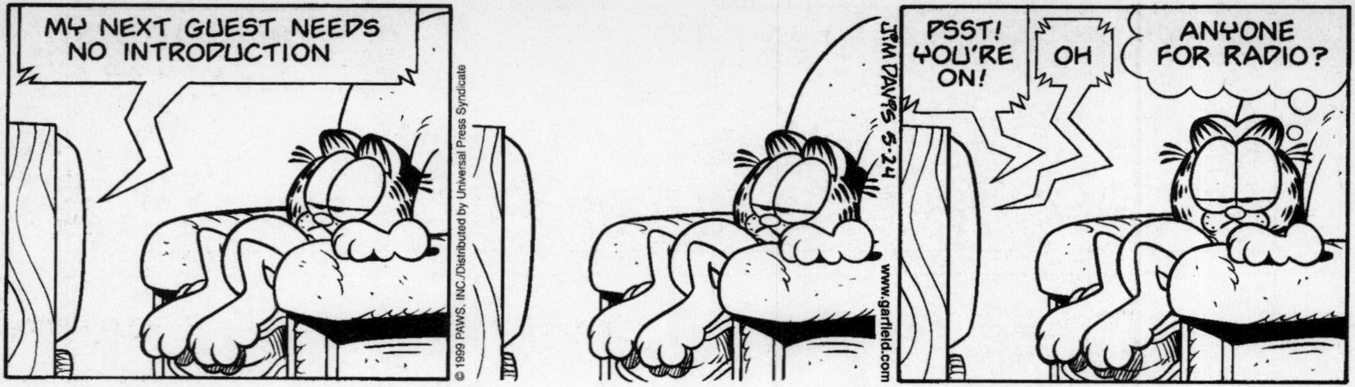

MY NEXT GUEST NEEDS NO INTRODUCTION
© 1999 PAWS, INC./Distributed by Universal Press Syndicate
JIM DAVIS 5·24
www.garfield.com
PSST! YOU'RE ON!
OH
ANYONE FOR RADIO?

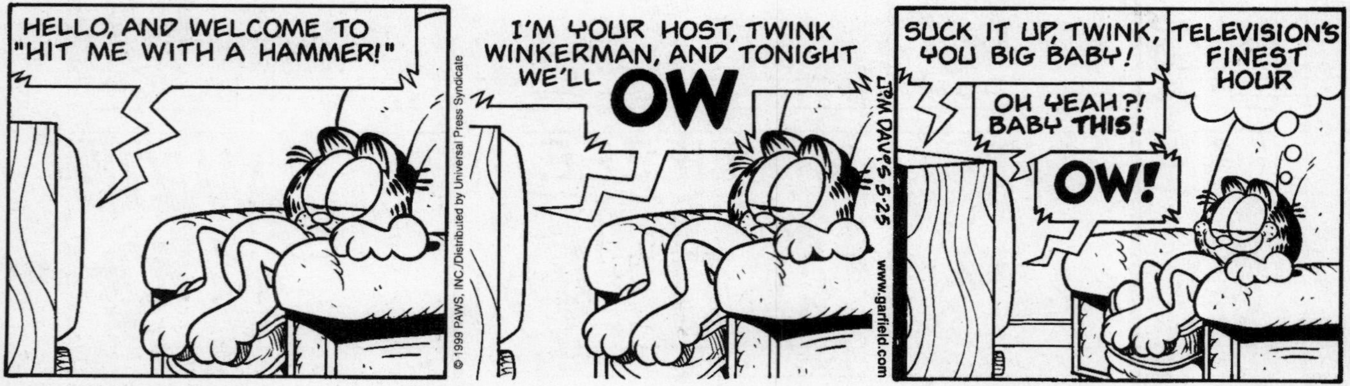

HELLO, AND WELCOME TO "HIT ME WITH A HAMMER!"
© 1999 PAWS, INC./Distributed by Universal Press Syndicate
I'M YOUR HOST, TWINK WINKERMAN, AND TONIGHT WE'LL OW
JIM DAVIS 5·25
www.garfield.com
SUCK IT UP, TWINK, YOU BIG BABY!
OH YEAH?! BABY THIS!
OW!
TELEVISION'S FINEST HOUR

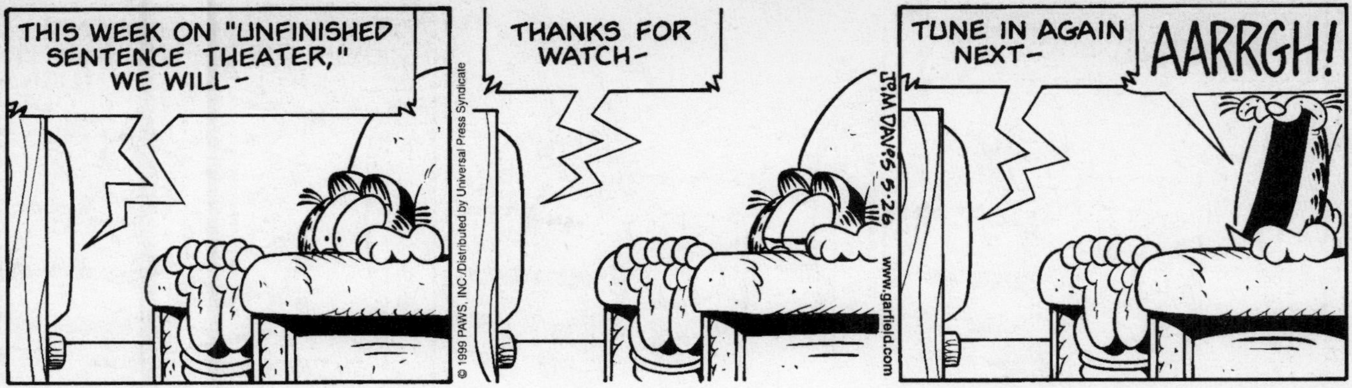
THIS WEEK ON "UNFINISHED SENTENCE THEATER," WE WILL-
THANKS FOR WATCH-
TUNE IN AGAIN NEXT-
AARRGH!
© 1999 PAWS, INC./Distributed by Universal Press Syndicate
JIM DAVIS 5-26
www.garfield.com

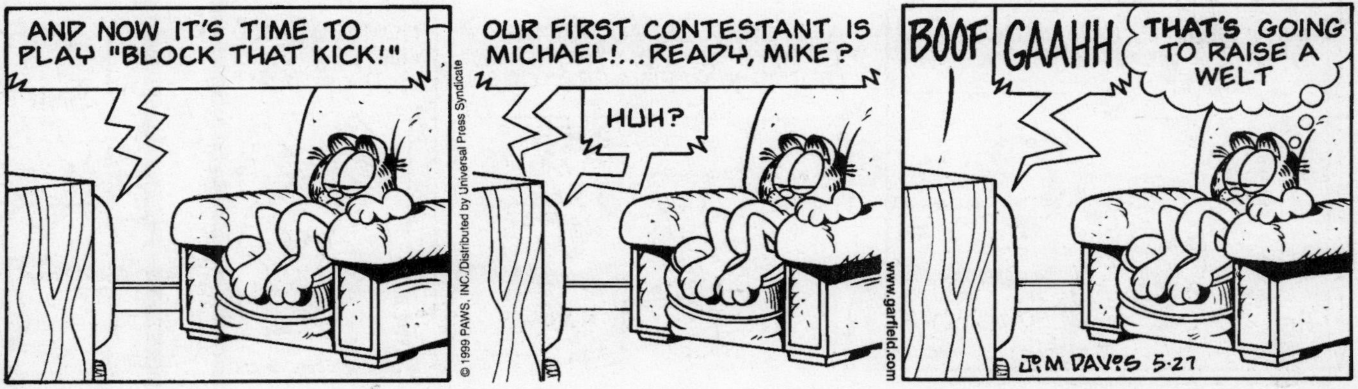
AND NOW IT'S TIME TO PLAY "BLOCK THAT KICK!"
OUR FIRST CONTESTANT IS MICHAEL!...READY, MIKE?
HUH?
BOOF
GAAHH
THAT'S GOING TO RAISE A WELT
© 1999 PAWS, INC./Distributed by Universal Press Syndicate
www.garfield.com
JIM DAVIS 5-27

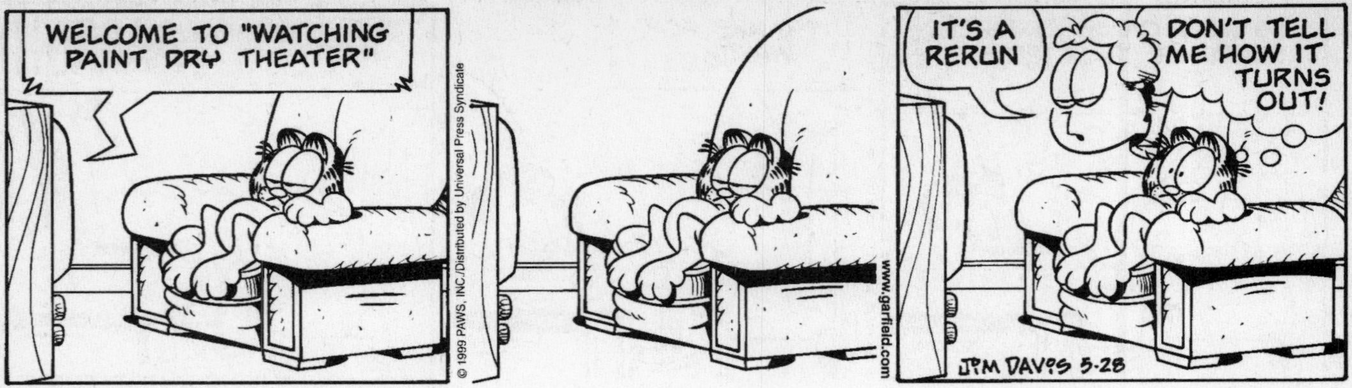

WELCOME TO "WATCHING PAINT DRY THEATER"
© 1999 PAWS, INC./Distributed by Universal Press Syndicate
www.garfield.com
IT'S A RERUN
DON'T TELL ME HOW IT TURNS OUT!
JIM DAVIS 5-28

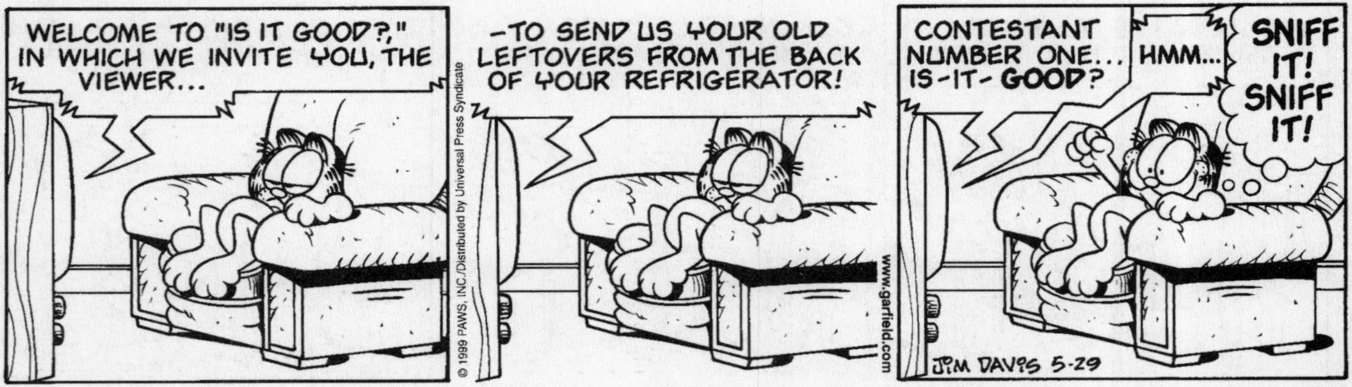

WELCOME TO "IS IT GOOD?," IN WHICH WE INVITE YOU, THE VIEWER...
© 1999 PAWS, INC./Distributed by Universal Press Syndicate
-TO SEND US YOUR OLD LEFTOVERS FROM THE BACK OF YOUR REFRIGERATOR!
www.garfield.com
CONTESTANT NUMBER ONE... IS-IT-GOOD?
HMM...
SNIFF IT! SNIFF IT!
JIM DAVIS 5-29

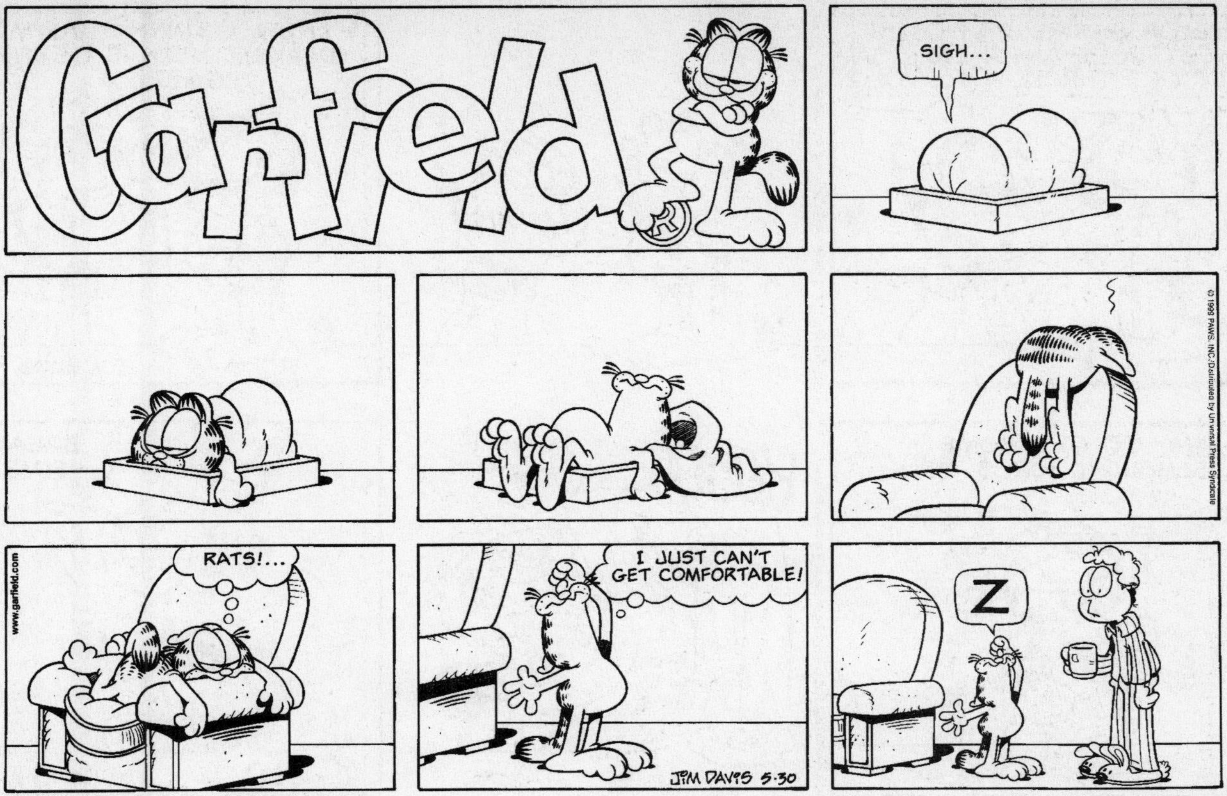
Garfield
SIGH...
RATS!...
I JUST CAN'T GET COMFORTABLE!
Z
JIM DAVIS 5-30
© 1999 PAWS, INC./Distributed by Universal Press Syndicate
www.garfield.com

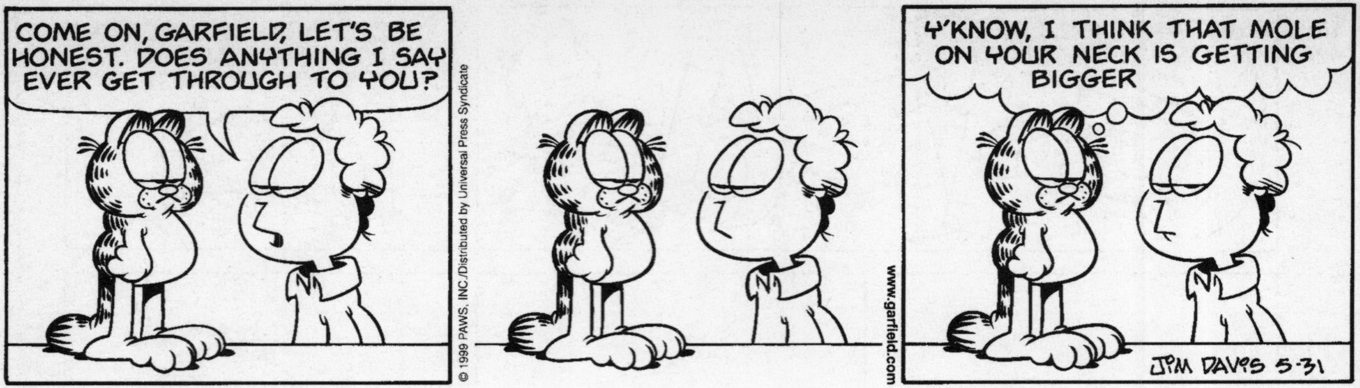
COME ON, GARFIELD, LET'S BE HONEST. DOES ANYTHING I SAY EVER GET THROUGH TO YOU?
Y'KNOW, I THINK THAT MOLE ON YOUR NECK IS GETTING BIGGER
JIM DAVIS 5-31

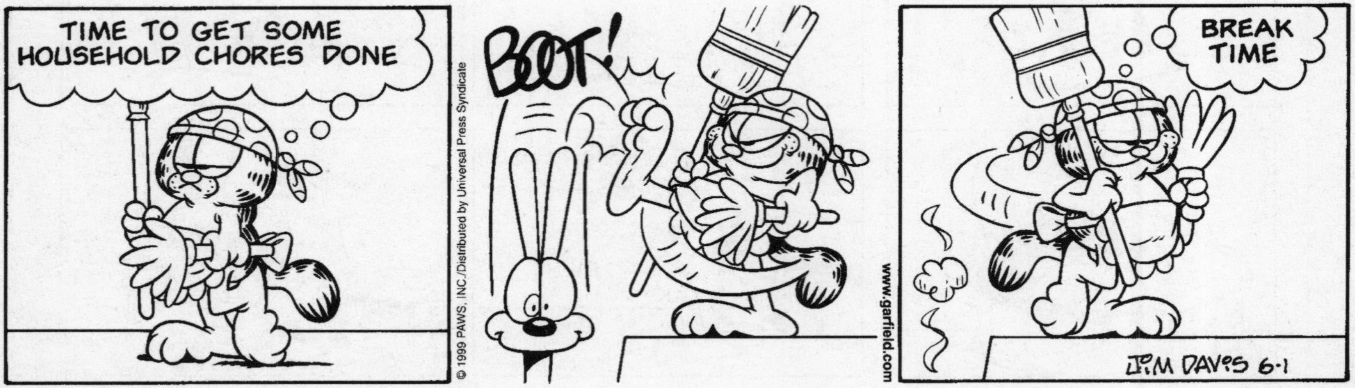
TIME TO GET SOME HOUSEHOLD CHORES DONE
BOOT!
BREAK TIME
JIM DAVIS 6-1

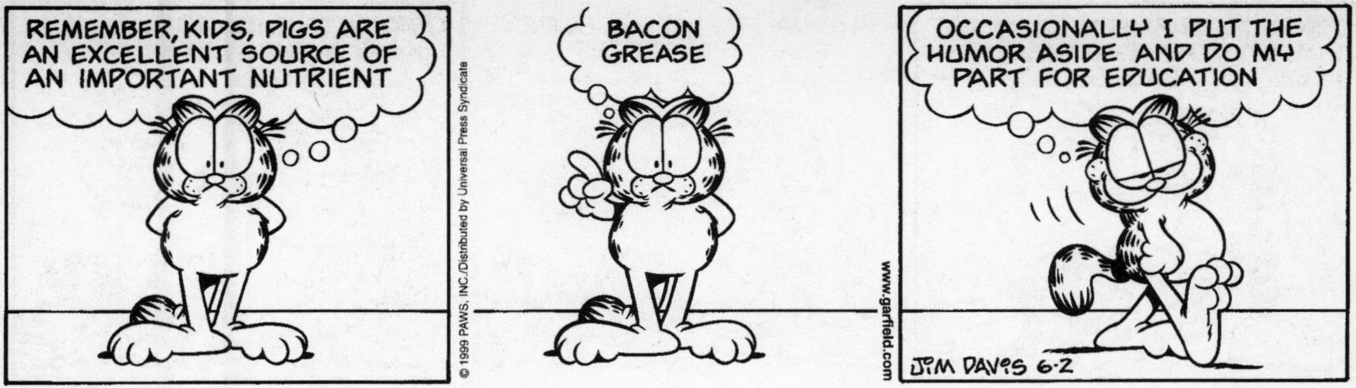
REMEMBER, KIDS, PIGS ARE AN EXCELLENT SOURCE OF AN IMPORTANT NUTRIENT
BACON GREASE
OCCASIONALLY I PUT THE HUMOR ASIDE AND DO MY PART FOR EDUCATION
© 1999 PAWS, INC./Distributed by Universal Press Syndicate
www.garfield.com
JIM DAVIS 6-2

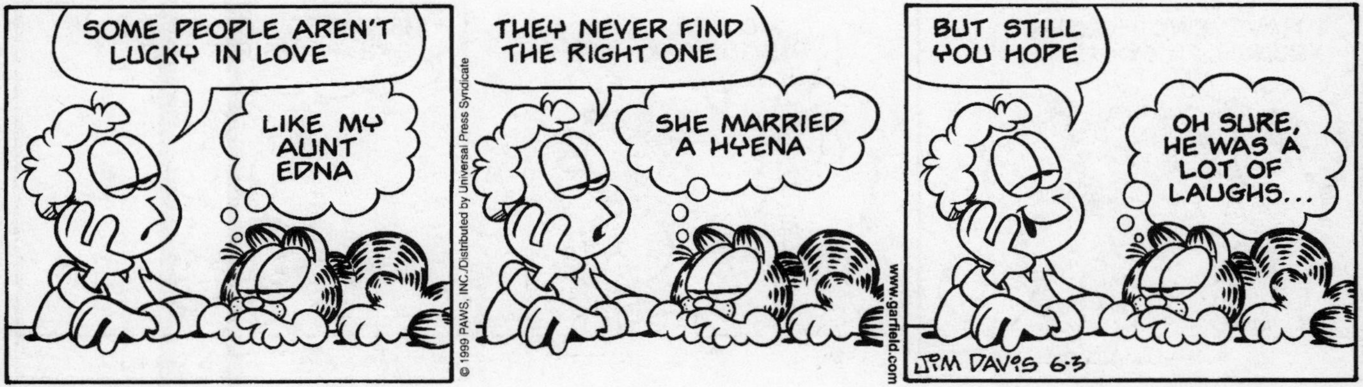
SOME PEOPLE AREN'T LUCKY IN LOVE
LIKE MY AUNT EDNA
THEY NEVER FIND THE RIGHT ONE
SHE MARRIED A HYENA
BUT STILL YOU HOPE
OH SURE, HE WAS A LOT OF LAUGHS...
© 1999 PAWS, INC./Distributed by Universal Press Syndicate
www.garfield.com
JIM DAVIS 6-3

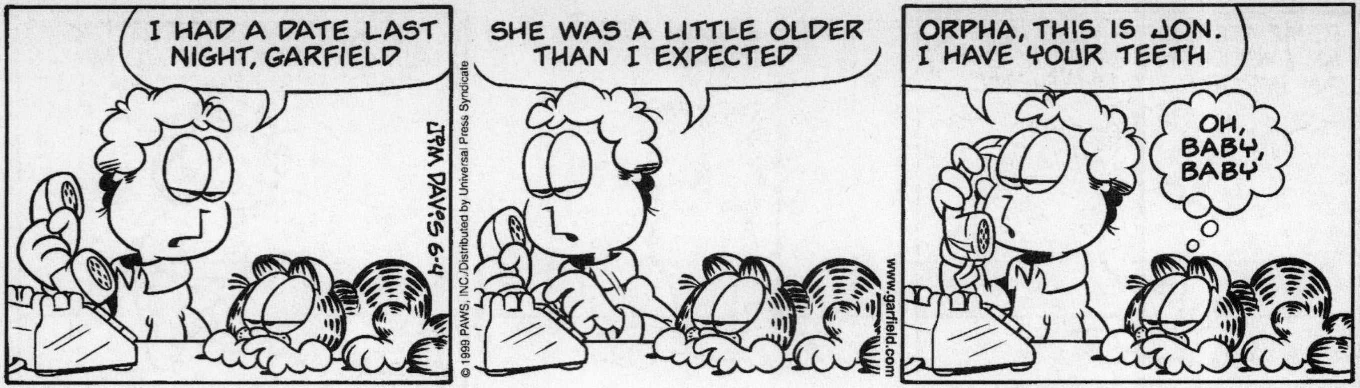
I HAD A DATE LAST NIGHT, GARFIELD
JIM DAVIS 6-4
© 1999 PAWS, INC./Distributed by Universal Press Syndicate
SHE WAS A LITTLE OLDER THAN I EXPECTED
www.garfield.com
ORPHA, THIS IS JON. I HAVE YOUR TEETH
OH, BABY, BABY

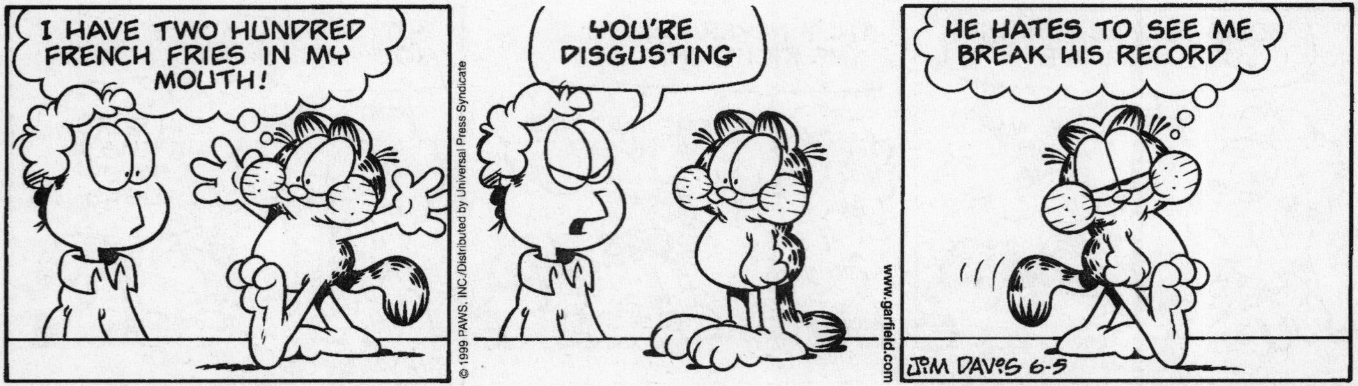
I HAVE TWO HUNDRED FRENCH FRIES IN MY MOUTH!
© 1999 PAWS, INC./Distributed by Universal Press Syndicate
YOU'RE DISGUSTING
www.garfield.com
HE HATES TO SEE ME BREAK HIS RECORD
JIM DAVIS 6-5

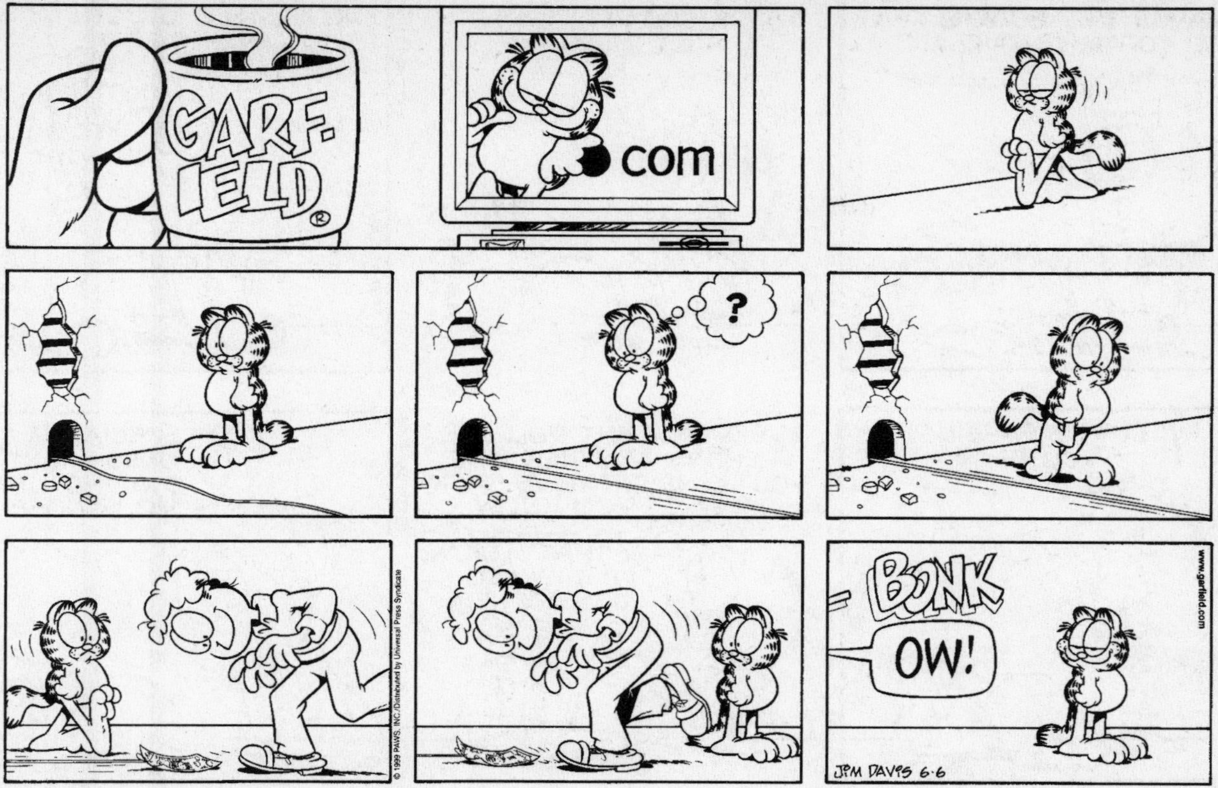
GARF. IELD ®
com
?
BONK
OW!
© 1999 PAWS, INC./Distributed by Universal Press Syndicate
www.garfield.com
JIM DAVIS 6-6

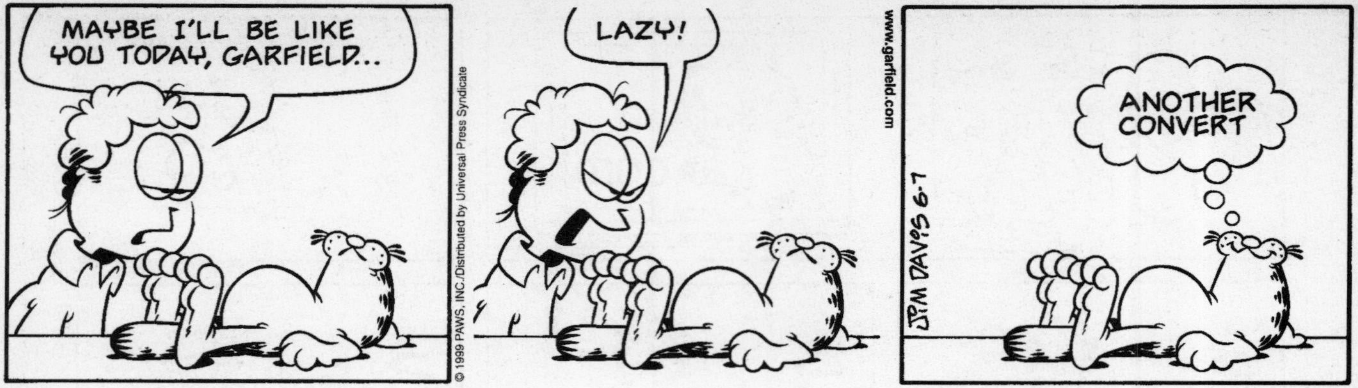
MAYBE I'LL BE LIKE YOU TODAY, GARFIELD...
LAZY!
ANOTHER CONVERT
JIM DAVIS 6-7

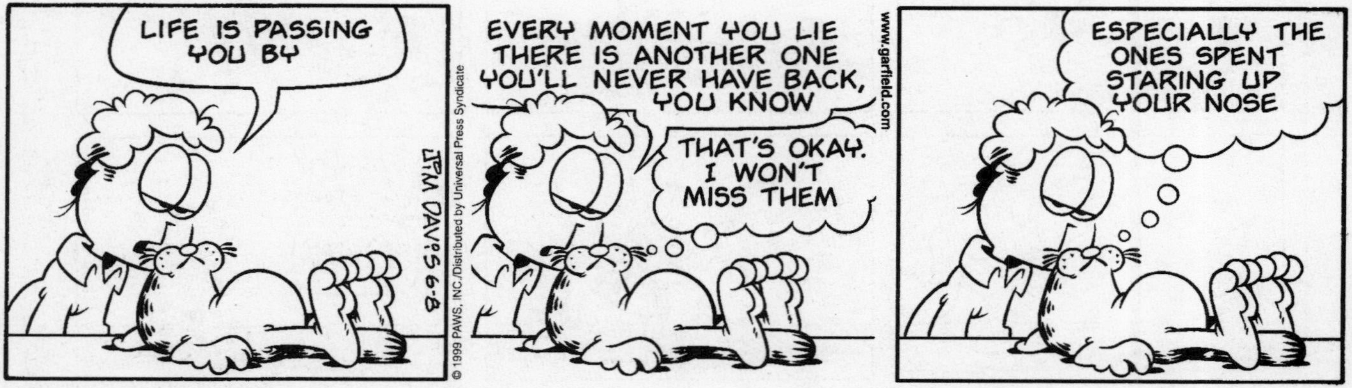
LIFE IS PASSING YOU BY
EVERY MOMENT YOU LIE THERE IS ANOTHER ONE YOU'LL NEVER HAVE BACK, YOU KNOW
THAT'S OKAY. I WON'T MISS THEM
ESPECIALLY THE ONES SPENT STARING UP YOUR NOSE
JIM DAVIS 6-8

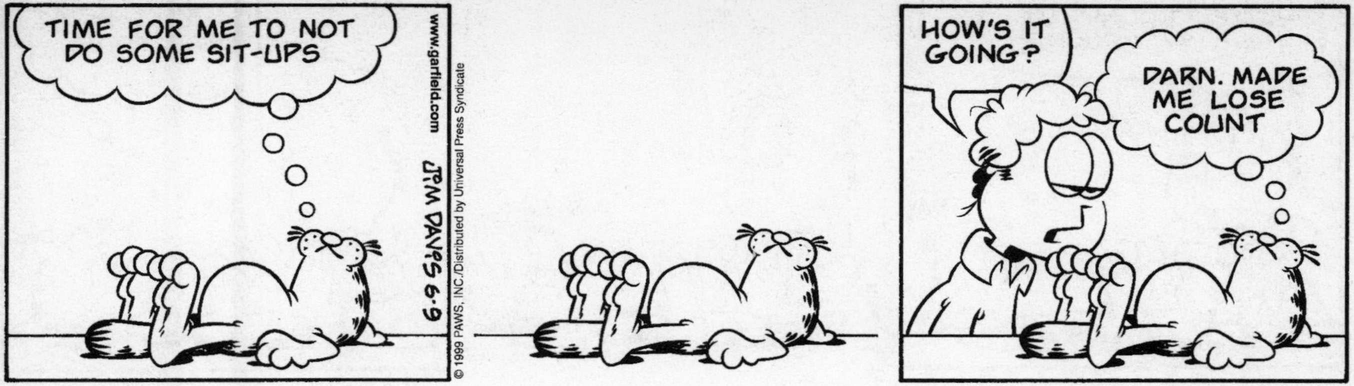
TIME FOR ME TO NOT DO SOME SIT-UPS
www.garfield.com
JIM DAVIS 6-9
© 1999 PAWS, INC./Distributed by Universal Press Syndicate
HOW'S IT GOING?
DARN. MADE ME LOSE COUNT

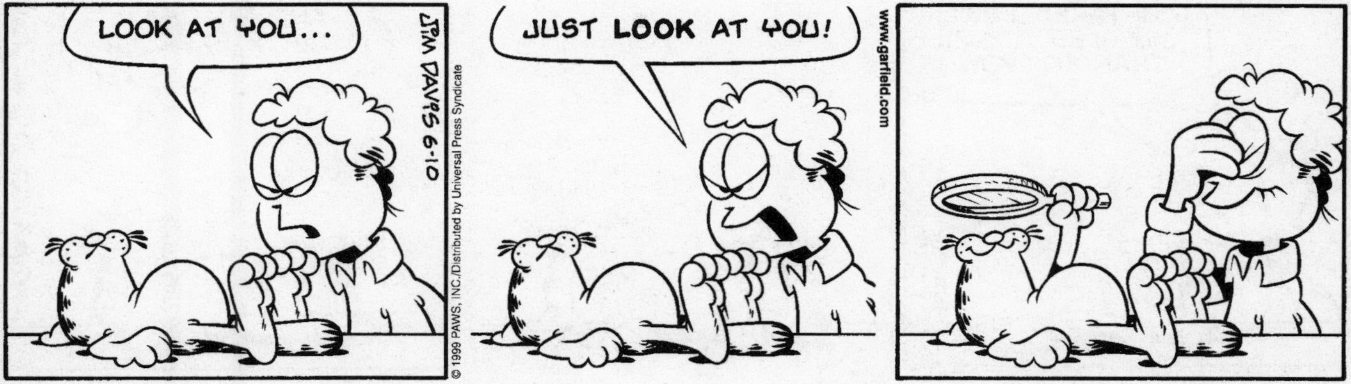
LOOK AT YOU...
JIM DAVIS 6-10
© 1999 PAWS, INC./Distributed by Universal Press Syndicate
JUST LOOK AT YOU!
www.garfield.com

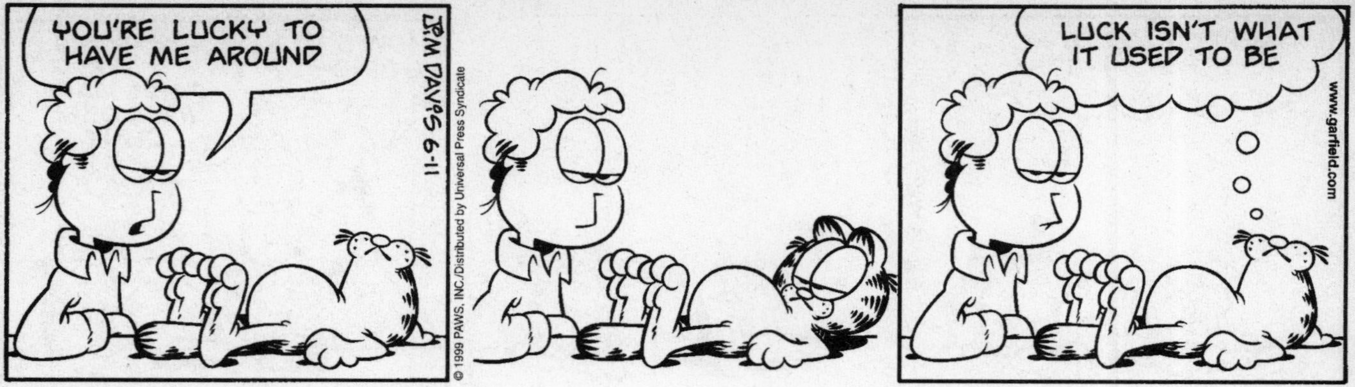
YOU'RE LUCKY TO HAVE ME AROUND
JIM DAVIS 6-11
© 1999 PAWS, INC./Distributed by Universal Press Syndicate
LUCK ISN'T WHAT IT USED TO BE
www.garfield.com

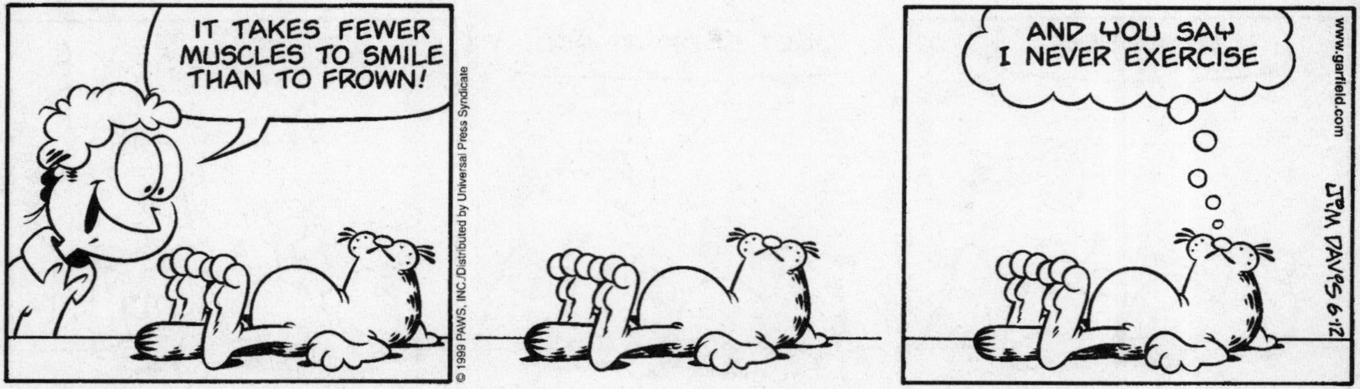
IT TAKES FEWER MUSCLES TO SMILE THAN TO FROWN!
© 1999 PAWS, INC./Distributed by Universal Press Syndicate
AND YOU SAY I NEVER EXERCISE
www.garfield.com
JIM DAVIS 6-12

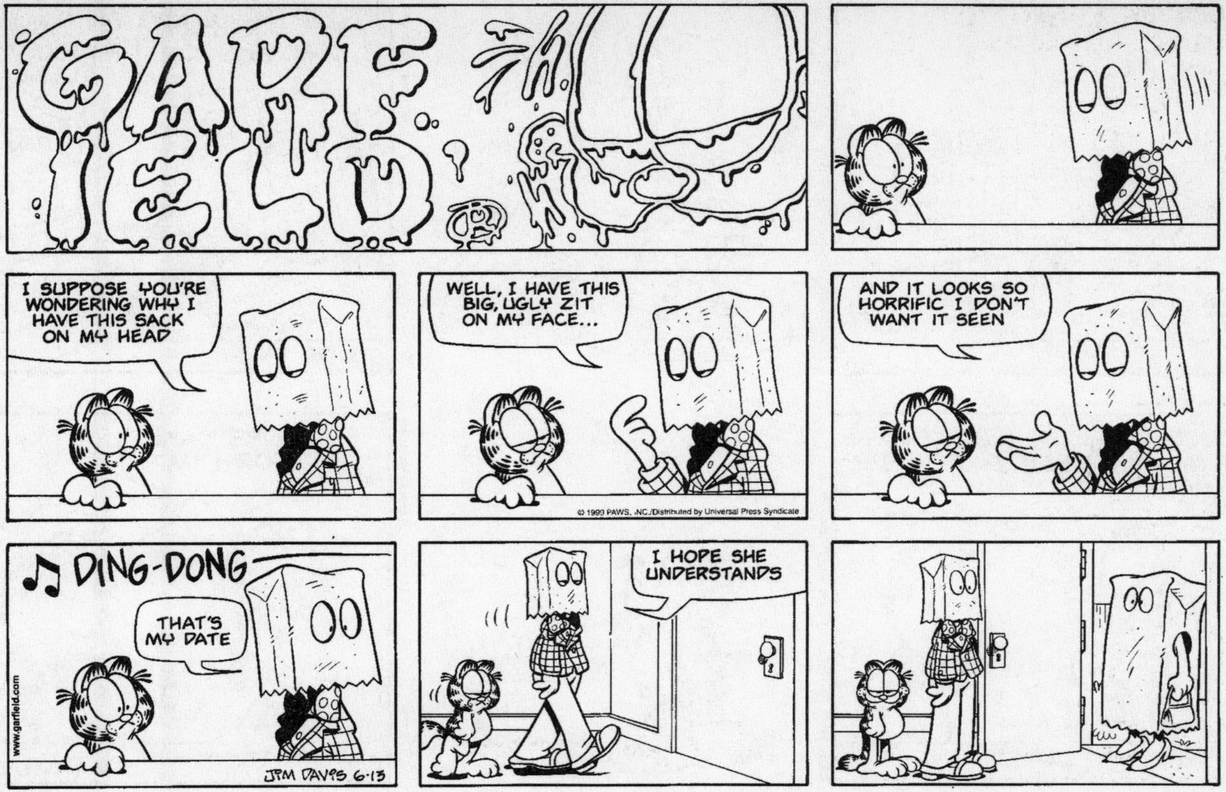
GARFIELD
I SUPPOSE YOU'RE WONDERING WHY I HAVE THIS SACK ON MY HEAD
WELL, I HAVE THIS BIG, UGLY ZIT ON MY FACE...
AND IT LOOKS SO HORRIFIC I DON'T WANT IT SEEN
© 1990 PAWS, INC./Distributed by Universal Press Syndicate
DING-DONG
THAT'S MY DATE
www.garfield.com
JIM DAVIS 6-13
I HOPE SHE UNDERSTANDS

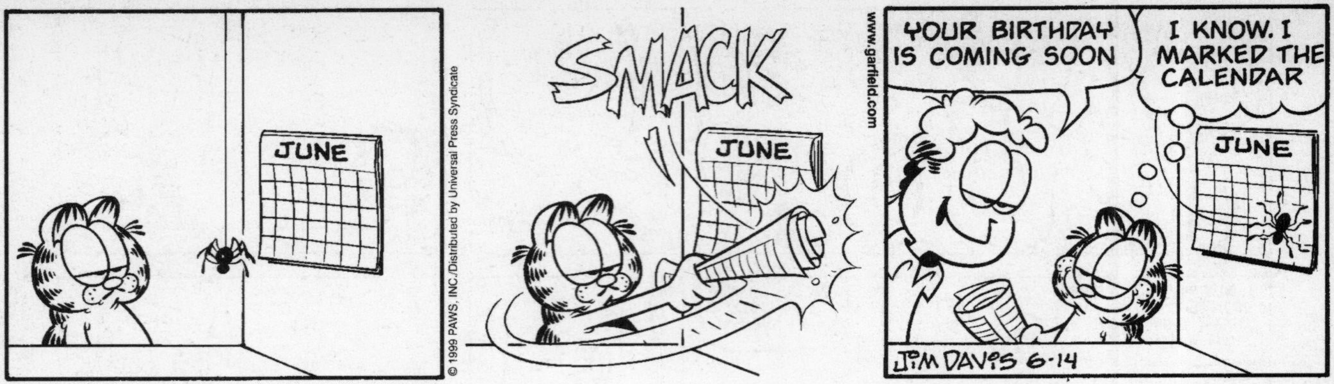
JUNE
SMACK
JUNE
YOUR BIRTHDAY IS COMING SOON
I KNOW. I MARKED THE CALENDAR
JUNE
JIM DAVIS 6-14
www.garfield.com

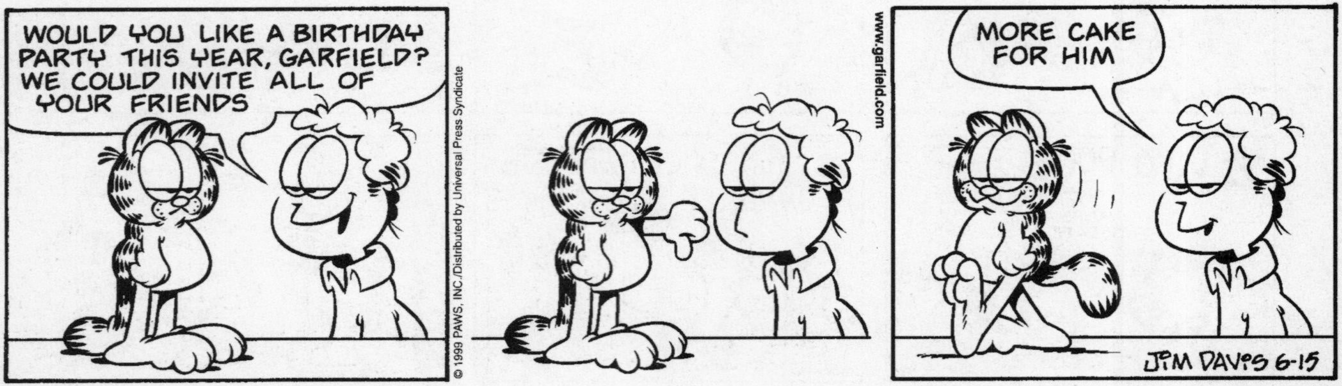
WOULD YOU LIKE A BIRTHDAY PARTY THIS YEAR, GARFIELD? WE COULD INVITE ALL OF YOUR FRIENDS
MORE CAKE FOR HIM
JIM DAVIS 6-15
www.garfield.com

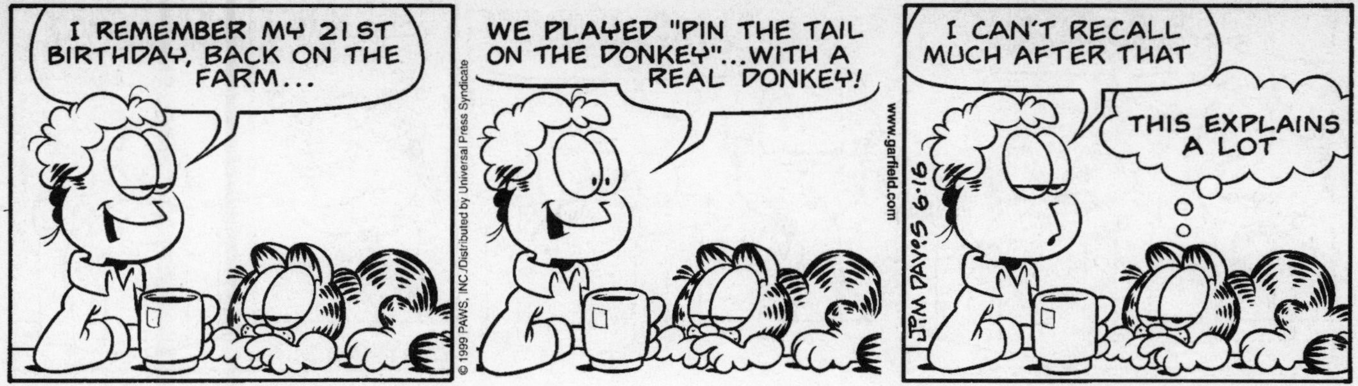
I REMEMBER MY 21 ST BIRTHDAY, BACK ON THE FARM...
WE PLAYED "PIN THE TAIL ON THE DONKEY"...WITH A REAL DONKEY!
I CAN'T RECALL MUCH AFTER THAT
THIS EXPLAINS A LOT
© 1999 PAWS, INC./Distributed by Universal Press Syndicate
www.garfield.com
JIM DAVIS 6·16

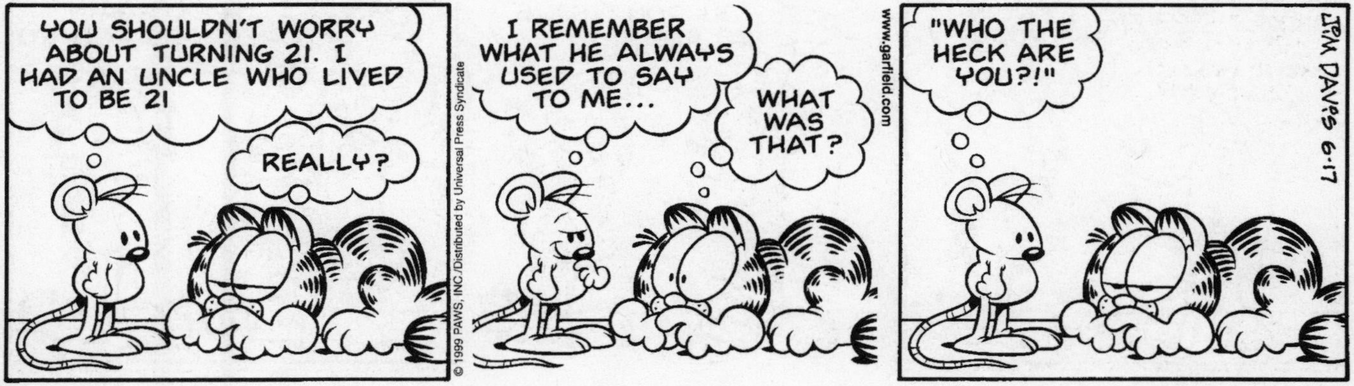
YOU SHOULDN'T WORRY ABOUT TURNING 21. I HAD AN UNCLE WHO LIVED TO BE 21
REALLY?
I REMEMBER WHAT HE ALWAYS USED TO SAY TO ME...
WHAT WAS THAT?
"WHO THE HECK ARE YOU?!"
© 1999 PAWS, INC./Distributed by Universal Press Syndicate
www.garfield.com
JIM DAVIS 6·17

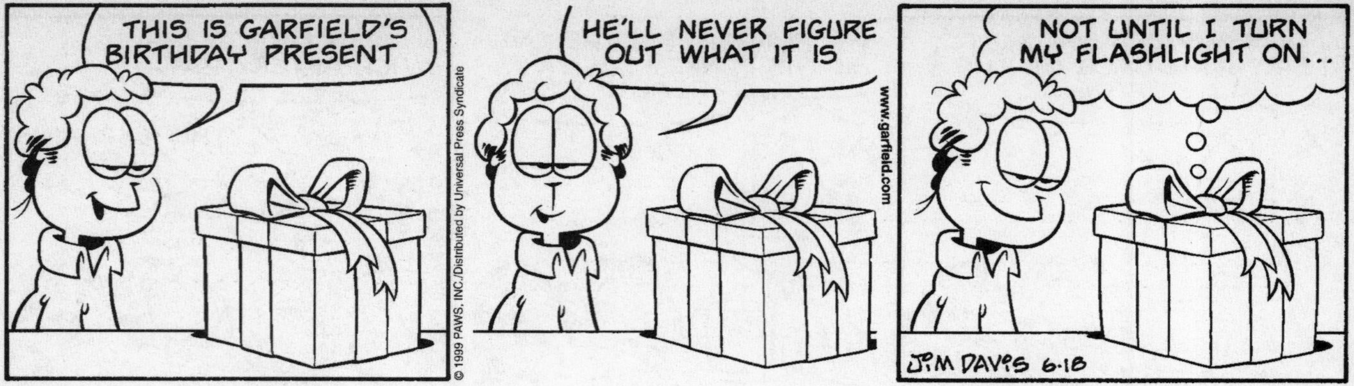
THIS IS GARFIELD'S BIRTHDAY PRESENT
HE'LL NEVER FIGURE OUT WHAT IT IS
NOT UNTIL I TURN MY FLASHLIGHT ON...
JIM DAVIS 6-18
© 1999 PAWS, INC./Distributed by Universal Press Syndicate
www.garfield.com

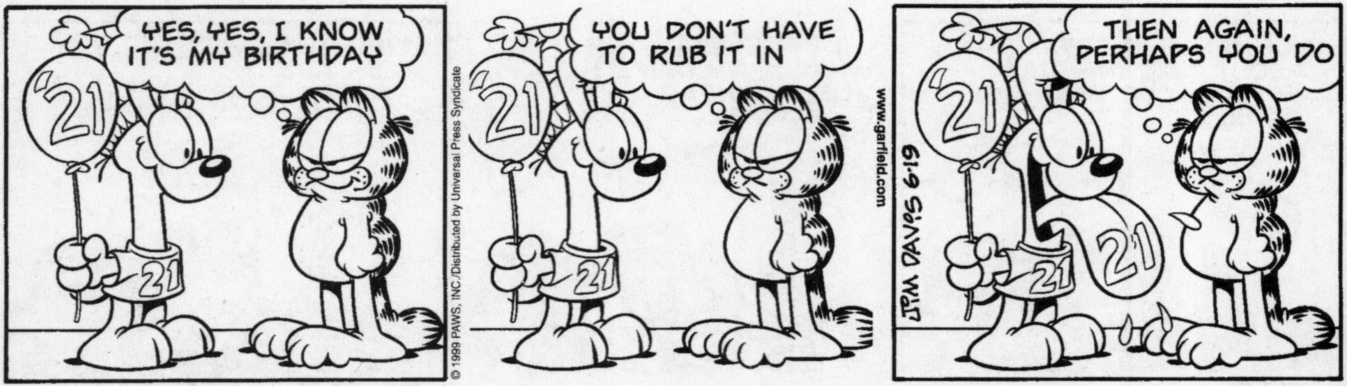
YES, YES, I KNOW IT'S MY BIRTHDAY
YOU DON'T HAVE TO RUB IT IN
THEN AGAIN, PERHAPS YOU DO
'21
21
JIM DAVIS 6-19
© 1999 PAWS, INC./Distributed by Universal Press Syndicate
www.garfield.com

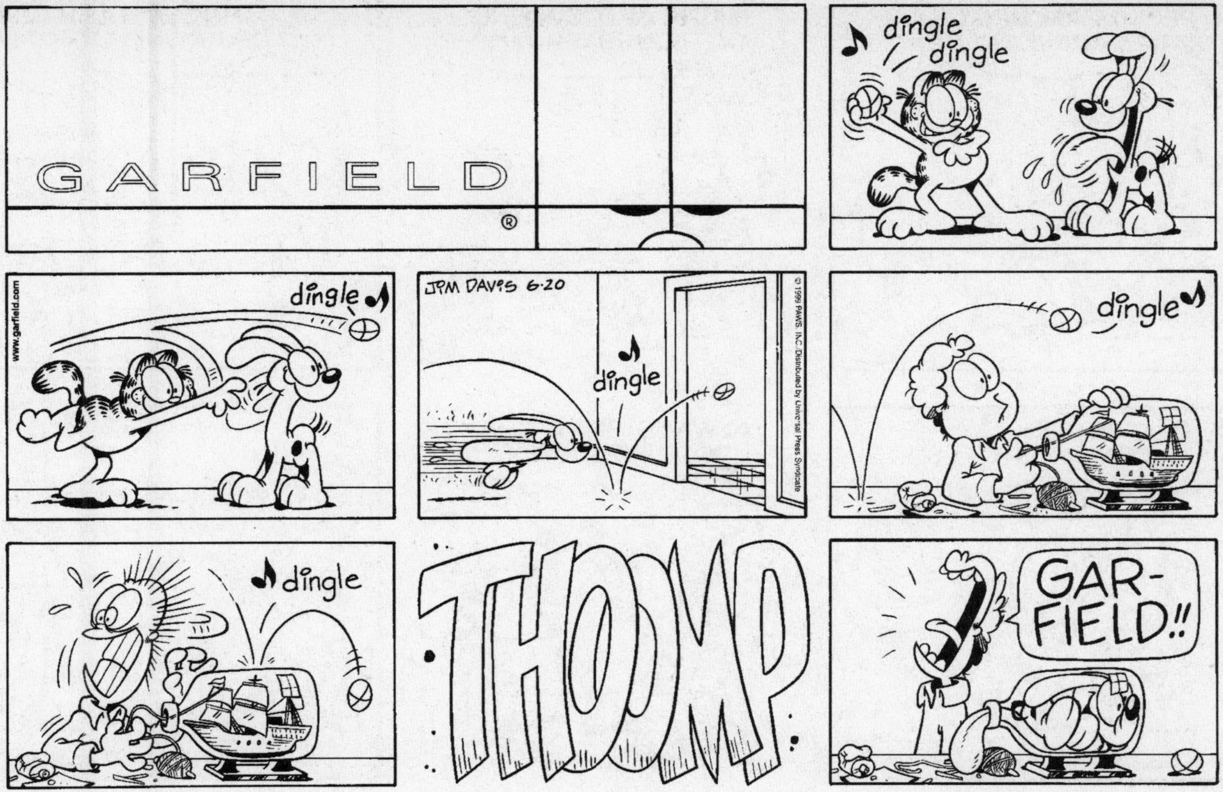
GARFIELD
dingle
dingle
www.garfield.com
dingle
JIM DAVIS 6·20
dingle
© 1999 PAWS, INC./Distributed by Universal Press Syndicate
dingle
dingle
THOOMP
GAR-
FIELD!!

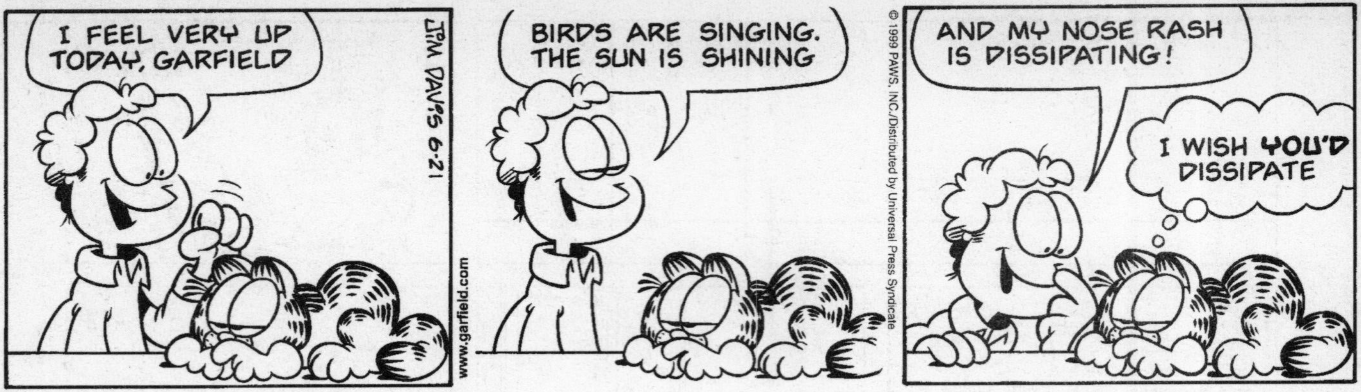
I FEEL VERY UP TODAY, GARFIELD
JIM DAVIS 6-21
www.garfield.com
BIRDS ARE SINGING. THE SUN IS SHINING
© 1999 PAWS, INC./Distributed by Universal Press Syndicate
AND MY NOSE RASH IS DISSIPATING!
I WISH YOU'D DISSIPATE

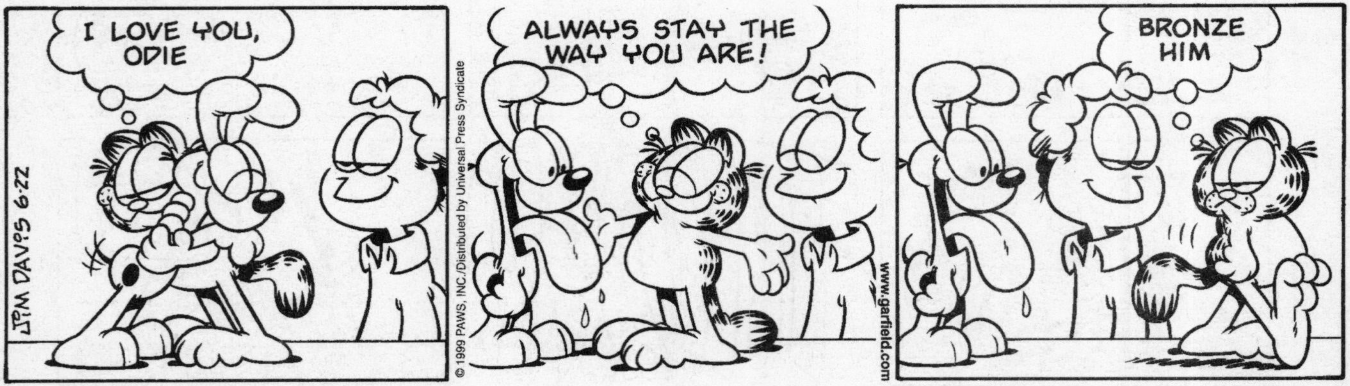
JIM DAVIS 6-22
I LOVE YOU, ODIE
© 1999 PAWS, INC./Distributed by Universal Press Syndicate
ALWAYS STAY THE WAY YOU ARE!
www.garfield.com
BRONZE HIM

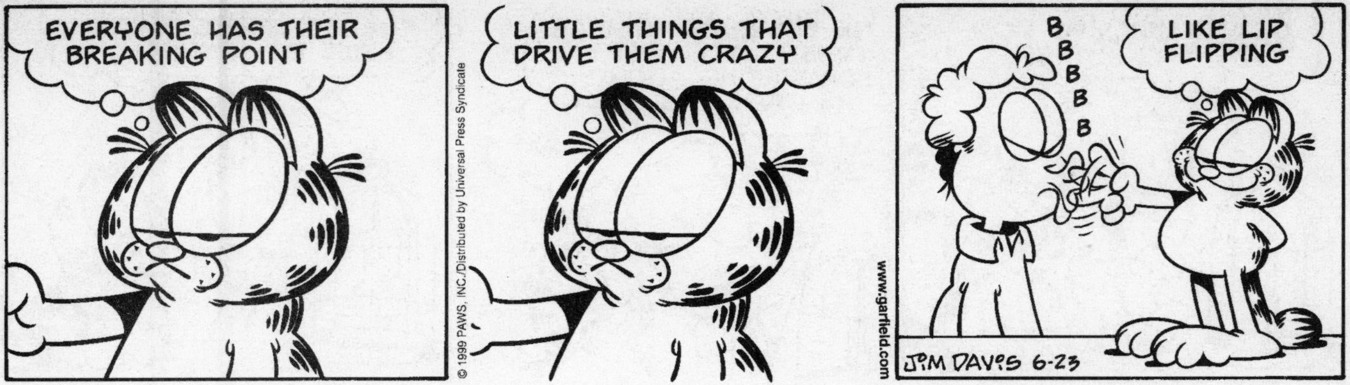
EVERYONE HAS THEIR BREAKING POINT
LITTLE THINGS THAT DRIVE THEM CRAZY
B B B B B
LIKE LIP FLIPPING
JIM DAVIS 6-23
© 1999 PAWS, INC./Distributed by Universal Press Syndicate
www.garfield.com

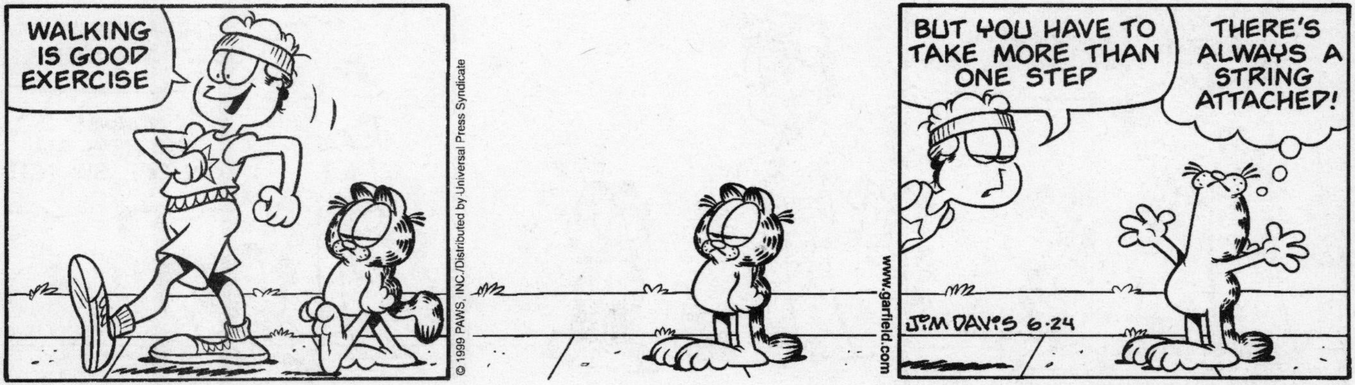
WALKING IS GOOD EXERCISE
BUT YOU HAVE TO TAKE MORE THAN ONE STEP
THERE'S ALWAYS A STRING ATTACHED!
JIM DAVIS 6-24
© 1999 PAWS, INC./Distributed by Universal Press Syndicate
www.garfield.com

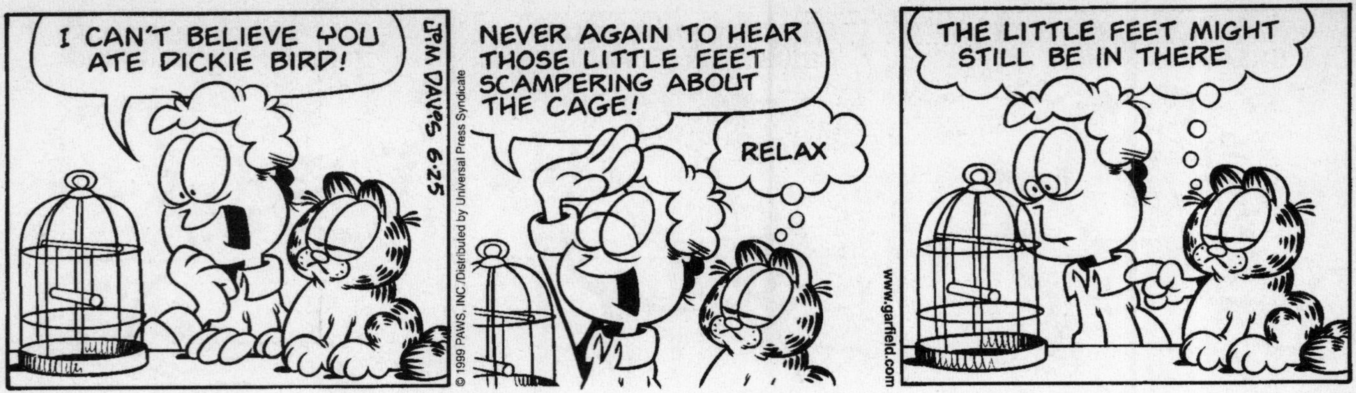
I CAN'T BELIEVE YOU ATE DICKIE BIRD!
JIM DAVIS 6-25
NEVER AGAIN TO HEAR THOSE LITTLE FEET SCAMPERING ABOUT THE CAGE!
RELAX
© 1999 PAWS, INC./Distributed by Universal Press Syndicate
THE LITTLE FEET MIGHT STILL BE IN THERE
www.garfield.com

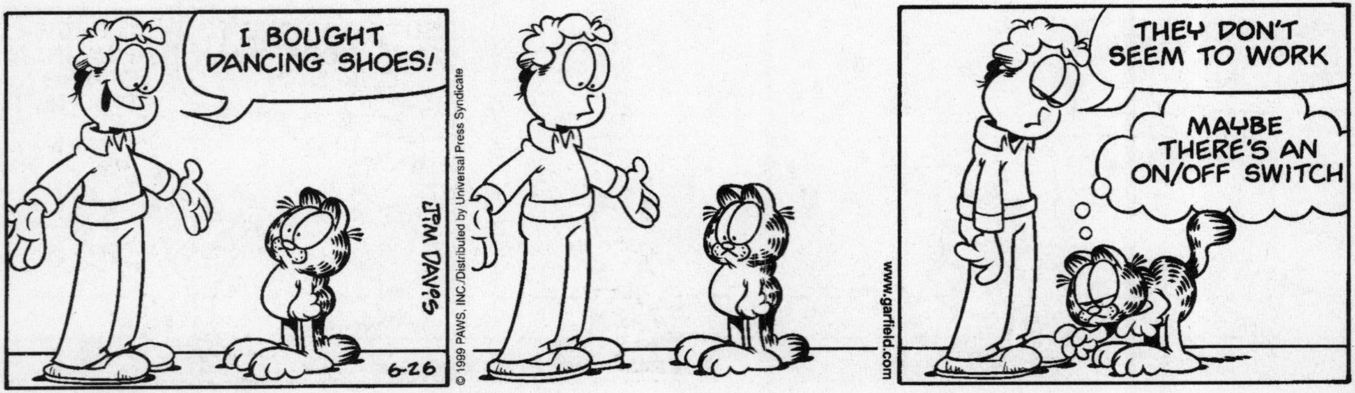
I BOUGHT DANCING SHOES!
JIM DAVIS
6-26
© 1999 PAWS, INC./Distributed by Universal Press Syndicate
THEY DON'T SEEM TO WORK
MAYBE THERE'S AN ON/OFF SWITCH
www.garfield.com

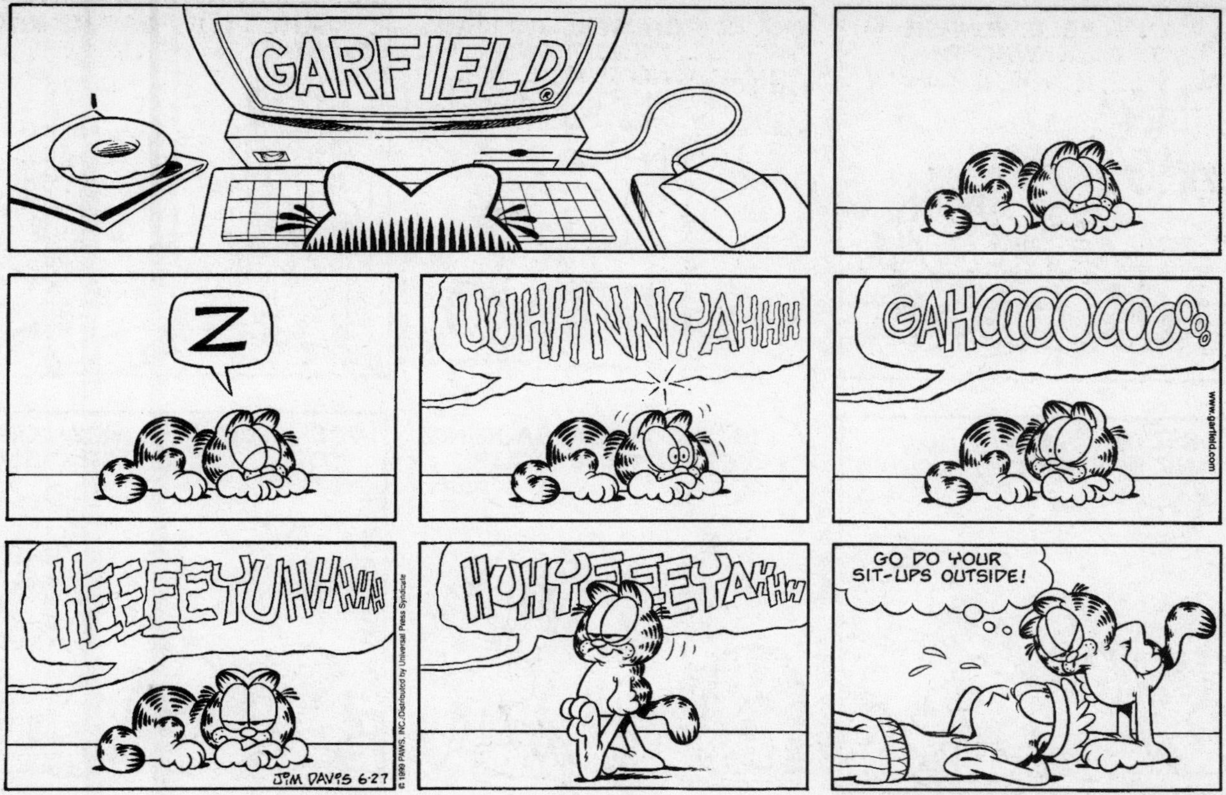
GARFIELD®
Z
UUHHNNYAHHH
GAHCOOOOOOOo
www.garfield.com
HEEEEEYUHHHHH
© 1999 PAWS, INC./Distributed by Universal Press Syndicate
JIM DAVIS 6·27
HUHYEEEEYAHHH
GO DO YOUR SIT-UPS OUTSIDE!

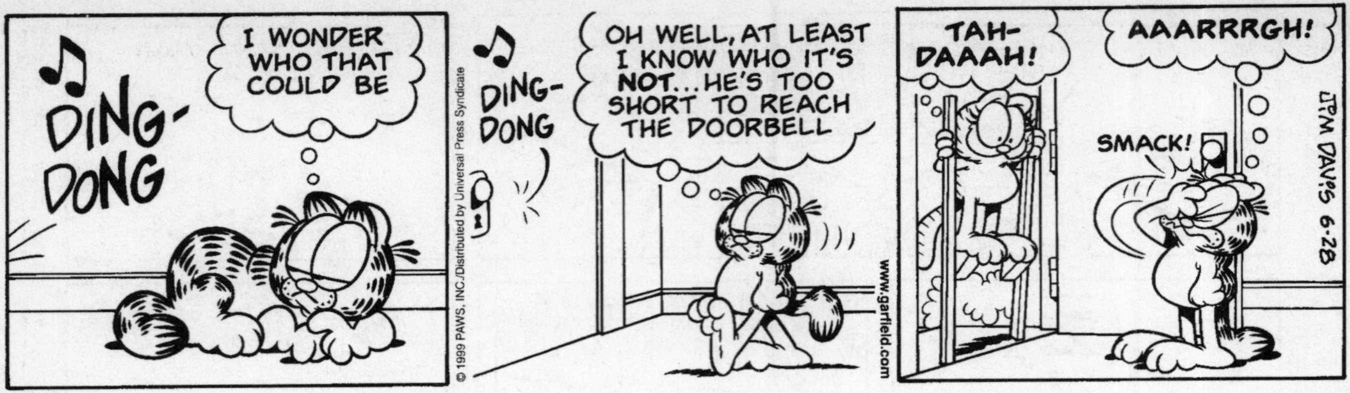
DING-DONG
I WONDER WHO THAT COULD BE
© 1999 PAWS, INC./Distributed by Universal Press Syndicate
DING-DONG
OH WELL, AT LEAST I KNOW WHO IT'S NOT...HE'S TOO SHORT TO REACH THE DOORBELL
www.garfield.com
TAH-DAAAH!
AAARRRGH!
SMACK!
JPM DAVPS 6-28

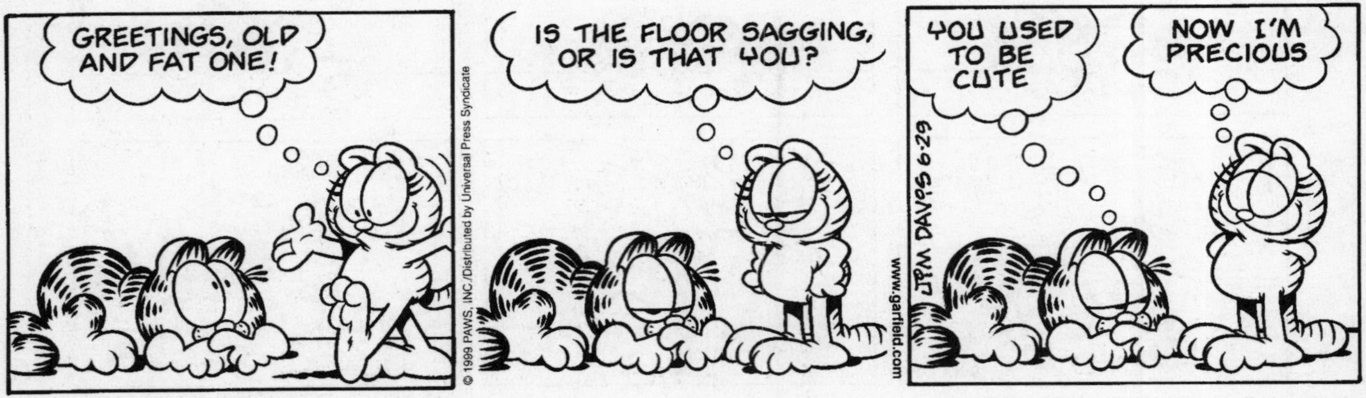
GREETINGS, OLD AND FAT ONE!
© 1999 PAWS, INC./Distributed by Universal Press Syndicate
IS THE FLOOR SAGGING, OR IS THAT YOU?
www.garfield.com
JPM DAVPS 6-29
YOU USED TO BE CUTE
NOW I'M PRECIOUS

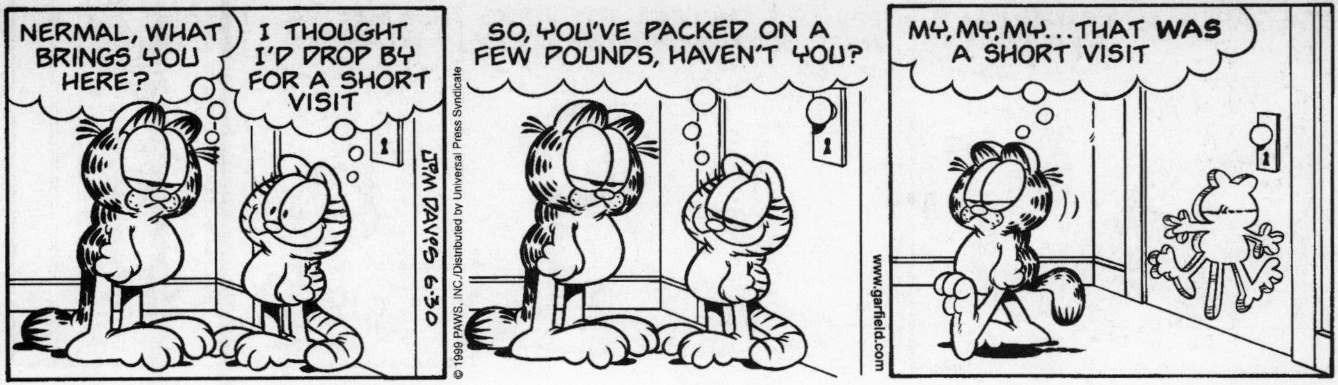
NERMAL, WHAT BRINGS YOU HERE?
I THOUGHT I'D DROP BY FOR A SHORT VISIT
JPM DAVIS 6-30
© 1999 PAWS, INC./Distributed by Universal Press Syndicate
SO, YOU'VE PACKED ON A FEW POUNDS, HAVEN'T YOU?
www.garfield.com
MY, MY, MY... THAT **WAS** A SHORT VISIT

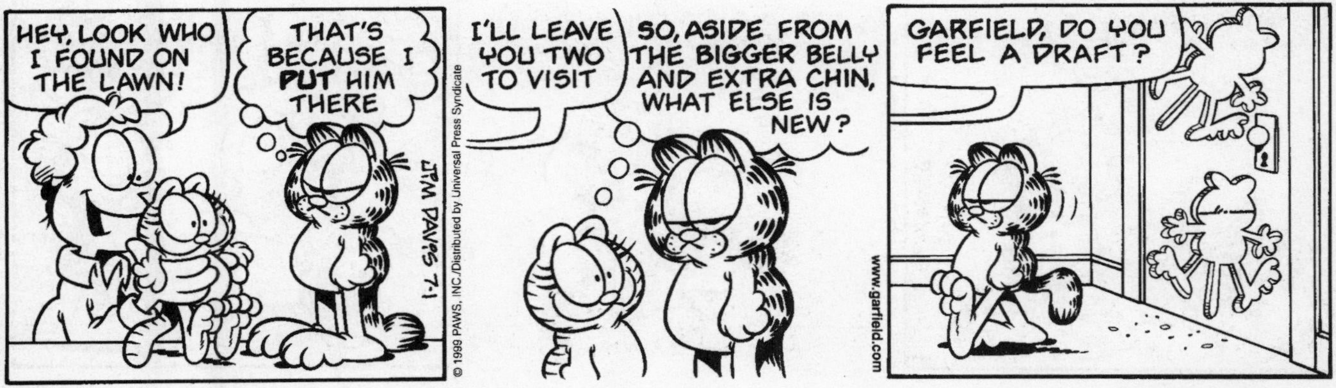
HEY, LOOK WHO I FOUND ON THE LAWN!
THAT'S BECAUSE I **PUT** HIM THERE
JPM DAVIS 7-1
© 1999 PAWS, INC./Distributed by Universal Press Syndicate
I'LL LEAVE YOU TWO TO VISIT
SO, ASIDE FROM THE BIGGER BELLY AND EXTRA CHIN, WHAT ELSE IS NEW?
www.garfield.com
GARFIELD, DO YOU FEEL A DRAFT?

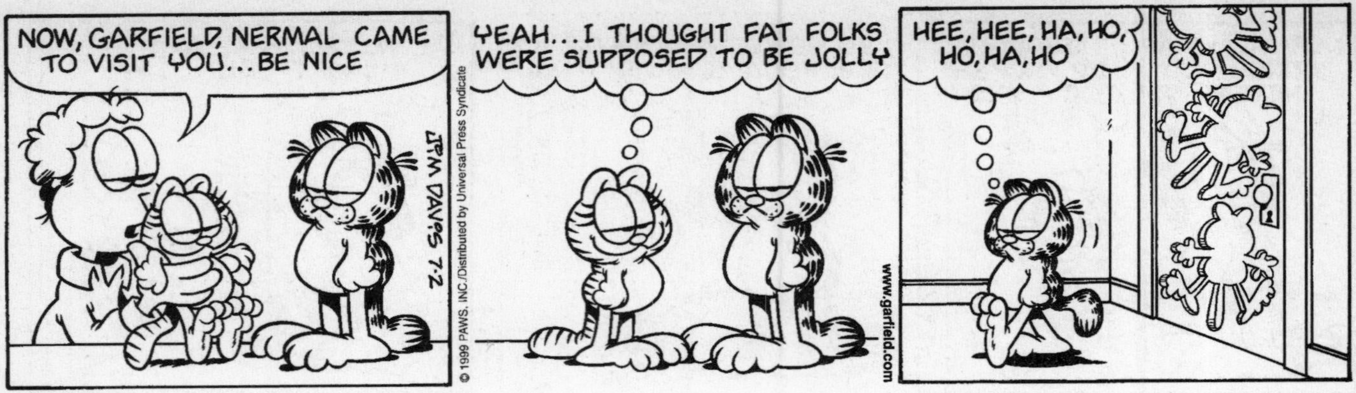
NOW, GARFIELD, NERMAL CAME TO VISIT YOU... BE NICE
JPM DAVPS 7-2
© 1999 PAWS, INC./Distributed by Universal Press Syndicate
YEAH... I THOUGHT FAT FOLKS WERE SUPPOSED TO BE JOLLY
www.garfield.com
HEE, HEE, HA, HO, HO, HA, HO

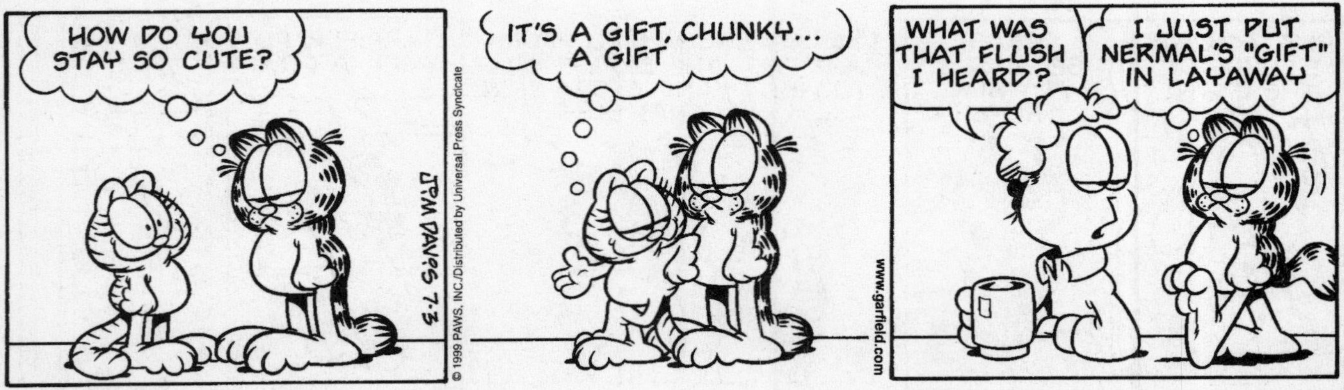
HOW DO YOU STAY SO CUTE?
JPM DAVPS 7-3
© 1999 PAWS, INC./Distributed by Universal Press Syndicate
IT'S A GIFT, CHUNKY... A GIFT
www.garfield.com
WHAT WAS THAT FLUSH I HEARD?
I JUST PUT NERMAL'S "GIFT" IN LAYAWAY

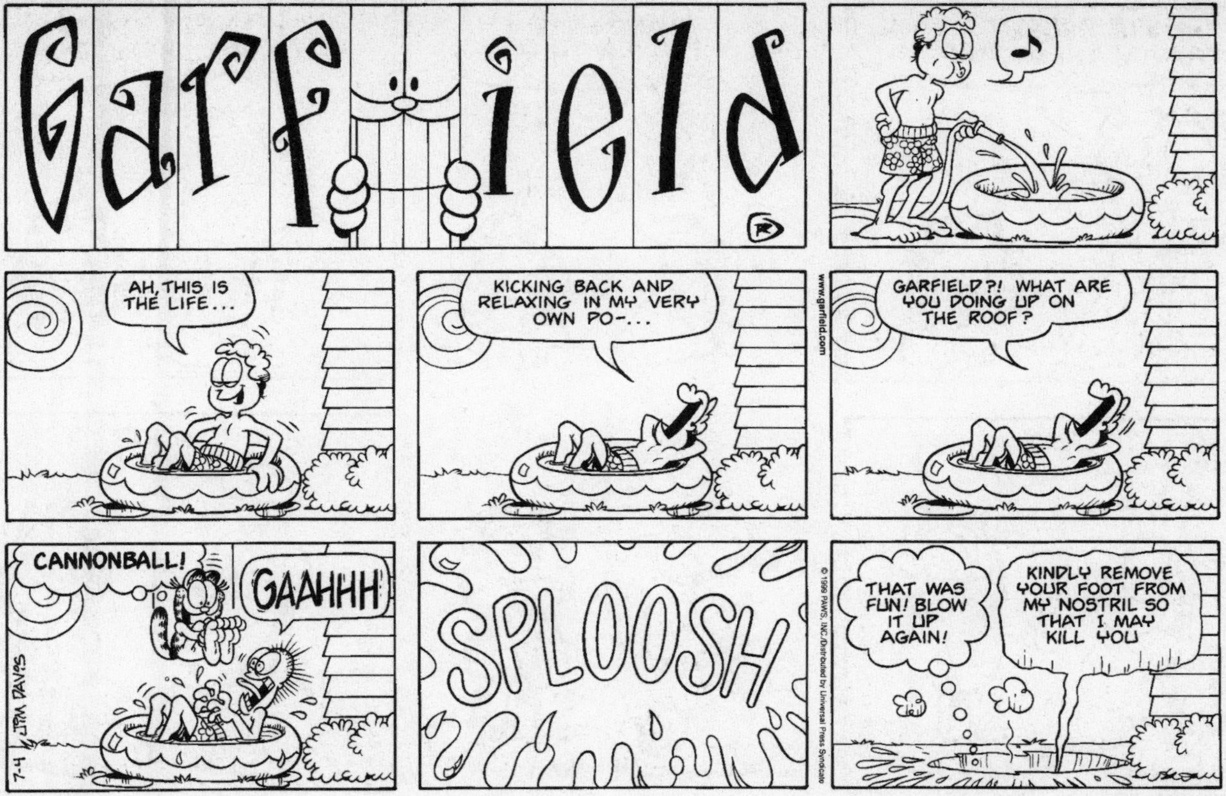
Garfield
AH, THIS IS THE LIFE...
KICKING BACK AND RELAXING IN MY VERY OWN PO-...
GARFIELD?! WHAT ARE YOU DOING UP ON THE ROOF?
CANNONBALL!
GAAHHH
SPLOOSH
THAT WAS FUN! BLOW IT UP AGAIN!
KINDLY REMOVE YOUR FOOT FROM MY NOSTRIL SO THAT I MAY KILL YOU
JIM DAVIS
7-4
www.garfield.com
© 1999 PAWS, INC./Distributed by Universal Press Syndicate

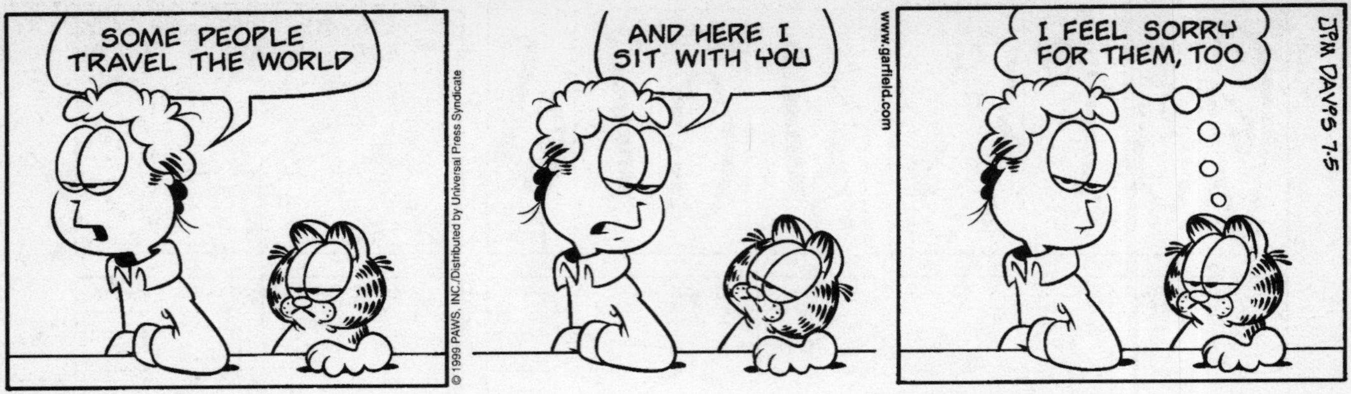
SOME PEOPLE TRAVEL THE WORLD
AND HERE I SIT WITH YOU
I FEEL SORRY FOR THEM, TOO
© 1999 PAWS, INC./Distributed by Universal Press Syndicate
www.garfield.com
JPM DAVIS 7-5

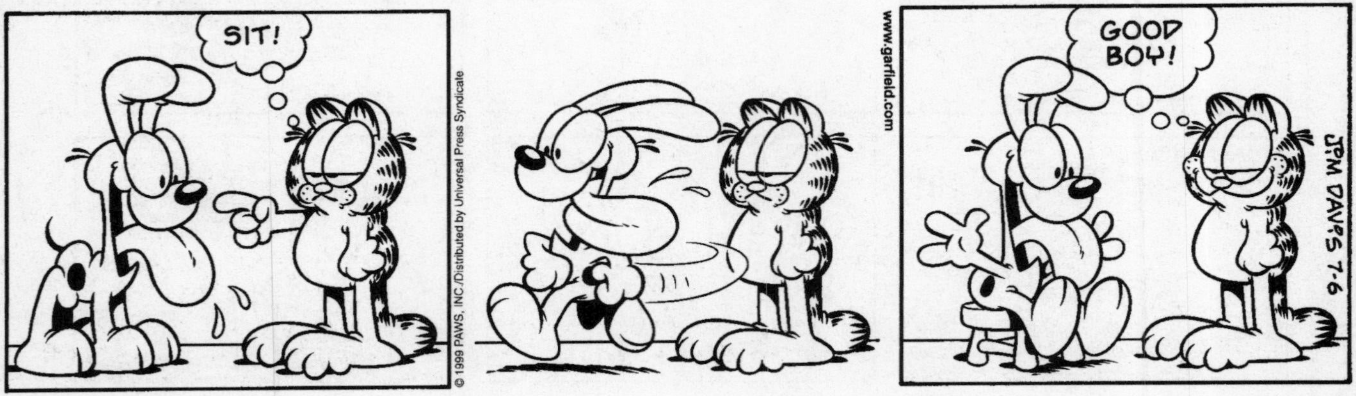
SIT!
GOOD BOY!
© 1999 PAWS, INC./Distributed by Universal Press Syndicate
www.garfield.com
JPM DAVIS 7-6

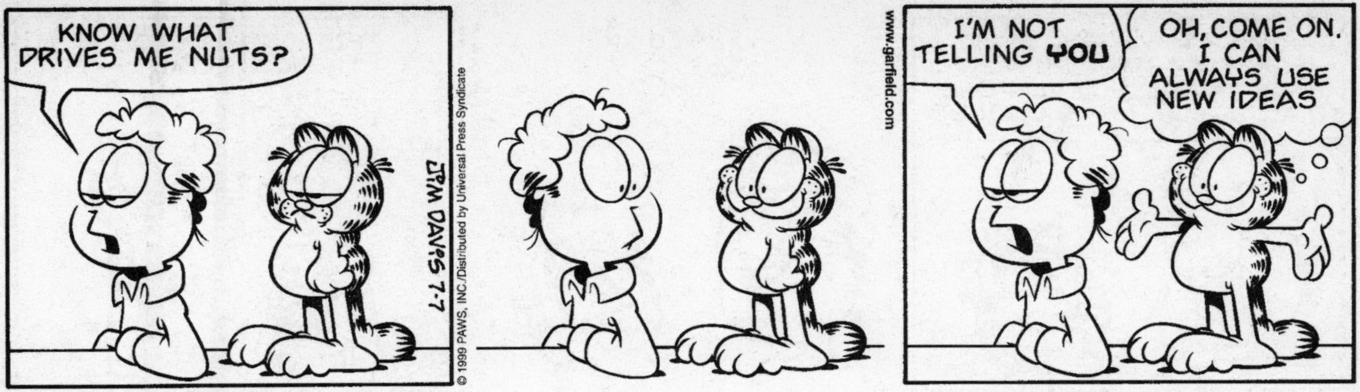
KNOW WHAT DRIVES ME NUTS?
JIM DAVIS 7-7
© 1999 PAWS, INC./Distributed by Universal Press Syndicate
www.garfield.com
I'M NOT TELLING **YOU**
OH, COME ON. I CAN ALWAYS USE NEW IDEAS

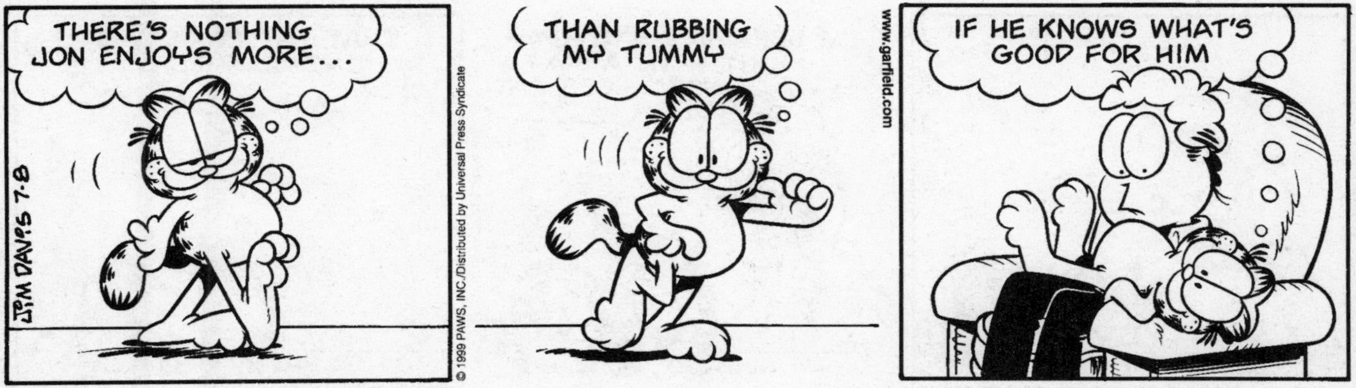
THERE'S NOTHING JON ENJOYS MORE...
JIM DAVIS 7-8
© 1999 PAWS, INC./Distributed by Universal Press Syndicate
THAN RUBBING MY TUMMY
www.garfield.com
IF HE KNOWS WHAT'S GOOD FOR HIM

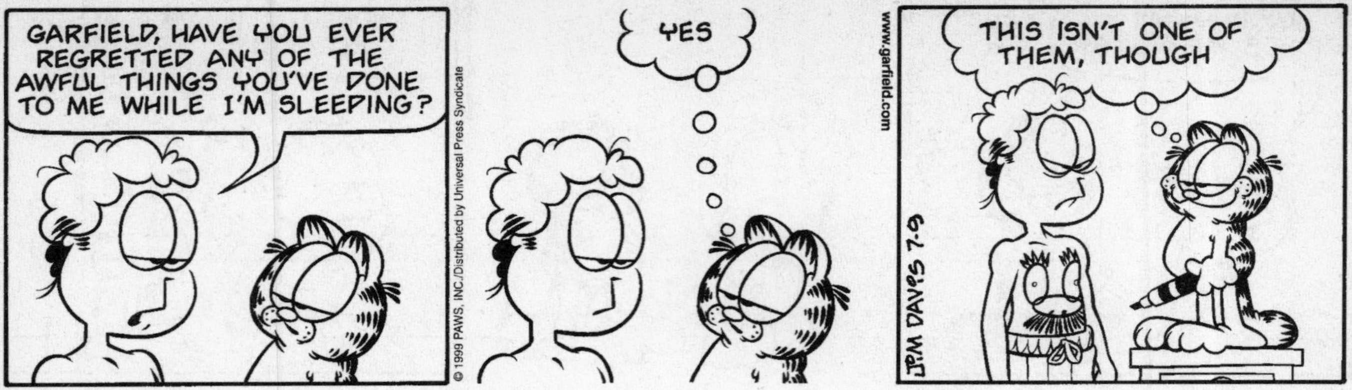
GARFIELD, HAVE YOU EVER REGRETTED ANY OF THE AWFUL THINGS YOU'VE DONE TO ME WHILE I'M SLEEPING?
© 1999 PAWS, INC./Distributed by Universal Press Syndicate
YES
www.garfield.com
THIS ISN'T ONE OF THEM, THOUGH
JPM DAVPS 7-9

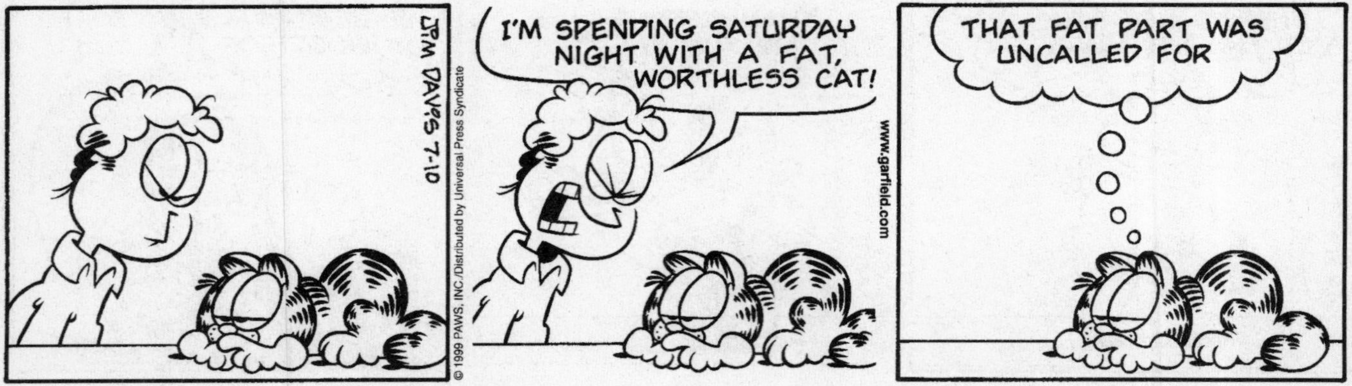
JPM DAVPS 7-10
© 1999 PAWS, INC./Distributed by Universal Press Syndicate
I'M SPENDING SATURDAY NIGHT WITH A FAT, WORTHLESS CAT!
www.garfield.com
THAT FAT PART WAS UNCALLED FOR

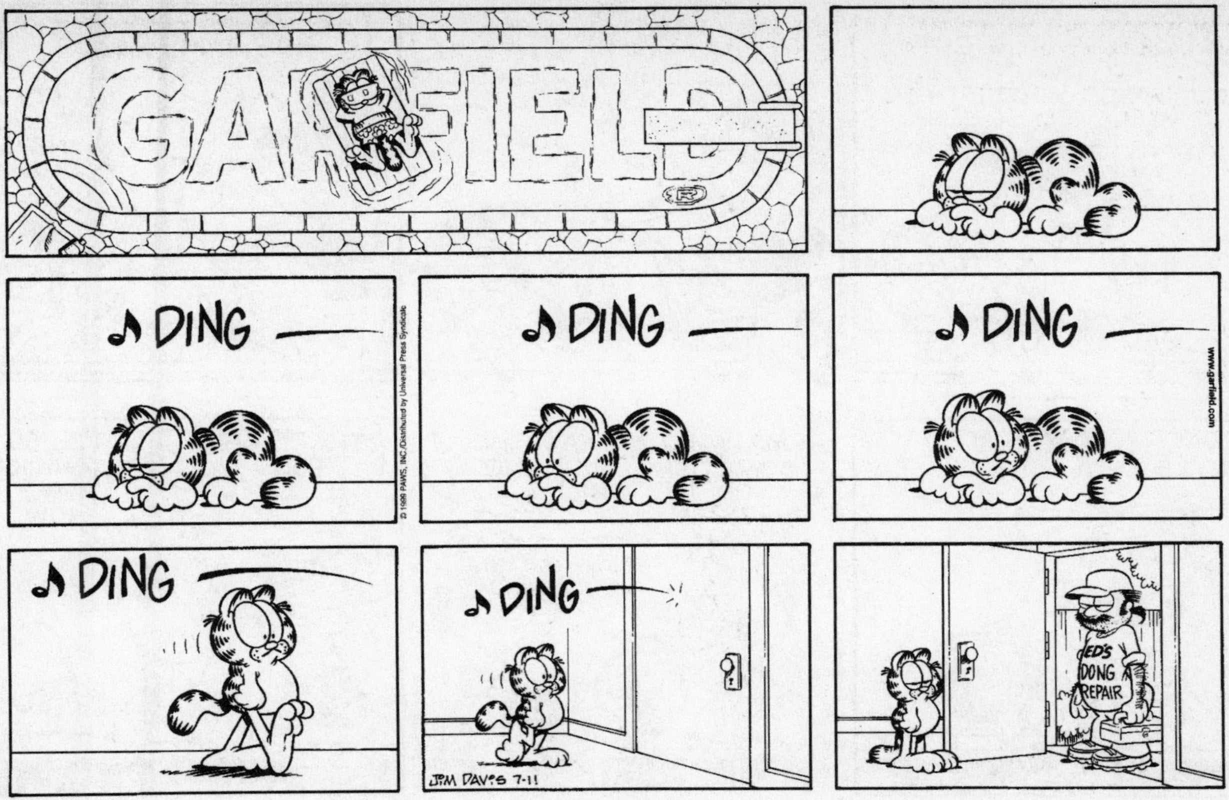
GARFIELD
♪ DING
♪ DING
♪ DING
♪ DING
♪ DING
ED'S
DONG
REPAIR
JIM DAVIS 7-11
© 1999 PAWS, INC./Distributed by Universal Press Syndicate
www.garfield.com

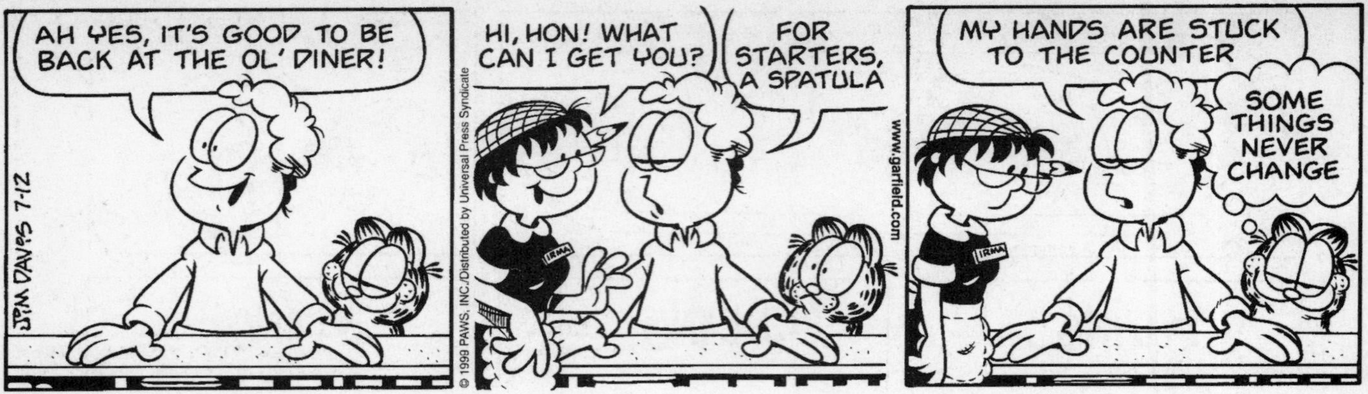
AH YES, IT'S GOOD TO BE BACK AT THE OL' DINER!
JIM DAVIS 7-12
HI, HON! WHAT CAN I GET YOU?
FOR STARTERS, A SPATULA
IRMA
© 1999 PAWS, INC./Distributed by Universal Press Syndicate
www.garfield.com
MY HANDS ARE STUCK TO THE COUNTER
SOME THINGS NEVER CHANGE
IRMA

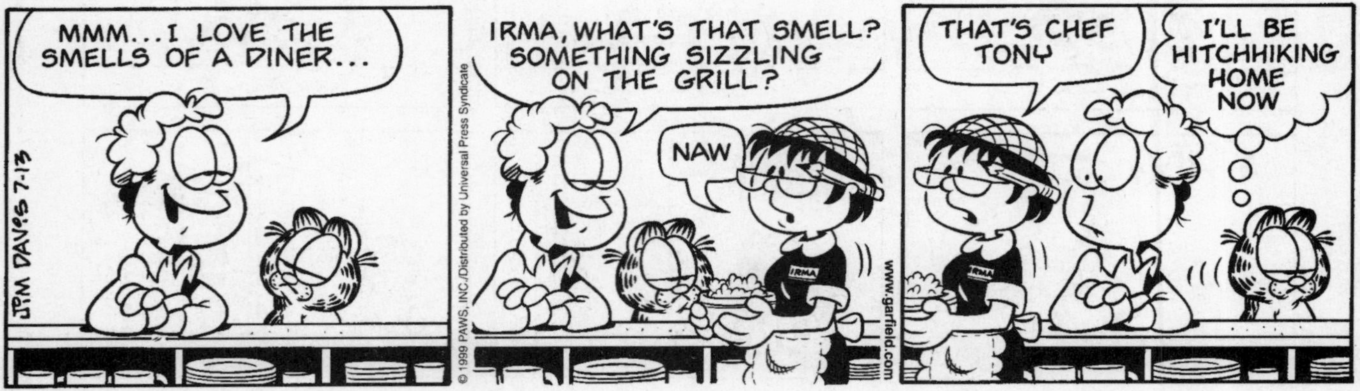
MMM... I LOVE THE SMELLS OF A DINER...
JIM DAVIS 7-13
IRMA, WHAT'S THAT SMELL? SOMETHING SIZZLING ON THE GRILL?
NAW
IRMA
© 1999 PAWS, INC./Distributed by Universal Press Syndicate
www.garfield.com
THAT'S CHEF TONY
I'LL BE HITCHHIKING HOME NOW
IRMA

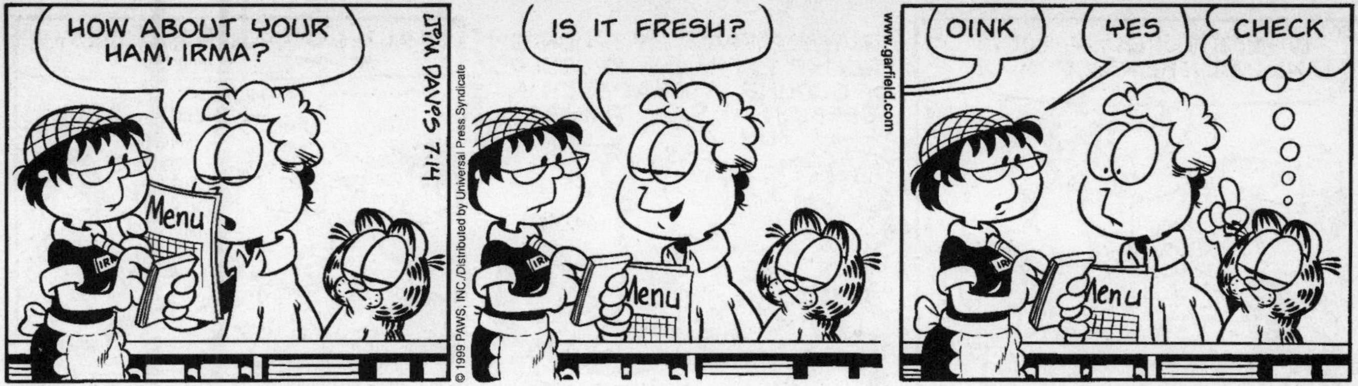
HOW ABOUT YOUR HAM, IRMA?
Menu
JIM DAVIS 7-14
© 1999 PAWS, INC./Distributed by Universal Press Syndicate
IS IT FRESH?
Menu
www.garfield.com
OINK
YES
CHECK
Menu

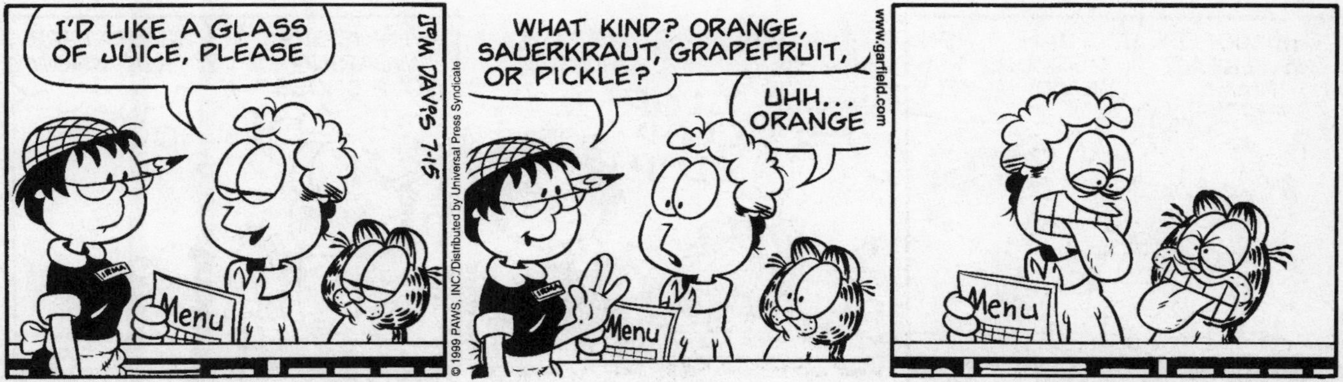
I'D LIKE A GLASS OF JUICE, PLEASE
IRMA
Menu
JIM DAVIS 7-15
© 1999 PAWS, INC./Distributed by Universal Press Syndicate
WHAT KIND? ORANGE, SAUERKRAUT, GRAPEFRUIT, OR PICKLE?
UHH... ORANGE
IRMA
Menu
www.garfield.com
Menu

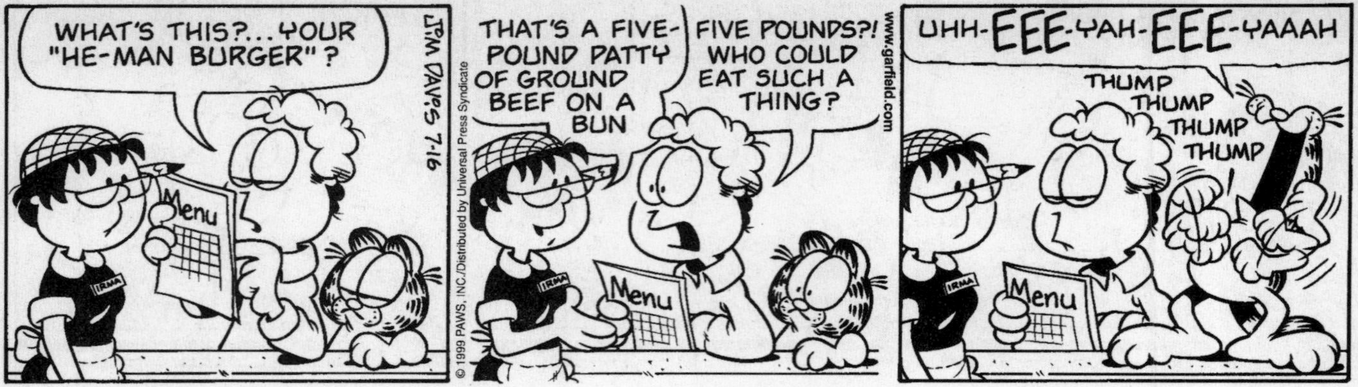
WHAT'S THIS?...YOUR "HE-MAN BURGER"?
JIM DAVIS 7-16
© 1999 PAWS, INC./Distributed by Universal Press Syndicate
Menu
THAT'S A FIVE-POUND PATTY OF GROUND BEEF ON A BUN
FIVE POUNDS?! WHO COULD EAT SUCH A THING?
www.garfield.com
UHH-EEE-YAH-EEE-YAAAH
THUMP
THUMP
THUMP
THUMP

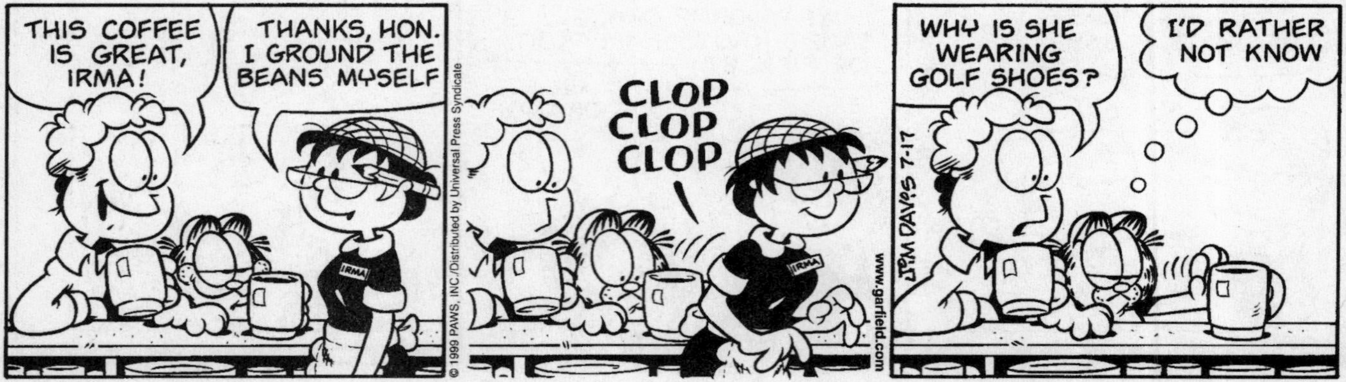
THIS COFFEE IS GREAT, IRMA!
THANKS, HON. I GROUND THE BEANS MYSELF
© 1999 PAWS, INC./Distributed by Universal Press Syndicate
CLOP
CLOP
CLOP
JIM DAVIS 7-17
www.garfield.com
WHY IS SHE WEARING GOLF SHOES?
I'D RATHER NOT KNOW

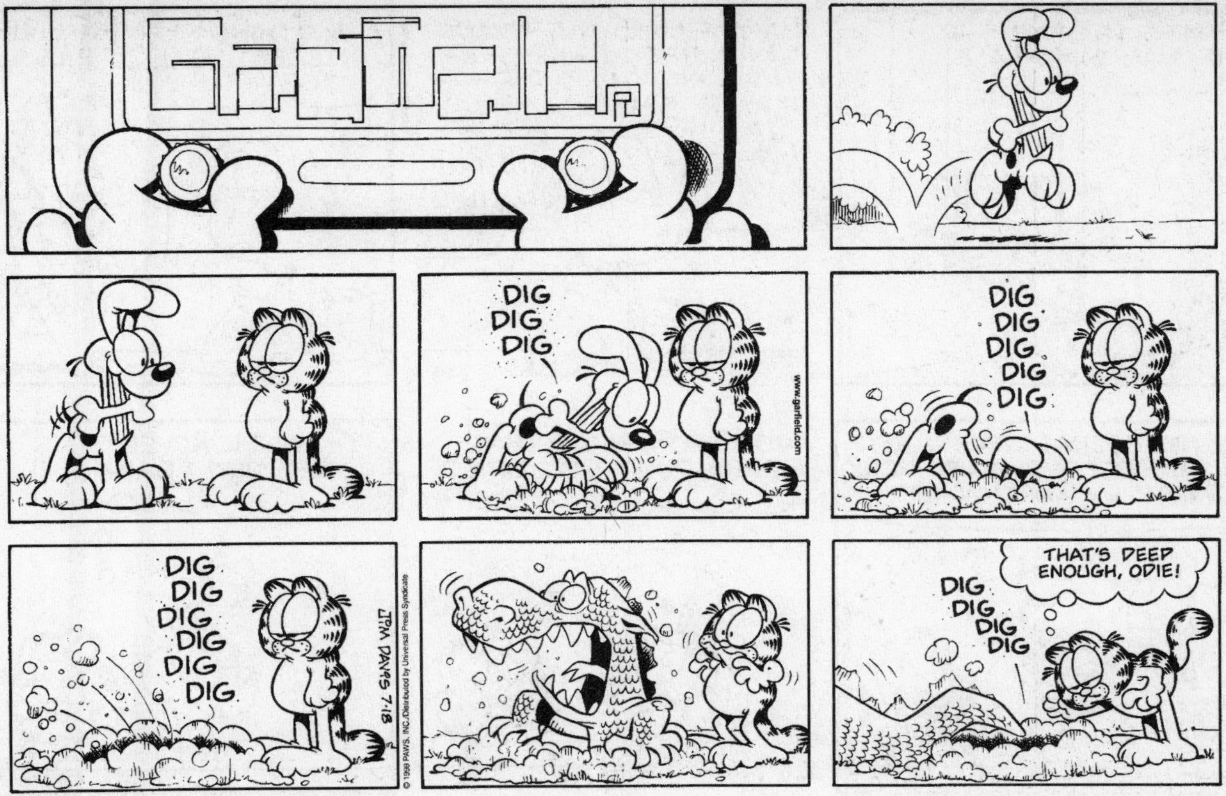

GARFIELD
DIG DIG DIG
www.garfield.com
DIG DIG DIG DIG DIG
DIG DIG DIG DIG DIG DIG
JPM DAVIS 7-18
© 1999 PAWS, INC./Distributed by Universal Press Syndicate
DIG DIG DIG DIG
THAT'S DEEP ENOUGH, ODIE!

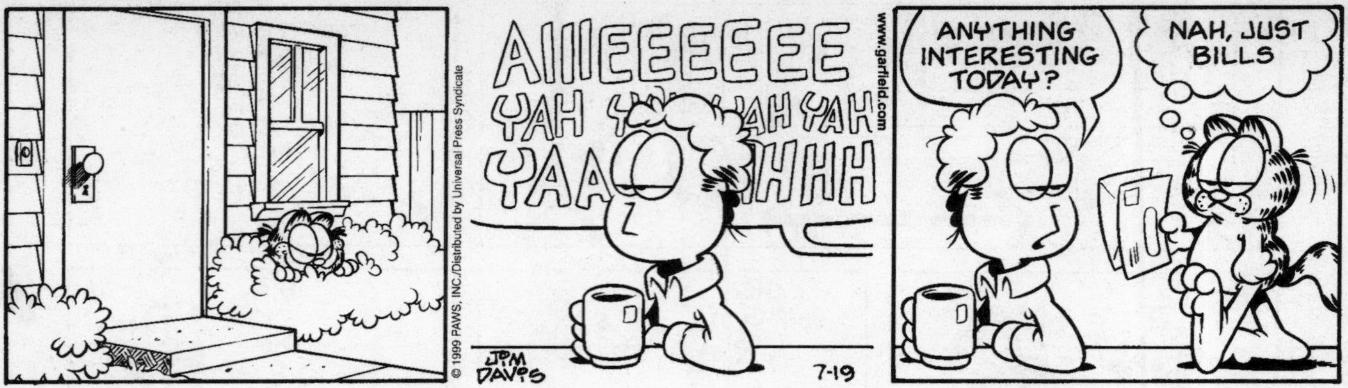
AIIIEEEEEEE
YAH
YAH YAH
YAA
HHH
JIM DAVIS 7-19
© 1999 PAWS, INC./Distributed by Universal Press Syndicate
www.garfield.com
ANYTHING INTERESTING TODAY?
NAH, JUST BILLS

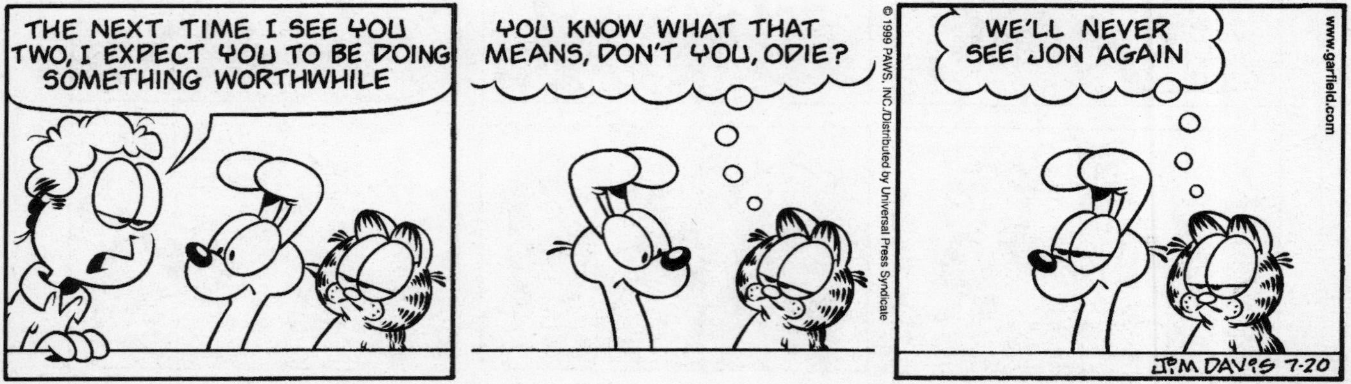
THE NEXT TIME I SEE YOU TWO, I EXPECT YOU TO BE DOING SOMETHING WORTHWHILE
YOU KNOW WHAT THAT MEANS, DON'T YOU, ODIE?
© 1999 PAWS, INC./Distributed by Universal Press Syndicate
WE'LL NEVER SEE JON AGAIN
www.garfield.com
JIM DAVIS 7-20

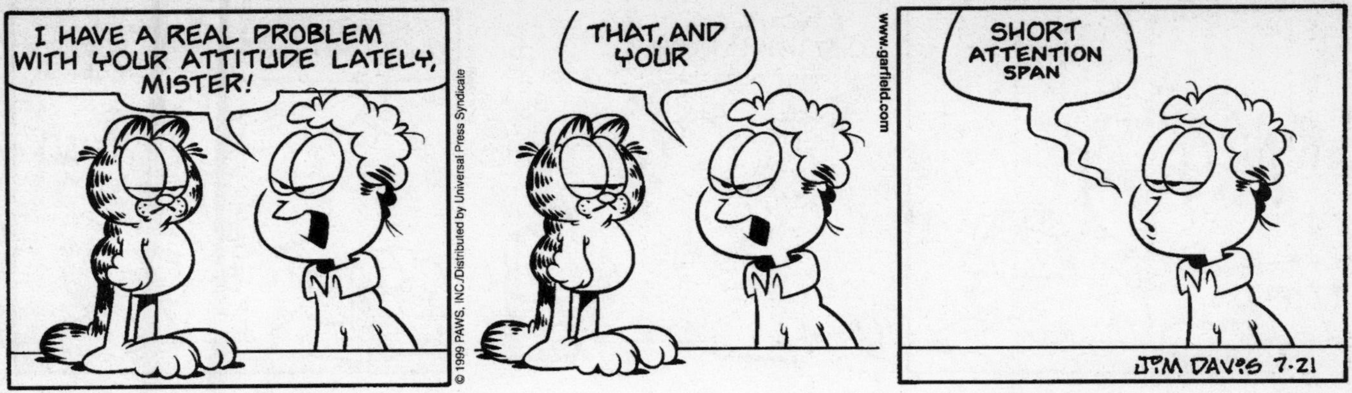
I HAVE A REAL PROBLEM WITH YOUR ATTITUDE LATELY, MISTER!
© 1999 PAWS, INC./Distributed by Universal Press Syndicate
THAT, AND YOUR
www.garfield.com
SHORT ATTENTION SPAN
JIM DAVIS 7-21

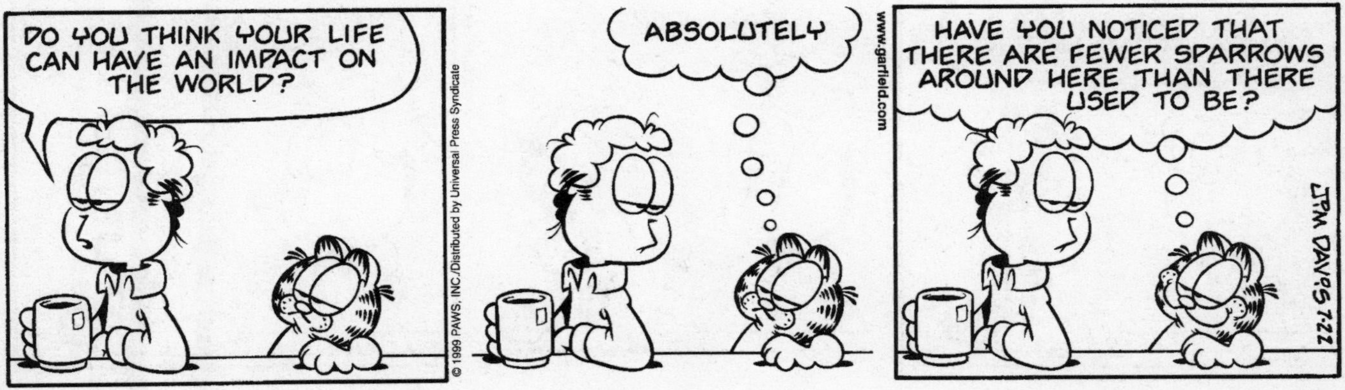
DO YOU THINK YOUR LIFE CAN HAVE AN IMPACT ON THE WORLD?
© 1999 PAWS, INC./Distributed by Universal Press Syndicate
ABSOLUTELY
www.garfield.com
HAVE YOU NOTICED THAT THERE ARE FEWER SPARROWS AROUND HERE THAN THERE USED TO BE?
JIM DAVIS 7-22

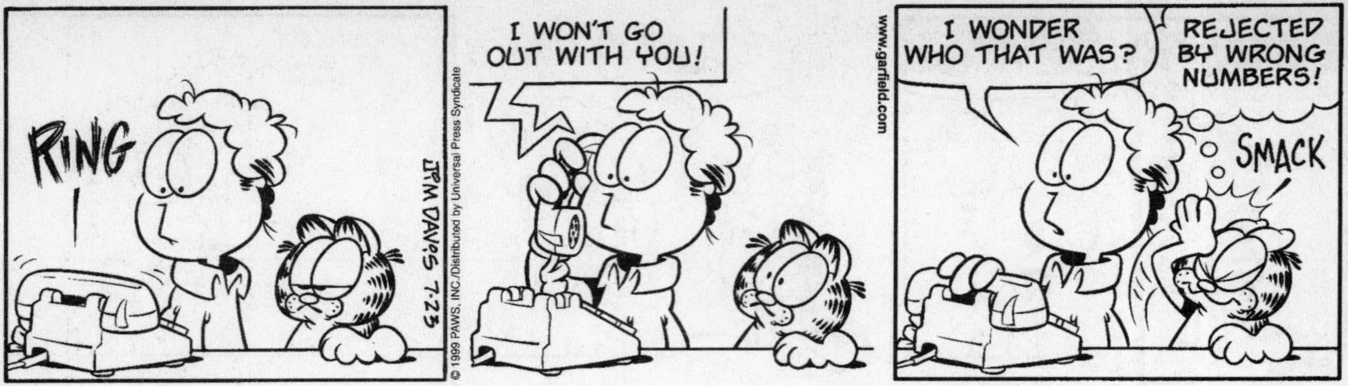
RING
JIM DAVIS 7-23
© 1999 PAWS, INC./Distributed by Universal Press Syndicate
I WON'T GO OUT WITH YOU!
www.garfield.com
I WONDER WHO THAT WAS?
REJECTED BY WRONG NUMBERS!
SMACK

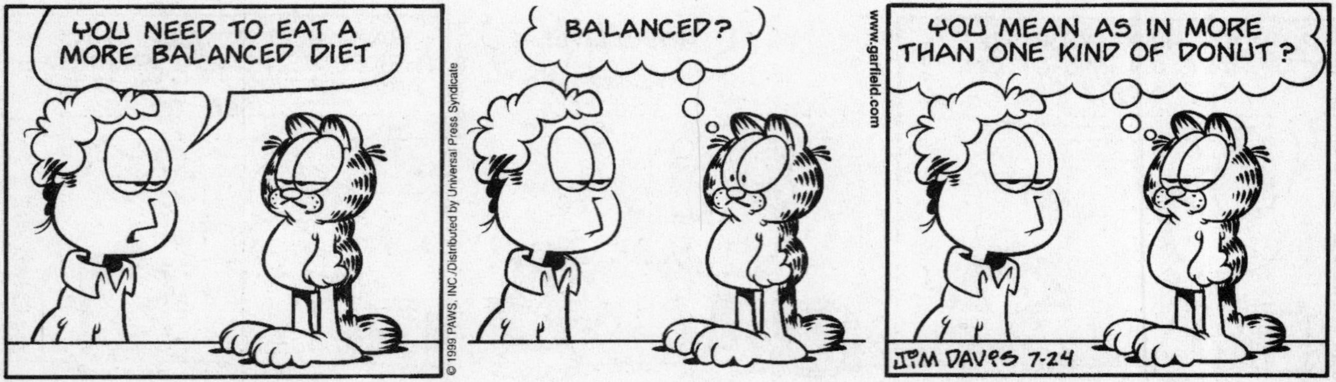
YOU NEED TO EAT A MORE BALANCED DIET
© 1999 PAWS, INC./Distributed by Universal Press Syndicate
BALANCED?
www.garfield.com
YOU MEAN AS IN MORE THAN ONE KIND OF DONUT?
JIM DAVIS 7-24

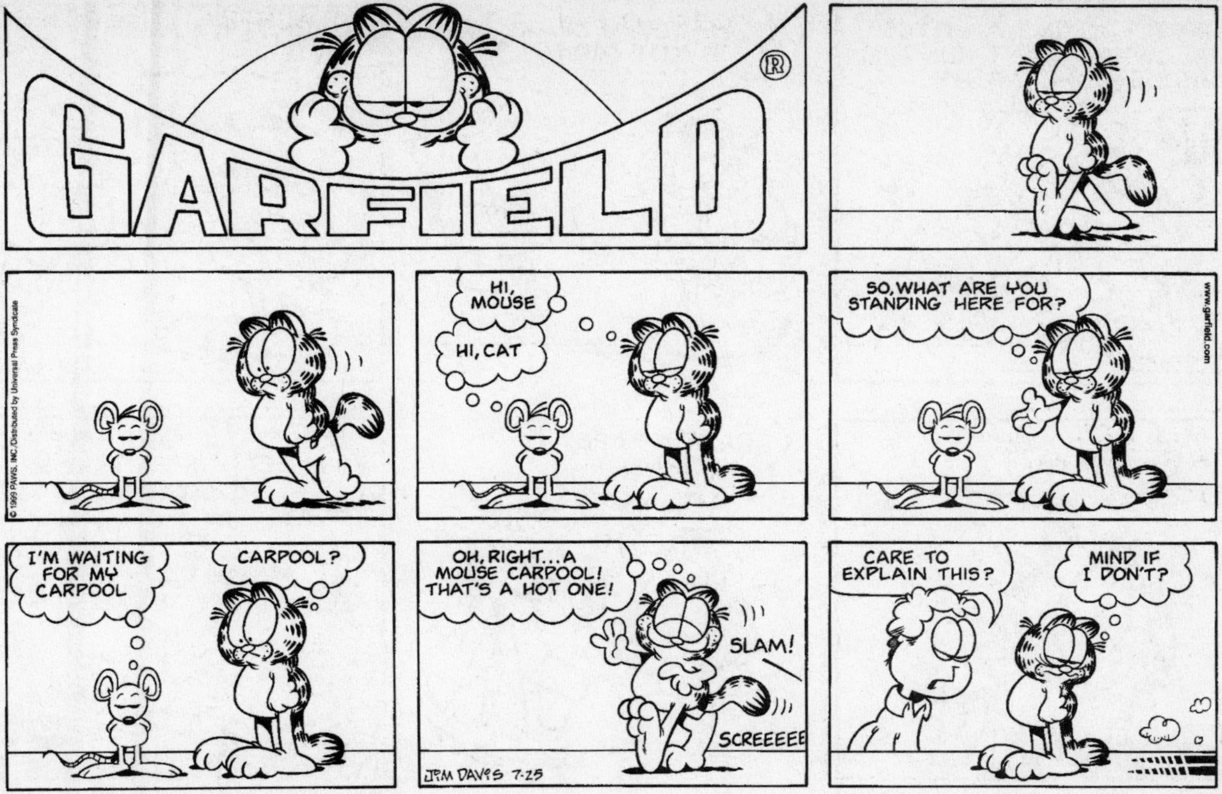
GARFIELD
© 1999 PAWS, INC./Distributed by Universal Press Syndicate
HI, MOUSE
HI, CAT
SO, WHAT ARE YOU STANDING HERE FOR?
www.garfield.com
I'M WAITING FOR MY CARPOOL
CARPOOL?
OH, RIGHT... A MOUSE CARPOOL! THAT'S A HOT ONE!
SLAM!
SCREEEEEE
JIM DAVIS 7-25
CARE TO EXPLAIN THIS?
MIND IF I DON'T?

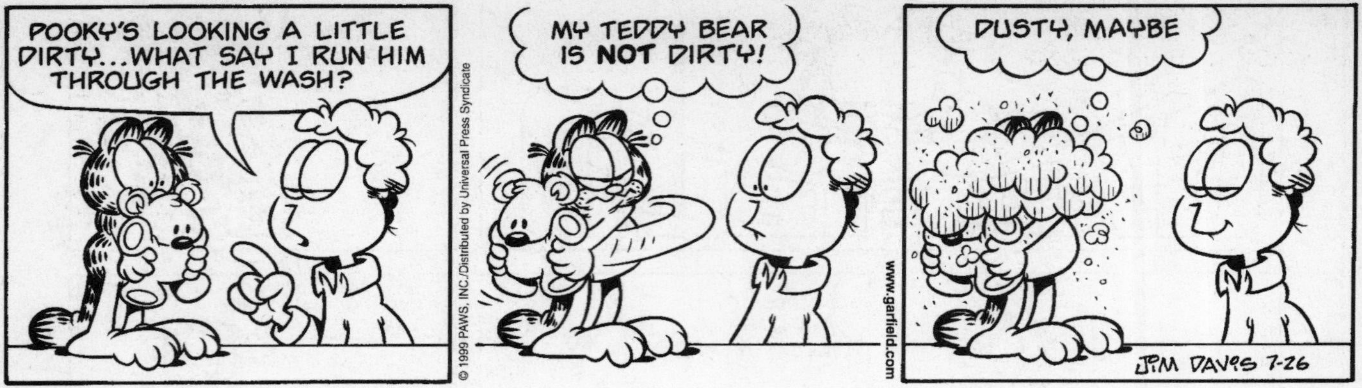
POOKY'S LOOKING A LITTLE DIRTY...WHAT SAY I RUN HIM THROUGH THE WASH?
MY TEDDY BEAR IS **NOT** DIRTY!
DUSTY, MAYBE
JIM DAVIS 7-26
© 1999 PAWS, INC./Distributed by Universal Press Syndicate
www.garfield.com

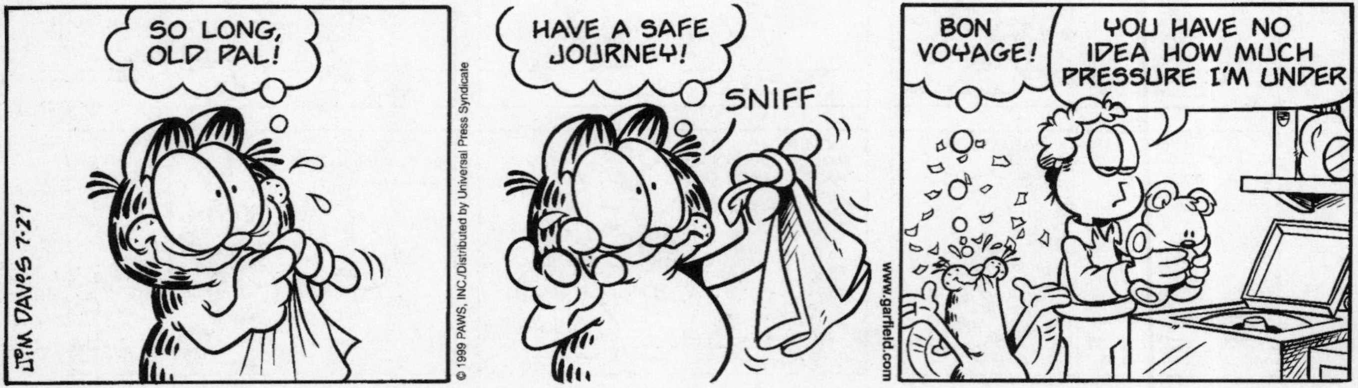
SO LONG, OLD PAL!
HAVE A SAFE JOURNEY!
SNIFF
BON VOYAGE!
YOU HAVE NO IDEA HOW MUCH PRESSURE I'M UNDER
JIM DAVIS 7-27
© 1999 PAWS, INC./Distributed by Universal Press Syndicate
www.garfield.com

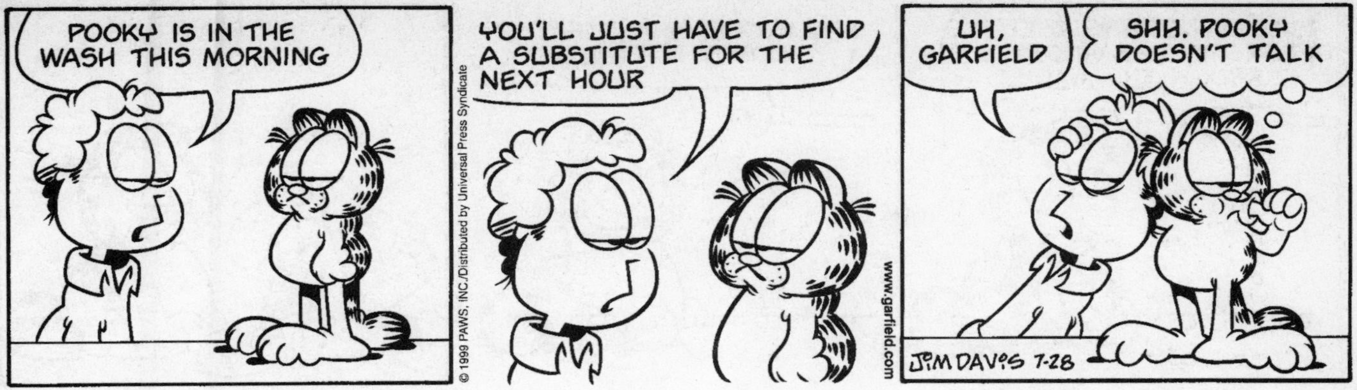
POOKY IS IN THE WASH THIS MORNING
YOU'LL JUST HAVE TO FIND A SUBSTITUTE FOR THE NEXT HOUR
UH, GARFIELD
SHH. POOKY DOESN'T TALK
JIM DAVIS 7-28
© 1999 PAWS, INC./Distributed by Universal Press Syndicate
www.garfield.com

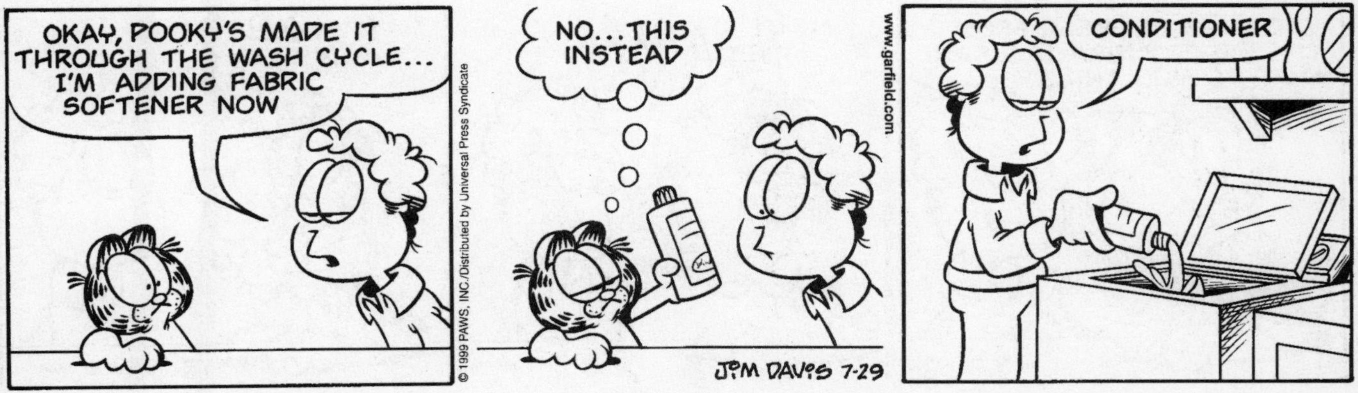
OKAY, POOKY'S MADE IT THROUGH THE WASH CYCLE... I'M ADDING FABRIC SOFTENER NOW
NO...THIS INSTEAD
CONDITIONER
JIM DAVIS 7-29
© 1999 PAWS, INC./Distributed by Universal Press Syndicate
www.garfield.com

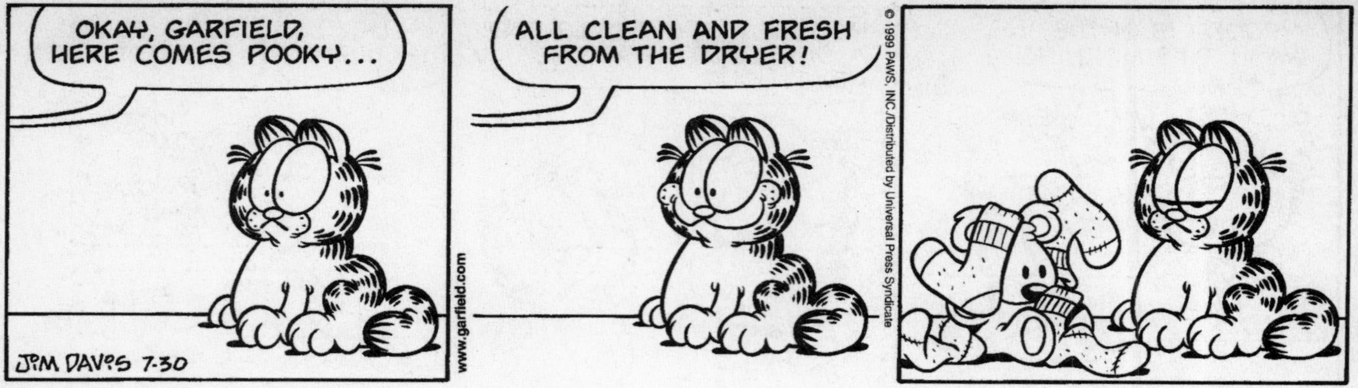
OKAY, GARFIELD, HERE COMES POOKY...
ALL CLEAN AND FRESH FROM THE DRYER!
JIM DAVIS 7-30
www.garfield.com
© 1999 PAWS, INC./Distributed by Universal Press Syndicate

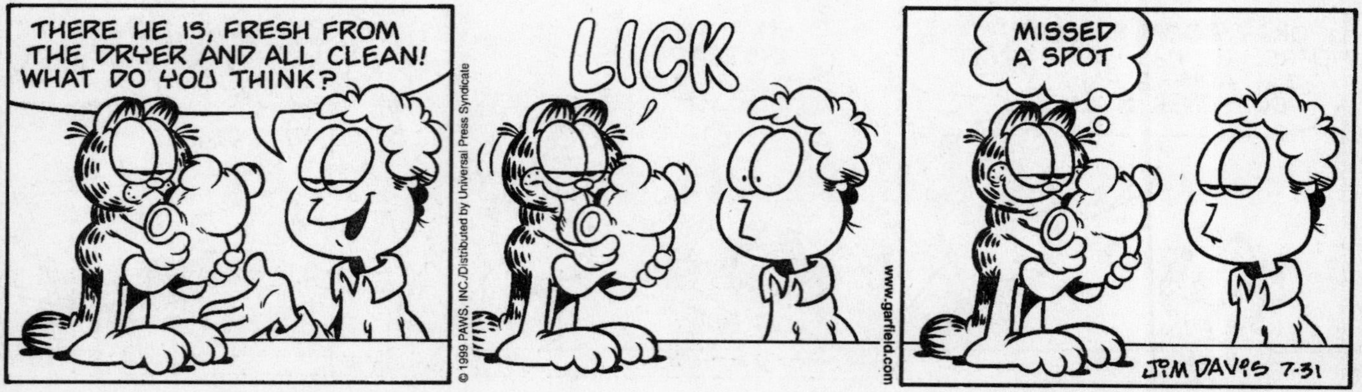
THERE HE IS, FRESH FROM THE DRYER AND ALL CLEAN! WHAT DO YOU THINK?
LICK
MISSED A SPOT
JIM DAVIS 7-31
© 1999 PAWS, INC./Distributed by Universal Press Syndicate
www.garfield.com

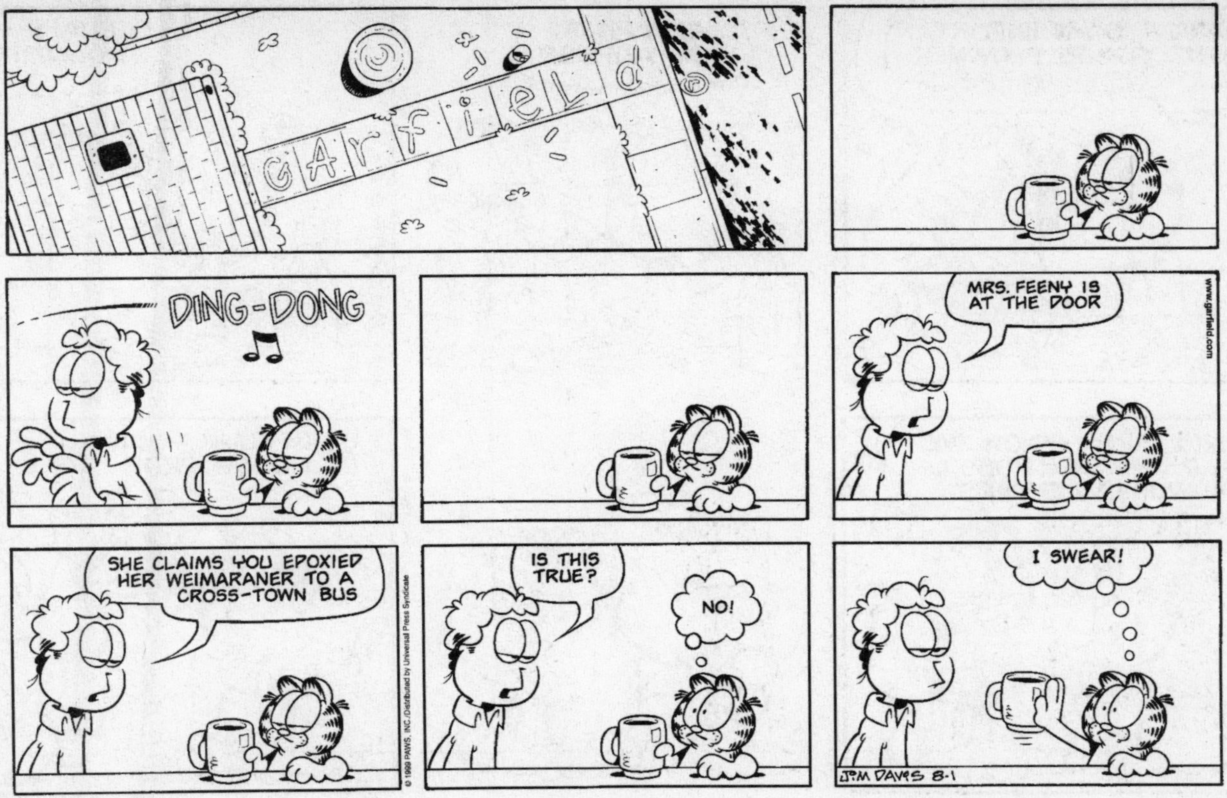
GARFIELD
DING-DONG
MRS. FEENY IS AT THE DOOR
www.garfield.com
SHE CLAIMS YOU EPOXIED HER WEIMARANER TO A CROSS-TOWN BUS
© 1999 PAWS, INC./Distributed by Universal Press Syndicate
IS THIS TRUE?
NO!
I SWEAR!
JIM DAVIS 8-1

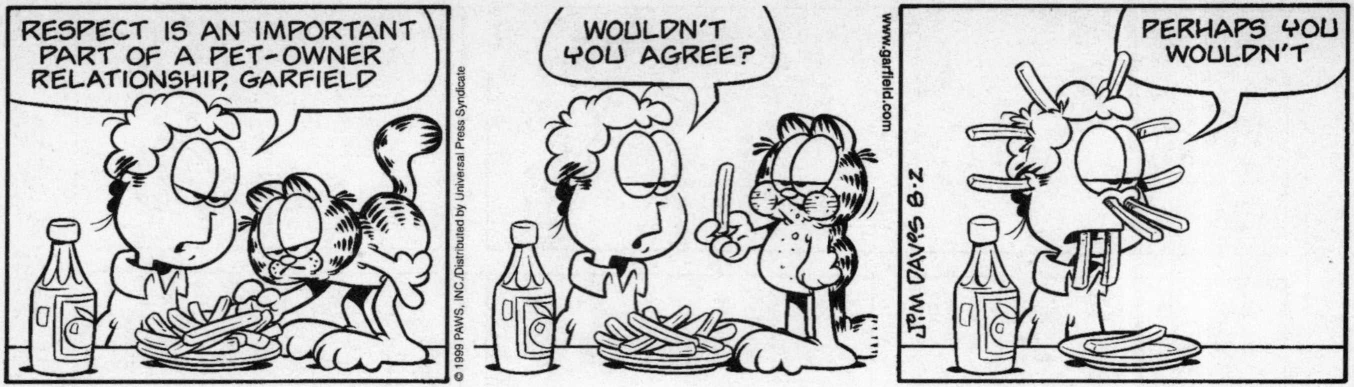
RESPECT IS AN IMPORTANT PART OF A PET-OWNER RELATIONSHIP, GARFIELD
© 1999 PAWS, INC./Distributed by Universal Press Syndicate
WOULDN'T YOU AGREE?
www.garfield.com
JIM DAVIS 8-2
PERHAPS YOU WOULDN'T

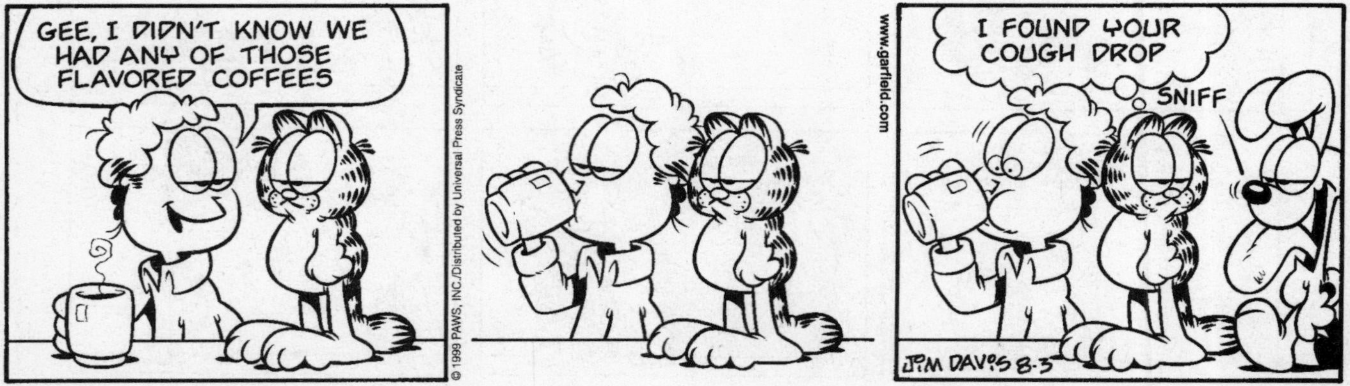
GEE, I DIDN'T KNOW WE HAD ANY OF THOSE FLAVORED COFFEES
© 1999 PAWS, INC./Distributed by Universal Press Syndicate
www.garfield.com
I FOUND YOUR COUGH DROP
SNIFF
JIM DAVIS 8-3

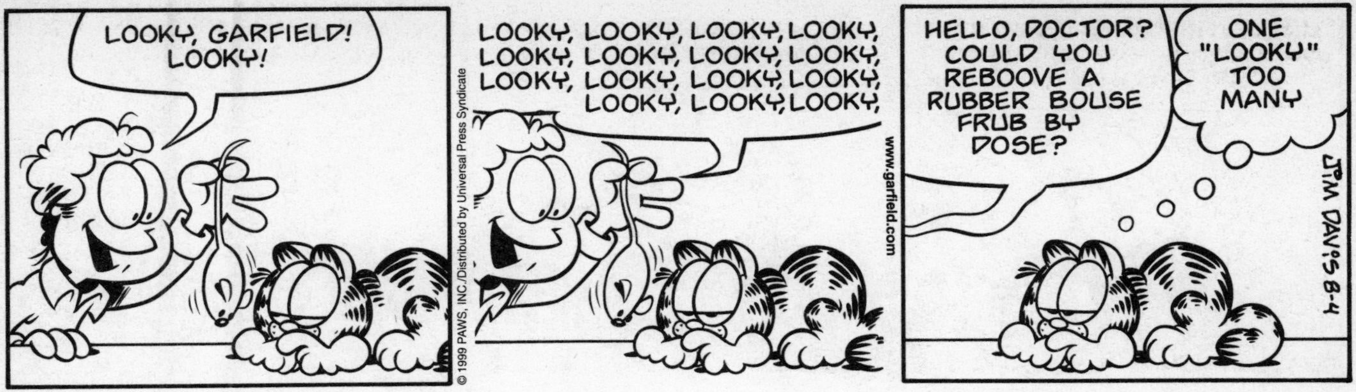
LOOKY, GARFIELD! LOOKY!
LOOKY, LOOKY, LOOKY, LOOKY, LOOKY, LOOKY, LOOKY, LOOKY, LOOKY, LOOKY, LOOKY, LOOKY, LOOKY, LOOKY, LOOKY,
© 1999 PAWS, INC./Distributed by Universal Press Syndicate
www.garfield.com
HELLO, DOCTOR? COULD YOU REBOOVE A RUBBER BOUSE FRUB BY DOSE?
ONE "LOOKY" TOO MANY
JIM DAVIS 8-4

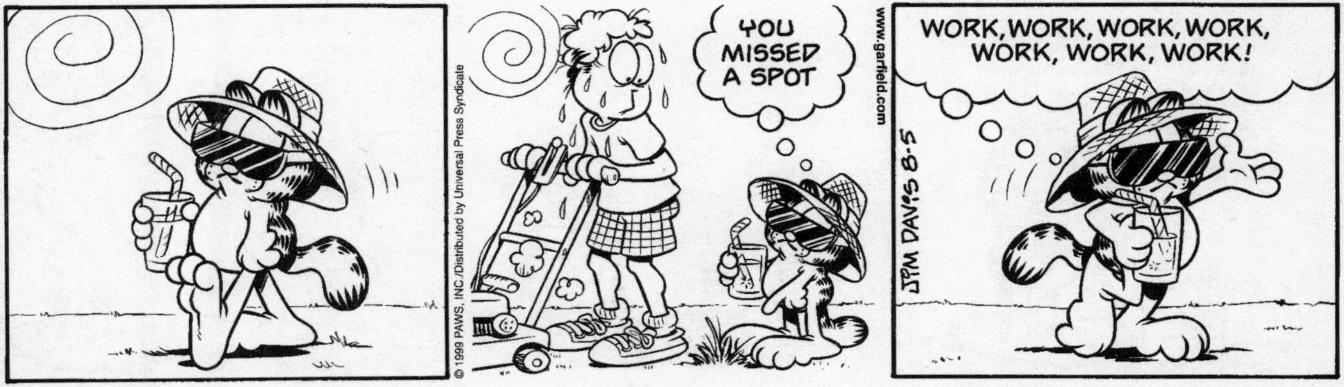
© 1999 PAWS, INC./Distributed by Universal Press Syndicate
YOU MISSED A SPOT
www.garfield.com
JIM DAVIS 8-5
WORK, WORK, WORK, WORK, WORK, WORK, WORK!

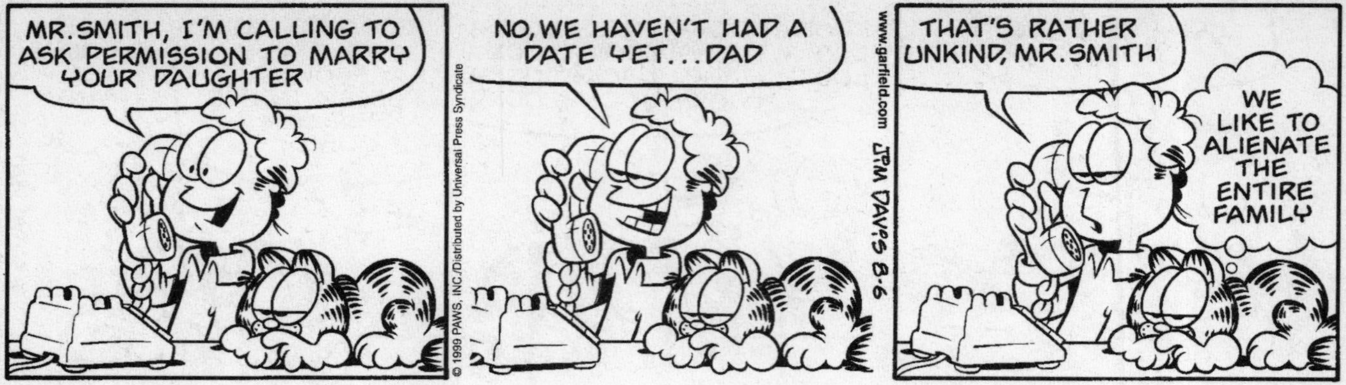
MR. SMITH, I'M CALLING TO ASK PERMISSION TO MARRY YOUR DAUGHTER
© 1999 PAWS, INC./Distributed by Universal Press Syndicate
NO, WE HAVEN'T HAD A DATE YET...DAD
www.garfield.com
JPM DAVIS 8-6
THAT'S RATHER UNKIND, MR. SMITH
WE LIKE TO ALIENATE THE ENTIRE FAMILY

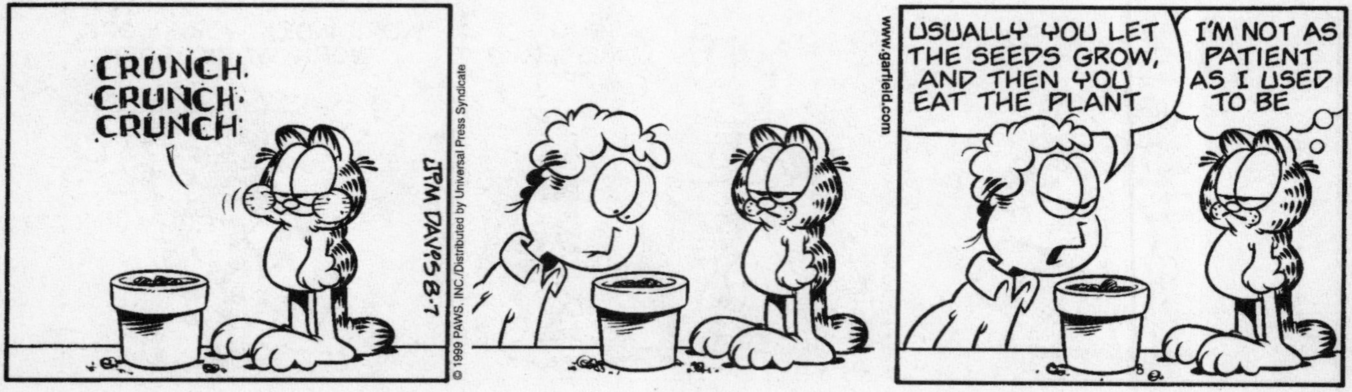
CRUNCH CRUNCH CRUNCH
JPM DAVIS 8-7
© 1999 PAWS, INC./Distributed by Universal Press Syndicate
www.garfield.com
USUALLY YOU LET THE SEEDS GROW, AND THEN YOU EAT THE PLANT
I'M NOT AS PATIENT AS I USED TO BE

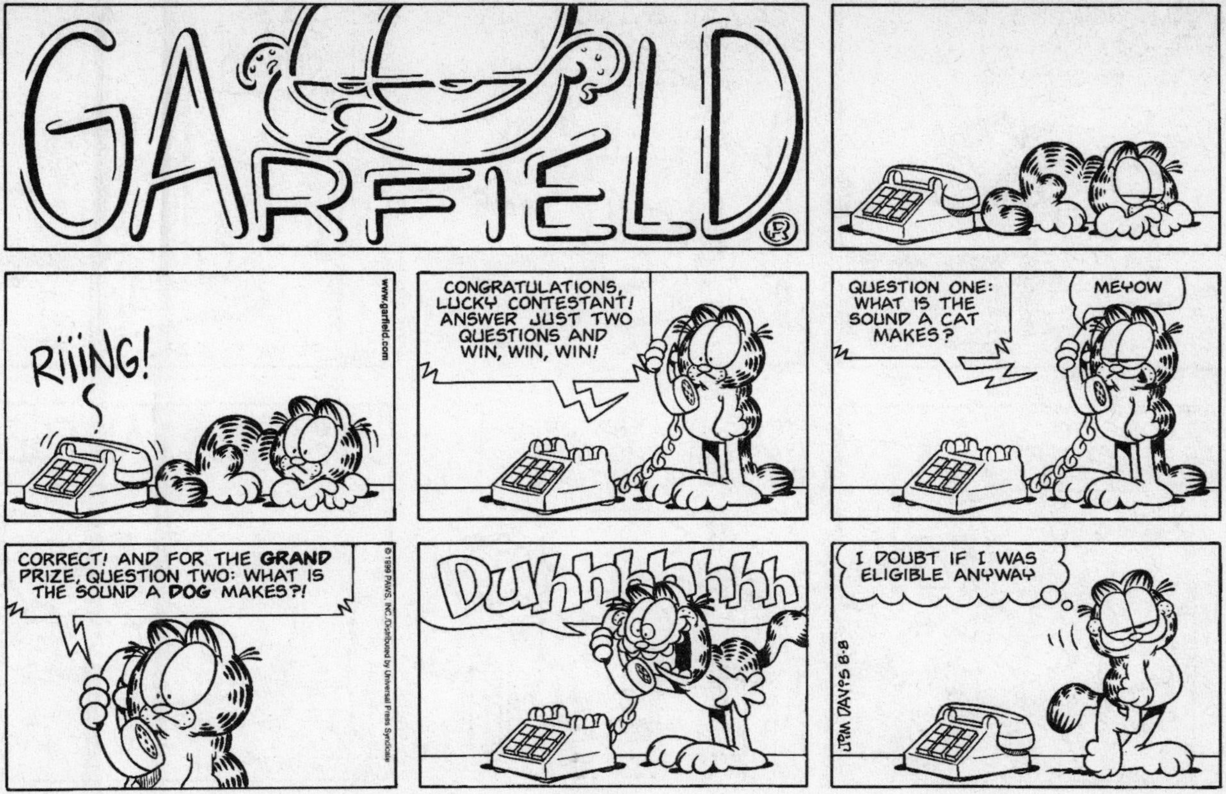
GARFIELD
RIIING!
www.garfield.com
CONGRATULATIONS, LUCKY CONTESTANT! ANSWER JUST TWO QUESTIONS AND WIN, WIN, WIN!
QUESTION ONE: WHAT IS THE SOUND A CAT MAKES?
MEYOW
CORRECT! AND FOR THE GRAND PRIZE, QUESTION TWO: WHAT IS THE SOUND A DOG MAKES?!
© 1999 PAWS, INC./Distributed by Universal Press Syndicate
Duhhhhhhh
JIM DAVIS 8-8
I DOUBT IF I WAS ELIGIBLE ANYWAY

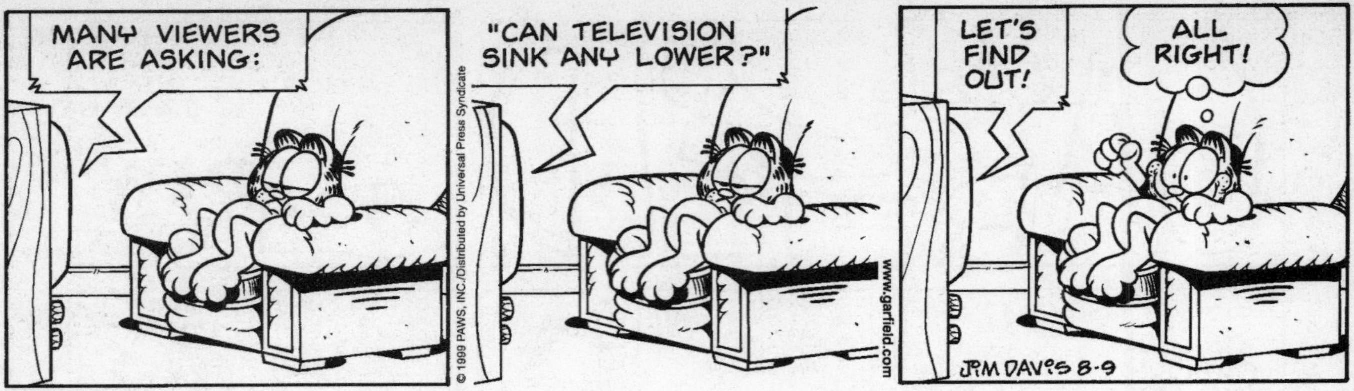
MANY VIEWERS ARE ASKING:
"CAN TELEVISION SINK ANY LOWER?"
LET'S FIND OUT!
ALL RIGHT!
© 1999 PAWS, INC./Distributed by Universal Press Syndicate
www.garfield.com
JIM DAVIS 8-9

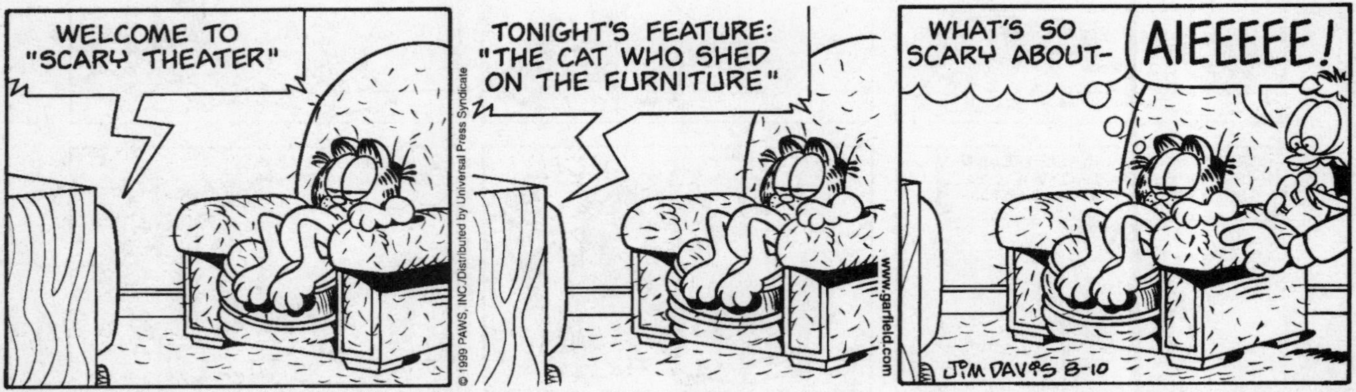
WELCOME TO "SCARY THEATER"
TONIGHT'S FEATURE: "THE CAT WHO SHED ON THE FURNITURE"
WHAT'S SO SCARY ABOUT-
AIEEEEE!
© 1999 PAWS, INC./Distributed by Universal Press Syndicate
www.garfield.com
JIM DAVIS 8-10

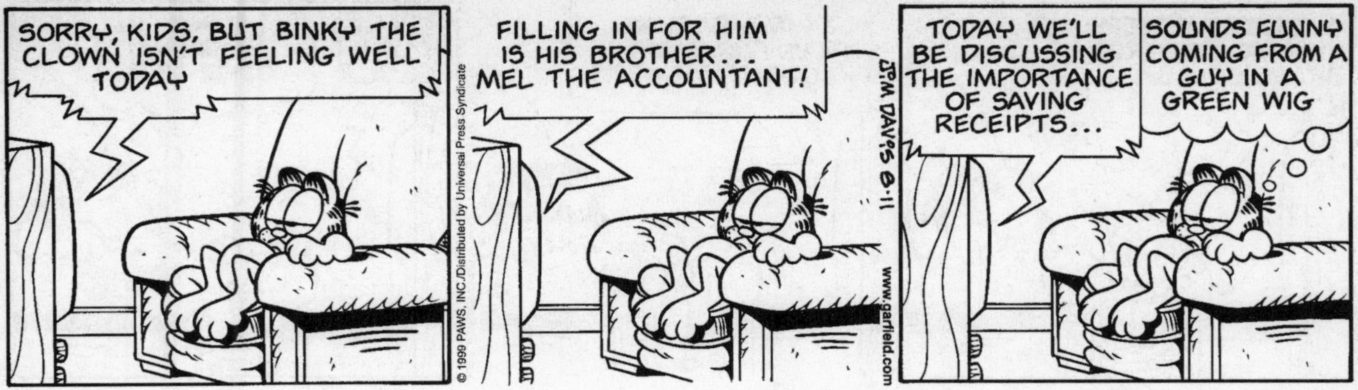
SORRY, KIDS, BUT BINKY THE CLOWN ISN'T FEELING WELL TODAY
FILLING IN FOR HIM IS HIS BROTHER... MEL THE ACCOUNTANT!
TODAY WE'LL BE DISCUSSING THE IMPORTANCE OF SAVING RECEIPTS...
SOUNDS FUNNY COMING FROM A GUY IN A GREEN WIG
© 1999 PAWS, INC./Distributed by Universal Press Syndicate
JIM DAVIS 8-11
www.garfield.com

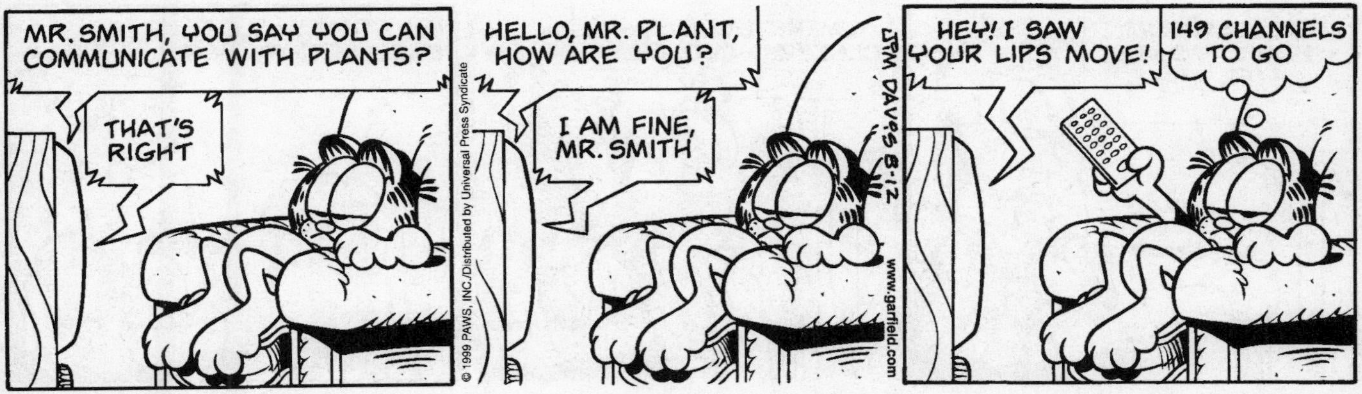
MR. SMITH, YOU SAY YOU CAN COMMUNICATE WITH PLANTS?
THAT'S RIGHT
HELLO, MR. PLANT, HOW ARE YOU?
I AM FINE, MR. SMITH
HEY! I SAW YOUR LIPS MOVE!
149 CHANNELS TO GO
© 1999 PAWS, INC./Distributed by Universal Press Syndicate
JIM DAVIS 8-12
www.garfield.com

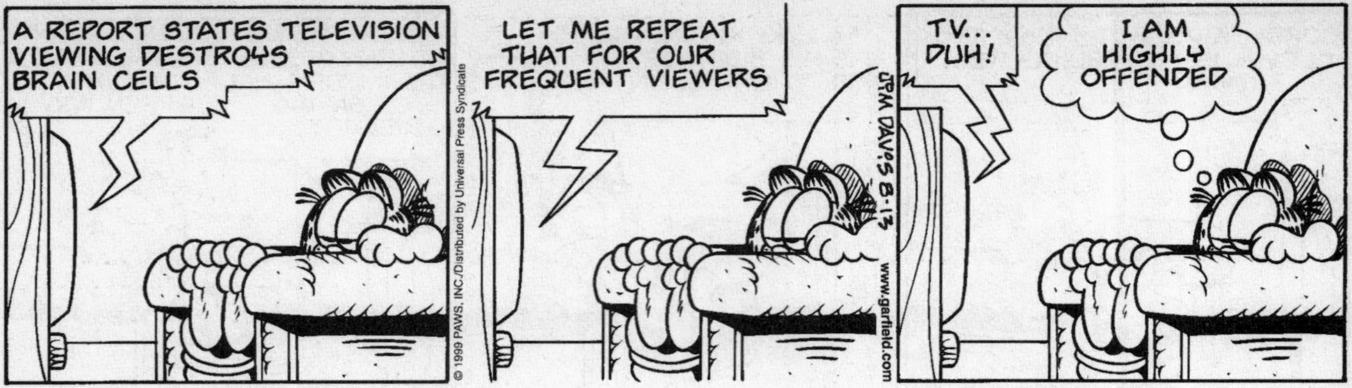
A REPORT STATES TELEVISION VIEWING DESTROYS BRAIN CELLS
© 1999 PAWS, INC./Distributed by Universal Press Syndicate
LET ME REPEAT THAT FOR OUR FREQUENT VIEWERS
JIM DAVIS 8-13
www.garfield.com
TV... DUH!
I AM HIGHLY OFFENDED

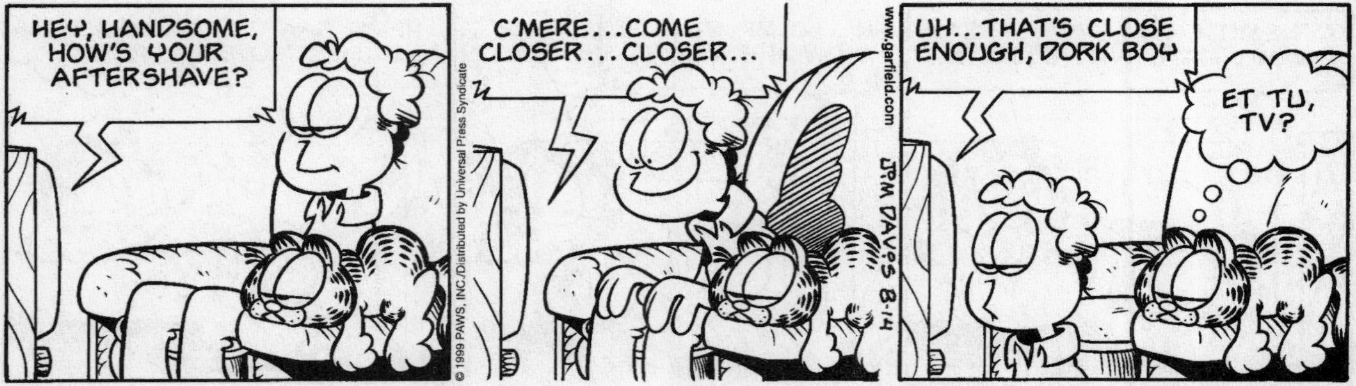
HEY, HANDSOME, HOW'S YOUR AFTERSHAVE?
© 1999 PAWS, INC./Distributed by Universal Press Syndicate
C'MERE...COME CLOSER...CLOSER...
JIM DAVIS 8-14
www.garfield.com
UH...THAT'S CLOSE ENOUGH, DORK BOY
ET TU, TV?

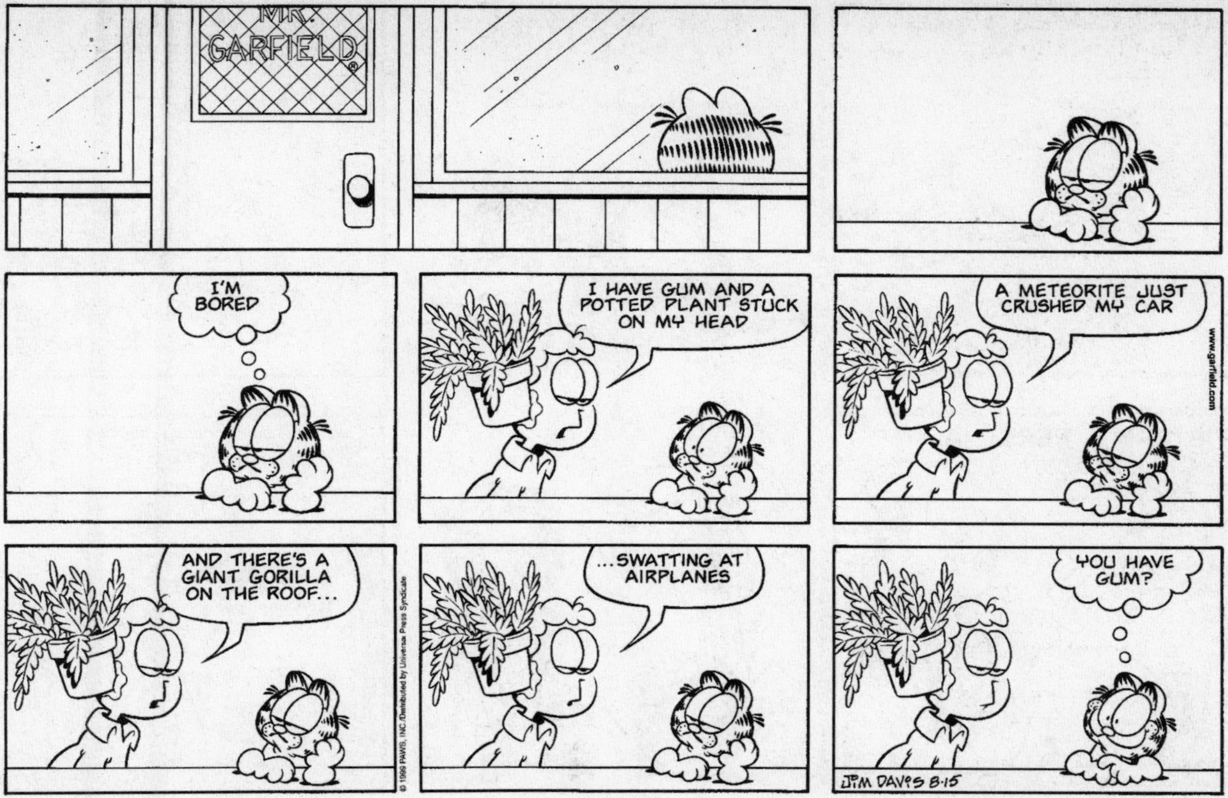
MR. GARFIELD®
I'M BORED
I HAVE GUM AND A POTTED PLANT STUCK ON MY HEAD
A METEORITE JUST CRUSHED MY CAR
www.garfield.com
AND THERE'S A GIANT GORILLA ON THE ROOF...
...SWATTING AT AIRPLANES
YOU HAVE GUM?
JIM DAVIS 8-15
© 1999 PAWS, INC./Distributed by Universal Press Syndicate

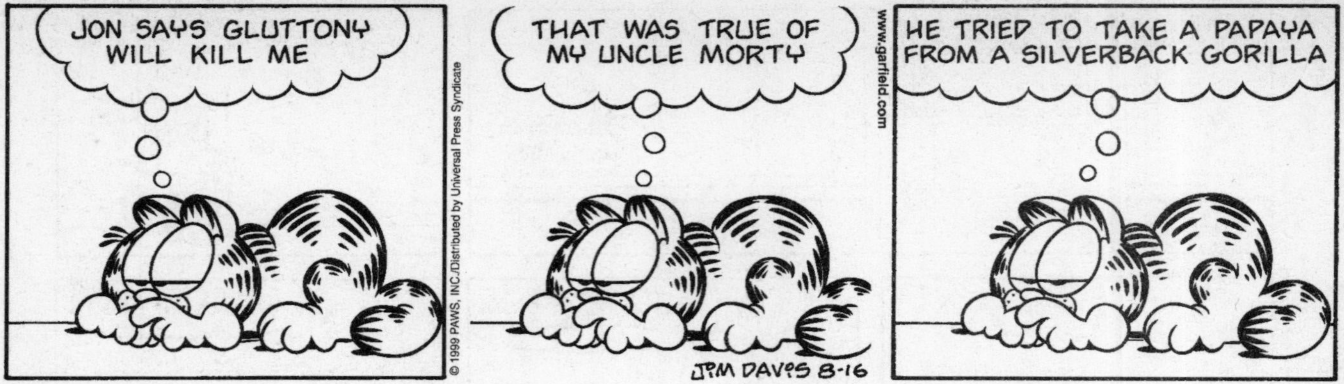
JON SAYS GLUTTONY WILL KILL ME
THAT WAS TRUE OF MY UNCLE MORTY
HE TRIED TO TAKE A PAPAYA FROM A SILVERBACK GORILLA
© 1999 PAWS, INC./Distributed by Universal Press Syndicate
www.garfield.com
JIM DAVIS 8-16

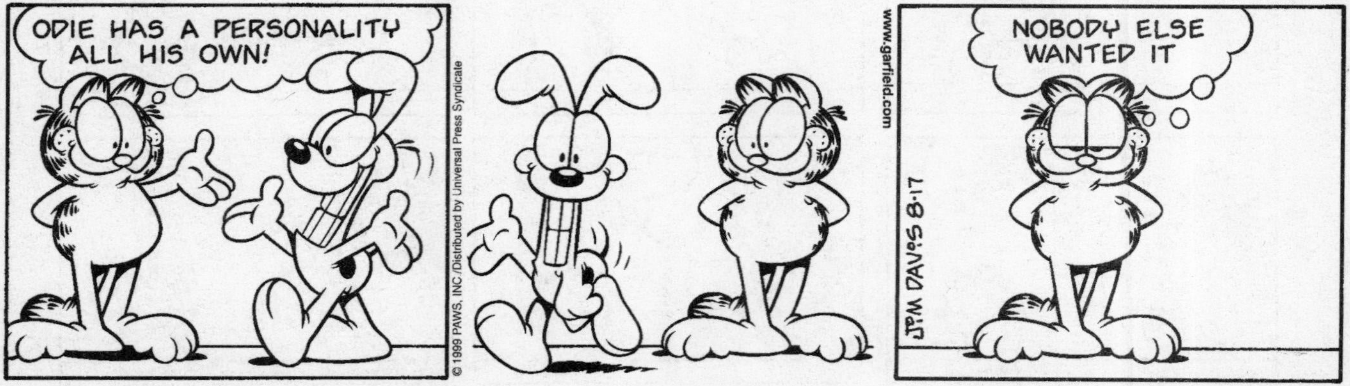
ODIE HAS A PERSONALITY ALL HIS OWN!
NOBODY ELSE WANTED IT
© 1999 PAWS, INC./Distributed by Universal Press Syndicate
www.garfield.com
JIM DAVIS 8-17

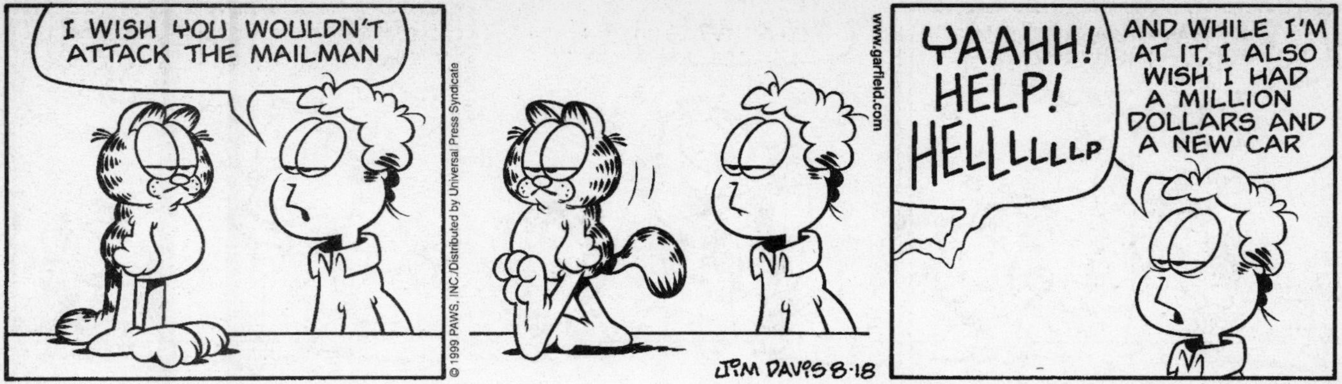
I WISH YOU WOULDN'T ATTACK THE MAILMAN
© 1999 PAWS, INC./Distributed by Universal Press Syndicate
JIM DAVIS 8-18
www.garfield.com
YAAHH! HELP! HELLLLLLLP
AND WHILE I'M AT IT, I ALSO WISH I HAD A MILLION DOLLARS AND A NEW CAR

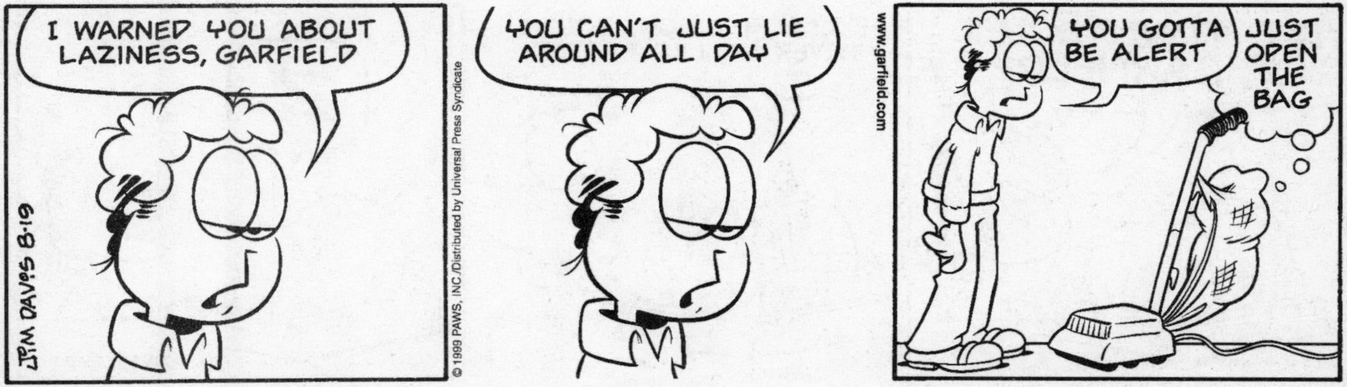
I WARNED YOU ABOUT LAZINESS, GARFIELD
JIM DAVIS 8-19
© 1999 PAWS, INC./Distributed by Universal Press Syndicate
YOU CAN'T JUST LIE AROUND ALL DAY
www.garfield.com
YOU GOTTA BE ALERT
JUST OPEN THE BAG

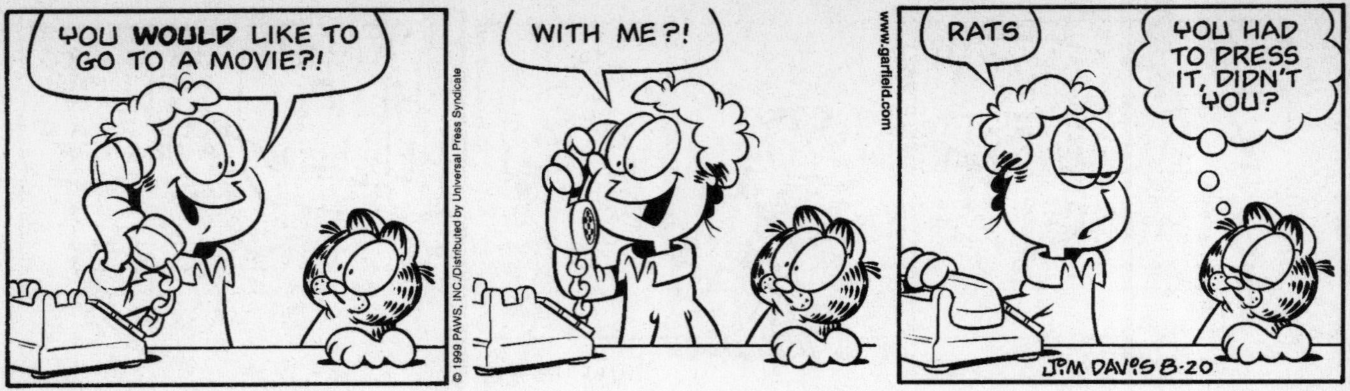
YOU WOULD LIKE TO GO TO A MOVIE?!
© 1999 PAWS, INC./Distributed by Universal Press Syndicate
WITH ME?!
www.garfield.com
RATS
YOU HAD TO PRESS IT, DIDN'T YOU?
JIM DAVIS 8-20

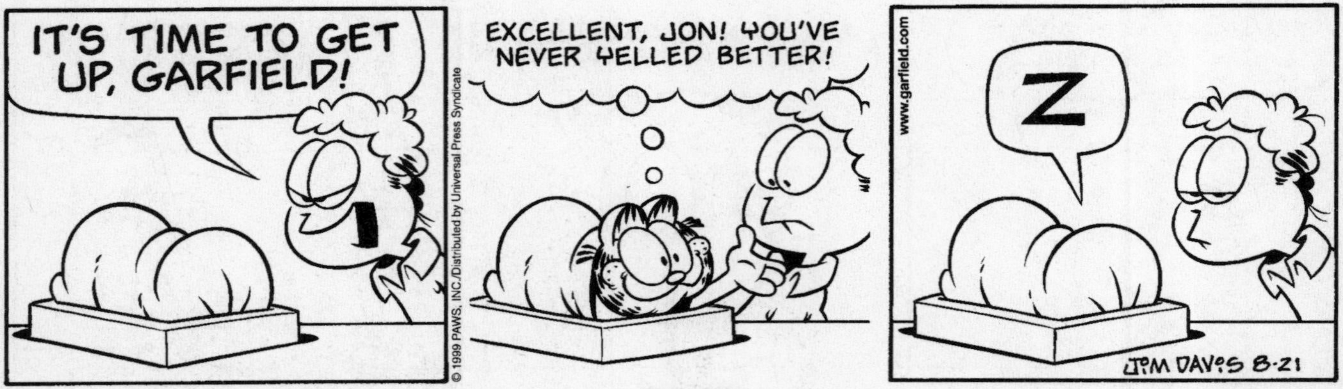
IT'S TIME TO GET UP, GARFIELD!
© 1999 PAWS, INC./Distributed by Universal Press Syndicate
EXCELLENT, JON! YOU'VE NEVER YELLED BETTER!
www.garfield.com
Z
JIM DAVIS 8-21

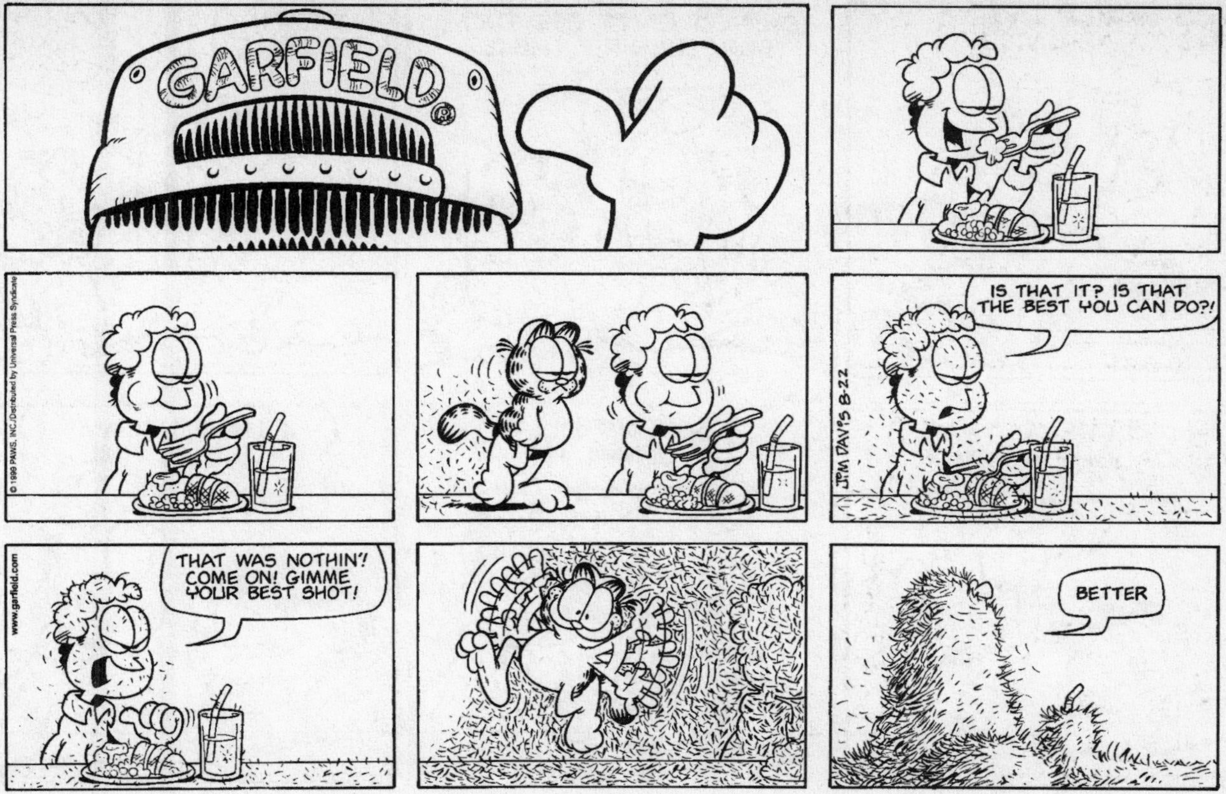
GARFIELD
© 1999 PAWS, INC./Distributed by Universal Press Syndicate
JPM DAVIS 8-22
IS THAT IT? IS THAT THE BEST YOU CAN DO?!
www.garfield.com
THAT WAS NOTHIN'! COME ON! GIMME YOUR BEST SHOT!
BETTER

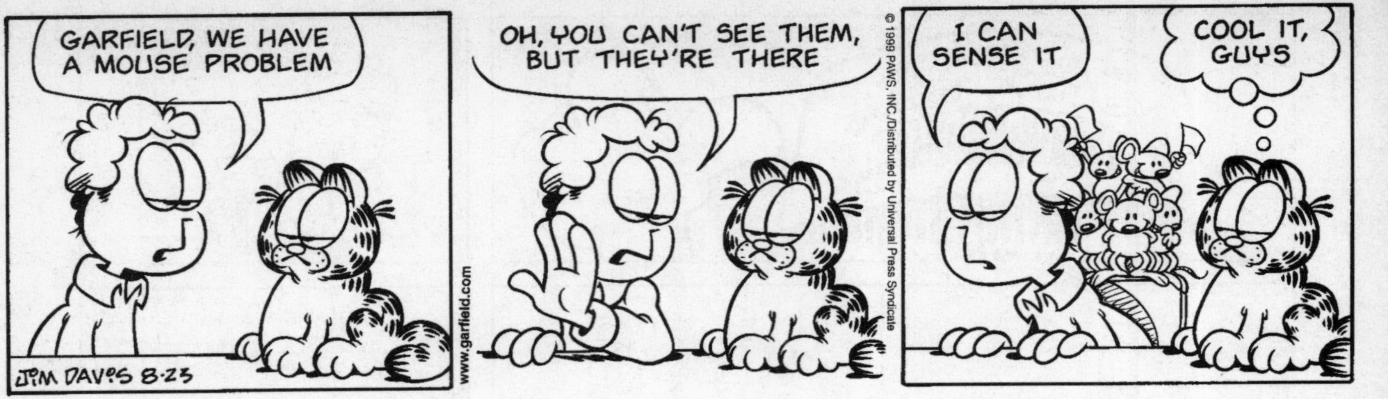
GARFIELD, WE HAVE A MOUSE PROBLEM
JIM DAVIS 8-23
www.garfield.com
OH, YOU CAN'T SEE THEM, BUT THEY'RE THERE
© 1999 PAWS, INC./Distributed by Universal Press Syndicate
I CAN SENSE IT
COOL IT, GUYS

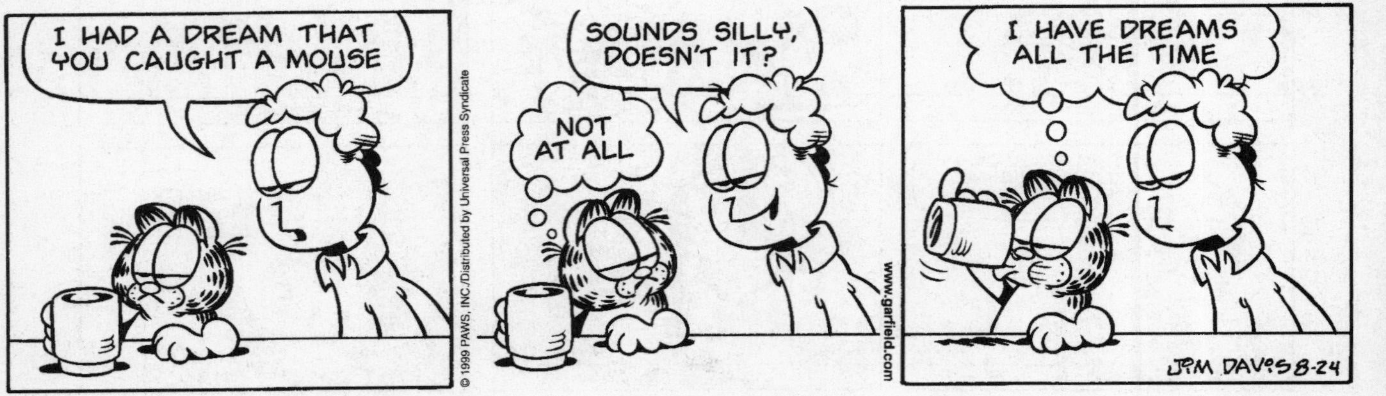
I HAD A DREAM THAT YOU CAUGHT A MOUSE
© 1999 PAWS, INC./Distributed by Universal Press Syndicate
SOUNDS SILLY, DOESN'T IT?
NOT AT ALL
www.garfield.com
I HAVE DREAMS ALL THE TIME
JIM DAVIS 8-24

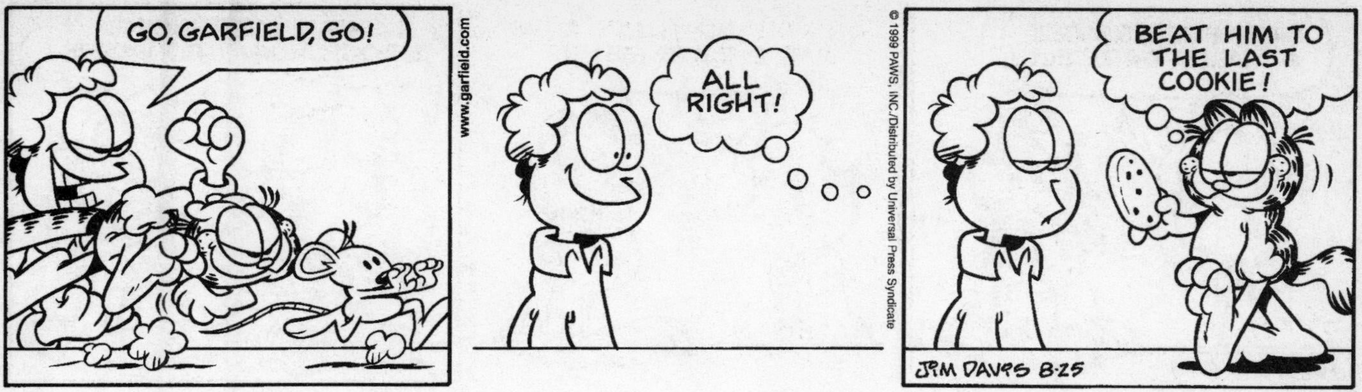
GO, GARFIELD, GO!
www.garfield.com
ALL RIGHT!
© 1999 PAWS, INC./Distributed by Universal Press Syndicate
BEAT HIM TO THE LAST COOKIE!
JIM DAVIS 8-25

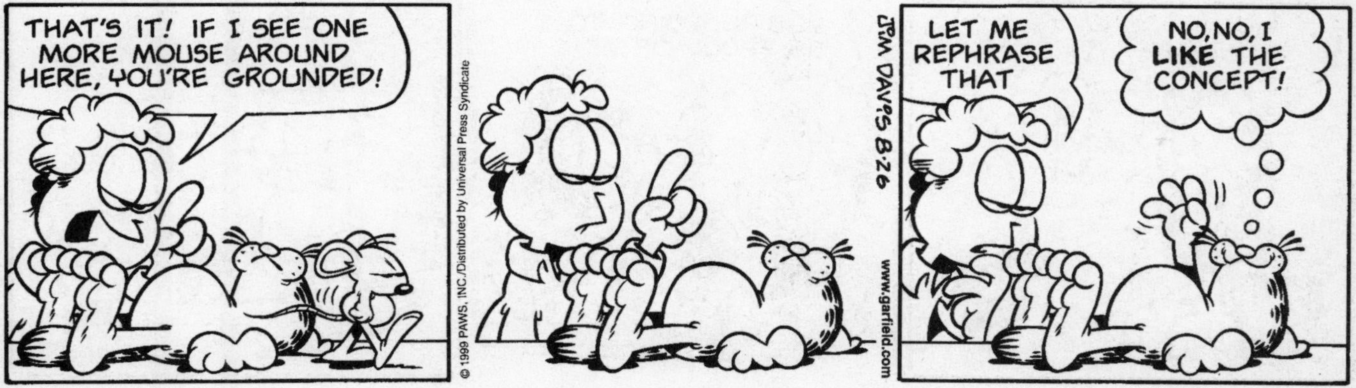
THAT'S IT! IF I SEE ONE MORE MOUSE AROUND HERE, YOU'RE GROUNDED!
© 1999 PAWS, INC./Distributed by Universal Press Syndicate
JIM DAVIS 8-26
www.garfield.com
LET ME REPHRASE THAT
NO, NO, I **LIKE** THE CONCEPT!

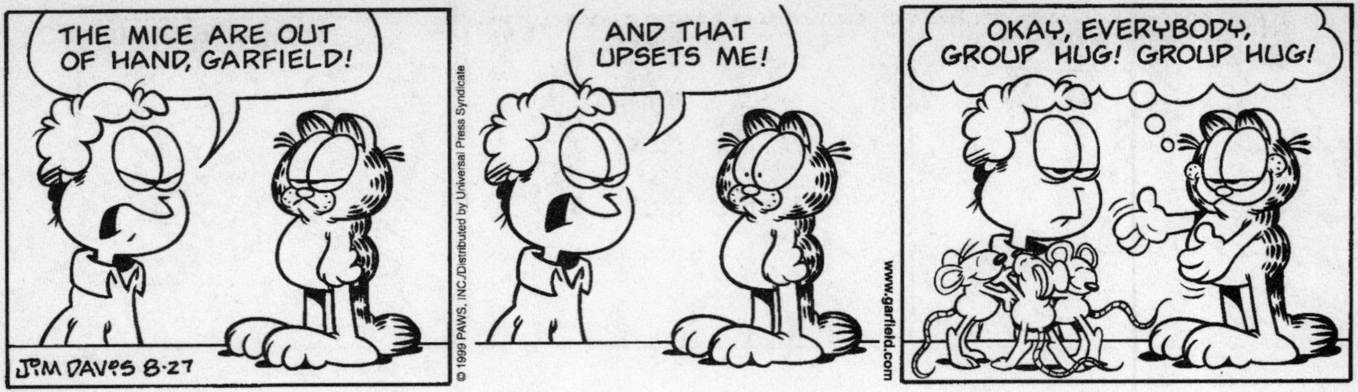
THE MICE ARE OUT OF HAND, GARFIELD!
JIM DAVIS 8-27
© 1999 PAWS, INC./Distributed by Universal Press Syndicate
AND THAT UPSETS ME!
www.garfield.com
OKAY, EVERYBODY, GROUP HUG! GROUP HUG!

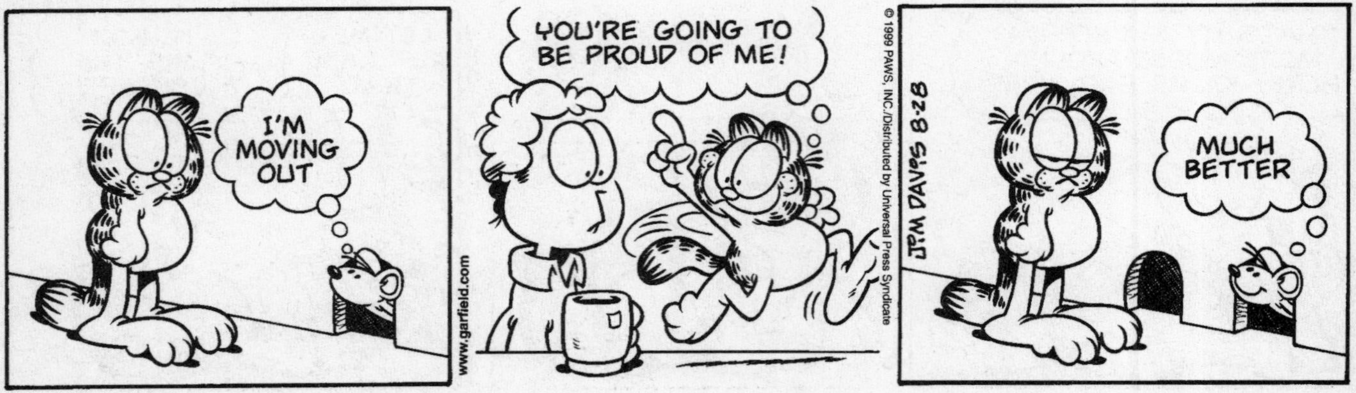
I'M MOVING OUT
www.garfield.com
YOU'RE GOING TO BE PROUD OF ME!
© 1999 PAWS, INC./Distributed by Universal Press Syndicate
JIM DAVIS 8-28
MUCH BETTER

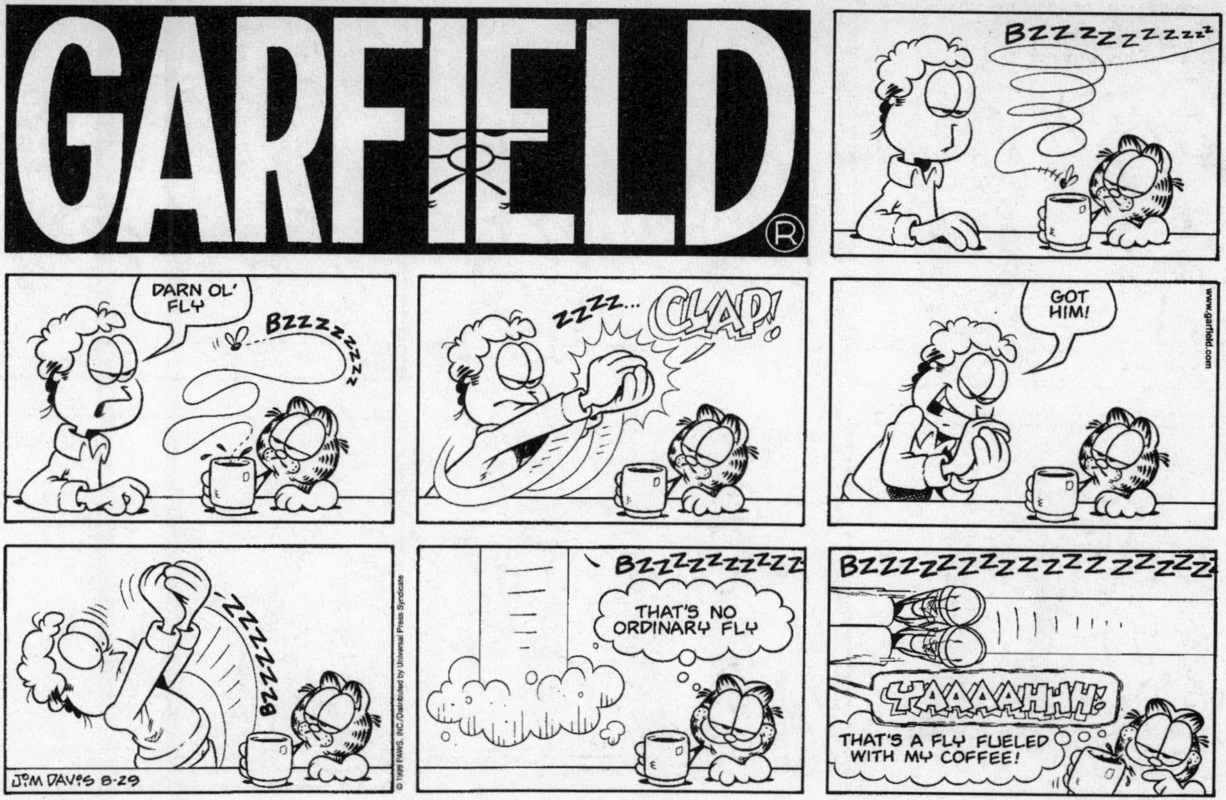
GARFIELD
BZZZZZZZZZZ
DARN OL' FLY
BZZZZZZZZZZ
ZZZZ... CLAP!
GOT HIM!
www.garfield.com
BZZZZZZZ
JIM DAVIS 8-29
© 1999 PAWS, INC./Distributed by Universal Press Syndicate
BZZZZZZZZZZZ
THAT'S NO ORDINARY FLY
BZZZZZZZZZZZZZZZZZZ
YAAAAHHH!
THAT'S A FLY FUELED WITH MY COFFEE!

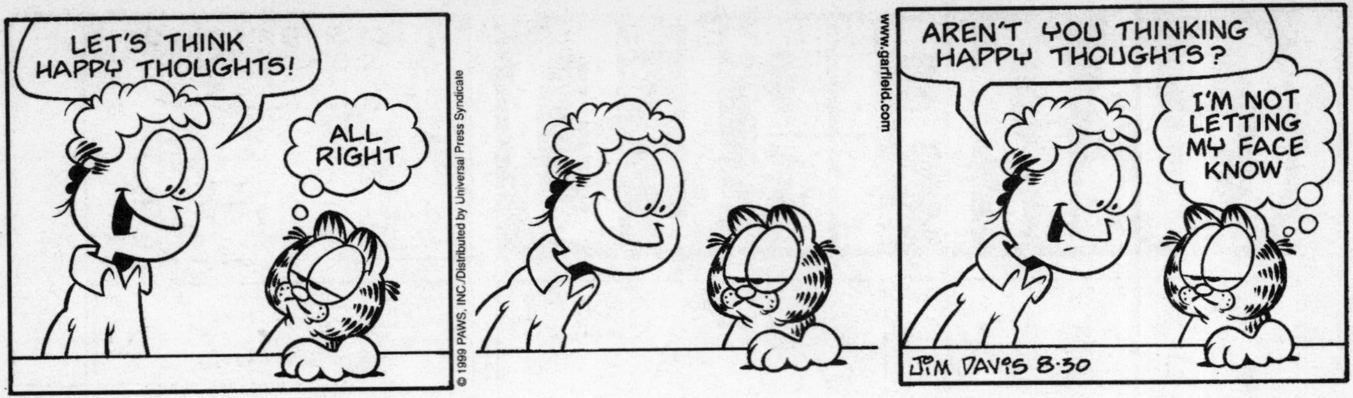
LET'S THINK HAPPY THOUGHTS!
ALL RIGHT
AREN'T YOU THINKING HAPPY THOUGHTS?
I'M NOT LETTING MY FACE KNOW
JIM DAVIS 8-30
© 1999 PAWS, INC./Distributed by Universal Press Syndicate
www.garfield.com

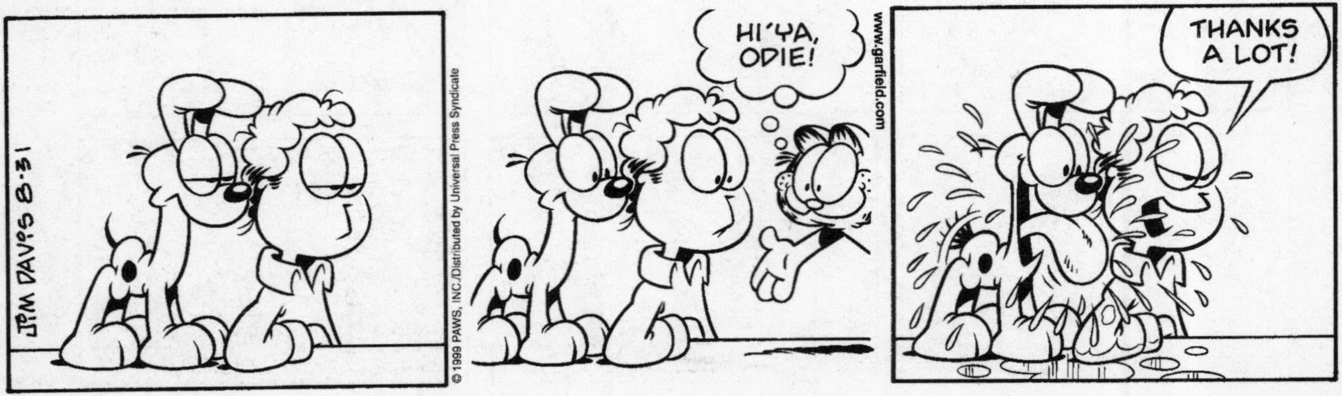
JIM DAVIS 8-31
HI'YA, ODIE!
THANKS A LOT!
© 1999 PAWS, INC./Distributed by Universal Press Syndicate
www.garfield.com

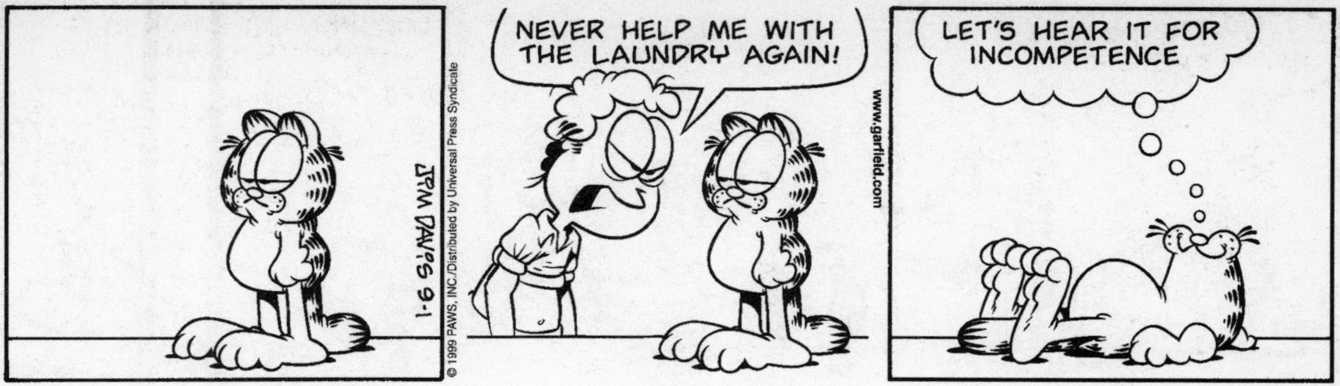
NEVER HELP ME WITH THE LAUNDRY AGAIN!
LET'S HEAR IT FOR INCOMPETENCE
JPM DAVPS 9-1
© 1999 PAWS, INC./Distributed by Universal Press Syndicate
www.garfield.com

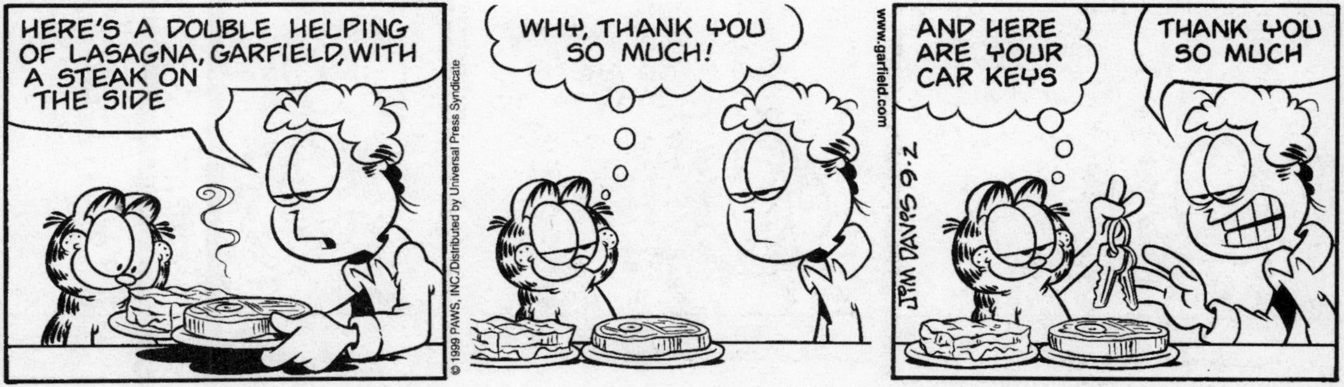
HERE'S A DOUBLE HELPING OF LASAGNA, GARFIELD, WITH A STEAK ON THE SIDE
WHY, THANK YOU SO MUCH!
AND HERE ARE YOUR CAR KEYS
THANK YOU SO MUCH
JPM DAVPS 9-2
© 1999 PAWS, INC./Distributed by Universal Press Syndicate
www.garfield.com

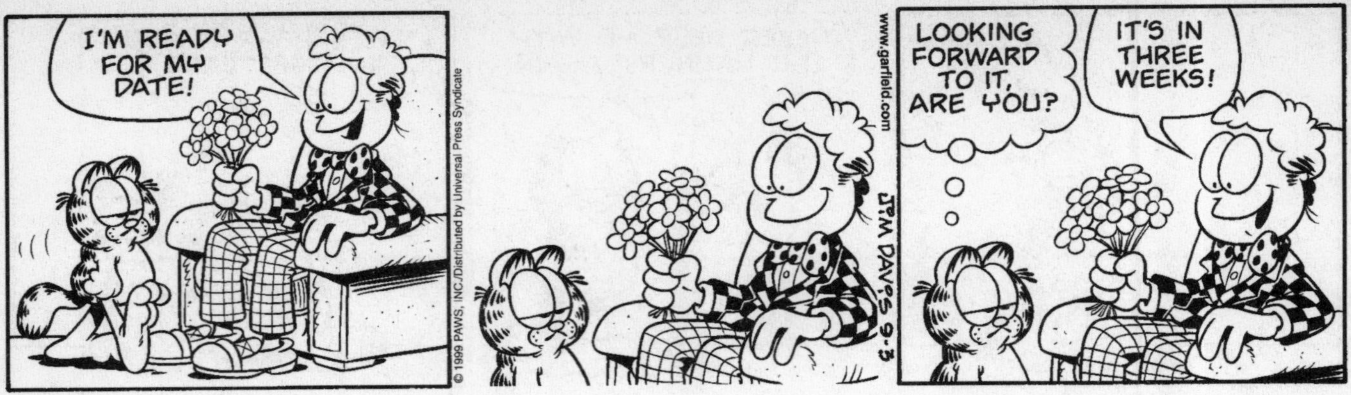
I'M READY FOR MY DATE!
© 1999 PAWS, INC./Distributed by Universal Press Syndicate
JIM DAVIS 9-3
www.garfield.com
LOOKING FORWARD TO IT, ARE YOU?
IT'S IN THREE WEEKS!

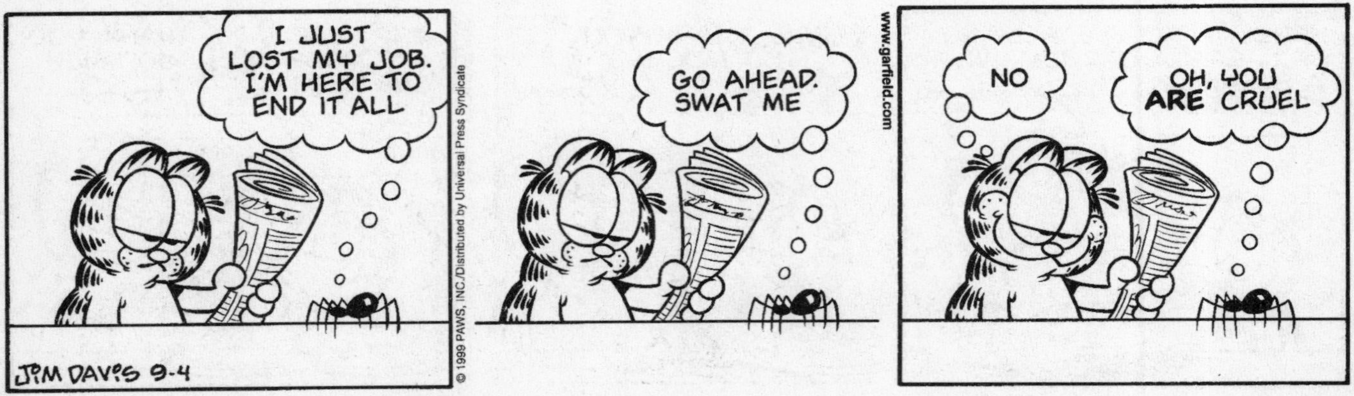
I JUST LOST MY JOB. I'M HERE TO END IT ALL
JIM DAVIS 9-4
© 1999 PAWS, INC./Distributed by Universal Press Syndicate
GO AHEAD. SWAT ME
www.garfield.com
NO
OH, YOU **ARE** CRUEL

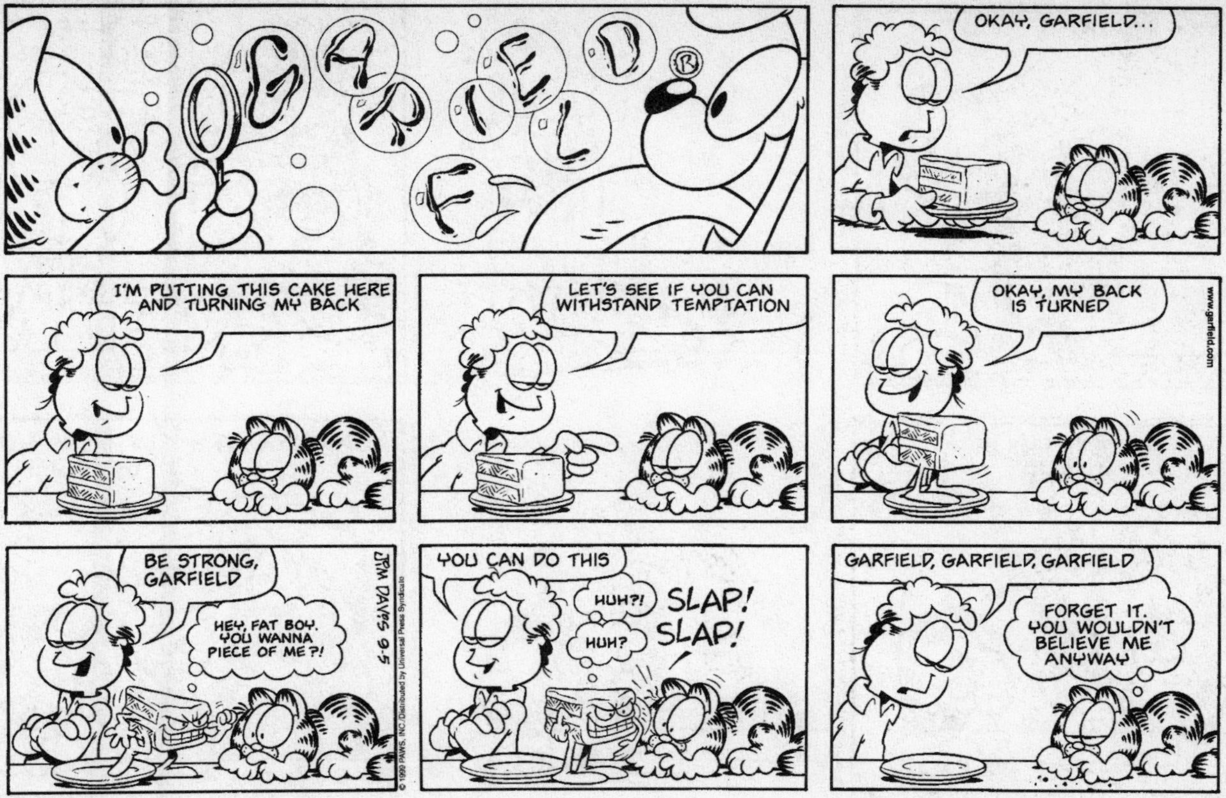
GARFIELD®
OKAY, GARFIELD...
I'M PUTTING THIS CAKE HERE AND TURNING MY BACK
LET'S SEE IF YOU CAN WITHSTAND TEMPTATION
OKAY, MY BACK IS TURNED
www.garfield.com
BE STRONG, GARFIELD
HEY, FAT BOY. YOU WANNA PIECE OF ME?!
JIM DAVIS 9-5
© 1999 PAWS, INC./Distributed by Universal Press Syndicate
YOU CAN DO THIS
HUH?
HUH?!
SLAP! SLAP!
GARFIELD, GARFIELD, GARFIELD
FORGET IT. YOU WOULDN'T BELIEVE ME ANYWAY

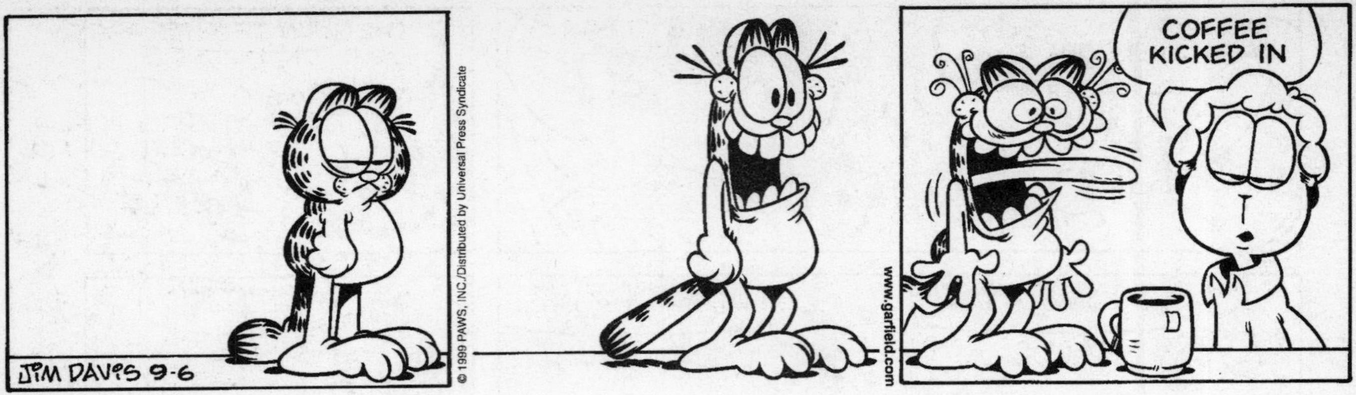
JIM DAVIS 9-6
© 1999 PAWS, INC./Distributed by Universal Press Syndicate
www.garfield.com
COFFEE KICKED IN

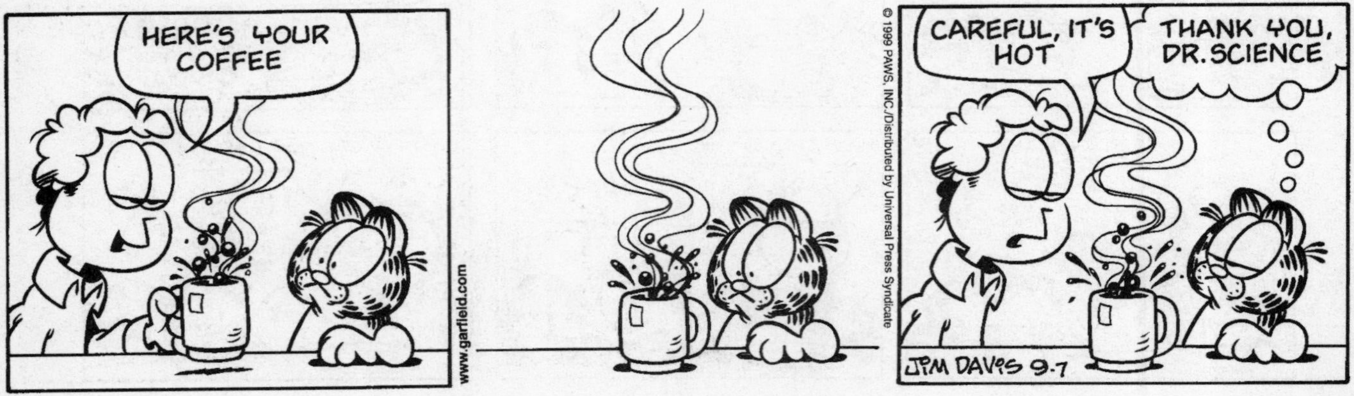
HERE'S YOUR COFFEE
www.garfield.com
© 1999 PAWS, INC./Distributed by Universal Press Syndicate
CAREFUL, IT'S HOT
THANK YOU, DR. SCIENCE
JIM DAVIS 9-7

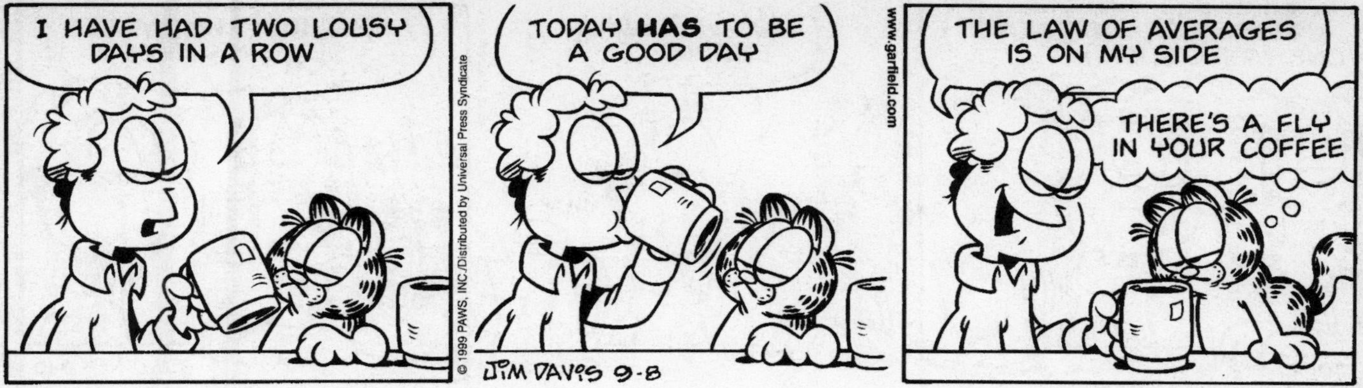
I HAVE HAD TWO LOUSY DAYS IN A ROW
TODAY **HAS** TO BE A GOOD DAY
THE LAW OF AVERAGES IS ON MY SIDE
THERE'S A FLY IN YOUR COFFEE
JIM DAVIS 9-8
© 1999 PAWS, INC./Distributed by Universal Press Syndicate
www.garfield.com

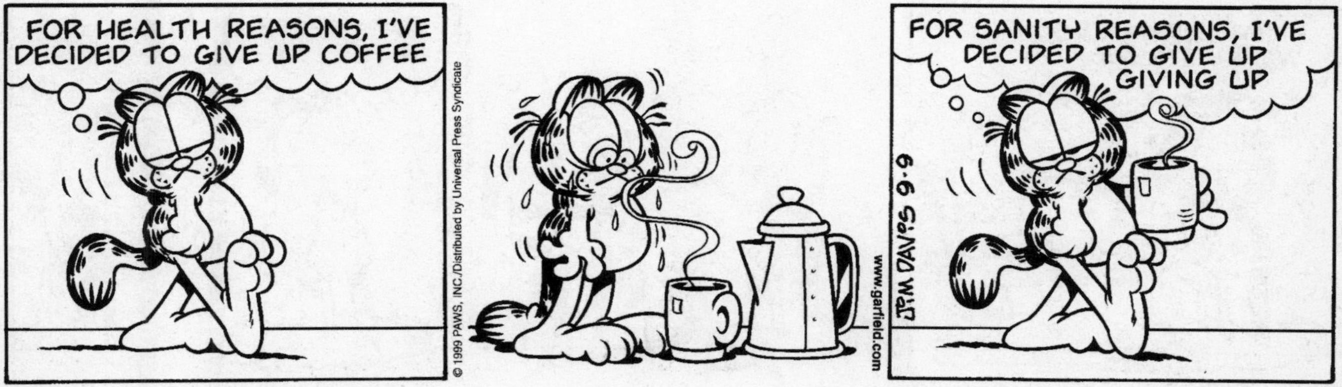
FOR HEALTH REASONS, I'VE DECIDED TO GIVE UP COFFEE
FOR SANITY REASONS, I'VE DECIDED TO GIVE UP GIVING UP
JIM DAVIS 9-9
© 1999 PAWS, INC./Distributed by Universal Press Syndicate
www.garfield.com

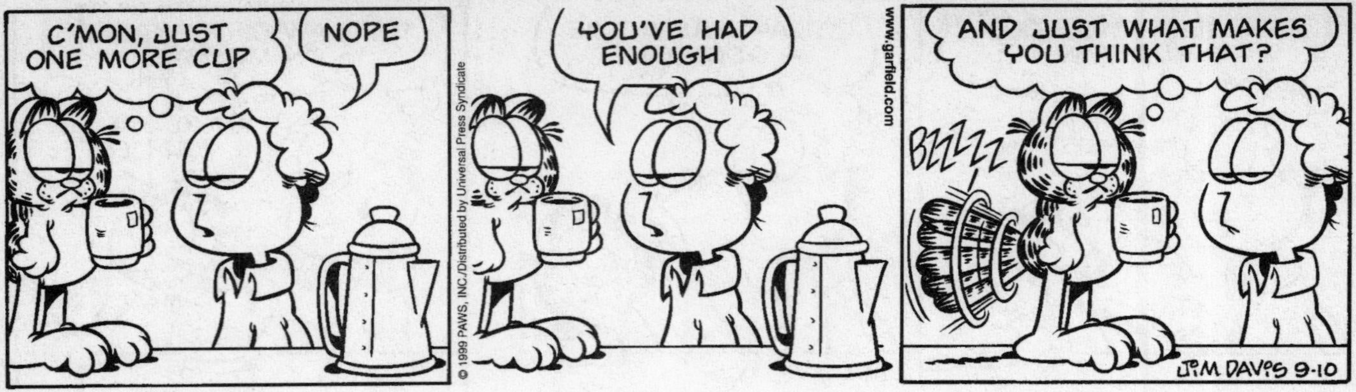
C'MON, JUST ONE MORE CUP
NOPE
YOU'VE HAD ENOUGH
AND JUST WHAT MAKES YOU THINK THAT?
BZZZZZ
JIM DAVIS 9-10
© 1999 PAWS, INC./Distributed by Universal Press Syndicate
www.garfield.com

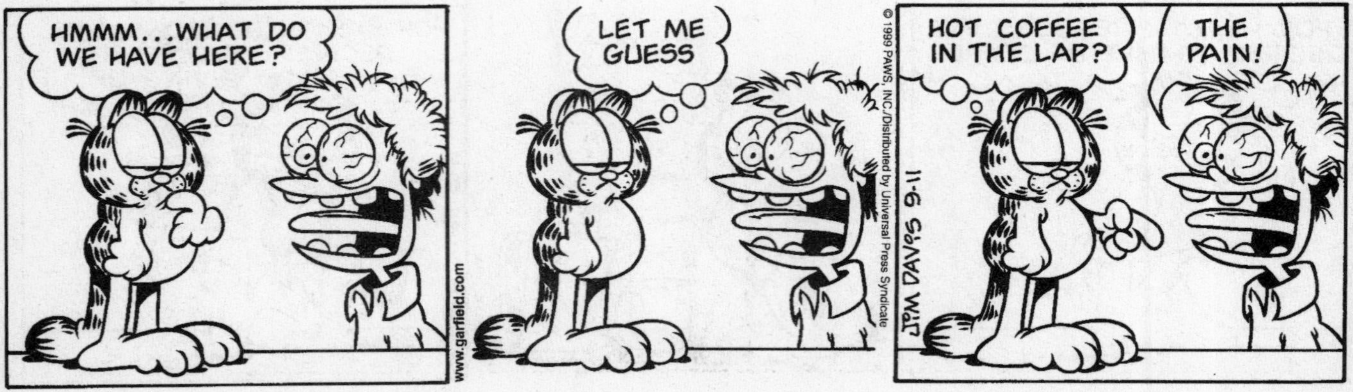
HMMM...WHAT DO WE HAVE HERE?
LET ME GUESS
HOT COFFEE IN THE LAP?
THE PAIN!
JIM DAVIS 9-11
© 1999 PAWS, INC./Distributed by Universal Press Syndicate
www.garfield.com

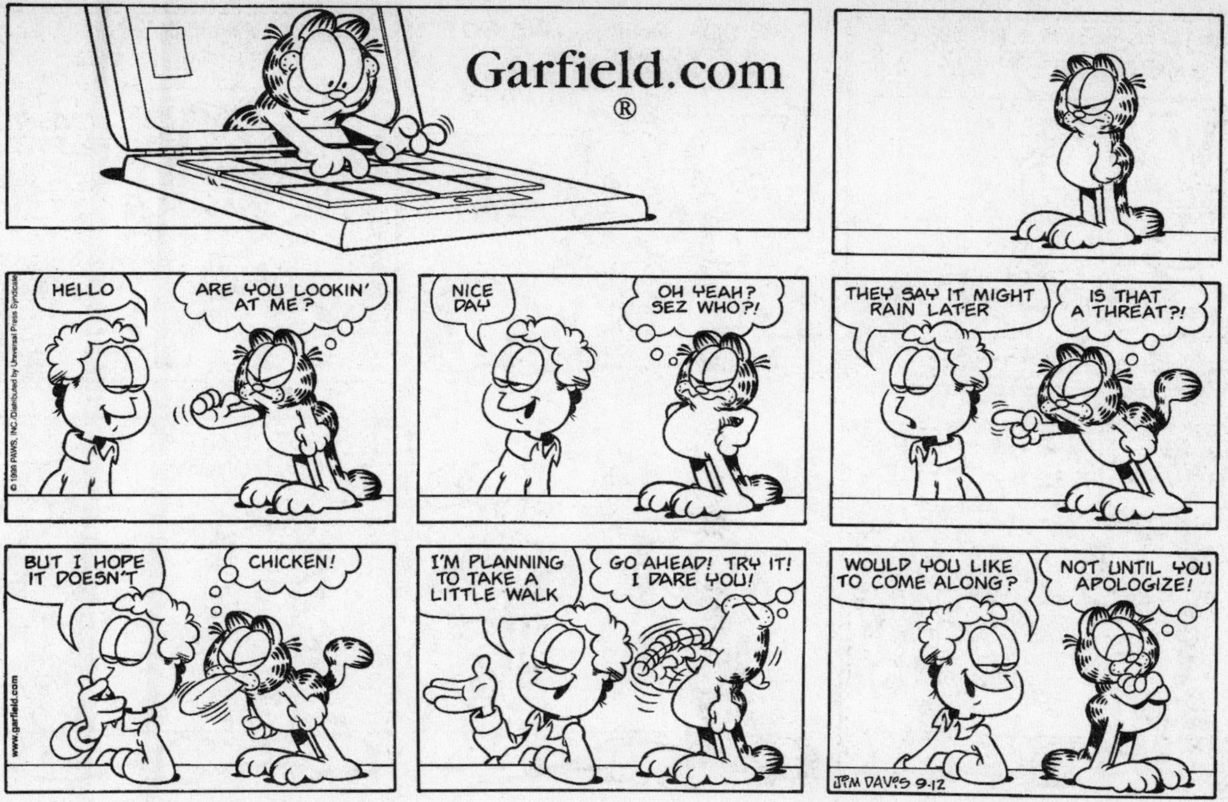
Garfield.com ®
© 1999 PAWS, INC./Distributed by Universal Press Syndicate
HELLO
ARE YOU LOOKIN' AT ME?
NICE DAY
OH YEAH? SEZ WHO?!
THEY SAY IT MIGHT RAIN LATER
IS THAT A THREAT?!
www.garfield.com
BUT I HOPE IT DOESN'T
CHICKEN!
I'M PLANNING TO TAKE A LITTLE WALK
GO AHEAD! TRY IT! I DARE YOU!
WOULD YOU LIKE TO COME ALONG?
NOT UNTIL YOU APOLOGIZE!
JIM DAVIS 9-12

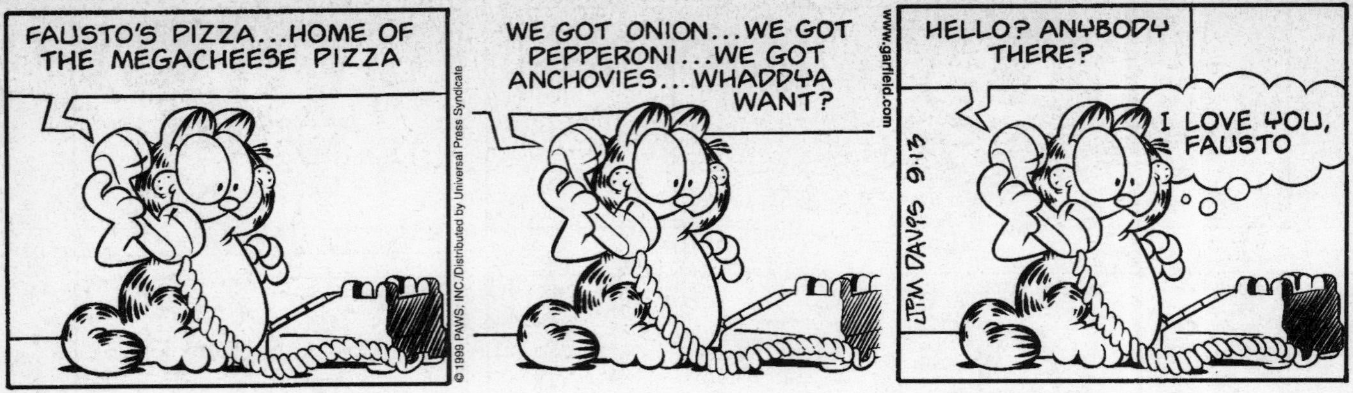
FAUSTO'S PIZZA...HOME OF THE MEGACHEESE PIZZA
© 1999 PAWS, INC./Distributed by Universal Press Syndicate
WE GOT ONION...WE GOT PEPPERONI...WE GOT ANCHOVIES...WHADDYA WANT?
www.garfield.com
HELLO? ANYBODY THERE?
I LOVE YOU, FAUSTO
JPM DAVPS 9-13

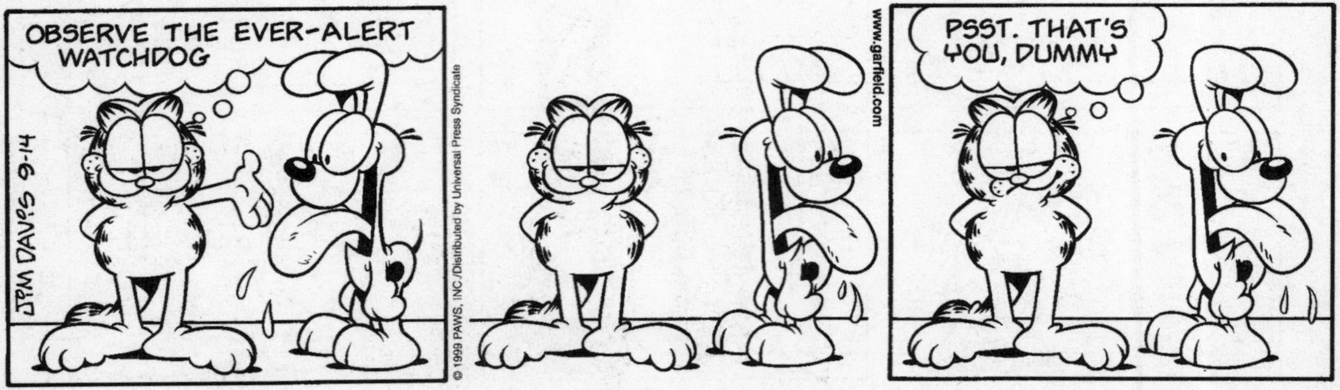
OBSERVE THE EVER-ALERT WATCHDOG
JPM DAVPS 9-14
© 1999 PAWS, INC./Distributed by Universal Press Syndicate
www.garfield.com
PSST. THAT'S YOU, DUMMY

Fat Cat Classics Vol. 2

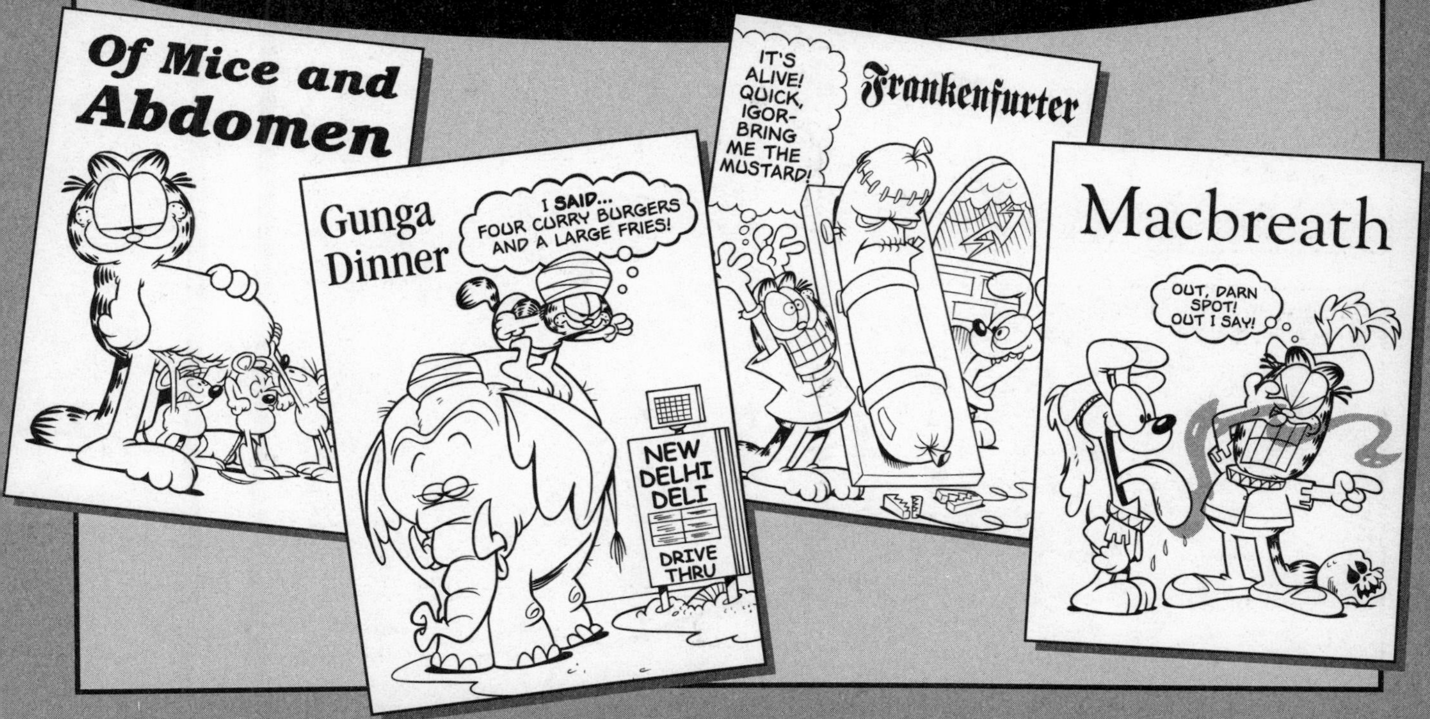
Of Mice and Abdomen
Gunga Dinner
I SAID... FOUR CURRY BURGERS AND A LARGE FRIES!
NEW DELHI DELI
DRIVE THRU
IT'S ALIVE! QUICK, IGOR- BRING ME THE MUSTARD!
Frankenfurter
Macbreath
OUT, DARN SPOT! OUT I SAY!